Trends and Applications in Information Systems and Technologies

Trends and Applications in Information Systems and Technologies

Editors

Galina Ilieva
George A. Tsihrintzis

MDPI

Basel • Beijing • Wuhan • Barcelona • Belgrade • Novi Sad • Cluj • Manchester

Editors

Galina Ilieva
Department of Management and Quantitative Methods in Economics Hilendarski
University of Plovdiv Paisii Hilendarski
Plovdiv, Bulgaria

George A. Tsihrintzis
Department of Informatics
University of Piraeus
Piraeus, Greece

Editorial Office
MDPI
St. Alban-Anlage 66
4052 Basel, Switzerland

This is a reprint of articles from the Special Issue published online in the open access journal *Electronics* (ISSN 2079-9292) (available at: https://www.mdpi.com/journal/electronics/special_issues/information_systems_technologies).

For citation purposes, cite each article independently as indicated on the article page online and as indicated below:

Lastname, A.A.; Lastname, B.B. Article Title. *Journal Name* **Year**, *Volume Number*, Page Range.

ISBN 978-3-0365-9568-9 (Hbk)
ISBN 978-3-0365-9569-6 (PDF)
doi.org/10.3390/books978-3-0365-9569-6

Cover image courtesy of George A. Tsihrintzis

Contents

About the Editors

Galina Ilieva

Galina Ilieva earned her diploma in Electrical Engineering (with honors) from the Technical University of Sofia, Bulgaria, and her Ph.D. from Plovdiv University Paisii Hilendarski (PU), specializing in agent-based solutions for electronic commerce negotiations. Since 2008, she has served as a lecturer at the Faculty of Economics and Social Sciences at PU. In 2011, she successfully defended her habilitation and now holds the position of a professor in Business Informatics at the Management and Quantitative Methods in Economics Department, PU. Currently, she is also serving as a member of the Supervisory Board at the Plovdiv University for a four-year term (2023–2027). A senior member of international scientific societies, including the Institute of Electrical and Electronics Engineers (IEEE) and the Association for Computing Machinery (ACM), she co-authored 47 papers, with an h-index of 12. Her current research focuses on the synthesis and properties of intelligent systems for decision making and machine learning.

George A. Tsihrintzis

George A. Tsihrintzis received Ph.D. degrees in Electrical and Computer Engineering from Northeastern University, Boston, Massachusetts, USA. He is currently a Professor in The University of Piraeus, Greece, and during 2016–2020, he served as the Head of its Department of Informatics. During the period 2016–2020, he was a member of the first Administration Council of the University of Piraeus. Currently, he is serving again as a Member of the Administration Council of the University of Piraeus for a four-year term (2022–2026). His current research interests include Artificial and Computational Intelligence, Machine Learning, Pattern Recognition, Decision Theory, and Statistical Signal Processing and their applications in Internet-of-Things Technologies, Multimedia Interactive Services, User Modeling, Knowledge-based Software Systems, Human–Computer Interaction, and Information Retrieval. He has authored or co-authored over 350 research publications in these areas. He has served as the principal investigator or co-investigator in several R&D projects. He is the Editor-in-Chief of the Intelligent Decision Technologies Journal (IOS Press). During 2012–2022, he was the Editor-in-Chief of the International Journal of Computational Intelligence Studies (Inderscience). He has been the Editor-in-Chief of Engineering Section of SpringerPlus. He is the founder and Editor-in-Chief of the Learning and Analytics in Intelligent Systems book series (Springer 2019-now) and the Artificial Intelligence-Enhanced Software and Systems Engineering book series (Springer 2022-now). He has organized and chaired 38 international conferences. He has received best paper awards from several international conferences and has been a keynote speaker at several international conferences. He is ranked among the top 2% of the most influential scientists worldwide of Scientists List at Stanford University ranking in the area of Artificial Intelligence for 2023.

Preface

In this Special Issue, we present a diverse collection of 14 articles spanning various domains within information systems and technologies. From the integration of oracles into blockchain platforms to innovative tools for measuring employee performance using emerging technologies like VR and AR, these contributions showcase the dynamic landscape of current research. The exploration of topics, such as IoT data sharing, machine learning applications and the adoption of digital business solutions, reflects the interdisciplinary nature of advancements in information systems. Each article delves into novel approaches, providing valuable insights and contributing to the ongoing evolution of the field.

Galina Ilieva and George A. Tsihrintzis
Editors

electronics

MDPI

Editorial

Editorial Note to the Special Issue: "Trends and Applications in Information Systems and Technologies"

Galina Ilieva [1,*] and George A. Tsihrintzis [2,*]

1 Department of Management and Quantitative Methods in Economics, University of Plovdiv Paisii Hilendarski, 4000 Plovdiv, Bulgaria
2 Department of Informatics, University of Piraeus, 18534 Piraeus, Greece
* Correspondence: galili@uni-plovdiv.bg (G.I.); geoatsi@unipi.gr (G.A.T.)

In today's fast-paced and competitive market, information technologies play a significant role in reshaping business models and enhancing company performance. A business can anticipate customer trends, streamline workflows, and improve its operational efficiency by digitally transforming its value chain. The swift adoption of information technologies has brought big data and business intelligence to the forefront, opening doors to innovative practices and improved productivity. The expansion of digital networks and distributed computing has also led to the rapid growth of information systems. However, these systems introduce new challenges, including cybersecurity issues, the need for advanced big data analysis, and reliance on data-centric decision-making processes.

Contrary to common belief, merely implementing information systems does not guarantee enhanced performance. This is because these systems are intricate, consisting of hardware, software, data, and a variety of use cases. Thus, inadequately designed systems or those failing to meet user requirements can result in subpar outcomes.

Addressing the primary challenges in creating and utilizing information systems is the main focus of this Special Issue of *Electronics*. These challenges include: (1) developing cutting-edge architecture (encompassing computers, networks, and software) to facilitate supply chain coordination and enable organizations to operate independently of geographical constraints; (2) processing and analyzing extensive data from IoT, transactions, and social interactions to aid in accurate business planning, forecasting, and monitoring; and (3) exploring the practical applications of information systems and analytical platforms in real-world scenarios.

Citation: Ilieva, G.; Tsihrintzis, G.A. Editorial Note to the Special Issue: "Trends and Applications in Information Systems and Technologies". *Electronics* **2023**, *12*, 4663. https://doi.org/10.3390/electronics12224663

Received: 8 November 2023
Accepted: 15 November 2023
Published: 15 November 2023

From the many papers submitted to this Special Issue, fourteen papers were selected for inclusion. The selection process was based on rigorous reviews of the submitted papers and considered a range of topics; papers that cover several aspects of information systems and technologies were selected. More specifically, the selected papers were grouped into three sets as follows: (1) three papers on the adoption and penetration of information systems and digital business technologies in various sectors, (2) six papers on advanced processing and information extraction in information systems, and (3) five papers on innovative streamline applications and services of information systems in various areas.

More specifically, the three papers on studies on adoption and penetration of information systems and digital business technologies in various sectors are as follows:

1. The paper entitled "Investigating the Factors Influencing the Adoption of Blockchain Technology across Different Countries and Industries: A Systematic Literature Review" conducts a systematic investigation into the influential factors impacting the adoption of blockchain technology. This research delves into the differences and commonalities of these factors across various countries and industries. After a comprehensive examination of both individual and organizational perspectives, the study identifies 152 unique factors that influence 25 different industries spanning 21 countries.

2. In the paper entitled "Adoption of Digital Business Solutions: Designing and Monitoring Critical Success Factors", the authors present an extensive framework that encompasses the end-to-end management of critical success factors, from their design to their monitoring, towards adopting a chosen digital business solution. Its applicability extends to businesses looking to undergo digital transformation, offering valuable insights and guidance throughout the adoption process.
3. The paper entitled "ICT Penetration and Insurance Sector Development: Evidence from the 10 New EU Member States" explores the intricate relationship between information and communication technologies, as represented by indicators such as mobile cellular subscriptions per 100 people, the percentage of individuals using the Internet, and the development of the insurance sector. Drawing upon data spanning the period from 2000 to 2020 in the context of the 10 new European Union member states, this study uncovers a dynamic interaction between indicators of ICT penetration and the evolution of the insurance sector.

The six papers on processing and information extraction in information systems are as follows:

1. In the paper entitled "An Extreme Value Analysis-Based Systemic Approach in Healthcare Information Systems: The Case of Dietary Intake", the authors employ extreme value theory to investigate outliers within health data, focusing on dietary intake and the standard biochemistry profile. This analysis showcases that, by utilizing extreme value analysis and implementing a systematic approach, it becomes possible to predict health trends. Consequently, health interventions can be (at least partially) automated.
2. The paper "Handling Class Imbalance and Class Overlap in Machine Learning Applications for Undeclared Work Prediction" addresses the challenges of class imbalance and class overlap in the context of automated undeclared work detection. The study identifies these issues and employs various data engineering techniques to mitigate them, underscoring the benefits for inspection authorities when integrating machine learning in the detection of undeclared work. The study found that performance was significantly enhanced when using data engineering approaches to tackle class imbalance and class overlap problems.
3. The paper entitled "An Incremental Learning Framework for Photovoltaic Production and Load Forecasting in Energy Microgrids" introduces an innovative online (or incremental) learning framework designed to adapt dynamically to evolving environments in energy-related time-series forecasting. This paradigm is specifically applied to energy forecasting problems, resulting in the development of models that flexibly adjust to emerging patterns in streaming data. Experimental evaluations highlight substantial performance improvements.
4. In the paper "A Multi-Attribute Decision-Making Approach for the Analysis of Vendor Management Using Novel Complex Picture Fuzzy Hamy Mean Operators", the performance of vendor management systems is assessed through multi-attribute decision-making techniques. The study utilizes Hany mean operators within the complex picture fuzzy sets framework and assesses their reliability by taking into account properties such as idempotency, monotonicity, and boundedness.
5. The paper "Investigating Trace Equivalences in Information Networks" introduces the concept of trace and trace equivalence within information networks, drawing inspiration from concurrent systems. The authors propose a computational method for determining whether two nodes exhibit trace equivalence in an information network. The study further derives trace-equivalent networks from the original networks. Real-data experiments demonstrate significant node reduction.
6. The paper "Improving Multi-Class Motor Imagery EEG Classification Using Overlapping Sliding Window and Deep Learning Model" presents a classification framework based on Long Short-Term Memory (LSTM) to enhance the accuracy of classifying

four-class motor imagery electroencephalography signals. The improved performance and robustness of the proposed framework are experimentally illustrated.

Finally, the five papers on innovative streamline applications and services of information systems in various areas are as follows:

1. The paper entitled "A Framework for Smart Home System with Voice Control Using NLP Methods" introduces an innovative IoT–fog–cloud framework. This framework leverages natural language processing methods and incorporates utterance-to-command transformation into existing cloud-based speech-to-text and text-to-speech services. The system testing has shown its reliability, user friendliness and its ability to enhance customer experience.
2. In the paper "Oracles Integration in Blockchain-Based Platform for Smart Crop Production Data Exchange", the authors discuss the seamless integration of oracles into an EOSIO blockchain-based platform. This integration facilitates the exchange of data related to smart crop production through the use of smart contracts. The paper provides in-depth insights into the design, implementation, and operational outcomes of the proposed platform modification.
3. In the paper entitled "Emotion-Based Literature Book Classification Using Online Reviews", the authors implement a scraper to create a new experimental dataset of reviews gathered from Goodreads. The system extracts emotions from the reviews and associates them with the reviewed book so that this information can be employed to identify similar books based on readers' impressions. The system is experimentally evaluated.
4. In the paper "An Innovative Tool to Measure Employee Performance through Customer Satisfaction: Pilot Research Using eWOM, VR, and AR Technologies", the authors present an innovative tool to enhance the efficiency of employee performance assessment systems. The tool focuses on assessing employee performance in relation to customer satisfaction in both service and industry sectors. Both theoretical and practical contributions are included, with the aim of continuously improving a company by utilizing applications in different fields.
5. The paper entitled "IoT Data Sharing Platform in Web 3.0 Using Blockchain Technology" introduces a novel open IoT data-sharing framework empowered by blockchain technology. This framework was built upon the capabilities of the interplanetary file system. A case-study-based approach was used to evaluate the proposed solution.

It is the hope of the guest editors that the readers will find this Special Issue of *Electronics*, "Trends and Applications in Information Systems and Technologies", informative and helpful, thus inspiring new research endeavors. Given that society is continuously striving for further innovation, not all challenges in the design and development of information systems can be identified and addressed in a single Special Issue. Thus, readers of *Electronics* may expect follow-up Special Issues on this topic to appear in due course.

Author Contributions: Writing—original draft preparation, G.I. and G.A.T.; writing—review and editing, G.I. and G.A.T. All authors have read and agreed to the published version of the manuscript.

Conflicts of Interest: The authors declare no conflict of interest.

List of Contributions

1. Marengo, A.; Pagano, A. Investigating the Factors Influencing the Adoption of Blockchain Technology across Different Countries and Industries: A Systematic Literature Review. *Electronics* **2023**, *12*, 3006. https://doi.org/10.3390/electronics12143006.
2. Doneva, R.; Gaftandzhieva, S. Adoption of Digital Business Solutions: Designing and Monitoring Critical Success Factors. *Electronics* **2022**, *11*, 3494. https://doi.org/10.3390/electronics11213494.
3. Bayar, Y.; Danuletiu, D.C.; Danuletiu, A.E.; Gavriletea, M.D. ICT Penetration and Insurance Sector Development: Evidence from the 10 New EU Member States. *Electronics* **2023**, *12*, 823. https://doi.org/10.3390/electronics12040823.

4. Panagoulias, D.P.; Sotiropoulos, D.N.; Tsihrintzis, G.A. An Extreme Value Analysis-Based Systemic Approach in Healthcare Information Systems: The Case of Dietary Intake. *Electronics* **2023**, *12*, 204. https://doi.org/10.3390/electronics12010204.
5. Alogogianni, E.; Virvou, M. Handling Class Imbalance and Class Overlap in Machine Learning Applications for Undeclared Work Prediction. *Electronics* **2023**, *12*, 913. https://doi.org/10.3390/electronics12040913.
6. Sarmas, E.; Strompolas, S.; Marinakis, V.; Santori, F.; Bucarelli, M.A.; Doukas, H. An Incremental Learning Framework for Photovoltaic Production and Load Forecasting in Energy Microgrids. *Electronics* **2022**, *11*, 3962. https://doi.org/10.3390/electronics11233962.
7. Hussain, A.; Ullah, K.; Pamucar, D.; Vranješ, D. A Multi-Attribute Decision-Making Approach for the Analysis of Vendor Management Using Novel Complex Picture Fuzzy Hamy Mean Operators. *Electronics* **2022**, *11*, 3841. https://doi.org/10.3390/electronics11233841.
8. Li, R.; Wu, J.; Hu, W. Investigating Trace Equivalences in Information Networks. *Electronics* **2023**, *12*, 865. https://doi.org/10.3390/electronics12040865.
9. Hwang, J.; Park, S.; Chi, J. Improving Multi-Class Motor Imagery EEG Classification Using Overlapping Sliding Window and Deep Learning Model. *Electronics* **2023**, *12*, 1186. https://doi.org/10.3390/electronics12051186.
10. Iliev, Y.; Ilieva, G. A Framework for Smart Home System with Voice Control Using NLP Methods. *Electronics* **2023**, *12*, 116. https://doi.org/10.3390/electronics12010116.
11. Popchev, I.; Radeva, I.; Doukovska, L. Oracles Integration in Blockchain-Based Platform for Smart Crop Production Data Exchange. *Electronics* **2023**, *12*, 2244. https://doi.org/10.3390/electronics12102244.
12. Luţan, E.R.; Bădică, C. Emotion-Based Literature Book Classification Using Online Reviews. *Electronics* **2022**, *11*, 3412. https://doi.org/10.3390/electronics11203412.
13. Legman, I.-D.; Gabor, M.R.; Kardos, M. An Innovative Tool to Measure Employee Performance through Customer Satisfaction: Pilot Research Using eWOM, VR, and AR Technologies. *Electronics* **2023**, *12*, 1158. https://doi.org/10.3390/electronics12051158.
14. Razzaq, A.; Altamimi, A.B.; Alreshidi, A.; Chayyur, S.A.K.; Khan, W; Alsaffar, M. IoT Data Sharing Platform in Web 3.0 Using Blockchain Technology. *Electronics* **2023**, *12*, 1233. https://doi.org/10.3390/electronics12051233.

electronics

MDPI

Article

Emotion-Based Literature Book Classification Using Online Reviews

Elena-Ruxandra Luţan * and Costin Bădică *

Department of Computers and Information Technology, University of Craiova, 200585 Craiova, Romania
* Correspondence: elena.ruxandra.lutan@gmail.com (E.-R.L.); costin.badica@edu.ucv.ro (C.B.)

Abstract: Reading is not only a recreational activity; it also shapes the emotional and cognitive competences of the reader. In this paper, we present a method and tools for the analysis of emotions extracted from online reviews of literature books. We implement a scraper to create a new experimental dataset of reviews gathered from Goodreads, a website dedicated to readers that contains a large database of books and readers' reviews. We propose a system which extracts the emotions from the reviews and associates them with the reviewed book. Afterwards, this information can be used to find similarities between the books based on readers' impressions. Lastly, we show the experimental setup, consisting of the user interface developed for the proposed system, together with the experimental results.

Keywords: natural language processing; Web scraping; emotion analysis

Citation: Luţan, E.-R.; Bădică, C. Emotion-Based Literature Book Classification Using Online Reviews. *Electronics* **2022**, *11*, 3412. https://doi.org/10.3390/electronics11203412

Academic Editors: Galina Ilieva and George A. Tsihrintzis

Received: 19 September 2022
Accepted: 19 October 2022
Published: 21 October 2022

1. Introduction

Nowadays, customer feedback plays a very important role for any producer of goods or provider of services. All companies aim to offer high-quality products that customers enjoy and are more likely to recommend to other peers, as this leads to attracting more and more customers, thus bringing an increased direct benefit for the well-being of the company.

E-marketing and digital branding techniques are highly used to promote products, but many studies have shown that the customers are usually mostly attracted by word-of-mouth [1] when making their purchase decisions. It has been observed that when a customer is satisfied with a company or product, he or she might tell other people about his or her experience. On the other hand, if the customer is dissatisfied, he or she is more likely to share the experience to all his acquaintances [2]. Considering this, companies are advised to regularly check their customers' feedback in order to see why customers are not content with their goods or services and, consequently, to improve in these sections.

In this paper, we focus on a specific category of products, literature books, and we are interested in analyzing the customer feedback related to them—book reviews.

Studies have shown that peers' opinions of a book is one of the top criteria on which people choose their next book to read [3,4]. Online reviews are very handy for readers who are interested in knowing about other peoples' experiences with reading certain books. This is because the reviews appreciate, critique or summarize the book, therefore giving the user the possibility to become familiar with the subject of the book and determine if it will be an enjoyable read [5].

In this context, we consider that it would be both interesting and useful to grasp how different aspects of online reviews, such as the emotions hidden behind the reviewers' words, contribute as general features of the book. Our aim is to identify the emotions triggered by reading books that are captured from online book reviews and use them in order to define an emotion-based categorization of books.

The main contribution of this paper is a new approach to book classification based on modeling and extracting emotions from book reviews. In particular, we provide new insights on how relevant the emotions are sentiment-wise by comparing them with the ground truth provided by the scaled rating attached to the review by the review author. Our results show that the emotions extracted from the reviews can be considered additional features of the book, and together with other relevant information, such as author and genre, can be used in our future work to generate better book recommendations.

Although our proposed method is not so computationally elaborate as other supervised ML techniques (including, for example, NN approaches), this is actually an advantage, as it offers good performance and low computation cost for accurately retrieving emotions from the reviews. In particular, there are no training and labelling costs as compared with the more complex supervised approaches.

We also propose an experimental system that extracts the emotions present in literature book reviews and assigns them as features of the reviewed book.

The paper is structured as follows. In Section 2, we present related works. Section 3 describes the design of the system, consisting of gathering the reviews, preprocessing the reviews' content, and extracting the emotions. In Section 4, we show the dataset overview and discuss the experimental results. Section 5 presents the conclusions and future work.

2. Related Works

Product reviews capture customers' evaluations of products or services. Online reviews are usually presented in a text form next to the product or service description on a website, sometimes accompanied by images and videos taken to support the review [6]. These reviews represent an important source of information for the provider, as well as for other potential customers, because they summarize the reasons for liking or disliking a product or service from the user perspective.

Performing an automated analysis of reviews assumes the availability of datasets that can be used for experiments in order to extract the user sentiments and emotions from the text. Therefore, we checked different datasets of books and reviews on the Internet. Ref. [7] offers a dataset of the 10 thousand most-rated books on the Goodreads website. The number of books and ratings in the dataset is impressive, but it does not help us because it only provides the number of ratings and not the review content. Ref. [8] provides a very good set of datasets for academic use, consisting of books, reviews and user information in JSON format, but it constrains us in choosing a certain book domain on which to perform the analysis.

After a short analysis, we concluded that existing datasets either did not include all the necessary details or the form in which the data were presented did not meet our needs and expectations. In this situation, we concluded that we needed to create our own scraping system to extract the necessary data from a website.

An analysis of how the books are classified into categories on the Goodreads website is provided by Melanie Walsh and Maria Antoniak in [9]. The Goodreads website offers a collaborative tagging system in which the users can group the books into virtual shelves; afterwards, these shelves or tags are used to classify the book into different literature genres. The article focuses on what determines the classification of a book as a "classic". Although limited in scope, this analysis still gave us a good background on the shelving system, the evolution of the website, and certain features of the reviews.

The same authors offer a scraper implementation [10], which collects the data used in the article [9] and stores it in JSON files. We consulted this implementation when developing our scraping system with regard to how we can overcome the problems caused by the windows popping up when loading the Goodreads pages, which hindered the automated scraping process.

In the article [11], M. Colhon et al. presented a method of analyzing sentiments of tourists' reviews. The dataset for experiments was extracted from the AmFostAcolo website, which is a Romanian website where tourists can share their travelling experiences. The authors proposed a method to compute the polarity of the review by counting positive and negative words inside the review. In order to define the positive and negative words, an English lexicon of words representing emotions was considered and translated into Romanian.

The research of M. Malik and A. Hussain [12] focused on the importance of emotions embedded in online reviews. They defined eight basic emotions for the text: four positive (joy, surprise, anticipation, trust) and four negative (angry, anxiety, sadness and disgust). For mapping the words from reviews with their corresponding emotions, they used a word-emotion association lexicon presented by The National Research Council Canada. For experiments, two different datasets were used, both referring to reviews of products belonging to a mixture of categories. The study highlights how emotions contribute to the helpfulness of online reviews.

An approach of classifying food restaurants using opinion mining was proposed by Y. Kumar et al. in [13]. The polarity of opinions is computed based on the attitude of public audiences or individuals in order to rate the review as positive or negative. The dataset for the experiments was retrieved from Kaggle, and it was split in two parts: 70% of reviews were used for training the data model, and the remaining 30% were used for making predictions. To compute the polarity of the review, the Text Blob library was used. The proposed model counts the words from the positive and negative reviews and assigns a rate to each word. These rates are later used to predict the polarity of a new review belonging to the test dataset.

Different methodologies of sentiment analysis of book reviews were presented by A. Mounika and Dr. S. Saraswathi in [14]. The authors described the stages of the sentiment analyzer which lead to categorizing the reviews into clusters. The clusters of reviews and their authors (users) can be used by a recommender system to provide personalized information.

K.S. Srujan et al. proposed a different approach based on supervised machine learning algorithms in [15] for classifying book reviews extracted from Amazon website. The idea was to map the reviews into numerical vectors based on techniques inspired from information retrieval and then apply machine learning classification algorithms to determine the sentiment score assigned to a review: positive, negative or neutral.

In [16], Valentina Franzoni et al. made a comparison between the emotions extracted from book blurbs and the emotion tags assigned by users through reviews. The dataset was extracted from Zazie, an Italian social network similar to Goodreads, which introduced emotional icon tagging as a new dimension for book descriptions. The idea of the research was to see if the emotions extracted from book blurbs are similar to the tags provided by the users and if an automated classification of books is possible with acceptable accuracy.

The authors R. Ganda and A. Mahmood [17] provided a model that uses pre-trained word vectors for sentence-level classification tasks together with recurrent neural networks. Although recurrent neural networks are efficient at capturing the semantics of the sentences, the computation incurred is a time-consuming task. The authors considered that using word vectors as an extra feature with recurrent neural networks can increase the performance of the system.

Zeng et al. [18] proposed an unsupervised model for sentiment classification that uses pairs of words composed of opinion words and target words. Using dependency parsers and a set of rules, the target-opinion words are extracted from reviews. The goal was to predict an opinion word given a target word.

In [19], David Robinson classified basic emotions depending on three attributes of the emotional experience and personality: emotions motivating a subjective quality, emotions that appear as a result of a certain event, and emotions that motivate a particular kind of behavior. Although the emotions were divided into detailed categories according to the three criteria of the mental experience, we are only interested into the subdivision of "positive emotions" and "negative emotions" presented in the article, which helps us classify our list of emotions into two categories.

The Human-Machine Interaction Network on Emotion (HUMAINE) [20] has proposed an emotion annotation and representation language (EARL) which classifies 48 emotions into the following categories: *negative and forceful, negative and not in control, negative thoughts, negative and passive, agitation, positive and lively, caring, positive thoughts, quiet positive, and reactive*. However, similarly to [19], we are interested only in the positive-negative classification, regardless of the other subcategories.

Emotions by groups is a concept developed by P. Shaver et al. [21] and also featured by W.G. Parrot [22]. This refers to the fact that starting from six primary emotions (*love, joy, surprise, anger, sadness, fear*), one can define related secondary and tertiary emotions. We use these emotion groups in order to map the secondary or tertiary emotions we have in the emotion file with the positive and negative emotions given by [19,20].

3. System Design

Conducting emotion analysis on a text refers to classifying the text based on the emotion carried by the words of the text. Then, this information can be used for different purposes, such as computing the emotions transmitted by a book, classifying the books into certain categories based on the emotions, or making recommendations of books that transmit similar sentiments. Our aim is to build a system for literature book classification based on the emotions that are present in online reviews of the books.

Figure 1 shows the system workflow containing the two main tasks performed by the system:

1. Data extraction from the Goodreads website and storage into CSV files;
2. Extraction of the emotions present in the reviews.

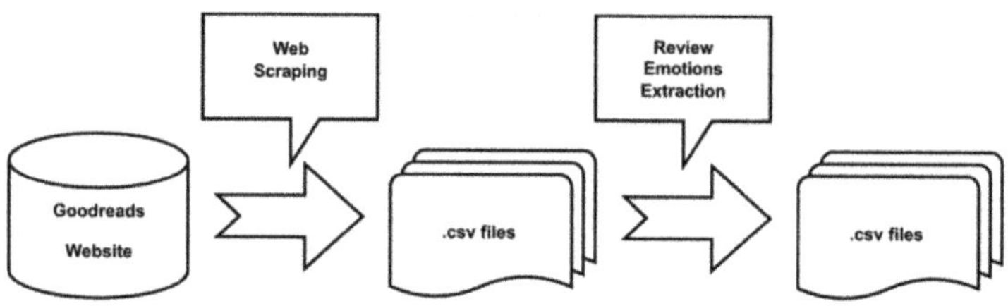

Figure 1. System workflow.

We propose the use of datasets extracted from the Goodreads website, which has a very large database. It is considered to be the world's largest website for readers and book recommendations with more than 3.5 billion books, 80 million comments and 125 million users [23]. It contains almost every existing book, and, depending on the popularity of the book, there are a great number of reviews to choose from.

After our initially visual and then more detailed manual inspection of the Goodreads Web pages, we noticed that their HTML content can be quite easy collected. The only disadvantage identified is that Goodreads does not provide much information about the users (book readers) that can be retrieved. This is caused by either the fact that either the user account is set to private or the user did not publish much information about him or herself. Because of this, we focused our analysis only on the contents of reviews and not on the users' information.

Three main entities that are relevant for our goal were identified on Goodreads Web pages: books, reviews, and users. For each entity, multiple attributes were extracted using Web page scraping. These attributes are illustrated in Figure 2.

Based on these entities, three different files are created using Web scraping, i.e., for each entity and its attributes, a separate file was created.

The goal of the first task was to collect the experimental dataset. We created a Python application to scrape the content of Goodreads website using Beautiful Soup [24]. We used a separate text file to specify which books have to be collected. For this, we wrote a book title on each line. The application goes through each line of the file and conducts a search on the Goodreads website using the available words in the book description. After accessing the page with the book specifications, the parser analyses the HTML content, extracts the fields of interest for the book description and creates a dictionary entry, which is stored inside the database of books.

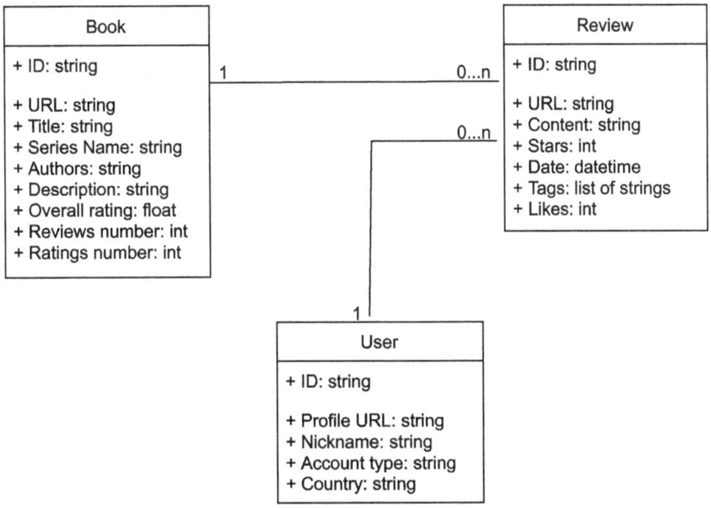

Figure 2. Entity and their relationships on Goodreads Web pages.

During its next step, the parser checks the comments section of the page in order to collect the reviews as well as other users' data. The fields that are retrieved for the two entities are described in Figure 2. By default, the Goodreads reviews are sorted by popularity, which is assessed by the reactions of other users to the respective reviews. On the website, a user has the possibility to react to a review by using a "like" button or by adding comments. We think it is an advantage for us to collect the reviews sorted by popularity, as we can assume that the most relevant reviews for analysis are the ones with the most reactions.

After the data are collected, we can start the sentiment and emotions analysis of the reviews. This refers to being able to classify the reviews as positive, negative or neutral and extracting the emotions from the text. The model uses a dimension of 35 emotions and a list of words associated with these emotions.

In order to perform a sentiment and emotion analysis of a text, it is necessary to prepare it by converting all letters into lowercase, removing punctuation and stop words. During the text preprocessing, we removed additional parts from the text, such as: duplicated letters to exaggerate the words (e.g., "ahhhhh", "I loooooove"), insertions of elements to create an atmosphere when reading the comment (e.g., *finally*, *spoiler alert*), and insertions of quotes from the book, URLs or emails. Algorithm 1 describes the complete process of preprocessing the review content for sentiment and emotion analysis.

Algorithm 1 Algorithm for preprocessing (cleaning) the review content

1: Convert letters to lowercase
2: Remove punctuation by replacing it with spaces
3: Remove duplicate letters used for exaggeration
4: Remove notes written between ** and ()
5: Remove quotes from the book
6: Remove URLs and emails
7: Remove new lines, tabs, multiple space characters
8: Remove stop words

Using the clean text, we compute the polarity of the review. The polarity is a real number in the range $[-1, 1]$, where 1 means positive and -1 means negative. By using the polarity, we can classify the comment as being positive (polarity > 0), negative (polarity < 0) or neutral (polarity = 0).

The polarity is computed using TextBlob, which is a Python library that offers a simple API to perform shallow NLP tasks [25]. The library uses a dictionary of English adjectives such that each adjective has a polarity value assigned according to its emotion. The overall polarity of the review is computed based on the polarities of the adjectives present in the review. Afterwards, the review polarity, together with the review classification (positive, negative or neutral) are added as new columns inside the review dataset.

The NLP Emotion Algorithm used in the project is inspired by [26]. It consists of cross-checking all the words of the review (clean text) with the words present inside an emotions file called *emotions.txt*. The emotions file contains a series of 517 adjectives from the English language. Each adjective is assigned an emotion. In total, there are 35 emotions considered: *'cheated', 'singled out', 'loved', 'attracted', 'sad', 'fearful', 'happy', 'angry', 'bored', 'esteemed', 'lustful', 'attached', 'independent', 'embarrassed', 'powerless', 'surprise', 'fearless', 'safe', 'adequate', 'belittled', 'hated', 'codependent', 'average', 'apathetic', 'obsessed', 'entitled', 'alone', 'focused', 'demoralized', 'derailed', 'anxious', 'ecstatic', 'free', 'lost', 'burdened'*.

In the implementation proposed by [26], each adjective from the *emotions.txt* file is checked for existence inside the review in order to compute the emotions list corresponding to the review. If the word is present in the review, the associated emotion is added into the emotions list. After analysis, for each review, we obtain a list of emotions in form of a counter object. This counter is useful because it provides us an image about the weight of a certain emotion inside the review.

Although the implementation [26] was able to extract emotions from the reviews, we realized that it provides only a light overview regarding the emotions present in the review.

The main disadvantage we observed is regarding repetitive words expressing emotions inside the review. In [26], the approach was to check if each adjective from *emotions.txt* is present inside the review, returning true or false output. This means that in case an adjective is used multiple times inside the review, the emotion expressed will only be counted once based on its first occurrence of the adjective. When conducting an emotion analysis, we consider this does not provide a good overview, because if a certain adjective occurs multiple times, the intensity of that emotion shall be taken into consideration in the analysis by increasing the weight of the respective emotion.

As a result of this observation, we decided to change the method of matching the words from the reviews with the adjectives from *emotions.txt* file. In our implementation, we split the review into words, check each of the words for presence inside *emotions.txt* and count the corresponding emotion if a match is found. In this way, each occurrence of emotion-relevant words inside the review will be taken into consideration when creating the emotion list of the review.

At this stage, we identified another aspect which can be improved regarding the counting of emotions. Because the *emotions.txt* file contains only adjectives, we are constrained by the occurrence of certain adjectives inside the review in order to determine the emotions. After an analysis, we observed that we can perform an approximate match regarding the words from the review and the adjectives from the *emotions.txt* file and therefore extract more detailed emotions specification.

As an example, before the approximate match update, the comment "I love this book. I appreciate the vision of the author." does not detect any emotion, because the *emotions.txt* file contains adjectives, and no exact match with the existing words can be done. On the other hand, after our improvement, the verb "love" was matched with the word "loved", and the verb "appreciate" with the word "appreciated", therefore extracting the associated emotions "esteemed attached loved".

Algorithm 2 shows the procedure used for extracting the emotions present inside a review.

With these changes, the time needed to analyze the comments was greatly increased, but we consider this a good compromise for obtaining a more detailed analysis of emotions of the comments.

Algorithm 2 Algorithm for extracting the emotions present in a review.

```
Clean the review content using Algorithm 1
Create an empty emotions list
for each word in review content do
    if word matches adjective in emotions.txt file then
        Extract the emotion associated with the word
        Add the emotion inside the emotions list
    end if
end for
Create a counter based on emotions list to reflect the weight of each emotion
```

The final step of the emotions analysis is to associate all the emotions found inside the reviews with the books. This refers to going through all the reviews for a book and creating an emotions list for the book by counting all the reviews' emotions and attaching them to the book.

4. Experiments and Discussions

4.1. Dataset Overview

For our project, we considered that it is important to execute the book selection in such way as to create a mini-universe to which we can apply the sentiment analysis algorithm in order to obtain a rich classification of the books based on their computed emotion-focused similarities.

The most important aspect for us when choosing the data for analysis is to have a large enough number of reviews. Therefore, we decided to select the books based on the top popular books available on the Internet. We used as inspiration the list of books provided in the article "100 books everyone should read before they die (ranked!)"[27].

In Table 1, we present a few quantitative figures regarding our dataset.

Table 1. Statistics of dataset collected from Goodreads website.

Entity	Number
Books	78
Reviews	6566
Users	2661

One of the attributes collected for each book is "review numbers", which represents the number of reviews available on Goodreads website for the respective book. In Figure 3, we can observe that 86% of the books contain more than ten thousand reviews.

Instead of a clear book categorization into genres, the Goodreads website uses the approach of shelves and tags to classify and organize the books. This shelves system is a collaborative tagging system where the users can give different tags for the same content (book) in order to categorize it. For each book, we considered the first 10 tags to determine the genre.

We created a word cloud to visualize the overall genre distribution of the books we have inside the dataset. This can be seen in Figure 4. We can see that most of the books belong to the same categories: classics, fantasy, fiction etc.

Note that, because of the collaborative tagging system, some of the genres are repeated, with small changes in naming, such as "Academic Read"—"Academic School", "Literature 19th"—"19th Century".

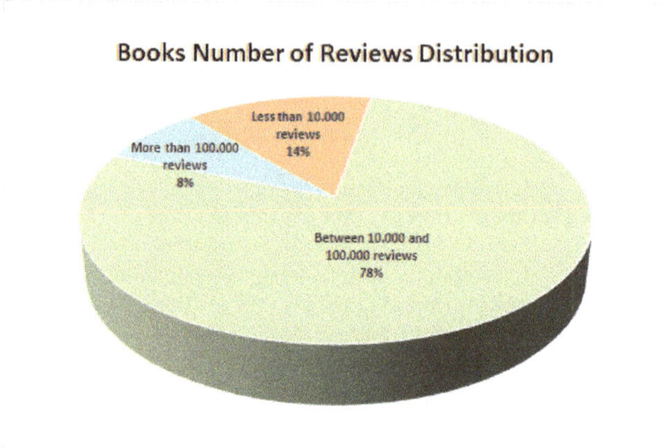

Figure 3. Books classification considering the number of reviews available on Goodreads website.

Figure 4. Genres of the collected books.

4.2. *Experimental Results*

We assumed that when doing the search, the first book that occurs in the search outcome will be the one we were looking for, since we are using well-known books, which should be at the top of the search. In practice, this depends on the query string used to perform the search. More specifically, we assumed that by using the combination of "book title" and "book author" for the search query, we would obtain the desired book. However, we noticed that rather often, other related books (especially literature guides to the books) were included in the list search results before the sought-after book.

Regarding the review dataset, we noticed that some of the reviews contained information written in languages other than English. Since we use the English language for the text analyzer, we had to remove comments and eventually parts of comments which were not written in English.

Another issue observed was that some of the comments, usually smaller ones, contained information which was not relevant for sentiment analysis or even had nothing to do with the book. For example, some of the reviews contained a short description of the pros or cons of the book, while others contained only links to review videos on other platforms.

We observe that the positive reviews are dominant in the dataset, with a percentage of 86%, followed by the negative reviews, representing 11% of the dataset; only 3% of the dataset consisted of neutral reviews (Figure 5). We consider that this distribution is also influenced by the way we collected the reviews. In the previous sections, we described that when collecting the reviews, we took the reviews ordered according to the default order present on Goodreads website; therefore, we expect the majority of reviews to be positive ones to influence the visiting user to read the respective book.

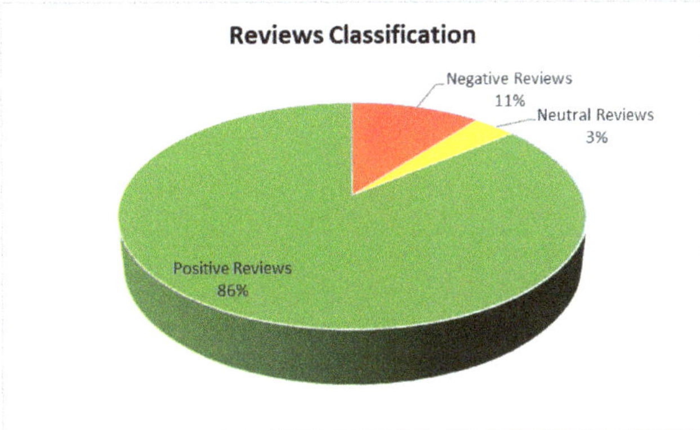

Figure 5. Classification of the reviews using polarity value.

In addition, we made an analysis consisting of the polarity classification combined with the number of stars given to the reviews, which can be seen in Figure 6. This is relevant in order to see the false positive or false negative classifications.

We can observe that we have a lot of reviews that received 1 or 2 stars, which were classified as "positive", although from the star number, we can consider that the user actually did not greatly enjoy the book. These are considered false-positive results. The number of false-negative results is lower, as we can see that a large part of the reviews with 3, 4 or 5 stars were classified as "positive", as expected.

Moreover, we also have reviews for which no star-scaled classification was done by the reviewer (column "0"). It can be seen that majority of these comments are positive ones, but we cannot consider them as good inputs for our sentiment analysis system.

	0	1	2	3	4	5
Negative	27	120	74	84	166	230
Neutral	19	13	15	20	58	108
Positive	126	210	226	581	1455	3034

Figure 6. Classification of the reviews using review stars and polarity.

Once the sentiments are extracted from the reviews, the sentiments are stored as an additional column inside the review dataset so that it can be easily accessed for future purposes. We decided to store the sentiments as counter objects because in this way we can see weight of each sentiment inside the review. An extract of the emotions column can be seen in Figure 7.

```
Emotions
[('happy', 7), ('attached', 4), ('fearful', 3), ('sad', 2), ('loved', 2), ('cheated', 2), ('fearless', 1), ('ecstatic', 1), ('attracted', 1), ('codependent', 1), ('lustful', 1), ('hated', 1), ('angry', 1)]
[('cheated', 7), ('attached', 5), ('happy', 4), ('fearful', 3), ('lustful', 3), ('fearless', 2), ('powerless', 2), ('sad', 2), ('apathetic', 2), ('entitled', 2), ('loved', 2), ('demoralized', 1), ('ecstatic', 1), ('hated', 1), ('singled out', 1), ('focused', 1)]
[]
[('cheated', 3), ('sad', 2), ('lustful', 2), ('happy', 2), ('loved', 1), ('powerless'. 1), ('obsessed', 1), ('entitled', 1), ('hated', 1), ('apathetic', 1), ('singled out', 1)]
[('bored', 1), ('powerless', 1), ('attached', 1)]
[('fearless', 18), ('fearful', 4), ('angry', 4), ('singled out', 3), ('independent', 3), ('cheated', 3), ('focused', 2), ('attracted', 2), ('attached', 2), ('happy', 2), ('entitled', 2), ('apathetic', 1), ('alone', 1), ('burdened', 1), ('esteemed', 1), ('pow
[('entitled', 14), ('happy', 13), ('sad', 11), ('cheated', 7), ('powerless', 7), ('fearful', 7), ('apathetic', 7), ('angry', 6), ('attracted', 5), ('hated', 3), ('loved', 3), ('singled out', 2), ('fearless', 2), ('belittled', 2), ('focused', 2), ('esteemed', 1), (
[('attracted', 8), ('sad', 8), ('angry', 5), ('happy', 5), ('attached', 5), ('powerless', 4), ('fearful', 4), ('hated', 4), ('average', 3), ('entitled', 3), ('singled out', 3), ('ecstatic', 2), ('alone', 2), ('codependent', 2), ('burdened', 2), ('fearless', 1), 
[('attached', 4), ('loved', 4), ('hated', 2), ('fearless', 1), ('sad', 1), ('apathetic', 1), ('happy', 1)]
[('powerless', 8), ('cheated', 7), ('entitled', 4), ('attracted', 3), ('happy', 3), ('fearful', 3), ('sad', 2), ('free', 2), ('attached', 1), ('lost', 1), ('esteemed', 1), ('surprise', 1)]
[('happy', 19), ('fearful', 14), ('sad', 11), ('powerless', 9), ('burdened', 9), ('angry', 9), ('attached', 8), ('anxious', 8), ('hated', 6), ('loved', 6), ('lustful', 4), ('apathetic', 4), ('safe', 4), ('entitled', 4), ('belittled', 1), ('attracted', 1), ('adequa
[('entitled', 4), ('happy', 4), ('attached', 3), ('fearless', 2), ('alone', 2), ('apathetic', 2), ('powerless', 2), ('cheated', 2), ('demoralized', 1), ('lost', 1), ('attracted', 1), ('codependent', 1), ('esteemed', 1), ('singled out', 1), ('loved', 1)]
[('happy', 5), ('fearful', 3), ('attracted', 2), ('sad', 2), ('bored', 2), ('apathetic', 2), ('attached', 2), ('entitled', 2), ('loved', 2), ('hated', 1), ('esteemed', 1), ('anxious', 1)]
[('attached', 6), ('happy', 2), ('loved', 2), ('sad', 1), ('hated', 1), ('free', 1), ('surprise', 1), ('lustful', 1)]
[('attached', 5), ('loved', 4), ('happy', 2), ('attracted', 1)]
[('happy', 3), ('cheated', 3), ('powerless', 1), ('attracted', 1), ('free', 1), ('sad', 1), ('apathetic', 1), ('hated', 1), ('attached', 1), ('angry', 1), ('lustful', 1), ('alone', 1), ('singled out', 1), ('loved', 1), ('anxious', 1)]
[('cheated', 4), ('singled out', 2), ('powerless', 1), ('lost', 1)]
[('happy', 2)]
```

Figure 7. Snapshot of the "emotions" column from the review dataset.

The book emotions were computed by adding the emotions present in all the reviews for the book. The counter of emotions for the book was added as an additional column called "emotions" to the books dataset, similarly to the one for reviews presented in Figure 7.

The last step in our analysis consisted of evaluating the emotions algorithm. For this, we divided the emotions into three categories (positive, negative and neutral) by considering a series of emotion classification studies ([19–22]), as follows: positive emotions—*'loved', 'attracted', 'happy', 'lustful', 'fearless', 'ecstatic', 'esteemed', 'safe', 'adequate', 'focused', 'entitled', 'independent', 'free', 'attached'*; negative emotions—*'sad', 'fearful', 'angry', 'bored', 'embarrassed', 'powerless', 'surprise', 'hated', 'alone', 'anxious', 'cheated', 'singled out', 'belittled', 'lost', 'burdened', 'alone', 'demoralized', 'apathetic', 'obsessed', 'derailed', 'codependent'*; neutral emotions—*'average', 'free'*.

Using the Eeotions column in the reviews dataset (Figure 7), for each review, we counted the total of positive, negative and neutral emotions whiel also taking into consideration their weight. In order to determine the correctness of our algorithm, we compared the emotion-based classification with the polarity-based classification. This is illustrated in Figure 8.

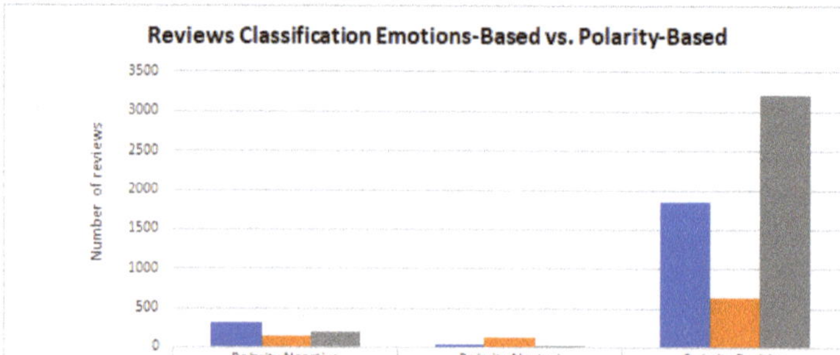

	Polarity Negative	Polarity Neutral	Polarity Positive
Emotions Negative	316	43	1853
Emotions Neutral	149	135	639
Emotions Positive	197	26	3208

Figure 8. Review classes considering emotion-based classification and polarity-based classification.

In Figure 8, we can observe that only 47,73% of the reviews classified as "negative" based on polarity are also classified as "negative" based on emotions. The remaining 52,27% seem to be classified as false positives if we consider that the polarity-based classification was conducted correctly. At a first glance, this would suggest our algorithm does not work correctly, but if we analyze their emotion-based classification with the review stars, we can observe that the emotion-based classification is actually correctly carried out (Figure 9).

The review stars are a valuable input because they are directly given by the user. In Figure 9, we can see that for a considerable number of "negative" reviews (polarity-based), the users have provided 4 or 5 stars, which suggests that the user has liked the book, so he or she actually provided a "positive" review.

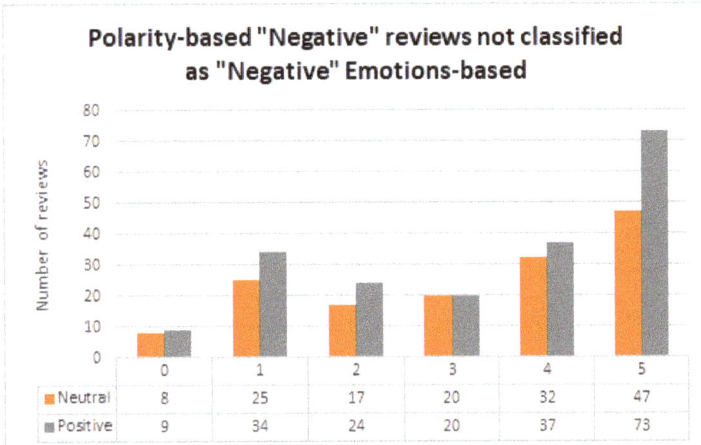

Figure 9. Review classes considering emotion-based classification and polarity-based classification.

Let us discuss some examples considering the two types of review classification, which are provided in Table 2. In the case of review 1917, we consider that the classification "neutral" reflects the 3-star rating provided by the user better than the "positive" classification assigned considering the polarity value, while for review 1915, the polarity-based classification better reflects the 4-star rating provided by the user. In review 1916, the user has given a 5-star rating to the book, so the expectation is that we have a positive review, which is the case for both the polarity-based classification and the emotion-based classification. Review 1918 is a clear example of a false-positive classification, because although the polarity-based classification and emotion-based classification are "positive", the used only provided a 2-star rating, which is unexpected.

Table 2. Extract of Reviews dataset.

Review Index	Review Stars	Polarity Classification	Emotions Classification
1915	4	Positive	Neutral
1916	5	Positive	Positive
1917	3	Positive	Neutral
1918	2	Positive	Positive

5. Conclusions and Future Work

In this paper, we presented a model of extracting the sentiment and emotions of literature books from online reviews. In the first stage, we designed the entities with the fields of interest and created a scraper to collect the dataset from the Goodreads website. The second stage consisted of retrieving the sentiments and emotions present in the online reviews. The sentiments were extracted using the TextBlob Python library. For the extraction of emotions, we used an implementation from Github as a starting point, which we improved in order to fulfill our needs. We re-worked the method of extracting the sentiments to take into consideration verbs or adjectives and arranging the extracted emotions such that they can be easily accessed for different use cases.

As future work, we aim to improve the extraction of emotions from the reviews by considering a larger emotions file or a library for emotions. Another future development refers to the usage of the emotion-based book classification with a particular scope, such as a recommender system, for providing literature recommendations to users or finding similarities between users who felt the same emotions when reading a certain book.

Author Contributions: Conceptualization, E.-R.L. and C.B.; methodology, E.-R.L. and C.B.; software, E.-R.L.; validation, E.-R.L. and C.B.; formal analysis, E.-R.L.; investigation, E.-R.L.; resources, E.-R.L.; data curation, E.-R.L.; writing—original draft preparation, E.-R.L.; writing—review and editing, E.-R.L. and C.B. All authors have read and agreed to the published version of the manuscript.

Funding: This research received no external funding.

Institutional Review Board Statement: Not applicable.

Informed Consent Statement: Not applicable.

Data Availability Statement: The source code and datasets are available at: https://drive.google.com/drive/folders/1aGTeWZRd4QK1t48u_0WAazu30Tla-jEc?usp=sharing (accessed on 18 September 2022).

Conflicts of Interest: The authors declare no conflict of interest.

References

1. Arndt, J. Role of Product-Related Conversations in the Diffusion of a New Product. *J. Mark. Res.* **1967**, *4*, 291–295. [CrossRef]
2. Chatterjee, P. Online Reviews: Do Consumers Use Them? In *Proceedings of the ACR 2001*; Association for Consumer Research: Provo, UT, USA, 2001; Volume 28, pp. 129–133.
3. Kragler, S. Choosing Books for Reading: An Analysis of Three Types of Readers. *J. Res. Child. Educ.* **2000**, *14*, 133–141. Available online: https://www.thefreelibrary.com/Choosing+Books+for+Reading%3A+An+Analysis+of+Three+Types+of+Readers.-a063567043 (accessed on 3 October 2022). [CrossRef]
4. Noblit, C. How Readers Pick What to Read Next. Available online: https://www.writtenwordmedia.com/how-readers-pick-what-to-read-next (accessed on 3 October 2022).
5. Woodard, G. Why Book Reviews Are Important to Authors and Readers. Available online: https://www.dudleycourtpress.com/book-reviews (accessed on 3 October 2022).
6. Lackermair, G.; Kailer, D.; Kanmaz, K. Importance of Online Product Reviews from a Consumer's Perspective. *Adv. Econ. Bus.* **2013**, *1*, 1–5. [CrossRef]
7. Zygmunt Zając. Github: Goodbooks-10k. Available online: https://github.com/zygmuntz/goodbooks-10k (accessed on 31 Augsut 2022).
8. UCSD Book Graph—Goodreads Datasets. Available online: https://sites.google.com/eng.ucsd.edu/ucsdbookgraph/home (accessed on 31 August 2022).
9. Walsh, M.; Antoniak, M. The Goodreads "Classics": A Computational Study of Readers, Amazon, and Crowdsourced Amateur Criticism. *J. Cult. Anal.* **2021**, *4*, 243–287. [CrossRef]
10. Antoniak, M. Goodreads Scraper. Available online: https://github.com/maria-antoniak/goodreads-scraper (accessed on 26 April 2022).
11. Colhon, M.; Bădică, C.; Sendre, A. Relating the Opinion Holder and the Review Accuracy in Sentiment Analysis of Tourist Reviews. In Proceedings of the 7th International Conference on Knowledge Science, Engineering and Management, KSEM, Sibiu, Romania, 16–18 October 2014; Lecture Notes in Computer Science; Springer: Cham, Switzerland, 2014; Volume 8793, pp. 246–257.
12. Malik, M.; Hussain, A. Helpfulness of product reviews as a function of discrete positive and negative emotions. *Comput. Hum. Behav.* **2017**, *73*, 290–302. [CrossRef]
13. Kumar, Y.; Sai, B.; Shailaja, V.; Renuka, S.; Panduri, B. Python NLTK Sentiment Inspection using Naïve Bayes Classifier. *Int. J. Recent Technol. Eng.* **2019**, *8*, 2S11.
14. Mounika, A.; Saraswathi, S. Classification of book reviews based on sentiment analysis: A survey. *Int. J. Res. Anal. Rev.* **2019**, *6*, 150–155.
15. Srujan, K.S.; Nikhil, S.S.; Raghav Rao, H.; Karthik, K.; Harish, B.; Keerthi Kumar, H. Classification of Amazon Book Reviews Based on Sentiment Analysis. In *Information Systems Design and Intelligent Applications*; Bhateja, V., Nguyen, B., Nguyen, N., Satapathy, S., Le, D.N., Eds.; Advances in Intelligent Systems and Computing; Springer: Singapore, 2018; Volume 672.
16. Franzoni, V.; Poggioni, V.; Zollo, F. Automated Classification of Book Blurbs According to the Emotional Tags of the Social Network Zazie. In Proceedings of the First International Workshop on Emotion and Sentiment in Social and Expressive Media: Approaches and perspectives from AI (ESSEM 2013), AI*IA 2013 Conference, Tourin, Italy, 3 December 2013; CEUR-WSAt: Turin, Italy, 2013; Volume 1096, pp. 83–94.
17. Ganda, R.; Mahmood, A. Sentiment Analysis with Recurrent Neural Network and Unsupervised Neural Language Model. In Proceedings of the 42nd IEEE International Conference on Acoustics, Speech, and Signal Processing (ICASSP), New Orleans, LA, USA, 5–9 March 2017.

18. Zeng, Z.; Zhou, W.; Liu, X.; Lin, Z.; Song, Y.; Kuo, M.D.; Chiu, W.H.K. A Variational Approach to Unsupervised Sentiment Analysis. *arXiv* **2020**, arXiv:2008.09394.
19. Robinson, D.L. Brain function, emotional experience and personality. *Neth. J. Psychol.* **2009**, *64*, 152–167. [CrossRef]
20. HUMAINE Emotion Annotation and Representation Language (EARL). Available online: https://web.archive.org/web/20080411092724/http://emotion-research.net/projects/humaine/earl (accessed on 8 September 2022).
21. Shaver, P.; Schwartz, J.; Kirson, D.; O'connor, C. Emotion knowledge: Further exploration of a prototype approach. *J. Personal. Soc. Psychol.* **1987**, *52*, 1061–1086. [CrossRef]
22. Shaver, P.; Schwartz, J.; Kirson, D.; O'connor, C.: Emotion Knowledge: Further Exploration of a Prototype Approach, In *Emotions in Social Psychology. Essential Readings*; Parrott, W.G., Ed.; Reading 1; Taylor & Francis: Abingdon, UK, 2001; pp. 26–56.
23. Goodreads Statistics, User Counts, Facts & News. Available online: https://expandedramblings.com/index.php/goodreads-facts-and-statistics/ (accessed on 31 August 2022).
24. Beautiful Soup Documentation. Available online: https://beautiful-soup-4.readthedocs.io/en/latest/ (accessed on 17 August 2022).
25. Loria, S. TextBlob: Simplified Text Processing. Available online: https://textblob.readthedocs.io/en/dev/ (accessed on 17 August 2022).
26. Bhatt, A. Twitter Sentiment Analysis. Available online: https://github.com/attreyabhatt/Sentiment-Analysis (accessed on 17 August 2022).
27. D'Onfro, J. 100 Books Everyone Should Read before They Die (Ranked!). Available online: https://www.businessinsider.com/100-books-everyone-should-read-amazon-goodreads-2015-3 (accessed on 17 August 2022).

electronics

MDPI

Article

Adoption of Digital Business Solutions: Designing and Monitoring Critical Success Factors

Rositsa Doneva [1] and Silvia Gaftandzhieva [2,*]

1 Faculty of Physics and Technology, University of Plovdiv "Paisii Hilendarski", 4000 Plovdiv, Bulgaria
2 Faculty of Mathematics and Informatics, University of Plovdiv "Paisii Hilendarski", 4000 Plovdiv, Bulgaria
* Correspondence: sissiy88@uni-plovdiv.bg

Abstract: The success of a business organization on its path to digital transformation depends on the success of the various stages of the project in order to adopt the selected digital business solutions. The success of this project is determined to a large extent by identifying and monitoring critical success factors (CSFs) for these stages. Based on the studies in the field of CSFs and consultations with experts from the ICT sector and academia, the paper presents a comprehensive framework for the overall management of CSFs (from CSFs' design to their monitoring). The framework helps business organizations conceptualize CSFs for different stages of a project for the adoption of a chosen digital business solution. Furthermore, the framework provides practical guidance in the form of a framework, a methodology on what organizations should do to identify, monitor and manage the proper CSFs so that they can take the most advantage of them. The proposed framework has broad practical application and can be used by companies implementing projects for the digitalization of their activity to improve the digital services offered and advance the organization's efficiency, etc. Currently, aiming to validate the presented framework, it will be applied for the adoption of a customer relationship management (CRM) digitalization solution, based on a cooperation agreement with a national company from the internet and TV service delivery industry. The framework can be further developed and applied to other project types.

Keywords: digital business solutions; adoption; project; CSFs; design; monitoring

Citation: Doneva, R.; Gaftandzhieva, S. Adoption of Digital Business Solutions: Designing and Monitoring Critical Success Factors. *Electronics* **2022**, *11*, 3494. https://doi.org/10.3390/electronics11213494

Academic Editor: Juan M. Corchado

Received: 1 October 2022
Accepted: 26 October 2022
Published: 28 October 2022

1. Introduction

The success of a business organization on its path to digital transformation depends on the success of the various stages of the project (such as adoption, implementation and use) in order to adopt the selected digital business solutions. The success of this project is determined to a large extent by identifying factors or prerequisites that are critical for these stages. These factors are known as critical success factors (CSFs).

Knowledge/identification of CSFs and understanding the interactions between them provides a positive, beneficial effect on the results of such innovative projects and the achievements of organizations [1–3].

CSFs for a company are such factors, the implementation of which allows the concentration of resources in areas where the company can achieve a significant benefit over its main competitors and gain a better position in the target market. The competitiveness of the company and the successful implementation of its various projects depend on the practical use of CSFs.

The concept of CSFs was proposed in the 1960s by R. Daniel [4]. Its main principles, steps for data collection and analysis needed to form the right set of CSFs, sources and goals of CSFs applications have been developed in detail by Rockart and his team at the Massachusetts Institute of Technology [5]. They define CSFs as a small number of key activity areas (issues, factors) in which achieving satisfactory results would ensure competitive success for an individual employee, unit or the entire organization. Their distinguishing feature is their small number—only really important, "critical" to the success areas of activity on which to focus.

The following main goals of the application of CSFs can be formulated as follows:

- to identify the individual information needs of top managers;
- for the needs of the strategic, long-term and annual planning process;
- when it is planned, to create an information system for the organization that meets the information needs of top managers.

Bullen and Rockart [5] assign to the fundamental sources of CSFs the characteristics of the general environment (political, social and technological) and the economic sector, the competitive strategy and the competitive position of the company, the time factors and the specifics of the company management structure. They propose a procedure for CSF formation, which requires a series of interviews with the organization's top management to be conducted. Initially, individual interviews are conducted with the top management to reveal their views on CSFs. Then, the results are analyzed and summarized by compiling a preliminary list of success factors. The list of CSFs is discussed, and based on this, the final set of CSFs is determined, which operate on a company-wide scale. Then, the management information systems, which are oriented to facilitate the work with the information related to these factors, are developed. It is important to note that in their studies in the field, Rockart and his team have focused mainly on identifying the information needs of managers and planning the development of information systems to meet these needs.

Over time, CSFs are used for more and more other application purposes related to the activities of economic subjects [6–10], e.g., in the process of strategic planning and analysis, to identify opportunities and threats to business, to measure people's productivity, as a tool used from the top management of organizations to achieve high efficiency [11–17] or in project management (incl. projects for the adoption of business applications, e.g., ERP systems [2,3,14,18,19], CRM systems [20–22], projects for digitalization and adoption of advanced manufacturing technologies [23–29], etc.). As a rule, CSFs are associated with various areas of the company's activity, such as technology, production, marketing, sales, management, and staff training. Moreover, the term CSF is adapted according to its application area, i.e., it is defined in the context of a specific domain. For example, some standards and documents in the field of Information Technology (IT) should be mentioned, (e.g., CobiT and ITIL [30]). The framework for IT management CobiT (Control Objectives for Information and Related Technologies) examines CFCs that identify the most important actions of managers to achieve control over IT processes [31]. The engines, goals, success factors and consequences of digital transformation are studied in [32] with a focus on information systems.

In regard to the various purposes of the application of CSFs, different methods and sources suitable for CSFs identification are proposed, e.g., analysis of the external environment, analysis of the industry structure, analysis of competition, expert surveys, internal analysis, and comparative research [5,12,13,33–35].

The literature addresses another significant problem related to CSFs: the usefulness of identified CFCs remains questionable if they are not monitored and managed [36]. The latter requires planning a logical sequence of activities (called a model for CSFs monitoring in this paper) to provide the process to ensure their management and impact on the improvement of the results and/or project success in the company [37]. Most often, the issue of monitoring and periodic evaluation of CSFs is considered in connection with the strategic management of companies [38]. However, a literature review indicates a lack of sufficient general studies in this area.

All the information mentioned thus far shows that at the moment, no universal (in terms of the purpose of application of CSFs, the business domain of the company and its areas of activity) way to determine CSFs, nor to monitor them cannot be specified. Therefore, the management of each company must be able to diagnose accurately and manage overtime factors that are most important for the company's success as a whole or for the success of a project based on the specific characteristics of its area and goals to which CFCs will apply.

The paper aims to answer the above need by proposing a comprehensive framework for the overall management of CSFs—from CSFs' design to their monitoring. The framework is dedicated to CSFs with a specific purpose, namely, the management of projects for the adoption of ICT solutions for digitalization. The framework helps business organizations conceptualize CSFs for different project stages for the adoption of a chosen digital business solution. Furthermore, the framework provides practical guidance, and a methodology on what organizations should do to identify, monitor and manage the proper CSFs so that they can take the most advantage of them. The type of projects to which the framework is applicable was not randomly chosen because the success of any company in today's digital transformation depends on the success of the almost daily implementation of various ICT digitalization solutions. The research and the resulting framework for designing and monitoring the CSFs presented here are based on the review of research in the field of CSFs, but the specifics of the digitalization on projects are also consulted with experts from the ICT sector and academia.

The following sections of the paper present the framework in two parts. Part 1 "CSFs Design" of the framework contains specific guidelines for identifying CSFs and their overall design (Section 2). Part 2 "CSFs Monitoring" is dedicated to the proper organization of the CSFs management and monitoring process (Section 3). A methodology for implementing the framework is also proposed (Section 4). The conclusion summarizes the research contribution and implications in the field, the limitations of the presented study and plans for future studies.

2. Framework Part 1. CSFs Design

Undoubtedly, the best business practices are evolving towards the use of CSFs. Since there is no unambiguous answer to the question of which internal factors are decisive for the success of the adoption of a chosen digital business solution, this section presents an approach that companies can follow to identify the sources and determine the right set of CSFs that would ensure the success of the individual stages of such a complex project.

2.1. CSFs Sources

Based on the research in the field of CSFs (see Section 1), the following primary sources of CSFs can be proposed in the adoption of a project for digital business solutions (Figure 1):

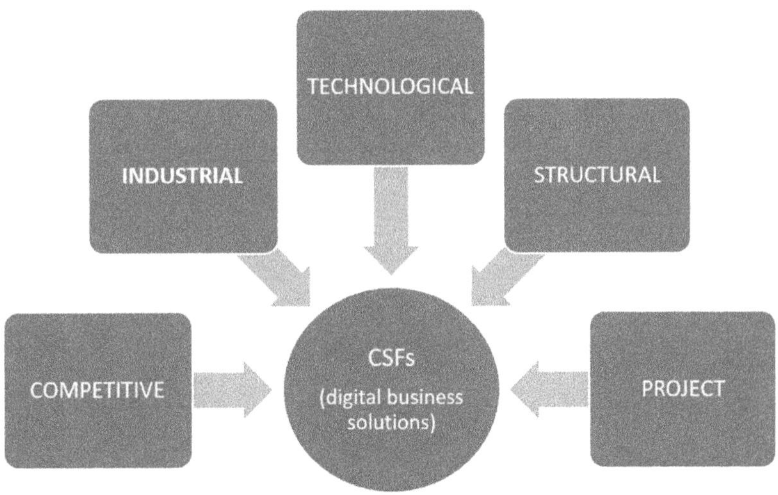

Figure 1. CSFs sources.

The characteristics of the industry/business domain of the company (industrial). Each industry has its CSFs, which must be realized and taken into account when developing the business strategy and projects for the company's digitalization. The organization's managers should focus their attention on these factors because the implementation of the branch CSFs largely determines the company's competitiveness. However, we should not forget that overtime sectoral CSFs may change under the influence of changes in the general situation in the industry.

- The competitive strategy and competitive position of the business organization to partners (competitive/partner). CSFs depend on the organization's rate in the industry compared to its competitors, its history and competitive strategies.
- The characteristics of the technological environment (technological)—in the classical theory related to CSFs, characteristics of the general environment (economic, political, social and technological) are taken into account here. However, the proposed framework mainly considers technological innovations in the digitalization field. These innovations should be important particularly in this case and have a significant impact on the adoption of projects for digital business solutions.
- The peculiarities of the management structure(structural)—this source determines the factors that depend on the internal organization's management structure and the managers' responsibilities at different levels (specific to the direction of the industry in which the organization operates).
- Requirements for the success of the project(project)—this source determines the internal factors (competencies and resources) that determine the success of the project and the related stages and activities.

In some cases, the so-called time factors can be considered. There may be periods in the company's operations when certain areas of activity prove be critical due to some exceptional circumstances, such as during a merger/separation of companies, when the company begins to operate in other areas or enters a new market. If the period of strategic planning of the organization, which is associated with the determination of CSFs, implies such circumstances, then the relevant CSFs must be determined. Under normal conditions, as in this case, CSFs are not determined in these areas.

The proposed set of CSFs sources is too general. It could be expanded to consider the specifics of a particular company.

To better understand the company's control capabilities and ensure the achievement of its goals, it is important to classify the sources and their respective CSFs into internal and external.

External sources of CSFs include the structure and general condition of the market; the current business climate; the economic, political and social situation; the level of demand/competence of the society concerning the product/service offered by the company; trends in the development of the industry.

The internal sources of CSFs can include the company's competitive strategy and position, time factors, the specifics of the company's management structure and the specifics of the direction of the industry in which the organization operates.

The macro-environment determines external CSFs, but the specific business organization must consider and ensure their availability to achieve its goals and fulfil the company's mission.

The micro-environment determines internal CSFs. They are in the field of issues on which decision-making is influenced significantly by the management activities of the company's governance.

CSFs can also be divided into factors oriented towards the monitoring of ongoing activities of the organization or improving and developing the business direction.

Attention should be paid to the fact that business organizations can develop and implement CFCs in their activities with different scope. Some CSFs are determined by strategic goals (corporate). Other CSFs relate to the level of departments, units, project teams or the level of individual heads of organizational units (collective). All of them are influenced by the more general, industrial CSFs.

2.2. Designing

When designing CSFs to successfully adopt a project for digital business solutions in a company, each of the above sources (see Section 2.1) is important to identify the correct set of CSFs. The company inherits a part of the CSFs from the industry in which it operates and the characteristics of the general environment. Another part of the CSFs is determined by internal sources. To be able to design CSFs and use them as a tool for managing success, it is important to systematize the factors identified by all these sources following four design stages (DS) and activities described below.

2.2.1. DS1. Defining the Scope of CSFs

There are two main activities at this stage (Figure 2). As CSFs exist for different levels of management in the organization, the scope of CSFs to be developed (i.e., corporate or for a separate operating unit) must be taken into account. Once the level of CSFs has been determined, participants who will be involved in the work on determining CSFs can be identified.

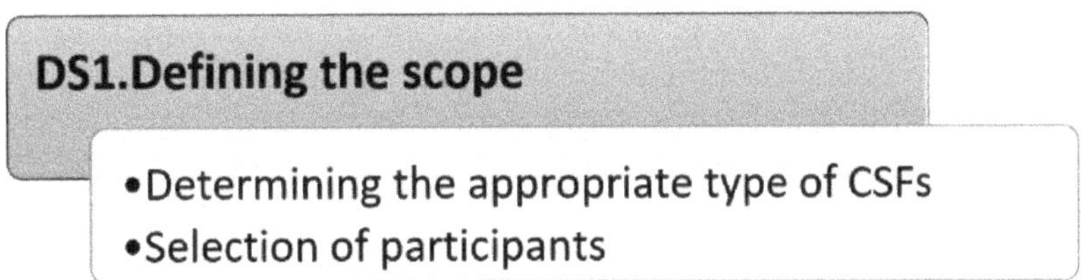

Figure 2. Design of CSFs: Stage 1.

The main reason for determining the scope of the designed CSFs in the discussed case is contained in the purpose of application of these CFCs (see Section 2)—for management of projects for the digital business solution adoption but also, in the nature of the particular solution itself. Depending on whether the solution chosen by the company aims to make changes in the whole company or only its separate unit/department/activity/team, it will need to develop corporate CFCs or collective CFCs, respectively.

Several other factors can be taken into account when determining the scope of CSFs:

- Corporate CSFs are strongly related to and are somewhat derived from the collective CSFs of the operational units of the organization. However, in the absence of time to determine the CSFs of each organization unit, a set of corporate CSFs may be created to be representative of all operational units.
- If the organization structure is flat (i.e., there are not many layers of management), a set of corporate CSFs can actually be highly representative and be applied instead of any necessary set of collective CSFs.
- On the other hand, the organization can have many layers of management and many divisions, sometimes even involved in different industries. Even in such cases, it is required to create corporate CSFs, it will be best to develop collective CSFs for individual divisions, as essentially each is a separate, functioning organization.

For example, if the digital business solution is related to digitalization and optimization of the company's internal processes to provide better products, the choice will be to develop collective CSFs. While if the digital business solution aims to improve the overall digital presence and company opportunities, then CSFs will have a corporate scope.

The type of CSFs strongly influences the decisions for selecting participants to be involved in their development.

For corporate CSFs, a more general view of CEOs and other organization's top managers is vital in creating a set of valid and representative CSFs.

The development of collective CFUs requires the involvement of high-level unit/team managers and top-level managers. It is also important to remember that the operational unit is part of a larger organization, so the involvement of some senior officials and roles can also be useful.

2.2.2. DS2. Providing the Necessary Data

At this stage (Figure 3), it is necessary to collect the raw data as a basis for CSFs extraction.

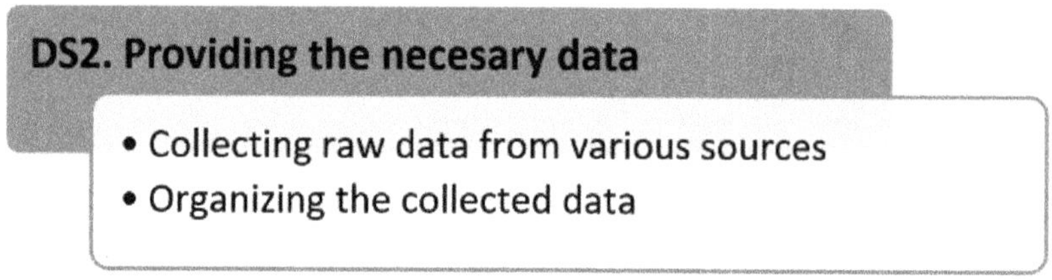

Figure 3. Design of CSFs: Stage 2.

Sources of relevant data to define CFUs may include the following:

- the stated, documented mission and vision of the organization and/or the operational unit;
- the indicated goals and tasks for the current year (fiscal or calendar) for the participants in the CSFs activities;
- performance indicators, collected about all stated goals and tasks;
- the short-term plan of the organization/operational unit or the long-term strategic plan;
- internal audit reports or other relevant documents;
- annual reports and other similar documents;
- industry reports for the primary industry to which the activity of the organization relates;
- scientific or technical literature representing existing related CSF sets or related analyses;
- CSFs of partner or branch organizations from the same branch;
- opinions on the CSFs of the staff of the company/unit.

All data collected from documents, interviews or other sources should be organized to facilitate subsequent analysis. This means grouping the same data type by certain characteristics, such as content, similar organizational functions, levels of management or problems. If notes are collected (e.g., from interviews), it is good to use a common format. To ensure that the collected data are ready for analysis, we have to check them for accuracy and completeness and, if necessary, to correct and supplement them.

Examples of approaches and sources for data collection to determine CSFs can be found in almost all literature sources cited in this paper. Although they do not affect projects for the adoption of digital business solutions, they can provide important guidance for the data collection phase in this particular case as well.

2.2.3. DS3. Data Analysis

This stage aims to categorize and analyze the raw data so that they can be used to extract CSFs. This requires some formatting and conversion of the raw data to the main components of CSFs. This "normalization" process prepares the data to meet the following requirements:

- independence—not to indicate which of the staff provided them (to avoid bias or influence);
- condensation—to be shortened to the level of their essential meaning or idea (to remove ambiguity);
- shape—to be converted into controllable pieces or units that can be analyzed.

The most basic approach that can be used for this stage is the direct analysis of the raw data by the participants in the development of CSFs, relying on their experience and intuition.

However, the above approach does not apply to CSFs related to larger and more complex companies, units or projects, such as the discussed digitalization project. In such cases, various structured tools, models, frameworks and methods are used to "normalize" the data, such as the method of interpretive structural modelling [11,39–42] or structured similarity analysis [43].

Based on the structured approaches to raw data analysis found in the literature and practice, this paper proposes a method for converting raw data to key components of CSFs for the success of a project for digital business solutions, which is an iterative process consisting of two recurring activities (Figure 4).

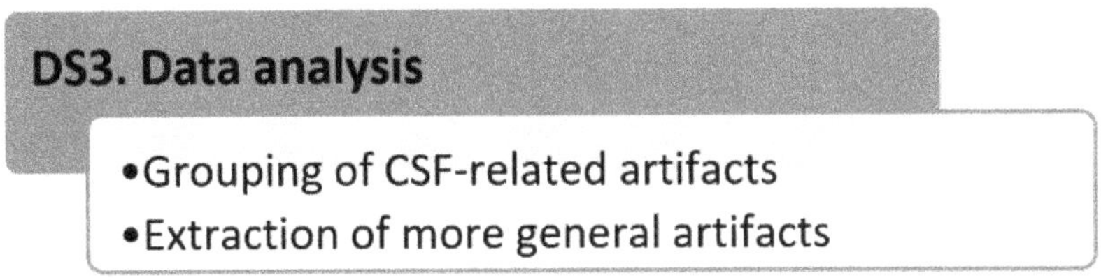

Figure 4. Design of CSFs: Stage 3.

At each step of the iteration, the available CSF-related artefacts are grouped by similarity (according to general characteristics or qualities) to reduce them by extracting more common artefacts from each group. In the first step, the available artefacts are all that can be found by reviewing the data collected (from documents, interviews, etc.) in the previous stage. The resulting (more general) artefacts from each step represent CSFs candidates and are input to the next step of the analysis.

The specific goal of the developed CSFs application and related basic concepts, intentions, etc., are leading in this categorization process. In this case, the subjects of this framework are digital business solutions, project management, and digital changes in the company or its unit. Business and operational goals and activities of their management in general and in connection with the chosen digital business solution must be added to them.

This iterative process continues until a sufficiently small number of artefacts are retrieved at a given step, which ultimately represents the desired set of CSFs candidates.

An example is considered (Table 1) for extracting artefacts from the mission of a randomly selected company (Legal Advice Company, Progressive Lawyers, https://progressive.legal/bg/nashata-misia-vision-and-values/ accessed on 1 October 2022) to illustrate the steps of the raw data analysis. The artefacts that are related to CSFs (for strategic management) are marked in the text of the mission (left column of Table 1), and more general artefacts that are candidates for CSFs (right column of Table 1) are derived from them.

Table 1. Design of CSFs: Illustration of Stage 3.

Mission	CSFs Artefacts (Candidates for CSFs)
Our mission is *to help our clients achieve their goals* by taking into account their interests, understanding their needs and meeting and even exceeding their expectations.	Customer relationship management.
We dare to *offer creative, practical and effective solutions*, with an emphasis on *effective communication*, responsiveness and attention to details.	Attracting and developing human resources (staff).
We dare to work hard for the success of our clients to *provide timely legal services* while *maintaining the highest standards of professional integrity*.	Provide high quality products and services to customers.
We dare to commit ourselves by *providing efficient and appropriate legal services*, applying *the advantages of modern technologies*.	Using modern IT strategically.

2.2.4. DS4. CSFs Identification

According to theoretical research on CSFs, they have greater clarity, usability and impact when they can be reduced to short and concise sentences that reflect the main intentions and essence of CSFs. In this direction, the last stage (Stage 4) of the CSFs' design is carried out. This stage includes two main activities (Figure 5). At this stage, to determine the final set of CSFs, it is recommended to perform a survey among top managers and/or heads of structural units to analyze the candidates for CSFs obtained as a result of Stage 3. Then, the final set of CSFs can be derived, and this set is to be used as a tool to ensure the successful adoption of a project for digital business solutions.

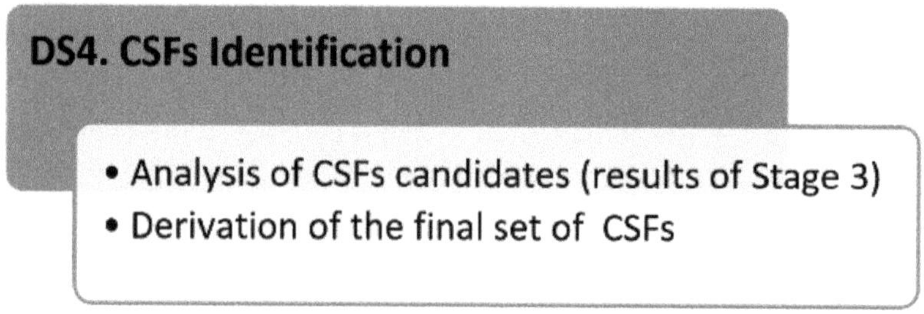

Figure 5. Design of CSFs: Stage 4.

The starting point for implementing these activities is considering the qualities that define CSF as excellent. To be considered as a qualitative, the CSF must:

- be worded clearly, concisely and be easy to understand. Interpretations by different managers are not relied upon to understand the CSFs' meaning;
- propose specific actions or activities performed by the organization/unit, typical for the operational work or the business domain;
- suggest improvements or recommendations which have to be made;
- begin with verbs describing actions or activities—attract, perform, expand, observe, manage, expand, etc.

Other additional general characteristics of CSFs of a project or organization are that they are specific, measurable, achievable, relevant and time-bounded [44].

Unfortunately, the number of existing literature sources addressing this topic is small. A large number of them are popular publications on online platforms, mostly dedicated to strategic CSFs for successful digital business transformation (e.g., Critical Success Factors for Each Phase of Digital Transformation [45]). The author has identified 14 CSFs (rather recommendations) for the successful implementing planning, design and development phases of the overall digital transformation of a company that seeks to make the transition from standard software systems to intelligent platforms to provide a modern level of connectivity with people, business networks, technologies such as the internet of things, big data and everything new that the future has to offer:

1. Planning:
    - Starting with the end in mind;
    - Identifying value drivers;
    - Discovering your potential;
    - Developing a plan for digital transformation;
    - Deploying in the cloud, on-premise, or hybrid;
    - Choosing greenfield or brownfield project investment;
    - Partnering to move ahead;
2. Design:
    - Jump-starting the design process;
    - Get a seat at the table;
    - Controlling complexity;
3. Development:
    - Sprinting to the finish line;
    - Taking a factory-like approach to configuration;
    - Automating the testing process;
    - Transitioning to operations.

Other publications on the subject are [46–52]. A specific example of CSFs that have a similar subject for development of those of this framework—digital business solutions—are the 10 CSFs identified for the needs of introduction of electronic payment systems in the bank sector [42]: coherence, complexity, customer demand, support from senior management, infrastructure, expert selection, security, cultural factors, government policies, awareness.

Adherence to the four main stages and the activities included in them (Figure 6) would ensure the design of the right set of CSFs for any CSF initiative, including the case covered by this paper.

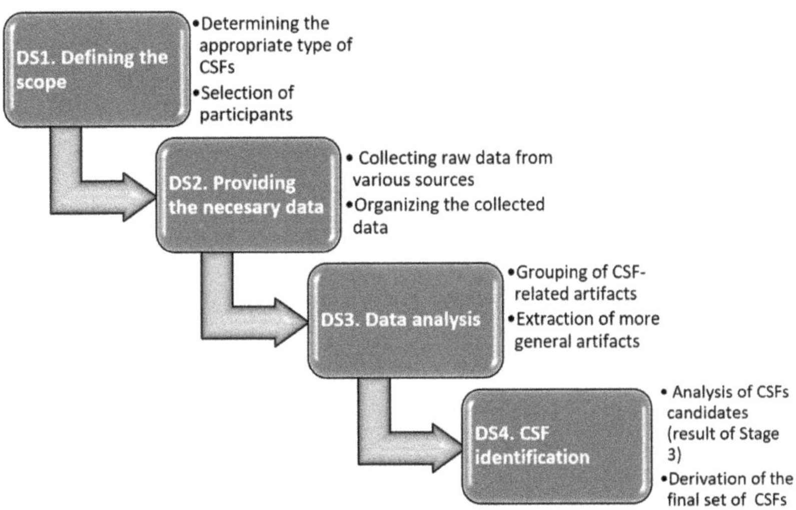

Figure 6. Design of CSFs: Stages 1–4.

3. Framework Part 2. CSFs Monitoring

The identification of CSFs is not enough—it is only part of the complete process of their establishment, management and monitoring to achieve the desired benefits and objectives for which they are developed. Undoubtedly, the advantages of CSFs would be "incomplete" without following a predetermined process of CSFs management and monitoring [37].

The literature review of the available sources indicates a lack of empirical and theoretically oriented research on CSFs management. This fact leads to a limited understanding of the actual benefit of CSFs, as the focus is only on identifying them. However, experts widely recognize the crucial importance and the need to provide such guidance to managers of organizations/units/projects that apply the methods of CSFs to achieve the goals of their initiatives.

It is necessary to go beyond the typical approach of simply identifying CFCs, providing resources and guidance on what action plan to follow in the process of management interventions based on CSFs to deploy the potential of the practical benefit of CSFs.

This section presents a theoretical model (see Section 1) for CSFs monitoring and overall management of the process for ensuring their impact on improving the results and (or) success of the venture/project of the company. The model covers four monitoring stages (MS) of activities (Figure 7), which are a natural continuation of the stages for CSFs design. Therefore, the monitoring process starts from the last stage of the CSFs design.

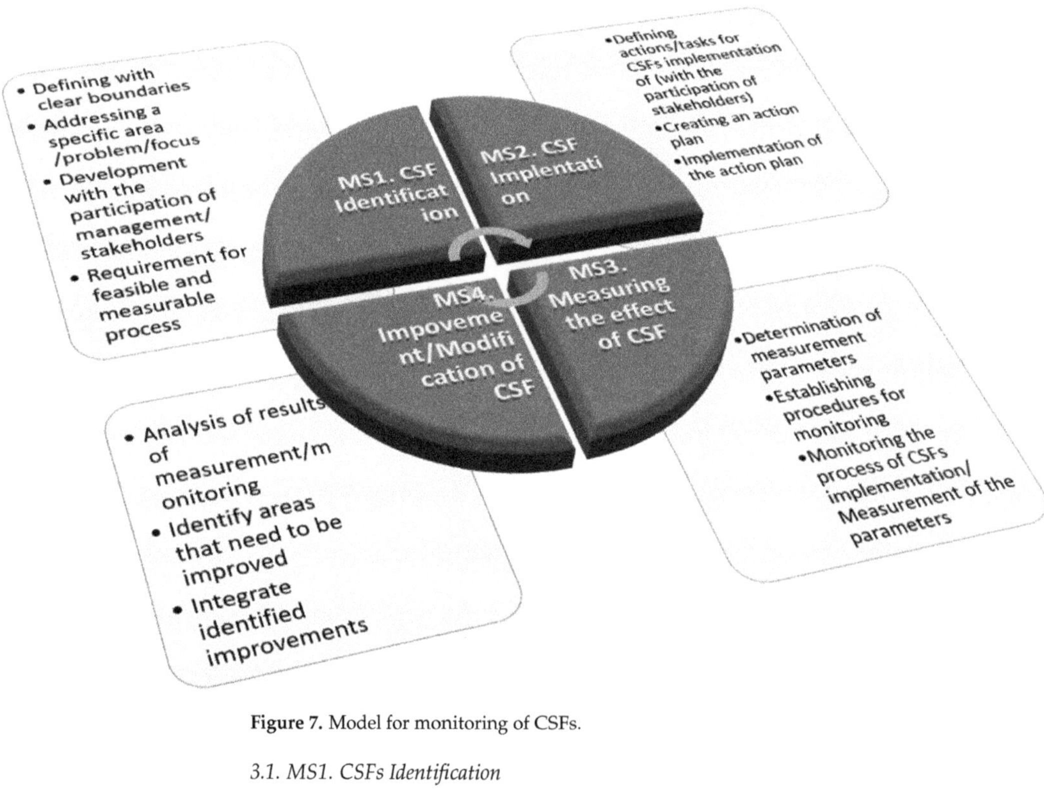

Figure 7. Model for monitoring of CSFs.

3.1. MS1. CSFs Identification

A crucial step in using the CSFs concept is CSFs identification. CFCs can be identified in many ways, some of which are described above. Several characteristics need special attention to improve the usefulness of CSFs from a monitoring point of view. In particular, each identified CSF must:

- have clear boundaries and a specific area of application, focus or problem to solve;

- allow the implementation of strategies and action plans of management/relevant stakeholders that address the underlying area/problem/focus;
- require a workable process with a measurable result regarding accepted benchmarks or performance criteria.

3.2. MS2. CSF Implementation

The second stage provides the actual benefit of CSFs. It requires planning and implementing who, what and when to take action to achieve the goals pursued in the process of CSFs identification. The issues that need attention at this stage are the definition of actions and (or) tasks to achieve the goals on which the CSFs are focused, involving relevant stakeholders in the discussions, creating an action plan with a schedule, necessary resources and people, and implementation of the action plan.

Taking a careful and thorough approach at this stage is vital to achieving the goals behind the CSFs identification.

3.3. MS3. Measuring the Effect of CSFs

In the first steps of this stage, the parameters (indicators) for measuring the effects of the implementation and appropriate procedures for monitoring the CSFs should be determined.

To assess whether the requirements of CSFs are met, as well as whether the set goals are achieved the so-called Key Performance Indicators (KPIs) [38,53] can be used. KPIs are specific and measurable criteria that managers use to assess the achievement of goals. For example, an organization may define the following as its CSF: "Increase sales of product X in the domestic market". Accordingly, the following can be identified as a KPI: "To increase sales of product X on the domestic market by 20% compared to the previous year".

Based on the measurement/evaluation of the defined parameters (e.g., KPIs), the actual monitoring of the CSF implementation process is carried out.

3.4. MS4. Improvement/Modification of CSF

The last stage in the monitoring process is related to the reassessment of the selected concept of CSFs. Based on the analysis of the results obtained from the measurement of the effects of CSFs application, according to defined goals and parameters, the areas in which CSFs should be improved/changed and even, if necessary, rejected should be identified. To integrate the identified improvements, the process of CSF monitoring and management must start again from the beginning, from MS1—the stage of CSFs identification.

The model for CSF monitoring described above can be illustrated briefly by the following example: often, the "Support from senior management" factor is involved in the identified CSFs. The model then requires the following: for this factor to be concretely defined, with a clear focus on attracting managerial attention; drawing up an action plan on how to look for and maintain support for its leadership; and assessing whether the perception of this factor as a CSF has achieved its goals.

The four stages from the model for monitoring, identification, implementation, measurement of efficiency and improvement of CSFs are repeated (Figure 7) periodically. This repetition ensures the maintenance of an always up-to-date set of CSFs (in unison with any change in the company's business goals, at the level of technology, etc.) that support the desired success.

It is important to note that stages MS2 (CSF Implementation) and MS3 (Measuring the effect of CSFs) are mutually justified, because if CSFs are not applied in practice, then the measurement of their effects would be pointless and vice versa.

4. Methodology for Implementing the Framework

Undoubtedly, for the success of any business venture, an essential role play experience, qualities and even the intuition managers of the organization.

The section systematizes the methods and tools appropriate for use in the various stages of the overall process of CSFs design and monitoring (DS1–4 and MS1–4).

DS1. Defining the scope of CSFs and participants—the project managers should discuss the following issues:

- the type of CSFs that are being developed (corporate or collective);
- the structure of the organization (multi-layered or flat structure);
- the specific working conditions of the organization (international presence, size of divisions, industry structure, etc.);
- the goal for CSF development.

DS2. Providing the necessary data

Many data collection methods are known, such as conducting staff interviews, questionnaires and other survey techniques, reviewing key company documents, and reviewing literature from primary and secondary sources in the field (in some cases even automated).

Where possible, it is good to apply several of these data collection techniques because they complement each other. However, if only one technique should be used, the preferred method is staff interview, which provides a dialogue.

The collection of data from documents and literature sources requires their in-depth study and analysis to understand the focus and direction of development of the specific organization/operational unit, of short-term and long-term strategies and related staff goals to achieve these strategies at the level of theoretical and applied developments in the field. All this is decisive about the developed CSFs. The large volume of researched sources can complicate the data collection process. Since most modern written sources are digital, it is easy to apply tools and methods to automate their collection and analysis (incl. search engines, computational linguistics methods and big data).

In some cases, data collection from written sources is not possible because these sources are not available. Such a problem can be mitigated by proper planning and conducting interviews with staff.

Data collection methods based on survey techniques are well-known and established due to their application in many other areas. For them, automated conducting and analysis of the results is also possible and recommended.

The most commonly used and most effective method is to collect data by conducting interviews with staff. It is known that for an effective interview, it is necessary to prepare and specify in advance the interviewing team, the interviewed staff members, the time and order of interviews and the questions. Important recommendations regarding the content of this type of interview are:

- indicate the purpose of the interview;
- clarify the participant's idea of the mission of the organization or unit;
- clarify the participant's opinion about his/her role in the organization or operational unit;
- discuss the goals and tasks of the participant;
- Ask a series of open-ended questions to retrieve data on the required CSFs, including for their priority and measurement.

Bullen and Rockhart [5] offer detailed instructions for conducting a CSF interview. These include a set of questions that directly intend to extract CSF.

DS3. Data Analysis

Some existing classification techniques, as mentioned, are suitable for performing Stage 3 of the CSFs design process related to raw data analysis. The need to apply formal techniques depends on factors such as: how many artefacts related to the target CSFs were found during the review of the raw data; the number of persons participating in the activity; and the required accuracy, etc.

In general, due to the complexity of such innovative projects, the success of which depends on many internal and external factors and covers almost all areas of the company's activity, it is necessary to analyze a significant number of sources of relevant data to define CSFs, and from there to identify an extraordinary large number of primary artefacts. This is well illustrated in the example in Table 1, where only in the mission of the company seven primary artefacts were found.

The Big Data technologies and specifically the MapReduce model for distributed processing of a large amount of data in computer clusters (where the internal and external sources of primary data are stored) are particularly suitable for carrying out Stage 3 according to the iterative method selected in this Framework. In this case, IT managers may predict developing a project to create a Hadoop MapReduce application providing automated extraction of the desired set of CSFs candidates through a series of MapReduce tasks. This would ensure the efficiency of the extraction process, the objectivity of analyses and the avoidance of bias.

DS4. CSF Identification

The basic approach that has been necessary to determine the final set of CSFs, i.e., for the implementation of the activities of DS4, is a survey among representatives of the top management related to the CSFs-initiative, concerning the actual applicability of the identified candidates for CSFs, as a final result of DS3.

This survey is often carried out based on one of the survey methods during a specially organized round table in which, in addition to representatives of the management of the organization/unit/project and the team who implement the CSFs initiative, it is good to use the help of experts in the business domain of the company. It is desirable that all participants be familiar in advance with the purpose of the digitalization project, the business goals and mission of the company/unit and the general requirements for the quality of CSFs (see DS4 in Section 2.2). Based on all this, they assess the extent to which each of the candidates for CSFs be included in the final set of factors, e.g., filling in the form developed for this purpose (see Table 2, where a short example of filling in is also given). In order to highlight the area of impact and the importance of individual CSFs, it is appropriate to group them according to the elements of appropriately selected leading signs (targeted improvements), which may vary depending on the purpose of the digitalization project. In this sense, the grouping can be according to the strategic goals of the company/unit, performance indicators, planned results, critical assets (in this case, these are mostly information assets and systems), the stages of the innovation process or the stages of the project life cycle.

Table 2. Design of CSFs: Form for DS4.

Leading Sign of CSF Grouping	Candidate for CSF	Should It Be Included in the Final Set of CSFs? (Yes/No)	Brief Justification
Sign 1. Customer satisfaction	CSF 1.1. Pricing and Services	Yes	Important factor
	CSF 1.2. Loyalty	Yes	Particularly important
	CSF 1.3. Honesty	No	Not important—it is part of the factor Loyalty
	...	...	
Sign 2.	CSF 2.1.	...	

In some cases, when there are pre-developed CSFs in the target area of application, it is possible to shorten the design process of CSFs and, after DS1, move directly to DS4. The developers of CSFs identified for implementing electronic payment systems in the banking sector [42] acted in a similar way (see the specific example of CSFs given at the end of Section 2.2).

Stages 1–4 of the CSF monitoring model (MS1–4)

In order to monitor CSFs identified with the goal of application discussed in this Framework, project managers who adopt digital business solutions must systematically follow a large number of interrelated activities of the CSF monitoring model (see Section 4).

This, in turn, would lead to meeting the requirements of and successfully implementing such a complex innovation project.

To ensure fully the process of CSFs monitoring and management, it is necessary to specify the activities/actions to be taken, the parameters for measuring the effect and all other preconditions determining the implementation of each of the four stages from the monitoring model for each of the identified CSFs. This includes:

- selection and use of formal methodologies, tools and techniques for project management;
- evaluation of the scope, location and necessary efforts for the project;
- judgement and decision-making on the approach for adoption of chosen digital business solutions;
- building knowledge by organizing joint teams of external consultants and experts in the field;
- constructing project team(s) that cover the organization and have a balance of business and IT skills;
- empowering the project team(s) to make changes.

In these activities, project managers can be facilitated, as there are already many software applications and tools that can automate one of the most time-consuming stages—measuring the effect of CSF (MS3). For example, BSC Designer is software that automates all elements of the so-called business continuity strategies, e.g., by automatically feeding KPI or generating analytical reports.

The entire process of CSFs design and monitoring of the framework with its eight stages (DS1–4 and MS1–4) is presented in Figure 8.

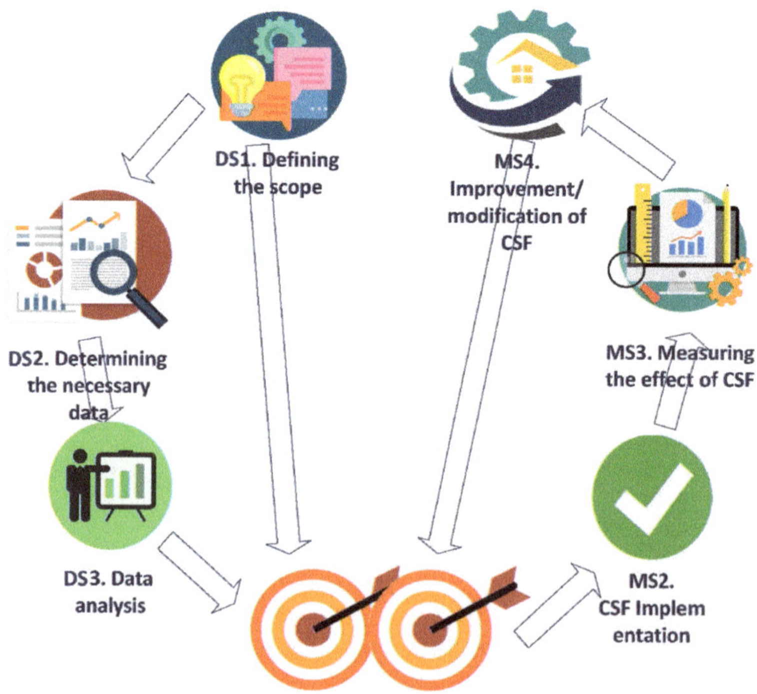

Figure 8. Methodology for application of the framework for design and monitoring of CSF.

5. Conclusions

The study presented in this paper aims to increase the understanding of how to identify and how to monitor CSFs affecting projects for the adoption of digital business solutions. It seeks to assist organizations and their managers in taking initiatives related to such kinds of projects by providing guidance on the use of CSF methods to orient resources to those activities that can ensure the initiative's success.

Based on the extensive review of research in the CSF field and on consultations with experts from the ICT sector and academia on the specifics of the field of digitalization, the present study provides a comprehensive framework for managing all interrelated activities for the proper identification and monitoring of CSFs in the field of the projects under consideration. If these activities are systematically undertaken, they can lead to the achievement of the relevant CSFs and the operational implementation of the chosen digitalization solution. Thus, the proposed framework has a broad practical application and can be used by companies implementing projects for the digitalization of their activity to improve the digital services offered and advance the organization's efficiency, etc.

This study also contributes to the research on the use of CSF methods in the digitalization sector and the widely established approach of identifying CSFs by proposing a framework for overall managing CSFs and providing valuable guidance for project managers in the adoption of digital business solutions.

Currently, aiming to validate the presented framework, it will be applied for the adoption of a customer relationship management (CRM) digitalization solution, based on a cooperation agreement with a national company from the internet and TV service delivery industry.

The incomplete validation of the framework and, accordingly, the impossibility to present the validation results can be considered somewhat of a limitation of the study. The limited research that specifically addresses the topic under consideration can also be attributed here.

In this regard, the most promising prospect for future development of the research is to finish the framework validation and analyze its results regarding the applicability of the framework. From a more long-term perspective, the framework can be further developed and applied to other project types. However, the most ambitious future goal is to develop an integrated software platform that automates the entire process of CSFs design and monitoring (Figure 8) presented in the eight stages of the framework (DS1–4 and MS1–4). This implies combining the means of state-of-the-art IT achievements, including search engines, computational linguistics methods, big data, cloud technologies, and intelligent data analysis, etc.

Author Contributions: Conceptualization, R.D. and S.G.; framework, R.D. and S.G.; methodology, R.D. and S.G.; writing—original draft preparation, R.D. and S.G.; writing—review and editing, R.D. and S.G.; visualization, R.D. and S.G. All authors have read and agreed to the published version of the manuscript.

Funding: This research was funded by the Scientific Research Fund at the University of Plovdiv "Paisii Hilendarski" grant number PP22-FTF-009.

Data Availability Statement: Not applicable.

Conflicts of Interest: The authors declare no conflict of interest.

References

1. Karimi, J.; Somers, T.M.; Bhattacherjee, A. The Role of Information Systems Resources in ERP Capability Building and Business Process Outcomes. *J. Manag. Inf. Syst.* **2007**, *24*, 221–260. [CrossRef]
2. Wijaya, M.I.; Suzanna; Utomo, D. Enterprise Resource Planning Modification: A Literature Review. *ComTech Comput. Math. Eng. Appl.* **2021**, *12*, 33–43. [CrossRef]
3. Marsudi, A.S.; Pambudi, R. The Effect of Enterprise Resource Planning (ERP) on Performance with Information Technology Capability as Moderating Variable. *J. Econ. Bus. Account. Ventur.* **2021**, *24*, 1–11. [CrossRef]
4. Daniel, R. *Management Information Crisis*; Harvard Business Review: Boston, MA, USA, 1961.
5. Bullen, C.V.; Rockart, J.F. *A Primer on Critical Success Factors*; CISR No. 69, Sloan WP No. 1220-81; Massachusetts Institute of Technology: Cambridge, MA, USA, 1981.

6. Dobbins, J.; Donnelly, R. Summary Research Report on Critical Success Factors in Federal Government Program Management. *Acquis. Rev. Q.* **1998**, *5*, 61–81.
7. Oliva, F.L.; Teberga, P.M.F.; Testi, L.I.O.; Kotabe, M.; Del Giudice, M.; Kelle, P.; Cunha, M.P. Risks and critical success factors in the internationalization of born global startups of industry 4.0: A social, environmental, economic, and institutional analysis. *Technol. Forecast. Soc. Chang.* **2021**, *175*, 121346. [CrossRef]
8. Pandey, N.; Bhatnagar, M.; Ghosh, D. An analysis of critical success factors towards sustainable supply chain management—In the context of an engine manufacturing industry. *Int. J. Sustain. Eng.* **2021**, *14*, 1496–1508. [CrossRef]
9. Handoyo, S.; Yudianto, I.; Fitriyah, F.K. Critical success factors for the internationalisation of small–medium enterprises in indonesia. *Cogent Bus. Manag.* **2021**, *8*, 1923358. [CrossRef]
10. Arman, H.; Ramadhan, M. Critical success factors for small and medium-sized enterprises in resource-rich country context. *Int. J. Glob. Small Bus.* **2021**, *12*, 299. [CrossRef]
11. Dwivedi, Y.K.; Janssen, M.; Slade, E.L.; Rana, N.P.; Weerakkody, V.; Millard, J.; Hidders, J.; Snijders, D. Driving innovation through big open linked data (BOLD): Exploring antecedents using interpretive structural modelling. *Inf. Syst. Front.* **2016**, *19*, 197–212. [CrossRef]
12. Strickland, A.; Thompson, A. *Strategic Management Concepts and Cases*; McGraw-Hill: Irvine, CA, USA, 2003.
13. Kaplan, R.; Norton, D. *The Balanced Scorecard: Translating Strategy into Action*; Harvard Business School Press: Boston, MA, USA, 1996.
14. Costa, C.J.; Aparicio, M.; Raposo, J. Determinants of the management learning performance in ERP context. *Heliyon* **2020**, *6*, e03689. [CrossRef]
15. Herath, S.; Chong, S. Key Components and Critical Success Factors for Project Management Success: A Literature Review. *Oper. Supply Chain. Manag. Int. J.* **2021**, *14*, 431–443. [CrossRef]
16. Sobieraj, J.; Metelski, D. Quantifying Critical Success Factors (CSFs) in Management of Investment-Construction Projects: Insights from Bayesian Model Averaging. *Buildings* **2021**, *11*, 360. [CrossRef]
17. Chen, M.-K.; Wu, S.-W.; Huang, Y.-P.; Chang, F.-J. The Key Success Factors for the Operation of SME Cluster Business Ecosystem. *Sustainability* **2022**, *14*, 8236. [CrossRef]
18. Barth, C.; Koch, S. Critical success factors in ERP upgrade projects. *Ind. Manag. Data Syst.* **2019**, *119*, 656–675. [CrossRef]
19. Adiasih, P.; Hatane, S.E.; Christyanto, S. The Role of Enterprise Resource Planning (ERP) in Improving Organization's Intellectual Capital. In Proceedings of the 2018 International Conference on Logistics and Business Innovation (ICLBI), Surabaya, Indonesia, 26–28 September 2018; pp. 159–178. [CrossRef]
20. Alireza, S. Critical Success Factors of CRM: Antecedents to successful implementation. *Manag. Innov.* **2015**, *8*, 105–131.
21. Parahita, A.N.; Eitiveni, I.; Nurchahyo, D.; Efendi, M.; Shafarina, R.; Aristio, A.P. Customer Relationship Management System Implementation Process and its Critical Success Factors: A Case Study. In Proceedings of the 2021 International Conference on Advanced Computer Science and Information Systems (ICACSIS), Virtual, 23–25 October 2021; pp. 1–7. [CrossRef]
22. Birau, R.; Spulbar, C.; Yazdi, A.; ShahrAeini, S. Critical success factors for CRM implementation in the Iranian banking sector: A conceptual analysis. *Revista Științe Politice* **2021**, *69*, 32–45.
23. Rahman, A.; Mohezar, S.; Habidin, N.; Fuzi, N. Critical success factors of the continued usage of digital library successful implementation in military-context: An organisational support perspective. *Digit. Libr. Perspect.* **2020**, *36*, 38–54. [CrossRef]
24. WHO. Global Strategy on Digital Health 2020–2024. 2020. Available online: https://www.who.int/docs/default-source/documents/gs4dhdaa2a9f352b0445bafbc79ca799dce4d.pdf?sfvrsn=f112ede5_38 (accessed on 1 October 2022).
25. Kabrilyants, R.; Obeidat, B.; Alshurideh, M.; Masadeh, R. The role of organizational capabilities on e-business suc-cessful implementation. *Int. J. Data Netw. Sci.* **2021**, *5*, 417–432. [CrossRef]
26. Sukathong, S.; Suksawang, P.; Naenna, T. Analyzing the importance of critical success factors for the adoption of advanced manufacturing technologies. *Int. J. Eng. Bus. Manag.* **2021**, *13*, 18479790211055057. [CrossRef]
27. Goyal, S.; Garg, D.; Luthra, S. Analyzing critical success factors to adopt sustainable consumption and production linked with circular economy. *Environ. Dev. Sustain.* **2021**, *24*, 5195–5224. [CrossRef]
28. Florek-Paszkowska, A.; Ujwary-Gil, A.; Godlewska-Dzioboń, B. Business innovation and critical success factors in the era of digital transformation and turbulent times. *J. Entrep. Manag. Innov.* **2021**, *17*, 7–28. [CrossRef]
29. Rohn, D.; Bican, P.M.; Brem, A.; Kraus, S.; Clauss, T. Digital platform-based business models—An exploration of critical success factors. *J. Eng. Technol. Manag.* **2021**, *60*, 101625. [CrossRef]
30. White, S.; Greiner, L. What is ITIL? Your guide to the IT Infrastructure Library. 2019. Available online: https://www.cio.com/article/2439501/infrastructure-it-infrastructure-library-itil-definition-and-solutions.html (accessed on 1 October 2022).
31. Haes, S.; Grembergen, W. Chapter 5: COBIT as a Framework for Enterprise Governance of IT. In *Enterprise Governance of Information Technology: Achieving Alignment and Value in Digital Organizations*; Featuring COBIT 5; Springer: Berlin/Heidelberg, Germany, 2015; pp. 103–128.
32. Osmundsen, K.; Iden, J.; Bygstad, B. Digital Transformation Drivers, Success Factors, and Implications. In Proceedings of the 12th Mediterranean Conference on Information Systems (MCIS), Corfu, Greece, 28–30 September 2018.
33. Fleischer, K.; Bensussan, B. *Strategic and Competitive Analysis: Methods and Techniques for Analyzing Business Competition*; Prentice Hall: Upper Saddle River, NJ, USA, 2003.
34. Levochkina, G.; Vasiliev, R. Key Success Factors in IT Consulting. *Qual. Educ. Innov.* **2012**, *91*, 57–65.

35. Gumay, L.A.; Purwandari, B.; Raharjo, T.; Wahyudi, A.; Purwaningsih, M. Identifying Critical Success Factors for Information Technology Projects with an Analytic Hierarchy Process: A Case of a Telco Company in Indonesia. In Proceedings of the 2020 2nd Asia Pacific Information Technology Conference, Bali Island, Indonesia, 17–19 January 2020. [CrossRef]
36. Ang, J.S.; Sum, C.-C.; Yeo, L.-N. A multiple-case design methodology for studying MRP success and CSFs. *Inf. Manag.* **2002**, *39*, 271–281. [CrossRef]
37. Françoise, O.; Bourgault, M.; Pellerin, R. ERP implementation through critical success factors' management. *Bus. Process Manag. J.* **2009**, *15*, 371–394. [CrossRef]
38. Hristov, T. Critical Success Factors, New Vision. 2020. Available online: https://www.novavizia.com/kritichni-faktori-za-uspeh/ (accessed on 1 October 2022).
39. Hughes, D.L.; Dwivedi, Y.K.; Rana, N.P. Mapping IS failure factors on PRINCE2®stages: An application of Interpretive Ranking Process (IRP). *Prod. Plan. Control* **2017**, *28*, 776–790. [CrossRef]
40. Hughes, D.L.; Dwivedi, Y.K.; Rana, N.; Simintiras, A.C. Information systems project failure—Analysis of causal links using interpretive structural modelling. *Prod. Plan. Control* **2016**, *27*, 1313–1333. [CrossRef]
41. Janssen, M.; Rana, N.; Slade, E.; Dwivcdi, Y. Trustworthiness of digital government services: Deriving a compre-hensive theory through interpretive structural modelling. *Public Manag. Rev.* **2017**, *20*, 647–671. [CrossRef]
42. Sahu, G.; Singh, M. Green information system adoption and sustainability: A ease study of select Indian Banks. In *Social Media: The Good, the Bad, and the Ugly, Proceedings of the 15th IFIP WG 6.11 Conference on e-Business, e-Services, and e-Society; Swansea, UK, 13–15 September 2016*; Springer International Publishing: Cham, Switzerland, 2016; pp. 292–304.
43. Caralli, R. *The Critical Success Factor Method: Establishing a Foundationfor Enterprise Security Management (CMU/SEI2004-TR-010)*; Software Engineering Institute, Carnegie Mellon University: Pittsburgh, PA, USA, 2004.
44. Sherman, F. Examples of Critical Success Factors, 2019. 2019. Available online: https://bizfluent.com/list-5968674-examples-critical-success-factors.html (accessed on 1 October 2022).
45. Hoeliner, R. Critical Success Factors For Each Phase Of Digital Transformation. 2018. Available online: https://www.digitalistmag.com/cio-knowledge/2018/11/13/critical-success-factors-for-each-phase-of-digital-transformation-06193854/ (accessed on 1 October 2022).
46. Holotiuk, F.; Beimborn, D. Critical Success Factors of Digital Business Strategy. In Proceedings of the 13th International Conference on Wirtschaftsinformatik, St.Gallen, Switzerland, 12–15 February 2017.
47. McKinsey. Unlocking Success in Digital Transformations. 2018. Available online: https://www.mckinsey.com/business-functions/organization/our-insights/unlocking-success-in-digital-transformations (accessed on 1 October 2022).
48. McKinsey. Digital Transformation in 2020: In-Depth guide for Executives. 2020. Available online: https://research.aimultiple.com/digital-transformation/ (accessed on 1 October 2022).
49. Rossi, B. The Critical Success Factors for Digital Transformation Programmes and How to Meet Them. 2015. Available online: https://www.information-age.com/critical-success-factors-digital-transformation-programmes-and-how-meet-them-123460348/ (accessed on 1 October 2022).
50. Reyero, D.; Garrido, J. Digitalization: 10 Key Success Factors. 2020. Available online: https://davidreyero.com/en/mythemes/people-mythemes/business-digitalization-10-keys-to-success-david-reyero-juncal-garrido-february-2017/ (accessed on 1 October 2022).
51. Adzmi, R.M.; Hassan, Z. A Theoretical Framework of Critical Success Factors on Information Technology Project Management During Project Planning. *Int. J. Eng. Technol.* **2018**, *7*, 650–655. [CrossRef]
52. Herglotz, Y. Success Factors for Digital Transformation in 2020. 2020. Available online: https://digitaltransformationtrends.com/2020/01/05/success-factors-for-digital-transformations-in-2020/ (accessed on 1 October 2022).
53. Braglia, M.; Gabbrielli, R.; Marrazzini, L.; Padellini, L. Key Performance Indicators and Industry 4.0—A structured approach for monitoring the implementation of digital technologies. *Procedia Comput. Sci.* **2022**, *200*, 1626–1635. [CrossRef]

electronics

MDPI

Article

A Multi-Attribute Decision-Making Approach for the Analysis of Vendor Management Using Novel Complex Picture Fuzzy Hamy Mean Operators

Abrar Hussain [1], Kifayat Ullah [1,*], Dragan Pamucar [2,*] and Đorđe Vranješ [3]

[1] Department of Mathematics, Lahore Campus, Riphah International University, Lahore 54000, Pakistan
[2] Department of Operations Research and Statistics, Faculty of Organizational Sciences, University of Belgrade, 11000 Belgrade, Serbia
[3] Academy of Technical and Art Applied Studies Belgrade, University of Belgrade, 11000 Belgrade, Serbia
* Correspondence: kifayat.khan.dr@gmail.com (K.U.); dragan.pamucar@fon.bg.ac.rs (D.P.)

Abstract: Vendor management systems (VMSs) are web-based software packages that can be used to manage businesses. The performance of the VMSs can be assessed using multi-attribute decision-making (MADM) techniques under uncertain situations. This article aims to analyze and assess the performance of VMSs using MADM techniques, especially when the uncertainty is of complex nature. To achieve the goals, we aim to explore Hany mean (HM) operators in the environment of complex picture fuzzy (CPF) sets (CPFSs). We introduce CPF Hamy mean (CPFHM) and CPF weighted HM (CPFWHM) operators. Moreover, the reliability of the newly proposed HM operators is examined by taking into account the properties of idempotency, monotonicity, and boundedness. A case study of VMS is briefly discussed, and a comprehensive numerical example is carried out to assess VMSs using the MADM technique based on CPFHM operators. The sensitivity analysis and comprehensive comparative analysis of the proposed work are discussed to point out the significance of the newly established results.

Keywords: ambiguous and vague information; complex picture fuzzy numbers; Hamy mean operators; multi-attribute decision-making technique; vendor management systems

Citation: Hussain, A.; Ullah, K.; Pamucar, D.; Vranješ, Đ. A Multi-Attribute Decision-Making Approach for the Analysis of Vendor Management Using Novel Complex Picture Fuzzy Hamy Mean Operators. *Electronics* **2022**, *11*, 3841. https://doi.org/10.3390/electronics11233841

Academic Editors: Galina Ilieva and George A. Tsihrintzis

Received: 21 October 2022
Accepted: 18 November 2022
Published: 22 November 2022

1. Introduction

The majority of fields, including engineering, economics, and management, involve some type of decision-making difficulties. All of the information about using the alternatives has been traditionally thought to be taken in the form of unambiguous numbers. The processing of the data fuzziness and uncertainty is essential because they change regularly in real-life scenarios. A VMS is a tool that allows businesses to manage every step of the vendor management process, from the initial point of interaction through the final steps of concluding a sale or establishing a new business relationship. They typically feature particular modules or apps that deal with procedures such as on-boarding new vendors or processing vendor payments because they have a modular approach. Many aspects can move in vendor relationship management. There are purchase orders, purchase requisitions, order confirmations, performance monitoring, vendor screening procedures, and so on.

The decision-making technique plays a vital role in the process of aggregating information and creates a lot of interactions for several research scholars. Every field is full of uncertain, imprecise, and hazy information. To deal with human opinion in the form of uncertain and vague information, Zadeh [1] gave the concept of a fuzzy set (FS) with a degree of truth index (TI). El-Bably and Abo-Tabl [2,3] presented an innovative concept of FSs in the frame work of a rough set under some topological reduction. El Sayed et al. [4] explored the theory of topological techniques to handle the current situations of COVID-19 by using the model of nano-topology. Atanassov [5] generalized the theory of FS in the framework of an intuitionistic fuzzy set (IFS) having TI and falsity index (FI), where the sum of TI $\breve{\mho}(\varrho)$ and FI $\tilde{\Upsilon}(\varrho)$ restricted is less and equal to 0 and 1, i.e., $0 \leq \breve{\mho}(\varrho) + \tilde{\Upsilon}(\varrho) \leq 1$. In some scenarios IFS has failed; if the TI is 0.65 and FI is 0.55, then the sum of TI and FI is $0.65 + 0.55 = 1.2 \notin [0,\ 1]$. To cope with this situation, Yager [6] presented the concepts of a Pythagorean fuzzy set (PyFS); according to PyFS, the sum of the square of TI and FI are less than or equal to 0 and 1, and from the above example, $0 \leq \breve{\mho}^2(\varrho) + \tilde{\Upsilon}^2(\varrho) \leq 1$, so $(0.65)^2 + (0.55)^2 = 0.73 \in [0,\ 1]$. Yager [7] also developed the concept of a q-rung orthopair fuzzy set (q-ROFS) by generalizing the idea of PyFS. Cuong [8,9] introduced a new concept of picture fuzzy (PF) set (PFS), which contains four types of characteristic functions, TI, abstinence index (AI), FI, and refusal index (RI). The structure of PFS has the sum of three terms, and TI, AI, and FI are restricted in $[0,\ 1]$. Lu et al. [10] generalized the concepts of PFSs in the framework of PF rough sets to solve real-life problems under the system of MADM techniques. Several research scholars worked in different fields of research to find the limitations of the above-discussed phenomenon seen in [11–14].

Aggregation operators are convenient mathematical models to investigate fuzzy information, for the study of above discussed existing AOs, we analyzed research works to recognize how to deal with ambiguity and uncertainty in complex information. Several research scholars presented their research methodologies to solve MADM techniques. For instance, Xu [15] presented some AOs of IFS to investigate fuzziness data. Xu and Xia [16] generalized IFSs and developed a list of AOs to solve the MADM process. Biswas and Deb [17] introduced a list of new AOs by utilizing the Schweizer and Sklar power operations under the system of PyFSs. Garg [18] presented some AOs of PyFSs by using the operations of Einstein T-norm (TNM) and T-conorm (TCNM). Mahmood and Ali [19] explained a new technique of AOs by using the VIKOR method in the environment of complex q-rung orthopair sets. Riaz and Hashmi [20] elaborated on AOs based on Linear Diophantine FSs and solve a MADM technique to investigate a suitable candidate for a multinational company. Liu [21] extended algebraic AOs and Einstein AOs to develop some new AOs by using the operations of Hamacher TNM and TCNM under the system interval-valued IFSs (IVIFSs). Hussain et al. [22] presented some AOs by utilizing the basic operations of Aczel Alsina TNM and TCNM to select a suitable candidate for a multinational company. Liu et al. [23] generalized similarity measures based on interval-valued PFS (IVPFS) and studied a MADM technique to solve real-life problems. Mahmood et al. [24] established a series of new AOs based on the bipolar valued fuzzy hesitant system and their special cases. Garg [25] explained some new AOs based on PFSs and also studied a MADM technique to solve a numerical example related to our daily life. Wei [26] presented some AOs of arithmetic and geometric operators by utilizing the basic operations of Hamacher TNM and TCNM. We also studied the theory of generalized FS in different fuzzy environments seen in references [27–30].

The preceding aggregation operators and their associated methodologies are frequently utilized by researchers, but it has been determined from these studies that these works consider the data under the FS, IFSs, or their modifications, which are only to handle the uncertainty and vagueness that exist in the data. The partial ignorance of the data and their variations at a specific point in the time during implementation, however, is something that none of the existing models is capable of recognizing. Additionally, in daily life, change in the phase (periodicity) of the data corresponds with uncertainty and ambiguity that is present in the data. There is information loss during the process as a result of the present theories' inability to adequately account for this information. To overcome this situation, Ramot et al. [31] introduced the complex fuzzy set (CFS), in which the range of the TI is expanding from real numbers to complex numbers with the unit circle. Traditionally, fuzzy logic was generalized to complex fuzzy logic by Ramot et al. [32] in which the sets employed in the reasoning process are CFSs, characterized by complex-valued TI functions. In a later study, Greenfield et al. expanded on the CFS idea by considering the TI as an interval number rather than a single integer. A systematic review of CFSs and logic was done by Yazdanbakhsh and Dick [33], and they explained their finding. Alkouri and Salleh [34] extended the concepts of CFS in the framework of complex IFS (CIFS) by adding the new term of FI in CFS. They extended the range of both TI and FI to a unit circle in a complex system. Furthermore, they defined fundamental operations of CIFS such as union, intersection, and complement of CIFSs. Garg and Rani [35] utilized the MADM technique to solve real life problems by using the AOs of complex IFSs. Ullah et al. [36] generalized the concepts of CFS and CIFS in the framework of complex PyFS to find distance measures by using the technique of pattern recognition. Liu et al. [37] presented a new concepts of complex q-ROFS (Cq-ROFS) by the generalization of CPyFSs with sum of qth power of TI and FI. Rong et al. [38] developed a new list of AOs of MacLaurin symmetric mean operators under the system of Cq-ROFS. Akram et al. [39] proposed a new theory of complex PFS (CPFS), as an extension of CFSs, CIFSs, CPyFSs, and Cq-ROFSs by utilizing the basic operations of Hamacher AOs.

The HM tools are used to aggregate uncertain and vague information in a different framework of fuzzy environment. Firstly, the theory of HM operators was discovered by Hara et al. [40] in 1998. He obtained different inequalities by classifying the arithmetic and geometric inequalities. Recently a lot of research done on this topic. Qin [41] explored the concept of HM operator to cope with vagueness and imprecision under the system of interval type 2-fuzzy and he also discussed their application based on MADM techniques. Wu et al. [42] expanded the ideas of HM operators in the framework of interval-valued intuitionistic fuzzy Dombi HM operators to find suitable tourism destinations. Li et al. [43] utilized the theory of HM operator to select a suitable supplier for a motor vehicle under the system of IFSs. Wu et al. [44] also explored the concepts of HM operators in a new research area to evaluate construction engineering schemes based on the 2-tuple linguistic neutrosophic system. Li et al. [45] provided some new AOs by using the operational laws of HM operators based on PyFSs and also established an application to find the best supplier system based on the MADM technique. Liu et al. [46] also introduced some new AOs of IF uncertain linguistic HM operators with an application of a healthcare waste administration authority. Wu et al. [47] elaborated the concept of HM and dual HM (DHM) operators to develop a series of new AOs based on IVIFSs and also discussed an application to find the best tourism place. Wang et al. [48] developed some AOs by using the idea of HM and DHM operators under the system of q-rung orthopair fuzzy sets and gave an application for the selection of enterprise resource management authority. Xing et al. [49] developed some AOs to handle uncertain and vague information by using new operational laws of interactive HM and DHM operators. Sinani et al. [50] introduced a series of AOs by using the operation operator based on rough numbers. Wei et al. [51] developed some AOs to fuse uncertain information under the system of dual hesitant PyFSs with the help of the MADM approaches. Liu et al. [52] presented some convenient AOs by generalizing the concept of HM and DHM tools in the framework of interval neutrosophic power sets. Garg et al. [53] illustrated a list of AOs by using the operations of HM operators in the framework of a q-rung orthopair fuzzy set (q-ROFS). Ali et al. [54] presented a series of AOs by utilizing the theory of HM operators under the system of complex interval-valued q-ROFS (CIVq-ROFSs).

Keeping in mind the significance of CPFSs, we developed some new AOs by using the concept of the HM tool in the framework of CPFS. A CPFS has two aspects of information in the form of amplitude terms and phase terms of TI, AI, and FI. In this article, a list of AOs discusses CPFHM, CPFWHM, CPFDHM and CPFWDHM operators with some basic properties such as idempotency, monotonicity, and boundedness. We also study some numerical examples to support our proposed methodologies. We established an application based on VMS to find the flexibility and reliability of our proposed techniques. With the help of a practical numerical example, we evaluate suitable software for VMS. To check validity and compatibility, we study a comprehensive comparative study to contrast the results of existing AOs with the results of the discussed technique.

The structure of this article is organized as follows: In Section 1, we review the history of our research work for the improvement of this article. In Section 2, we study all the notions related to PFSs, CPFSs, and their basic operations. In Section 3, we recall existing concepts of HM and GHM operators and also discuss their basic properties. In Section 4, we utilize the basic operations of HM operators to introduce some new AOs such as CPFHM and CPFWHM operators with their characteristics. In Section 5, we also present some new AOs of CPFGHM and CPFWGHM operators. We also present some numerical examples to find the feasibility of our proposed approaches. In Section 6, we establish a strategy for the MADM process under the system of CPFSs. We also provide an application in the framework of VMS. To check the competitiveness and flexibility of our proposed AOs, we illustrate a numerical example based on CPF information. In Section 7, to find the validity and rationality of our proposed work, we make comparison results of our proposed approaches with some existing AOs. In Section 8, we summarize the whole article in a paragraph.

2. Preliminaries

This section aims to recall notions of PFSs, CPFSs, and their basic operational laws. We applied these operational laws to develop our proposed methodology. First, we want to define the meaning of some symbols and letters in Table 1, as follows.

Table 1. Symbols and their meanings.

Symbols	Meanings	Symbols	Meanings
$\tilde{\text{Ŭ}}$	Universal set	ϕ_v	Falsity Index of phase term
ϱ	Element belonging to Universal set	$\hat{\text{S}}$	Score function
$\breve{\text{u}}_\mu$	Truth Index/(TI) of amplitude term	Ą	Accuracy function
$\hat{\text{ɛ}}_A$	Abstinence Index /(AI) of amplitude term	$\mathfrak{N}_{i_j}$	Weight vector
$\tilde{\Upsilon}_v$	Falsity Index/(FI) of amplitude term	$C_n^{\text{ш}}$	Binomial Coefficient
$\mathfrak{E}$	CPFS	$\sqrt{-1}$	Unit circle
ψ_μ	Truth Index of phase term	$\mathfrak{f}_{\mathfrak{E}}$	Hesitancy Index
φ_A	Abstinence Index of phase term	$\overline{I}$	Complement of CPFV

The concepts of PFSs were developed by Cuong [8] and is given as follows:

Definition 1. *[8] Consider* $\tilde{\text{Ŭ}}$ *to be an empty set. A PFS* $\mathcal{Y}$ *is defined as:*

$$\mathcal{Y} = \{(\varrho,\ \breve{\text{u}}_\mu(\varrho),\ \hat{\text{ɛ}}_A(\varrho), \tilde{\Upsilon}_v(\varrho))|\varrho\}$$

where $\breve{\text{u}}_\mu(\varrho),\ \tilde{\Upsilon}_A(\varrho), \tilde{\Upsilon}_v(\varrho) \in [0,1]$. *Truth index is denoted (TI) by the* $\breve{\text{u}}_\mu(\varrho)$, *abstinence index (AI) is denoted by the* $\hat{\text{ɛ}}_A(\varrho)$, *and falsity index (FI) is denoted by the* $\tilde{\Upsilon}_v(\varrho)$, *such that:*

$$0 < \breve{\text{u}}_\mu(\varrho) + \hat{\text{ɛ}}_A(\varrho) + \tilde{\Upsilon}_v(\varrho) < 1$$

A picture fuzzy value (PFV) represented by $\mathcal{T} = (\breve{\text{u}}_\mu(\varrho),\ \hat{\text{ɛ}}_A(\varrho), \tilde{\Upsilon}_v(\varrho))$.

The theory of the following Definition was proposed by Akram et al. [39].

Definition 2. *[39] A CPFS is formed as:*

$$\mathfrak{E} = \left\{\left(\varrho,\ \breve{\text{u}}_\mu(\varrho)e^{2i\pi\psi_\mu(\varrho)},\ \hat{\text{ɛ}}_A(\varrho)e^{2i\pi\varphi_A(\varrho)}, \tilde{\Upsilon}_v(\varrho)e^{2i\pi\phi_v(\varrho)}\right)\middle|\varrho \in \tilde{\text{Ŭ}}\right\},\ i = \sqrt{-1}$$

where $\breve{\text{u}}_\mu(\varrho)$, $\hat{\text{ɛ}}_A(\varrho)$ *and* $\tilde{\Upsilon}_v(\varrho) \in [0,1]$ *be amplitude terms and* $\psi_\mu(\varrho)$, $\varphi_A(\varrho)$, *and* $\phi_v(\varrho) \in [0,1]$ *be the phase terms. TI, AI, and FI for amplitude terms are represented by the* $\breve{\text{u}}_\mu(\varrho)$, $\hat{\text{ɛ}}_A(\varrho)$ *and*

$\tilde{\Upsilon}_v(\varrho)$, *respectively. Similarly, TI, AI and FI for phase terms are represented by the* $\psi_\mu(\varrho)$, $\varphi_A(\varrho)$, *and* $\phi_v(\varrho)$, *respectively. A CPFS must satisfy the following condition:*

$$0 \leq \breve{\upsilon}_\mu(\varrho) + \hat{\varepsilon}_A(\varrho) + \tilde{\Upsilon}_v(\varrho) \leq 1, \text{ and } 0 \leq \psi_\mu(\varrho) + \varphi_A(\varrho) + \phi_v(\varrho) \leq 1, \ \forall \varrho \in \bar{\breve{U}},$$

A hesitancy index of a CPFS $\mathfrak{r}_{\mathfrak{E}}$ *is denoted by* $\mathfrak{r}_{\mathfrak{E}} = 1 - (\breve{\upsilon}_\mu(\varrho) + \hat{\varepsilon}_A(\varrho) + \tilde{\Upsilon}_v(\varrho))\, e^{2\pi i(1-(\psi_\mu(\varrho)+\varphi_A(\varrho)+\phi_v(\varrho)))}$. *Let a complex PFV (CPFV) be denoted by* $I = (\breve{\upsilon}_\mu(\varrho)e^{2\pi i\psi_\mu(\varrho)}, \hat{\varepsilon}_A(\varrho)e^{2\pi i\varphi_A(\varrho)}, \tilde{\Upsilon}_v(\varrho)e^{2\pi i\phi_v(\varrho)})$.

Definition 3. *[55] Consider* $I = (\breve{\upsilon}_\mu(\varrho)e^{2i\pi\psi_\mu(\varrho)}, \hat{\varepsilon}_A(\varrho)e^{2i\pi\varphi_A(\varrho)}, \tilde{\Upsilon}_v(\varrho)e^{2i\pi\phi_v(\varrho)})$, $I_1 = (\breve{\upsilon}_{\mu_1}(\varrho)e^{2i\pi\psi_{\mu_1}(\varrho)}, \hat{\varepsilon}_{A_1}(\varrho)e^{2i\pi\varphi_{A_1}(\varrho)}, \tilde{\Upsilon}_{v_1}(\varrho)e^{2i\pi\phi_{v_1}(\varrho)})$ *and* $I_2 = (\breve{\upsilon}_{\mu_2}(\varrho)e^{2i\pi\psi_{\mu_2}(\varrho)}, \hat{\varepsilon}_{A_2}(\varrho)\, e^{2i\pi\varphi_{A_2}(\varrho)}, \tilde{\Upsilon}_{v_2}(\varrho)e^{2i\pi\phi_{v_2}(\varrho)})$ *be any three CPFSs. Then some basic operational laws are defined as:*

1. $I_1 \subseteq I_2$ *, if and only if* $\breve{\upsilon}_{\mu_1}(\varrho) \leq \breve{\upsilon}_{\mu_2}(\varrho)$, $\hat{\varepsilon}_{A_1}(\varrho) \leq \hat{\varepsilon}_{A_2}(\varrho)$ *and* $\tilde{\Upsilon}_{v_1}(\varrho) \geq \tilde{\Upsilon}_{v_2}(\varrho)$ *for amplitude terms and* $\psi_{\mu_1}(\varrho) \leq \psi_{\mu_2}(\varrho)$, $\varphi_{A_1}(\varrho) \leq \varphi_{A_2}(\varrho)$ *, and* $\phi_{v_1}(\varrho) \geq \phi_{v_2}(\varrho)$ *for phase terms. For all* $\varrho \in \bar{\breve{U}}$
2. $\bar{I} = \{(\varrho, \breve{\upsilon}_{\mu_I}(\varrho)e^{2i\pi\psi_{\mu_I}(\varrho)}, \hat{\varepsilon}_{AI}(\varrho)e^{2i\pi\varphi_{A_I}(\varrho)}, \tilde{\Upsilon}_{v_I}(\varrho)e^{2i\pi\phi_{v_I}(\varrho)}) | \varrho \in \bar{\breve{U}}\}$
3. $I_1 \cap I_2 = \{(\varrho, (\breve{\upsilon}_{\mu_1}(\varrho) \wedge \breve{\upsilon}_{\mu_2}(\varrho))\, e^{2i\pi(\psi_{\mu_1}(\varrho)\wedge\psi_{\mu_2}(\varrho))}, (\hat{\varepsilon}_{A_1}(\varrho) \vee \hat{\varepsilon}_{A_2}(\varrho))e^{2i\pi(\varphi_{A_1}(\varrho)\vee\varphi_{A_2}(\varrho))}, (\tilde{\Upsilon}_{v_1}(\varrho) \vee \tilde{\Upsilon}_{v_2}(\varrho))e^{2i\pi(\phi_{v_1}(\varrho)\vee\phi_{v_2}(\varrho))}) | \varrho \in \bar{\breve{U}}\}$
4. $I_1 \uplus I_2 = \{(\varrho, (\breve{\upsilon}_{\mu_1}(\varrho) \vee \breve{\upsilon}_{\mu_2}(\varrho))\, e^{2i\pi(\psi_{\mu_1}(\varrho)\vee\psi_{\mu_2}(\varrho))}, (\hat{\varepsilon}_{A_1}(\varrho) \wedge \hat{\varepsilon}_{A_2}(\varrho))e^{2i\pi(\varphi_{A_1}(\varrho)\wedge\varphi_{A_2}(\varrho))}, (\tilde{\Upsilon}_{v_1}(\varrho) \wedge \tilde{\Upsilon}_{v_2}(\varrho))e^{2i\pi(\phi_{v_1}(\varrho)\wedge\phi_{v_2}(\varrho))}) | \varrho \in \bar{\breve{U}}\}$
where symbol $\wedge$ and $\vee$ *represent the minimum and maximum respectively.*

Definition 4. *Consider* $I = \left(\breve{\upsilon}_\mu(\varrho)e^{2\pi i\psi_\mu(\varrho)}, \hat{\varepsilon}_A(\varrho)e^{2\pi i\varphi_A(\varrho)}, \tilde{\Upsilon}_v(\varrho)e^{2\pi i\phi_v(\varrho)}\right)$ *is a CPFV. Then score functions are defined as:*

$$\hat{S}(I) = \frac{(3 + (\breve{\upsilon}_\mu(\varrho) - \hat{\varepsilon}_A(\varrho) - \tilde{\Upsilon}_v(\varrho)) + (\psi_\mu(\varrho) - \varphi_A(\varrho) - \phi_v(\varrho)))}{6}$$

where $\hat{S}(I) \in [-1, 1]$.

Definition 5. *Consider* $I = \left(\breve{\upsilon}_\mu(\varrho)e^{2\pi i\psi_\mu(\varrho)}, \hat{\varepsilon}_A(\varrho)e^{2\pi i\varphi_A(\varrho)}, \tilde{\Upsilon}_v(\varrho)e^{2\pi i\phi_v(\varrho)}\right)$ *is a CPFV. Then accuracy functions are defined as:*

$$\mathrm{A}(I) = \frac{(\breve{\upsilon}_\mu(\varrho) + \hat{\varepsilon}_A(\varrho) + \tilde{\Upsilon}_v(\varrho)) + (\psi_\mu(\varrho) + \varphi_A(\varrho) + \phi_v(\varrho))}{3}$$

where $\mathrm{A}(I) \in [0, 2]$.

Example 1. *Let* $I_1 = \left(0.30e^{2\pi i(0.09)}, 0.17e^{2\pi i(0.12)}, 0.42e^{2\pi i(0.32)}\right)$, $I_2 = \left(0.68e^{2\pi i(0.29)}, 0.07e^{2\pi i(0.52)}, 0.16e^{2\pi i(0.06)}\right)$ *and* $I_3 = \left(0.37e^{2\pi i(0.22)}, 0.25e^{2\pi i(0.32)}, 0.17e^{2\pi i(0.09)}\right)$ *be three CPFVs. The score function and accuracy function is defined as follows:*

$$\hat{S}(I_1) = \frac{(3 + (0.30 - 0.17 - 0.42) + (0.09 - 0.12 - 0.32))}{6} = 0.3050 \in [0, 1]$$

$$\hat{S}(I_2) = \frac{(3 + (0.68 - 0.07 - 0.16) + (0.29 - 0.52 - 0.06))}{6} = 0.3550 \in [0, 1]$$

$$\hat{S}(I_3) = \frac{(3 + (0.37 - 0.25 - 0.17) + (0.22 - 0.32 - 0.09))}{6} = 0.5433 \in [0, 1]$$

and

$$\mathrm{A}(I_1) = \frac{(0.30 + 0.17 + 0.42) + (0.09 + 0.12 + 0.32)}{3} = 0.6500 \in [0, 1]$$

$$Ą(I_2) = \frac{(0.68 + 0.07 + 0.16) + (0.29 + 0.52 + 0.06)}{3} = 0.4833 \in [0,1]$$

$$Ą(I_3) = \frac{(0.37 + 0.25 + 0.17) + (0.22 + 0.32 + 0.09)}{3} = 0.4067 \in [0,1]$$

Remark 1. *Consider* $I_1 = \left(\breve{\upsilon}_{\mu_1}(\varrho)e^{2\pi i\psi_{\mu_1}(\varrho)}, \hat{\varepsilon}_{A_1}(\varrho)e^{2\pi i\varphi_{A_1}(\varrho)}, \tilde{\Upsilon}_{v_1}(\varrho)e^{2\pi i\phi_{v_1}(\varrho)}\right)$ *and* $I_2 = \left(\breve{\upsilon}_{\mu_2}(\varrho)e^{2\pi i\psi_{\mu_2}(\varrho)}, \hat{\varepsilon}_{A_2}(\varrho)e^{2\pi i\varphi_{A_2}(\varrho)}, \tilde{\Upsilon}_{v_2}(\varrho)e^{2\pi i\phi_{v_2}(\varrho)}\right)$ *are two CPFVs. Then some rules of score function and accuracy function such as if* $I_1 < I_2$ *, then* $\hat{S}(I_1) < \hat{S}(I_2)$*, if* $I_1 > I_2$*, then* $\hat{S}(I_1) > \hat{S}(I_2)$*. Similarly, if* $\hat{S}(I_1) = \hat{S}(I_2)$*, then following conditions must be satisfied:*

I. If $Ą(I_1) < Ą(I_2)$, then $I_1 < I_2$.
II. If $Ą(I_1) = Ą(I_2)$, then $I_1 = I_2$.

Definition 6. *Consider* $I = \left(\breve{\upsilon}_{\mu}(\varrho)e^{2\pi i\psi_{\mu}(\varrho)}, \hat{\varepsilon}_{A}(\varrho)e^{2\pi i\varphi_{A}(\varrho)}, \tilde{\Upsilon}_{v}(\varrho)e^{2\pi i\phi_{v}(\varrho)}\right)$, $I_1 = \left(\breve{\upsilon}_{\mu_1}(\varrho)e^{2\pi i\psi_{\mu_1}(\varrho)}, \hat{\varepsilon}_{A_1}(\varrho)e^{2\pi i\varphi_{A_1}(\varrho)}, \tilde{\Upsilon}_{v_1}(\varrho)e^{2\pi i\phi_{v_1}(\varrho)}\right)$ *and* $I_2 = \left(\breve{\upsilon}_{\mu_2}(\varrho)e^{2\pi i\psi_{\mu_2}(\varrho)}, \hat{\varepsilon}_{A_2}(\varrho) e^{2\pi i\varphi_{A_2}(\varrho)}, \tilde{\Upsilon}_{v_2}(\varrho)e^{2\pi i\phi_{v_2}(\varrho)}\right)$ *are three CPFVs. The fundamental operations of CPFSs are defined as:*

I. $$I_1 \oplus I_2 = \begin{pmatrix} \left(\breve{\upsilon}_{\mu_1}(\varrho) + \breve{\upsilon}_{\mu_2}(\varrho) - \breve{\upsilon}_{\mu_1}(\varrho).\breve{\upsilon}_{\mu_2}(\varrho)\right)e^{2\pi i(\psi_{\mu_1}(\varrho)+\psi_{\mu_2}(\varrho)-\psi_{\mu_1}(\varrho).\psi_{\mu_2}(\varrho))}, \\ \left(\hat{\varepsilon}_{A_1}(\varrho).\hat{\varepsilon}_{A_2}(\varrho)\right)e^{2\pi i(\varphi_{A_1}(\varrho).\varphi_{A_2}(\varrho))}, \\ \left(\tilde{\Upsilon}_{v_1}(\varrho).\tilde{\Upsilon}_{v_2}(\varrho)\right)e^{2\pi i(\phi_{v_1}(\varrho).\phi_{v_2}(\varrho))} \end{pmatrix}$$

II. $$I_1 \otimes I_2 = \begin{pmatrix} \left(\breve{\upsilon}_{\mu_1}(\varrho).\breve{\upsilon}_{\mu_2}(\varrho)\right)e^{2\pi i(\psi_{\mu_1}(\varrho).\psi_{\mu_2}(\varrho))}, \\ \left(\hat{\varepsilon}_{A_1}(\varrho) + \hat{\varepsilon}_{A_2}(\varrho) - \hat{\varepsilon}_{A_1}(\varrho).\hat{\varepsilon}_{AI_2}(\varrho)\right)e^{2\pi i(\varphi_{A_1}(\varrho)+\varphi_{A_2}(\varrho)-\varphi_{A_1}(\varrho).\varphi_{A_2}(\varrho))}, \\ \left(\tilde{\Upsilon}_{v_1}(\varrho) + \tilde{\Upsilon}_{v_2}(\varrho) - \tilde{\Upsilon}_{v_1}(\varrho).\tilde{\Upsilon}_{v_2}(\varrho)\right)e^{2\pi i(\phi_{v_1}(\varrho)+\phi_{v_2}(\varrho)-\phi_{v_1}(\varrho).\phi_{v_2}(\varrho))} \end{pmatrix}$$

III. $$''\Omega.I = \begin{pmatrix} \left(1 - \left(1 - \breve{\upsilon}_{\mu_I}(\varrho)\right)^{''\Omega}\right)e^{2\pi i(1-(1-\psi_{\mu_I}(\varrho))^{''\Omega})}, \\ \left(\hat{\varepsilon}_{A_I}(\varrho)\right)^{''\Omega}e^{2\pi i(\varphi_{A_I}(\varrho))^{''\Omega}}, \\ \left(\tilde{\Upsilon}_{v_I}(\varrho)\right)^{''\Omega}e^{2\pi i(\phi_{v_I}(\varrho))^{''\Omega}} \end{pmatrix}, \; ''\Omega > 0$$

IV. $$I^{''\Omega} = \begin{pmatrix} \left(\breve{\upsilon}_{\mu I}(\varrho)\right)^{''\Omega}e^{2\pi i(\psi_{\mu_I}(\varrho))^{''\Omega}}, \\ \left(1 - \left(1 - \hat{\varepsilon}_{A_I}(\varrho)\right)^{''\Omega}\right)e^{2\pi i(1-(1-\varphi_{A_I}(\varrho))^{''\Omega})}, \\ \left(1 - \left(1 - \tilde{\Upsilon}_{v_I}(\varrho)\right)^{''\Omega}\right)e^{2\pi i(1-(1-\phi_{v_I}(\varrho))^{''\Omega})} \end{pmatrix}, \; ''\Omega > 0$$

3. Previous Study

This section aims to recall the concepts of the HM operator since the HM operator is a very useful tool to aggregate real numbers. Moreover, we use the concepts of HM operator for further development of this article.

Definition 7. *[40] The HM operator is defined as:*

$$HM^{(ꙡ)}(I_1, I_2, \ldots, I_n) = \frac{\sum_{1 \le i_1 <, \ldots, < i_ꙡ \le n}\left(\prod_{i=1}^{ꙡ} I_{i_j}\right)^{\frac{1}{ꙡ}}}{C_n^{ꙡ}} \tag{1}$$

where $C_k^{ꙡ}$ *denotes the binomial coefficient, i.e.,* $C_n^{ꙡ} = \frac{n!}{ꙡ!(n-ꙡ)!}$*, and* ꙡ *is such that* $1 \le ꙡ \le n$*.*

The HM operator must satisfy the following axioms.

1. $HM^{(ꙡ)}(I_1, I_2, \ldots, I_k) = I$ if $I_i = I$, $(i = 1, 2, 3, \ldots, k)$.
2. $HM^{(ꙡ)}(I_1, I_2, \ldots, I_k) \le HM^{(ꙡ)}(\acute{\omega}_1, \acute{\omega}_2, \ldots, \acute{\omega}_k)$ if $I_i \le \acute{\omega}_i$, $(i = 1, 2, 3, \ldots, k)$.

3. $min(I_i) \leq HM^{(ɰ)}(I_1, I_2, \ldots, I_k) \leq max I_i$.
4. For arithmetic mean operator $HM^{(ɰ)}(I_1, I_2, \ldots, I_k) = \frac{1}{k}\sum_{i=1}^{k} I_i$
5. For geometric mean operator $HM^{(ɰ)}(I_1, I_2, \ldots, I_k) = (\prod_{i=1}^{k} I_i)^{\frac{1}{ɰ}}$

Now we study the notion of DHM operators given by the [56].

Definition 8. *[56] The DHM operator is particularized as:*

$$DHM^{(ɰ)}(I_1, I_2, \ldots, I_n) = \left(\prod_{1 \leq i_1 <, \ldots, < i_ɰ \leq n} \left(\frac{\sum_{j=1}^{ɰ} I_j}{ɰ} \right) \right)^{\frac{1}{C_n^{ɰ}}} \tag{2}$$

Definition 9. *[45] Consider* $I_j = \left(\breve{\mathrm{o}}_{\mu_j}(\varrho), \Upsilon_{v_j}(\varrho) \right), j = 1, 2, \ldots, k$ *be the family of PyFVs. Then PyF Hamy mean (PyFHM) operator is particularized as:*

$$PyFHM^{(ɰ)}(I_1, I_2, \ldots, I_n) = \frac{\underset{1 \leq i_1 <, \ldots, < i_ɰ \leq n}{\oplus} \left(\overset{ɰ}{\underset{i=1}{\otimes}} I_{i_j} \right)^{\frac{1}{ɰ}}}{C_n^{ɰ}}$$

$$= \left(\begin{array}{c} \sqrt{1 - \left(\prod_{1 \leq i_1 <, \ldots, < i_ɰ \leq n} \left(1 - \left(\left(\prod_{j=1}^{ɰ} \breve{\mathrm{o}}_{\mu_j}(\varrho) \right)^{\frac{1}{ɰ}} \right)^2 \right) \right)^{\frac{1}{C_n^{ɰ}}}}, \\ \left(\prod_{1 \leq i_1 <, \ldots, < i_ɰ \leq n} \sqrt{\left(1 - \left(\prod_{j=1}^{ɰ} \left(1 - \left(\Upsilon_{v_j}(\varrho) \right)^2 \right) \right)^{\frac{1}{ɰ}} \right)} \right)^{\frac{1}{C_n^{ɰ}}} \end{array} \right)$$

Definition 10. *[47] Consider* $I_j = \left(\left[\breve{\mathrm{o}}_{\mu j}(\varrho), \Upsilon_{v_j}(\varrho) \right], \left[t_j(\varrho), u_j(\varrho) \right] \right), j = 1, 2, \ldots, k$, *to be any collection of interval-valued IFNs (IVIFNs). Then IVIF Hamy mean (IVIFHM) operator is particularized as:*

$$IVIFHM^{(ɰ)}(I_1, I_2, \ldots, I_n) = \frac{\underset{1 \leq i_1 <, \ldots, < i_ɰ \leq n}{\oplus} \left(\overset{ɰ}{\underset{i=1}{\otimes}} I_{i_j} \right)^{\frac{1}{ɰ}}}{C_n^{ɰ}}$$

$$IVIFHM^{(ɰ)}(I_1, I_2, \ldots, I_n) = \left(\begin{array}{c} \left[\begin{array}{c} 1 - \left(\prod_{1 \leq i_1 <, \ldots, < i_ɰ \leq n} \left(1 - \left(\prod_{j=1}^{ɰ} \breve{\mathrm{o}}_{\mu_j}(\varrho) \right)^{\frac{1}{ɰ}} \right) \right)^{\frac{1}{C_n^{ɰ}}}, \\ 1 - \left(\prod_{1 \leq i_1 <, \ldots, < i_ɰ \leq n} \left(1 - \left(\prod_{j=1}^{ɰ} \Upsilon_{v_j}(\varrho) \right)^{\frac{1}{ɰ}} \right) \right)^{\frac{1}{C_n^{ɰ}}} \end{array} \right], \\ \left[\begin{array}{c} \left(\prod_{1 \leq i_1 <, \ldots, < i_ɰ \leq n} \left(1 - \left(\prod_{j=1}^{ɰ} \left(1 - t_{\mu_j}(\varrho) \right) \right)^{\frac{1}{ɰ}} \right) \right)^{\frac{1}{C_n^{ɰ}}}, \\ \left(\prod_{1 \leq i_1 <, \ldots, < i_ɰ \leq n} \left(1 - \left(\prod_{j=1}^{ɰ} \left(1 - u_{v_j}(\varrho) \right) \right)^{\frac{1}{ɰ}} \right) \right)^{\frac{1}{C_n^{ɰ}}} \end{array} \right] \end{array} \right)$$

By utilizing theory of HM tool, we generalized concepts of CPFSs having two aspects of TI, AI, and FI in amplitude and phase terms. We also introduced some new AOs such as CPFHM and CPFWHM operators with their basic properties.

4. Complex Picture Fuzzy Hamy Mean Operators

Now we utilize the concept of HM operator to discover some new AOs under the system of CPF information. We establish AOs of CPFHM and CPFWHM operators with their basic properties of idempotency, monotonicity, and boundedness.

Definition 11. *Consider* $I_j = \left(\breve{\upsilon}_{\mu_j}(\varrho)e^{2i\pi\psi_{\mu j}(\varrho)},\ \mathfrak{E}_{A_j}(\varrho)e^{2i\pi\varphi_{Aj}(\varrho)},\ \Upsilon_{v_j}(\varrho)e^{2i\pi\phi_{v_j}(\varrho)}\right), j = 1, 2, \ldots, k$, *to be the any family of CPFVs. Then, the CPFHM operator is given as:*

$$CPFHM^{(ɰ)}(I_1, I_2, \ldots, I_n) = \frac{\oplus_{1\le i_1<,\ldots,<i_ɰ\le n}\left(\bigotimes_{i=1}^{ɰ} I_j\right)^{\frac{1}{ɰ}}}{C_n^{ɰ}} \tag{3}$$

Theorem 1. *Consider* $I_j = \left(\breve{\upsilon}_{\mu_j}(\varrho)e^{2i\pi\psi_{\mu j}(\varrho)},\ \mathfrak{E}_{A_j}(\varrho)e^{2i\pi\varphi_{Aj}(\varrho)},\ \Upsilon_{v_j}(\varrho)e^{2i\pi\phi_{v_j}(\varrho)}\right), j = 1, 2, \ldots, k$ *to be any family of CPFVs. Then, accumulated value is also a CPFV.*

$$CPFHM^{(ɰ)}(I_1, I_2, \ldots, I_n) = \begin{pmatrix} 1-\left(\prod_{1\le i_1<,\ldots,<i_ɰ\le n}\left(1-\left(\prod_{j=1}^{ɰ}\breve{\upsilon}_{\mu_j}(\varrho)\right)^{\frac{1}{ɰ}}\right)\right)^{\frac{1}{C_n^{ɰ}}}. \\ e^{2\pi i\left(1-\left(\prod_{1\le i_1<,\ldots,<i_ɰ\le n}\left(1-\left(\prod_{j=1}^{ɰ}\psi_{\mu_j}(\varrho)\right)^{\frac{1}{ɰ}}\right)\right)^{\frac{1}{C_n^{ɰ}}}\right)}, \\ \left(\prod_{1\le i_1<,\ldots,<i_ɰ\le n}\left(1-\left(\prod_{j=1}^{ɰ}\left(1-\mathfrak{E}_{A_j}(\varrho)\right)\right)^{\frac{1}{ɰ}}\right)\right)^{\frac{1}{C_n^{ɰ}}}. \\ e^{2\pi i\left(\left(\prod_{1\le i_1<,\ldots,<i_ɰ\le n}\left(1-\left(\prod_{j=1}^{ɰ}\left(1-\varphi_{Aj}(\varrho)\right)\right)^{\frac{1}{ɰ}}\right)\right)^{\frac{1}{C_n^{ɰ}}}\right)} \\ \left(\prod_{1\le i_1<,\ldots,<i_ɰ\le n}\left(1-\left(\prod_{j=1}^{ɰ}\left(1-\Upsilon_{v_j}(\varrho)\right)\right)^{\frac{1}{ɰ}}\right)\right)^{\frac{1}{C_n^{ɰ}}}. \\ e^{2\pi i\left(\left(\prod_{1\le i_1<,\ldots,<i_ɰ\le n}\left(1-\left(\prod_{j=1}^{ɰ}\left(1-\phi_{v_j}(\varrho)\right)\right)^{\frac{1}{ɰ}}\right)\right)^{\frac{1}{C_n^{ɰ}}}\right)} \end{pmatrix} \tag{4}$$

Proof of this theorem given in Appendix A.

Further, we have to prove the basic properties of CPFHM operators such as idempotency, monotonicity, and boundedness under the basic operations of CPFHM.

Theorem 2. *(Idempotency Property) Consider* $I_j = \left(\breve{\upsilon}_{\mu_j}(\varrho)e^{2i\pi\psi_{\mu j}(\varrho)},\ \mathfrak{E}_{A_j}(\varrho)e^{2i\pi\varphi_{Aj}(\varrho)},\ \Upsilon_{v_j}(\varrho)e^{2i\pi\phi_{v_j}(\varrho)}\right), j = 1, 2, \ldots, k$ *to be the family of all same CPFVs. Then, CPFHM is given as:*

$$CPFHM^{ɰ}(I_1, I_2, \ldots, I_n) = I$$

We studied the proof of this theorem in Appendix A.

Theorem 3. *(Monotonicity Property), Consider* $I_j = \left(\breve{\upsilon}_{\mu_j}(\varrho)e^{2i\pi\psi_{\mu j}(\varrho)},\ \hat{\varepsilon}_{A_j}(\varrho)e^{2i\pi\varphi_{Aj}(\varrho)},\ \tilde{\Upsilon}_{v_j}(\varrho)e^{2i\pi\phi_{v_j}(\varrho)}\right)$, *and* $R_j(\varrho) = \left(g_{\mu_j}(\varrho)e^{2i\pi\alpha_{\mu j}(\varrho)},\ t_{A_j}(\varrho)e^{2i\pi\gamma_{Aj}(\varrho)}, h_{vj}(\varrho)e^{2i\pi\beta_{vj}(\varrho)}\right), j = 1, 2, \ldots, k$ *are any two CPFSs. If* $I_j(\varrho) \le R_j(\varrho)$. $\breve{\upsilon}_{\mu_j}(\varrho) \le g_{\mu_j}(\varrho)$, $\psi_{\mu j}(\varrho) \le \alpha_{\mu_j}(\varrho)$, $\hat{\varepsilon}_{A_j}(\varrho) \le t_{A_j}(\varrho)$, $\varphi_{Aj}(\varrho) \le \gamma_{Aj}(\varrho)$ *and* $\tilde{\Upsilon}_{vj}(\varrho) \le h_{vj}(\varrho)$, $\phi_{vj}(\varrho) \le \beta_{vj}(\varrho)$ *then:*

$$CPFHM^{\varrho}(I_1, I_2, \ldots, I_n) \le CPFHM^{\varrho}(R_1, R_2, \ldots, R_n)$$

We discussed the proof of the Theorem 3 in Appendix A.

Theorem 4. *(Boundedness Property), Consider* $I_j = \left(\breve{\upsilon}_{\mu_j}(\varrho)e^{2i\pi\psi_{\mu j}(\varrho)},\ \hat{\varepsilon}_{A_j}(\varrho)e^{2i\pi\varphi_{Aj}(\varrho)},\ \tilde{\Upsilon}_{v_j}(\varrho)e^{2i\pi\phi_{v_j}(\varrho)}\right), j = 1, 2, \ldots, k$, *to be the family of CPFVs, if* $I_j^- = min(I_1,\ I_2,\ I_3,\ \ldots,\ I_n)$ *and* $I_j^+ = max(I_1,\ I_2,\ I_3,\ \ldots,\ I_n)$ *Then:*

$$I^- \le CPFHM^{щ}(I_1, I_2, \ldots, I_n) \le I^+$$

Proof: From the Theorem 2:

$$CPFHM^{щ}(I_1, I_2, \ldots, I_n) = I^-$$

$$CPFHM^{щ}(I_1, I_2, \ldots, I_n) = I^+$$

□

From The Theorem 3,

$$I^- \le CPFHM^{щ}(I_1, I_2, \ldots, I_n) \le I^+$$

Now we discuss the CPFWHM operator by utilizing the basic operations of the HM operator. To solve the MADM techniques, the decision maker uses a weight vector of all attributes given by the experts.

Definition 12. *Consider* $I_j = \left(\breve{\upsilon}_{\mu_j}(\varrho)e^{2i\pi\psi_{\mu j}(\varrho)},\ \hat{\varepsilon}_{A_j}(\varrho)e^{2i\pi\varphi_{Aj}(\varrho)}, \tilde{\Upsilon}_{v_j}(\varrho)e^{2i\pi\phi_{v_j}(\varrho)}\right), j = 1, 2, \ldots, k$, *to be the family of CPFVs and corresponding weight vectors* $\mathfrak{N}_i = (\mathfrak{N}_1, \mathfrak{N}_2,\ \ldots,\ \mathfrak{N}_n)^T$, $\mathfrak{N}_i \in [0,1]$ *and* $\sum_{i=1}^{n} \mathfrak{N}_i = 1$. *Then:*

$$CPFWHM^{(щ)}(I_1, I_2, \ldots, I_n) = \frac{\underset{1 \le i_1 <, \ldots, < i_щ \le n}{\oplus} \left(1 - \prod_{j=1}^{щ} \mathfrak{N}_{i_j}\right)\left(\overset{щ}{\underset{j=1}{\otimes}}\left(I_{i_j}\right)\right)^{\frac{1}{щ}}}{C_n^{щ}} \tag{5}$$

Theorem 5. *Consider* $I_j = \left(\breve{\upsilon}_{\mu_j}(\varrho)e^{2i\pi\psi_{\mu j}(\varrho)},\ \hat{\varepsilon}_{A_j}(\varrho)e^{2i\pi\varphi_{Aj}(\varrho)}, \tilde{\Upsilon}_{v_j}(\varrho)e^{2i\pi\phi_{v_j}(\varrho)}\right), j = 1, 2, \ldots, k$, *to be the family of CPFVs, Then the accumulated index of the CPFWHM operator is also a CPFV:*

$$CPFWHM^{(\text{ч})}(I_1, I_2, \ldots, I_n) = \left(\begin{array}{c} 1 - \left(\prod_{1 \le i_1 <, \ldots, < i_{\text{ч}} \le n} \left(1 - \left(\prod_{j=1}^{\text{ч}} \breve{\upsilon}_{\mu_{i_j}}(\varrho) \right)^{\frac{1}{\text{ч}}} \right)^{(1 - \prod_{j=1}^{\text{ч}} \mathfrak{N}_{i_j})} \right)^{\frac{1}{C_n^{\text{ч}}}} \\ e^{2\pi i \left(1 - \left(\prod_{1 \le i_1 <, \ldots, < i_{\text{ч}} \le n} \left(1 - \left(\prod_{j=1}^{\text{ч}} \psi_{\mu_{i_j}}(\varrho) \right)^{\frac{1}{\text{ч}}} \right)^{(1 - \prod_{j=1}^{\text{ч}} \mathfrak{N}_{i_j})} \right)^{\frac{1}{C_n^{\text{ч}}}} \right)}, \\ \left(\prod_{1 \le i_1 <, \ldots, < i_{\text{ч}} \le n} \left(1 - \left(\prod_{j=1}^{\text{ч}} \left(1 - \left(\mathfrak{E}_{A_j}(\varrho) \right) \right) \right)^{\frac{1}{\text{ч}}} \right)^{(1 - \prod_{j=1}^{\text{ч}} \mathfrak{N}_{i_j})} \right)^{\frac{1}{C_n^{\text{ч}}}} \\ e^{2\pi i \left(\left(\prod_{1 \le i_1 <, \ldots, < i_{\text{ч}} \le n} \left(1 - \left(\prod_{j=1}^{\text{ч}} \left(1 - (\varphi_{Aj}(\varrho)) \right) \right)^{\frac{1}{\text{ч}}} \right)^{(1 - \prod_{j=1}^{\text{ч}} \mathfrak{N}_{i_j})} \right)^{\frac{1}{C_n^{\text{ч}}}} \right)}, \\ \left(\prod_{1 \le i_1 <, \ldots, < i_{\text{ч}} \le n} \left(1 - \left(\prod_{j=1}^{\text{ч}} \left(1 - \left(\tilde{\Upsilon}_{v_{i_j}}(\varrho) \right) \right) \right)^{\frac{1}{\text{ч}}} \right)^{(1 - \prod_{j=1}^{\text{ч}} \mathfrak{N}_{i_j})} \right)^{\frac{1}{C_n^{\text{ч}}}} \\ e^{2\pi i \left(\left(\prod_{1 \le i_1 <, \ldots, < i_{\text{ч}} \le n} \left(1 - \left(\prod_{j=1}^{\text{ч}} \left(1 - (\phi_{v_{i_j}}(\varrho)) \right) \right)^{\frac{1}{\text{ч}}} \right)^{(1 - \prod_{j=1}^{\text{ч}} \mathfrak{N}_{i_j})} \right)^{\frac{1}{C_n^{\text{ч}}}} \right)} \end{array} \right) \tag{6}$$

Proof of this theorem is given in Appendix A.

We established a numerical example to support the CPFWHM operator by using the methodology of the Definition 12.

Example 2. *Let* $I_1 = \left(0.28e^{2\pi i(0.42)}, 0.36e^{2\pi i(0.18)}, 0.33e^{2\pi i(0.19)}\right)$, $I_2 = \left(0.15e^{2\pi i(0.07)}, 0.52e^{2\pi i(0.09)}, 0.15e^{2\pi i(0.66)}\right)$, $I_3 = \left(0.64e^{2\pi i(0.15)}, 0.09e^{2\pi i(0.42)}, 0.16e^{2\pi i(0.15)}\right)$ *are three CPFVs with corresponding weight vectors* $\mathfrak{N} = (0.45,\ 0.35,\ 20)$, *suppose that* $\text{ч} = 2$. *Then,*

$$CPFWHM^{(\text{ч})}(I_1, I_2, \ldots, I_n) = \left(\begin{array}{c} \left(1 - \left(\prod_{1 \le i_1 <, \ldots, < i_{\text{ч}} \le n} \left(1 - \left(\prod_{j=1}^{\text{ч}} \breve{\upsilon}_{\mu_{i_j}}(\varrho) \right)^{\frac{1}{\text{ч}}} \right)^{(1 - \prod_{j=1}^{\text{ч}} \mathfrak{N}_{i_j})} \right)^{\frac{1}{C_n^{\text{ч}}}} \right) \\ e^{2\pi i \left(\left(1 - \left(\prod_{1 \le i_1 <, \ldots, < i_{\text{ч}} \le n} \left(1 - \left(\prod_{j=1}^{\text{ч}} \psi_{\mu_{i_j}}(\varrho) \right)^{\frac{1}{\text{ч}}} \right)^{(1 - \prod_{j=1}^{\text{ч}} \mathfrak{N}_{i_j})} \right)^{\frac{1}{C_n^{\text{ч}}}} \right) \right)}, \\ \left(\prod_{1 \le i_1 <, \ldots, < i_{\text{ч}} \le n} \left(1 - \left(\prod_{j=1}^{\text{ч}} \left(1 - \mathfrak{E}_{A_j}(\varrho) \right) \right)^{\frac{1}{\text{ч}}} \right)^{(1 - \prod_{j=1}^{\text{ч}} \mathfrak{N}_{i_j})} \right)^{\frac{1}{C_n^{\text{ч}}}} \\ e^{2\pi i \left(\left(\prod_{1 \le i_1 <, \ldots, < i_{\text{ч}} \le n} \left(1 - \left(\prod_{j=1}^{\text{ч}} (1 - \varphi_{Aj}(\varrho)) \right)^{\frac{1}{\text{ч}}} \right)^{(1 - \prod_{j=1}^{\text{ч}} \mathfrak{N}_{i_j})} \right)^{\frac{1}{C_n^{\text{ч}}}} \right)}, \\ \left(\prod_{1 \le i_1 <, \ldots, < i_{\text{ч}} \le n} \left(1 - \left(\prod_{j=1}^{\text{ч}} \left(1 - \tilde{\Upsilon}_{v_{i_j}}(\varrho) \right) \right)^{\frac{1}{\text{ч}}} \right)^{(1 - \prod_{j=1}^{\text{ч}} \mathfrak{N}_{i_j})} \right)^{\frac{1}{C_n^{\text{ч}}}} \\ e^{2\pi i \left(\left(\left(\prod_{1 \le i_1 <, \ldots, < i_{\text{ч}} \le n} \left(1 - \left(\prod_{j=1}^{\text{ч}} (1 - \phi_{v_{i_j}}(\varrho)) \right)^{\frac{1}{\text{ч}}} \right)^{(1 - \prod_{j=1}^{\text{ч}} \mathfrak{N}_{i_j})} \right) \right)^{\frac{1}{C_n^{\text{ч}}}} \right)} \end{array} \right)$$

$$= \left(\begin{array}{c} 1 - \left(\begin{array}{c} \left(1-(0.28\times 0.15)^{0.5}\right)^{(1-(0.45\times 0.35))}. \\ \left(1-(0.28\times 0.64)^{0.5}\right)^{(1-(0.45\times 0.20))} \\ \left(1-(0.15\times 0.64)^{0.5}\right)^{(1-(0.35\times 0.20))} \end{array} \right)^{\frac{1}{6}} \\ e^{2\pi i \left(1 - \left(\begin{array}{c} (1-(0.42\times 0.07)^{0.5})^{(1-(1-0.20\times 0.15))}. \\ (1-(0.42\times 0.15)^{0.5})^{(1-(0.45\times 0.20))} \\ (1-(0.07\times 0.15)^{0.5})^{(1-(0.35\times 0.20))} \end{array} \right)^{\frac{1}{6}} \right)}, \\ \left(\begin{array}{c} \left(1-((1-0.36)\times(1-0.52))^{0.5}\right)^{(1-(0.45\times 0.35))}. \\ \left(1-((1-0.36)\times(1-0.09))^{0.5}\right)^{(1-(0.45\times 0.20))} \\ \left(1-((1-0.52)\times(1-0.09))^{0.5}\right)^{(1-(0.35\times 0.20))} \end{array} \right)^{\frac{1}{6}} \\ e^{2\pi i \left(\left(\begin{array}{c} (1-((1-0.18)\times(1-0.09))^{0.5})^{(1-(0.45\times 0.35))}. \\ (1-((1-0.18)\times(1-0.42))^{0.5})^{(1-(0.45\times 0.20))} \\ (1-((1-0.09)\times(1-0.42))^{0.5})^{(1-(0.35\times 0.20))} \end{array} \right)^{\frac{1}{6}} \right)}, \\ \left(\begin{array}{c} \left(1-((1-0.33)\times(1-0.15))^{0.5}\right)^{(1-(0.45\times 0.35))}. \\ \left(1-((1-0.33)\times(1-0.16))^{0.5}\right)^{(1-(0.45\times 0.20))} \\ \left(1-((1-0.15)\times(1-0.16))^{0.5}\right)^{(1-(0.35\times 0.20))} \end{array} \right)^{\frac{1}{6}} \\ e^{2\pi i \left(\left(\begin{array}{c} (1-((1-0.19)\times(1-0.66))^{0.5})^{(1-(0.45\times 0.35))}. \\ (1-((1-0.19)\times(1-0.15))^{0.5})^{(1-(0.45\times 0.20))} \\ (1-((1-0.66)\times(1-0.15))^{0.5})^{(1-(0.35\times 0.20))} \end{array} \right)^{\frac{1}{6}} \right)} \end{array} \right)$$

$$= \left(0.0981e^{2\pi i(0.0309)}, 0.5793e^{2\pi i(0.4433)}, 0.4166e^{2\pi i(0.5770)}\right)$$

Theorem 6. *(Idempotency Property), Consider* $I_j = \left(\text{ʊ}_{\mu_j}(\varrho)e^{2\pi i\psi_{\mu j}(\varrho)}, \text{ȇ}_{A_j}(\varrho)e^{2\pi i\varphi_{Aj}(\varrho)}, \Upsilon_{v_j}(\varrho)e^{2\pi i\phi_{v_j}(\varrho)}\right), j = 1, 2, \ldots, k$*, to be the family of all identical CPFVs. Then:*

$$CPFWHM^{\text{ɰ}}(I_1, I_2, \ldots, I_n) = I$$

Proof: Proof is analogously. □

Theorem 7. *(Monotonicity Property), Consider* $I_j = \left(\text{ʊ}_{\mu_j}(\varrho)e^{2\pi i\psi_{\mu j}(\varrho)}, \text{ȇ}_{A_j}(\varrho)e^{2\pi i\varphi_{Aj}(\varrho)}, \Upsilon_{v_j}(\varrho)e^{2\pi i\phi_{v_j}(\varrho)}\right)$*, and* $R_j(\varrho) = \left(g_{\mu_j}(\varrho)e^{2\pi i\alpha_{\mu j}(\varrho)}, t_{A_j}(\varrho)e^{2\pi i\gamma_{Aj}(\varrho)}, h_{vj}(\varrho)e^{2\pi i\beta_{vj}(\varrho)}\right), j = 1, 2, \ldots, k$ *are any two CPFSs. If* $I_j(\varrho) \le R_j(\varrho)$*.* $\text{ʊ}_{\mu_j}(\varrho) \le g_{\mu_j}(\varrho)$, $\psi_{\mu j}(\varrho) \le \alpha_{\mu_j}(\varrho)$, $\text{ȇ}_{A_j}(\varrho) \le t_{A_j}(\varrho)$, $\varphi_{Aj}(\varrho) \le \gamma_{Aj}(\varrho)$ *and* $\Upsilon_{vj}(\varrho) \le h_{vj}(\varrho)$, $\phi_{vj}(\varrho) \le \beta_{vj}(\varrho)$ *. Then:*

Proof: Straightforward. □

Theorem 8. *(Boundedness Property),*

Consider $I_j = \left(\breve{\upsilon}_{\mu_j}(\varrho)e^{2\pi i\psi_{\mu j}(\varrho)},\ \mathfrak{E}_{A_j}(\varrho)e^{2\pi i\varphi_{Aj}(\varrho)}, \Upsilon_{v_j}(\varrho)e^{2\pi i\phi_{v_j}(\varrho)}\right), j = 1,2,\ldots,k,$ *to be the family of CPFVs, if:*

$$I_j^- = min(I_1,\ I_2,\ I_3,\ \ldots,\ I_n)$$

and

$$I_j^+ = max(I_1,\ I_2,\ I_3,\ \ldots,\ I_n)$$

then

$$I^- \leq CPFWHM^{ɰ}(I_1, I_2, \ldots, I_n) \leq I^+$$

From boundedness property:

$$CPFWHM^{ɰ}(I_1, I_2, \ldots, I_n) = I^-$$
$$CPFWHM^{ɰ}(I_1, I_2, \ldots, I_n) = I^+$$

From monotonicity property

$$I^- \leq CPFWHM^{ɰ}(I_1, I_2, \ldots, I_n) \leq I^+$$

We explored the proof of the Theorem 8 in Appendix A.

5. Complex Picture Fuzzy Dual Hamy Mean Operators

We establish AOs of CPFDHM and CPFWDHM operators by using the basic idea of DHM operator under the system of CPF information. To find the validity of our discussion strategy, we gave a numerical example.

Definition 13. *Consider* $I_j = \left(\breve{\upsilon}_{\mu_j}(\varrho)e^{2\pi i\psi_{\mu j}(\varrho)},\ \mathfrak{E}_{A_j}(\varrho)e^{2\pi i\varphi_{Aj}(\varrho)}, \Upsilon_{v_j}(\varrho)e^{2\pi i\phi_{v_j}(\varrho)}\right), j = 1,$ $2,\ldots,k,$ *to be the family of CPFVs. Then CPFDHM operator is given as:*

$$CPFDHM^{(ɰ)}(I_1, I_2, \ldots, I_n) = \left(\prod_{1\leq i_1<,\ldots,<i_{ɰ}\leq n}\left(\frac{\sum_{j=1}^{ɰ} I_{i_j}}{ɰ}\right)\right)^{\frac{1}{C_n^{ɰ}}} \tag{7}$$

Theorem 9. *Consider* $I_j = \left(\breve{\upsilon}_{\mu_j}(\varrho)e^{2\pi i\psi_{\mu j}(\varrho)},\ \mathfrak{E}_{A_j}(\varrho)e^{2\pi i\varphi_{Aj}(\varrho)}, \Upsilon_{v_j}(\varrho)e^{2\pi i\phi_{v_j}(\varrho)}\right), j = 1,2,\ldots,k,$ *to be the family of CPFVs. Then CPFDHM operator is given as:*

$$CPFDHM^{(ɰ)}(I_1, I_2, \ldots, I_n) = \left(\prod_{1\leq i_1<,\ldots,<i_{ɰ}\leq n}\left(\frac{\sum_{j=1}^{ɰ} I_{i_j}}{ɰ}\right)\right)^{\frac{1}{C_n^{ɰ}}} \tag{8}$$

Proof: The proof is analogous to the proof of Theorem 1. □

Remark 2. *All the properties of CPFWHM operator such as idempotency, monotonicity, and boundedness are prove similar to Theorems 2, 3 and 4.*

We elaborated the concept of DHM tool to establish a new AOs of CPFDHM operator under the system of CPFSs.

Definition 14. *Consider* $I_j = \left(\breve{\upsilon}_{\mu_j}(\varrho)e^{2\pi i\psi_{\mu j}(\varrho)}, \mathfrak{E}_{A_j}(\varrho)e^{2\pi i\varphi_{Aj}(\varrho)}, \tilde{\Upsilon}_{v_j}(\varrho)e^{2\pi i\phi_{v_j}(\varrho)}\right), j = 1, 2, \ldots, k$, *to be the family of CPFVs, with corresponding weight vectors* $\mathfrak{N}_i = (\mathfrak{N}_1, \mathfrak{N}_2, \ldots, \mathfrak{N}_n)^T$, $\mathfrak{N}_i \in [0,1]$ *and* $\sum_{i=1}^{n} \mathfrak{N}_i = 1$. *Then:*

$$CPFWDHM^{(\text{ щ})}(I_1, I_2, \ldots, I_n) = \frac{\underset{1\le i_1<,\ldots,<i_{щ}\le n}{\otimes}\left(1-\prod_{j=1}^{щ}\mathfrak{N}_{i_j}\right)\left(\underset{j=1}{\overset{щ}{\oplus}}\left(I_{i_j}\right)\right)^{\frac{1}{щ}}}{C_n^{щ}} \tag{9}$$

Theorem 10. *Consider* $I_j = \left(\breve{\upsilon}_{\mu_j}(\varrho)e^{2i\pi\psi_{\mu j}(\varrho)}, \mathfrak{E}_{A_j}(\varrho)e^{2i\pi\varphi_{Aj}(\varrho)}, \tilde{\Upsilon}_{v_j}(\varrho)e^{2i\pi\phi_{v_j}(\varrho)}\right), j = 1, 2, \ldots, k$, *to be the family of CPFV, then:*

$$CPFWDHM^{(щ)}(I_1, I_2, \ldots, I_n) = \left(\begin{array}{c} \left(\prod_{1\le i_1<,\ldots,<i_{щ}\le n}\left(1-\left(\prod_{j=1}^{щ}\left(1-\left(\breve{\upsilon}_{\mu_{i_j}}(\varrho)\right)\right)\right)^{\frac{1}{щ}}\right)^{(1-\prod_{j=1}^{щ}\mathfrak{N}_{i_j})}\right)^{\frac{1}{C_n^{щ}}} e^{2\pi i\left(\left(\prod_{1\le i_1<,\ldots,<i_{щ}\le n}\left(1-\left(\prod_{j=1}^{щ}\left(1-\left(\psi_{\mu_{i_j}}(\varrho)\right)\right)\right)^{\frac{1}{щ}}\right)^{(1-\prod_{j=1}^{щ}\mathfrak{N}_{i_j})}\right)^{\frac{1}{C_n^{щ}}}\right)}, \\ 1-\left(\prod_{1\le i_1<,\ldots,<i_{щ}\le n}\left(1-\left(\prod_{j=1}^{щ}\mathfrak{E}_{A_j}(\varrho)\right)^{\frac{1}{щ}}\right)^{(1-\prod_{j=1}^{щ}\mathfrak{N}_{i_j})}\right)^{\frac{1}{C_n^{щ}}} e^{2\pi i\left(1-\left(\prod_{1\le i_1<,\ldots,<i_{щ}\le n}\left(1-\left(\prod_{j=1}^{щ}\varphi_{Aj}(\varrho)\right)^{\frac{1}{щ}}\right)^{(1-\prod_{j=1}^{щ}\mathfrak{N}_{i_j})}\right)^{\frac{1}{C_n^{щ}}}\right)}, \\ 1-\left(\prod_{1\le i_1<,\ldots,<i_{щ}\le n}\left(1-\left(\prod_{j=1}^{щ}\tilde{\Upsilon}_{v_{i_j}}(\varrho)\right)^{\frac{1}{щ}}\right)^{(1-\prod_{j=1}^{щ}\mathfrak{N}_{i_j})}\right)^{\frac{1}{C_n^{щ}}} e^{2\pi i\left(1-\left(\prod_{1\le i_1<,\ldots,<i_{щ}\le n}\left(1-\left(\prod_{j=1}^{щ}\phi_{v_{i_j}}(\varrho)\right)^{\frac{1}{щ}}\right)^{(1-\prod_{j=1}^{щ}\mathfrak{N}_{i_j})}\right)^{\frac{1}{C_n^{щ}}}\right)} \end{array}\right) \tag{10}$$

Proof: The proof is similar to the proof of Theorem 5. □

To support Definition 14, we establish the following practice Example 3 by utilizing the idea of CPFWDHM operator.

Example 3. *Let* $I_1 = \left(0.42e^{2\pi i(0.18)}, 0.04e^{2\pi i(0.36)}, 0.16e^{2\pi i(0.23)}\right)$, $I_2 = \left(0.08e^{2\pi i(0.16)}, 0.62e^{2\pi i(0.27)}, 0.26e^{2\pi i(0.19)}\right)$, $I_3 = \left(0.53e^{2\pi i(0.22)}, 0.12e^{2\pi i(0.32)}, 0.33e^{2\pi i(0.22)}\right)$ *are three CPFVs with corresponding weight vectors* $\mathfrak{N} = (0.45, 0.35, 0.20)$, *and suppose that* $щ = 2$. *Then*

$$CPFWDHM^{(щ)}(I_1, I_2, \ldots, I_n) = \begin{pmatrix} \left(\prod_{1\le i_1<,\ldots,<i_щ\le n}\left(1-\left(\prod_{j=1}^{щ}\left(1-\left(ὒ_{\mu_{i_j}}(\varrho)\right)\right)\right)^{\frac{1}{щ}}\right)^{(1-\prod_{j=1}^{щ}\mathfrak{N}_{i_j})}\right)^{\frac{1}{C_n^{щ}}} e^{2\pi i\left(\left(\prod_{1\le i_1<,\ldots,<i_щ\le n}\left(1-\left(\prod_{j=1}^{щ}\left(1-\left(\psi_{\mu_{i_j}}(\varrho)\right)\right)\right)^{\frac{1}{щ}}\right)^{(1-\prod_{j=1}^{щ}\mathfrak{N}_{i_j})}\right)^{\frac{1}{C_n^{щ}}}\right)}, \\ 1-\left(\prod_{1\le i_1<,\ldots,<i_щ\le n}\left(1-\left(\prod_{j=1}^{щ}ȿ_{A_j}(\varrho)\right)^{\frac{1}{щ}}\right)^{(1-\prod_{j=1}^{щ}\mathfrak{N}_{i_j})}\right)^{\frac{1}{C_n^{щ}}} e^{2\pi i\left(1-\left(\prod_{1\le i_1<,\ldots,<i_щ\le n}\left(1-\left(\prod_{j=1}^{щ}\varphi_{A_j}(\varrho)\right)^{\frac{1}{щ}}\right)^{(1-\prod_{j=1}^{щ}\mathfrak{N}_{i_j})}\right)^{\frac{1}{C_n^{щ}}}\right)}, \\ 1-\left(\prod_{1\le i_1<,\ldots,<i_щ\le n}\left(1-\left(\prod_{j=1}^{щ}\Upsilon_{v_{i_j}}(\varrho)\right)^{\frac{1}{щ}}\right)^{(1-\prod_{j=1}^{щ}\mathfrak{N}_{i_j})}\right)^{\frac{1}{C_n^{щ}}} e^{2\pi i\left(1-\left(\prod_{1\le i_1<,\ldots,<i_щ\le n}\left(1-\left(\prod_{j=1}^{щ}\phi_{v_{i_j}}(\varrho)\right)^{\frac{1}{щ}}\right)^{(1-\prod_{j=1}^{щ}\mathfrak{N}_{i_j})}\right)^{\frac{1}{C_n^{щ}}}\right)} \end{pmatrix}$$

$$= \left(0.6149e^{2\pi i(0.3800)}, 0.0320e^{2\pi i(0.0896)}, 0.0546e^{2\pi i(0.0407)}\right)$$

Remark 3. *All the properties of CPFWDHM operator like idempotency, monotonicity, and boundedness are proved similar to Theorems 2, 3 and 4.*

6. MADM Techniques and Its Algorithm

In this section, we study a method to solve the procedure of the MADM technique under the system of PFSs. We also apply our discussed approaches like CPFWHM and CPFWDHM operators. Consider $ϰ = (ϰ_1, ϰ_2, \ldots, ϰ_n)$ be a discrete set of alternatives, which can be evaluated by using characteristics (set of attributes) $Æ = (Æ_1, Æ_2, \ldots, Æ_n)$ with corresponding weight vectors $Æ = (\mathfrak{N}_1, \mathfrak{N}_2, \ldots, \mathfrak{N}_n)^T, \mathfrak{N}, \in [0,1]$ and $\sum_{i=1}^{n} \mathfrak{N}_i = 1$. Each alternative has information on the environment of CPFSs. After accumulation of the information results in the state of CPFVs,

$I_{i_j} = \left(ὒ_{\mu_j}(\varrho)e^{2\pi i\psi_{\mu j}(\varrho)}, ȿ_{A_j}(\varrho)e^{2\pi i\varphi_{A j}(\varrho)}, \Upsilon_{v_j}(\varrho)e^{2\pi i\phi_{v_j}(\varrho)}\right), j = 1,2,\ldots,k$, these results must satisfy such conditions:

$0 \le ὒ_{\mu_j}(\varrho) + ȿ_{A_j}(\varrho) + \Upsilon_{v_j}(\varrho) \le 1$ and $0 \le \psi_{\mu j}(\varrho) + \varphi_{A j}(\varrho) + \phi_{v_j}(\varrho) \le 1$.

A decision matrix $Đ = (å_{ij})_{m\times n}$ is depicted in the following form:

$$Đ = \begin{bmatrix} I_{11} & I_{12} & \cdots & I_{1n} \\ I_{21} & I_{22} & \cdots & I_{2n} \\ \vdots & \vdots & \ddots & \vdots \\ I_{m1} & I_{m2} & \cdots & I_{mn} \end{bmatrix}$$

To solve a MADM technique, we follow the steps of the following algorithm.

Steps 1: A decision maker constructs a decision matrix having information in form of alternative $щ = (щ_1, щ_2, \ldots, щ_n)$ and attributes $Æ = (Æ_1, Æ_2, \ldots, Æ_n)$ with corresponding weight vectors $\mathfrak{N}_i = (\mathfrak{N}_1, \mathfrak{N}_2, \ldots, \mathfrak{N}_n)^T$, $i = 1, 2, 3, \ldots, n$. All above-discussed information is packed in a decision matrix $Đ = (å_{ij})_{m\times n}$.

Step 2: Transformation of a decision matrix into a normalization matrix. The attributes can be divided into two types of criteria, cost type, and benefit type. If the cost factor involves then we have to transform the decision matrix into a normalizing matrix otherwise there is no need to transform the decision matrix. We can normalize the decision matrix by using the following technique.

$$Ð = (\mathring{a}_{ij}) = \begin{Bmatrix} \left(\tilde{\Upsilon}_{v_j}(\varrho)e^{2\pi i\phi_{v_j}(\varrho)}, \hat{\varepsilon}_{A_j}(\varrho)e^{2\pi i\varphi_{Aj}(\varrho)}, \breve{\upsilon}_{\mu_j}(\varrho)e^{2\pi i\psi_{\mu j}(\varrho)}\right) & if\ j\ is\ cost\ factor \\ \left(\breve{\upsilon}_{\mu_j}(\varrho)e^{2\pi i\psi_{\mu j}(\varrho)}, \hat{\varepsilon}_{A_j}(\varrho)e^{2\pi i\varphi_{Aj}(\varrho)}, \tilde{\Upsilon}_{v_j}(\varrho)e^{2\pi i\phi_{v_j}(\varrho)}\right) & if\ j\ is\ benefit\ factor \end{Bmatrix}$$

Steps 3: Accumulate CPF information depicted in the decision matrix by using our discussed approaches of CPFWHM and CPFWDHM operators.

Step 4: Investigate score values of the consequences of CPFWHM and CPFWDHM operators by using Definition 4.

Step 5: To find a suitable alternative, we have to make ranking and ordering of the score values.

A compressive flowchart explaining all the steps of algorithm is given below in Figure 1.

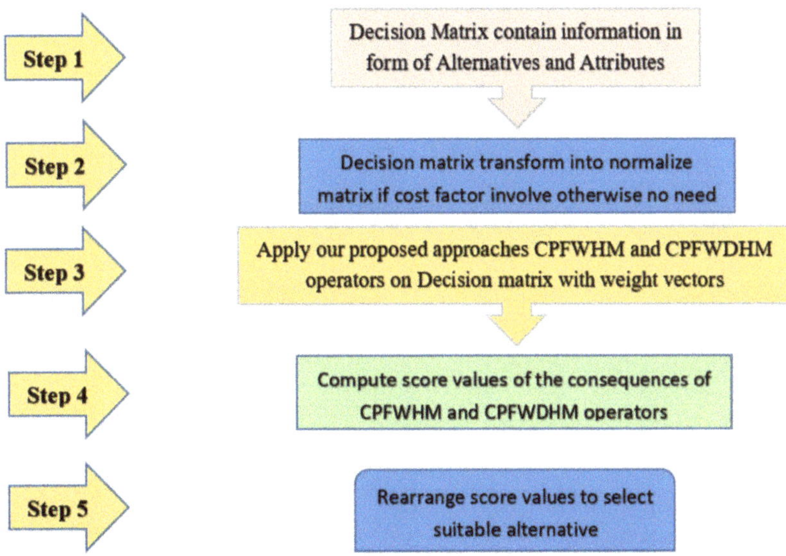

Figure 1. Flowchart of algorithm.

6.1. Application

A VMS is a program or piece of software that automates all of an organization's vendor-related tasks. An organization's communication and collaboration with vendors can be an important mechanism for these systems. On a VMS, a business can also effectively approve and monitor a vendor's portfolio and performance. A VMS enables your business to collect purchase orders from managers, optimize flexible worker onboarding, automate transactions, save and collect data from every stage of your contingent worker hiring process, and compile key performance indicators such as spending tracking, candidate information, payroll and invoice data. A vendor management system is often adopted by a business directly to manage its independent talent pool or by an MSP on its behalf. By improving the supply chain system and reducing the risk of operational disruptions, vendor management also enables firms to better controls and management of vendors. Additionally, it helps businesses ensure quality and timely delivery of various goods and services, which improves customer satisfaction levels. As a last advantage, the vendor management process enables companies in developing long-lasting and reputable relationships with their vendors, which leads to better rates being secured. A lot of research scholars worked on the theory of VMS to try to improve the mechanism of the VMS. Savaşaneril and Erkip [57] analyzed the purpose and advantages of vendor management software. Solyal and Süral [58] proposed the solution for inventory control under the system of VMS.

6.2. Numerical Example

In this numerical example, we evaluate the suitable software for VMS by observing the various qualities of different software presented by different multinational companies. The reliability and lifespan of a software for VMS depend on manufacturing and the degree of testing qualities. Consider we have to choose a suitable software for VMS from four different types of software $\beta_{þ}$, $(þ = 1, 2, 3, 4)$ according to observing a few qualities (attributes) $\eta_{þ}$, $(þ = 1, 2, 3)$ by assigning the experts. We select the best software for VMS based on the following characteristics: η_1 represents ease of navigation and setup; η_2 represents a large capacity to manage, order, invoices, deliveries, and payments; and η_3 represents product performance and warranty.

The experts assign different weight vectors $\mathfrak{N} = (0.35, 0.40, 0.25)$ to the attributes according to their characteristics. By using our proposed methodology, we select a suitable object from the given information by the decision maker. To investigate the best software for a VMS, we follow the above-discussed algorithm and its steps.

Step 1: The decision maker collects information under the system of CPFNs (this information is present in Table 2 which contains alternative and attributes).

Step 2: There is no need to transform the decision matrix because the cost factor does not involve the types of attributes.

Step 3: Accumulate the given information of CPFNs which is displayed in Table 2 by using CPFWHM and CPFWDHM operators. These AOs are used to deduce results of alternatives in form of CPFNs depicted in Table 3. The results of CPFNs representing in Table 3 for the parametric value of $ɰ = 2$.

Table 2. The decision matrix in the form of CPFVs.

	η_1		η_2
β_1	$\left(0.36e^{2\pi i(0.09)}, 0.15e^{2\pi i(0.36)}, 0.09e^{2\pi i(0.19)}\right)$	β_1	$\left(0.56e^{2\pi i(0.09)}, 0.12e^{2\pi i(0.44)}, 0.17e^{2\pi i(0.23)}\right)$
β_2	$\left(0.17e^{2\pi i(0.46)}, 0.35e^{2\pi i(0.09)}, 0.45e^{2\pi i(0.32)}\right)$	β_2	$\left(0.24e^{2\pi i(0.42)}, 0.17e^{2\pi i(0.38)}, 0.42e^{2\pi i(0.16)}\right)$
β_3	$\left(0.15e^{2\pi i(0.08)}, 0.45e^{2\pi i(0.36)}, 0.18e^{2\pi i(0.43)}\right)$	β_3	$\left(0.03e^{2\pi i(0.39)}, 0.07e^{2\pi i(0.15)}, 0.35e^{2\pi i(0.41)}\right)$
β_4	$\left(0.48e^{2\pi i(0.47)}, 0.07e^{2\pi i(0.15)}, 0.25e^{2\pi i(0.28)}\right)$	β_4	$\left(0.23e^{2\pi i(0.37)}, 0.17e^{2\pi i(0.34)}, 0.07e^{2\pi i(0.26)}\right)$
	η_3		
β_1	$\left(0.43e^{2\pi i(0.42)}, 0.15e^{2\pi i(0.27)}, 0.06e^{2\pi i(0.09)}\right)$		
β_2	$\left(0.09e^{2\pi i(0.12)}, 0.09e^{2\pi i(0.06)}, 0.42e^{2\pi i(0.24)}\right)$		
β_3	$\left(0.33e^{2\pi i(0.17)}, 0.28e^{2\pi i(0.33)}, 0.07e^{2\pi i(0.38)}\right)$		
β_4	$\left(0.38e^{2\pi i(0.62)}, 0.37e^{2\pi i(0.26)}, 0.05e^{2\pi i(0.07)}\right)$		

Table 3. Aggregated values by the CPFWHM and CPFWDHM.

CPFWHM	**CPFWDHM**
$\left(0.4087e^{2\pi i(0.1459)}, 0.1736e^{2\pi i(0.3995)}, 0.1334e^{2\pi i(0.2047)}\right)$	$\left(0.4931e^{2\pi i(0.2291)}, 0.1254e^{2\pi i(0.3202)}, 0.0888e^{2\pi i(0.1448)}\right)$
$\left(0.1415e^{2\pi i(0.2765)}, 0.2379e^{2\pi i(0.1982)}, 0.4715e^{2\pi i(0.2804)}\right)$	$\left(0.2007e^{2\pi i(0.3803)}, 0.1641e^{2\pi i(0.1227)}, 0.3938e^{2\pi i(0.2115)}\right)$
$\left(0.1201e^{2\pi i(0.1670)}, 0.3093e^{2\pi i(0.3235)}, 0.2335e^{2\pi i(0.4486)}\right)$	$\left(0.1201e^{2\pi i(0.1670)}, 0.3093e^{2\pi i(0.3235)}, 0.2335e^{2\pi i(0.4486)}\right)$
$\left(0.3232e^{2\pi i(0.4436)}, 0.2391e^{2\pi i(0.2907)}, 0.1457e^{2\pi i(0.2406)}\right)$	$\left(0.4088e^{2\pi i(0.5326)}, 0.1590e^{2\pi i(0.2182)}, 0.0907e^{2\pi i(0.1643)}\right)$

Step 4: Evaluate score values by using the results of CPFWHM and CPFWDHM operators depicted in Table 3. Computed score values are presented in Table 4.

Table 4. Score values of different software applications for a VMS.

Operators	$\hat{S}(ß_1)$	$\hat{S}(ß_2)$	$\hat{S}(ß_3)$	$\hat{S}(ß_4)$	Ranking and Ordering
CPFWHM	0.4406	0.3717	0.3287	0.4751	$ß_4 > ß_1 > ß_2 > ß_3$
CPFWDHM	0.5072	0.4482	0.4112	0.5515	$ß_4 > ß_1 > ß_2 > ß_3$

Step 5: Rearrange the results of score values to determine a suitable alternative by ordering and ranking the score values.

The following graphical representation explores the results of score values of CPFWHM and CPFWDHM operators in Figure 2.

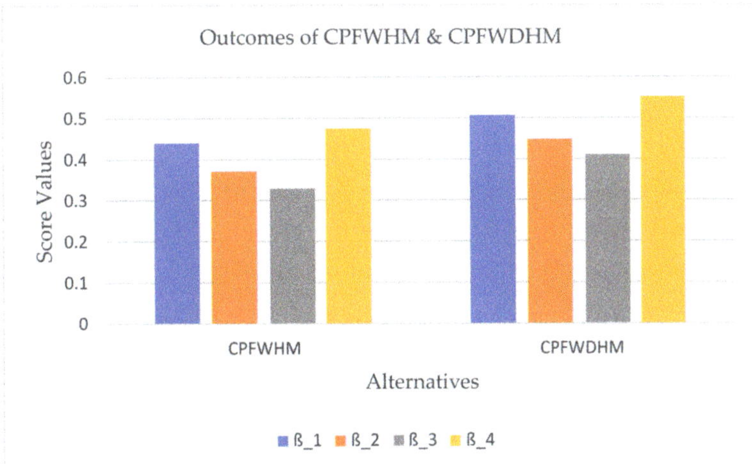

Figure 2. Score values of tourist destinations.

6.3. Influence Study

To find flexibility and reliability of our proposed methodologies, we use a different value of ɰ in binomial coefficient $C_n^{ɰ} = \frac{n!}{ɰ!(n-ɰ)!}$. We observe if the parametric value of ɰ increases, then the score values are obtained by the CPFWHM and CPFWDHM operators. We also observed if we increase the magnitude of the parametric value of ɰ, then there is no change in the ordering and ranking of the score values. All the score values which are obtained by the CPFWHM and CPFWDHM operators are shown in the following Table 5. After evaluating the score values, we see $ß_4$ is a suitable alternative for both AOs. Moreover, we represent score values geometrically in Figures 3 and 4 obtained by the CPFWHM and CPFWDHM operators, respectively.

Table 5. Ranking and ordering of the consequences of CPFWHM and CPFWDHM operators.

Operators	Parameters	$\hat{S}(ß_1)$	$\hat{S}(ß_2)$	$\hat{S}(ß_3)$	$\hat{S}(ß_4)$	Ranking and Ordering
CPFWHM	ɰ = 1	0.3734	0.3093	0.2788	0.4087	$ß_4 > ß_1 > ß_2 > ß_3$
	ɰ = 2	0.4406	0.3717	0.3287	0.4751	$ß_4 > ß_1 > ß_2 > ß_3$
	ɰ = 3	0.4589	0.3838	0.3407	0.4919	$ß_4 > ß_1 > ß_2 > ß_3$
CPFWDHM	ɰ = 1	0.5565	0.4916	0.4533	0.5935	$ß_4 > ß_1 > ß_2 > ß_3$
	ɰ = 2	0.5072	0.4482	0.4112	0.5515	$ß_4 > ß_1 > ß_2 > ß_3$
	ɰ = 3	0.4817	0.4569	0.3974	0.5181	$ß_4 > ß_1 > ß_2 > ß_3$

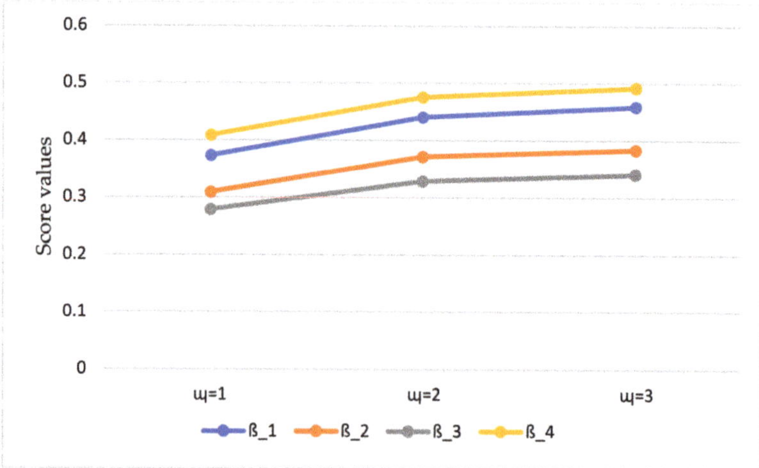

Figure 3. Results of the CPFWHM operator for different values of ɰ.

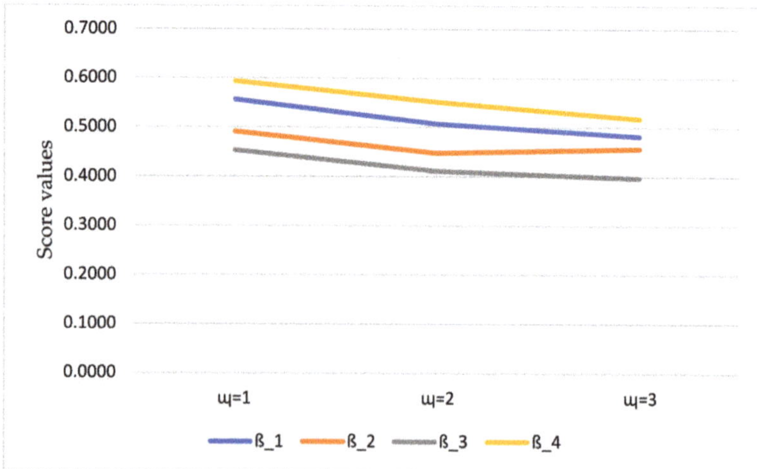

Figure 4. Results of the CPFWDHM operator for different values of ɰ.

7. Comparative Analysis

In this section, we contrast the results of existing AOs with the results of our proposed methodology. We applied existing AOs to the decision matrix developed by Garg and Rani [59], Akram et al. [39,60], Zhang et al. [61] and Ullah et al. [36]. We observed some existing AOs are unable to deal with the decision matrix shown in Table 2. The existing AOs [59–61] and [36] failed with the information given by the decision maker. We also study the consequences of AOs [39] shown in the following Table 6, which is obtained by the decision matrix shown in Table 2.

Table 6. Results of the comparative study.

Operator	Environment	Results
CIFWHM operator (current work)	CPFSs	$ß_3 > ß_3 > ß_3 > ß_3$
CIFWDHM operator (current work)	CPFSs	$ß_3 > ß_3 > ß_3 > ß_3$
CPFHWA Akram et al. [39]	CPFSs	$ß_4 > ß_1 > ß_2 > ß_3$
CPFHWG Akram et al. [39]	CPFSs	$ß_4 > ß_1 > ß_2 > ß_3$
Akram et al. [60]	CIFSs	Failed
Akram et al. [60]	CIFSs	Failed
Ullah et al. [36]	CPyFSs	Failed
Garg and Rani [59]	CIVIFSs	Failed
Zhang et al. [61]	PFSs	Failed

The following graphical interpretation shows results of our proposed AOs and CPF Hamacher weighted (CPFHW) averaging (CPFHWA) and CPFHW geometric (CPFHWG) operators in the Figure 5.

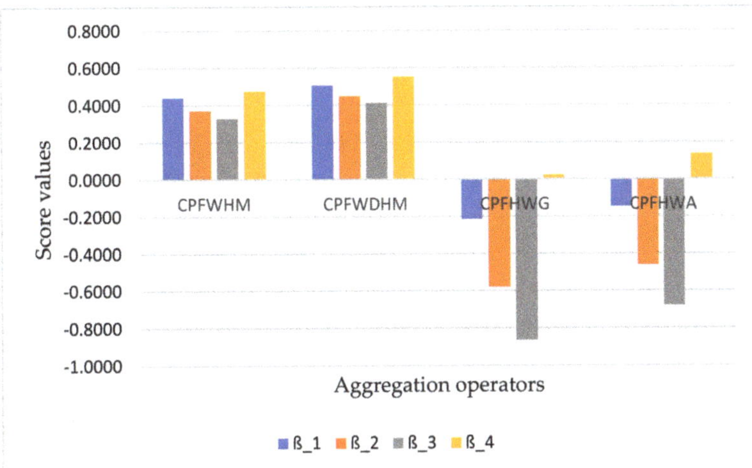

Figure 5. Comparison of existing AOs with our proposed methodologies.

8. Conclusions

To cope with uncertainty and vagueness, we established a series of new AOs under the system of CPFSs. A CPFS contains two aspects of MV, AV, and NMV in the form of amplitude and phase terms. A CPFS is superior and flexible because CPFSs are the extension of IFSs, PyFSs, q-ROFSs, CIFSs, CPyFSs, and PFSs. We deduced some new AOs of CPFHM and CPFWDHM operators by using the operational laws of the HM tool under the environment of CPFS with some basic characteristics such as idempotency, monotonicity, and boundedness. We also generalized concepts of HM operators in the framework of CPFDHM and CPFWDHM operators. To support our proposed methodology, we interpreted some examples. We established an application based on VMS under the system of CPFSs. A VMS is a software application that is utilized to handle vendors, ordering, invoices, and delivery procedures in several shopping malls, restaurants, and other numerous companies. To find the reliability and validity of our proposed AOs, we evaluated a numerical example to show usefulness and compatibility by using the technique of the MADM process under VMS. We also demonstrated a comprehensive comparative study to compare the results of our proposed methodology with existing AOs.

In future, we will elaborate our proposed work in the framework of picture fuzzy Maclaurin symmetric operators [62] and a further extension in the environment of a bipolar soft set [63]. Further, we will also extend our invented approaches in the framework of rough sets under the system of topological techniques [64].

Author Contributions: Conceptualization, A.H., D.P., Đ.V. and K.U.; methodology, A.H. and Đ.V.; software, A.H.; validation, D.P. and A.H.; formal analysis, K.U.; investigation, A.H.; resources, K.U.; data curation, K.U.; writing—original draft preparation, A.H.; writing—review and editing, A.H.; visualization, A.H.; supervision, K.U.; project administration, D.P.; funding acquisition, Đ.V. All authors have read and agreed to the published version of the manuscript.

Funding: This research received no external funding.

Conflicts of Interest: The authors declare no conflict of interest.

Appendix A

Proof of Theorem 1. This theorem has two parts. First, we derive the formula given in Equation (6) as follows:

$$\bigotimes_{i=1}^{ɰ} I_j = \begin{pmatrix} \prod_{j=1}^{ɰ} \breve{\upsilon}_{\mu_j}(\varrho) e^{2\pi i \left(\prod_{j=1}^{ɰ} \psi_{\mu_j}(\varrho)\right)}, \\ \left(1-\prod_{j=1}^{ɰ}\left(1-\hat{\varepsilon}_{A_j}(\varrho)\right)\right).e^{2\pi i \left(1-\prod_{j=1}^{ɰ}\left(1-\varphi_{A_j}(\varrho)\right)\right)}, \\ \left(1-\prod_{j=1}^{ɰ}\left(1-\tilde{\Upsilon}_{v_j}(\varrho)\right)\right).e^{2\pi i \left(1-\prod_{j=1}^{ɰ}\left(1-\phi_{v_j}(\varrho)\right)\right)} \end{pmatrix}$$

$$\left(\bigotimes_{i=1}^{ɰ} I_j\right)^{\frac{1}{ɰ}} = \begin{pmatrix} \left(\left(\prod_{j=1}^{X} \breve{\upsilon}_{\mu_j}(\varrho)\right)^{\frac{1}{ɰ}} e^{2\pi i \left(\prod_{j=1}^{ɰ} \psi_{\mu j}(\varrho)\right)^{\frac{1}{ɰ}}}\right), \\ \left(1-\prod_{j=1}^{ɰ}\left(1-\hat{\varepsilon}_{A_j}(\varrho)\right)^{\frac{1}{ɰ}} e^{2\pi i \left(1-\prod_{j=1}^{ɰ}\left(1-\varphi_{A j}(\varrho)\right)\right)^{\frac{1}{ɰ}}}\right) \\ \left(1-\prod_{j=1}^{X}\left(1-\tilde{\Upsilon}_{v_j}(\varrho)\right)^{\frac{1}{ɰ}} e^{2\pi i \left(1-\prod_{j=1}^{ɰ}\left(1-\phi_{v_j}(\varrho)\right)\right)^{\frac{1}{ɰ}}}\right) \end{pmatrix}$$

$$\bigoplus_{1\le i_t <,\ldots,< i_t} \left(\bigotimes_{i=1}^{n} I_j\right)^{\frac{1}{ɰ}}$$

$$= \begin{pmatrix} \left(\left(1-\prod_{1\le i_t<,\ldots,<i_t}\left(1-\left(\prod_{j=1}^{ɰ} \breve{\upsilon}_{\mu_j}(\varrho)\right)^{\frac{1}{ɰ}}\right) e^{2\pi i \left(1-\prod_{1\le i_t<,\ldots,<i_t}\left(1-\left(\prod_{j=1}^{ɰ}\psi_{\mu j}(\varrho)\right)^{\frac{1}{ɰ}}\right)\right)}\right)\right), \\ \left(\prod_{1\le i_t<,\ldots,<i_t}\left(1-\prod_{j=1}^{X}\left(\hat{\varepsilon}_{A_j}(\varrho)\right)^{\frac{1}{ɰ}}\right) e^{2\pi i \left(\prod_{1\le i_t<,\ldots,<i_t}\left(1-\left(\prod_{j=1}^{ɰ}\varphi_{A j}(\varrho)\right)^{\frac{1}{ɰ}}\right)\right)}\right) \\ \left(\prod_{1\le i_t<,\ldots,<i_t}\left(1-\prod_{j=1}^{X}\left(\tilde{\Upsilon}_{v_j}(\varrho)\right)^{\frac{1}{ɰ}}\right) e^{2\pi i \left(\prod_{1\le i_t<,\ldots,<i_t}\left(1-\left(\prod_{j=1}^{ɰ}\phi_{v_j}(\varrho)\right)^{\frac{1}{ɰ}}\right)\right)}\right) \end{pmatrix}$$

$$CPFHM^{\text{щ}}(I_1, I_2, \ldots, I_n) = \left(\begin{array}{c} 1 - \left(\prod_{1 \le i_1 <, \ldots, < i_{\text{щ}} \le n} \left(1 - \left(\prod_{j=1}^{\text{щ}} \breve{\upsilon}_{\mu_j}(\varrho) \right)^{\frac{1}{\text{щ}}} \right) \right)^{\frac{1}{C_n^{\text{щ}}}} \\ e^{2\pi i \left(1 - \left(\prod_{1 \le i_1 <, \ldots, < i_{\text{щ}} \le n} \left(1 - \left(\prod_{j=1}^{\text{щ}} \psi_{\mu j}(\varrho) \right)^{\frac{1}{\text{щ}}} \right) \right)^{\frac{1}{C_n^{\text{щ}}}} \right)}, \\ \left(\prod_{1 \le i_1 <, \ldots, < i_{\text{щ}} \le n} \left(1 - \left(\prod_{j=1}^{\text{щ}} \left(1 - \hat{\varepsilon}_{A_j}(\varrho) \right) \right)^{\frac{1}{\text{щ}}} \right) \right)^{\frac{1}{C_n^{\text{щ}}}} \\ e^{2\pi i \left(\prod_{1 \le i_1 <, \ldots, < i_{\text{щ}} \le n} \left(1 - \left(\prod_{j=1}^{\text{щ}} \left(1 - \varphi_{Aj}(\varrho) \right) \right)^{\frac{1}{\text{щ}}} \right) \right)^{\frac{1}{C_n^{\text{щ}}}}} \\ \left(\prod_{1 \le i_1 <, \ldots, < i_{\text{щ}} \le n} \left(1 - \left(\prod_{j=1}^{n} \left(1 - \tilde{\Upsilon}_{\nu_j}(\varrho) \right) \right)^{\frac{1}{\text{щ}}} \right) \right)^{\frac{1}{C_n^{\text{щ}}}} \\ e^{2\pi i \left(\prod_{1 \le i_1 <, \ldots, < i_{\text{щ}} \le n} \left(1 - \left(\prod_{j=1}^{\text{щ}} \left(1 - \phi_{\nu_j}(\varrho) \right) \right)^{\frac{1}{\text{щ}}} \right) \right)^{\frac{1}{C_n^{\text{щ}}}}} \end{array} \right)$$

Now, we prove that Equation (6) represents a CPFV, as follows:

(1) $\breve{\upsilon}_\mu(\varrho), \hat{\varepsilon}_A(\varrho), \tilde{\Upsilon}_\nu(\varrho) \in [0,1], \psi_\mu(\varrho), \varphi_A(\varrho), \phi_\nu(\varrho) \in [0,1]$

(2) $0 \le \breve{\upsilon}_\mu(\varrho) + \hat{\varepsilon}_A(\varrho) + \tilde{\Upsilon}_\nu(\varrho) \le 1$ and $0 \le \psi_\mu(\varrho) + \varphi_A(\varrho) + \phi_\nu(\varrho) \le 1$

$$\breve{\upsilon}_\mu(\varrho) = 1 - \left(\prod_{1 \le i_1 <, \ldots, < i_{\text{щ}} \le n} \left(1 - \left(\prod_{j=1}^{\text{щ}} \breve{\upsilon}_{\mu_j}(\varrho) \right)^{\frac{1}{\text{щ}}} \right) \right)^{\frac{1}{C_n^{\text{щ}}}}$$

$$\psi_\mu(\varrho) = 1 - \left(\prod_{1 \le i_1 <, \ldots, < i_{\text{щ}} \le n} \left(1 - \left(\prod_{j=1}^{\text{щ}} \psi_{\mu j}(\varrho) \right)^{\frac{1}{\text{щ}}} \right) \right)^{\frac{1}{C_n^{\text{щ}}}}$$

$$\hat{\varepsilon}_A(\varrho) = \left(\prod_{1 \le i_1 <, \ldots, < i_{\text{щ}} \le n} \left(1 - \left(\prod_{j=1}^{\text{щ}} \left(1 - \hat{\varepsilon}_{A_j}(\varrho) \right) \right)^{\frac{1}{\text{щ}}} \right) \right)^{\frac{1}{C_n^{\text{щ}}}}$$

$$\varphi_A(\varrho) = \left(\prod_{1 \le i_1 <, \ldots, < i_{\text{щ}} \le n} \left(1 - \left(\prod_{j=1}^{\text{щ}} (1 - \varphi_{Aj}(\varrho)) \right)^{\frac{1}{\text{щ}}} \right) \right)^{\frac{1}{C_n^{\text{щ}}}}$$

$$\tilde{\Upsilon}_\nu(\varrho) = \left(\prod_{1 \le i_1 <, \ldots, < i_{\text{щ}} \le n} \left(1 - \left(\prod_{j=1}^{\text{щ}} \left(1 - \tilde{\Upsilon}_{\nu_j}(\varrho) \right) \right)^{\frac{1}{\text{щ}}} \right) \right)^{\frac{1}{C_n^{\text{щ}}}}$$

$$\phi_\nu(\varrho) = \left(\prod_{1 \le i_1 <, \ldots, < i_{\text{щ}} \le n} \left(1 - \left(\prod_{j=1}^{\text{щ}} \left(1 - \phi_{\nu_j}(\varrho) \right) \right)^{\frac{1}{\text{щ}}} \right) \right)^{\frac{1}{C_n^{\text{щ}}}}$$

Since $0 \le \breve{\upsilon}_\mu(\varrho) \le 1$ and $0 \le \psi_\mu(\varrho) \le 1$.

$$0 \le \breve{\upsilon}_\mu(\varrho) e^{2\pi i \psi_\mu(\varrho)} \le 1$$

$$0 \leq \prod_{j=1}^{ш} \mho_{\mu_j}(\varrho) e^{2\pi i (\prod_{j=1}^{ш} \psi_{\mu_j}(\varrho))} \leq 1$$

$$0 \leq \prod_{j=1}^{ш} \mho_{\mu_j}(\varrho) e^{2\pi i (\prod_{j=1}^{ш} \psi_{\mu_j}(\varrho))} \leq 1$$

$$0 \leq 1 - \left(\prod_{j=1}^{X} \mho_{\mu_j}(\varrho) \right)^{\frac{1}{ш}} e^{2\pi i (1 - (\prod_{j=1}^{ш} \psi_{\mu_j}(\varrho))^{\frac{1}{ш}})} \leq 1$$

$$0 \leq \prod_{1 \leq i_1 <, \ldots, < i_ш \leq n} \left(1 - \left(\prod_{j=1}^{X} \mho_{\mu_j}(\varrho) \right)^{\frac{1}{ш}} \right) . e^{2\pi i (\prod_{1 \leq i_1 <, \ldots, < i_ш \leq n} (1 - (\prod_{j=1}^{ш} \psi_{\mu_j}(\varrho))^{\frac{1}{ш}}))} \leq 1$$

$$0 \leq \left(1 - \prod_{1 \leq i_1 <, \ldots, < i_ш \leq n} \left(1 - \left(\prod_{j=1}^{ш} \left(1 - \mho_{\mu_j}(\varrho) \right) \right)^{\frac{1}{ш}} \right) \right)^{\frac{1}{C_n^ш}}$$

$$e^{2\pi i \left(\left(1 - \prod_{1 \leq i_1 <, \ldots, < i_ш \leq n} \left(1 - \left(\prod_{j=1}^{ш} \left(1 - \psi_{\mu_j}(\varrho) \right) \right)^{\frac{1}{ш}} \right) \right)^{\frac{1}{C_n^ш}} \right)} \leq 1$$

In a similar way,

$$0 \leq \mathfrak{E}_A(\varrho) e^{2\pi i \varphi_A(\varrho)} \leq 1$$

and

$$0 \leq \Upsilon_v(\varrho) e^{2\pi i \phi_v(\varrho)} \leq 1$$

Since $0 \leq \mho_\mu(\varrho) e^{2\pi i \psi_\mu(\varrho)} \leq 1$, $0 \leq \mathfrak{E}_A(\varrho) e^{2\pi i \varphi_A(\varrho)} \leq 1$ and $0 \leq \Upsilon_v(\varrho) e^{2\pi i \phi_v(\varrho)} \leq 1$, therefore,

$$0 \leq \mho_\mu(\varrho) e^{2\pi i \psi_\mu(\varrho)} + \mathfrak{E}_A(\varrho) e^{2\pi i \varphi_A(\varrho)} + \Upsilon_v(\varrho) e^{2\pi i \phi_v(\varrho)} \leq 1$$

□

Proof of Theorem 2. Let $I_j = \left(\mho_{\mu_j}(\varrho) e^{2i\pi \psi_{\mu_j}(\varrho)}, \mathfrak{E}_{A_j}(\varrho) e^{2i\pi \varphi_{A_j}(\varrho)}, \Upsilon_{v_j}(\varrho) e^{2i\pi \phi_{v_j}(\varrho)} \right), j = 1, 2, \ldots, k$ be the family of all same CPFVs. Then CPFHM operator is as follows:

$$CPFHM^{(ш)}(I_1, I_2, \ldots, I_n) = \begin{pmatrix} 1 - \left(\prod_{1 \leq i_1 <, \ldots, < i_ш \leq n} \left(1 - \left(\prod_{j=1}^{ш} \mho_{\mu_j}(\varrho) \right)^{\frac{1}{ш}} \right) \right)^{\frac{1}{C_n^ш}} \\ e^{2\pi i \left(1 - \left(\prod_{1 \leq i_1 <, \ldots, < i_ш \leq n} \left(1 - \left(\prod_{j=1}^{ш} \psi_{\mu j}(\varrho) \right)^{\frac{1}{ш}} \right) \right)^{\frac{1}{C_n^ш}} \right)}, \\ \left(\prod_{1 \leq i_1 <, \ldots, < i_ш \leq n} \left(1 - \left(\prod_{j=1}^{ш} \left(1 - \mathfrak{E}_{A_j}(\varrho) \right) \right)^{\frac{1}{ш}} \right) \right)^{\frac{1}{C_n^ш}} \\ e^{2\pi i \left(\prod_{1 \leq i_1 <, \ldots, < i_ш \leq n} \left(1 - \left(\prod_{j=1}^{ш} \left(1 - \varphi_{A j}(\varrho) \right) \right)^{\frac{1}{ш}} \right) \right)^{\frac{1}{C_n^ш}}} \\ \left(\prod_{1 \leq i_1 <, \ldots, < i_ш \leq n} \left(1 - \left(\prod_{j=1}^{n} \left(1 - \Upsilon_{v_j}(\varrho) \right) \right)^{\frac{1}{ш}} \right) \right)^{\frac{1}{C_n^ш}} \\ e^{2\pi i \left(\prod_{1 \leq i_1 <, \ldots, < i_ш \leq n} \left(1 - \left(\prod_{j=1}^{ш} \left(1 - \phi_{v_j}(\varrho) \right) \right)^{\frac{1}{ш}} \right) \right)^{\frac{1}{C_n^ш}}} \end{pmatrix}$$

$$= \begin{pmatrix} 1-\left(\left(1-\left(\prod_{j=1}^{\text{щ}} \breve{\upsilon}_{\mu}(\varrho)\right)^{\frac{1}{\text{щ}}}\right)\right)^{\frac{1}{C_n^{\text{щ}}}} .e^{2\pi i\left(1-\left(\left(1-\left(\prod_{j=1}^{\text{щ}} \psi_{\mu}(\varrho)\right)^{\frac{1}{\text{щ}}}\right)\right)^{\frac{1}{C_n^{\text{щ}}}}\right)}, \\ \left(\left(1-\left(\prod_{j=1}^{\text{щ}} (1-\hat{\varepsilon}_A(\varrho))\right)^{\frac{1}{\text{щ}}}\right)\right)^{\frac{1}{C_n^{\text{щ}}}} .e^{2\pi i\left(\left(\left(1-\left(\prod_{j=1}^{\text{щ}} (1-\varphi_A(\varrho))\right)^{\frac{1}{\text{щ}}}\right)\right)^{\frac{1}{C_n^{\text{щ}}}}\right)} \\ \left(\left(1-\left(\prod_{j=1}^{\text{щ}} (1-\tilde{\Upsilon}_{\nu}(\varrho))\right)^{\frac{1}{\text{щ}}}\right)\right)^{\frac{1}{C_n^{\text{щ}}}} .e^{2\pi i\left(\left(\left(1-\left(\prod_{j=1}^{\text{щ}} (1-\phi_{\nu}(\varrho))\right)^{\frac{1}{\text{щ}}}\right)\right)^{\frac{1}{C_n^{\text{щ}}}}\right)} \end{pmatrix}$$

$$= \left(\breve{\upsilon}_{\mu}(\varrho)e^{2i\pi\psi_{\mu}}, \hat{\varepsilon}_A(\varrho)e^{2i\pi\varphi_A}, \tilde{\Upsilon}_{\nu}(\varrho)e^{2i\pi\phi_{\nu}}\right) = I$$

□

Proof of Theorem 3. Since $I_j(\varrho) \leq R_j(\varrho)$, $\breve{\upsilon}_{\mu_j}(\varrho) \leq g_{\mu_j}(\varrho)$, $\psi_{\mu j}(\varrho) \leq \alpha_{\mu_j}(\varrho)$, $\hat{\varepsilon}_{A_j}(\varrho) \leq t_{A_j}(\varrho)$, $\varphi_{Aj}(\varrho) \leq \gamma_{Aj}(\varrho)$ and $\tilde{\Upsilon}_{\nu j}(\varrho) \leq h_{\nu j}(\varrho)$, $\phi_{\nu j}(\varrho) \leq \beta_{\nu j}(\varrho)$, then:

$$\prod_{j=1}^{\text{щ}} \breve{\upsilon}_{\mu_j}(\varrho)e^{2\pi i(\prod_{j=1}^{\text{щ}} \psi_{\mu j}(\varrho))} \leq \prod_{j=1}^{\text{щ}} g_{\mu_j}e^{2\pi i(\prod_{j=1}^{\text{щ}} \alpha_{\mu j}(\varrho))}$$

$$1-\left(\prod_{j=1}^{\text{щ}} \breve{\upsilon}_{\mu_j}(\varrho)\right)^{\frac{1}{\text{щ}}} e^{2\pi i\left(1-\left(\prod_{j=1}^{\text{щ}} \psi_{\mu j}(\varrho)\right)^{\frac{1}{\text{щ}}}\right)} \geq 1-\left(\prod_{j=1}^{\text{щ}} g_{\mu_j}(\varrho)\right)^{\frac{1}{\text{щ}}} e^{2\pi i\left(1-\left(\prod_{j=1}^{\text{щ}} \alpha_{\mu j}(\varrho)\right)^{\frac{1}{\text{щ}}}\right)}$$

$$\left(\prod_{1\leq i_1<,\ldots,<i_{\text{щ}}\leq i_n}\left(1-\left(\prod_{j=1}^{\text{щ}} \breve{\upsilon}_{\mu_j}(\varrho)\right)^{\frac{1}{\text{щ}}}\right)^{\frac{1}{C_n^{\text{щ}}}}\right)$$

$$e^{2\pi i\left(\prod_{1\leq i_1<,\ldots,<i_{\text{щ}}\leq i_n}\left(1-\left(\prod_{j=1}^{\text{щ}} \psi_{\mu j}(\varrho)\right)^{\frac{1}{\text{щ}}}\right)^{\frac{1}{C_n^{\text{щ}}}}\right)} \geq \left(\prod_{1\leq i_1<,\ldots,<i_{\text{щ}}\leq i_n}\left(1-\left(\prod_{j=1}^{\text{щ}} g_{\mu_j}(\varrho)\right)^{\frac{1}{\text{щ}}}\right)^{\frac{1}{C_n^{\text{щ}}}}\right)$$

$$e^{2\pi i\left(\prod_{1\leq i_1<,\ldots,<i_{\text{щ}}\leq i_n}\left(1-\left(\prod_{j=1}^{\text{щ}} \alpha_{\mu j}(\varrho)\right)^{\frac{1}{\text{щ}}}\right)^{\frac{1}{C_n^{\text{щ}}}}\right)}$$

$$1-\left(\prod_{1\leq i_1<,\ldots,<i_{\text{щ}}\leq i_n}\left(1-\left(\prod_{j=1}^{\text{щ}} \breve{\upsilon}_{\mu_j}(\varrho)\right)^{\frac{1}{\text{щ}}}\right)^{\frac{1}{C_n^{\text{щ}}}}\right) e^{2\pi i\left(1-\left(\prod_{1\leq i_1<,\ldots,<i_{\text{щ}}\leq i_n}\left(1-\left(\prod_{j=1}^{\text{щ}} \psi_{\mu j}(\varrho)\right)^{\frac{1}{\text{щ}}}\right)^{\frac{1}{C_n^{\text{щ}}}}\right)\right)} \leq$$

$$1-\left(\prod_{1\leq i_1<,\ldots,<i_{\text{щ}}\leq i_n}\left(1-\left(\prod_{j=1}^{\text{щ}} g_{\mu_j}(\varrho)\right)^{\frac{1}{\text{щ}}}\right)^{\frac{1}{C_n^{\text{щ}}}}\right) e^{2\pi i\left(1-\left(\prod_{1\leq i_1<,\ldots,<i_{\text{щ}}\leq i_n}\left(1-\left(\prod_{j=1}^{\text{щ}} \alpha_{\mu j}(\varrho)\right)^{\frac{1}{\text{щ}}}\right)^{\frac{1}{C_n^{\text{щ}}}}\right)\right)}$$

Thus, the above equation can be written as $\breve{\upsilon}_{\mu_j}(\varrho)e^{2\pi i\psi_{\mu}(\varrho)} \leq g e^{2\pi i\alpha_{\mu}(\varrho)}$. We also investigate the value of $\hat{\varepsilon}_{A_j}(\varrho)e^{2\pi i\varphi_{Aj}(\varrho)} \geq t_{A_j}(\varrho)e^{2\pi i\varphi_{Aj}(\varrho)}$ and $\tilde{\Upsilon}_{\nu_j}(\varrho)e^{2\pi i\phi_{\nu}(\varrho)} \geq h_{\nu}(\varrho)e^{2\pi i\beta_{\nu}(\varrho)}$, keeping in mind the step of the above equations.

1. If $\breve{\upsilon}_{\mu_j}(\varrho)e^{2\pi i\psi_{\mu}(\varrho)} < g_{\mu_j}(\varrho)e^{2\pi i\alpha_{\mu}(\varrho)}$, $\hat{\varepsilon}_{A_j}(\varrho)e^{2\pi i\varphi_{Aj}(\varrho)} \geq t_{A_j}(\varrho)e^{2\pi i\varphi_{Aj}(\varrho)}$ and $\tilde{\Upsilon}_{\nu}(\varrho)e^{2\pi i\phi_{\nu}(\varrho)} > h_{\nu}(\varrho)e^{2\pi i\beta_{\nu}(\varrho)}$, then:

$$CPFHM^{\text{щ}}(I_1, I_2, \ldots, I_n) < CPFHM^{\text{щ}}(R_1, R_2, \ldots, R_n)$$

2. If $\breve{\upsilon}_{\mu_j}(\varrho)e^{2\pi i\psi_\mu(\varrho)} = g_{\mu_j}(\varrho)e^{2\pi i\alpha_\mu(\varrho)}$, $\hat{\varepsilon}_{A_j}(\varrho)e^{2\pi i\varphi_{Aj}(\varrho)} = t_{A_j}(\varrho)e^{2\pi i\varphi_{Aj}(\varrho)}$ and $\tilde{\Upsilon}_v(\varrho)e^{2\pi i\phi_v(\varrho)} > h_v(\varrho)e^{2\pi i\beta_v(\varrho)}$, then:

$$CPFHM^{ɰ}(I_1, I_2, \ldots, I_n) = CPFHM^{ɰ}(R_1, R_2, \ldots, R_n)$$

□

Proof of Theorem 5. We have

$$\bigotimes_{j=1}^{ɰ}\left(I_{i_j}\right) = \begin{pmatrix} \left(\prod_{j=1}^{ɰ}\breve{\upsilon}_{\mu_{i_j}}(\varrho)\right)e^{2\pi i\left(\prod_{j=1}^{ɰ}\psi_{\mu_{i_j}}(\varrho)\right)}, \\ 1-\prod_{j=1}^{ɰ}\left(1-\left(\hat{\varepsilon}_{A_j}(\varrho)\right)^n\right)e^{2\pi i\left(1-\prod_{j=1}^{ɰ}\left(1-\left(\varphi_{Aj}(\varrho)\right)^n\right)\right)}, \\ 1-\prod_{j=1}^{ɰ}\left(1-\left(\tilde{\Upsilon}_{v_{i_j}}(\varrho)\right)^n\right)e^{2\pi i\left(1-\prod_{j=1}^{ɰ}\left(1-\left(\phi_{v_{i_j}}(\varrho)\right)^n\right)\right)} \end{pmatrix}$$

$$\left(\bigotimes_{j=1}^{ɰ}\left(I_{i_j}\right)\right)^{\frac{1}{ɰ}} = \begin{pmatrix} \left(\prod_{j=1}^{ɰ}\breve{\upsilon}_{\mu_{i_j}}(\varrho)\right)^{\frac{1}{ɰ}}e^{2\pi i\left(\prod_{j=1}^{ɰ}\psi_{\mu_{i_j}}(\varrho)\right)^{\frac{1}{ɰ}}}, \\ \left(1-\left(\prod_{j=1}^{ɰ}\left(1-\left(\hat{\varepsilon}_{A_j}(\varrho)\right)^n\right)\right)^{\frac{1}{ɰ}}\right)e^{2\pi i\left(\left(1-\left(\prod_{j=1}^{ɰ}\left(1-\left(\varphi_{Aj}(\varrho)\right)^n\right)\right)^{\frac{1}{ɰ}}\right)\right)}, \\ \left(1-\left(\prod_{j=1}^{ɰ}\left(1-\left(\tilde{\Upsilon}_{v_{i_j}}(\varrho)\right)^n\right)\right)^{\frac{1}{ɰ}}\right)e^{2\pi i\left(1-\left(\prod_{j=1}^{ɰ}\left(1-\left(\phi_{v_{i_j}}(\varrho)\right)^n\right)\right)^{\frac{1}{ɰ}}\right)} \end{pmatrix}$$

$$\left(1-\prod_{j=1}^{ɰ}\mathfrak{N}_{i_j}\right)\left(\bigotimes_{j=1}^{ɰ}\left(I_{i_j}\right)\right)^{\frac{1}{ɰ}} = \begin{pmatrix} \left(1-\left(\left(1-\left(\prod_{j=1}^{ɰ}\breve{\upsilon}_{\mu_{i_j}}(\varrho)\right)^{\frac{1}{ɰ}}\right)^{\left(1-\prod_{j=1}^{ɰ}\mathfrak{N}_{i_j}\right)}\right)\right) \\ e^{2\pi i\left(1-\left(\left(1-\left(\prod_{j=1}^{ɰ}\psi_{\mu_{i_j}}(\varrho)\right)^{\frac{1}{ɰ}}\right)^{\left(1-\prod_{j=1}^{ɰ}\mathfrak{N}_{i_j}\right)}\right)\right)}, \\ \left(1-\left(\prod_{j=1}^{ɰ}\left(1-\hat{\varepsilon}_{A_j}(\varrho)\right)\right)^{\frac{1}{ɰ}}\right)^{\left(1-\prod_{j=1}^{ɰ}\mathfrak{N}_{i_j}\right)} \\ e^{2\pi i\left(\left(1-\left(\prod_{j=1}^{ɰ}\left(1-\varphi_{Aj}(\varrho)\right)\right)^{\frac{1}{ɰ}}\right)^{\left(1-\prod_{j=1}^{ɰ}\mathfrak{N}_{i_j}\right)}\right)}, \\ \left(1-\left(\prod_{j=1}^{ɰ}\left(1-\tilde{\Upsilon}_{v_{i_j}}(\varrho)\right)\right)^{\frac{1}{ɰ}}\right)^{\left(1-\prod_{j=1}^{ɰ}\mathfrak{N}_{i_j}\right)} \\ e^{2\pi i\left(\left(1-\left(\prod_{j=1}^{ɰ}\left(1-\phi_{v_{i_j}}(\varrho)\right)\right)^{\frac{1}{ɰ}}\right)^{\left(1-\prod_{j=1}^{ɰ}\mathfrak{N}_{i_j}\right)}\right)} \end{pmatrix}$$

$$\underset{1\le i_1<,\ldots,<i_{\text{щ}}\le n}{\oplus}\left(1-\prod_{j=1}^{\text{щ}}\mathfrak{N}_{i_j}\right)\left(\bigotimes_{j=1}^{\text{щ}}\left(I_{i_j}\right)\right)^{\frac{1}{\text{щ}}}=\begin{pmatrix}\left(1-\left(\prod_{1\le i_1<,\ldots,<i_{\text{щ}}\le n}\left(1-\left(\prod_{j=1}^{\text{щ}}\breve{\mho}_{\mu_{i_j}}(\varrho)\right)^{\frac{1}{\text{щ}}}\right)^{\left(1-\prod_{j=1}^{\text{щ}}\mathfrak{N}_{i_j}\right)}\right)\right)\\ e^{2\pi i\left(1-\left(\prod_{1\le i_1<,\ldots,<i_{\text{щ}}\le n}\left(1-\left(\prod_{j=1}^{\text{щ}}\psi_{\mu_{i_j}}(\varrho)\right)^{\frac{1}{\text{щ}}}\right)^{\left(1-\prod_{j=1}^{\text{щ}}\mathfrak{N}_{i_j}\right)}\right)\right)},\\ \left(\prod_{1\le i_1<,\ldots,<i_{\text{щ}}\le n}\left(1-\left(\prod_{j=1}^{\text{щ}}\left(1-\hat{\hat{\varepsilon}}_{A_j}(\varrho)\right)\right)^{\frac{1}{\text{щ}}}\right)^{\left(1-\prod_{j=1}^{\text{щ}}\mathfrak{N}_{i_j}\right)}\right),\\ e^{2\pi i\left(\left(\prod_{1\le i_1<,\ldots,<i_{\text{щ}}\le n}\left(1-\left(\prod_{j=1}^{\text{щ}}\left(1-\varphi_{Aj}(\varrho)\right)\right)^{\frac{1}{\text{щ}}}\right)^{\left(1-\prod_{j=1}^{\text{щ}}\mathfrak{N}_{i_j}\right)}\right)\right)}\\ \left(\prod_{1\le i_1<,\ldots,<i_{\text{щ}}\le n}\left(1-\left(\prod_{j=1}^{\text{щ}}\left(1-\tilde{\Upsilon}_{v_{i_j}}(\varrho)\right)\right)^{\frac{1}{\text{щ}}}\right)^{\left(1-\prod_{j=1}^{\text{щ}}\mathfrak{N}_{i_j}\right)}\right)\\ e^{2\pi i\left(\left(\prod_{1\le i_1<,\ldots,<i_{\text{щ}}\le n}\left(1-\left(\prod_{j=1}^{\text{щ}}\left(1-\phi_{v_{i_j}}(\varrho)\right)\right)^{\frac{1}{\text{щ}}}\right)^{\left(1-\prod_{j=1}^{\text{щ}}\mathfrak{N}_{i_j}\right)}\right)\right)}\end{pmatrix}$$

$$\frac{\underset{1\le i_1<,\ldots,<i_{\text{щ}}\le n}{\oplus}\left(1-\prod_{j=1}^{\text{щ}}\mathfrak{N}_{i_j}\right)\left(\bigotimes_{j=1}^{\text{щ}}\left(I_{i_j}\right)\right)^{\frac{1}{\text{щ}}}}{C_n^{\text{щ}}}=\begin{pmatrix}\left(1-\left(\prod_{1\le i_1<,\ldots,<i_{\text{щ}}\le n}\left(1-\left(\prod_{j=1}^{\text{щ}}\breve{\mho}_{\mu_{i_j}}(\varrho)\right)^{\frac{1}{\text{щ}}}\right)^{\left(1-\prod_{j=1}^{\text{щ}}\mathfrak{N}_{i_j}\right)}\right)^{\frac{1}{C_n^{\text{щ}}}}\right)\\ e^{2\pi i\left(\left(1-\left(\prod_{1\le i_1<,\ldots,<i_{\text{щ}}\le n}\left(1-\left(\prod_{j=1}^{\text{щ}}\psi_{\mu_{i_j}}(\varrho)\right)^{\frac{1}{\text{щ}}}\right)^{\left(1-\prod_{j=1}^{\text{щ}}\mathfrak{N}_{i_j}\right)}\right)^{\frac{1}{C_n^{\text{щ}}}}\right)\right)},\\ \left(\prod_{1\le i_1<,\ldots,<i_{\text{щ}}\le n}\left(1-\left(\prod_{j=1}^{\text{щ}}\left(1-\hat{\hat{\varepsilon}}_{A_j}(\varrho)\right)\right)^{\frac{1}{\text{щ}}}\right)^{\left(1-\prod_{j=1}^{\text{щ}}\mathfrak{N}_{i_j}\right)}\right)^{\frac{1}{C_n^{\text{щ}}}}\\ e^{2\pi i\left(\left(\prod_{1\le i_1<,\ldots,<i_{\text{щ}}\le n}\left(1-\left(\prod_{j=1}^{\text{щ}}\left(1-\varphi_{Aj}(\varrho)\right)\right)^{\frac{1}{\text{щ}}}\right)^{\left(1-\prod_{j=1}^{\text{щ}}\mathfrak{N}_{i_j}\right)}\right)^{\frac{1}{C_n^{\text{щ}}}}\right)},\\ \left(\prod_{1\le i_1<,\ldots,<i_{\text{щ}}\le n}\left(1-\left(\prod_{j=1}^{\text{щ}}\left(1-\tilde{\Upsilon}_{v_{i_j}}(\varrho)\right)\right)^{\frac{1}{\text{щ}}}\right)^{\left(1-\prod_{j=1}^{\text{щ}}\mathfrak{N}_{i_j}\right)}\right)^{\frac{1}{C_n^{\text{щ}}}}\\ e^{2\pi i\left(\left(\left(\prod_{1\le i_1<,\ldots,<i_{\text{щ}}\le n}\left(1-\left(\prod_{j=1}^{\text{щ}}\left(1-\phi_{v_{i_j}}(\varrho)\right)\right)^{\frac{1}{\text{щ}}}\right)^{\left(1-\prod_{j=1}^{\text{щ}}\mathfrak{N}_{i_j}\right)}\right)\right)^{\frac{1}{C_n^{\text{щ}}}}\right)}\end{pmatrix}$$

$$CPFWHM^{(\text{щ})}(I_1,I_2,\ldots,I_n)=\begin{pmatrix}\left(1-\left(\prod_{1\le i_1<,\ldots,<i_{\text{щ}}\le n}\left(1-\left(\prod_{j=1}^{\text{щ}}\breve{\mho}_{\mu_{i_j}}(\varrho)\right)^{\frac{1}{\text{щ}}}\right)^{\left(1-\prod_{j=1}^{\text{щ}}\mathfrak{N}_{i_j}\right)}\right)^{\frac{1}{C_n^{\text{щ}}}}\right)\\ e^{2\pi i\left(\left(1-\left(\prod_{1\le i_1<,\ldots,<i_{\text{щ}}\le n}\left(1-\left(\prod_{j=1}^{\text{щ}}\psi_{\mu_{i_j}}(\varrho)\right)^{\frac{1}{\text{щ}}}\right)^{\left(1-\prod_{j=1}^{\text{щ}}\mathfrak{N}_{i_j}\right)}\right)^{\frac{1}{C_n^{\text{щ}}}}\right)\right)},\\ \left(\prod_{1\le i_1<,\ldots,<i_{\text{щ}}\le n}\left(1-\left(\prod_{j=1}^{\text{щ}}\left(1-\hat{\hat{\varepsilon}}_{A_j}(\varrho)\right)\right)^{\frac{1}{\text{щ}}}\right)^{\left(1-\prod_{j=1}^{\text{щ}}\mathfrak{N}_{i_j}\right)}\right)^{\frac{1}{C_n^{\text{щ}}}}\\ e^{2\pi i\left(\left(\prod_{1\le i_1<,\ldots,<i_{\text{щ}}\le n}\left(1-\left(\prod_{j=1}^{\text{щ}}\left(1-\varphi_{Aj}(\varrho)\right)\right)^{\frac{1}{\text{щ}}}\right)^{\left(1-\prod_{j=1}^{\text{щ}}\mathfrak{N}_{i_j}\right)}\right)^{\frac{1}{C_n^{\text{щ}}}}\right)},\\ \left(\prod_{1\le i_1<,\ldots,<i_{\text{щ}}\le n}\left(1-\left(\prod_{j=1}^{\text{щ}}\left(1-\tilde{\Upsilon}_{v_{i_j}}(\varrho)\right)\right)^{\frac{1}{\text{щ}}}\right)^{\left(1-\prod_{j=1}^{\text{щ}}\mathfrak{N}_{i_j}\right)}\right)^{\frac{1}{C_n^{\text{щ}}}}\\ e^{2\pi i\left(\left(\left(\prod_{1\le i_1<,\ldots,<i_{\text{щ}}\le n}\left(1-\left(\prod_{j=1}^{\text{щ}}\left(1-\phi_{v_{i_j}}(\varrho)\right)\right)^{\frac{1}{\text{щ}}}\right)^{\left(1-\prod_{j=1}^{\text{щ}}\mathfrak{N}_{i_j}\right)}\right)\right)^{\frac{1}{C_n^{\text{щ}}}}\right)}\end{pmatrix}$$

Now, we have to show that is a CPFV.

(1) $\breve{\upsilon}_\mu(\varrho),\ \hat{\varepsilon}_A(\varrho),\ \tilde{\Upsilon}_v(\varrho) \in [0,1], \psi_\mu(\varrho), \varphi_A(\varrho),\ \phi_v(\varrho) \in [0,1]$

(2) $0 \le \breve{\upsilon}_\mu(\varrho) + \hat{\varepsilon}_A(\varrho) + \tilde{\Upsilon}_v(\varrho) \le 1$ and $0 \le \psi_\mu(\varrho) + \varphi_A(\varrho) + \phi_v(\varrho) \le 1$

$$\breve{\upsilon}_\mu(\varrho) = \left(1 - \left(\prod_{1 \le i_1 <, \ldots, < i_{ш} \le n} \left(1 - \left(\prod_{j=1}^{ш} \breve{\upsilon}_{\mu_{i_j}}(\varrho)\right)^{\frac{1}{ш}}\right)^{(1-\prod_{j=1}^{ш} \mathfrak{N}_{i_j})}\right)^{\frac{1}{C_n^{ш}}}\right)$$

$$\psi_\mu(\varrho) = \left(\left(1 - \left(\prod_{1 \le i_1 <, \ldots, < i_{ш} \le n} \left(1 - \left(\prod_{j=1}^{ш} \psi_{\mu_{i_j}}(\varrho)\right)^{\frac{1}{ш}}\right)^{(1-\prod_{j=1}^{ш} \mathfrak{N}_{i_j})}\right)^{\frac{1}{C_n^{ш}}}\right)\right)$$

$$\hat{\varepsilon}_A = \left(\prod_{1 \le i_1 <, \ldots, < i_{ш} \le n} \left(1 - \left(\prod_{j=1}^{ш} \left(1 - \hat{\varepsilon}_{A_j}(\varrho)\right)\right)^{\frac{1}{ш}}\right)^{(1-\prod_{j=1}^{ш} \mathfrak{N}_{i_j})}\right)^{\frac{1}{C_n^{ш}}}$$

$$\varphi_A = \left(\left(\prod_{1 \le i_1 <, \ldots, < i_{ш} \le n} \left(1 - \left(\prod_{j=1}^{ш} (1 - \varphi_{Aj}(\varrho))\right)^{\frac{1}{ш}}\right)^{(1-\prod_{j=1}^{ш} \mathfrak{N}_{i_j})}\right)^{\frac{1}{C_n^{ш}}}\right)$$

$$\tilde{\Upsilon}_v(\varrho) = \left(\prod_{1 \le i_1 <, \ldots, < i_{ш} \le n} \left(1 - \left(\prod_{j=1}^{ш} \left(1 - \tilde{\Upsilon}_{v_{i_j}}(\varrho)\right)\right)^{\frac{1}{ш}}\right)^{(1-\prod_{j=1}^{ш} \mathfrak{N}_{i_j})}\right)^{\frac{1}{C_n^{ш}}}$$

$$\phi_v(\varrho) = \left(\left(\left(\prod_{1 \le i_1 <, \ldots, < i_{ш} \le n} \left(1 - \left(\prod_{j=1}^{ш} \left(1 - \phi_{v_{i_j}}(\varrho)\right)\right)^{\frac{1}{ш}}\right)^{(1-\prod_{j=1}^{ш} \mathfrak{N}_{i_j})}\right)\right)^{\frac{1}{C_n^{ш}}}\right)^{\frac{1}{C_n^{ш}}}$$

Since $0 \le \breve{\upsilon}_\mu(\varrho) \le 1$ and $0 \le \psi_\mu(\varrho) \le 1$, we have:

$$0 \le \breve{\upsilon}_\mu(\varrho) e^{2\pi i \psi_\mu(\varrho)} \le 1$$

$$0 \le \prod_{j=1}^{ш} \breve{\upsilon}_{\mu_j}(\varrho) e^{2\pi i \left(\prod_{j=1}^{ш} \psi_{\mu_j}(\varrho)\right)} \le 1$$

$$0 \le \left(\prod_{j=1}^{ш} \breve{\upsilon}_{\mu_j}(\varrho)\right)^{\frac{1}{ш}} e^{2\pi i \left(\left(\prod_{j=1}^{ш} \psi_{\mu_j}(\varrho)\right)^{\frac{1}{ш}}\right)} \le 1$$

$$0 \le \left(\left(\prod_{j=1}^{ш} \breve{\upsilon}_{\mu_j}(\varrho)\right)^{\frac{1}{ш}}\right)^{1-\sum_{j=1}^{ш} \mathfrak{N}_{i_j}} e^{2\pi i \left(\left(\left(\prod_{j=1}^{ш} \psi_{\mu_j}(\varrho)\right)^{\frac{1}{ш}}\right)^{(1-\prod_{j=1}^{ш} \mathfrak{N}_{i_j})}\right)} \le 1$$

$$0 \le \prod_{1 \le i_1 <, \ldots, < i_{ш} \le n} \left(\left(\prod_{j=1}^{ш} \breve{\upsilon}_{\mu_j}(\varrho)\right)^{\frac{1}{ш}}\right)^{(1-\prod_{j=1}^{ш} \mathfrak{N}_{i_j})} e^{2\pi i \left(\prod_{1 \le i_1 <, \ldots, < i_{ш} \le n} \left(\left(\prod_{j=1}^{ш} \psi_{\mu_j}(\varrho)\right)^{\frac{1}{ш}}\right)^{(1-\prod_{j=1}^{ш} \mathfrak{N}_{i_j})}\right)} \le 1$$

$$0 \le 1 - \left(\prod_{1 \le i_1 <, \ldots, < i_{ш} \le n} \left(\left(\prod_{j=1}^{ш} \breve{\upsilon}_{\mu_j}(\varrho)\right)^{\frac{1}{ш}}\right)^{(1-\prod_{j=1}^{ш} \mathfrak{N}_{i_j})}\right)^{\frac{1}{C_n^{ш}}} e^{2\pi i \left(\left(1 - \left(\prod_{1 \le i_1 <, \ldots, < i_{ш} \le n} \left(\left(\left(\prod_{j=1}^{ш} \psi_{\mu_j}(\varrho)\right)^{\frac{1}{ш}}\right)^n\right)^{(1-\prod_{j=1}^{ш} \mathfrak{N}_{i_j})}\right)^{\frac{1}{C_n^{ш}}}\right)^{\frac{1}{n}}\right)} \le 1$$

Similarly, we can prove the following equations.

$$0 \leq \Upsilon_v(\varrho)e^{2\pi i\phi_v(\varrho)} \leq 1, \text{ and } 0 \leq \mathfrak{E}_A(\varrho)e^{2\pi i\varphi_A(\varrho)} \leq 1$$

Since $0 \leq \ddot{\mathrm{U}}_\mu(\varrho)e^{2\pi i\psi_\mu(\varrho)} \leq 1$, $0 \leq \mathfrak{E}_A(\varrho)e^{2\pi i\varphi_A(\varrho)} \leq 1$ and $0 \leq \Upsilon_v(\varrho)e^{2\pi i\phi_v(\varrho)} \leq 1$, therefore,

$$0 \leq \ddot{\mathrm{U}}_\mu(\varrho)e^{2\pi i\psi_\mu(\varrho)} + \mathfrak{E}_A(\varrho)e^{2\pi i\varphi_A(\varrho)} + \Upsilon_v(\varrho)e^{2\pi i\phi_v(\varrho)} \leq 1$$

□

Proof of Theorem 8. We prove this theorem by using previous Theorems 2 and 3.

From Theorem 5, we have:

$$CPFWHM^{(ɰ)}(I_1^-, I_2^-, \ldots, I_n^-) = \begin{pmatrix} \left(1 - \left(\prod_{1\leq i_1<,\ldots,<i_ɰ\leq n}\left(1 - \left(\prod_{j=1}^{ɰ}\min\left(\ddot{\mathrm{U}}_{\mu_{i_j}}(\varrho)\right)\right)^{\frac{1}{ɰ}}\right)^{(1-\prod_{j=1}^{ɰ}\mathfrak{N}_{i_j})}\right)^{\frac{1}{C_n^ɰ}}\right) \\ e^{2\pi i\left(\left(1 - \left(\prod_{1\leq i_1<,\ldots,<i_ɰ\leq n}\left(1 - \left(\prod_{j=1}^{ɰ} min(\psi_{\mu_{i_j}}(\varrho))\right)^{\frac{1}{ɰ}}\right)^{(1-\prod_{j=1}^{ɰ}\mathfrak{N}_{i_j})}\right)^{\frac{1}{C_n^ɰ}}\right)\right)}, \\ \left(\prod_{1\leq i_1<,\ldots,<i_ɰ\leq n}\left(1 - \left(\prod_{j=1}^{ɰ}\left(1 - max\left(\mathfrak{E}_{A_j}(\varrho)\right)\right)\right)^{\frac{1}{ɰ}}\right)^{(1-\prod_{j=1}^{ɰ}\mathfrak{N}_{i_j})}\right)^{\frac{1}{C_n^ɰ}} \\ e^{2\pi i\left(\left(\prod_{1\leq i_1<,\ldots,<i_ɰ\leq n}\left(1 - \left(\prod_{j=1}^{ɰ}(1 - max(\varphi_{Aj}(\varrho)))\right)^{\frac{1}{ɰ}}\right)^{(1-\prod_{j=1}^{ɰ}\mathfrak{N}_{i_j})}\right)^{\frac{1}{C_n^ɰ}}\right)}, \\ \left(\prod_{1\leq i_1<,\ldots,<i_ɰ\leq n}\left(1 - \left(\prod_{j=1}^{ɰ}\left(1 - max\left(\Upsilon_{v_{i_j}}(\varrho)\right)\right)\right)^{\frac{1}{ɰ}}\right)^{(1-\prod_{j=1}^{ɰ}\mathfrak{N}_{i_j})}\right)^{\frac{1}{C_n^ɰ}} \\ e^{2\pi i\left(\left(\left(\prod_{1\leq i_1<,\ldots,<i_ɰ\leq n}\left(1 - \left(\prod_{j=1}^{ɰ}(1 - max(\phi_{v_{i_j}}(\varrho)))\right)^{\frac{1}{ɰ}}\right)^{(1-\prod_{j=1}^{ɰ}\mathfrak{N}_{i_j})}\right)\right)^{\frac{1}{C_n^ɰ}}\right)} \end{pmatrix}$$

$$CPFWHM^{(ɰ)}(I_1^+, I_2^+, \ldots, I_n^+) = \begin{pmatrix} \left(1 - \left(\prod_{1\leq i_1<,\ldots,<i_ɰ\leq n}\left(1 - \left(\prod_{j=1}^{ɰ} max\left(\ddot{\mathrm{U}}_{\mu_{i_j}}(\varrho)\right)\right)^{\frac{1}{ɰ}}\right)^{(1-\prod_{j=1}^{ɰ}\mathfrak{N}_{i_j})}\right)^{\frac{1}{C_n^ɰ}}\right) \\ e^{2\pi i\left(\left(1 - \left(\prod_{1\leq i_1<,\ldots,<i_ɰ\leq n}\left(1 - \left(\prod_{j=1}^{ɰ} max(\psi_{\mu_{i_j}}(\varrho))\right)^{\frac{1}{ɰ}}\right)^{(1-\prod_{j=1}^{ɰ}\mathfrak{N}_{i_j})}\right)^{\frac{1}{C_n^ɰ}}\right)\right)}, \\ \left(\prod_{1\leq i_1<,\ldots,<i_ɰ\leq n}\left(1 - \left(\prod_{j=1}^{ɰ}\left(1 - min\left(\mathfrak{E}_{A_j}(\varrho)\right)\right)\right)^{\frac{1}{ɰ}}\right)^{(1-\prod_{j=1}^{ɰ}\mathfrak{N}_{i_j})}\right)^{\frac{1}{C_n^ɰ}} \\ e^{2\pi i\left(\left(\prod_{1\leq i_1<,\ldots,<i_ɰ\leq n}\left(1 - \left(\prod_{j=1}^{ɰ}(1 - min(\varphi_{Aj}(\varrho)))\right)^{\frac{1}{ɰ}}\right)^{(1-\prod_{j=1}^{ɰ}\mathfrak{N}_{i_j})}\right)^{\frac{1}{C_n^ɰ}}\right)} \\ \left(\prod_{1\leq i_1<,\ldots,<i_ɰ\leq n}\left(1 - \left(\prod_{j=1}^{ɰ}\left(1 - min\left(\Upsilon_{v_{i_j}}(\varrho)\right)\right)\right)^{\frac{1}{ɰ}}\right)^{(1-\prod_{j=1}^{ɰ}\mathfrak{N}_{i_j})}\right)^{\frac{1}{C_n^ɰ}} \\ e^{2\pi i\left(\left(\left(\prod_{1\leq i_1<,\ldots,<i_ɰ\leq n}\left(1 - \left(\prod_{j=1}^{ɰ}(1 - min(\phi_{v_{i_j}}(\varrho)))\right)^{\frac{1}{ɰ}}\right)^{(1-\prod_{j=1}^{ɰ}\mathfrak{N}_{i_j})}\right)\right)^{\frac{1}{C_n^ɰ}}\right)} \end{pmatrix}$$

From property 4 we have:

$$I^- \leq CPFWHM^{ɰ}(I_1, I_2, \ldots, I_n) \leq I^+$$

□

References

1. Zadeh, L.A. Fuzzy sets. *Inf. Control* **1965**, *8*, 338–353. [CrossRef]
2. El-Bably, M.K.; Abo-Tabl, E.A. A topological reduction for predicting of a lung cancer disease based on generalized rough sets. *J. Intell. Fuzzy Syst.* **2021**, *41*, 3045–3060. [CrossRef]
3. Abu-Gdairi, R.; El-Gayar, M.A.; Al-Shami, T.M.; Nawar, A.S.; El-Bably, M.K. Some Topological Approaches for Generalized Rough Sets and Their Decision-Making Applications. *Symmetry* **2022**, *14*, 95. [CrossRef]
4. El Sayed, M.; El Safty, M.A.; El-Bably, M.K. Topological approach for decision-making of COVID-19 infection via a nano-topology model. *AIMS Math.* **2021**, *6*, 7872–7894. [CrossRef]
5. Atanassov, K. Intuitionistic fuzzy sets. *Fuzzy Sets Syst.* **1986**, *20*, 87–96. [CrossRef]
6. Yager, R.R. Pythagorean fuzzy subsets. In Proceedings of the 2013 Joint IFSA World Congress and NAFIPS Annual Meeting (IFSA/NAFIPS), Edmonton, AB, Canada, 24–28 June 2013; pp. 57–61.
7. Yager, R.R. Generalized Orthopair Fuzzy Sets. *IEEE Trans. Fuzzy Syst.* **2016**, *25*, 1222–1230. [CrossRef]
8. Cường, B.C. Picture fuzzy sets. *J. Comput. Sci. Cybern.* **2015**, *30*, 409–420. [CrossRef]
9. Cuong, B.C.; Kreinovich, V. Picture fuzzy sets—A new concept for computational intelligence problems. In Proceedings of the 2013 Third World Congress on Information and Communication Technologies (WICT 2013), Hanoi, Vietnam, 15–18 December 2013; pp. 1–6. [CrossRef]
10. Lu, H.; Khalil, A.M.; Alharbi, W.; El-Gayar, M.A. A new type of generalized picture fuzzy soft set and its application in decision making. *J. Intell. Fuzzy Syst.* **2021**, *40*, 12459–12475. [CrossRef]
11. Riaz, M.; Athar Farid, H.M. Picture fuzzy aggregation approach with application to third-party logistic provider selection process. *Rep. Mech. Eng.* **2022**, *3*, 318–327. [CrossRef]
12. Rasoulzadeh, M.; Edalatpanah, S.A.; Fallah, M.; Najafi, S.E. A multi-objective approach based on Markowitz and DEA cross-efficiency models for the intuitionistic fuzzy portfolio selection problem. *Decis. Mak. Appl. Manag. Eng.* **2022**, *5*, 241–259. [CrossRef]
13. Limboo, B.; Dutta, P. A q-rung orthopair basic probability assignment and its application in medical diagnosis. *Decis. Mak. Appl. Manag. Eng.* **2022**, *5*, 290–308. [CrossRef]
14. Ashraf, A.; Ullah, K.; Hussain, A.; Bari, M. Interval-Valued Picture Fuzzy Maclaurin Symmetric Mean Operator with application in Multiple Attribute Decision-Making. *Rep. Mech. Eng.* **2022**, *3*, 301–317. [CrossRef]
15. Xu, Z. Intuitionistic Fuzzy Aggregation Operators. *IEEE Trans. Fuzzy Syst.* **2007**, *15*, 1179–1187.
16. Xu, Z.; Xia, M. Induced generalized intuitionistic fuzzy operators. *Knowl. Based Syst.* **2011**, *24*, 197–209. [CrossRef]
17. Biswas, A.; Deb, N. Pythagorean fuzzy Schweizer and Sklar power aggregation operators for solving multi-attribute decision-making problems. *Granul. Comput.* **2021**, *6*, 991–1007. [CrossRef]
18. Garg, H. Generalized Pythagorean fuzzy geometric aggregation operators using Einstein t-norm and t-conorm for multicriteria decision-making process. *Int. J. Intell. Syst.* **2017**, *32*, 597–630. [CrossRef]
19. Mahmood, T.; Ali, Z. Aggregation operators and VIKOR method based on complex q-rung orthopair uncertain linguistic informations and their applications in multi-attribute decision making. *Comput. Appl. Math.* **2020**, *39*, 306. [CrossRef]
20. Riaz, M.; Hashmi, M.R. Linear Diophantine fuzzy set and its applications towards multi-attribute decision-making problems. *J. Intell. Fuzzy Syst.* **2019**, *37*, 5417–5439. [CrossRef]
21. Liu, P. Some Hamacher Aggregation Operators Based on the Interval-Valued Intuitionistic Fuzzy Numbers and Their Application to Group Decision Making. *IEEE Trans. Fuzzy Syst.* **2013**, *22*, 83–97. [CrossRef]
22. Hussain, A.; Ullah, K.; Alshahrani, M.N.; Yang, M.-S.; Pamucar, D. Novel Aczel–Alsina Operators for Pythagorean Fuzzy Sets with Application in Multi-Attribute Decision Making. *Symmetry* **2022**, *14*, 940. [CrossRef]
23. Liu, P.; Munir, M.; Mahmood, T.; Ullah, K. Some Similarity Measures for Interval-Valued Picture Fuzzy Sets and Their Applications in Decision Making. *Information* **2019**, *10*, 369. [CrossRef]
24. Mahmood, T.; Ullah, K.; Khan, Q. Some aggregation operators for bipolar-valued hesitant fuzzy information. *J. Eng. Appl. Sci.* **2018**, *10*, 240–245.
25. Garg, H. Some Picture Fuzzy Aggregation Operators and Their Applications to Multicriteria Decision-Making. *Arab. J. Sci. Eng.* **2017**, *42*, 5275–5290. [CrossRef]
26. Wei, G. Picture Fuzzy Hamacher Aggregation Operators and their Application to Multiple Attribute Decision Making. *Fundam. Inform.* **2018**, *157*, 271–320. [CrossRef]
27. El-Bably, M.K.; El-Sayed, M. Three methods to generalize Pawlak approximations via simply open concepts with economic applications. *Soft Comput.* **2022**, *26*, 4685–4700. [CrossRef]
28. Božanić, D.; Milić, A.; Tešić, D.; Salabun, W.; Pamučar, D. D Numbers–Fucom–Fuzzy Rafsi Model for Selecting The Group Of Construction Machines For Enabling Mobility. *Facta Univ. Ser. Mech. Eng.* **2021**, *19*, 447–471. [CrossRef]
29. Hussain, A.; Ullah, K.; Ahmad, J.; Karamti, H.; Pamucar, D.; Wang, H. Applications of the Multiattribute Decision-Making for the Development of the Tourism Industry Using Complex Intuitionistic Fuzzy Hamy Mean Operators. *Comput. Intell. Neurosci.* **2022**, *2022*, 8562390. [CrossRef] [PubMed]
30. Zhou, B.; Chen, J.; Wu, Q.; Pamucar, D.; Wang, W.; Zhou, L. Risk priority evaluation of power transformer parts based on hybrid FMEA framework under hesitant fuzzy environment. *Facta Univ. Ser. Mech. Eng.* **2021**, *20*, 399–420. [CrossRef]
31. Ramot, D.; Milo, R.; Friedman, M.; Kandel, A. Complex fuzzy sets. *IEEE Trans. Fuzzy Syst.* **2002**, *10*, 171–186. [CrossRef]

32. Ramot, D.; Friedman, M.; Langholz, G.; Kandel, A. Complex fuzzy logic. *IEEE Trans. Fuzzy Syst.* **2003**, *11*, 450–461. [CrossRef]
33. Yazdanbakhsh, O.; Dick, S. Multi-variate timeseries forecasting using complex fuzzy logic. In Proceedings of the 2015 Annual Conference of the North American Fuzzy Information Processing Society (NAFIPS) Held Jointly with 2015 5th World Conference on Soft Computing (WConSC), Redmond, WA, USA, 17–19 August 2015; pp. 1–6.
34. Alkouri, A.M.D.J.S.; Salleh, A.R. Complex intuitionistic fuzzy sets. In *AIP Conference Proceedings*; American Institute of Physics: College Park, MD, USA, 2012; Volume 1482, pp. 464–470.
35. Garg, H.; Rani, D. Some generalized complex intuitionistic fuzzy aggregation operators and their application to multicriteria decision-making process. *Arab. J. Sci. Eng.* **2019**, *44*, 2679–2698. [CrossRef]
36. Ullah, K.; Mahmood, T.; Ali, Z.; Jan, N. On some distance measures of complex Pythagorean fuzzy sets and their applications in pattern recognition. *Complex Intell. Syst.* **2020**, *6*, 15–27. [CrossRef]
37. Liu, P.; Mahmood, T.; Ali, Z. Complex q-rung orthopair fuzzy aggregation operators and their applications in multi-attribute group decision making. *Information* **2020**, *11*, 5. [CrossRef]
38. Rong, Y.; Liu, Y.; Pei, Z. Complex q-rung orthopair fuzzy 2-tuple linguistic Maclaurin symmetric mean operators and its application to emergency program selection. *Int. J. Intell. Syst.* **2020**, *35*, 1749–1790. [CrossRef]
39. Akram, M.; Bashir, A.; Garg, H. Decision-making model under complex picture fuzzy Hamacher aggregation operators. *Comput. Appl. Math.* **2020**, *39*, 226. [CrossRef]
40. Hara, T.; Uchiyama, M.; Takahasi, S.-E. A refinement of various mean inequalities. *J. Inequal. Appl.* **1998**, *1998*, 932025. [CrossRef]
41. Qin, J. Interval type-2 fuzzy Hamy mean operators and their application in multiple criteria decision making. *Granul. Comput.* **2017**, *2*, 249–269. [CrossRef]
42. Wu, L.; Wei, G.; Gao, H.; Wei, Y. Some Interval-Valued Intuitionistic Fuzzy Dombi Hamy Mean Operators and Their Application for Evaluating the Elderly Tourism Service Quality in Tourism Destination. *Mathematics* **2018**, *6*, 294. [CrossRef]
43. Li, Z.; Gao, H.; Wei, G. Methods for Multiple Attribute Group Decision Making Based on Intuitionistic Fuzzy Dombi Hamy Mean Operators. *Symmetry* **2018**, *10*, 574. [CrossRef]
44. Wu, S.; Wang, J.; Wei, G.; Wei, Y. Research on Construction Engineering Project Risk Assessment with Some 2-Tuple Linguistic Neutrosophic Hamy Mean Operators. *Sustainability* **2018**, *10*, 1536. [CrossRef]
45. Li, Z.; Wei, G.; Lu, M. Pythagorean Fuzzy Hamy Mean Operators in Multiple Attribute Group Decision Making and Their Application to Supplier Selection. *Symmetry* **2018**, *10*, 505. [CrossRef]
46. Liu, Z.; Xu, H.; Zhao, X.; Liu, P.; Li, J. Multi-Attribute Group Decision Making Based on Intuitionistic Uncertain Linguistic Hamy Mean Operators with Linguistic Scale Functions and Its Application to Health-Care Waste Treatment Technology Selection. *IEEE Access* **2019**, *7*, 20–46. [CrossRef]
47. Wu, L.; Wang, J.; Gao, H. Models for competiveness evaluation of tourist destination with some interval-valued intuitionistic fuzzy Hamy mean operators. *J. Intell. Fuzzy Syst.* **2019**, *36*, 5693–5709. [CrossRef]
48. Wang, J.; Wei, G.; Lu, J.; Alsaadi, F.E.; Hayat, T.; Wei, C.; Zhang, Y. Some *q*-rung orthopair fuzzy Hamy mean operators in multiple attribute decision-making and their application to enterprise resource planning systems selection. *Int. J. Intell. Syst.* **2019**, *34*, 2429–2458. [CrossRef]
49. Xing, Y.; Zhang, R.; Wang, J.; Bai, K.; Xue, J. A new multi-criteria group decision-making approach based on q-rung orthopair fuzzy interaction Hamy mean operators. *Neural Comput. Appl.* **2020**, *32*, 7465–7488. [CrossRef]
50. Sinani, F.; Erceg, Z.; Vasiljević, M. An evaluation of a third-party logistics provider: The application of the rough Dombi-Hamy mean operator. *Decis. Mak. Appl. Manag. Eng.* **2020**, *3*, 92–107. [CrossRef]
51. Wei, G.; Wang, J.; Wei, C.; Wei, Y.; Zhang, Y. Dual Hesitant Pythagorean Fuzzy Hamy Mean Operators in Multiple Attribute Decision Making. *IEEE Access* **2019**, *7*, 86697–86716. [CrossRef]
52. Liu, P.; Khan, Q.; Mahmood, T. Application of Interval Neutrosophic Power Hamy Mean Operators in MAGDM. *Informatica* **2019**, *30*, 293–325. [CrossRef]
53. Garg, H.; Sirbiladze, G.; Ali, Z.; Mahmood, T. Hamy Mean Operators Based on Complex q-Rung Orthopair Fuzzy Setting and Their Application in Multi-Attribute Decision Making. *Mathematics* **2021**, *9*, 2312. [CrossRef]
54. Ali, Z.; Mahmood, T.; Pamucar, D.; Wei, C. Complex Interval-Valued q-Rung Orthopair Fuzzy Hamy Mean Operators and Their Application in Decision-Making Strategy. *Symmetry* **2022**, *14*, 592. [CrossRef]
55. Mahmood, T.; Rehman, U.U.; Ahmmad, J. Complex picture fuzzy N-soft sets and their decision-making algorithm. *Soft Comput.* **2021**, *25*, 13657–13678. [CrossRef]
56. 'Ele-Math—Journal of Mathematical Inequalities: Some Properties of Dual form of the Hamy's Symmetric Function'. Available online: http://jmi.ele-math.com/01-12/Some-properties-of-dual-form-of-the-Hamy-s-symmetric-function (accessed on 27 September 2022).
57. Savasaneril, S.; Erkip, N.K. An analysis of manufacturer benefits under vendor-managed systems. *IIE Trans.* **2010**, *42*, 455–477. [CrossRef]
58. Solyalı, O.; Süral, H. A Relaxation Based Solution Approach for the Inventory Control and Vehicle Routing Problem in Vendor Managed Systems. In *Modeling, Computation and Optimization*; World Scientific: London, UK, 2009; Volume 6, pp. 171–189. [CrossRef]
59. Garg, H.; Rani, D. Complex Interval-valued Intuitionistic Fuzzy Sets and their Aggregation Operators. *Fundam. Inform.* **2019**, *164*, 61–101. [CrossRef]

60. Akram, M.; Peng, X.; Sattar, A. A new decision-making model using complex intuitionistic fuzzy Hamacher aggregation operators. *Soft Comput.* **2021**, *25*, 7059–7086. [CrossRef]
61. Zhang, H.; Zhang, R.; Huang, H.; Wang, J. Some Picture Fuzzy Dombi Heronian Mean Operators with Their Application to Multi-Attribute Decision-Making. *Symmetry* **2018**, *10*, 593. [CrossRef]
62. Ullah, K. Picture fuzzy maclaurin symmetric mean operators and their applications in solving multiattribute decision-making problems. *Math. Probl. Eng.* **2021**, *2021*, 1098631. [CrossRef]
63. Mahmood, T. A Novel Approach towards Bipolar Soft Sets and Their Applications. *J. Math.* **2020**, *2020*, 4690808. [CrossRef]
64. El-Bably, M.K.; Ali, M.I.; Abo-Tabl, E.-S.A. New Topological Approaches to Generalized Soft Rough Approximations with Medical Applications. *J. Math.* **2021**, *2021*, 2559495. [CrossRef]

electronics

MDPI

Article

An Incremental Learning Framework for Photovoltaic Production and Load Forecasting in Energy Microgrids

Elissaios Sarmas [1,*], Sofoklis Strompolas [1], Vangelis Marinakis [1], Francesca Santori [2], Marco Antonio Bucarelli [2] and Haris Doukas [1]

1 Decision Support Systems Laboratory, School of Electrical & Computer Engineering, National Technical University of Athens, 15780 Athens, Greece
2 ASM Terni S.p.A., 05100 Terni, Italy
* Correspondence: esarmas@epu.ntua.gr; Tel.: +30-6977-8714-23

Abstract: Energy management is crucial for various activities in the energy sector, such as effective exploitation of energy resources, reliability in supply, energy conservation, and integrated energy systems. In this context, several machine learning and deep learning models have been developed during the last decades focusing on energy demand and renewable energy source (RES) production forecasting. However, most forecasting models are trained using batch learning, ingesting all data to build a model in a static fashion. The main drawback of models trained offline is that they tend to mis-calibrate after launch. In this study, we propose a novel, integrated online (or incremental) learning framework that recognizes the dynamic nature of learning environments in energy-related time-series forecasting problems. The proposed paradigm is applied to the problem of energy forecasting, resulting in the construction of models that dynamically adapt to new patterns of streaming data. The evaluation process is realized using a real use case consisting of an energy demand and a RES production forecasting problem. Experimental results indicate that online learning models outperform offline learning models by 8.6% in the case of energy demand and by 11.9% in the case of RES forecasting in terms of mean absolute error (MAE), highlighting the benefits of incremental learning.

Keywords: incremental learning; machine learning; energy forecasting; renewable energy sources; energy demand

Citation: Sarmas, E.; Strompolas, S.; Marinakis, V.; Santori, F.; Bucarelli, M.A.; Doukas, H. An Incremental Learning Framework for Photovoltaic Production and Load Forecasting in Energy Microgrids. *Electronics* **2022**, *11*, 3962. https://doi.org/10.3390/electronics11233962

Academic Editors: Galina Ilieva and George A. Tsihrintzis

Received: 10 November 2022
Accepted: 28 November 2022
Published: 29 November 2022

1. Introduction

Forecasting is a key branch for the proper and smooth operation of the energy industry. As a matter of fact, energy forecasting may refer to various quantities in the energy environment, the main ones being grid-level or building-level load forecasting [1], energy production forecasting from renewable energy sources (RES) such as photovoltaic (PV) parks, wind farms and hybrid systems [2], and energy price forecasting [3], among others. The generated forecasts are used by different stakeholders in all segments of the energy sector for planning and operation purposes, both from the aspect of the power system and from the aspect of a business entity [4]. Moreover, the formation of energy communities during the last years also intensifies the need for accurate forecasts, as local energy communities are heavily reliant upon load demand forecasts to schedule energy usage ahead of time in order to achieve higher self-sufficiency levels [5].

On the one hand, forecasting consumption in buildings is very important to maintain an optimal level of energy performance [6]. The immense technological progress in terms of equipment with the evolution of Internet of things (IoT) devices and smart metering sensors has resulted in a digital transformation of buildings, which can be monitored by smart energy management systems and digital twin platforms [7,8]. However, the existence of all this data generated needs to be supported by intelligent algorithms and models offering prescriptive and descriptive and predictive analytics. In this context, many time-series forecasting models have been developed for consumption prediction in buildings, so as to provide continuous monitoring and facilitate the development of data-driven operational strategies.

On the other hand, RES forecasting is vital for several key activities of the energy sector. As the penetration of RES and especially wind and solar energy has increased in the last few years due to decarbonization goals set at the European and global levels [9], solid forecasting models lead to a reliable integration process of RES production [10]. More specifically, solar-based generated power accounted for 3.6% of the electricity mix in 2021, remaining the third largest renewable electricity technology behind hydropower and wind, and this percentage is expected to rapidly increase in the next few years [11]. In this context, forecasting of PV production can be exploited for several purposes and tasks, including energy management of smart grids, ensuring power unit commitment, scheduling and dispatching [12], dynamic pricing, and predictive maintenance [13].

In the case of both RES production forecasting and building consumption forecasting, several studies can be found in the existing literature [14,15]. In general, there are two broad categories of methods: physical methods and data-driven methods. Physical methods rely on weather data, such as surface roughness, temperature, relative humidity, and wind speed, as well as key design parameters of the building or the PV panel, and they use physical equations to generate the forecasts [16]. On the contrary, data-driven methods rely on historical data of time series in order to provide predictions, and they are split into statistical models and machine learning (ML) models, which may be combined with the development of hybrid models to achieve increased accuracy [17].

Although the breakthrough in model development has been rapid and the predictive performance of models is constantly improving, there is a significant gap in the field of ML and DL model development. Most of the studies in the field focus on developing models in a static fashion. This means that models are trained once using a set of training data and they are evaluated on another set of hidden data, which is called test set. This is the most common approach for evaluating the potential of an ML/DL model, but it fails to address the aspect of online re-training of the model to further improve its accuracy. This also creates another gap, as there is not any evidence on how the proposed models would operate as part of a service or application. The process of employing a model in an intelligent service by applying incremental re-training is a fundamental step towards the successful deployment in production.

This study aims to address the above-mentioned gap by assessing the impact of applying incremental (or online) learning to DL models in the energy domain. In this context, an integrated methodological framework is provided describing the whole data life cycle, from connection to the smart-metering equipment to the generation of the forecasts through incrementally trained models in a unified architectural schema. Moreover, the proposed training procedure is applied to a real use case, i.e., a microgrid in Italy composed of a multi-story building and a PV system. One of the most popular DL algorithms, the multilayer perceptron (MLP), is used to develop energy forecasting models for the consumption of the building and the production of the PV system. The online training framework is compared with the traditional training process in order to evaluate the benefits of incremental learning in these time-series forecasting problems.

Apart from this introductory section, the rest of the paper is structured as follows. Section 2 introduces the problems of RES forecasting and building consumption forecasting and provides a short literature review on these topics. Section 3 presents the methodological approach in more detail, presenting the MLP used for developing the models, the basic principles of incremental learning, and the proposed architecture for incremental learning. Section 4 includes the experimental application of incremental learning in PV production and building consumption forecasting. Finally, Section 5 concludes the paper and provides directions for future research.

2. Related Work

2.1. RES Forecasting

Over the last decade the number of forecasting methods that have been proposed to forecast energy generation from RES has significantly increased. This is quite reasonable considering that RES forecasting is a key analytic service for the support of several decisions related to microgrid management, flexibility planning, demand-response mechanisms development, pricing in the energy market, and many others. Most methods have focused on wing and solar power forecasting, as these two sources are the most cost-efficient, resulting in their high degree of penetration.

Focusing on PV production forecasting, many popular regression models have been proposed, including traditional time-series ARIMA models [18], decision-tree-based models [19], support vector machines (SVM) [20], and artificial neural networks (ANNs) [21], among others. Recent studies indicate that DL models result in better forecasting accuracy compared to purely statistical models and simple ML models, but this cannot be generalized for all cases [22]. Moreover, various techniques have also been tested, either with the aim of increasing forecasting accuracy through ensembling [23] or meta-learning [24], or with the aim of addressing data scarcity [25].

In terms of determining the most influencing factors for PV production models, literature has shown that, as expected, global horizontal irradiance (GHI) is the main driver for estimating the energy produced by a solar panel [26]. However, solar radiation is not the only factor exploited for predicting PV production, as other variables such as air temperature, cloud coverage, and humidity also affect the operation of the PV system through complex nonlinear relationships [27,28]. Apart from these, it is evident that for DL models, a significant input feature is historical data from the PV production time series. Finally, another distinction of ML/DL models for PV forecasting is their dependence on numerical weather predictions (NWP). Short-term forecasting models are usually trained and used without NWP, while models with longer forecasting horizons require integration with a weather prediction service [29].

2.2. Building Consumption Forecasting

Buildings account for 40% of the global energy consumption and greenhouse gas (GHG) emissions, giving them a pivotal role in the recent climate crisis and global warming [30,31]. Thus, the ability to predict the electrical consumption of a building or a specific area of the building is extremely useful in the context of the effort made to increase energy efficiency. However, accurately forecasting a building's energy consumption is not a simplistic task, as there are a great variety of factors that influence the energy needs such as the building's enclosed structure, the occupancy and energy use patterns of the occupants, and outdoor air temperature and humidity levels [32].

Many studies can be found in the existing literature proposing forecasting methods for short-term and mid-term consumption forecasting [33]. Some recent specialized reviews for electrical energy forecasting in buildings have been provided by Amasyali and El-Gohari [34] and Sun et al. [29]. More specifically, as stated in Section 1, there are two main approaches for predicting a building's energy consumption: the physical modeling approach and the data-driven approach. On the one hand, physical models apply thermodynamic equations in order to calculate the consumption of an energy subsystem through energy simulations. Such models are implemented in specific energy simulation tools (e.g., EnergyPlus). Although they can be very accurate, they require specific information as input that is not always available to the user. On the other hand, data-driven models do not calculate the consumption via complex equations, but they rely on historical consumption data to extract usage patterns of the building using statistical or ML/DL-based models [35].

Regarding the second category, several models have been evaluated and tested for this problem. For example, in [36], the authors compare SVMs and ANNs to predict a building's lighting energy consumption, while in [37], the authors compare a purely statistical auto-regressive model and an SVR to forecast building consumption. Literature has not indicated that a specific model outperforms the others as a rule of thumb but, as in most forecasting tasks, DL models are expected to perform better if there are plenty of data available.

2.3. The Need for an Incremental Learning Approach

In the last few years, the amount of generated data has been continuously increasing. The energy sector is not an exception, since the multitude of synchronously installed smart meters generate a large amount of energy consumption data, RES generation data, grid energy flows data, and other energy data [38,39]. Furthermore, according to Sarmas et al. [23], access to open data has been simplified, opening new opportunities for the development of ML models and data-driven approaches. At the same time, however, the generated data from all these heterogeneous IoT devices bring new challenges, as well as opportunities to develop multi-scale systems and data analytics to enhance decision making [40].

A significant dimension of developing intelligent systems is their ability to continuously learn and adapt to new conditions in their environment. According to Bouchachia et al. [41], these systems must incorporate adaptable learning algorithms and continuous adaptation processes, making them capable of responding to new conditions as part of their learning process, just like any intelligent living organism that learns incrementally and dynamically from any changes in its environment [42]. In order to enable the above-mentioned behavior, ML models should be periodically re-trained when new data are available, thus adjusting their behavior when new patterns are detected.

However, although several studies have focused on developing forecasting models for energy-related time-series problems, only few of them have focused on the impact of incremental learning on the forecasting accuracy of the models. One of these studies has developed an incremental learning algorithm called regression enhanced incremental self-organizing neural network (RE-SOINN) in order to predict solar irradiance, finding that the proposed algorithm achieves higher accuracy compared to widely used models such as the persistence model, the exponential smoothing model, and ANNs [43]. Similarly, Qiu et al. [44] used incremental learning to increase accuracy in electrical load forecasting. More specifically, the authors proposed a hybrid incremental learning approach composed of discrete wavelet transform (DWT), empirical mode decomposition (EMD) and random vector functional link networks (RVFL), which demonstrated better forecasting accuracy compared to eight benchmark models.

Summarizing all the above statements, there is a clear gap in evaluating how incremental learning can enhance the accuracy of energy forecasting models, considering both RES production and building load. More specifically, most of the above-mentioned studies have focused on comparing different models and algorithms, on evaluating the influence of different input features, and on testing models on different forecasting horizons. However, they do not assess the possibility of incrementally training the developed models in order to further increase their abilities. Thus, the novelty of this study lies in the evaluation of how continuous periodic re-training boosts ML models for short-term time-series forecasting problems in the energy sector.

3. Methodological Approach

The studies presented in Section 2 pave the way towards further examining the impact of incremental learning in forecasting problems. In this section, the methodological approach is described in detail. Firstly, the MLP model is presented in detail, as it is the basis of the incremental learning approach. Then, the incremental learning approach is analyzed along with the proposed architecture.

3.1. Multi-Layer Perceptron

The multi-layer perceptron (MLP) is a feedforward ANN consisting of a system of interconnected neurons, which are generally referred to as nodes. These nodes are connected by weights and they are activated by a simple non-linear activation function.

Since the activation function is non-linear, the MLP is able to provide solutions to non-linear problems. The architecture of the MLP includes an input layer and an output layer, as well as one or more hidden layers. Each node of the MLP is connected to every node in the next layer and the previous layer; thus, it can be considered as a fully connected network [45]. An example of an MLP network with two hidden layers is presented in Figure 1. As a general rule, the output of each hidden and output node is determined by the sum of all the weighted values of the preceding layer's nodes. Afterwards, the result passes through the activation function [46]. The training of the MLP determines the values for each weight and resolves the network's modeling. It is based on an algorithm called backpropagation, which computes the gradient of the cost function with respect to the weights of the nodes, aiming to minimize the cost function by adjusting the network's weights and biases [47].

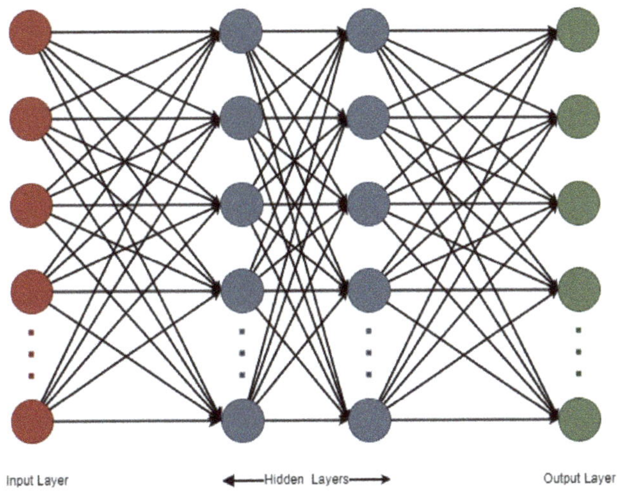

Figure 1. The architecture of the MLP, which is a fully connected network that includes an input layer, two hidden layers, and an output layer.

The main MLP application goal is to find a function f that associates the input nodes in X to the output vectors in $Y(Y = f(X))$. In that case, $X = [n \times k]$, $Y = [n \times j]$, n is number of training patterns, k the number of input nodes/variables, and j the number of output nodes/variables. During the process of training the model, the function f is optimized. The optimization comes by achieving the lowest possible margin in the output given the input vectors in X to the target values in Y. The function f is based on the adjustable weights of the network's nodes, and the matrices X, Y represent the training data. The ideas behind the method used for the approximation and prediction are very much alike. The MLP only has one output node, and the dimensions of matrices X and Y in the generic application are $n \times k$ and $n \times 1$, respectively, since one variable is modeled from the input data. The prediction requires training the model to output the future value of a variable given an input vector containing earlier values [45].

By selecting a suitable set of connecting weights and transfer functions, it has been shown that an MLP is able to estimate all the perceptible functions within the input and output nodes after choosing the appropriate activation/transfer functions and weights [48]. By training the MLP, the network learns the current set of training data, which formulates the input and related output nodes. During this process of training, the MLP is constantly introduced to the training data; by adjusting the weights, the optimal input–output mapping occurs. The training/learning process of a MLP is performed in a supervised approach, and when the desired output is not met during a certain input vector, an error signal is identified as the difference between the desired and real output. During the training process, this error signal is used to establish the adjustable weights in order to reduce the error signal. As a result, the MLP is able to extrapolate to unknown but related input data when trained with the appropriate training data [45].

3.2. Incremental Learning

Most traditional ML and DL methods use offline learning, meaning they ingest training data at once to construct a static model. Incremental learning, or online learning, is a branch of ML that involves processing incoming data from a data stream continuously and in real time. Thus, a model can be trained multiple times and can be iteratively re-adjusted to new data, while still considering older data as well.

Training the model incrementally offers multiple advantages and solves many problems of the traditional training methods. Incremental learning algorithms can be used to solve the problem of shortages in computation power. By providing the data in the form of batches, the model is able to fit to data quickly and efficiently, without the need for a computationally powerful machine. Additionally, at several occasions, the size of training data may be unknown or of very large volume, thus making storage impossible. Exploiting incremental learning, a substantial solution is provided by offering the ability to ingest data in batches and re-train the model. As a result, the whole dataset does not need to be stored and can be gradually stockpiled and used. This method is also beneficial when dealing with streaming data or with data that is provided in small chunks and not in one unified pile. Furthermore, incremental learning helps to implement a system that gradually improves in terms of accuracy whenever new examples emerge, offering an appealing approach to real life problems and actual scenarios, where changes in the data distribution are continuous and real-time monitoring of environments is important [49].

However, incremental learning brings some difficulties that are important to acknowledge. In the process of training and learning new data, one of the main challenges faced by incremental learning algorithms is catastrophic forgetting, which is the tendency of an ANN to completely and abruptly forget previously learned information upon learning new information [50]. For that reason, the behavior of the new obtained values should be monitored closely. Some simple solutions include rehearsal and pseudo-rehearsal methods, i.e., re-training the model on a part of old data when new data is introduced [51]. Another obstacle of online learning is the concept drift. Concept drift means that the properties of the target variable, which the model is trying to predict, change over time in unforeseen ways. This causes problems because the predictions become less accurate as time passes. Concept drift can be avoided by using tracking solutions and updating the set using features of the data in old classes [52].

3.3. Proposed Framework

In this section, we introduce the proposed methodological framework that satisfies the needs for incrementally training the proposed ML models, as well as the methods used to implement it. A high-level representation of the incremental learning framework is presented in Figure 2. Firstly, the framework includes a continuous connection to an MQ telemetry transport (MQTT) broker for collecting data streams in real time, as well as the operations of data pre-processing, cleaning, and analysis. The collected data is aggregated to an hourly format and stored in a database. Thus, data can be loaded from the database once per day in order to periodically re-train the models. The re-training process requires only the most recent data and not the whole dataset, thus offering scalability and reduced training time. The updated models are then stored and can be used directly to produce hourly day-ahead forecasts. More details on the process of online learning are given in the following paragraphs.

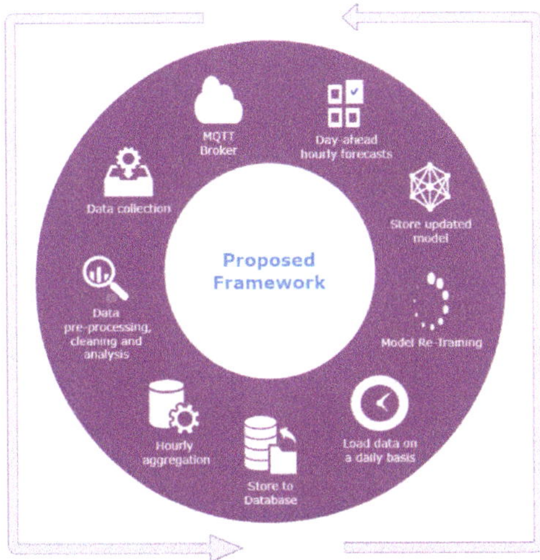

Figure 2. The proposed framework for incremental learning.

First, as noted above, a connection to a continuous data stream in real time is required, which, in our case is provided via an MQTT broker. The MQTT is a lightweight, publish–subscribe, machine to machine network protocol for message queue/message queuing service. This software component communicates with smart metering equipment and runs on a computing machine on-premises or in the cloud. The broker acts as a post office, since it sends and receives information [53]. Connecting to an MQTT broker is done by using the broker's address and credentials. In the next step, all collected data are aggregated hourly and pre-processed to detect any unusual details. In this use case, the pre-processing operations focus on missing data and outliers. For instance, when data are missing for a specific hour, missing values are filled by using a special type of linear interpolation averaging past days' data during the same hour. Additionally, since data originate from a smart meter, some false data may be detected. In order to handle these outliers, a check is performed, replacing negative or unjustifiably high values. This pre-processing routine results in a uniform dataset that can be fed to the ML models.

Consequently, data are stored in a time-series database to allow for easy and direct querying. In this specific use case, a PostgreSQL database is used to store and retrieve the hourly aggregated information. Thus, data can be loaded on a daily basis to re-train ML models. Regarding ML models, the "MLPRegressor" model of the sklearn.neural_network library is used [54]. The proposed framework involves fitting the model to a chunk of already collected data (one year of data), creating a solid baseline model that has learned the patterns of a calendar year. After that period, the baseline model is periodically re-trained once per day using the continuous flow of data previously stored in the time-series database. Stored data is given to the model on a daily basis in mini-batches of 24 values. Consequently, the model is re-trained with the most recent data at the end of the day. As a result of this process, the model keeps adjusting to new data every day and is able to cope with changes in the data distribution in near real time. At the same time, the stored model generates day ahead-forecasts by using the most recent records of the database.

Moving to the core of the incremental learning process, it is noteworthy that in order to perform the training process in an incremental fashion, the function partial_fit() is used instead of the traditional fit() method. The traditional fit method clears the model and provides a different initialization of the weights each time used. On the contrary, the partial_fit method does not completely clear and re-initialize the model, but it updates it with respect to the data provided [55]. The small portion of data (usually a data stream) that is provided as input to the partial_fit method is called a mini-batch. Thus, the ability to learn incrementally from a mini-batch of instances is key to out-of-core learning, as it guarantees that at any given time there will be only a small amount of instances in the main memory [56].

As mentioned above, the algorithm used for evaluating incremental learning is the MLP regressor of Scikit-Learn. The selection of the MLP regressor was made because of its ability to support online learning in mini-batches, as compared to several other ML models. A very important step of the learning process is the selection of optimal model hyper-parameters, as this offers a significant boost to the accuracy of the ML models. The selected hyper-parameters for the case of PV production and electricity consumption are presented in Table 1.

Table 1. The selected hyper-parameters for the PV production and the electricity consumption forecasting models.

Measure	PV Production	Electricity Consumption
Number of Hidden Layers	4	3
Neurons per Layer	641,286,432	6,412,832
Learning Rate	0.001	0.001
Solver	*adam*	*adam*

4. Use Case

The incremental learning framework was evaluated on a real case study located in the distribution grid owned by ASM Terni S.p.A. ASM is a public utility owned by the municipality of the city of Terni, in Umbria, Italy, operating in the electrical, gas, water, and waste management sectors. Through its business unit Terni Distributione Elettrica (TDE), it covers the role of distribution system operator (DSO), managing about 65,000 end users, 700 secondary substations, and three primary substations. Every year TDE supplies electric users with about 400 GWh, half of which is produced by RES.

In the context of this study, a portion of Terni's low-voltage electricity grid is used to test the proposed models, including two secondary substations: a building, namely, the headquarters of ASM, and a PV production plant of 185 kW. The headquarters of ASM comprise a 4050 m^2 three-story office, a 2790 m^2 single-story space, consisting of technical offices, a computer center, an operation control center, and a 1350 m^2 warehouse. The annual building consumption is about 650 MWh, mainly due to lighting, HVAC, and powering computers and data servers.

The infrastructure for data sharing consists of a supervisory control and data acquisition (SCADA) system used by ASM specifically for research and innovation activities. Data are transmitted from the sensors via the MQTT and Modbus protocol to the broker located in ASM's headquarters. The sensors communicate in near real-time with a time resolution of 1 second. Data are then transmitted, again via the MQTT protocol, to an AVEVA Historian database, which is capable of collecting up to 2 million tags, storing and aggregating the data, guaranteeing the authenticity of the original data, and preventing manipulation of historical data. To access this data, the Microsoft SQL Server interface is used.

4.1. Datasets

Two different dataset were used in the context of this study. The first dataset is a PV production time series, accompanied by weather data for the respective dates, while the second dataset includes the consumption of the investigated building. Although raw PV production and building consumption data comes at irregular time intervals through the MQTT protocol, appropriate aggregations have been applied transforming the data resolution to hourly level. On the other hand, weather data (air temperature, humidity, cloud coverage, and solar radiation) were obtained in hourly resolution from a weather service. Therefore, all the data used are hourly and have a duration of about 2 years and nine months (23,616 h). A visualization of the PV production time series is presented in Figure 3, while the consumption of the building is visualized in Figure 4.

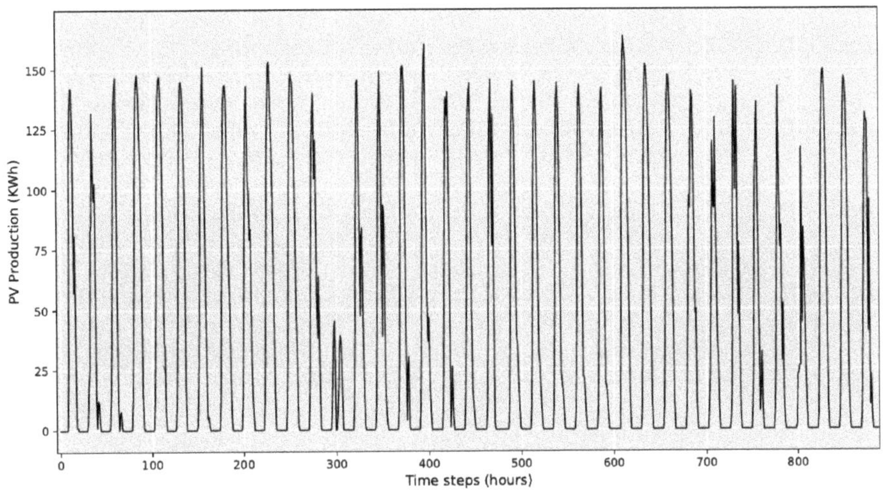

Figure 3. A visualization of the PV production time series.

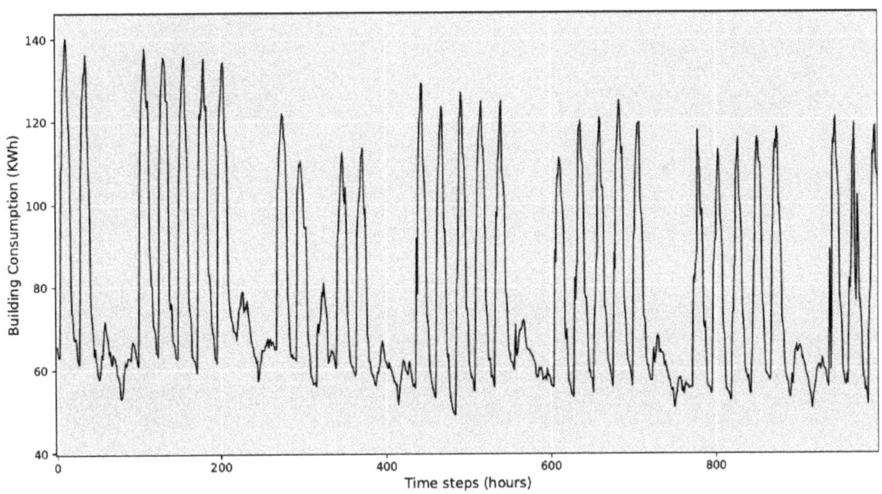

Figure 4. A visualization of the building consumption time series.

It is obvious that the PV production time series has both daily and yearly patterns due to its dependency on solar radiation. Thus, the position of the sun during the day directly affects the performance of the PV system, and at the same time, seasonal weather differences affect the production at a yearly level, resulting in much more energy production during the summer period compared to winter. On the other hand, as seen in Figure 4, the building consumption time series is more irregular in general, being affected by human factors. An indicative example is the difference observed between weekdays and weekends due to the difference in occupancy levels (during the weekends, the offices are closed and the building is vacant). The same applies for holidays periods.

In general, PV production is stochastic and is mainly influenced by weather conditions. Consequently, the main features driving the performance of the PV forecasting model are seasonal features, such as the hour of the day and the month of the year, as well as weather features, mainly solar radiation. The correlation plots between the PV production and the weather features time series are presented in Figure 5. These plots confirm that PV production is strongly related with solar radiation. On the other hand, the other weather features, namely air temperature, cloud coverage, and relative humidity, are also related with PV production, but to a much weaker extent. Considering all these factors and after experimenting with several combinations of input features, the selected input features for the PV production forecasting model are the following: (a) air temperature, (b) relative humidity, (c) global radiation, (d) month of the year, and (e) hour of the day.

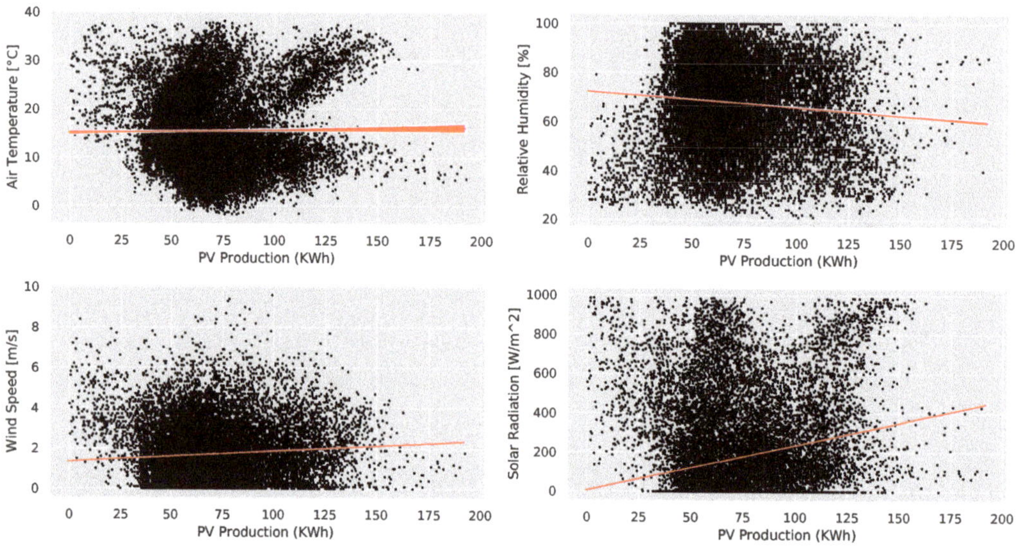

Figure 5. PV capacity factor (%) compared with solar radiation (W/m^2), temperature (°C), cloud coverage, and wind speed (m/s).

On the other hand, the consumption of the building is not strongly affected by weather features. As seen in Figure 4, the consumption time series is more stochastic than the PV production one, as it is influenced mainly by human behavior and use patterns of the building. Thus, consumption patterns vary during the two years and nine months time span. Nevertheless, electricity consumption demonstrates strong seasonality patterns. Figure 6 presents the auto-correlation function (ACF) of the electricity consumption time series across a week (168 h lag). The most interesting insight is that consumption patterns tend to repeat for the same hour of different days. This has led to using past electricity consumption data as input features in the consumption forecasting model. Another useful observation is that similar patterns are detected during weekends and weekdays, highlighting that the day of the week is another useful feature. With respect to the above insights, the selected input features for the electricity consumption forecasting model are the following: (a) hour of the day, (b) day of the week, (c) month of the year. (d) electricity consumption at the same hour last two days, and (e) electricity consumption at the same hour and same day last week.

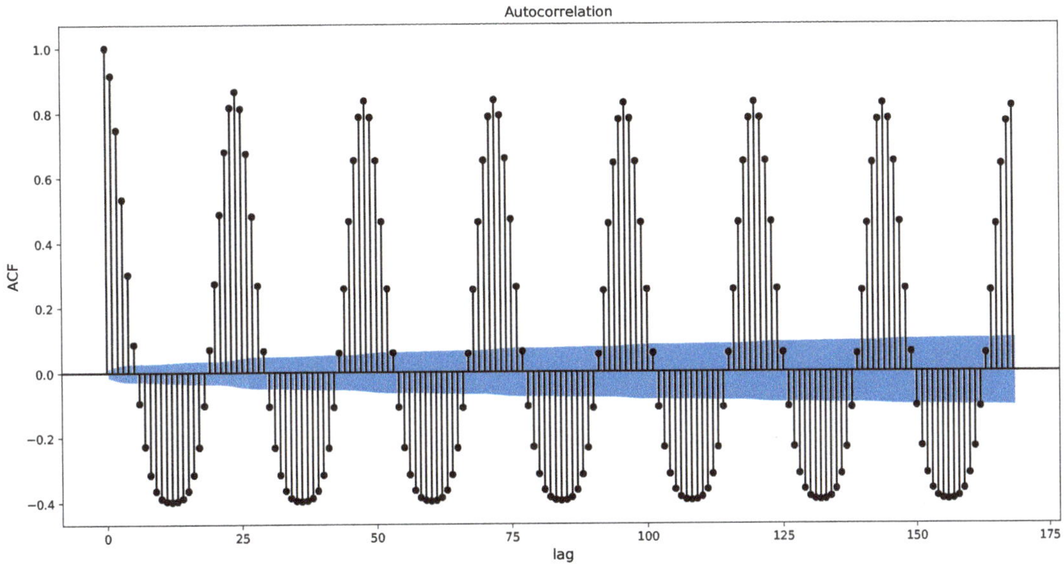

Figure 6. Auto-correlation function (ACF) of the building's electricity consumption across the week (168 h lag).

4.2. Evaluation Metrics

Ensuring that the proposed model can achieve accurate forecasts is a prerequisite for evaluating the potential of exploiting incremental learning. In this context, the performance of the MLP models for both PV production and building consumption is evaluated with the following procedure. The dataset is split into a training dataset and an evaluation dataset using a 63–37% split to allow the models to learn the patterns of more than a calendar year (since the month of the year is given as input) and to be evaluated under a whole calendar year as well. Thus, the first 63% of the dataset (14,856 hourly observations or 619 days) is used for the training process and the remaining 37% (8760 hourly observations or 365 days) is used for testing the models.

The accuracy of the models is evaluated by computing the root mean squared error (RMSE) and the mean absolute error (MAE) of the respective forecasts across the evaluation period considered. The mathematical formula for these two metrics is presented as follows:

$$RMSE = \sqrt{\frac{1}{n}\sum_{t=1}^{n}(y_t - \hat{y}_t)^2} \quad (1)$$

$$MAE = \frac{1}{n}\sum_{t=1}^{n}|y_t - \hat{y}_t| \quad (2)$$

where y_t is the real value of the PV production or the building consumption time series at hourly interval t of the evaluation period and $\hat{y}_t$ is the produced forecast of the respective model. Alon with these two evaluation metrics, one additional error metric is considered in order to make the model evaluation process more complete: the normalized root mean squared error (NRMSE). NRMSE is an appropriate metric for comparing models of different scales, connecting the RMSE value with the observed range of the variable [25]. It is calculated as follows:

$$NRMSE = \frac{RMSE}{\bar{y}} \quad (3)$$

where $\bar{y}$ is the average of the real values.

4.3. Results and Discussion

In this section, we present the results of the experimental application, comparing the models that were traditionally trained and the ones that were incrementally trained in terms of forecasting accuracy based on the above-mentioned error metrics. Results are presented separately for the case of PV production forecasting and for the case of the building's electricity consumption forecasting.

A comparative plot of the predictions of the two forecasting models for PV production is presented in Figure 7. It can be observed that the MLP model that was periodically re-trained during the evaluation period is more accurate than the traditionally trained one. This can be attributed to the ability of the first to better adjust to changes in the data distribution or possible trends. If, for example, a PV system has some major performance changes due to anomalies such as PV cell internal damages or cracks in panels, then a traditional model will not be able to adjust to these changes. On the contrary, an incrementally trained model is capable of detecting such patterns in the PV production time series, adjusting and thus accurately forecasting even in these difficult cases.

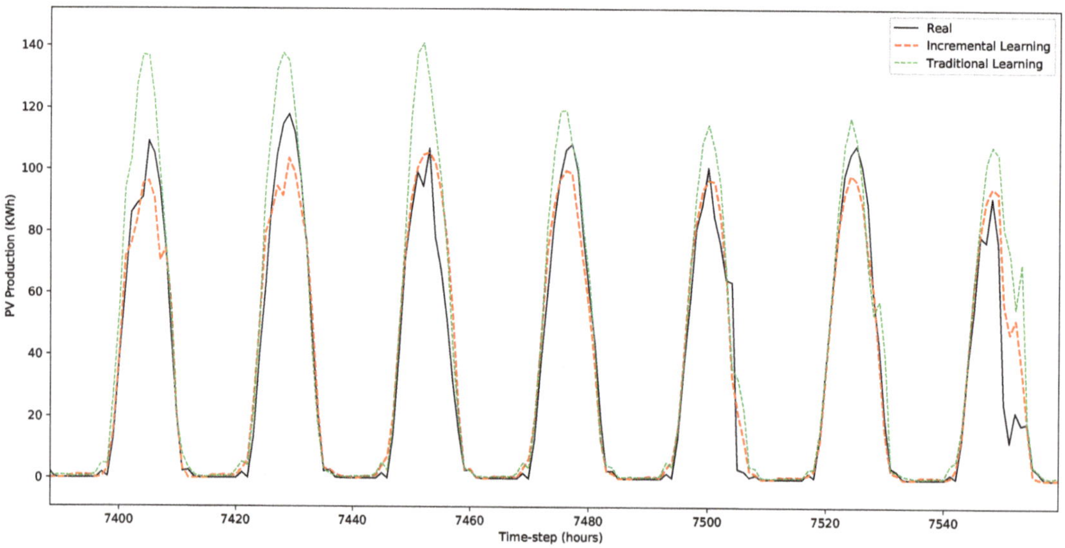

Figure 7. Comparative plot of the traditional and the online learning frameworks for the PV production forecasting task.

In the case of PV production forecasting, the incrementally trained model demonstrated an MAE index equal to 6.697 KWh, an RMSE index equal to 13.260 KWh and an NRMSE index equal to 0.527. On the contrary, the traditional ML model demonstrated an MAE index equal to 7.273 KWh, an RMSE index equal to 13.340 KWh and an NRMSE index equal to 0.570, as presented in Table 2. Thus, the incrementally trained model outperforms the traditional one by 8.6% in terms of MAE and 8.1% in terms of RMSE, further highlighting the importance of periodical re-training in the predictive task of PV forecasting.

Table 2. Error metrics for the PV production forecasting models in the cases of traditional and incremental learning.

Measure	Incremental Learning	Traditional Learning
MAE	6.697	7.273
RMSE	13.260	14.340
nRMSE	0.527	0.570

Considering the case of electricity forecasting in buildings, the impact of re-training the models is even higher. This could be attributed to the fact that electricity consumption is more stochastic in nature compared to the mainly weather-driven PV production forecasting task. This results in a more variant time series influenced by human habits, which, as expected, is more difficult to predict. In this context, incremental re-training allows for the model to adapt in real time to changes in the data distribution. The results of the models for a typical week of the evaluation set are demonstrated in Figure 8.

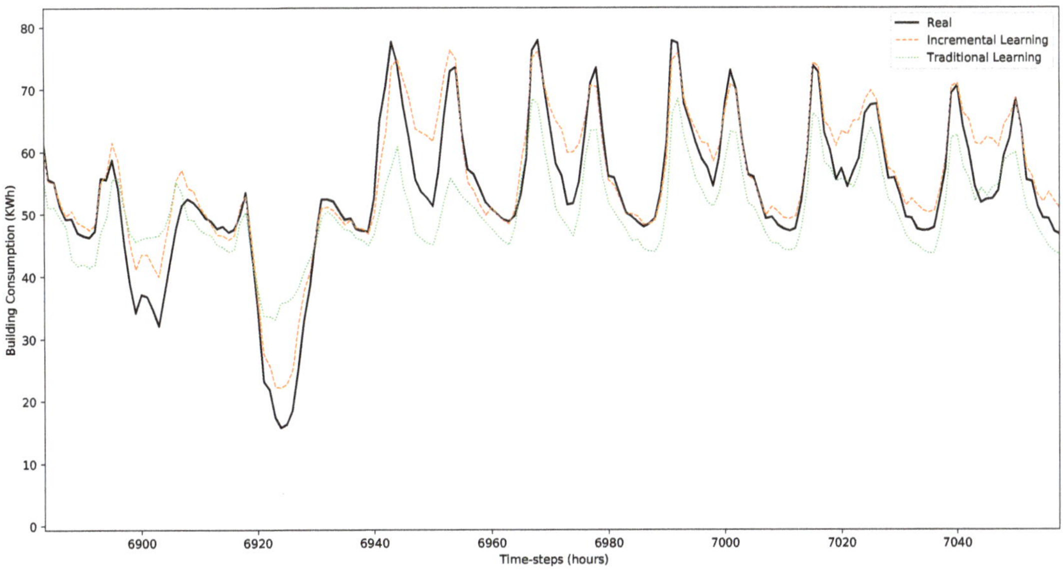

Figure 8. Comparative plot of the traditional and the online learning framework for the electricity consumption forecasting task.

With regard to accuracy metrics, the incrementally trained MLP model outperforms the traditional MLP, considering both the MAE error index (8.082 KWh for the incremental one against 9.048 KWh for the traditional one) and the RMSE index (12.391 KWh for the incremental one against 13.429 KWh for the traditional one), as presented in Table 3. The respective percentages of improvement are 11.9% for MAE and 8.4% for RMSE.

Table 3. Error metrics for the electricity consumption forecasting models in the cases of traditional and incremental learning.

Measure	Incremental Learning	Traditional Learning
MAE	8.082	9.048
RMSE	12.391	13.429
nRMSE	0.214	0.232

It can be observed that the impact of incremental learning is higher on the building electricity consumption task compared to the PV production forecasting task. As expected, this can be attributed to the more stochastic nature of the electricity consumption time series, which is highly influenced by human behavior.

Regarding the benefits in terms of complexity, the incremental learning approach requires over 600 times less memory space than the standard learning process in the examined use case. This can be attributed to the incremental learning architecture, which consumes only a single batch of data each time. In terms of time complexity, the incremental models were trained in significantly less time than the traditional ones, although the training time difference depends on the computational system used.

Consequently, using standard training methods makes storage and manipulation more difficult and time consuming. On the contrary, training a model incrementally offers the option to use batches of data. Thus, the required space is reduced, being equal to the size of a single batch. As for time complexity, incremental training is more efficient and quicker, since the training time required when using a single batch is significantly lower than the respective time when using the whole dataset in standard methods.

5. Conclusions

Progress in measurement devices and data engineering has resulted in an abundance of generated data. In this paper an incremental learning architecture is introduced that is suitable for real-time data streams, recognizing the dynamic nature of learning environments in time-series problems and adjusting to changes in the data distribution. The proposed incremental learning framework was applied on two separate energy forecasting problems with streaming data from a real use case in Italy composed of a PV system and a building. The findings of this study have highlighted the need for incrementally trained ML models, especially for production, as the incrementally trained models have been found to be more robust, showing increased accuracy even when the patterns of incoming data change. Furthermore, except for the increased forecasting accuracy, it should be highlighted that the proposed approach does not require the whole dataset to be held in memory, contrary to offline training procedures. Future research should involve evaluating the proposed framework on other ML and DL models in order to conclude which models are the most suitable for incremental learning processes. Furthermore, it would be beneficial to evaluate the framework with datasets of greater volume in order to gain more insight about the impact of online learning in forecasting accuracy and memory use. Finally, research efforts could also focus on the periodicity with which the re-training process should take place.

Author Contributions: Conceptualization, E.S., H.D. and V.M.; methodology, E.S. and H.D.; software, E.S. and S.S.; validation, M.A.B., F.S. and V.M.; formal analysis, E.S., M.A.B. and S.S.; investigation, E.S, F.S. and S.S.; resources, M.A.B. and F.S.; writing—original draft preparation, E.S., M.A.B. and S.S.; writing—review and editing, V.M., F.S. and H.D.; visualization, E.S. and S.S.; supervision, V.M. and H.D.; project administration, H.D. All authors have read and agreed to the published version of the manuscript.

Funding: The work presented is based on research conducted within the framework of the H2020 European Commission project BD4NRG (grant agreement no. 872613). The content of the paper is the sole responsibility of its author and does not necessary reflect the views of the EC.

Conflicts of Interest: The authors declare no conflict of interest.

Abbreviations

ACF	Auto-Correlation Function
ANN	Artificial Neural Network
ARIMA	Autoregressive Integrated Moving Average
DL	Deep Learning
DSO	Distribution System Operator
DWT	Discrete Wavelet Transform
EMD	Empirical Mode Decomposition
GHG	Greenhouse Gas
HVAC	Heating, Ventilation, Air-Conditioning
IoT	Internet of Things

MAE	Mean Absolute Error
ML	Machine Learning
MLP	Multilayer Perceptron
MQTT	MQ Telemetry Transport
NRMSE	Normalized Root Mean Squared Error
NWP	Numerical Weather Prediction
PV	Photovoltaic
RE-SOINN	Regression Enhanced Self-organizing Incremental Neural Network
RES	Renewable Energy Sources
RMSE	Root Mean Squared Error
RVFL	Random Vector Functional Link
SCADA	Supervisory Control And Data Acquisition
SVM	Support Vector Machine

References

1. Marino, D.L.; Amarasinghe, K.; Manic, M. Building energy load forecasting using deep neural networks. In Proceedings of the IECON 2016-42nd Annual Conference of the IEEE Industrial Electronics Society, Florence, Italy, 23–26 October 2016; IEEE: Piscataway, NJ, USA, 2016; pp. 7046–7051.
2. Wang, H.; Lei, Z.; Zhang, X.; Zhou, B.; Peng, J. A review of deep learning for renewable energy forecasting. *Energy Convers. Manag.* **2019**, *198*, 111799. [CrossRef]
3. Tang, L.; Wu, Y.; Yu, L. A randomized-algorithm-based decomposition-ensemble learning methodology for energy price forecasting. *Energy* **2018**, *157*, 526–538. [CrossRef]
4. Hong, T.; Pinson, P.; Wang, Y.; Weron, R.; Yang, D.; Zareipour, H. Energy forecasting: A review and outlook. *IEEE Open Access J. Power Energy* **2020**, *7*, 376–388. [CrossRef]
5. Coignard, J.; Janvier, M.; Debusschere, V.; Moreau, G.; Chollet, S.; Caire, R. Evaluating forecasting methods in the context of local energy communities. *Int. J. Electr. Power Energy Syst.* **2021**, *131*, 106956. [CrossRef]
6. Deb, C.; Zhang, F.; Yang, J.; Lee, S.E.; Shah, K.W. A review on time series forecasting techniques for building energy consumption. *Renew. Sustain. Energy Rev.* **2017**, *74*, 902–924. [CrossRef]
7. Henzel, J.; Wróbel, Ł.; Fice, M.; Sikora, M. Energy consumption forecasting for the digital-twin model of the building. *Energies* **2022**, *15*, 4318. [CrossRef]
8. Sarmas, E.; Dimitropoulos, N.; Strompolas, S.; Mylona, Z.; Marinakis, V.; Giannadakis, A.; Romaios, A.; Doukas, H. A web-based Building Automation and Control Service. In Proceedings of the 2022 13th International Conference on Information, Intelligence, Systems & Applications (IISA), Corfu, Greece, 18–20 July 2022; IEEE: Piscataway, NJ, USA, 2022; pp. 1–6.
9. Fitch-Roy, O.; Fairbrass, J. *Negotiating the EU's 2030 Climate and Energy Framework*; Springer: Berlin/Heidelberg, Germany, 2018.
10. Sweeney, C.; Bessa, R.J.; Browell, J.; Pinson, P. The future of forecasting for renewable energy. *Wiley Interdiscip. Rev. Energy Environ.* **2020**, *9*, e365. [CrossRef]
11. IEA. Solar PV, Paris. 2022. Available online: https://www.iea.org/reports/solar-pv (accessed on 9 November 2022).
12. Das, U.K.; Tey, K.S.; Seyedmahmoudian, M.; Mekhilef, S.; Idris, M.Y.I.; Van Deventer, W.; Horan, B.; Stojcevski, A. Forecasting of photovoltaic power generation and model optimization: A review. *Renew. Sustain. Energy Rev.* **2018**, *81*, 912–928. [CrossRef]
13. Spiliotis, E.; Legaki, N.Z.; Assimakopoulos, V.; Doukas, H.; El Moursi, M.S. Tracking the performance of photovoltaic systems: A tool for minimising the risk of malfunctions and deterioration. *IET Renew. Power Gener.* **2018**, *12*, 815–822. [CrossRef]
14. Ssekulima, E.B.; Anwar, M.B.; Al Hinai, A.; El Moursi, M.S. Wind speed and solar irradiance forecasting techniques for enhanced renewable energy integration with the grid: A review. *IET Renew. Power Gener.* **2016**, *10*, 885–989. [CrossRef]
15. Ahmad, A.S.; Hassan, M.Y.; Abdullah, M.P.; Rahman, H.A.; Hussin, F.; Abdullah, H.; Saidur, R. A review on applications of ANN and SVM for building electrical energy consumption forecasting. *Renew. Sustain. Energy Rev.* **2014**, *33*, 102–109. [CrossRef]
16. Ahmed, R.; Sreeram, V.; Mishra, Y.; Arif, M. A review and evaluation of the state-of-the-art in PV solar power forecasting: Techniques and optimization. *Renew. Sustain. Energy Rev.* **2020**, *124*, 109792.
17. Mayer, M.J. Benefits of physical and machine learning hybridization for photovoltaic power forecasting. *Renew. Sustain. Energy Rev.* **2022**, *168*, 112772. [CrossRef]
18. Fara, L.; Diaconu, A.; Craciunescu, D.; Fara, S. Forecasting of energy production for photovoltaic systems based on ARIMA and ANN advanced models. *Int. J. Photoenergy* **2021**, *2021*. [CrossRef]
19. Hassan, M.A.; Khalil, A.; Kaseb, S.; Kassem, M. Exploring the potential of tree-based ensemble methods in solar radiation modeling. *Appl. Energy* **2017**, *203*, 897–916. [CrossRef]
20. Shi, J.; Lee, W.J.; Liu, Y.; Yang, Y.; Wang, P. Forecasting power output of photovoltaic systems based on weather classification and support vector machines. *IEEE Trans. Ind. Appl.* **2012**, *48*, 1064–1069. [CrossRef]
21. Pazikadin, A.R.; Rifai, D.; Ali, K.; Malik, M.Z.; Abdalla, A.N.; Faraj, M.A. Solar irradiance measurement instrumentation and power solar generation forecasting based on Artificial Neural Networks (ANN): A review of five years research trend. *Sci. Total Environ.* **2020**, *715*, 136848. [CrossRef]

22. Li, P.; Zhou, K.; Lu, X.; Yang, S. A hybrid deep learning model for short-term PV power forecasting. *Appl. Energy* **2020**, *259*, 114216. [CrossRef]
23. Sarmas, E.; Spiliotis, E.; Marinakis, V.; Tzanes, G.; Kaldellis, J.K.; Doukas, H. ML-based energy management of water pumping systems for the application of peak shaving in small-scale islands. *Sustain. Cities Soc.* **2022**, *82*, 103873. [CrossRef]
24. Zang, H.; Cheng, L.; Ding, T.; Cheung, K.W.; Wei, Z.; Sun, G. Day-ahead photovoltaic power forecasting approach based on deep convolutional neural networks and meta learning. *Int. J. Electr. Power Energy Syst.* **2020**, *118*, 105790. [CrossRef]
25. Sarmas, E.; Dimitropoulos, N.; Marinakis, V.; Mylona, Z.; Doukas, H. Transfer learning strategies for solar power forecasting under data scarcity. *Sci. Rep.* **2022**, *12*, 1–13. [CrossRef] [PubMed]
26. De Giorgi, M.G.; Congedo, P.M.; Malvoni, M. Photovoltaic power forecasting using statistical methods: Impact of weather data. *IET Sci. Meas. Technol.* **2014**, *8*, 90–97. [CrossRef]
27. Yu, T.C.; Chang, H.T. The forecast of the electrical energy generated by photovoltaic systems using neural network method. In Proceedings of the 2011 International Conference on Electric Information and Control Engineering, Wuhan, China, 15–17 April 2011; IEEE: Piscataway, NJ, USA, 2011; pp. 2758–2761.
28. Raza, M.Q.; Nadarajah, M.; Ekanayake, C. On recent advances in PV output power forecast. *Sol. Energy* **2016**, *136*, 125–144. [CrossRef]
29. Sun, X.; Zhang, T. Solar power prediction in smart grid based on NWP data and an improved boosting method. In Proceedings of the 2017 IEEE International Conference on Energy Internet (ICEI), Beijing, China, 17–21 April 2017; IEEE: Piscataway, NJ, USA, 2017; pp. 89–94.
30. Akeiber, H.; Nejat, P.; Majid, M.Z.A.; Wahid, M.A.; Jomehzadeh, F.; Famileh, I.Z.; Calautit, J.K.; Hughes, B.R.; Zaki, S.A. A review on phase change material (PCM) for sustainable passive cooling in building envelopes. *Renew. Sustain. Energy Rev.* **2016**, *60*, 1470–1497. [CrossRef]
31. Sarmas, E.; Marinakis, V.; Doukas, H. A data-driven multicriteria decision making tool for assessing investments in energy efficiency. *Oper. Res.* **2022**, *22*, 5597–5616. [CrossRef]
32. Kwok, S.S.; Lee, E.W. A study of the importance of occupancy to building cooling load in prediction by intelligent approach. *Energy Convers. Manag.* **2011**, *52*, 2555–2564. [CrossRef]
33. Suganthi, L.; Samuel, A.A. Energy models for demand forecasting—A review. *Renew. Sustain. Energy Rev.* **2012**, *16*, 1223–1240. [CrossRef]
34. Amasyali, K.; El-Gohary, N.M. A review of data-driven building energy consumption prediction studies. *Renew. Sustain. Energy Rev.* **2018**, *81*, 1192–1205. [CrossRef]
35. Li, Q.; Ren, P.; Meng, Q. Prediction model of annual energy consumption of residential buildings. In Proceedings of the 2010 International Conference on Advances in Energy Engineering, Beijing, China, 19–20 June 2010; IEEE: Piscataway, NJ, USA, 2010; pp. 223–226.
36. Liu, D.; Chen, Q. Prediction of building lighting energy consumption based on support vector regression. In Proceedings of the 2013 9th Asian Control Conference (ASCC), Istanbul, Turkey, 23–26 June 2013; IEEE: Piscataway, NJ, USA, 2013; pp. 1–5.
37. Borges, C.E.; Penya, Y.K.; Fernández, I.; Prieto, J.; Bretos, O. Assessing tolerance-based robust short-term load forecasting in buildings. *Energies* **2013**, *6*, 2110–2129. [CrossRef]
38. Saadi, M.; Noor, M.T.; Imran, A.; Toor, W.T.; Mumtaz, S.; Wuttisittikulkij, L. IoT enabled quality of experience measurement for next generation networks in smart cities. *Sustain. Cities Soc.* **2020**, *60*, 102266. [CrossRef]
39. Sarmas, E.; Spiliotis, E.; Marinakis, V.; Koutselis, T.; Doukas, H. A meta-learning classification model for supporting decisions on energy efficiency investments. *Energy Build.* **2022**, *258*, 111836. [CrossRef]
40. Marinakis, V. Big data for energy management and energy-efficient buildings. *Energies* **2020**, *13*, 1555. [CrossRef]
41. Bouchachia, A.; Gabrys, B.; Sahel, Z. Overview of some incremental learning algorithms. In Proceedings of the 2007 IEEE International Fuzzy Systems Conference, London, UK, 23–26 July 2007; IEEE: Piscataway, NJ, USA, 2007; pp. 1–6.
42. Ksieniewicz, P.; Zyblewski, P. Stream-learn—Open-source Python library for difficult data stream batch analysis. *Neurocomputing* **2022**, *478*, 11–21. [CrossRef]
43. Puah, B.K.; Chong, L.W.; Wong, Y.W.; Begam, K.; Khan, N.; Juman, M.A.; Rajkumar, R.K. A regression unsupervised incremental learning algorithm for solar irradiance prediction. *Renew. Energy* **2021**, *164*, 908–925. [CrossRef]
44. Qiu, X.; Suganthan, P.N.; Amaratunga, G.A. Ensemble incremental learning random vector functional link network for short-term electric load forecasting. *Knowl.-Based Syst.* **2018**, *145*, 182–196. [CrossRef]
45. Gardner, M.W.; Dorling, S. Artificial neural networks (the multilayer perceptron)—A review of applications in the atmospheric sciences. *Atmos. Environ.* **1998**, *32*, 2627–2636. [CrossRef]
46. Bourlard, H.; Kamp, Y. Auto-association by multilayer perceptrons and singular value decomposition. *Biol. Cybern.* **1988**, *59*, 291–294. [CrossRef]
47. Rumelhart, D.E.; Hinton, G.E.; Williams, R.J. Learning representations by back-propagating errors. *Nature* **1986**, *323*, 533–536. [CrossRef]
48. Hornik, K.; Stinchcombe, M.; White, H. Multilayer feedforward networks are universal approximators. *Neural Netw.* **1989**, *2*, 359–366. [CrossRef]
49. Bifet, A.; Gavalda, R.; Holmes, G.; Pfahringer, B. *Machine Learning for Data Streams: With Practical Examples in MOA*; MIT Press: Cambridge, MA, USA, 2018.

50. Ratcliff, R. Connectionist models of recognition memory: Constraints imposed by learning and forgetting functions. *Psychol. Rev.* **1990**, *97*, 285. [CrossRef]
51. Robins, A. Catastrophic forgetting, rehearsal and pseudorehearsal. *Connect. Sci.* **1995**, *7*, 123–146. [CrossRef]
52. He, J.; Mao, R.; Shao, Z.; Zhu, F. Incremental Learning in Online Scenario. In Proceedings of the IEEE/CVF Conference on Computer Vision and Pattern Recognition (CVPR), Seattle, WA, USA, 16–19 June 2020.
53. MQTT. Available online: https://docs.oasis-open.org/mqtt/mqtt/v5.0/mqtt-v5.0.html (accessed on 25 November 2022).
54. Buitinck, L.; Louppe, G.; Blondel, M.; Pedregosa, F.; Mueller, A.; Grisel, O.; Niculae, V.; Prettenhofer, P.; Gramfort, A.; Grobler, J.; et al. API design for machine learning software: Experiences from the scikit-learn project. In Proceedings of the ECML PKDD Workshop: Languages for Data Mining and Machine Learning, Prague, Czech Republic, 23–27 September 2013; pp. 108–122.
55. Pedregosa, F.; Varoquaux, G.; Gramfort, A.; Michel, V.; Thirion, B.; Grisel, O.; Blondel, M.; Prettenhofer, P.; Weiss, R.; Dubourg, V.; et al. Scikit-learn: Machine learning in Python. *J. Mach. Learn. Res.* **2011**, *12*, 2825–2830.
56. Scitkit-Learn 6. Strategies to Scale Computationally: Bigger Data. Available online: https://scikit-learn.org/0.15/modules/scaling_strategies.html#strategies-to-scale-computationally-bigger-data (accessed on 3 November 2022).

electronics

MDPI

Article

A Framework for Smart Home System with Voice Control Using NLP Methods

Yuliy Iliev [1] and Galina Ilieva [2,*]

[1] Teletek Electronics, 1407 Sofia, Bulgaria
[2] Department of Management and Quantitative Methods in Economics, University of Plovdiv Paisii Hilendarski, 4000 Plovdiv, Bulgaria
* Correspondence: galili@uni-plovdiv.bg

Abstract: The proliferation of information technologies and the emergence of ubiquitous computing have quickly transformed electronic devices from isolated islands of data and control into interconnected parts of intelligent systems. These network-based systems have advanced features, including Internet of Things (IoT) sensors and actuators, multiple connectivity options and multimodal user interfaces, and they also enable remote monitoring and management. In order to develop a human machine interface of smart home systems with speech recognition, we propose a new IoT-fog-cloud framework using natural language processing (NLP) methods. The new methodology adds utterance to command transformation to the existing cloud-based speech-to-text and text-to-speech services. This approach is flexible and can be easily adapted for different types of automation systems and consumer electronics as well as to almost every non-tonal language not currently supported by online platforms for intent detection and classification. The proposed framework has been employed in the development of prototypes of voice user interface extension of existing smart security system via new service for speech intent recognition. Tests on the system were carried out and the obtained results show the effectiveness of the new voice communication option. The speech-based interface is reliable; it facilitates customers and improves their experience with smart home devices.

Keywords: smart system; smart home; voice user interface; speech command recognition; natural language processing; natural language understanding; under-resourced languages

Citation: Iliev, Y.; Ilieva, G. A Framework for Smart Home System with Voice Control Using NLP Methods. *Electronics* **2023**, *12*, 116. https://doi.org/10.3390/electronics12010116

Academic Editor: Juan M. Corchado

Received: 30 November 2022
Revised: 21 December 2022
Accepted: 23 December 2022
Published: 27 December 2022

1. Introduction

A home automation system (smart home, smart house) is a communication network comprising of home sensors, devices and appliances (lighting, fans, air conditioners, entertainment systems, surveillance cameras, electronic doors, alarm systems, etc.) for access and monitoring of home environment without human intervention [1]. If smart home components (usually Internet of Things—IoT devices) are connected to the Internet, they can send and receive data from the global network and thus be controlled remotely via different communication protocols [2,3].

Typically, smart home systems employ three different computing layers for data collection: processing and storage—edge, fog and cloud, respectively. The middle layer (fog) of smart home architecture lies between physical IoT devices (edge) and traditional data storage (cloud) levels. This intermediate layer extends the cloud infrastructure and brings computations and storage closer to their data source, i.e., the edge. Distinct from centralised cloud computing infrastructure [4,5], the fog layer consists of multiple nodes which can build a decentralised computing ecosystem. When a fog node receives data, it can decide whether to process it locally or send it to the cloud. In addition, the data can be accessed offline as it can be stored locally. This is another key difference between fog and cloud computing, where data processing and storage are only carried out by remote servers [6–8]. Therefore, the fog layer is more effective than the cloud one in solving local tasks in real time, since it minimises transmission latency, improves response time, decreases bandwidth consumption and reduces some cyber security risks [9,10].

In this study, we combine sensors and actuators, fog and cloud services in a single information space to extend the capabilities of user interface of smart systems. Human-machine interaction is an important factor for the adoption of new products by consumer electronics market worldwide. On the one hand, smart user interface (SUI) increases sales and improves the corporate image of smart system manufacturers and vendors. On the other hand, an innovative human-machine communication is also useful for customers, as they quickly appreciate the capabilities of new technologies that enter their everyday lives. According to International Data Corporation (IDC), a market research company, worldwide smart home devices market grew by 11.7% in 2021, with double-digit growth forecast as we approach 2026 [11]. The results of Juniper Research study of digital technologies market [12] show that there will be almost 13.5 billion home automation systems in active use by 2025 and voice capabilities are an increasingly common way to control digital devices, linking them into the smart home ecosystem.

In the last decade, the spread of IoT and speech recognition technologies has led to the development of a variety of smart devices that can be controlled from a distance by voice. The advantages of Voice User Interface (VUI) compared to the classical interaction modes are numerous:

1. VUI provides an additional control channel offering hands-free and eyes-free interaction (multi-modality);
2. It enables users to perform multiple actions while communicating (multi-tasking);
3. VUI is analogous to everyday conversation (intuitiveness and ease of use);
4. It is also beneficial to people with physical and cognitive disabilities, who have difficulties interacting with electronic devices through a conventional interface (accessible design) [13].

There are several ecosystems for voice-based technologies that dominate the voice control market such as Google DialogFlow (2014) [14,15], Microsoft Language Understanding (LUIS) (2018) [16,17], IBM Watson Natural Language Understanding (2018) [18,19] and Alibaba Cloud Intelligent Speech Interaction (2020) [20]. These platforms offer a plethora of services, such as transcribing speech to text and vice versa, setting up reminders, searching the Internet and responding to simple queries (weather, traffic or route navigation, playing music or TV) in several languages. The above-mentioned voice service platforms, differing from their predecessors (smart voice speakers and traditional voice assistants). are not limited to specific hardware or operating systems. Instead, they are accessible on any device that is connected to the corresponding cloud platform. The voice platforms also have vertical integrations across multiple industries (retail, transportation, entertainment and media, health) but unfortunately, they have some drawbacks:

1. Speech-to-Text (STT), Text-to-Speech (TTS) and especially natural language understanding (NLU) services are only available for a small subset of the world's 7000+ languages and their variants, and often these services are paid (subscription is needed);
2. Service integration into smart home systems often requires computer science competences (especially in the case of on-premises deployment), a significant amount of time and effort, as well as technical support;
3. The list of recognised commands (skills) is usually domain-specific and needs to be expanded.

The main goal of this research is to develop a new conceptual framework for enhanced voice user interface in smart home systems. The proposed framework incorporates real-time remote monitoring and control through various channels and supports voice interface even for under-resourced languages.

The advantages of the new framework for home automation with voice control are as follows:

1. It allows for the implementation of intelligent user interface (IUI) with "understanding" of domain-specific voice commands in natural language. This option is especially important for under-resourced languages as there is no alternative online service for their automatic intent recognition;
2. The proposed approach is a free of charge alternative to existing paid online NLU services for the most widely used languages;
3. The new speech recognition service for voice control can be deployed in any layer of the IoT-Fog-Cloud (IoTFC) architecture and in the case of positioning in edge or fog level, it can minimise bandwidth loads, improve communication security and increase the intelligent system's efficacy.

The structure of the paper is as follows: in the next section, existing approaches for development of voice user interface for smart devices have been analysed and discussed. The third section presents the features of the proposed new framework for voice control of smart house systems using NLP methods. The next section describes the prototypes implemented to verify the new methodology and discusses its advantages. The last section concludes and outlines our future research directions.

2. Related Work

2.1. Literature Review on IoTFC Architecture

The recent research topics on smart systems architectures can be categorised in two main areas: (1) multi-layer frameworks and business processes for decentralised and real-time data processing and (2) practical implementations of customer electronics systems.

Sun et al. [21] have formulated the computation offloading and resource allocation in general IoTFC architecture as an energy and time cost minimisation problem. Then, they proposed a new algorithm to solve this problem, improving the energy consumption and completion time of application requests. In order to cope with big data and heterogeneity challenges in an IoTFC ecosystem, Chegini et al. [22] designed automatic components for fog resiliency. The advantage of the proposed approach is that it makes the processing of IoT tasks independent of the cloud layer.

Kallel et al. [23] modelled and implemented two IoT-aware business processes. The first one monitors behaviour of children with disabilities to guarantee their safety and facilitate their parents' intervention. The second model facilitates and accelerates the detection of persons infected with coronavirus as well as monitors their movements to reduce disease spread. Bhatia et al. [24] have employed a Multi-scaled Long Short Term Memory (M-LSTM)-based vulnerability prediction for preventive veterinary healthcare services. Moreover, a fog-assisted real-time alert generation module has been presented in the authors' framework to notify the concerned veterinary doctor in the case of medical emergency.

The overview of existing approaches for the development of multi-layered architectures for smart systems shows that the intelligent and coordinated management of the three-layer IoTFC model has been the subject of many studies. In such an ecosystem, if a task requires a large amount of computing resources or data storage space, the processing should be performed in the cloud layer. In the case of a task needing low latency, the sensors and devices should send the data to servers or computing devices in the fog layer.

2.2. Literature Review on Design Peculiarities of Smart Home Systems with NLU Interface

Many authors have developed smart home systems with voice recognition interface using classical and machine learning approaches. Intent classification from utterances is typically performed in a two-stage pipeline: first, extraction of transcriptions using Automatic Speech Recognition (ASR) and second, intent recognition. In order to reduce the errors accumulated at the ASR stage and their negative impact on the intent classifier, Desot et al. [25] have proposed an end-to-end model based on deep neural networks to perform intent classification directly from raw speech input. Liu et al. [26] have applied deep learning model to multi-intent detection task. Klaib et al. [27] have used Amazon

Alexa in the new smart home system to a receive user's verbal commands and then send the request to Azure cloud to control home appliances. Yang [28] has designed and implemented a new voice recognition smart home system with client-server architecture. The intelligent terminal (client) interprets the voice signal as a specific voice command using a hidden Markov model and a dynamic time warping algorithm. The control node finds the system's command corresponding to the voice command, sends it to the home devices, and responds to the system's control panel. Amin [29] has presented a smart home system as a single portable unit that uses a voice-controlled Android application to operate home devices. The new system utilises ThingSpeak cloud platform to collect, review and store data from home appliances. A web server retrieves data from ThingSpeak cloud and saves it into MySQL database. The new home automation system applies a Google voice recognition service and a microcontroller to execute certain voice commands. Stefanenko et al. [30] described a method for voice commands recognition based on fuzzy logic. The developed fuzzy system has been employed to execute linguistically inaccurate commands. The obtained results show that the proposed method increases the expressiveness of the voice control of a moving robot.

In the above-mentioned studies, the positive and negative characteristics of VUI have been identified and various applications of VUI based on different speech recognition methods have been presented. After the analysis of the literature review for the development of intelligent voice interface, the following conclusions can be drawn:

1. Voice user interface can be implemented only by integration of methods covering all aspects of natural language processing (voice data entry, tokenisation, lemmatisation, tagging, semantic analysis);
2. Intent detection methods can be categorised into three main groups:
    - Methods using statistical features (hidden Markov model, dynamic time warping, naive Bayes, AdaBoost, support vector machines, logistic regression) [28];
    - Neural networks (convolutional neural networks, recurrent neural networks) and deep learning (LSTM), distance-based (Term Frequency-Inverse Document Frequency–TF-IDF) methods or combination of several deep learning methods [25,26];
    - Other intelligent methods for semantic recognition of voice commands (fuzzy logic [30], semantic patterns).
3. Since advanced-level voice recognition devices are costly for mainstream household appliances, the developers preferred commercial speech recognition services, such as Amazon Alexa [27], Google Assistant [29].
4. The implemented interactive user interfaces are only focused in a specific subject area [25,27,28].

In summary, the authors of the above-mentioned studies have employed statistical and machine learning methods for voice command classification in the most widely used natural languages. The first issue of existing approaches is the limited number of supported natural languages. There are several commercial NLU platforms available in the market at affordable prices such as Alexa Skills (2015) [31], Azure Cognitive Services (2018) [32], Watson Assistant (2020) [33] and Dialogflow CX (2021) [34]. Despite the fact that these platforms offer general-purpose natural language services with a lot of functionality, they have some disadvantages: (1) Their NLU services only support several languages (a maximum of 13 to 87). Bulgarian and many other under-resourced languages are not supported. (2) Natural language processing services are quite complex to test, set up and maintain. Further challenges are as follows: time delays due to remote data processing in the cloud, increased costs (as voice services are paid), and privacy and security issues due the risk of personal data breach.

In order to achieve the goal of our research, it is necessary to develop a new NLU service for speech recognition of domain-specific commands in an under-resourced language. For this purpose:

1. Each input user's utterance needs to be converted to its semantic equivalent (intent).
2. Specific syntax for encoding structured semantic templates must be defined for smart home commands (nodes, patterns and slots);
3. Speech-To-Text and Text-To-Speech services offered by Microsoft, Google and other speech service providers are among the building blocks of the new intelligent voice user interface. In the case of normal speed and reliable Internet connection, they could be employed via the cloud or otherwise as on-premises software.

The same approach can be applied for any language with available STT and TTS services and not supported intent recognition.

3. New Framework for Voice-Based User Interface

In order to achieve interconnection and interoperability of multiple devices, services and applications in intelligent home systems, there are two main requirements for their architectural design.

1. Smart home systems have to provide intelligent user interface, aimed at maximum user convenience.

Intelligent user interface can personalise and guide interaction. IUI is one of the most important and distinguishing characteristics that determines, to a large extent, new products adoption, especially in regional markets. Voice communication options improve customer experience, increase consumer loyalty and create a competitive advantage for new products. It also enables initial installation and configuration, periodic diagnostics and maintenance, reconfiguration and optimisation of smart systems.

2. Home automation systems should guarantee effective remote communication between the control panel and other control systems (IoT networks, building management system, etc.).

In order to meet this second requirement, data has to be transferred via a gateway. In this case, the control panel of a smart home system should be transformed into a hub, supporting standardised IoT communication protocols, such as WiFi and KNX, a communication protocol developed for and widely used in home automation. The voice control of smart home systems could be implemented through an Alexa Skills mechanism or similar.

According to the two aforementioned aspects of smart home connectivity, the new framework needs to combine an innovative user interface and diverse communication capabilities between the control panel and other (external) control systems.

As pointed out in the previous section, the voice user interface can be implemented in two ways:

- The functionality is embedded in the control panel of the smart home systems, which has a secured a connection to the cloud infrastructure;
- The functionality is located in a separate layer within the structure of smart home systems.

The new conceptual framework for smart home systems with VUI follows the second approach (Figure 1).

The diagram in Figure 1 visualizes the communications of smart home components with system's panel via two types of channels: (1) direct: to the peripheral devices and external computer networks and mobile networks; and (2) indirect: to IP sensors, devices and appliances, other control systems (KNX) and voice-based interface.

In the proposed framework, an integration server (a fog structure) is introduced as an additional communication node. It allows for both the deployment of the intelligent user interface as well as integration with existing IoT devices and control systems.

Another novel element in the proposed framework is that communications between users (left) and external control systems (right) can be realised via virtual channels to a variety of services offered by different providers, including by smart automation company.

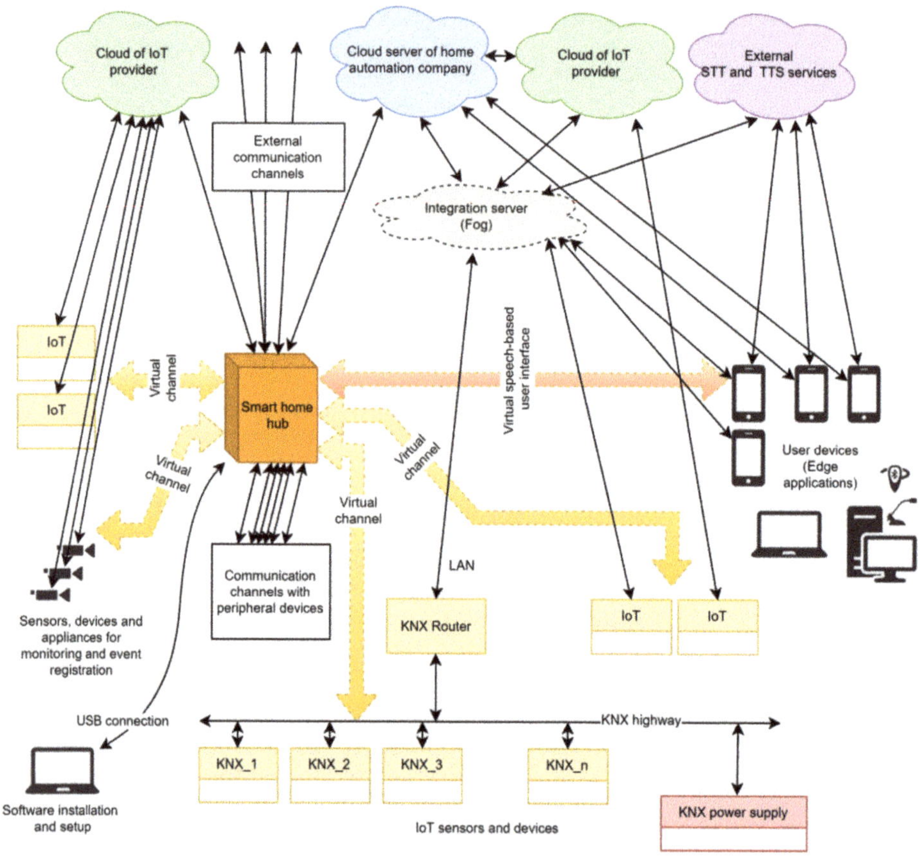

Figure 1. Framework for voice-based user interface. Note: Black arrows indicate direct communications between central panel (hub) and system's elements, while yellow arrows show indirect ones. The indirect communications consist of multiple requests to services.

The new software module implementing a dialog-based IUI can be deployed in any layer of the smart home architecture. Placing the voice interface in a separate architectural level offloads the control panel from non-core functionality and distributes computations between different devices. This approach is preferred because:

- IUI development is relatively independent from system panel limitations;
- The risks of security breaches are shifted away from the system core.

Another advantage of this approach is that multiplier effect can be utilised by implementing the same intelligent interface module for an entire product family and in different languages.

The proposed distributed multi-layer framework expands the capabilities of smart home systems in comparison with classical IoTFC approach. Edge or fog voice services can provide quick responses to requests with minimal delays because processing is located where data is available or needed.

4. System Prototype Design, Implementation and Evaluation

This section presents the implementation of a smart home system in line with the proposed framework for voice control combining local and remote natural language services for under-resourced languages with visual illustrations and algorithms' descriptions.

4.1. Design of Interactions between User and a Smart Home System

The flowchart in Figure 2a and corresponding steps in Algorithm 1 represent the voice-based interactions between a user and a smart home system as a sequence of requests and responses.

Algorithm 1 User–smart home system interactions via speech command as a part of SUI

1. Smart home user enters an utterance (speech) with a certain meaning (a1);
2. The user device (computer, laptop, tablet, smartphone or wearable) records the speech and transmits it as an audio stream (a2) to a service provided by the integration server;
3. IUI software module receives the message. The module sends a request (a3) to STT cloud service, forwarding the audio data;
4. IUI receives a response (a4) to its request. It is a text that corresponds to the sent audio data.
5. IUI extracts the meaning of the input user utterance and generates a request containing the obtained command for the smart home hub. The request (a5) is sent to the server in Cloud of Home Automation Company (CHAC);
6. CHAC receives the request, verifies its authenticity and correctness, prepares and sends the command (a6) to the smart home sub-system specified for it;
7. The smart home sub-system receives the command, executes it and returns the corresponding response (a7);
8. The response is received by CHAC, which transforms it to an answer to an IUI re-quest and sends this answer (a8) to IUI;
9. IUI receives the response from CHAC, prepares its own text response and sends it through a request (a9) for conversion to TTS cloud service;
10. IUI receives the result of its request as an audio file (a10);
11. IUI prepares a response specifying the URI of the received audio file and sends it (a11) to the user device;
12. The user device plays the audio file (a12) received as a result of their request and the user hears a speech response by the system to their utterance.

In some cases, several steps of Algorithm 1 can be omitted and/or added (Figure 2b):

1. Audio data from the user device can be sent directly to STT service (skipping step a2), and the received response is then submitted to IUI service (step b4 is added).
2. During the preparation of a response as an audio file, the call to TTS service might be skipped (steps a9 and a10 can be omitted) if such response has already been made and catalogued on the integration server. In this case, the URI to the already created audio file is sent as a response to the user device.

The flowchart in Figure 2b visualises the shortest version of this interaction process. In this way, the communication between user and smart home system takes less time and is more efficient.

The proposed Algorithm 1 is composed according to the classical five-stage structure of voice-controlled dialogue [35] (Table 1).

Table 1. Description of voice-controlled dialog in a smart home system (in two versions; a more detailed and the shortest one).

Stage	Detailed Version	The Shortest Version
Voice Activity Detection	a1	b1
ASR	a2–a4, a9–a10	b2–b3
NLU	a5	b5
Decision Stage	a6–a7	b6–b7
Communication Stage	a8, a11–a12	b8, b9–b10

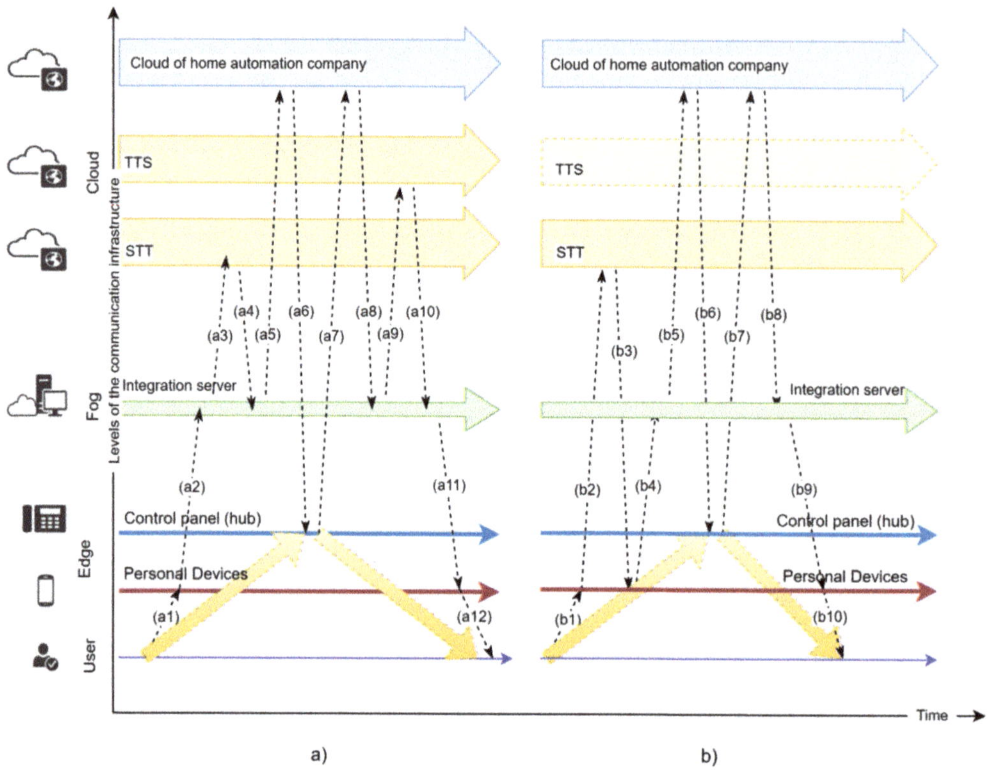

Figure 2. Step-by-step voice communication between user and smart home system, (**a**) long and (**b**) short version, respectively.

The flowchart in Figure 3 and corresponding steps in Algorithm 2 depict the proposed intent detection method (Algorithm 1, Step 5). In the algorithm description, a node represents a collection of predefined information structures, which is necessary to recognise each possible executable command. They are stored as a list of nodes. Each node contains a list of structural patterns, a list of slots, and command generation mechanism.

Each command structural pattern is defined by a specialised syntax and contains word lemmas, synonym groups, parameter slots, etc. It defines the permissible positions of keywords and parameter slots in the utterance. It is used as a basis for detecting the correspondence between the utterance and the pattern.

Each slot corresponds to one parameter required by the command. Specific questions for requesting the value of the corresponding parameter from the user are defined for it.

Command generation mechanism is a procedure in which the received command parameter values are processed and a formal command is generated for the hub. It can include other procedures, links to external services and URL references.

The list of commands can be easily extended with no coding required.

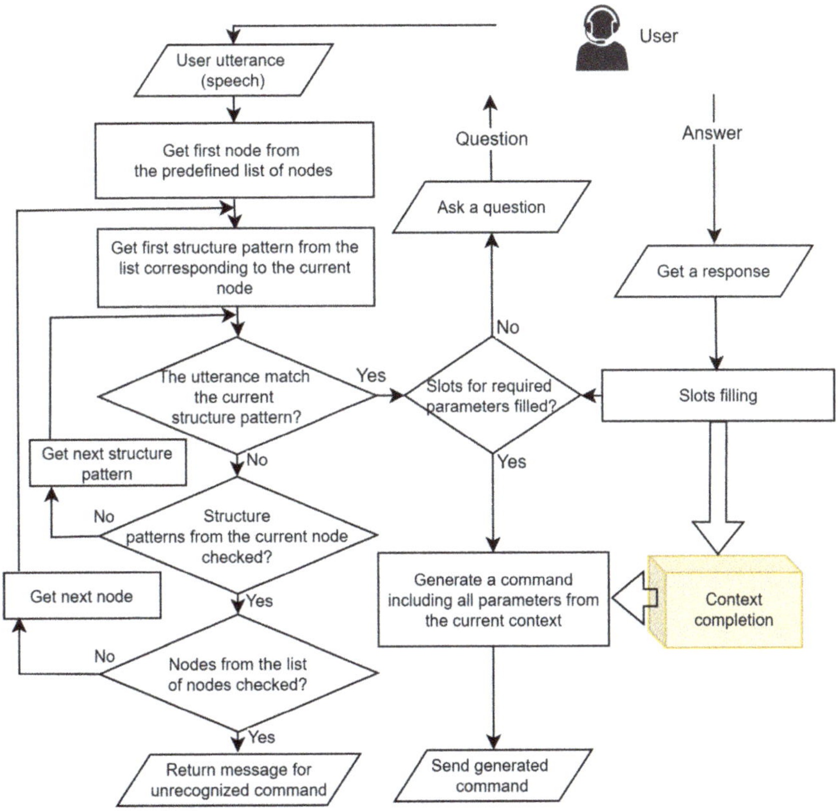

Figure 3. Flowchart of intent-based voice command recognition.

Algorithm 2 Intent-based voice command detection from user utterance

---

1. User utterance is entered;
2. All nodes from the list of predefined application nodes are traversed sequentially. The process starts with the first one in the list;
3. For each node, all structural patterns associated with this node are traversed sequentially;
4. The utterance is compared with the current structural pattern;
5. If there is a match, the traversal of the nodes stops and the command corresponding to the current node is considered as recognised;
6. If there is a recognised command, it is checked whether all required parameters are available in the utterance or in the current context;

6a. If the context still does not contain values for all required parameters, the user is asked clarifying questions about each missing value and upon receiving the answers, the values are filled in the context;

6b. If all required parameters have corresponding values in the context, a command is generated, including the parameter values accumulated in the context, and it is sent to the execution device;

7. In the case of missing match after traversing of all nodes and all their structural patterns, an unrecognised command message is generated and sent to the user.

In the next subsection, we present the peculiarities of software implementation of new VUI for existing smart security system and the results obtained from demonstration of new system prototypes in an operational environment.

4.2. Implementation Details and Evaluation

In order to validate the functionality of the new voice user interface, the existing smart security system has been extended with additional embedded software and software modules on the server as follows:

1. System software for integration server has been developed.

The integration server has been positioned in the intermediate (fog) layer of the proposed IoTFC framework. On this server, new software for voice command interface in domain-specific Bulgarian has been deployed. The new user interface has been implemented as a Web application. The interface has been connected to STT and TTS cloud services (both in Bulgarian). The program code has been created in Node.js environment;

2. Several additional services have been added to the existing cloud of smart home automation company;
3. New services have been created to handle remote users' requests for control and monitoring of the smart home system including from third party applications;
4. An add-on has also been created to employ Alexa Skills and other similar applications for mobile access and control of system devices.

The main challenge during the development process of our smart voice interface was intent extraction from the users' utterances and its conversion into a specific structured command. The issues that must be overcome are as follows:

1. The computing power of personal and mobile devices is limited;
2. The computational complexity of STT, TTS and natural language understanding tasks is significant.

The implemented algorithm also employs a deep learning neural network, which is pre-trained to recognise wake-up words through TensorFlow platform (in its JavaScript version), installed on user devices. This approach eliminates redundant traffic that would occur if user devices "listen" to any noise and forward it for recognition somewhere in the network. The rest of the natural language understanding (Algorithm 2) is performed on the server side. In this way, personal devices are unloaded from some tasks and the know-how of manufacturer of smart security system is protected.

After the implementation of VUI for smart security system and its connections to local and remote services, a demonstration of system prototypes in operational environment was organised. Two different prototypes of wireless smart security system were presented. They were configured to work with various wireless devices: passive infrared (PIR) sensors in different zones, magnetic sensors, external siren, remote control devices, etc. During the demonstration using voice control in Bulgarian, the following system components and features were tested:

- Wake-up of listening modules with a predefined word;
- Activation (turn on) of security system in arm mode; an indication has been received on the panel display that arm mode is turned on;
- Lights control in different rooms, with visual and verbal confirmation of recognised and executed commands;
- Hints are provided for command options when a dialogue has already been started but some slots are still empty;
- Providing information about the projects (distribution of projects information);
- Speech commands responses by two synthetic voice types (male and female);
- Several command variations have been executed with different keywords, keywords' derivatives and paraphrases and the extracted intent has been validated.

New services based on the proposed framework for VUI have been built into an existing smart security system and the systems' prototypes has been demonstrated in an operative environment. The test results have shown that the system can successfully control security facilities through a predefined set of voice commands, taking into account real-time environmental data. The experimental results also demonstrate that the new VUI is reliable and flexible; it can execute speech commands with different variations in users' utterances and voice nuances.

In this section, an intelligent home system, which employs the proposed IoTFC framework, has been presented. The new system can react immediately to all events that are signalled, i.e., the system operates normally in isolated (local) mode. This smart home system can collect and process data generated by its peripheral (edge) devices (sensors, devices and appliances) and control them remotely in real time. It can also communicate with user's smartphones and wearable devices, but in these cases, Bluetooth communication protocol is required. The proposed architecture for smart home allows for integration with other external systems (for example, systems for building automation), acting as a hub connecting different systems. The smart system can transmit IoT data to the fog layer via REST HTTP protocol, which provides flexibility and interoperability in building RESTful services. This feature ensures backward compatibility with legacy systems running in the computational infrastructure of smart home automation company. Local computing entities (fog nodes) can filter received data and either process it locally or send it to the cloud for further processing. The voice user interface provides control and monitoring services using real-time data about devices' state and events occurring in the home environment. It can be deployed in any layer of the smart home architecture. The voice user interface can be implemented in any non-tonal language, including under-resourced ones, if STT and TTS services are available for it.

5. Conclusions

Edge-Fog-Cloud computing and automatic speech recognition are among the most dynamic areas of today's computer science. In our manuscript, we combine IoT-Fog-Cloud architecture and speech recognition methods to develop a new distributed framework for smart home systems with voice user interface for under-resourced languages. The new framework incorporates existing STT and TTS cloud services in speech recognition method in a particular (smart home) domain.

The limitations of our study are as follows: (1) Defining patterns for smart home commands requires very good knowledge in the respective language(s). For example, since Bulgarian and the other Slavic languages belong to the group of morphologically rich languages, special attention is needed to different word forms (morphological derivation) in patterns of smart home commands. (2) The prototype implementation can only handle a predefined set of domain-specific voice commands; for smart security system, in only one language (Bulgarian). (3) The proposed methodology does not support VUI in tonal languages and in languages without available STT and TTS services. (4) The commands happen only at the sentence level.

Our future research directions are as follows: (1) implement the proposed framework using small single-board computers; (2) modify the proposed framework for voice command interface for industrial automation systems; (3) enhance the prototype by adding more voice commands for monitoring and controlling of smart home devices and appliances in several natural languages. In the future, we also plan to apply fuzzy multi-criteria decision-making methods in voice-controlled human-machine dialogues.

Author Contributions: Conceptualisation, Y.I.; software, Y.I.; validation, G.I. and Y.I.; resources, G.I. and Y.I.; writing—original draft preparation, G.I.; writing—review and editing, G.I. and Y.I.; visualization, G.I and Y.I.; supervision, G.I.; project administration, Y.I.; funding acquisition, G.I. and Y.I. All authors have read and agreed to the published version of the manuscript.

Funding: This research was funded by the National Innovation Fund, Grant No. 11IF-02-5/01.12.2020 "Scientific and applied research for the development of a wireless security system with universal connectivity" and by the Ministry of Education and Science and by the National Science Fund, co-founded by the European Regional Development Fund, Grant No. BG05M2OP001-1.002-0002 "Digitization of the Economy in Big Data Environment".

Data Availability Statement: Not applicable.

Acknowledgments: The authors thank the academic editors and anonymous reviewers for their insightful comments and suggestions.

Conflicts of Interest: The authors declare no conflict of interest.

References

1. Schiefer, M. Smart home definition and security threats. In Proceedings of the 2015 Ninth international conference on IT security incident management & IT forensics, Magdeburg, Germany, 18–20 May 2015. [CrossRef]
2. Domb, M. Smart home systems based on internet of things. In *Internet of Things (IoT) for Automated and Smart Applications*; Ismail, Y., Ed.; IntechOpen: London, UK, 2019; pp. 25–40. [CrossRef]
3. Stojkoska, B.L.R.; Trivodaliev, K.V. A review of Internet of Things for smart home: Challenges and solutions. *J. Clean. Prod.* **2017**, *140*, 1454–1464. [CrossRef]
4. Wei, Z.; Qin, S.; Jia, D.; Yang, Y. Research and design of cloud architecture for smart home. In Proceedings of the 2010 IEEE International Conference on Software Engineering and Service Sciences, Beijing, China, 16–18 July 2010. [CrossRef]
5. Soliman, M.; Abiodun, T.; Hamouda, T.; Zhou, J.; Lung, C.H. Smart home: Integrating internet of things with web services and cloud computing. In Proceedings of the 2013 IEEE 5th International Conference on Cloud Computing Technology and Science, Bristol, UK, 2–5 December 2013. [CrossRef]
6. Wadhwa, H.; Aron, R. Fog computing with the integration of internet of things: Architecture, applications and future directions. In Proceedings of the 2018 IEEE International Conference on Parallel & Distributed Processing with Applications, Ubiquitous Computing & Communications, Big Data & Cloud Computing, Social Computing & Networking, Sustainable Computing & Communications, Melbourne, Australia, 11–13 December 2018. [CrossRef]
7. Atlam, H.F.; Walters, R.J.; Wills, G.B. Fog Computing and the Internet of Things: A Review. *Big Data Cogn. Comput.* **2018**, *2*, 10. [CrossRef]
8. Rahimi, M.; Songhorabadi, M.; Kashani, M.H. Fog-based smart homes: A systematic review. *J. Netw. Comput. Appl.* **2020**, *153*, 102531. [CrossRef]
9. Shukla, S.; Hassan, M.F.; Khan, M.K.; Jung, L.T.; Awang, A. An analytical model to minimize the latency in healthcare internet-of-things in fog computing environment. *PLoS ONE* **2019**, *14*, e0224934. [CrossRef] [PubMed]
10. La, Q.D.; Ngo, M.V.; Dinh, T.Q.; Quek, T.Q.; Shin, H. Enabling intelligence in fog computing to achieve energy and latency reduction. *Digit. Commun. Netw.* **2019**, *5*, 3–9. [CrossRef]
11. Worldwide Smart Home Devices Market Grew 11.7% in 2021 with Double-Digit Growth Forecast Through 2026. According to IDC. Available online: https://www.idc.com/getdoc.jsp?containerId=prUS49051622 (accessed on 30 November 2022).
12. Smart Home Devices to Exceed 13 Billion in Active Use by 2025, with Entertainment Devices Leading Way. Available online: https://www.juniperresearch.com/press/smart-home-devices-to-exceed-13-billion-in-active (accessed on 30 November 2022).
13. Sovacool, B.K.; Del Rio, D.D.F. Smart home technologies in Europe: A critical review of concepts, benefits, risks and policies. *Renew. Sust. Energ. Rev.* **2020**, *120*, 109663. [CrossRef]
14. DialogFlow. Available online: https://cloud.google.com/dialogflow/ (accessed on 30 November 2022).
15. Sabharwal, N.; Agrawal, A. Introduction to Google Dialogflow. In *Cognitive Virtual Assistants Using Google Dialogflow*; Apress: Berkeley, CA, USA, 2020; pp. 13–54.
16. What is Language Understanding (LUIS)? Available online: https://learn.microsoft.com/en-us/azure/cognitive-services/luis/what-is-luis (accessed on 30 November 2022).
17. Rozga, S. Language Understanding Intelligent Service (LUIS). In *Practical Bot Development*; Apress: Berkeley, CA, USA, 2018; pp. 47–128.
18. Watson Natural Language Understanding. Available online: https://www.ibm.com/cloud/watson-natural-language-understanding (accessed on 30 November 2022).
19. Vergara, S.; El-Khouly, M.; El Tantawi, M.; Marla, S.; Sri, L. *Building Cognitive Applications with IBM Watson Services: Volume 7 Natural Language Understanding*; IBM Redbooks: Armonk, NY, USA, 2017; pp. 1–57.
20. Alibaba Cloud Intelligent Speech Interaction. Available online: https://www.alibabacloud.com/product/intelligent-speech-interaction (accessed on 30 November 2022).
21. Sun, H.; Yu, H.; Fan, G.; Chen, L. Energy and time efficient task offloading and resource allocation on the generic IoT-fog-cloud architecture. *Peer Peer Netw. Appl.* **2020**, *13*, 548–563. [CrossRef]
22. Chegini, H.; Naha, R.K.; Mahanti, A.; Thulasiraman, P. Process automation in an IoT–fog–cloud ecosystem: A survey and taxonomy. *IoT* **2021**, *2*, 6. [CrossRef]
23. Kallel, A.; Rekik, M.; Khemakhem, M. IoT-fog-cloud based architecture for smart systems: Prototypes of autism and COVID-19 monitoring systems. *Softw. Pract. Exp.* **2021**, *51*, 91–116. [CrossRef]

24. Bhatia, M.; Sood, S.K.; Manocha, A. Fog-inspired smart home environment for domestic animal healthcare. *Comput. Commun.* **2020**, *160*, 521–533. [CrossRef]
25. Desot, T.; Portet, F.; Vacher, M. Towards end-to-end spoken intent recognition in smart home. In Proceedings of the 2019 International Conference on Speech Technology and Human-Computer Dialogue, Timisoara, Romania, 10–12 October 2019.
26. Liu, J.; Li, Y.; Lin, M. Review of intent detection methods in the human-machine dialogue system. *J. Phys. Conf. Ser.* **2019**, *1267*, 012059. [CrossRef]
27. Klaib, A.F.; Alsrehin, N.O.; Melhem, W.Y.; Bashtawi, H.O. IoT Smart Home Using Eye Tracking and Voice Interfaces for Elderly and Special Needs People. *J. Commun.* **2019**, *14*, 614–621. [CrossRef]
28. Yang, C. Design of smart home control system based on wireless voice sensor. *J. Sens.* **2021**, *2021*, 8254478. [CrossRef]
29. Amin, D.H.M. Voice Controlled Home Automation System. *Int. J. Electr. Comput. Eng.* **2022**, *7*, 1–11. [CrossRef]
30. Stefanenko, O.S.; Lipinskiy, L.V.; Polyakova, A.S.; Khudonogova, J.A.; Semenkin, E.S. An intelligent voice recognition system based on fuzzy logic and the bag-of-words technique. *IOP Conf. Ser.: Mater. Sci. Eng.* **2020**, *1230*, 012020. [CrossRef]
31. Alexa Skills. Available online: https://developer.amazon.com/en-US/alexa/alexa-skills-kit/ (accessed on 30 November 2022).
32. Azure Cognitive Services. Available online: https://azure.microsoft.com/en-us/products/cognitive-services/ (accessed on 30 November 2022).
33. Watson Assistant. Available online: https://www.ibm.com/products/watson-assistant (accessed on 30 November 2022).
34. Dialogflow CX. Available online: https://cloud.google.com/dialogflow/cx/docs/ (accessed on 30 November 2022).
35. Vacher, M.; Caffiau, S.; Portet, F.; Meillon, B.; Roux, C.; Elias, E.; Lecouteux, B.; Chahuara, P. Evaluation of a Context-Aware voice interface for ambient assisted living: Qualitative user study vs. quantitative system evaluation. *ACM Trans. Access. Comput.* **2015**, *7*, 1–36. [CrossRef]

electronics

MDPI

Article

An Extreme Value Analysis-Based Systemic Approach in Healthcare Information Systems: The Case of Dietary Intake

Dimitrios P. Panagoulias, Dionisios N. Sotiropoulos and George A. Tsihrintzis *

Department of Informatics, University of Piraeus, Karaoli ke Dimitriou 80, 185 34 Piraeus, Greece
* Correspondence: geoatsi@unipi.gr

Abstract: Biomarkers are measurements of biological variables that can determine a state of health. They consist of measuring a single variable or a combination of variables related to the state of health that these variables represent. Biomarkers can provide an early warning of a health problem in relation to an individual patient or group of patients, and thus trigger actions and lead to interventions. Nutritional biomarkers measure the biological consequences of one's diet. In our recent work, we have used machine learning to predict weight, metabolic syndrome and blood pressure, using blood-exam-based biomarkers. In the current work, we use extreme value theory to examine the significance of outliers in health data, with a focus on diet and the standard biochemistry profile. Specifically, we show that, using extreme value analysis and by applying a systemisation of the process, health trends can be predicted, and thus, health interventions can be (at least partially) automated. For that purpose, public access datasets have been used, which were retrieved from the National Health and Nutrition Examination Survey. The NHANES is a program of studies designed to assess the health and nutritional status of the population in the United States. In total, about 70,000 datapoints were analysed, covering about a decade's worth of observations.

Keywords: biomarkers; bioinformatics; extreme value theory; extreme value analysis; health prediction; machine learning; artificial intelligence; information systems

Citation: Panagoulias, D.P.; Sotiropoulos, D.N.; Tsihrintzis, G.A. An Extreme Value Analysis-Based Systemic Approach in Healthcare Information Systems: The Case of Dietary Intake. *Electronics* **2023**, *12*, 204. https://doi.org/10.3390/electronics12010204

Academic Editor: Yue Wu

Received: 28 November 2022
Revised: 24 December 2022
Accepted: 26 December 2022
Published: 31 December 2022

1. Introduction

Predictive medicine is based on the forecasting of a disease via biomarker analysis and the instigation of preventive measures to decrease the impact of that disease or avoid it altogether. It is often utilised in cancer treatment and diagnosis. Biomarker can offer precise evaluation pathways and more effective treatment strategies by focusing them on individuals or groups of individuals with similar biological characteristics. A familiar and recognisable biometric and biomarker is the resting heart rate. Resting heart rate is the indicator of heart functionality and is considered a measurement of overall physical fitness. An immediate outcome of high heart rate is that of coronary heart disease. Another known biomarker related to heart attacks, congenital heart defects, coronary artery disease and pancreatitis is the level of triglycerides, which is retrieved via blood examinations. T-cells, which are white blood cells that protect against pathogens and tumours, are related to cancer, death, atherosclerosis and Alzheimer's disease.

1.1. Nutritional Variables and Data Collection Strategies

Diet and nutrition are closely related to health. Assessing though the impact and the relation is a vigorous task from an analytical and a data-collection standpoint. Nutritional assessment involves collecting information about food and liquids consumed over a specific time period, which is encoded and processed in order to calculate intake of energy, nutrients and other dietary components using food composition tables. The available nutritional assessment methods have different strengths and weaknesses, and the purpose of the data collection is essential for the more adequate method to be chosen [1].

The food frequency questionnaire (FFQ), using single or recurring 24 h recall, is a frequently used methodology for dietary assessment. Food records and/or food diaries are also utilised. The portion size is estimated using standardisation or population-average portion sizes, images and food models, among other methods. Diet history, diet checklist, direct observation, and dietary screening are methodologies also used for data collection purposes [1]. For the recurring 24 h recall method, the dietary intake is recorded by a trained interviewer or via automated self-administered systems. The detailed information on food and beverages consumed, including quantity, brand and preparation method, is logged. The preparation method may include ingredients, recipe and the addition of fats. The process includes structured questionnaires and memory-aiding images that are non-leading about the foods and beverages consumed over the previous 24 h period. Adoption of food-based dietary guidelines (F.B.D.G), should be considered a preventive approach to malnutrition and health optimisation through a balanced diet, while at the same time ensuring a positive environmental imprint [2]. F.B.D.G intends to influence consumer behaviour, through education about nutrients, foods and beverages [3]. As will be more thoroughly explained in Section 4, we have used publicly available data collected by the National Health and Nutrition Examination Survey. The NHANES is a set of studies designed to assess the health and nutritional status of the population in the United States. For the dietary data, the FFQ was used with 24 h recall.

1.2. Scope of the Study

Nutritional biomarkers can belong to one or more of three categories. They can be used as validators of dietary interventions or as substitute indicators of dietary habits or as measures for a nutrient. In cases where generic biomarkers are not sufficient to derive conclusions for some food ingredients, dietary intake methods and nutritional biomarkers can carry more information [4]. In this paper, we identify trends in nutrient intake and in the distribution of the extreme values. Seventy-thousand datapoints have been analysed, covering more than a decade (2000–2014) of observations. Specifically, we applied methodologies based on extreme value theory and correlation techniques to analyse dietary variables for different weight classes. Our goal is to automate the identification of patterns in nutrient intake as related to weight, and thus provide personalised interventions in nutrition management via intelligent information systems. In turn, this will educate and influence consumer behaviour. To better outline the characteristics of the examined hypothesis, we used our machine learning framework for the what, why and how [5].

More precisely, this paper is organised as follows: In Section 2, the basics of nutritional biomarkers and nutritional epidemiology are summarised, and an overview of application highlights of extreme value theory in the medical field is included. Section 3 outlines key issues and challenges related to our research, and the methodology used is analysed in Section 4. In Section 5, the implementation of the methodology is explained, and we report its results for select cases to better outline its usability aspects. In this section, the results of the described process are also discussed. Finally, in Section 6, conclusions are drawn and future research endeavours are considered.

2. Literature Review and Related Work

2.1. Nutritional Biomarkers and Bioinformatics

According to the Global Burden of Disease study, a sub-optimal diet is considered as the main risk factor for morbidity and mortality, surpassing smoking [6]. Disability-adjusted life years (DALYs) is a time-based metric that assumes years of life lost caused by premature mortality (Y.L.L) and years of life lost due to time lived in a sub-optimal health condition. Another similar metric is the years lost due to disability (Y.L.D.) and is determined by the number of years living disabled weighted by the level of disability. Both are used to assess the overall burden of a disease [7]. According to Herforth et al. [6], in 2019, about 8 million deaths and 180 million DALYs were attributable to dietary risk factors.

2.2. Epidemiology and Nutrition

Traditional epidemiology has contributed significantly to identifying many key lifestyle and environmental risk factors for chronic disease. "Systems epidemiology" is the research discipline that combines standard epidemiological methodologies and modern technologies to amplify the understanding of biological and metabolic pathways. Similarly, nutrition research offers another ideal domain, where traditional approaches and technological advances can optimise knowledge creation and knowledge sharing. Diet is a very important parameter of good health, and the data collection methods for dietary records have been instrumental to building awareness [8].

There is little evidence to suggest that metabolic effects interfere with weight loss [9]. On the contrary, compliance with dietary prescription is considered the main issue that affects weight loss. Indeed, recent studies that examined different diet plans with varying macro-nutrient content concluded that adherence to the prescribed diet is the strongest predictor of success [9]. Preventative dietary strategies could benefit eating behaviour and thus affect weight at the population level, when they are adopted as part of public health guidelines [10].

2.3. Research Continuity

In our previous related study, leading to the current one, we achieved high precision in predicting important health states. Namely, using blood-exam-based features, and more specifically, the standard biochemistry profile, we can predict weight class with 85% accuracy [11–14]. Moreover, using the same features, we can predict metabolic syndrome with 86% accuracy and high systolic blood pressure with 74% accuracy, as can be seen in Figure 1. The corresponding methodologies have been adapted in a system that can receive blood exams as input, assess the health state, offer recommendations and automate strategic health interventions [15–17]. Regulators, as stakeholders, have been examined in [5], where regulation and validation of methodologies were recognised as important factors in the development of health applications.

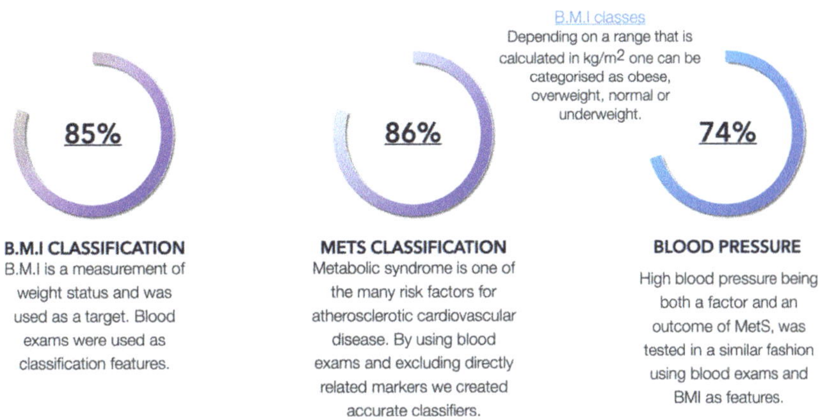

Figure 1. Developed methodologies and outcomes.

2.4. Theory and Application Highlights of Extreme Value Analysis

In this section, the key characteristics of extreme value theory are highlighted. Extreme value analysis (EVA) can be approached from two different angles. The first one refers to the block maxima (minima) series. According to block maxima (minima), the annual maximum (minimum) of time series data is extracted, generating an annual maxima or minima series, simply referred as AMS. The analysis of the AMS datasets are most frequently based on the results of the Fisher–Tippett–Gnedenko theorem, which leads to the fitting of the generalised extreme value distribution. A wide range of distributions can also be applied. The limiting of distributions for the maximum (minimum) of a collection of random variables from the same distribution is the basis of the examined theorem [18].

The peak-over-threshold (POT) methodology is the second approach used in EVA In POT, a sorted series is analysed, first identifying the peak values that exceed a given threshold in a given set of records. The analysis usually involves the fitting of two distributions. One concerns the number of events covering the time period or space analysed, and the other concerns the selected size of extracted peaks. As per the Pickands–Balkema–De Haan theorem, the POT extreme values asymptotically follow the generalised Pareto distribution family, and a Poisson distribution is used for the total number of events [19]. The return level (R.V.) of the extreme values can be approximated from the fitted distribution. The value expected or return value is equal to or exceeds the threshold on average once every interval T of time or space with a probability of $1/T$. P.D.F. refers to the probability density function of the continuous random variable, which, at any given point in the examined space, can provide the relative likelihood that the random variable is located near the sample space [18].

In medical data analysis, extreme value theory (EVT) is frequently utilised. In [20], Maud et al. predicted the weekly rates of deaths from pneumonia and influenza over a given time series. The daily number of emergency department visits was examined to determine the probability of extreme occurrences. In [21], Chiu et al. investigated mortality and morbidity using EVT. In [22], Flegal et al. examined age-specific extreme values of body mass index, using growth charts of the 2000 Centers for Disease Control and Prevention. Estimators based on asymptotic extreme value theory have been proposed, and their performances were theoretically evaluated and verified via Monte Carlo simulation as faster alternatives for estimation of the parameters of alpha-stable impulsive interference in [23].

In [24], Arsenault et al. used extreme value theory for the estimation of risk in finite-time systems, especially for cases when data collection is either expensive and/or impossible. For the monitoring of rare and damaging consequences of high blood glucose, EVA has been deployed using the block maxima approach [25]. More examples of application of EVT can be found in the recent literature, and here we only report those considered more relevant to our research.

The shape of the probability distribution is calculated via the L-moments. The L-moments represent linear combinations of order statistics (L-statistics) similar to conventional moments. They are used to calculate quantities analogous to standard deviation, skewness and kurtosis, and can thus be termed L-scale, L-skewness and L-kurtosis. Therefore, they summarise the shape of the probability distribution:

$L_4 = \frac{n*\Sigma n_i(Y_i-\tilde{Y})^4}{(\Sigma n_i(Y_i-\tilde{Y})^2)^2}$.

L_4 = L-kurtosis.

Y_i: ith Variable of the distribution.

$\tilde{Y}$: Mean of the distribution.

n: Number of Variables in the distribution.

$\tilde{\mu}_3 = \frac{\Sigma_i^N(X_i-\tilde{X})^3}{(N-1)*\sigma^3}$.

$\tilde{\mu}_3$ = L-skewness .

N = number of variables in the distribution.

X_i = random variables.

$\tilde{X}$ = mean of the distribution.

σ = standard deviation. namely.

3. Key Issues and Challenges

3.1. Patient's Journey

The patient's journey refers to the nonlinear process that integrates different parts of the healthcare ecosystem. Various stakeholders interact with each other, both directly and indirectly. In the micro-space, the relationships among the patients, the physician and the healthcare staff, which may include nursing and administrating personnel, are considered direct. Other indirect relationships may include the government, insurance agencies, academic regulating bodies, big pharmaceutical companies and others that fall outside the scope of this study. A systemic approach that involves automating a process in the healthcare ecosystem is considered an intervention in the patient's journey [5].

Symptom identification is regarded as a starting point for the patient's journey, followed by a visit to the doctor. As can be seen in Figure 2, for diagnosis of a health problem, the patient will visit a laboratory for generic and special examinations, and a treatment if deemed necessary by a specialist. A treatment follow-up may be required, which includes a general assessment of the patient's health by the doctor, in order to determine if further treatment is required and what treatment could potentially improve the patient's health state. Lifestyle changes can be suggested by the doctor, or more specialised treatment and continuous monitoring may be required [5,15]. The various steps are characterised by different emotions. Better alignment between patients and the other stakeholders of the ecosystem increases the likelihood that the patients will engage more, follow instructions and become more aware and proactive towards their health [16].

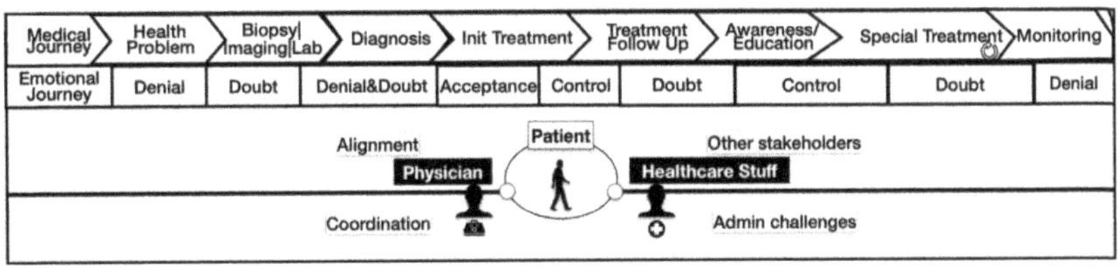

Figure 2. Patient's journey.

The use of big data and artificial intelligence technologies can support decision making, especially when incorporated as parts of intelligent knowledge systems [5]. New foundations in diagnostics and pathology analytics can be laid through more advanced machine learning pipelines [26]. On the other hand, extreme values and outliers in the medical domain provide considerable opportunities, where new pathways can be located and interventions can be engineered.

3.2. The Golden Circle of Innovation Adapted for Machine Learning

The golden circle of innovation as a process consists of three features, namely, the what, why and how [27]. To outline the problem at hand and define an adequate solution to it, we employ the golden circle of innovation as adapted for machine learning [5].

3.2.1. The What

Having obtained a first assessment of weight and metabolic status by analysing blood exams [11–14,28], it has become apparent that each weight class shows different characteristics. Since the outliers of each weight cluster form the gateway from one weight class to the next, the outliers of those characteristics can be analysed for additional patterns to be identified. The differences in those characteristics and the related distributions can also be examined and interpreted.

3.2.2. The Why

If patterns can be recognised in the distribution of the dietary variables, then recommendations and dietary strategies can be automated.

3.2.3. The How

Extreme values (otherwise known as "outliers") are data points that are sparsely distributed in the tails of a univariate or a multivariate distribution. The understanding and management of extreme values is a key part of data management. Through their exploitation, dietary intake can be fine-tuned based on personalised and specific parameters.

In the following sections, we outline our methodology to tackle the issues defined here using EVA The implementation of the methodology will illustrate the capacity of the proposed system and the utility of the system outcome.

4. Methodology

4.1. Technical Overview

The independent variable examined using the EVA methodology is the BMI, and the corresponding dependent variable is the dietary intake. The analysis was performed for the different weight classes defined by the BMI ranges shown in Table 1.

Table 1. BMI classification.

Range	Category
less than 18	underweight
between 18 and 25	normal
between 25 and 30	overweight
above 30	obese

The POT method was utilised, with which the BMI observations were sorted in ascending order. Three scenarios wereexamined per weight class. For the first scenario, the examined dietary variable exceeded the threshold that has been set. For the second scenario, the dietary variable fell below the threshold but lay above zero, and zero indicates that no consumption of the specific variable exists. Finally, for the third scenario, the dietary intake was equal to 0.

Dietary EVA Algorithm

In Figure 3, the designed algorithm is exhibited. As a first step, the BMI class to be analysed was chosen, and the dietary variable to be examined is set. A descriptive statistical analysis allows a first peek in the data examined as per the dietary variable and the weight class. The threshold was set for the peaks over it to be determined. The extreme values were plotted, and the corresponding *L*-moments were calculated. The results were then inspected, and the threshold was evaluated. If the results are not accepted, the process is repeated and the threshold is reset. Finally, the return values (R.V.) are extracted and plotted, and predictions based on trend can be proposed. For the implementation of the proposed EVA methodology, corresponding available Python libraries [29] were used, with the necessary modifications and adjustments.

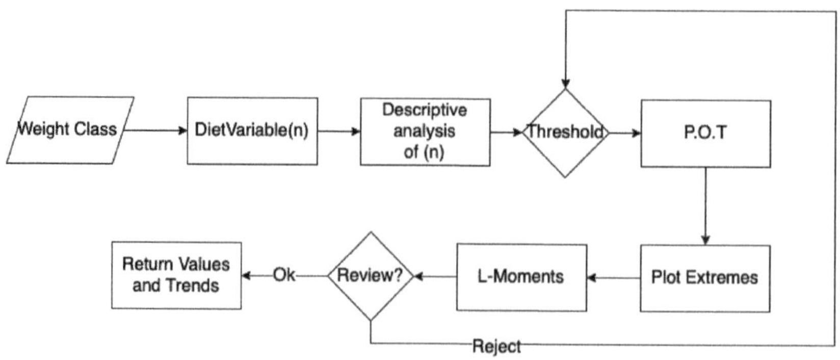

Figure 3. Dietary variable analysis and diet intervention algorithm.

4.2. EVA-Based Decision-Making Algorithm

In order to produce actionable insights, decision-making algorithms assimilate task-related information from the environment. In the healthcare domain, a decision-making algorithm can use a patient's vital markers and return a diagnosis. In [30], a decision-making algorithm is implemented for the suggestion of alternative foods, using a hybrid clustering food recommendation method based on chronic disease clustering. According to Kochenderfer et al. [31], agents are entities that can act based on observations from the environment. When implemented completely through software, those agents are non-physical and interact with the environment based on actions suggested by decision-making algorithms.

In Figure 4, a decision-making algorithm is proposed which uses EVA. Firstly, the dietary EVA algorithm is applied as previously described and output plots, and return values are produced. Following that, three different clusters are extracted based on three different scenarios, as can be seen in Figure 4, which are related to the threshold that defines the peaks in the examined data. Scenario (e) refers to the observations that are above the threshold, and scenario (o) refers to those below the threshold and greater than zero. Finally, scenario (z) refers to the cluster where the consumption of the examined dietary variable is equal to zero. Then, for the different scenarios examined, the correlations among the blood variables were analysed to identify how the body may react in each dietary context. The correlations were then filtered, setting a (−,+) threshold. For example, the threshold may be set according to whether correlation is below (−) or above (+) 55 percent. The filtered outputs for the different scenarios were then compared, and if the observed correlations for scenario (e′) increase compared to scenario (o′), more analysis is extracted related to unique demographic characteristics, weight differences and dietary consumption totals per scenario. If Total (e′) is greater than Total (o′), the Pearson correlation coefficient (PCC) between the dietary variable and blood exams is extracted for both scenarios. The difference is calculated to determine if the mean relation is negative or positive. The more prominent blood exams related to the mean are filtered.

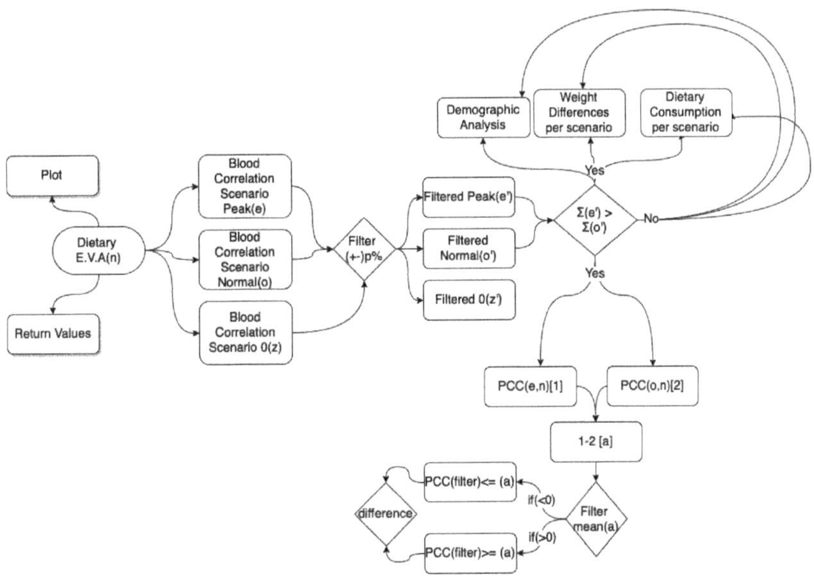

Figure 4. EVA–based decision-making algorithm.

If the observed correlations are equal, or if (e′) is less than (o′), then only the dietary consumption per scenario is examined. To summarise the process, decision-making algorithms can offer predictions based on weight trend and pinpoint a possible consumption level of the dietary variable, based on the EVA algorithm. Moreover, the progressive impact on the health state of an individual is outlined as determined by the blood exams. By outlining the demographic characteristics per scenario, an added layer of explainability is constructed. The patient/user can recognise and compare how a change in dietary behaviour can benefit his/her life. For example, if the normal consumption of a dietary intake leads to a better health state as indicated by better balanced blood metrics, then the goal of a dietary intervention is better-defined and explained.

4.3. Business Issue and Systemisation

A system is a series of explicit processes and operations that can be repeated. Systemisation is the process of creating a unique system by combining different operational activities and actions. Via systemisation, each process is outlined, examined and optimised.

In Figure 5, the EVA decision-making process is systematised. Moreover, we utilised the what, why and how of our adapted-for-machine-learning golden circle approach, which we analysed in Section 3.2. As per the "what", the intelligent system returns a trend analysis and cluster characteristics based on EVA. The process is automated, and the system returns actionable insights. As per the "why", the systemisation of health-related enquiries facilitates interventions to the patient's journey. EVA can add precision to the decision making. As per the "how", user input is received and analysed in the form of dietary intake. Via comparative analysis, a series of returns retrieved from EVA offer useful insights for a better dietary strategy and an overview of the relation of diet with a generic health state. Explainability of the process is a system option, where the user can view how the system works and the related procedure on which the decision–making algorithm is based. As a first step, the patient/user will input his/her dietary intake. The user can use the weight class predictor [5] to estimate his/her weight class, which will have to be validated or correctly manually inserted, to move on to the succeeding analytical procedure based on EVA. From there, the system return is shown to the user in the form of a report, where actionable insights can drive user engagement.

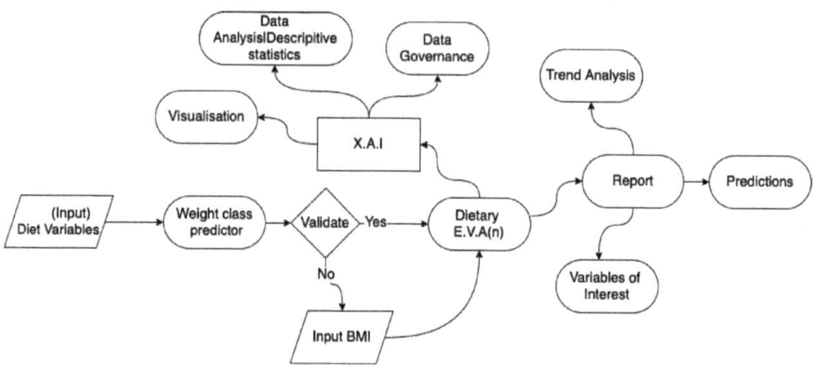

Figure 5. EVA process systemisation.

5. Implementation

5.1. Overview

The examined diet-related data reflect nutrients obtained from foods, beverages and tap or bottled water. Nutrients obtained from other sources, such as supplements or medications, are not included. The data collection was conducted in the U.S.A. via two 24 h dietary recall interviews (see Section 1.1). All parameters and criteria were determined by the National Health and Nutrition Examination Survey, which operates under the Centers for Disease Control and Prevention (CDC) [32]. A complete list of analysed dietary intake can be seen in Table 2. A complete list of the examined blood variables, alongside their aliases used in this paper and their respective measurement units, can be found in Table A1 in Appendix A. In this section, we present a precise descriptive analysis of the data used. The results of the implemented EVA pipeline are analysed in Figure 3, and the outputs of the EVA-based decision-making algorithm were extracted. The following dietary variables are analysed in this paper as an example of the proposed methodology:

- Vitamin C for the overweight category.
- Alcohol for the obese category.

Table 2. Dietary variables examined—system input data.

Name	Name
Alpha-carotene (mcg)	Alcohol (gm)
Vitamin E (mg)	vitamin B12 (mg)
Beta-carotene (mcg)	Caffeine (mg)
Calcium (mg)	Carbohydrate (gm
Total choline (mg)	Cholesterol (mg)
Copper (mg)	Beta-cryptoxanthin (mcg)
Folic acid (mcg)	Folate equivalents (mcg)
Food folate (mcg)	Dietary fiber (gm)
Total folate (mcg)	Iron (mg)
Energy (kcal)	Lycopene (mcg)
Lutein + zeaxanthin (mcg)	MFA (16–22):1 (gm)
Magnesium (mg)	fatty acids (gm)
Moisture (gm)	Niacin (mg)
Phosphorus (mg)	Potassium (mg)
Protein (gm)	Retinol (mcg)
Selenium (mcg)	fatty acids (gm)
Sodium (mg)	Total sugars (gm)
Total fat (gm)	Theobromine (mg)
Vitamin A (mcg)	Vitamin B1 (mg)
Vitamin B12 (mcg)	Vitamin C (mg)
Vitamin D (D2 + D3) (mcg)	Vitamin K (mcg)
Selenium (mcg)	Zinc (mg)

5.2. Descriptive Analytics

In Figure 6, selected metrics are shown of the analysed data. In this section, the generic and descriptive data analysis is detailed. The results of the EVA algorithm are reported and discussed. Finally, a proposed user report is examined, as produced by the systemisation algorithm (Figure 5). The dataset is separated based on weight class, which is defined by the ranges of the BMI (Table 1). The "obese", "overweight", "normal" and "underweight" categories are composed of about 23,000, 21,000, 20,000 and 2100 data-points. Moreover, our dataset consists of equally distributed females and males. The data were also analysed by age, educational level, whether the interviewee is pregnant and/or married and so on. Those data were used either for training the EVA algorithm or for categorising the patients, with regard to his/her relation to the different clusters that are defined by the data.

In the following section, the data are analysed using the algorithms described in Section 4. Some variables are examined more closely, in order to illustrate in more detail how a system works and how EVA is used as a decision making tool.

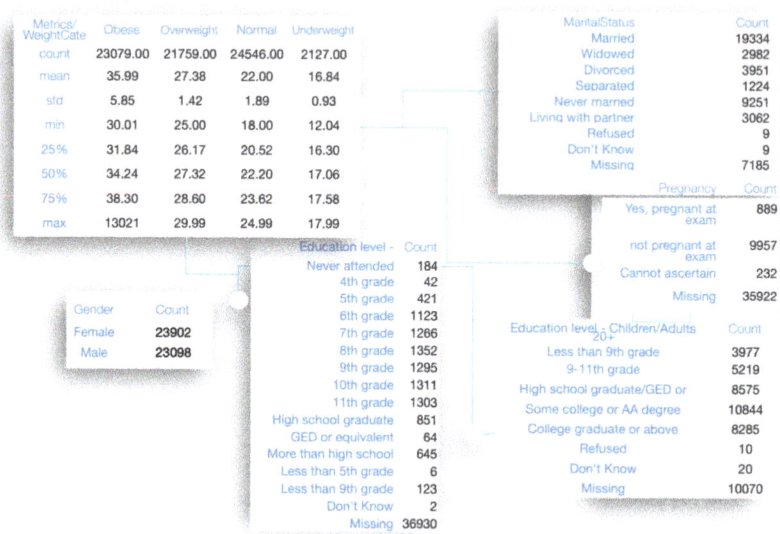

Metrics/ WeightCate	Obese	Overweight	Normal	Underweight
count	23079.00	21759.00	24546.00	2127.00
mean	35.99	27.38	22.00	16.84
std	5.85	1.42	1.89	0.93
min	30.01	25.00	18.00	12.04
25%	31.84	26.17	20.52	16.30
50%	34.24	27.32	22.20	17.06
75%	38.30	28.60	23.62	17.58
max	13021	29.99	24.99	17.99

Gender	Count
Female	23902
Male	23098

Education level -	Count
Never attended	184
4th grade	42
5th grade	421
6th grade	1123
7th grade	1266
8th grade	1352
9th grade	1295
10th grade	1311
11th grade	1303
High school graduate	851
GED or equivalent	64
More than high school	645
Less than 5th grade	6
Less than 9th grade	123
Don't Know	2
Missing	36930

MaritalStatus	Count
Married	19334
Widowed	2982
Divorced	3951
Separated	1224
Never married	9251
Living with partner	3062
Refused	9
Don't Know	9
Missing	7185

Pregnancy	Count
Yes, pregnant at exam	889
not pregnant at exam	9957
Cannot ascertain	232
Missing	35922

Education level - Children/Adults 20+	Count
Less than 9th grade	3977
9-11th grade	5219
High school graduate/GED or	8575
Some college or AA degree	10844
College graduate or above	8285
Refused	10
Don't Know	20
Missing	10070

Figure 6. Descriptive analysis of data and selected demographics.

5.3. Results

The results of the analysis consist of three parts: (i) the outputs of the EVA methodology, where the peaks over threshold are defined and plotted; (ii) the return value plot and probability density plot, derived by extreme value theory, and the related L-moments that define the distribution of the extremes; and (iii) the correlations among the blood variables for the different scenarios defined by the threshold examined. Finally, a comparison is given between each scenario as per the BMI and the general consumption and the related demographic characteristics.

In the next section, some examples are shown of how the data are analysed and can be utilised by an external user according to the systemisation algorithm in Figure 5.

5.4. System Analysis and Pipeline Outputs

5.4.1. Vitamin C–Overweight Status

In Figure 7, the consumption of vitamin C is analysed for the overweight category using the proposed algorithm. The formula used for defining the threshold (t) and thus getting the peaks from the dataset is the percentage (p) of the maximum of the examined sample ($t = \max(\Sigma X_n) * p$). When applying the algorithm in Figure 3 to the overweight category, percentage p was set to 0.34 and the threshold t was equal to 668 mg. The examined data were sorted in ascending order based on the value of the BMI of each observation. For $T = 1.6$, where T is BMI, the extreme consumption (return value) of the examined nutrient can increase to 1017 mg (with a confidence interval between 1010 and 1047), once every T with a probability of $1/T$ and vice versa. When comparing the correlation between blood variables (Figure 8 for each scenario, following the decision-making algorithm (Figure 4), an increase in correlation in the extreme scenario (e′) as compared to the normal scenario (i.e., in normal consumption of dietary variable for the examined weight class) can be seen.

In Figure 9, the related demographics and the key findings are shown, which can be employed as decision-making benchmarks. More precisely, these are the related demographics per scenario, the most prominent correlations between the blood variables and the dietary variable and the average dietary consumption per scenario. The statistics and demographics of the normal consumption for the normal weight category are also presented and can be used as a benchmark that an intelligent system can utilise to offer recommendations and suggestions related to better weight and health management. Based on the decision-making algorithm based on EVA, where PCC for scenario (e′) is compared with PCC for scenario (o′), the more prominent blood exam correlations are the following: aspartate aminotransferase, globulin, glucose, gamma glutamyl transferase, iron, phosphorus and triglycerides. The more immediate relation is with the following organs where a multiplier is added, depending on how many blood variables are related to it: heart (2×), liver (6×), kidneys (3×), pancreas, teeth, bones, parathyroid and intestines. In Figure 10, a semantic map is shown of the relationship between the blood variables and affected organs.

As per Figure 9, the impact of extreme consumption to BMI is too small. More precisely, when in the normal range of consumption, the BMI is greater than when in the extreme range and equal to 0.074. There is a generally positive relation between blood exams and the examined dietary variable: when the dietary intake increases, the value of the blood variables mostly increase and that increase is greater when consumption is extreme. The extreme average consumption is greater than the normal average consumption by 795 mg. The related demographics per scenario show that the average age for scenario (e′) is 37 years, and the average education level was lower than that of scenario (o′) but greater than that of scenario (z′). The average age of scenario (o′) was 46.6, and it had the highest percentage of being married or in a relationship. For the normal weight category where consumption of the examined dietary intake is also normal, the average age is 35. Average consumption of the dietary variable was equal to 86 mg.

5.4.2. Alcohol–Obese Status

In Figure 11, the consumption of alcohol is analysed for the obese category, using the proposed algorithm. The formula used for defining the threshold (t), and thus, getting the peaks from the dataset, is the percentage (p) of the maximum of the examined sample ($t = \max(\Sigma X_n) * p$). Following the algorithm shown in Figure 3, for the obese category, p is set to 0.36. The data examined are sorted in ascending order based on the value of the BMI of each observation. For $T = 15.8$, where T is BMI, the extreme consumption (return value) of the examined nutrient can reach 366.21 gm (with a confidence interval being between 365 and 393), once every T with a probability of $1/T$ and vice versa. When comparing the correlations among blood variables (Figure 12) for each scenario, following the decision-making algorithm (Figure 4), an increase can be seen as a correlation in the extreme scenario (e′) as compared to the normal scenario (normal consumption of dietary variable for examined weight class).

In Figure 13, the related demographics and the key findings are shown, which can be employed as decision-making benchmarks. More precisely, these are the related demographics per scenario, the most prominent correlated blood variables, the dietary variable and the average dietary consumption per scenario. The statistics and demographics of the normal consumption for the normal weight category are also presented and are used as benchmarks that an intelligent system can utilise to offer recommendations and suggestions related to better weight and health management.

According to the decision-making algorithm based on EVA, where PCC for scenario (e′) is compared with PCC for scenario (o′), the more prominent blood exam correlations are the following: bicarbonate, chloride, creatinine, gamma glutamyl transferase, iron, bilirubin and uric acid. The more immediate relation is with the following organs where a multiplier is added depending on how many blood variables are related to it: muscles (2×), lungs, kidneys (5×), heart (2×), liver (3×), red blood cells, pancreas, intestines and vascular endothelium.

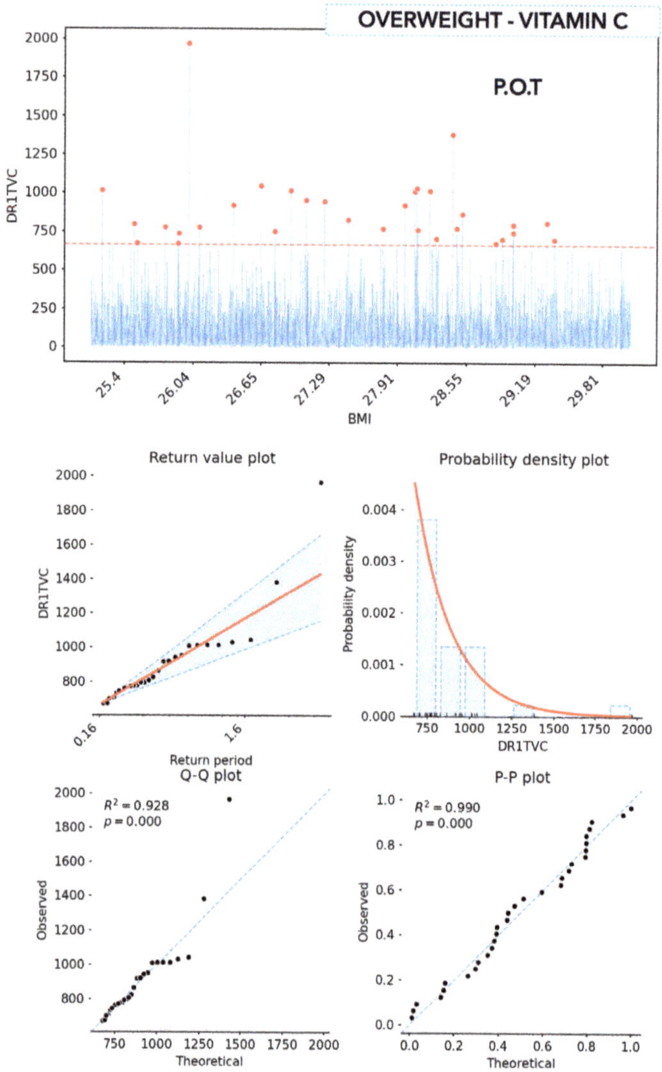

Return Intervals	return value	lower ci	upper ci
0.16	-inf	NaN	NaN
0.32	816.15	813.39	828.87
0.80	1017.27	1010.75	1047.30
1.60	1169.42	1160.06	1212.54
4.00	1370.54	1357.42	1430.98
8.00	1522.68	1506.72	1596.22
16.00	1674.83	1656.02	1761.46
40.00	1875.95	1853.39	1979.90
80.00	2028.09	2002.69	2145.14
160.00	2180.24	2151.99	2310.38

Figure 7. Overweight category–EVA of vitamin C (DR1TVC).

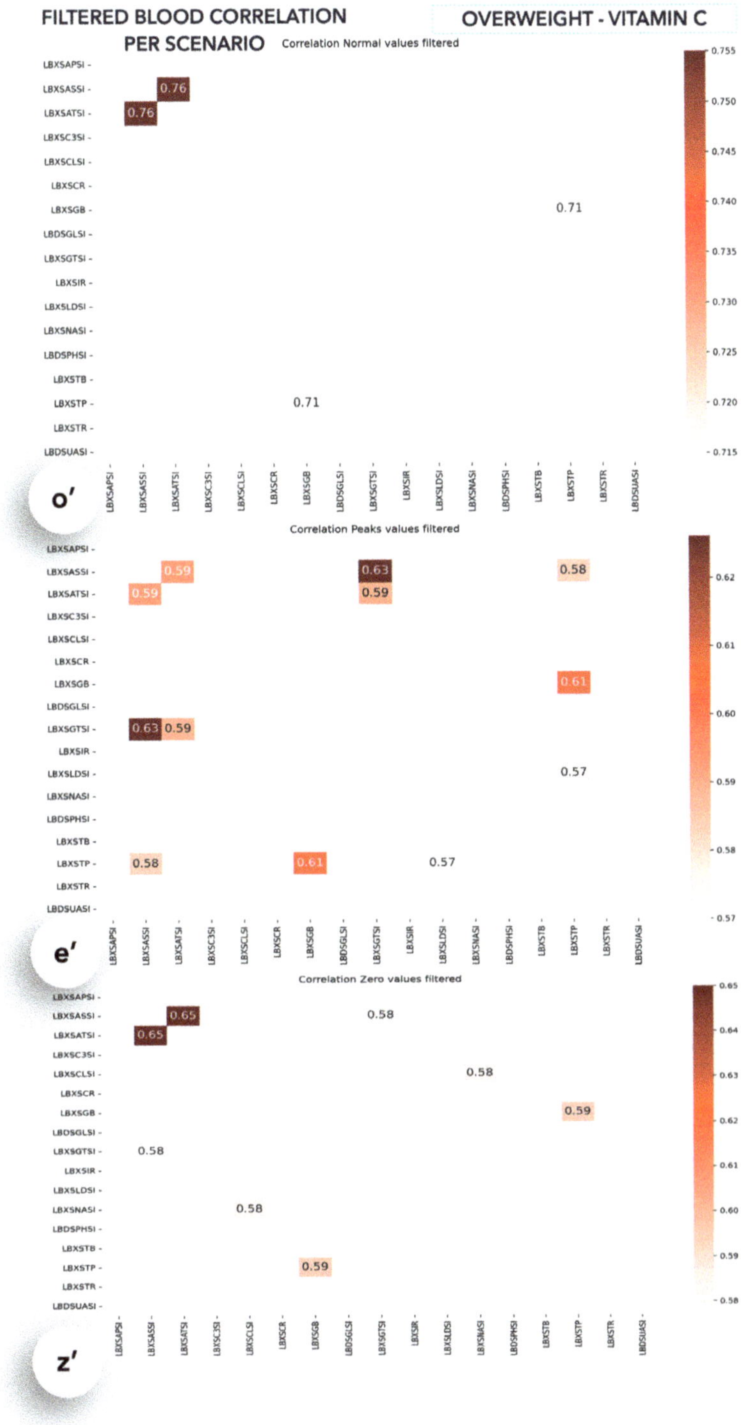

Figure 8. Overweight category–vitamin C. Filtered blood variable correlation as per EVA pipeline.

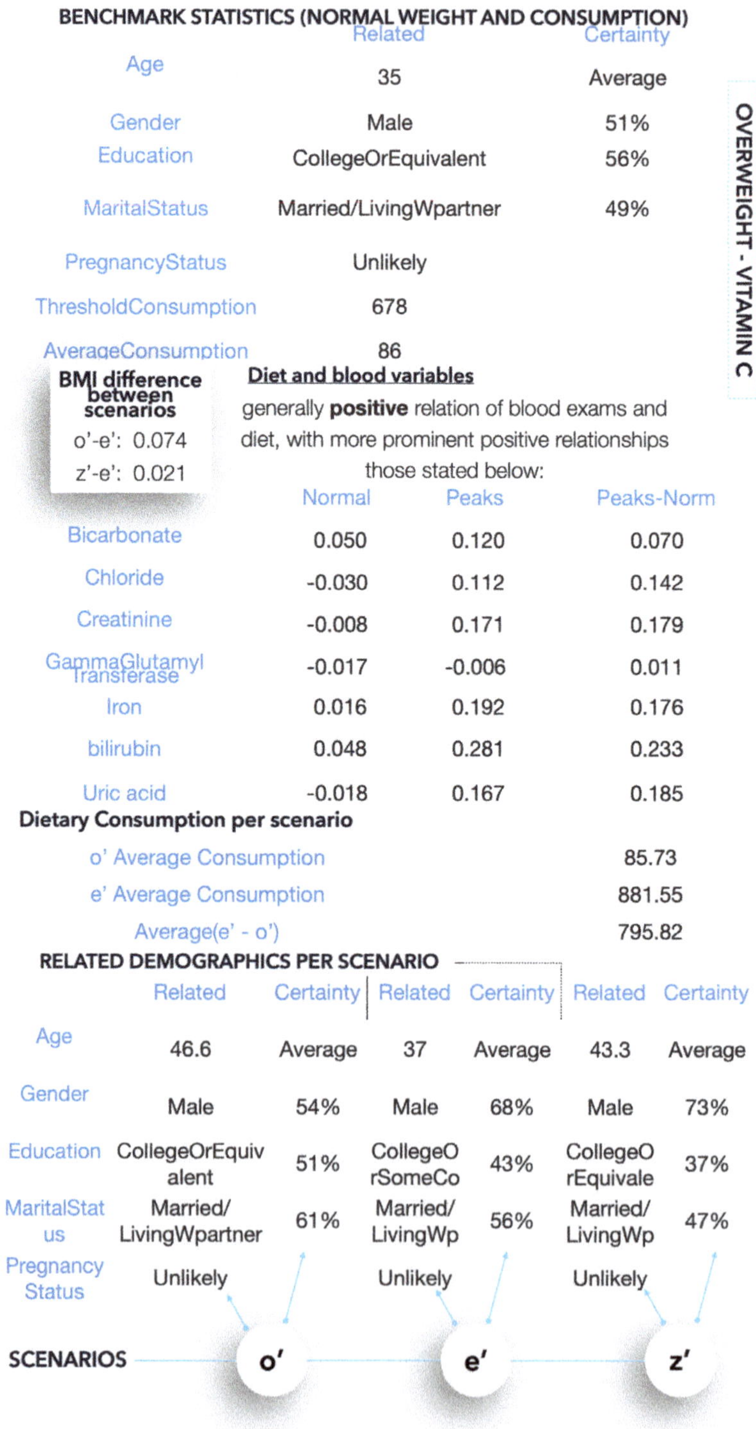

Figure 9. Vitamin C, related demographics and key findings.

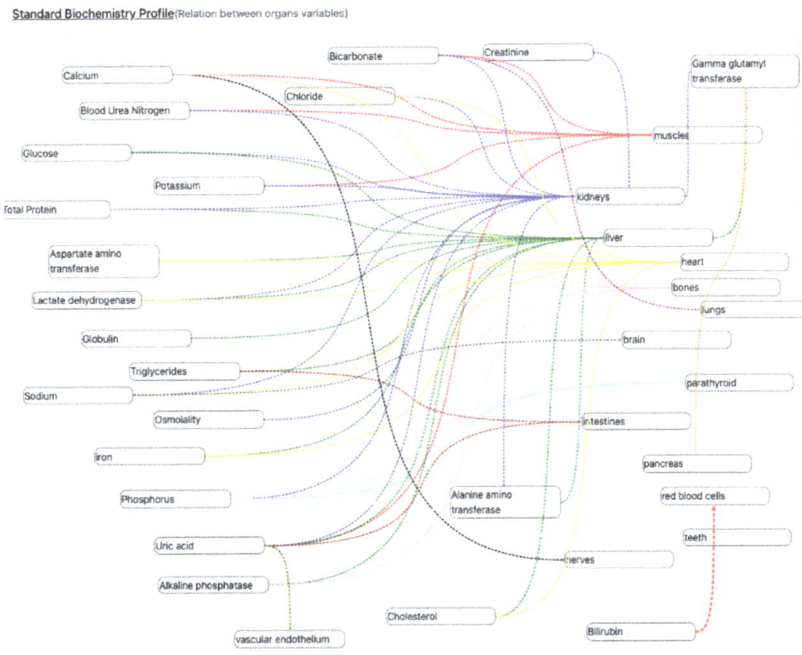

Figure 10. Blood, diet and organ functionality (screenshot from NUHealthSoft [16]).

As per Figure 13, the impact of extreme consumption on BMI is negative, meaning that when consumption is normal, the BMI is greater. More precisely, when in the normal range of consumption, the BMI is 0.59 greater than when in the extreme range, and when consumption is zero, the BMI is 1.7 greater than when extreme. There is a generally positive relation between blood exams and the examined dietary variable. When the dietary intake increases, the values of the blood variables mostly increase, and that increase is greater when consumption is extreme. The extreme average consumption is greater than the normal average consumption by 240.62 gm.

The related demographics per scenario show that the average age for scenario (e′) is 37 years, and it has a significantly lower average education level than scenario (o′) and scenario (z′). The average age of scenario (o′) is 39, and it has a lower percentage of being married or in a relationship. For the normal weight category where consumption of the examined dietary intake is also normal, the average age is 45 and the average consumption of the dietary variable is 38 gm—less than that of the examined weight category.

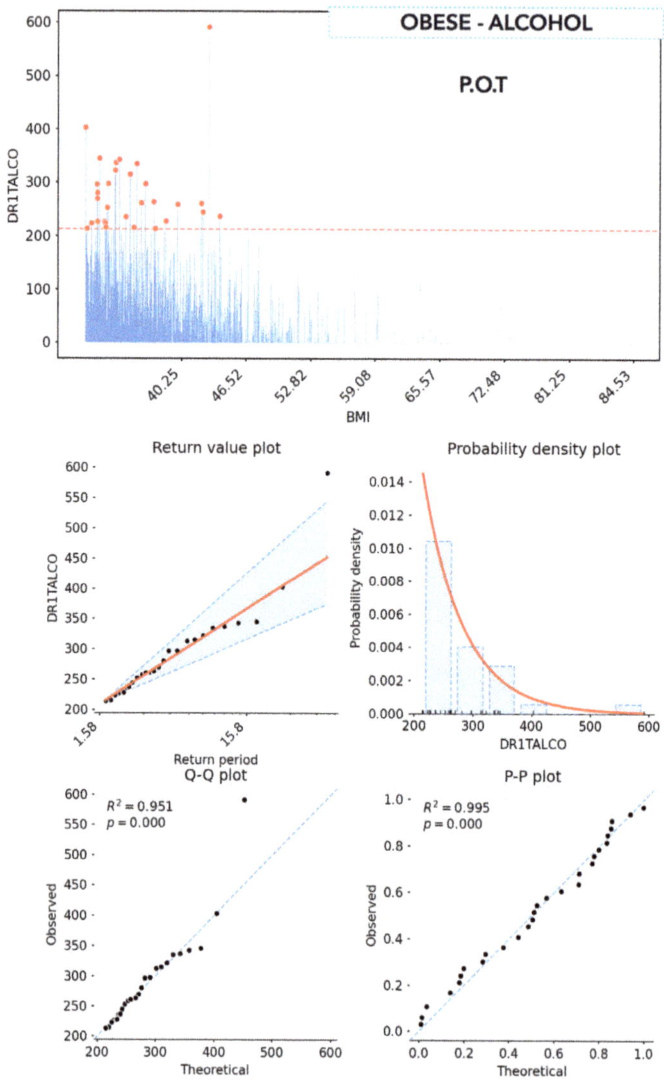

Return Intervals	return value	lower ci	upper ci
1.58	-inf	NaN	NaN
3.16	256.25	256.07	264.04
7.90	318.86	318.40	337.89
15.80	366.21	365.56	393.75
39.50	428.81	427.89	467.60
79.00	476.17	475.05	523.46
158.00	523.53	522.20	579.32
395.00	586.13	584.54	653.17
790.00	633.49	631.69	709.03
1580.00	680.84	678.85	764.90

Figure 11. Obese category–EVA of alcohol (DR1TALCO).

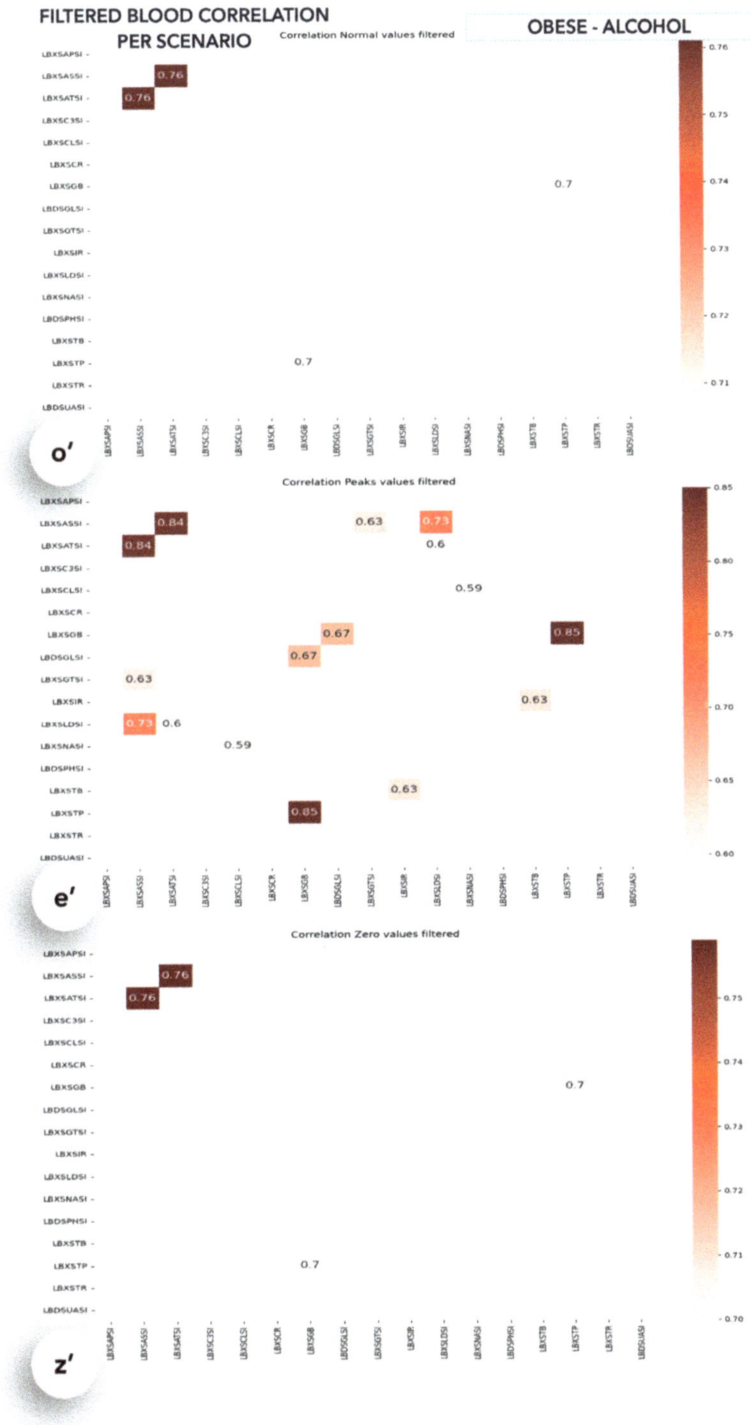

Figure 12. Obese category–alcohol. Filtered blood variable correlation as per EVA pipeline.

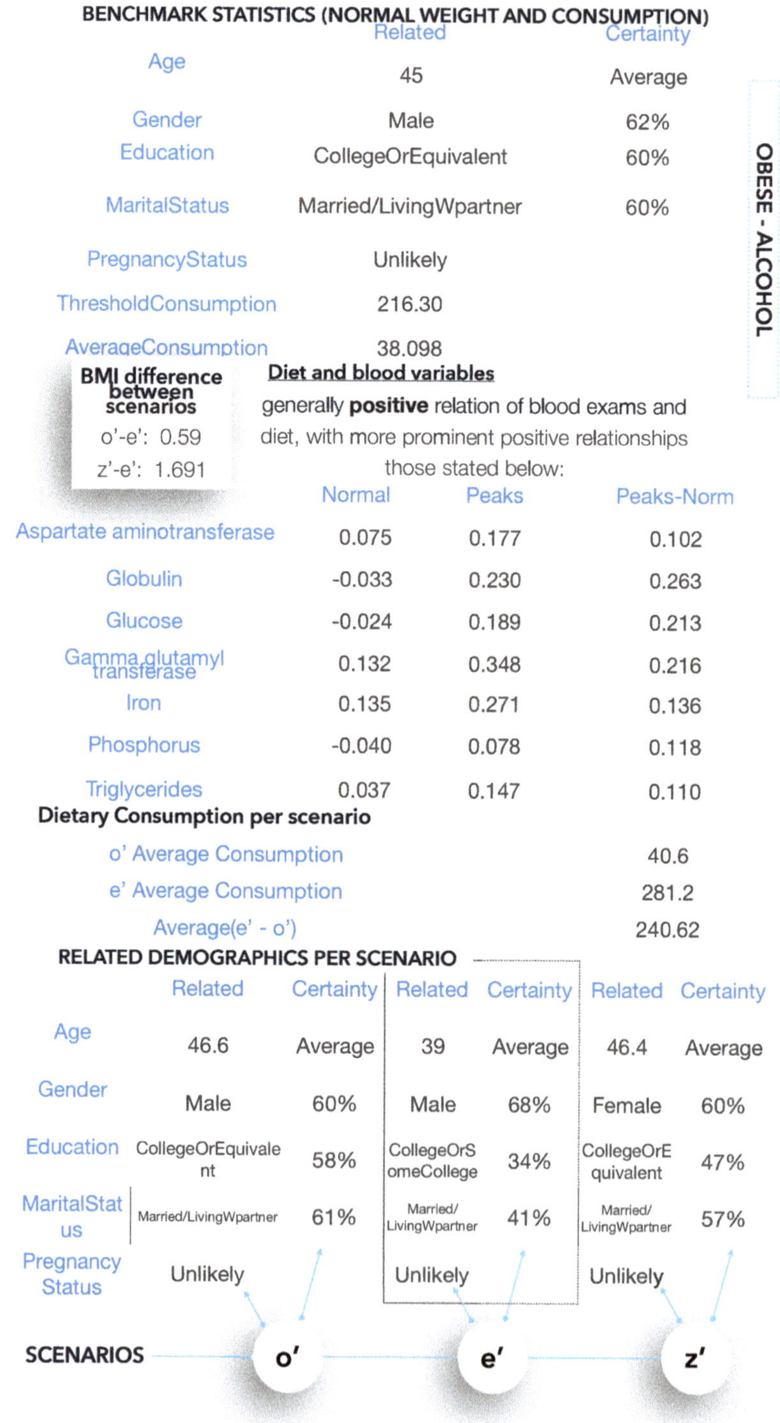

Figure 13. Alcohol, related demographics and key–findings.

5.5. Proposed Report and Recommendation Prototype

In this section, the system report is outlined:

1. There is extreme consumption of the dietary variable (x), as per the EVA pipeline. When the dietary intake of (x) is greater than that of (n) for weight class (g), for a BMI increase by (s), dietary intake may increase by (s′) and vice versa.
2. When consumption of dietary variable (x) decreases by (s″), BMI can decrease by (s‴).
3. When dietary intake of (x) is extreme, the most affected blood variables are (Bn).
4. When dietary intake (x) is extreme, there is a stronger correlation between blood variables B(n) and B(n′).
5. The blood variables, B(n), are mostly associated with organs, O(n).
6. There is generally a positive (negative) relation between blood variable B(n) and dietary variable (x); the more prominent relations are dietary variable (x) and blood exam B-filtered(n).
7. Your related age is AGE your gender is GENDER, your education is EDU, your marital status is STATUS and you are a (non)smoker.

5.6. Discussion of Results and Medical Ontologies

New knowledge can be inferred through formal semantics that underlie an ontology and thus allow the automatic processing and extraction of targeted information. According to Cedeno-Moreno et al. [33] and Studer et al. [34], an ontology can be considered as an explicit specification of a shared conceptualisation. In this section, we extract some still unstructured concepts related to the variables analysed previously that can be presented as an add-on to the proposed report.

5.6.1. Knowledge Extraction—Vitamin C and Overweight Status

According to the pipelines proposed in this paper, some interesting findings are outlined. First of all, the average age of the population that belongs to the extreme (e′) consumption cluster (Figure 9) was lower than the average age of the normal consumption cluster for the overweight category. Secondly, the BMI differences between the two clusters suggest that, for the extreme scenario (e′), the weight was lower than that of the normal (o′) scenario. According to our pipelines, the demographic examined when consumption of vitamin C was extreme showed a desire for weight loss and a change in the dietary lifestyle, since vitamin C is mostly found in fruits and fruits—dietary choices that are considered healthy. It is probably also connected with more dietary changes that may be implemented without the assistance of a healthcare professional. Even though in the data analysed in this paper, the average weight was lower, overconsumption of any dietary variable can lead to unpleasant outcomes.

To sum up the conclusions and new knowledge, we can identify a will for a lifestyle change and at the same time the necessity of professional intervention. That intervention can assist in avoiding unnecessary health burdens and effectively empower an already made decision for a healthier outlook.

5.6.2. Overconsumption of Vitamin C

Even though vitamin C is an essential part of daily nutrition, extreme consumption can have some undesirable effects. Vitamin C is mostly derived from fruits and vegetables, such as oranges, strawberries, chopped red pepper and broccoli. It helps the body absorb iron and supports growth and development. The recommended daily amount is 75 milligrams (mg) a day for women and 90 mg for men. During pregnancy, an amount of 120 mg is suggested. The upper limit for all adults is 2000 mg per day. Large doses of vitamin C might cause: diarrhoea, nausea, vomiting, heartburn, stomach cramps and headaches [35].

5.6.3. Knowledge Extraction—Alcohol and Obese Status

In the second case examined, by the proposed pipelines, some interesting facts were extracted. First of all, the average BMI when consumption was extreme (e′) was lower

(Figure 13) than in the normal (o′) consumption cluster. The average age was also lower 36.6 for the e′ scenario and 46.6 for scenario o′. Another interesting finding resides in the fact that scenario e′ concerns males (68% chance) that are more likely to be unmarried. Additionally, zero consumption (z′) was more likely to be found in the female population. By outlining a group based on well-defined population characteristics, targeted interventions and health awareness campaigns [36] for the particular population can have greater impact and be more effective, and thus improve health outcomes.

5.6.4. Alcohol and Obesity

Excessive drinking is defined as consuming four or more drinks during a single occasion for women and five or more drinks for men. Heavy drinking is considered to be when 8 or more drinks are consumed per week for women and 15 or more drinks per week for men. Excessive alcohol consumption can lead to harmful health conditions and result in injuries, violence, poisoning, kidney failure, miscarriage and stillbirth and heart attacks [37].

5.6.5. How Diet Affects Blood Variables

Diet affects all bodily functions, and dietary intake, when not normal, is usually displayed in blood exams. Essential minerals, such as sodium, potassium, calcium and chloride, and the macro-nutrients protein and carbohydrate, are necessary for the central nervous system to function. Muscles require energy from nutrients. Under- or over-nutrition can compromise endocrine and immune system functions. Inflammatory disorders are also symptoms of an imbalanced diet [38].

6. Conclusions and Future Research Endeavours

Intelligent health knowledge systems, when integrated with tracking devices and social media outlets, can revolutionise the creation of medical ontologies and the representation of medical data. The utilisation of such technologies can increase self-knowledge and data sharing [39,40], empower change, improve health and better communicate a health intervention or strategy.

EVA produces numerous tools that can improve the understanding of human biology and behaviour. The medical domain and the human biology are characterised by high complexity. The decoupling of that complexity and its transformation into useful and easy-to-understand information and actionable insights can simplify the development of systems that can add value to users and patients alike. Extreme value analysis can offer insights for dependable variables adapted to conditions that deviate from the normal distribution. With regard to health data, the management of medication dosage or quantity of nutritional intake is of outmost importance. EVA can add precision when proposing an optimisation strategy for a particular demographic. It can be utilised for biomarker discovery, since measurements can offer insights on outcomes of intervention and can be used as predictive and preventive tools.

By defining the usability aspects of EVA, using the machine-learning-adapted golden circle of innovation discussed in Section 3.2, we have outlined a suitable algorithm (Figures 3 and 4) for health data analysis and knowledge retention. Using that algorithm, we can better understand the relations among nutrients, weight and impact of diet on health and also proposed ways for that algorithm to be adapted into an interactive system (Figure 5). The return levels (R.V.), alongside the thresholds set (for POT-based EVA), defined with precision which value should be referred to as the nutritional limit and which values lead to an increase in weight and impact blood values, and subsequently, the body (Figure 10).

In our future research, the product of this study will be adapted to an interactive system that will use the analytical pipelines described, in order to automate interventions and strategies and increase its users′ self knowledge about their health. The impact of dietary habits can be explained using the benchmark demographic statistics shown in the previous section, improving self knowledge and adherence to health interventions.

Author Contributions: Conceptualization, D.P.P. and G.A.T.; Data curation, D.P.P.; Methodology, D.P.P., D.N.S. and G.A.T.; project administration, G.A.T.; Software, D.P.P.; Supervision, G.A.T. and D.N.S.; Validation, D.P.P., G.A.T. and D.N.S.; Visualization, D.P.P.; Writing - original draft, D.P.P.; Writing review and editing, D.P.P. and G.A.T. All authors have read and agreed to the published version of the manuscript.

Funding: This work has been partly supported by the University of Piraeus Research Center.

Institutional Review Board Statement: Not applicable.

Informed Consent Statement: Publicly available data were used, where anonymity was ensured by the provider of the data. "Information from NHANES is made available through an extensive series of publications and articles in scientific and technical journals. For data users and researchers throughout the world, survey data are available on the internet and on easy-to-use CD-ROMs [41]".

Data Availability Statement: All data are available in the digital library of the Centers for Disease Control and Prevention (CDC), from which the National Health and Nutrition Examination Survey (NHANES) was utilised [32] for the purposes of this research.

Acknowledgments: Theoretical/medical support and technical/medical advice as per the validity of our hypothesis was provided on 30 October 2022 by the medical doctors of Dermacen S.A https://www.dermatologikokentro.gr (Accessed on 30 October 2022). For the implementation of the project and the analysis of the data, the scikit-learn python libraries were used [42].

Conflicts of Interest: The authors declare no conflict of interest.

Abbreviations

The following abbreviations are used in this manuscript:

BMI	Body mass index
EVA	Extreme value analysis
EVT	Extreme value theory
POT	Peaks over threshold
A.M.S.	Annual maxima series
P.D.F.	Probability density plot
R.V.	Return value-level
FFQ	Food frequency questionnaires
DALYs	Disability-adjusted life years
F.B.D.G.	Food-based dietary guidelines
Y.L.L.	Years of life lost from mortality
Y.L.D.	Years lost due to disability
CDC	Center for Disease Control and Prevention
NHANES	National Health and Nutrition Examination Survey
WHO	World Health Organisation
PCC	Pearson correlation coefficient

Appendix A

Table A1. Standard Biochemistry Profile.

Alias	Name (Measurement)
LBXSAPSI	Alkaline phosphatase (IU/L)
LBXSASSI	Aspartate aminotransferase AST (IU/L)
LBXSATSI	Alanine aminotransferase ALT (IU/L)
LBXSC3SI	Bicarbonate (mmol/L)
LBXSCLSI	Chloride (mmol/L)
LBXSCR	Creatinine (mg/dL)
LBXSGB	Globulin (g/dL)
LBDSGLSI	Glucose, refrigerated serum (mmol/L)
LBXSGTSI	Gamma glutamyl transferase (U/L)
LBXSIR	Iron, refrigerated serum (ug/dL)
LBXSLDSI	Lactate dehydrogenase (U/L)
LBXSNASI	Sodium (mmol/L)
LBDSPHSI	Phosphorus (mmol/L)
LBXSTB	Total bilirubin (mg/dL)
LBXSTP	Total protein (g/dL)
LBXSTR	Triglycerides, refrigerated (mg/dL)
LBDSUASI	Uric acid (umol/L)

References

1. Dao, M.C.; Subar, A.F.; Warthon-Medina, M.; Cade, J.E.; Burrows, T.; Golley, R.K.; Forouhi, N.G.; Pearce, M.; Holmes, B.A. Dietary assessment toolkits: An overview. *Public Health Nutr.* **2019**, *22*, 404–418. [CrossRef] [PubMed]
2. Cámara, M.; Giner, R.M.; González-Fandos, E.; López-García, E.; Mañes, J.; Portillo, M.P.; Rafecas, M.; Domínguez, L.; Martínez, J.A. Food-Based Dietary Guidelines around the World: A Comparative Analysis to Update AESAN Scientific Committee Dietary Recommendations. *Nutrients* **2021**, *13*, 3131. [CrossRef] [PubMed]
3. Herforth, A.; Arimond, M.; Álvarez-Sánchez, C.; Coates, J.; Christianson, K.; Muehlhoff, E. A global review of food-based dietary guidelines. *Adv. Nutr.* **2019**, *10*, 590–605. [CrossRef] [PubMed]
4. Potischman, N.; Freudenheim, J.L. Biomarkers of nutritional exposure and nutritional status: An overview. *J. Nutr.* **2003**, *133*, 873S–874S. [CrossRef] [PubMed]
5. Panagoulias, D.P.; Virvou, M.; Tsihrintzis, G.A. Regulation and Validation Challenges in Artificial Intelligence-empowered Healthcare Applications—The Case of Blood-retrieved Biomarkers. In Proceedings of the 14th International Joint Conference on Knowledge-Based Software Engineering (JCKBSE 2022), Larnaca, Cyprus, 22–24 August 2022.
6. Qiao, J.; Lin, X.; Wu, Y.; Huang, X.; Pan, X.; Xu, J.; Wu, J.; Ren, Y.; Shan, P.F. Global burden of non-communicable diseases attributable to dietary risks in 1990–2019. *J. Hum. Nutr. Diet.* **2022**, *35*, 202–213. [CrossRef] [PubMed]
7. World Health Organization—Disability-Adjusted Life Years. Available online: https://www.who.int/data/gho/indicator-metadata-registry/imr-details/158 (accessed on 17 November 2022).
8. Cornelis, M.C.; Hu, F.B. Systems epidemiology: A new direction in nutrition and metabolic disease research. *Curr. Nutr. Rep.* **2013**, *2*, 225–235. [CrossRef]
9. Dansinger, M.L.; Gleason, J.A.; Griffith, J.L.; Selker, H.P.; Schaefer, E.J. Comparison of the Atkins, Ornish, Weight Watchers, and Zone diets for weight loss and heart disease risk reduction: A randomized trial. *JAMA* **2005**, *293*, 43–53. [CrossRef]
10. Jebb, S.A. Dietary strategies for the prevention of obesity. *Proc. Nutr. Soc.* **2005**, *64*, 217–227. [CrossRef] [PubMed]
11. Panagoulias, D.P.; Sotiropoulos, D.N.; Tsihrintzis, G.A. Biomarker-based deep learning for personalized nutrition. In Proceedings of the 2021 IEEE 33rd International Conference on Tools with Artificial Intelligence (ICTAI), Washington, DC, USA, 1–3 November 2021; pp. 306–313.
12. Panagoulias, D.P.; Sotiropoulos, D.N.; Tsihrintzis, G.A. Nutritional biomarkers and machine learning for personalized nutrition applications and health optimization. In Proceedings of the 2021 12th International Conference on Information, Intelligence, Systems & Applications (IISA), Chania Crete, Greece, 12–14 July 2021; pp. 1–6.

13. Panagoulias, D.P.; Sotiropoulos, D.N.; Tsihrintzis, G.A. Nutritional biomarkers and machine learning for personalized nutrition applications and health optimization (extended journal version). *Intell. Decis. Technol.* **2021**, *15*, 645–653. [CrossRef]
14. Panagoulias, D.P.; Sotiropoulos, D.N.; Tsihrintzis, G.A. SVM-Based Blood Exam Classification for Predicting Defining Factors in Metabolic Syndrome Diagnosis. *Electronics* **2022**, *11*, 857. [CrossRef]
15. Panagoulias, D.P.; Virvou, M.; Tsihrintzis, G.A. A microservices-based iterative development approach for usable, reliable and explainable A.I.-infused medical applications using R.U.P. In Proceedings of the 34th IEEE Conference on Tools with Artificial Intelligence (ICTAI 2022), Conference Proceedings, Virtually, 31 October–2 November 2022.
16. Panagoulias, D.P.; Virvou, M.; Tsihrintzis, G.A. NUHEALTHSOFT: A Nutritional and Health Data Processing Software Tool. In Proceedings of the 2022 16th International Conference on Signal Image Technology and Internet based Systems (SITIS), Dijon, France, 19–21 October 2022.
17. Panagoulias, D.P.; Sotiropoulos, D.N.; Tsihrintzis, G.A. Extreme value analysis for dietary intake based on weight class. In Proceedings of the 2022 13th International Conference on Information, Intelligence, Systems & Applications (IISA), Corfu, Greece, 18–20 July 2022.
18. Coles, S.; Bawa, J.; Trenner, L.; Dorazio, P. *An Introduction to Statistical Modeling of Extreme Values*; Springer: Berlin/Heidelberg, Germany, 2001; Volume 208.
19. Xu, S. *Proceedings of 2013 World Agricultural Outlook Conference*; Springer: Berlin/Heidelberg, Germany, 2014.
20. Thomas, M.; Lemaitre, M.; Wilson, M.L.; Viboud, C.; Yordanov, Y.; Wackernagel, H.; Carrat, F. Applications of extreme value theory in public health. *PLoS ONE* **2016**, *11*, e0159312. [CrossRef] [PubMed]
21. Chiu, Y.; Chebana, F.; Abdous, B.; Bélanger, D.; Gosselin, P. Mortality and morbidity peaks modeling: An extreme value theory approach. *Stat. Methods Med. Res.* **2018**, *27*, 1498–1512. [CrossRef] [PubMed]
22. Flegal, K.M.; Wei, R.; Ogden, C.L.; Freedman, D.S.; Johnson, C.L.; Curtin, L.R. Characterizing extreme values of body mass index–for-age by using the 2000 Centers for Disease Control and Prevention growth charts. *Am. J. Clin. Nutr.* **2009**, *90*, 1314–1320. [CrossRef] [PubMed]
23. Tsihrintzis, G.A.; Nikias, C.L. Fast estimation of the parameters of alpha-stable impulsive interference. *IEEE Trans. Signal Process.* **1996**, *44*, 1492–1503. [CrossRef]
24. Arsenault, E.; Wang, Y.; Chapman, M.P. Towards Scalable Risk Analysis for Stochastic Systems Using Extreme Value Theory. *arXiv* **2022**, arXiv:2203.12689.
25. Szigeti, M.; Ferenci, T.; Kovács, L. The use of block maxima method of extreme value statistics to characterise blood glucose curves. In Proceedings of the 2020 IEEE 15th International Conference of System of Systems Engineering (SoSE), Budapest, Hungary, 2–4 June 2020; pp. 433–438.
26. Huss, R.; Grunkin, M. *Artificial Intelligence Applications in Human Pathology*; WSPC: London, UK, 2022.
27. Spruijt, J.; Spanjaard, T.; Demouge, K. The Golden Circle of Innovation: What Companies Can Learn from NGOs When It Comes to Innovation. In *Modern Marketing for Non-Profit Organizations: International Perspectives*; Smyczek, S., Ed.; University of Economics in Katowice Publishing House, Forthcoming: Katowice, Poland, 2013.
28. Panagoulias, D.P.; Sotiropoulos, D.N.; Tsihrintzis, G.A. Towards Personalized Nutrition Applications with Nutritional Biomarkers and Machine Learning. In *Advances in Assistive Technologies: Selected Papers in Honour of Professor Nikolaos G. Bourbakis*; Tsihrintzis, G.A., Virvou, M., Esposito, A., Jain, L.C., Eds.; Springer: Berlin/Heidelberg, Germany, 2022; pp. 73–122.
29. Pyextremes—Python Library. Available online: https://georgebv.github.io/pyextremes/ (accessed on 28 May 2022).
30. Baek, J.W.; Kim, J.C.; Chun, J.; Chung, K. Hybrid clustering based health decision-making for improving dietary habits. *Technol. Health Care* **2019**, *27*, 459–472. [CrossRef] [PubMed]
31. Kochenderfer, M.J.; Wheeler, T.A.; Wray, K.H. *Algorithms for Decision Making*; MIT Press: Cambridge, MA, USA, 2022.
32. Johnson, C.L.; Dohrmann, S.M.; Burt, V.L.; Mohadjer, L.K. *National Health and Nutrition Examination Survey: Sample Design, 2011–2014*; Number 2014, US Department of Health and Human Services, Centers for Disease Control and Prevention: Atlanta, GA, USA, 2014.
33. Cedeno-Moreno, D.; Vargas-Lombardo, M. An ontology-based knowledge methodology in the medical domain in the Latin america: The study case of republic of Panama. *Acta Inform. Med.* **2018**, *26*, 98. [CrossRef] [PubMed]
34. Studer, R.; Benjamins, V.R.; Fensel, D. Knowledge engineering: Principles and methods. *Data Knowl. Eng.* **1998**, *25*, 161–197. [CrossRef]
35. Mayo Clinic—Nutrition and Healthy Eating. Available online: https://www.mayoclinic.org/healthy-lifestyle/nutrition-and-healthy-eating/expert-answers/vitamin-c/faq-20058030/ (accessed on 17 November 2022).
36. Hoschar, S.; Albarqouni, L.; Ladwig, K.H. A systematic review of educational interventions aiming to reduce prehospital delay in patients with acute coronary syndrome. *Open Heart* **2020**, *7*, e001175. [CrossRef] [PubMed]
37. World health Organization—Alcohol Use and Your Health. Available online: https://www.cdc.gov/alcohol/fact-sheets/alcohol-use.htm/ (accessed on 17 November 2022).
38. Libre Texts Medicine—Nutrients Are Essential for Organ Function. Available online: https://tinyurl.com/yxsf45bs/ (accessed on 17 November 2022).
39. Papacharissi, Z. *A Networked Self: Identity, Community, and Culture on Social Network Sites*; Routledge: London, UK, 2010 .
40. Kent, R. Social media and self-tracking: Representing the 'health self'. In *Self-Tracking*; Springer: Berlin/Heidelberg, Germany, 2018; pp. 61–76.

41. Uses of the Data. Available online: https://www.cdc.gov/nchs/nhanes/about_nhanes.htm#data/ (accessed on 17 November 2022).
42. Pedregosa, F.; Varoquaux, G.; Gramfort, A.; Michel, V.; Thirion, B.; Grisel, O.; Blondel, M.; Prettenhofer, P.; Weiss, R.; Dubourg, V.; et al. Scikit-learn: Machine learning in Python. *J. Mach. Learn. Res.* **2011**, *12*, 2825–2830.

electronics

Article

ICT Penetration and Insurance Sector Development: Evidence from the 10 New EU Member States

Yilmaz Bayar [1], Dan Constantin Danuletiu [2], Adina Elena Danuletiu [2] and Marius Dan Gavriletea [3,*]

1 Department of Public Finance, Faculty of Economics and Administrative Sciences, Bandirma Onyedi Eylul University, Bandirma 102000, Türkiye
2 Department of Finance–Accounting, Faculty of Economic Sciences, "1 Decembrie 1918" University of Alba Iulia, 510009 Alba Iulia, Romania
3 Department of Business, Faculty of Business, Babeș-Bolyai University, 400174 Cluj-Napoca, Romania
* Correspondence: marius.gavriletea@ubbcluj.ro

Abstract: The insurance sector provides protection to individuals and businesses against many types of risks and also promotes economic growth, being an important source of long-term capital. Analyzing factors that facilitate insurance sector development is important for both individuals and the entire economy. The purpose of this study is to investigate the relationship between information and communication technologies (ICT) represented by mobile cellular subscriptions per 100 people and individuals using the Internet (% of population) and insurance sector development represented by insurance company assets to GDP (%). Using data from 10 new member states of the European Union for the period 2000–2020, this study reveals a mutual interaction between ICT penetration indicators and insurance sector development. Furthermore, a regression analysis reveals that Internet penetration has a significant positive influence on insurance sector growth. Specifically, at the country level, the results indicate the existence of bidirectional causality between mobile cellular subscriptions and the insurance sector in Latvia, Poland, and Slovakia, and unidirectional causality between insurance and mobile cellular subscriptions in Estonia and Hungary.

Keywords: ICT penetration; insurance sector development; causality analysis; regression analysis

Citation: Bayar, Y.; Danuletiu, D.C.; Danuletiu, A.E.; Gavriletea, M.D. ICT Penetration and Insurance Sector Development: Evidence from the 10 New EU Member States. *Electronics* **2023**, *12*, 823. https://doi.org/10.3390/electronics12040823

Academic Editors: Galina Ilieva and George A. Tsihrintzis

Received: 19 January 2023
Revised: 31 January 2023
Accepted: 2 February 2023
Published: 6 February 2023

1. Introduction

In a world full of uncertainties, even when people take measures to protect themselves from various risks, different types of loss (e.g., assets, life, health, business income) can occur. It is the role of insurance to reduce the financial impact of these risks and to compensate these types of losses by providing financial support to the people affected. However, insurance's role is more complex because insurance companies are consider large investors, providing long-term finance for governments, banks, and other institutions. In addition, insurance stimulates the population to adopt responsible financial behavior and to increase financial literacy levels. Through these actions, the insurance sector, together with the other components of the financial markets, can exert a significant contribution to economic development. In modern economies, information and communication technologies (ICT) have been integrated into most activities and have generated significant changes in every domain, including financial markets. Consequently, the researchers started to explore the relationship between ICT and financial development [1–9]. Several studies argue that ICT improves financial inclusion by allowing access to different financial services to the poor or to marginalized people [1,9–12]. On the other hand, there are studies suggesting that financial inclusion generates improvements in ICT infrastructure [3,12] as a result of a higher demand for digital financial services generated by the initial access of the poor or marginalized people to such services that facilitated the improvement of the economic status of these people and the acquisition of more technology.

Previous studies that analysed the relationship between ICT and financial development have focused mainly on banking or financial market variables, without taking the insurance sector into account, despite the fact that insurance is a significant financial service in developed economies. One of the reasons for this situation is that, as Cappielo [13] argues, traditional insurance was resilient and adopted digitization very slowly, but once adopted this generated a profound transformation of the entire business [14].

Studies that investigate the determinants of insurance development generally found that macroeconomic (GDP growth, inflation, the unemployment rate, balance of payments as a percentage of GDP, trade openness, foreign direct investments, financial development), institutional (property rights, corruption control, government stability, law enforcement), demographic or social (educational attainment, tertiary education level, life expectancy, youth dependency ratio, urbanization) variables have various effects on insurance development [15–20].

Interaction between ICT and Insurance

The adoption of information and communication technologies by participants in the insurance market has a significant impact on the entire insurance value chain [21–23]. ICT generates changes in product design, offering the possibility of providing personalized instead of standard products and services and achieving a better risk assessment and, consequently, a more adapted insurance premium [14,21]. Additionally, ICT generates benefits for insurer marketing activities; the data obtained through ICT could be used for market and customer research and could generate better customer segmentation and a detailed overview of the customer needs and preferences [24]. Based on this information, insurers could develop a more suitable pricing strategy, design an appropriate communication and advertisement strategy, or could use the best suitable technologies such as websites, social media, and videos [25]. According to Cappielo [22], the most affected component of insurance by ICT development are sales and distribution. Online sales by using websites, apps or different social media platforms in the acquisition process are the significant implication of ICT in insurance distribution [14,25]. The use of ICT allows a vast amount of information to be shared with consumers that can provide a competitive advantage to insurance companies. Many companies operating in the insurance sector introduced chatbots or robo-advisors in their interaction with customers in order to collect data about clients' needs and used them to customize their products and services, and to provide advice for choosing the best insurance policies that suit customers' needs and financial situation. Video calls or phone conversations are used more and more by insurers to analyze emotions based on image and video processing and to generate new models to be used in product design [21]. The claim management process is also affected by the use of ICT. Filing an insurance claim using digital technologies improves not only company performance but also customer experience. By using Big Data and predictive analytics [14], insurers can improve the claim process and prevent insurance fraud.

By adopting digitalization, insurers can increase speed and efficiency by automating processes and decisions, generating simpler, more efficient and faster workflows. They can reduce operating costs and by issuing and delivering insurance policies in digital format, by automating the claim process, and by using digital archives and reducing the cost of storage, they can become more sustainable [26] and inclusive. Digitalization affects not only the core processes, but also the support services such as management, human resources, IT, and legal departments [25], inducing the transformation of insurers.

The crisis caused by COVID-19 forced insurers to implement digital transformation. Based on a study that involved the top 30 global insurers, Lanfranchi and Grassi [27] noted that during the COVID-19 pandemic, these companies adopted specific initiatives. There were cases of product adaptation that require no ICT involvement (inclusion of COVID-19 into the insurance coverage), but numerous initiatives were related to ICT use (improving existing technologies or adopting new technologies). Innovative initiatives such as realizing visual inspection using AI to deliver useful information for insurance underwriting, evaluating property or vehicle damages with AI, improving customer service communication by using call centers, using chatbots and specific applications for COVID-19 symptom checkers, using mobile apps for health care assessment, and providing access at no cost to telemedicine for all insured people have been implemented in the insurance sector recently.

Shevchuc et al. [28] investigated the digital transformations due to the coronavirus pandemic in the insurance sector of Ukraine and noticed that the most important processes became digital, here referring to the adoption of the electronic document management systems and significant transformations in distribution which consist in a dynamic shift from traditional to digital distribution, etc.

As Eling and Lehman [25] and Cappielo [22] argue, the digitalization generated by improving the ICT infrastructure and increasing the use of this infrastructure significantly impact the evolution of insurance activity in different ways: by providing innovative goods or services or new ways to deliver them, by generating lower costs or higher levels of efficiency and productivity, and also by helping insurers and their contracts to be more accessible to different categories of customers.

In a world dominated by technological innovations, customers, especially individual ones, press the insurers to provide simpler and more flexible products and buying opportunities and to develop new channels of communication [24]. With all of the changes mentioned above, insurers moved to a more customer-centric business in a tentative way in order to meet client needs adequately.

The customers' answer to the insurers' innovations depends on various factors. Different studies argue that ICT use reduces acquisition costs and insurance premiums [29], which will impact insurance customers' satisfaction [30], which is the main determinant of purchasing intention [31]. Eckert et al. [30] indicated that customer-focused digital strategies can improve customer satisfaction, and Dash and Chakraborty [32] suggested that search engine optimization and search engine marketing practices display marketing and electronic customer relationship management practices that have a major influence on consumer satisfaction and purchase intention.

However, on the other side, Mau et al. [33] emphasized that there are some characteristics of the customer that influence research-shopper behavior, referring to the fact that there are still many customers that use a channel to search for a product or a service and another one for purchasing. Bryzgalov and Tsyganov [34] noted that digital sales are exclusively related to insurance products regulated by the state.

Time and financial savings create unforgettable and meaningful experiences for customers [35], which can contribute to consumer satisfaction and can lead to customer loyalty. New technologies erase boundaries and improve customer relations, therefore insurance companies along with other financial institutions must understand that the transition from a hot trend to a must-have technology needs to be done quickly.

As can be seen, the use of ICT infrastructure could generate benefits for insurance activity, both tangible (adequate information storage facilities, timeliness of insurance operations through rapid communication, the reduced effort required for individual tasks) and intangible (customer satisfaction and a strong corporate image) [36,37].

The insurance industry, like other industries, has experienced a major transformation due to the development of ICT. However, there is not only a unidirectional interaction, as the digitalized insurance industry can also affect ICT development, as argued by Pradhan et al. [3] and Pradhan and Sahoo [12]. Therefore, a bidirectional interaction between ICT indicators and insurance sector development is theoretically expected.

Our paper examines the relationship between the development of ICT infrastructure and the insurance market in the 10 new EU member states. We focus mainly on this specific group of countries that have certain characteristics in common. Due to European integration, selected countries changed their "political, market and economic conditions" [38] (p. 74), and now share common visions and goals. To the best of our knowledge, for this group of countries, this is the first paper that attempts to analyse the link between ICT penetration indicators and the growth of the insurance sector.

2. Literature Review

In one of the first papers dealing with the implications of the Internet on insurance markets and institutions, Garven [39] identified some trends and highlighted that one of the main effects of Internet use in the insurance area will be lower insurance premiums. This effect is a consequence of reducing administrative costs and of the higher competition between insurers that is a result of the amount of information available to consumers. Another important aspect of using the Internet in the insurance sector involves the capacity of insurers to offer flexible coverage options by offering their clients products adapted to their unique situations. Based on these transformations, marketing strategies must evolve, and insurers need to rethink their business strategies and adopt a customer-centric approach.

The effect of ICT on the level of health insurance premiums paid by consumers was investigated by Pauly et al. [40] in an attempt to see which category would benefit most from the use of ICT. As a consequence of using the Internet, a decrease in search costs was noted, but the results of Pauly et al. [40] show that by using new technologies, not all categories of customers will pay lower premiums for private health insurance, only the younger ones.

More empirical papers have been developed in the last period that endeavored to investigate the ICT–insurance nexus. These could be divided into four categories, keeping their approach in mind.

The first category of studies includes papers that try to investigate the impact of ICT penetration on people's participation on the insurance market. These studies start from the hypothesis that information is important in determining higher participation in the financial markets [41–43]. Considering that the Internet is an important information channel for people in their attempt to minimize premium costs and obtain the best coverage through insurance, Liu et al. [44], Chen et al. [45], Hu et al. [46] and Lin et al. [47] argue that insurance market participation is positively influenced by the ICT infrastructure and its use, but differs for various types of insurance.

The second category of studies analyzes the reactions of people working in the insurance services towards using information and communications technology, trying to see their reactions related to the use of ICT. In this sense, Lee et al. [48] examine the suitability of mobile commerce systems based on personal digital assistant technology in the insurance sector from the perspective of the task-technology fit theory, and the authors argue that mobile commerce using PDA technology "is suitable for insurance tasks" [48] (p. 108) and that "the PDA technology provides different degrees of assistance to different types of insurance tasks" [48] (p. 108). Odoyo and Nyangosi [49] analyzed the opinions of employees and insurance agents regarding the perceived benefits of implementing ICT in insurance companies and Naicker and Van Der Merwe [50] analyzed the opinions of IT managers from South-African insurance companies in an attempt to identify factors that influence the adoption of mobile technology in the life insurance industry. In an attempt to see the impact of COVID-19 on the use of ICT in insurance, Eckert, Eckert and Zitzmann [51] analyzed the factors that influence the use of digital technologies in the sale of insurance for different intermediaries: exclusive agents, independent agents, and independent brokers. Their study used a questionnaire applied to persons acting in the German insurance market after the first wave of COVID-19 and concluded that the use of digital technologies in insurance sales is rather underdeveloped. The results of the survey underline that about 50% to 60% of the sales units use technology to interact with customers in the sales process; messenger services are the main used digital technologies, followed by video meetings.

In addition to this, technology is more frequently used in the underwriting process or for claims management, as more than 75% of the business transactions related to these aspects used digitalization. This situation confirms the idea that at least one cause of this conservative approach regarding digital technology comes from the consumers, as some of them still prefer face-to-face interactions. Another conclusion of the study highlights the fact that exclusive agents are more open to using digital technologies than independent agents or brokers, and also that younger people are using more digital technology than older ones.

The third category of studies evaluates the impact of ICT infrastructure on insurance companies' transformations. Neirotti and Paolucci [52] used study cases and econometric techniques to highlight the importance of IT management practices in order to determine better financial results for insurance companies. Lyskawa et al. [53] analyzed the effect of ICT investments determined by digitalization in four major European insurance groups on the results of their activity. They suggested that the impact of ICT investments is diverse for the four insurers, suggesting that just investing in more developed technology does not by itself lead to better financial results. Eckert and Osterrieder [54] analyzed the previous literature to describe the major digital technologies that have significant importance for insurers' transformation. Based on the benefits and opportunities of such technologies for the insurance activities, the authors suggest that by using these technologies, insurers could provide more customer-centric products and services, and in order for this to be achieved, it is necessary to integrate the digital transformation of the company into a strategic plan.

The fourth strand of studies tried to quantify the effect of ICT penetration on the development of the entire insurance market or on specific types of insurance, and is closely related to our approach.

Using a sample of average income countries from 2002 to 2011, Salatin et al. [37] examined the relationship between ICT use (seen as the number of mobile users) and the insurance industry, and indicated that the number of mobile users positively and significantly influences the insurance industry. Their explanations are based on the fact that sales/claims adjusting in the insurance industry will grow because of ICT use and the activities will be more specialized and, as a result, a higher speed and a better quality of services will be offered to the clients.

More studies were developed for African countries, and different results were revealed. Asongu and Odhiambo [55] noticed that an enhancement of mobile phone penetration and fixed broadband subscriptions generates a positive net effect on life insurance consumption, while a positive net effect on non-life insurance is obtained through an enhancement of fixed broadband subscriptions. Akinlo [8] established that the classic telephone positively influences non-life and life insurance but, on the other hand, mobile phones negatively affect the evolution of all segments of the insurance market. The Internet has a slightly different impact on non-life insurance (which is significantly positively influenced) than on life insurance, where the impact is also positive, but insignificant. Sibindi [56] found that all types of ICT analyzed (mobile, fixed phones, broadband or Internet) have a positive and significant impact on the life insurance market.

Benlagha and Hemrit [57] empirically analyzed the impact of Internet usage on insurance demand using a panel of 24 OECD countries for the 2007–2017 period. They noticed different results between life and general insurance: a positive effect of Internet use on non-life insurance and no effect on the demand for life insurance. The results can be explained by the fact that non-life policies have generally short-term coverage and are more adaptable to the distribution channels agreed by insured people.

Pradhan et al. [6] investigated the short-run link between ICT infrastructure use and the insurance market for a sample of high and medium-income countries, and their results indicate a significant number of cases of insurance market-led ICT infrastructure hypotheses and also relatively similar cases of ICT infrastructure–led insurance market hypotheses, but are also found some cases when the insurance market and ICT infrastructure influence each other or when there are no links between them. They concluded that the ICT infrastructure use in insurance activities is desired in order to supply better or more targeted products to different categories of people by the insurers, and also government policies toward more access to ICT infrastructure are necessary to increase the addressability of insurance products. As suggested by the authors, ICT infrastructure for insurance purposes could also be used in volatile market conditions and periods of high uncertainty, generating reduced risk for clients.

There are studies that analyze just one type of insurance, such as that of Xu et al. [58], which investigated the effect of Internet use on commercial health insurance purchases in China based on the data provided by a survey from 2017. The results show that even the use of Internet significantly influenced commercial health insurance purchases for all residents, but the effect was higher in the case of rural residents.

3. Data and Methods

This paper investigates the interaction between ICT penetration indicators and insurance sector growth in the 10 new member states of the European Union (EU) by a causality test and regression analysis. In econometric analyses, insurance sector development (INSURANCE) is represented by insurance company assets to GDP (%). On the other hand, ICT penetration is proxied by indicators of mobile cellular subscriptions (per 100 people) (MOBILE), and individuals using the Internet (% of population) (INTERNET). The ICT indicators are obtained from the World Bank database [59,60], and the insurance sector data is procured from the World Bank Global Financial Development Database by Mare et al. [61]. On the basis of limited available data for the insurance sector for countries selected, the study covers the period 2000–2020.

The panel comprised the 10 new EU member states: Bulgaria, Croatia, Czechia, Estonia, Hungary, Latvia, Lithuania, Poland, Slovakia, and Slovenia. Romania is not included in the analysis due to the absence of its insurance data. Econometric tests are performed using the statistical programmes E-Views 12.0, Stata 16.0, and Gauss 11.0.

The main characteristics of the series are displayed in Table 1. The mean value of INSURANCE, MOBILE, and INTERNET are 7.068, 104.707, and 56.427, respectively. However, the variables of MOBILE and INTERNET particularly displayed a significant variation among the analysed countries. Furthermore, the size of the insurance sector differs considerably among selected countries, as we can see from the data presented in Table 1. On the other hand, the mean of mobile cellular subscriptions (per 100 people) is very high in all countries, and the mean of Internet penetration as a percentage of the population is above 50%, except for Bulgaria. The correlation matrix in Table 2 also reveals a positive correlation between insurance sector growth and both ICT indicators and also supports the absence of multicollinearity problem.

Table 1. Dataset Characteristics.

Characteristics		INSURANCE	MOBILE	INTERNET
Mean		7.068	104.707	56.427
Std. Dev.		3.766	34.200	23.519
Maximum		17.500	163.131	90.229
Minimum		1.380	9.114	5.371
Bulgaria	Mean	3.651	102.619	40.716
	Std. Dev.	1.058	43.151	21.523
	Maximum	5.750	143.967	70.162
	Minimum	2.190	9.114	5.371
Croatia	Mean	8.521	91.878	50.044
	Std. Dev.	2.521	27.717	22.803
	Maximum	12.560	117.539	79.079
	Minimum	4.770	22.711	6.645

Table 1. *Cont.*

Characteristics		INSURANCE	MOBILE	INTERNET
Czechia	Mean	9.238	113.385	57.885
	Std. Dev.	1.815	23.081	23.291
	Maximum	11.570	132.775	81.339
	Minimum	4.690	42.463	9.781
Estonia	Mean	5.841	118.423	69.524
	Std. Dev.	2.468	34.693	19.459
	Maximum	9.130	151.189	90.228
	Minimum	1.900	39.875	28.576
Hungary	Mean	7.215	98.133	55.803
	Std. Dev.	1.064	24.264	24.765
	Maximum	9.030	121.955	84.771
	Minimum	5.530	30.154	6.999
Latvia	Mean	2.307	95.815	59.534
	Std. Dev.	1.020	34.645	25.513
	Maximum	5.050	134.295	88.898
	Minimum	1.380	16.772	6.319
Lithuania	Mean	3.132	122.376	54.035
	Std. Dev.	0.928	45.611	24.458
	Maximum	4.700	163.131	83.056
	Minimum	1.530	14.557	6.427
Poland	Mean	9.122	103.283	53.062
	Std. Dev.	1.548	42.199	22.876
	Maximum	10.730	147.569	83.185
	Minimum	5.070	17.523	7.285
Slovak Republic	Mean	8.213	100.414	64.039
	Std. Dev.	1.557	31.779	22.211
	Maximum	10.070	135.674	89.921
	Minimum	4.860	23.132	9.427
Slovenia	Mean	13.439	100.738	59.631
	Std. Dev.	3.736	15.752	20.317
	Maximum	17.500	120.459	86.601
	Minimum	6.020	61.259	15.110

Source: Author's calculations.

Table 2. Correlation matrix.

	LNINSURANCE	LNINTERNET	LNMOBILE
LNINSURANCE	-	0.196	0.136
LNINTERNET	0.196	-	0.386
LNMOBILE	0.136	0.386	-

Source: Author's calculations.

The causal interaction between ICT penetration indicators and insurance sector development is examined with Emirmahmutoglu and Kose's [62] causality test in view of the cross-sectional and heterogeneity presence among the variables. Emirmahmutoglu and Kose's [62] causality test performs the causality analysis for each cross-section by applying the bootstrap method to Fisher statistics. The stationarity of the variable (d_{max_i}) and optimal lag length (p_i) are specified before the causality analysis. The error terms for each cross-section are then obtained by the following regression:

$$LNINSURANCE_{i,t} = \alpha_{i,t} + \sum_{j=1}^{p_i+d_{max_i}} \beta_{ij} LNINSURANCE_{i,t-j} + \sum_{j=1}^{p_i+d_{max_i}} \gamma_{ij} LNICT_{i,t-j} + \varepsilon_{it} \quad (1)$$

$$LNICT_{i,t} = \alpha_{i,t} + \sum_{j=1}^{p_i+d_{max_i}} \beta_{ij} LNICT_{i,t-j} + \sum_{j=1}^{p_i+d_{max_i}} \gamma_{ij} LNINSURANCE_{i,t-j} + \varepsilon_{it} \quad (2)$$

The null hypothesis of the test suggests the absence of causality between two variables.

Furthermore, the influence of ICT indicators on insurance sector growth is analyzed through the following regression analysis (i (i = 1, . . . , 10) indicates the countries, and t (t = 2000, . . . , 2020) indicates the yearly time period):

$$LNINSURANCE_{it} = \alpha_i + \beta_1 LNINTERNET_{it} + \beta_2 LNMOBILE_{it} + \varepsilon_{it} \quad (3)$$

4. Empirical Analyses

The causal interaction between ICT indicators and insurance sector development for the selected countries is investigated by a causality test with cross-sectional dependence. In the econometric analysis, the presence of cross-sectional dependence and heterogeneity is firstly tested with tests of LM, LM CD and LMadj, and the results are reported in Table 3. The null hypothesis of cross-sectional independence was denied at a 1% significance level, and the test results reveal the subsistence of cross-sectional dependence. In other words, ICT indicators and the insurance sector in one country of the panel can influence the other countries of the panel due to close economic and social relations. Homogeneity is then examined with the delta tilde test of Pesaran and Yamagata [63], and the test results disclosed in Table 3 reveal the presence of heterogeneity. In other words, there exists a country-specific heterogeneity.

Table 3. Cross-Sectional Dependence and Homogeneity Test Results.

Test	Statistic	p Value
LM test [64]	164.5	0.0000
LM CD * [65]	2.484	0.0130
LM adjusted test * [66]	28.22	0.0000
$\tilde{\Delta}$ test	13.982	0.000
$\tilde{\Delta}_{adj}$ test	15.540	0.000

* two-sided test.

The integration levels of the variables should be determined before the implementation of causality and regression analyses, because it is an input for causality analysis and is also necessary in order to avoid a spurious regression. The stationarity analysis of LNINSURANCE, LNMOBILE, and LNINTERNET are examined with the unit root test of Pesaran [67] CIPS (Cross-sectionally augmented IPS [68]) with cross-sectional dependence, and the unit root test results are displayed in Table 4. All variables are nonstationary for their level values, but they become stationary for their first-differenced values.

Table 4. CIPS Panel Unit Root Test Results.

Variables	Constant	Constant + Trend
LNINSURANCE	1.353	0.707
d(LNINSURANCE)	−2.927 ***	−3.189 ***
LNMOBILE	1.369	1.611
d(LNMOBILE)	−2.586 ***	−4.664 ***
LNINTERNET	−1.124	−0.584
d(LNINTERNET)	−3.214 ***	−5.646

*** it is significant at 1%.

The Granger causality test investigates whether one variable is useful for forecasting another variable, and the null hypothesis suggests that there exists no causality from one variable to another [62]. The interaction between mobile cellular subscriptions and insurance sector development is investigated through Emirmahmutoglu and Kose's [62] causality test, and the results of the causality analysis are displayed in Table 5. The panel-level causality analysis reveals a bidirectional causality between two variables. In another words, both variables are useful in explaining the other. On the other hand, the country-level causality analysis uncovers a bidirectional causality between LNMOBILE and LNINSURANCE in Latvia, Poland, and Slovakia, and a unidirectional causality from LNINSURANCE to LNMOBILE in Estonia and Hungary.

Table 5. Panel Causality Test Results.

Countries	LNMOBILE ↛ LNINSURANCE		LNINSURANCE↛ LNMOBILE	
	Test Statistic	p Value	Test Statistic	p Value
Bulgaria	3.349	0.187	0.526	0.769
Croatia	0.054	0.816	0.047	0.828
Czechia	0.021	0.886	0.001	0.976
Estonia	1.109	0.574	5.203	0.074
Hungary	0.163	0.686	6.707	0.01
Latvia	9.814	0.007	7.135	0.028
Lithuania	0.006	0.94	0.043	0.837
Poland	10.845	0.004	10.731	0.005
Slovakia	11.597	0.003	5.941	0.051
Slovenia	0.079	0.779	0	0.99
Panel	38.739	0.007	39.632	0.006

Source: Author's calculations.

The bidirectional causality between insurance and mobile penetration is sustained by Pradhan et al. [6], but, on the other hand, Asongu and Odhiambo [55] and Sibindi [56] noticed a positive impact of mobile penetration on life insurance, and Akinlo [8] indicated that mobile has a negative effect on insurance development.

The interaction between Internet access and insurance sector development is investigated through the Emirmahmutoglu and Kose [62] causality test, and the results of the causality analysis are displayed in Table 6. The panel level causality analysis reveals a bidirectional causality between these two variables. On the other hand, the country-level causality analysis uncovers a unidirectional causality from LNINTERNET to LNINSURANCE in Croatia and Hungary, and unidirectional causality from LNINSURANCE to LNINTERNET in Czechia and Slovenia.

Table 6. Panel Causality Test Results.

Countries	LNINTERNET ↛ LNINSURANCE		LNINSURANCE ↛ LNINTERNET	
	Test Statistic	***p* Value**	**Test Statistic**	***p* Value**
Bulgaria	1.072	0.301	0.002	0.962
Croatia	11.527	0.009	1.135	0.769
Czechia	6.198	0.102	11.089	0.011
Estonia	0.482	0.786	0.067	0.967
Hungary	3.088	0.079	0.973	0.324
Latvia	0.647	0.886	3.041	0.385
Lithuania	2.116	0.347	3.432	0.180
Poland	1.601	0.206	0.277	0.599
Slovakia	0.040	0.998	5.555	0.135
Slovenia	1.000	0.801	28.271	0.000
Panel	37.871	0.012	47.576	0.000

Source: own processing.

A bidirectional causality between insurance and Internet use was reported by Pradhan et al. [6], for life insurance (when penetration was used) and non-life insurance (when the density is used); but generally, a positive impact of the Internet on insurance was found for life insurance [6,8,56] and for the case of non-life insurance [57]. In addition, an impact of insurance on the Internet was found by Pradhan et al. [6] for the case of life insurance when density is used.

Lastly, the influence of ICT indicators on insurance sector growth is investigated through regression analysis. In this context, the Chow (F) test [69] and the Breusch and Pagan LM test [64] are employed for regression model selection, and their results are displayed in Table 7. The null hypothesis of the Chow test [69] indicates that pooled regression is appropriate and the alternative hypothesis suggests that the fixed effects model is appropriate. The alternative hypothesis is accepted because the p value is found to be lower than 5%. On the other hand, the Breusch and Pagan LM test [64] is conducted to make a selection between pooled regression and the random effects model, and the p value is found to be lower than 5%, and in turn an alternative hypothesis suggesting that the random effects model is appropriate is accepted. At the last stage, the Hausman test [70] is implemented to make a selection between the fixed effects model and the random effects model, and the p value is found to be higher than 5%. Therefore, the null hypothesis suggesting that the random effects model is appropriate is accepted.

Table 7. Results of Panel Regression Model Selection Pretests.

Test	*p* Value	Decision
Chow (F) test	0.0000	Alternative hypothesis is accepted. (Fixed effects model is appropriate.)
BP (χ^2) test	0.0000	Alternative hypothesis is accepted. (Random effects model is appropriate.)
Hausman test	0.8807	Null hypothesis is accepted and random effects model is appropriate.

Source: Author's calculations.

The influence of ICT indicators on insurance sector growth is estimated through the random effects model, and the coefficients in Table 8 indicate that both ICT indicators have a positive influence on insurance sector growth, but the impact of Internet penetration on the insurance sector is revealed to be significant. In other words, Internet penetration has a positive influence on insurance sector growth. Endogeneity is also checked considering the presence of panel level bilateral causality between the series, but no endogeneity is revealed. Furthermore, autocorrelation and heteroskedasticity problems are respectively questioned by Wooldridge autocorrelation test [71] and the Greene test [72], and the results of both tests indicate that there exist no problems of autocorrelation or heteroskedasticity.

Table 8. Results of Panel Regression Estimation.

Variables	Coefficient	*p* Value
D(LNMOBILE)	0.018	0.820
D(LNINTERNET)	0.346	0.000
C	0.362	0.000
R-squared	0.543	
Adjusted R-squared	0.538	
F-statistics	122.910 (0.0000)	
Woolridge endogeneity test	2.345 (0.1834)	
Greene heterockedasticity test	205.13 (0.3254)	

Source: own processing.

The causal analysis revealed at the panel level, a bidirectional relationship between the ICT penetration indicators (mobile cellular subscriptions and individuals using the Internet) and the insurance sector development.. These results suggest that the ICT penetration and insurance sector development influence each other, so the measures that are taken to develop one side (for example, more regions covered by mobile networks or by Internet providers, for ICT indicators or the introduction of deductible revenues for specific types of insurance or new mandatory insurance, or for insurance sector development) will generate the same effect on the other side. However, at the country level, the situations are various as a result of the different structures of the insurance markets under analysis, but also because of different evolutions of ICT penetration. The Internet is usually more important in countries where MTPL, travel policies and not-so-complex property policies are more significant because these types of policies are the first offered through electronic channels. Mobile is generally used for contacting insured persons or prospects, for reminders about deadlines, for payments, so it is necessary not only for basic products but also for more complex ones. As Akinlo [8] suggests, the high intermediation of insurance products could also limit the influence of mobile on insurance, because intermediaries have significant personal interactions with the insured persons.

Considering the impact of both mobile cellular subscriptions and individuals using the Internet on insurance sector development, we discovered that only Internet penetration has a significant positive effect on insurance. This result suggests that for the countries analyzed, the measures that determine the growth of the number of individuals using the Internet are more important for the development of the insurance sector.

5. Conclusions

We have tested the causal relationship between various types of ICT penetration and insurance development for the 10 new member states of the European Union using a panel data set covering the period between 2000–2020, and the results revealed a bidirectional causality between ICT penetration indicators and insurance sector development. These results suggest that by creating a constructive environment for increasing Internet usage and mobile phone subscriptions, we can stimulate insurance sector development.

In the financial and insurance services industry, technological transformation is not just something inevitable, but is a major force behind development and innovation. Managers in the insurance sector must understand that they need to take appropriate measures to modernize and expand their technological infrastructure. This requires more resources and significant efforts for all involved in the transformation process, but will reshape operations, reduce costs, and increase profitability.

Policymakers should understand the key role of the Internet for many sectors and ensure an optimal environment for Internet development. Policies and programmes specifically targeting companies with the purpose of improving ICT adoption can help insurers to build resilient innovative strategies and to accelerate the adoption of both hardware and software technologies. Demand-oriented innovation policies can create a supportive environment that encourages innovation in the insurance industry. Insurers can automate information submission, quoting, underwriting and renewal processes, and can improve risk management systems, etc.

The measures adopted to develop the insurance market (such as the improvement of insurers' websites, the use of robo-advisors or chatbots, laws that favor the distribution of insurance through the Internet, and campaigns of awareness of the insurance role for people and businesses, etc.) will contribute to more mobile subscriptions and Internet users and will enhance ICT penetration. For various countries, the causal relations are different, suggesting that country-specific factors (macroeconomic, demographic or institutional ones) can also have a significant impact on insurance market development. A significant limitation of the study, because of the lack of some data, is that it does only cover the first period of the pandemic, when the use of ICT was more intense, and therefore future studies will be focused on a more extended period of time.

Author Contributions: Conceptualization and methodology—Y.B., D.C.D., A.E.D. and M.D.G.; formal analysis, Y.B., D.C.D., A.E.D. and M.D.G.; software, Y.B.; resources, Y.B. and M.D.G.; writing—original draft preparation, Y.B., D.C.D., A.E.D. and M.D.G.; writing—review and editing, Y.B., D.C.D., A.E.D. and M.D.G.; supervision, Y.B. and M.D.G.; funding acquisition, A.E.D. All authors have read and agreed to the published version of the manuscript.

Funding: This study was conducted with financial support from the scientific research funds of the "1 Decembrie 1918" University of Alba Iulia, Romania.

Conflicts of Interest: The authors declare that they have no conflict of interest.

References

1. Kpodar, K.; Andrianaivo, M. ICT, Financial Inclusion, and Growth: Evidence from African Countries, Working Paper No. 11/73, International Monetary Fund, IMF Working Paper. Available online: https://www.imf.org/en/Publications/WP/Issues/2016/12/31/ICT-Financial-Inclusion-and-Growth-Evidence-from-African-Countries-24771 (accessed on 11 October 2022).
2. Sassi, S.; Goaied, M. Financial Development, ICT Diffusion, and Economic Growth: Lessons from MENA Region. *Telecommun. Policy* **2013**, *37*, 252–261. [CrossRef]
3. Pradhan, R.P.; Arvin, M.B.; Hall, J.H.; Bennett, S.E. Mobile telephony, economic growth, financial development, foreign direct investment, and imports of ICT goods: The case of the G-20 countries. *Econ. Polit. Ind.* **2018**, *45*, 279–310. [CrossRef]
4. Alshubiri, F.; Jamil, S.A.; Elheddad, M. The impact of ICT on financial development: Empirical evidence from the Gulf Cooperation Council countries. *Int. J. Eng. Bus. Manag.* **2019**, *11*, 1847979019870670. [CrossRef]
5. Chien, M.S.; Cheng, C.Y.; Kurniawati, M.A. The non-linear relationship between ICT diffusion and financial development. *Telecommun. Policy* **2020**, *44*, 102023. [CrossRef]
6. Pradhan, R.P.; Bahmani, S.; Abraham, R.; Hall, J.H. Insurance Market and Economic Growth in an Information-Driven Economy: Evidence from a Panel of High- and Middle-Income Countries? *Asia-Pac. Financ. Mark.* **2022**. [CrossRef]
7. Verma, A.; Giri, A.K. ICT diffusion, financial development, and economic growth: Panel evidence from SAARC countries. *J. Public Aff.* **2022**, *22*, e2557. [CrossRef]
8. Akinlo, T. Information technology and insurance development in Sub-Saharan Africa. *Inf. Dev.* **2023**, *39*, 169–183. [CrossRef]
9. Bayar, Y.; Gavriletea, M.D.; Păun, D. Impact of mobile phones and Internet use on financial inclusion: Empirical evidence from the EU post-communist countries. *Technol. Econ. Dev. Econ.* **2021**, *27*, 722–741. [CrossRef]
10. Asongu, S.A. How has mobile phone penetration stimulated financial development in Africa? *J. Afr. Bus.* **2013**, *14*, 7–18. [CrossRef]
11. Kim, M.; Zoo, H.; Lee, H.; Kang, J. Mobile financial services, financial inclusion, and development: A systematic review of academic literature. *Electron. J. Inf. Syst. Dev. Count.* **2018**, *84*, e12044. [CrossRef]

12. Pradhan, R.P.; Sahoo, P.P. Are there links between financial inclusion, mobile telephony, and economic growth? Evidence from Indian states. *Appl. Econ. Lett.* **2021**, *28*, 310–314. [CrossRef]
13. Cappiello, A. Technology and Insurance. In *Technology and the Insurance Industry*; Palgrave Pivot: Cham, Switzerland, 2018; pp. 7–28. [CrossRef]
14. Njegomir, V.; Demko-Rihter, J.; Bojanić, T. Disruptive Technologies in the Operation of Insurance Industry. *Teh. Vjesn.* **2021**, *28*, 1797–1805.
15. Brokešová, Z.; Vachálková, I. Macroeconomic environment and insurance industry development: The case of Visegrad group countries. *Ekon. Rev.—Cent. Eur. Rev. Econ. Issues* **2016**, *19*, 63–72.
16. Lee, H.S.; Cheng, F.F.; Chong, S.C.; Sia, B.K. Influence of macroeconomics factors and legal stability to insurance growth in the ASEAN-5 Countries. *J. Ekon. Malays.* **2018**, *52*, 219–229. [CrossRef]
17. Lee, H.S.; Chong, S.C.; Sia, B.K. Influence of secondary and tertiary literacy on life insurance consumption: Case of selected ASEAN countries. *Geneva Pap. Risk Insur.-Issues Pract.* **2018**, *43*, 1–15. [CrossRef]
18. Guerineau, S.; Sawadogo, R. On the Determinants of Life Insurance Development in SubSaharan Africa: The Role of the Institutions Quality in the Effect of Economic Development. 2015. Available online: https://halshs.archives-ouvertes.fr/halshs-01178838/document (accessed on 28 December 2022).
19. Zerriaa, M.; Noubbigh, H. Determinants of life insurance demand in the MENA region. *Geneva Pap. Risk Insur.-Issues Pract.* **2016**, *41*, 491–511. [CrossRef]
20. Ben Dhiab, L.; Dkhili, H. Legal Stability and Determinants of Insurance Development in the Middle East and North Africa Region (MENA). *J. Asian Financ. Econ. Bus.* **2022**, *9*, 141–149.
21. Albrecher, H.; Bommier, A.; Filipović, D.; Koch-Medina, P.; Loisel, S.; Schmeiser, H. Insurance: Models, digitalization, and data science. *Eur. Actuar. J.* **2019**, *9*, 349–360. [CrossRef]
22. Cappiello, A. The Technological Disruption of Insurance Industry: A Review. *Int. J. Bus. Soc. Sci.* **2020**, *11*, 1–11. [CrossRef]
23. Swiss Re Institute. Technology and Insurance: Themes and Challenges. 2017. Available online: https://www.swissre.com/institute/research/topics-and-risk-dialogues/digital-business-model-and-cyber-risk/technology-and-insurance-themes-and-challenges.html (accessed on 2 December 2022).
24. Naujoks, H.; Mueller, F.; Kotalakidis, N. Digitalization in Insurance: The Multibillion Dollar Opportunity. Available online: https://www.bain.com/insights/digitalization-in-insurance/ (accessed on 2 December 2022).
25. Eling, M.; Lehmann, M. The Impact of Digitalization on the Insurance Value Chain and the Insurability of Risks. *Geneva Pap. Risk Insur. Issues Pract.* **2018**, *43*, 359–396. [CrossRef]
26. Lăzăroiu, G.; Ionescu, L.; Andronie, M.; Dijmărescu, I. Sustainability Management and Performance in the Urban Corporate Economy: A Systematic Literature Review. *Sustainability* **2020**, *12*, 7705. [CrossRef]
27. Lanfranchi, D.; Grassi, L. Examining insurance companies' use of technology for innovation. *Geneva Pap. Risk Insur. Issues Pract.* **2022**, *47*, 520–537. [CrossRef] [PubMed]
28. Shevchuk, O.; Kondrat, I.; Stanienda, J. Pandemic as an accelerator of digital transformation in the insurance industry: Evidence from Ukraine. *Insur. Mark. Co.* **2020**, *11*, 30–41. [CrossRef]
29. Tiwari, A.; Patro, A.; Shaikh, I. Information communication technology-enabled platforms and P&C insurance consumption: Evidence from emerging & developing economies. *Rev. Econ. Financ.* **2019**, *15*, 81–95.
30. Eckert, C.; Neunsinger, C.; Osterrieder, K. Managing customer satisfaction: Digital applications for insurance companies. *Geneva Pap. Risk Insur. Issues Pract.* **2022**, *47*, 569–602. [CrossRef]
31. Chimedtseren, E.; Safari, M. Service Quality Factors Affecting Purchase Intention of Life Insurance Products. *J. Insur. Financ. Manag.* **2016**, *1*, 1–12.
32. Dash, G.; Chakraborty, D. Digital Transformation of Marketing Strategies during a Pandemic: Evidence from an Emerging Economy during COVID-19. *Sustainability* **2021**, *13*, 6735. [CrossRef]
33. Mau, S.; Cvijikj, I.; Wagner, J. From research to purchase: An empirical analysis of research-shopping behaviour in the insurance sector. *Z. Für Die Gesamte Versicher.* **2015**, *104*, 573–593. [CrossRef]
34. Bryzgalov, D.V.; Tsyganov, A.A. Consumer Limitations on the Digitalization of the Insurance Market and Ways to Overcome Them. *Stud. Russ. Econ. Dev.* **2022**, *33*, 539–546. [CrossRef]
35. Barbu, C.M.; Florea, D.L.; Dabija, D.-C.; Barbu, M.C.R. Customer Experience in Fintech. *J. Theor. Appl. Electron. Commer. Res.* **2021**, *16*, 1415–1433. [CrossRef]
36. Bazini, E.; Madani, F. ICT Application in the Insurance Industry: Its Impact in Customer Relationship Management. *Acad. J. Interdiscip. Stud.* **2015**, *4*, 307–311. [CrossRef]
37. Salatin, P.; Yadollahi, F.; Eslambolchi, S. The effect of ICT on insurance industry in selected countries. *Res. J. Econ. Bus. ICT* **2014**, *9*, 2045–3345.
38. Kliestik, T.; Valaskova, K.; Lăzăroiu, G.; Kovacova, M.; Vrbka, J. Remaining Financially Healthy and Competitive: The Role of Financial Predictors. *J. Compet.* **2020**, *12*, 74–92. [CrossRef]
39. Garven, J.R. On the Implications of the Internet for Insurance Markets and Institutions. *Risk Manag. Insur. Rev.* **2002**, *5*, 105–116. [CrossRef]

40. Pauly, M.V.; Herring, B.; Song, D. Information technology and consumer search for health insurance. *Int. J. Econ. Bus.* **2006**, *13*, 45–63. [CrossRef]
41. Moran, J.R.; Kubik, J.D.; Beiseitov, E. Social Interactions and the Health Insurance Choices of the Elderly: Evidence from the Health and Retirement Study. Available online: https://papers.ssrn.com/sol3/papers.cfm?abstract_id=1809901 (accessed on 17 November 2022).
42. Liu, H.; Sun, Q.; Zhao, Z. Social learning and health insurance enrollment: Evidence from China's new cooperative medical scheme. *J. Econ. Behav. Organ.* **2014**, *97*, 84–102. [CrossRef]
43. Butler, R.J. Information access and homeowners insurance purchases. *Geneva Pap. Risk Insur. Issues Pract.* **2021**, *46*, 649–663. [CrossRef]
44. Liu, Z.; Li, W.; Zhang, T. Internet and private insurance participation. *Int. J. Financ. Econ.* **2022**, *27*, 1495–1509. [CrossRef]
45. Chen, A.; Chen, Y.; Finbarr, M.; Wei, X.; Xian, X. How Does the Insurer's Mobile Application Sales Strategy Perform? Available online: https://ssrn.com/abstract=3985977 (accessed on 20 November 2022).
46. Hu, X.; Wang, Z.; Liu, J. The impact of digital finance on household insurance purchases: Evidence from micro data in China. *Geneva Pap. Risk Insur. Issues Pract.* **2022**, *47*, 538–568. [CrossRef]
47. Lin, C.; Hsiao, Y.J.; Yeh, C.Y. Financial literacy, financial advisors, and information sources on demand for life insurance. *Pac.-Basin Financ. J.* **2017**, *43*, 218–237. [CrossRef]
48. Lee, C.C.; Cheng, H.K.; Cheng, H.H. An empirical study of mobile commerce in insurance industry: Task–technology fit and individual differences. *Decis. Support Syst.* **2007**, *43*, 95–110. [CrossRef]
49. Odoyo, F.S.; Nyangosi, R. E-Insurance: An Empirical Study of Perceived Benefits. *Int. J. Bus. Soc. Sci.* **2011**, *2*, 167–171.
50. Naicker, V.; Van Der Merwe, D.B. Managers' perception of mobile technology adoption in the Life Insurance industry. *Inf. Technol. People* **2018**, *31*, 507–526. [CrossRef]
51. Eckert, C.; Eckert, J.; Zitzmann, A. The status quo of digital transformation in insurance sales: An empirical analysis of the german insurance industry. *Z. Für Die Gesamte Versicher.* **2021**, *110*, 133–155. [CrossRef]
52. Neirotti, P.; Paolucci, E. Assessing the strategic value of Information Technology: An analysis on the insurance sector. *Inf. Manag.* **2007**, *44*, 568–582. [CrossRef]
53. Łyskawa, K.; Kędra, A.; Klapkiv, L.; Klapkiv, J. Digitalization in Insurance Companies. In Proceedings of the International Scientific Conference Contemporary Issues In Business, Management and Economics Engineering, Vilnius, Lithuania, 9–10 May 2019; Vilnius Gediminas Technical University: Vilnius, Lithuania, 2019; pp. 842–852.
54. Eckert, C.; Osterrieder, K. How digitalization affects insurance companies: Overview and use cases of digital technologies. *Z. Für Die Gesamte Versicher.* **2020**, *109*, 333–360. [CrossRef]
55. Asongu, S.; Odhiambo, N. Enhancing ICT for Insurance in Africa. *Rev. Dev. Financ.* **2019**, *9*, 16–27. [CrossRef]
56. Sibindi, A.B. Information and Communication Technology Adoption and Life Insurance Market Development: Evidence from Sub-Saharan Africa. *J. Risk Financ. Manag.* **2022**, *15*, 568. [CrossRef]
57. Benlagha, N.; Hemrit, W. Internet use and insurance growth: Evidence from a panel of OECD countries. *Technol. Soc.* **2020**, *62*, 101289. [CrossRef]
58. Xu, B.-C.; Xu, X.-N.; Zhao, J.-C.; Zhang, M. Influence of Internet Use on Commercial Health Insurance of Chinese Residents. *Front. Public Health* **2022**, *10*, 907124. [CrossRef]
59. World Bank. Mobile Cellular Subscriptions (Per 100 People). 2022. Available online: https://data.worldbank.org/indicator/IT.CEL.SETS.P2 (accessed on 10 October 2022).
60. World Bank. Individuals Using the Internet (% of Population). 2022. Available online: https://data.worldbank.org/indicator/IT.NET.USER.ZS (accessed on 10 October 2022).
61. Mare, D.S.; Bertay, A.C.; Zhou, N. Global Financial Development Database. 2022. Available online: https://www.worldbank.org/en/publication/gfdr/data/global-financial-development-database (accessed on 10 October 2022).
62. Emirmahmutoglu, F.; Kose, N. Testing for granger causality in heterogeneous mixed panels. *Econ. Model.* **2011**, *28*, 870–876. [CrossRef]
63. Pesaran, M.H.; Yamagata, T. Testing Slope Homogeneity in Large Panels. *J. Econom.* **2008**, *142*, 50–93. [CrossRef]
64. Breusch, T.S.; Pagan, A.R. The Lagrange Multiplier Test and Its Applications to Model Specification Tests in Econometrics. *Rev. Econ. Stud.* **1980**, *47*, 39–53. [CrossRef]
65. Pesaran, M.H. General Diagnostic Tests for Cross-Section Dependence in Panels; CESifo Working Papers No. 1229. Available online: https://www.cesifo.org/en/publications/2004/working-paper/general-diagnostic-tests-cross-section-dependence-panels (accessed on 10 October 2022).
66. Pesaran, M.H.; Ullah, A.; Yamagata, T. A Bias-adjusted LM Test of Error Cross-section Independence. *Econom. J.* **2008**, *11*, 105–127. [CrossRef]
67. Pesaran, M.H. A Simple Panel Unit Root Test in the Presence of Cross-section Dependence. *J. Appl. Econom.* **2007**, *22*, 265–312. [CrossRef]
68. Im, K.S.; Pesaran, M.H.; Shin, Y. Testing for Unit Roots in Heterogeneous Panels. *J. Econom.* **2003**, *115*, 53–74. [CrossRef]
69. Chow, G.C. Tests of Equality between Sets of Coefficients in Two Linear Regressions. *Econometrica* **1960**, *28*, 591–605. [CrossRef]
70. Hausman, J.A. Specification Tests in Econometrics. *Econometrica* **1978**, *46*, 1251–1271. [CrossRef]

71. Wooldridge, J.M. *Econometric Analysis of Cross Section and Panel Data*; MIT Press: Cambridge, MA, USA, 2002.
72. Greene, W.H. *Econometric Analysis*, 5th ed; Prentice Hall: Upper Saddle River, NJ, USA, 2003.

electronics

Article

Investigating Trace Equivalences in Information Networks

Run Li [1], Jinzhao Wu [1,2,*] and Wujie Hu [3]

[1] School of Computer and Electronic Information, Guangxi University, Nanning 530004, China; li_run@st.gxu.edu.cn
[2] Guangxi Key Laboratory of Hybrid Computation and IC Design Analysis, Guangxi University for Nationalities, Nanning 530006, China
[3] School of Electric Engineering, Guangxi University, Nanning 530004, China; 15578093929@163.com
* Correspondence: himrwujzh@aliyun.com or wujinzhao163@163.com

Abstract: Equivalences are widely used and have achieved much success in concurrent systems. Meanwhile, information networks are ubiquitous for representing many complex systems and have similar characteristics and properties to concurrent systems such that they both can be described by graphs. In order to simplify information networks, we introduce equivalence to information networks, specifically leveraging the trace equivalence to reduce the complexity of these networks. In this paper, we first define the concept of trace and trace equivalence in information networks, drawing on the similar concept of concurrent systems. We then propose a computational method for determining whether two nodes are trace equivalent in an information network. With the help of this method, we derive trace-equivalent networks from original networks. Experiments show that we are able to reduce the number of nodes in the ACM and DBLP datasets by at most 65.21% and 46.68%, respectively. Running the PathSim algorithm on the original and derived networks, the mean error is 0.0728 in ACM and 0.0446 in DBLP. Overall, the results indicate that the derived networks have fewer nodes and edges than the original networks, yet still capture the same or similar information. By using trace equivalence, we are able to simplify information networks and improve their efficiency while preserving most of their informational content.

Keywords: equivalences; trace semantics; information networks; information technologies; data analytics

Citation: Li, R.; Wu, J.; Hu, W. Investigating Trace Equivalences in Information Networks. *Electronics* **2023**, *12*, 865. https://doi.org/10.3390/electronics12040865

Academic Editors: Galina Ilieva and George A. Tsihrintzis

Received: 13 January 2023
Revised: 2 February 2023
Accepted: 3 February 2023
Published: 8 February 2023

1. Introduction

In concurrent systems, a process is the behavior of a system, and the study of process is referred to as process theory [1,2]. Process theory is concerned with two main activities: modeling and verification. Modeling is about representing processes, and verification is about proving statements of processes. Labeled transition systems and process graphs are commonly used to represent processes. To prove that the actual behavior of a system matches its intended behavior, semantics are used as a criterion to determine whether two processes are equal. Furthermore, the linear time-branching time spectrum [3] illustrates various semantics that can be used to simplify systems. This spectrum is formed by semantics that is partially ordered by the relation "makes strictly more identifications on processes than" [1,3,4]. Based on certain semantics, equivalence indicates that two processes behave similarly and can be used to simplify systems by reducing duplicate or similar branches of behaviors in concurrent systems [5], while still preserving information of the system.

Trace semantics [6–8] is the coarsest in the linear time-branching time spectrum, meaning that it makes the most identifications of any of the other semantics. In trace semantics, the behavior of a system is represented as a sequence of actions, called a trace, that is generated by the system as it executes. According to trace semantics, two processes are considered equivalent if they allow the same set of traces. Trace equivalence is based on trace semantics and can capture identical or similar behaviors, allowing concurrent systems to be simplified by removing redundant or unnecessary branches. Trace equivalences have been applied in a variety of fields, such as linear algebraic hybrid systems [5], security properties of cryptographic protocols [9], and polynomial algebraic event structure [10,11].

Information networks have gained a lot of attention from researchers in recent years for their ability to model real-world systems. These networks can represent a wide range of scenarios, from molecules and social networks to bibliography networks, e-commerce, and advertising. Due to powerful representation ability, various tasks have achieved good performance results, including node classification, link prediction, and recommendation [12–16]. Most of the state-of-the-art research has employed graph neural network techniques [17–24]. Graph neural networks are a class of neural networks that are designed to process data with a graph structure and use a message-passing mechanism to continuously aggregate the information from nodes and their neighborhoods. Through this approach, each node contains a summary of information from its neighboring nodes. The adjacency matrix and the features of each node are then fed into the graph neural network for training to obtain the final embedding of each node. With the final embedding of each node, we can do downstream tasks, such as classifications, predictions, and recommendations.

As modern society becomes more complex, information networks are becoming increasingly complicated due to the vast amount of information they contain. This results in these networks having a larger number of identical or similar pieces of information. For example, in an e-commerce scenario, different users are more likely to buy or click on the best-selling products on the website, leading to similar or even identical purchase information. Graph neural networks do not explicitly distinguish nodes with identical or similar information, and this can cause problems with information duplication. When nodes with similar information are aggregated and processed, it can lead to information redundancy in the final results, which can harm the accuracy of downstream tasks. To address this issue, it is important to consider similar information between nodes when performing information aggregation and graph neural network training. Additionally, as information networks become more complex, the number of nodes and edges in these networks is also increasing. This reminds us of the "state explosion" problem in concurrent systems, where the large number of possible states can make it difficult to analyze and verify the behavior of the system. Trace equivalence in concurrent systems can alleviate the "state explosion" problem by removing duplicate branches of processes. The relationships among entities in information networks indicate the transmission of information in these networks, which can be thought of as traces in concurrent systems. Based on this intuition, trace equivalence can be applied to remove duplicate information in information networks that consist of relationships. This can help to simplify information networks and improve the accuracy of downstream tasks.

In this paper, we propose the use of trace equivalence to simplify information networks. To do this, we first need to clarify which objects of information networks can be reduced through equivalence. In concurrent systems, these objects are known as "states" and "transitions". With these objects in mind, we define the concepts of trace and trace equivalence in information networks. We also provide a method for determining when two nodes are trace equivalent. By applying trace equivalence to the nodes of information networks, we can obtain trace-equivalent networks that are simplified versions of the original information networks. Finally, to verify that the trace-equivalent network maintains the information of the original network, we perform the same data mining tasks on both networks and compare the results to ensure that the output of the data mining algorithms is consistent or similar.

The main contributions of this paper are as follows:

1. We provide a characterization of trace semantics and trace equivalence in information networks, and we give a computational method for computing trace equivalence in information networks.

2. We conduct trace equivalence computational tasks on information networks to obtain trace-equivalent networks from the original networks, and show that these derived networks have a smaller number of nodes and edges.
3. We show that conventional data mining algorithms can achieve the same or similar results on both the original networks and their trace-equivalent networks.

2. Materials and Methods

2.1. Review of Information Networks

In this section, we recall some concepts and notations used throughout the paper.

An information network [14] can be modeled as a graph $G = (V, E, O, R)$, in which V is the set of entities(nodes), E is the set of relations(edges) among these entities. $|O| = m$ represents the number of entities, $|E| = n$ represents the number of relations, and O and R are the set of node types and edge types, respectively. Mapping function $\varphi : V \to O$ maps each node $v \in V$ to a node type $o \in O$ and mapping function $\psi : E \to R$ maps each edge $e \in E$ to an edge type. In the situation that $|O| + |R| > 2$, the information network is named heterogeneous information networks. Otherwise, it is homogeneous information network.

Adjacency matrix [14] is represented as $A \subseteq \mathbb{R}^{n\times n}$, n is the number of nodes in information networks. $A_{i,j} = 1$ indicates that there is an edge between node i and node j. Otherwise, $A_{i,j} = 0$ indicates no edge.

It is shown in Figure 1 that a small information network abstracts from the DBLP information network. There are seven entities in this network, including three authors, two papers ,and two venues. The set of entities of this network is formally denoted as $V = \{a_1, a_2, a_3, p_1, p_2, v_1, v_2\}$. And the set of relations is $E = \{a_1 \xrightarrow{write} p_1, a_2 \xrightarrow{write} p_1, a_2 \xrightarrow{write} p_2, a_3 \xrightarrow{write} p_1, a_3 \xrightarrow{write} p_2, p_1 \xrightarrow{publish} v_1, p_2 \xrightarrow{publsh} v_2\}$. The set of entity types O and relation types R is $\{author, paper, venue\}$ and $\{write, publish\}$, respectively. Furthermore, the adjacency matrix of this network is illustrated in Figure 2 in which each row and each column represents an entity, and each element of this matrix represents the relation of the corresponding pair of entities. The notations used in this paper are illustrated in Table 1.

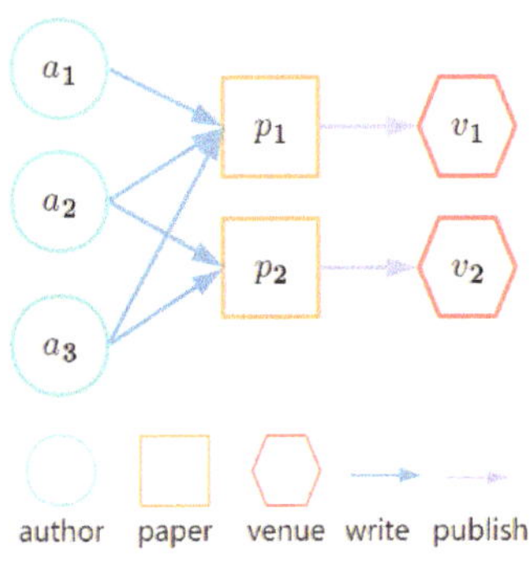

Figure 1. A small example abstracts from DBLP information network.

2.2. Methods

In this section, we theoretically introduce the idea of trace equivalence to information networks. We first give the concept of "states" and "actions" in information networks. Employing these concepts, we come up with the trace semantics of information networks inspired by the trace semantics of process theory in concurrent systems. Further, we show the computational method to determine whether two nodes are trace equivalent in information networks for deriving trace-equivalent networks from original networks. Moreover, to verify the maintainability of information in trace-equivalent networks, we conduct experiments on both the original networks and their trace-equivalent networks.

Table 1. Notations.

Notation	Explanations
G	an Information Network
V	set of nodes
E	set of edges
O	set of node types
R	set of edge types
A	adjacency matrix
v, v_i	node
e, e_i	edge
$P(v_i)$	path set of node v_i
$T(v_i)$	trace set of node v_i
$=_T$	trace equivalence

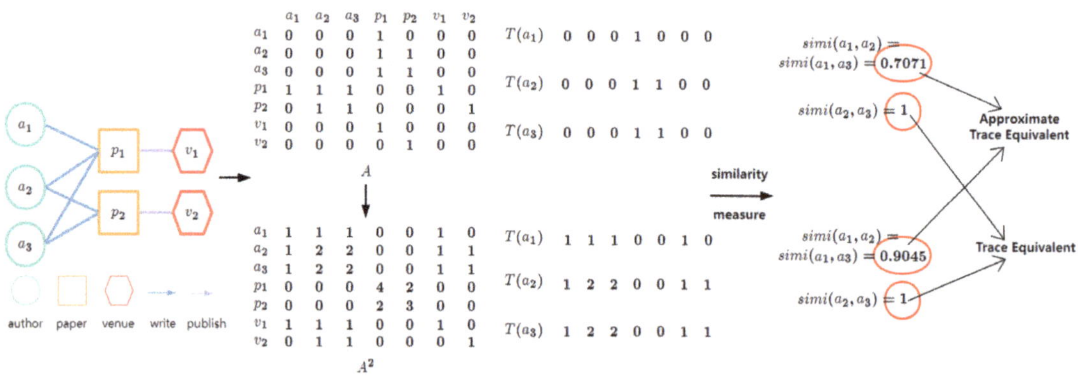

Figure 2. Illustration of computational methods of trace equivalence assisted by adjacency matrix.

2.2.1. Trace Semantics of Information Networks

In the process graph, states and transitions are the node and edges. Equivalences are then used to reduce the duplicate branches by removing equivalent states. Inspired by this, we leverage equivalence by treating nodes in information networks as states and edges as transitions in information networks. Nevertheless, we still use nodes and edges in the subsequent sections for the generality of research.

To begin, we come up with the concept of the trace in information networks according to the concepts in concurrent systems [4]. Information networks are usually represented as graphs, where nodes are entities and edges are relations between entities. Regarding nodes in information networks as states in process theory, the concept of trace in information networks is defined as follows according to the trace semantics of process theory.

Definition 1. ***Trace in information networks.*** *Given an information network $G = (V, E, O, R)$, a path starting from node $v \in V$ is represented as $p : v \xrightarrow{e_1} v_1 \cdots \xrightarrow{e_n} v_n$, where $v_i \in V$ and $e_i \in E$. A trace of this path is formally denoted as $e_1e_2 \cdots e_n$ based on the path. The set of paths starting from node v is denoted as $P(v)$, and the set of traces is denoted as $T(v)$, respectively.*

Note that a path is in the form of a node followed by an edge repeatedly, while continual edges composite a trace. Consequently, a trace describes and focuses on the relationship between two nodes since a trace is the edge sequence of a path starting from one node to another node, i.e., in a social network, if two people follow the same one, their relationship is common-follow, or if they follow each other, their relationship is mutual-follow.

Trace semantics of process is based on the idea that two processes are identified if they allow the same set of sequences of actions. In information networks, similarly, trace semantics are described as two nodes to be identified if they have the same set of relationships with other nodes. Moreover, it is significant that two nodes be identified if and only if they are of the same type. With Definition 1, we define trace equivalence as follows.

Definition 2. ***Trace equivalence in information networks.*** *Given an information network* $G = (V, E, O, R)$*, two nodes* v*,* w *are* ***trace equivalent*** *if and only if they are of the same type and their sets of traces are equal. Trace equivalence is formally represented as* $T(v) = T(w) \wedge \varphi(v) = \varphi(w)$ *and, for simplicity, notated as* $T(v) = T(w)$ *or* $v =_T w$.

For example, in Figure 1, we show that in a small example abstracting from the DBLP bibliography network, in which there are three authors a_1, a_2 and a_3, two papers p_1, p_2, and two venues v_1, v_2, the path set of a_1 is

$$P(a_1) = \{a_1 \xrightarrow{write} p_1, a_1 \xrightarrow{write} p_1 \xrightarrow{publish} v_1\},$$

then the trace of author a_1 is

$$T(a_1) = \{write(p_1), write(p_1) \circ publish(v_1)\},$$

similarly, the path set of a_2 is

$$P(a_2) = \{a_2 \xrightarrow{witer} p_1, a_2 \xrightarrow{write} p_1 \xrightarrow{publish} v_1, a_2 \xrightarrow{write} p_2, a_2 \xrightarrow{write} p_2 \xrightarrow{publish} v_2\},$$

and the path of a_3 is

$$P(a_3) = \{a_3 \xrightarrow{write} p_1, a_3 \xrightarrow{write} p_1 \xrightarrow{publish} v_1, a_3 \xrightarrow{write} p_2, a_3 \xrightarrow{write} p_2 \xrightarrow{publish} v_2\},$$

and it is significant that authors a_2 and a_3 are trace equivalent since they are of the same type of *author* and their sets of traces both are

$$T(a_2) = T(a_3) = \{write(p1), write(p2), write(p_1) \circ publish(v_1), write(p_2) \circ publish(v_2)\}.$$

Moreover, $T(a_1) \subset T(a_2)$ reveals that the interactions of author a_2 with other nodes contain the interactions of author a_1. We stipulate this situation as approximate trace equivalent because their sets of traces have common items but are not totally equal.

2.2.2. Computational Method of Trace Equivalences

Continuing with the concept of trace equivalence between nodes, we further give the computational method of trace equivalences in a mathematical way. In this regard, we need to represent an information network in mathematical form so that we leverage the adjacency matrix of an information network to reflect the messages we need mathematically. Given an information network $G = (V, E, O, R)$, an adjacency matrix of G is represented as $A \in \mathbb{R}^{n \times n}$. $A_{i,j} = 1$ if there is an edge between node i and node j such that these two nodes are connected and related; otherwise, $A_{i,j} = 0$ means node i and node j have no edges, yet they are not related. A_i can be used to depict all the paths whose start node is node i. Adjacency matrix A illustrates the relationships of every node with other nodes in the network, and with the adjacency matrix, we can describe the path information and further the trace information of every node.

A primitive adjacency matrix A not only describes the relationship of each node but also reflects all the paths in the network, where the length of all these paths is equal to 1. Moreover, the trace sets of these paths can also be described by the adjacency matrix A. $A_{i,j}$ means that there is a trace of node i indicating its relationships with node j. Furthermore, the matrix A multiplied by itself can be seen as a concatenation of two 1-length paths, where the end node of the former path is the same as the first node of the latter path. In this way, we can obtain the 2-length paths of the network. Repeating this procedure n times, we can acquire the n-length paths of the network. Formally, we use A^n to represent all the n-length paths of the network and yet traces.

Cosine Similarity [25] Cosine similarity is a measure of similarity between two non-zero vectors of an inner product space that measures the cosine of the angle between them. In other words, it determines the orientation of the vectors rather than their magnitude. The smaller the angle between the vectors, the higher the cosine similarity. Formally, given two vectors A and B, the cosine similarity score of A and B can be calculated by

$$similarity(A, B) = \frac{A \cdot B}{|A||B|} = \frac{\sum_{i=1}^{n} A_i B_i}{\sqrt{\sum_{i=1}^{n} A_i^2}\sqrt{\sum_{i=1}^{n} B_i^2}} \tag{1}$$

According to this equation, cosine similarity requires normalizing firstly the length of the two vectors A, B, then measuring the direction of the two vectors and finally resulting in a score of similarity of the two vectors. Cosine similarity is widely used in many research fields, such as natural language processing, information retrieval, and recommendation systems [25,26]. It has the advantageous feature that it is equal to 1 for identical vectors and 0 for orthogonal vectors when all elements of the vector are greater than 0.

In this paper, with adjacency matrix A of an information network indicating the traces deriving from 1-length paths of this network, we use A to show how to calculate the cosine similarity of traces. For two nodes i and j of an information network, their similarity score can be directly calculated by performing cosine similarity of the two vectors A_i and A_j, then the similarity score of these two nodes is calculated by the equation $similarity(A_i, A_j) = \frac{A_i \cdot A_j}{|A_i||A_j|}$.

With the similarity score of traces of two nodes, we can say that two nodes are trace equivalent if and only if $similarity(A_i, A_j) = 1$. Furthermore, since these vectors are used to represent sets of traces, elements of these vectors are usually greater than or equal to 0. The similarity score of each node pair is thus greater than or equal to 0. Based on this property, we stipulate that two nodes i and j are approximate trace equivalent if and only if $0 < similarity(A_i, A_j) < 1$.

Alongside the example in Figure 1, we show the computation steps in Figure 2. Considering three authors in this figure, the adjacency matrix A shows the relations held by three authors and describes the 1-length path of three authors and the traces corresponding to these paths. For the longest meaningful path with a length equal to two in this example, we iterate the matrix multiplication one time to obtain A^2 and obtain the 2-length paths of the information network. We then obtain the vectors representing the traces of every node from these paths. The trace sets of three authors are represented by vectors as follows.

For author a_1, the trace sets are

$$\begin{bmatrix} 0 & 0 & 0 & 1 & 0 & 0 & 0 \end{bmatrix},$$
$$\begin{bmatrix} 1 & 1 & 1 & 0 & 0 & 1 & 0 \end{bmatrix},$$

for author a_2, the trace sets are

$$\begin{bmatrix} 0 & 0 & 0 & 1 & 1 & 0 & 0 \end{bmatrix},$$
$$\begin{bmatrix} 1 & 2 & 2 & 0 & 0 & 1 & 1 \end{bmatrix},$$

and for author a_3, the trace sets are

$$\begin{bmatrix} 0 & 0 & 0 & 1 & 1 & 0 & 0 \end{bmatrix},$$
$$\begin{bmatrix} 1 & 2 & 2 & 0 & 0 & 1 & 1 \end{bmatrix},$$

Applying the cosine similarity measure on each pair of three authors, we obtain the similarity score of each pair:

$$similarity(a_1, a_2) < 1,$$
$$similarity(a_1, a_3) < 1,$$
$$similarity(a_2, a_3) = 1.$$

The results exhibit that authors a_2 and a_3 are trace equivalent since their similarity score is 1, a_1 and a_2 are approximate trace equivalent since their scores are less than 1, and a_1 and a_3 are approximate trace equivalent as well.

For more complex networks, we will iterate the matrix multiplication of adjacency matrix more than two times to fetch more traces and provide more details when determining whether two nodes are trace equivalent. For an information network, we will iterate n times to get $\{A, A^2, \cdots, A^n\}$, which also describes the traces of this information network, and based on traces of every node, we can calculate the similarity score by applying the similarity score function (cosine similarity in this paper).

2.2.3. Derive Trace-Equivalent Networks

With the computational method of trace equivalence, we determine whether two nodes are trace equivalent by computing the similarity score between them in an information network. This section will investigate how to derive a trace-equivalent network from a given information network. Given an information network $G = (V, E, O, R)$, after performing the similarity measure of an information network, we acquire many tuples of trace equivalent nodes in a mathematical way such that (i, j) where i and j are the nodes of information network G, and $T(i) = T(j)$. We use $TE(G)$ to denote the set of all the tuples of trace-equivalent nodes of information network G, formally as

$$TE(G) = \{(i, j) | T(i) = T(j), i \in V, j \in V\}$$

where $TE(G)$ encapsulates the rough trace equivalent node tuples of an information network. In $TE(G)$ of an information network G, the same node can appear in different tuples. The nodes in these different tuples are trace equivalent by the transitive of trace equivalence. We group these nodes by trace equivalence and merge all nodes in these tuples into the same set, which is named the trace-equivalence class.

We use $TEClass$ to formally represent these trace-equivalence classes of the information network G. Each element of $TEClass$ is a group of nodes that are trace equivalent to one another, meaning they have the same trace in the network. The $TEClass$ can be formally noted as

$$TEClass = \{N | \forall i, j \in N, T(i) = T(j), N \subset V\}$$

With the concept of trace-equivalence classes $TEClass$, we are able to simplify the representation of the information network G. By reducing nodes based on these trace-equivalence classes, we can derive a trace-equivalent network. To accomplish this, we select a representative node from each set in $TEClass$, which will be used to replace all nodes in that particular set. The generated trace-equivalent network not only simplifies the original network, but also maintains the essential information. It is a smaller and more manageable network, while still accurately reflecting the trace relationships between nodes. With this basis, we optimize the $TEClass$ as

$$TEClass = \{i \to N | i \in N, \forall j \in N, T(i) = T(j), N \subset V\},$$

where i is the representative node of a trace-equivalence class N. The optimized formula can be easily used in the process of node reduction by using i to replace N.

In Figure 3, continuing with the example in Figure 2, we demonstrate the procedure of generating equivalence classes and choose one representative node of each equivalence class on behalf of the whole class. Subsequently, we can derive the trace-equivalent network from the original information network. In this simple example, $TE(G) = (a_2, a_3)$ only contains one tuple, and hence, it is also the only equivalence class of this network. We choose a_2 to represent the whole equivalence class, and the result shows that one node and two edges are reduced in the new trace-equivalent network.

We use $G_{TE} = G \mod TE(G)$ to formally represent the derived network in which notation mod represents the procedure of reducing nodes by trace equivalences. G_{TE} encapsulates the complete structural information of the original network, which describes the relationships of the network, representing each equivalence class with one specific node, making it possible to reduce duplicate nodes and edges of the information network while preserving structural information. The representative nodes and edges of the same equivalence class hold the information of reduced nodes and edges. To state the method of deriving trace-equivalent networks more clearly, we summarize the above steps into Algorithm 1.

Algorithm 1: Deriving trace-equivalent network from an given network.

Input: Information Network $G = (V, E, O, R)$, Adjacency Matrix A, Threshold T
Output: Trace-equivalent Network G_{TE}

Pre calculate $A^2, A^3, \cdots, A^n$;
$TE(G) = \emptyset$;
$TEClass = \{\}$;
`/* Calculate the set of trace equivalent tuples` $TE(G)$ `*/`
for $i = 1$ *to* n **do**
    for $a_j, a_k \in A_i, a_j \neq a_k$ **do**
        Calculate the cosine similarity score $similarity(a_j, a_k)$;
        if $similarity(a_j, a_k) > T$ **then**
            Append (j, k) to $TE(G)$;
        end
    end
end
`/* Refine` $TE(G)$ `into trace equivalent classes */`
for *Tuple* $tetuple = (j, k) \in TE(G)$ **do**
    Merge all tuples that are not *tetuple* which contains the element j or k into *tetuple* ;
    Choose one representative node $tNode$ in $tetuple$;
    Append $tNode \rightarrow tetuple$ to $TEClass$;
    Remove nodes in $tetuple$ that are not $tNode$ from Graph G ;
end
Constitute $G_{TE} = G \mod TEClass$.

With the G_{TE} having fewer nodes and edges than the original, it is possible to accelerate data mining algorithms since less information leads to fewer computations while executing these algorithms. Another problem we need to figure out is, though less information leads to fewer computations, the accuracy of these algorithms while maintaining consistent or approximate accuracy of the original network. In this paper, we choose the Pathsim algorithm to verify the maintainability of data mining algorithms on both G and G_{TE}. We prove that the accuracy of Pathsim algorithms on G and G_{TE} is consistent.

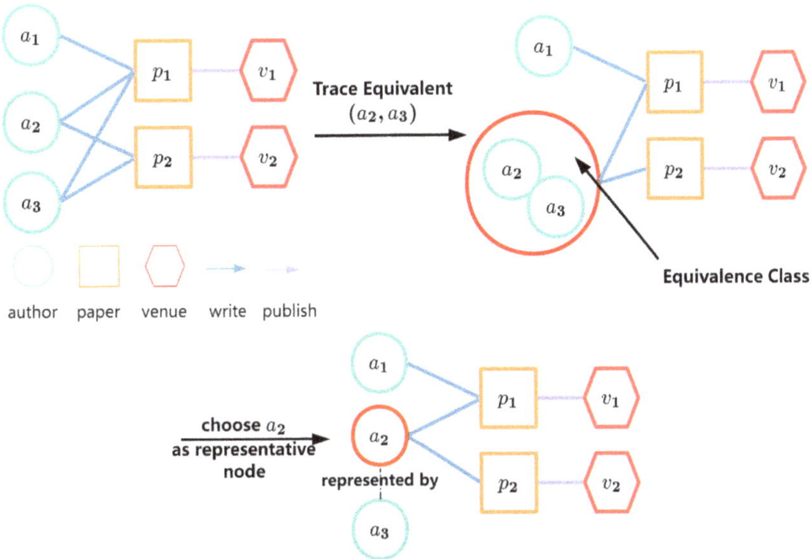

Figure 3. Procedure of generating equivalence class and choosing one representative node of equivalence class on behalf of the whole class.

Definition 3. ***Pathsim*** *[27]. Given an information network G, Pathsim measures the correlation of two entities x and y under a meta-path $\mathcal{P}$. The core component of the Pathsim algorithm is as follows.*

$$s(x,y) = \frac{2 \times |\{p_{x \rightsquigarrow y} : p_{x \rightsquigarrow y} \in \mathcal{P}\}|}{|\{p_{x \rightsquigarrow x} : p_{x \rightsquigarrow x} \in \mathcal{P}\}| + |\{p_{y \rightsquigarrow y} : p_{y \rightsquigarrow y} \in \mathcal{P}\}|} \tag{2}$$

where $p_{x \rightsquigarrow y}$ is a path instance between x and y, $p_{x \rightsquigarrow x}$ is a path instance between x and x and $p_{y \rightsquigarrow y}$ is a path instance between y and y. For elaboration, a meta path $\mathcal{P}$ is defined on (O, R) and denoted as $O_1 \xrightarrow{R_1} O_2 \xrightarrow{R_2} \cdots \xrightarrow{R_l} O_{l+1}$ so that it illustrates the relation between node types.

Theorem 1. *The results of Pathsim are consistent on the original network G and its trace-equivalent network G_{TE}, i.e., the results of Pathsim are maintainable.*

Proof. Given an information network $G = (V, E, O, R)$, node $v_1 \in V$ and node $v_2 \in V$ are trace equivalent. Then, for every reachable node $v_r \in V$ from node v_1 and v_2, $v_r \neq v_1 \neq v_2$,

$Pathsim(v_1, v_r) = \frac{2 \times |\{p_{v_1 \rightsquigarrow v_r}\}|}{|\{p_{v_1 \rightsquigarrow v_1}\}| + |\{p_{v_r \rightsquigarrow v_r}\}|}$,

$Pathsim(v_2, v_r) = \frac{2 \times |\{p_{v_2 \rightsquigarrow v_r}\}|}{|\{p_{v_2 \rightsquigarrow v_2}\}| + |\{p_{v_r \rightsquigarrow v_r}\}|}$,

Because node v_1 and node v_2 are trace equivalent,

$T(v_1) = T(v_2)$,

then for node v_r, the trace from node v_1 to node v_r and the trace from node v_2 to node v_r are equal.

Based on Definition 1, the paths from node v_1 to node v_r and the paths from node v_2 to node v_r are identical.

Then, $|\{p_{v_1 \rightsquigarrow v_r}\}| = |\{p_{v_2 \rightsquigarrow v_r}\}|$.

Similarly, we can obtain $|\{p_{v_1 \rightsquigarrow v_1}\} = |\{p_{v_2 \rightsquigarrow v_2}\}$,

So, $Pathsim(v_1, v_r) = Pathsim(v_2, v_r)$.

In $G's$ trace-equivalent network G_{TE}, v_1 and v_2 are in the same equivalence class. We choose v_1 to represent this equivalence class. With $Pathsim(v_1, v_r) = Pathsim(v_2, v_r)$, the results of Pathsim are consistent.

Therefore, the results of Pathsim are maintainable. □

Trace equivalence indicates that $similarity(v_1, v_2) = 1$. Meanwhile, approximate trace equivalence indicates $similarity(v_1, v_2) < 1$. The smaller the $similarity(v_1, v_2)$, the greater the difference of the Pathsim results between them. In the next section, we verify that our proof is correct through experiments.

3. Experiments and Discussion

In this section, we experiment on public real-world datasets to verify the availability of reduction by trace equivalence in information networks and verify the maintainability of data mining algorithms between trace-equivalent networks and original networks.

3.1. Datasets

We use the public ACM and DBLP datasets in [28]. ACM and DBLP datasets are both bibliographic networks of academic publications. These two datasets are representative information networks and are widely used in various tasks.

ACM. The ACM dataset from [28], also known as HGBn-ACM, is utilized in this study. It consists of four types of entities: 5959 authors (A), 3025 papers (P), 1902 terms (T), and 56 subjects (S). The relationships in the dataset are established through connections, such as 9949 paper–author (P-A), 5343 paper–paper (P-P), 3025 paper–subject (P-S), and 225,619 paper–term (P-T) connections. This paper focuses on the author (A) type due to the availability of labeled nodes, allowing for a further investigation into their label consistency under trace equivalence. Our task is to reduce the number of author nodes in the dataset through trace equivalence.

DBLP. The DBLP dataset, originating from [28], is known as HGNn-DBLP. It consists of four types of entities: 4057 authors (A), 14,328 papers (P), 7723 terms (T), and 56 venues (V). The relationships in the dataset are established through connections such as 19,645 author–paper (P-A), 85,810 paper–term (P-T), and 14,328 paper–venue (P-V) connections. Similar to the focus in the ACM dataset, this study concentrates on the author (A) type in the DBLP dataset due to the labeled nodes in this type of entity. Our task is also to reduce the number of author nodes in the dataset.

Statistics of these datasets are illustrated in Table 2.

Table 2. Statistics of ACM and DBLP Datasets.

Datasets	Nodes				Edges			
ACM	author 5959	paper 3025	term 1902	subject 56	paper-author 9949	paper-paper 5343	paper-subject 3025	paper-term 225,619
DBLP	author 4057	paper 14,328	term 7723	venue 20	author-paper 19,645	paper-term 85,810	paper-venue 14,328	

3.2. Reduction of Nodes by Trace Equivalence

In this subsection, we test the reduction of nodes in information networks by trace equivalence. According to Algorithm 1, we first calculate $A^2, A_3, \cdots, A_n$ for the subsequent similarity measure. The parameter n should be designed for different datasets according to their structures. In this paper, we set $n = 2$ for the ACM dataset and $n = 3$ for the DBLP dataset. Then the cosine similarity is utilized to measure the similarity of each pair of nodes in these networks. The threshold is pre-defined and used to filter the pairs of nodes whose similarity score is greater than or equal to the pre-defined threshold. Consequently, we leverage these pairs of nodes to constitute the final trace-equivalence class. Those nodes that are in the same trace-equivalence class will be replaced by a representative node inside this class and eventually will be reduced in the final trace-equivalent network. We record the number of the replaced nodes and show the ability of trace equivalence to simplify information networks.

Through the above steps, we record the number of reduced nodes in ACM and DBLP datasets. The results of the experiments are shown in Table 3. Results prove that it is feasible to reduce nodes and edges by leveraging trace equivalence. The results also reflect the duplicate information problem of these two information networks such that these datasets have duplicate nodes under trace equivalence.

Table 3. Results of node reduction by trace equivalence. RN: number of nodes reduced, Ra: ratio of reduced nodes to the total number of nodes, T: threshold.

Datasets	RN	Ra(%)	T	Datasets	RN	Ra(%)	T
	1603	26.90	1.0		150	3.70	1.0
	1634	27.42	0.9		166	4.09	0.9
	1830	30.71	0.8		233	5.74	0.8
	2267	38.04	0.7		355	8.75	0.7
ACM	2642	44.33	0.6	DBLP	503	12.40	0.6
	2960	49.67	0.5		757	18.66	0.5
	3259	54.69	0.4		1030	25.39	0.4
	3482	58.43	0.3		1361	33.55	0.3
	3720	62.42	0.2		1659	40.89	0.2
	3886	65.21	0.1		1894	46.68	0.1

Focusing on the trace-equivalent scenario, the similarity threshold equals 1.0. The number of reduction nodes is 1603 in the ACM dataset and 150 in the DBLP dataset. The number of all author nodes in the ACM dataset is 5959, and the corresponding number in the DBLP dataset is 4057 so that the ratio of nodes that are reduced to the total nodes is 26.90% and 3.70%, respectively. The difference in the number of reduction nodes and the ratio of reduced nodes reflects the varying degrees of duplication present in the original networks. The trace equivalence thus serves as a metric to reflect the degree of duplication in the datasets. The higher the number of reduction nodes and the ratio of reduced nodes, the greater the similarity between nodes, indicating a higher degree of duplication. This information can be useful in various fields, such as data science, network analysis, and graph theory, where it is important to identify the degree of duplication in a network and make decisions based on that information.

Moreover, the exact threshold of 1.0 for each dataset may lead to different results for different datasets. This is due to the nature of the data and the structure of the network. Therefore, it is important to understand the characteristics of the data and the network structure to determine the most appropriate threshold value. This will ensure that the results are accurate and relevant to the specific network being analyzed.

In addition to the trace-equivalence scenario, the experiments also consider the approximate trace-equivalence scenario. In this scenario, the cosine similarity score, which measures the similarity between nodes, ranges from 0 to 1. To determine the approximate trace equivalence, the range of similarity scores is divided into ten equal pieces, and the right boundary of each piece is used as a threshold to compare pairs of nodes.

The results, as shown in Table 3 and Figures 4 and 5, provide a comprehensive understanding of the node reduction process. The detailed statistics of the node reduction on both ACM and DBLP datasets are clearly presented in Table 3. This provides a clear picture of the number of nodes that have been reduced and the ratio of reduced nodes to the total nodes. Moreover, the visual representations in Figures 4 and 5 further support the information presented in Table 3 by providing an intuitive understanding of the data. The visual representation clearly shows that as the similarity threshold increases, the number of reduced nodes decreases. This highlights the trade-off between accuracy and efficiency in network reduction. By increasing the similarity threshold, a higher degree of similarity is required for node reduction, leading to a smaller number of reduced nodes but a more accurate representation of the network. This highlights the trade-off between accuracy and efficiency in network reduction. By using a higher similarity threshold, a higher degree of similarity is required for node reduction, leading to a smaller number of reduced nodes but a more accurate representation of the network.

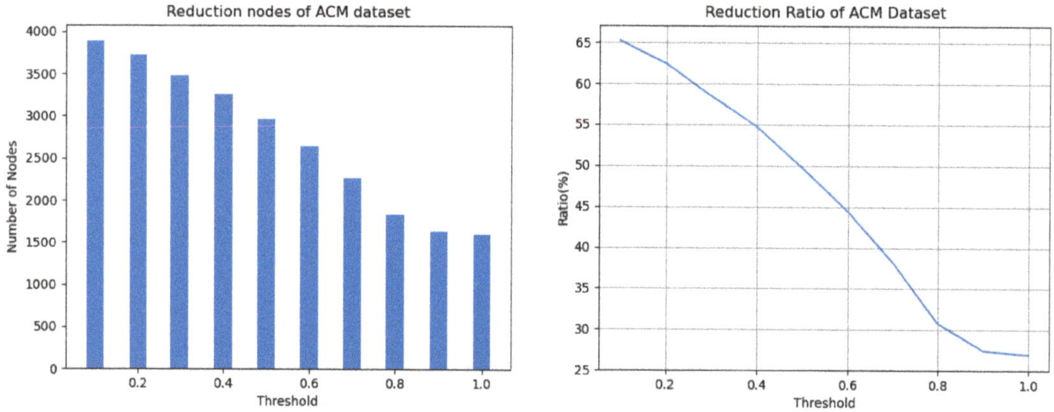

Figure 4. Histogram of the number of nodes reduced by trace equivalence (**Left**) and trend of the ratio of reduced nodes to total nodes (**Right**) on ACM dataset.

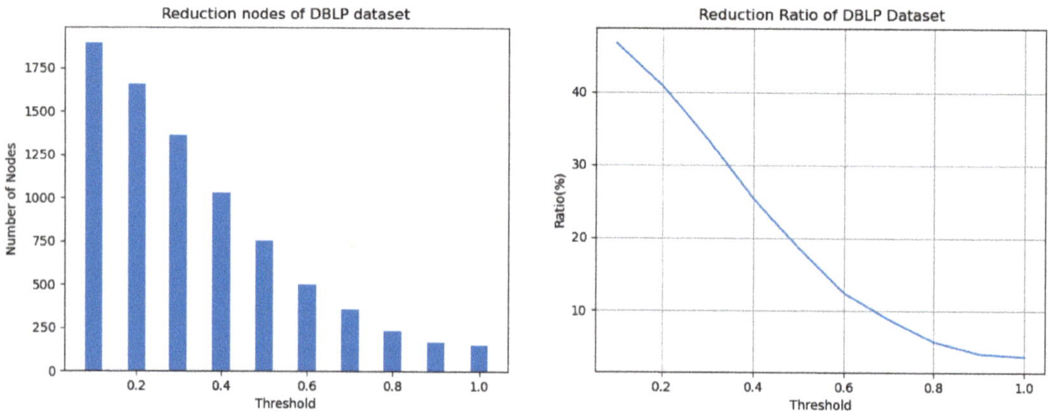

Figure 5. Histogram of the number of nodes reduced by trace equivalence (**Left**) and trend of the ratio of reduced nodes to total nodes (**Right**) on DBLP dataset.

In conclusion, the results of the node reduction experiments on ACM and DBLP datasets demonstrate the effectiveness of the trace-equivalence scenario and approximate trace-equivalence scenario in reducing duplicated nodes in networks. The statistics and visual representations in Table 3, Figures 4 and 5 highlight the trade-off between accuracy and efficiency in the network reduction. The results show that as the similarity threshold increases, the number of reduced nodes decreases, providing a more accurate representation of the network. This information is also valuable for various fields, where identifying the degree of duplication in a network is crucial. For example, in bibliographic network analysis, it can help to eliminate duplicate author nodes, resulting in a more comprehensive and cleaner network representation. In data analysis, it can be used to identify and remove duplicate records in a dataset, leading to a more accurate representation of the data. Moreover, there are also various ways to further extend and improve the methodology and techniques used in this study. For example, one can consider using different similarity measures or combining multiple similarity measures to provide a more comprehensive and accurate representation of node similarity.

3.3. Maintainability of Pathsim Algorithm

In this subsection, we assess the maintainability of data mining algorithms in both the original network and its trace-equivalent network. The maintainability of data mining algorithms refers to the ability to retain the precision and reliability of the results obtained from the algorithms when they are applied to the trace-equivalent network. To do so, we utilize a derived network that has fewer nodes and edges and compare the results of the data mining algorithms to ensure they are either identical or approximate.

We rigorously evaluate the performance of our approach through the application of the PathSim algorithm [27] on the ACM and DBLP datasets in this experiment. Our analysis involves running the PathSim algorithm on both the original network and its trace-equivalent network, and measuring the error between the results produced by the original network and those produced by the trace-equivalent network. To provide a comprehensive evaluation, we record the highest error value as the maximum error, the lowest error value as the minimum error, and the average of all error values as the mean error. Moreover, we meticulously analyze the maximum error, minimum error, and mean error under a range of threshold values to gain a deeper understanding of our approach's effectiveness. Our findings are presented in Table 4.

Table 4. Results of maintainability mining by PathSim algorithms. Max-E: maximum error, Min-E: minimum error, Mean-E: mean error, T: threshold.

Datasets	Max-E	Min-E	Mean-E	T	Datasets	Max-E	Min-E	Mean-E	T
ACM	0	0	0	1.0	DBLP	0	0	0	1.0
	0	0	0	0.99		0	0	0	**0.99**
	0	0	0	0.98		3.33×10^{-2}	2×10^{-4}	1.28×10^{-2}	0.98
	0	0	0	0.97		7.2×10^{-2}	5.7924×10^{-6}	7.2×10^{-3}	0.97
	0	0	0	0.96		9.59×10^{-2}	7.7896×10^{-7}	1.66×10^{-2}	0.96
	0	0	0	**0.95**		9.59×10^{-2}	7.79×10^{-7}	1.66×10^{-2}	0.95
	0.1	1.4818×10^{-5}	6.43×10^{-2}	0.94		0.1	7.7896×10^{-7}	2.44×10^{-2}	0.94
	0.17	5.0402×10^{-6}	6×10^{-2}	0.93		0.16	7.7896×10^{-7}	2.59×10^{-2}	0.93
	0.17	5.0402×10^{-6}	5.71×10^{-2}	0.92		0.17	1.7609×10^{-7}	3.72×10^{-2}	0.92
	0.2	1.3144×10^{-6}	6.34×10^{-2}	0.91		0.2	1.5792×10^{-7}	3.68×10^{-2}	0.91
	0.2	1.3144×10^{-6}	7.28×10^{-2}	0.90		0.2	1.5792×10^{-7}	4.46×10^{-2}	0.90

Our results reveal that when the threshold value is set above 0.95 for ACM and 0.99 for DBLP, the PathSim algorithms produce identical results on both the original network and its trace-equivalent network, with 100% consistency. This confirms the maintainability of data mining algorithms, demonstrating that the trace-equivalent network can serve as a reliable substitute for the original network while maintaining the accuracy and dependability of the results obtained from the algorithms.

Continuing from our previous experiment, we divide $[0.90, 1.00]$ into ten pieces and use each boundary as the threshold value. Our findings, displayed in Table 4 and Figures 6 and 7, reveal that the degree of inconsistency, mainly indicated by the mean error, increases as the threshold value decreases. Although 0.99 and 0.95 are considered threshold values that indicate approximate trace equivalence instead of trace equivalence, we discovered that approximate trace equivalence can sometimes serve as a substitute for trace equivalence, enabling us to simplify the network further by reducing even more nodes. This highlights the potential trade-off between network simplicity and consistency of the results, and underscores the importance of considering the appropriate threshold value when evaluating trace-equivalent networks.

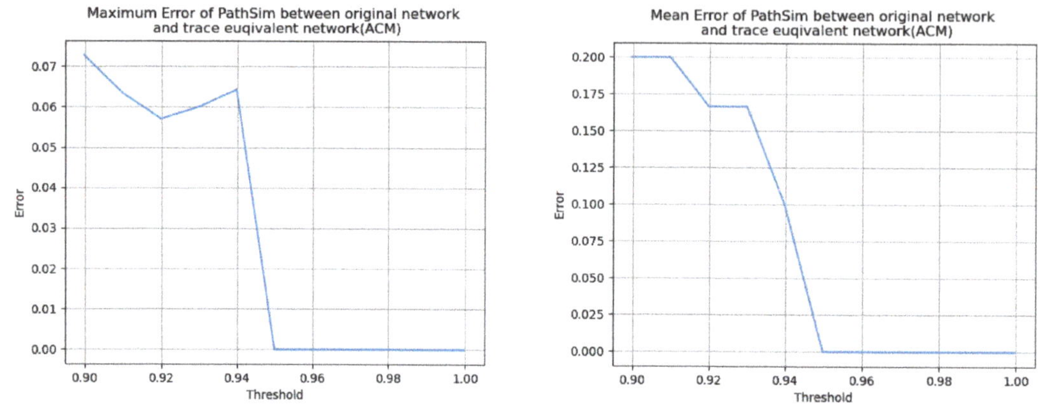

Figure 6. Trend of maximum error (**Left**) and mean error (**Right**) of PathSim on ACM between original network and trace-equivalent network.

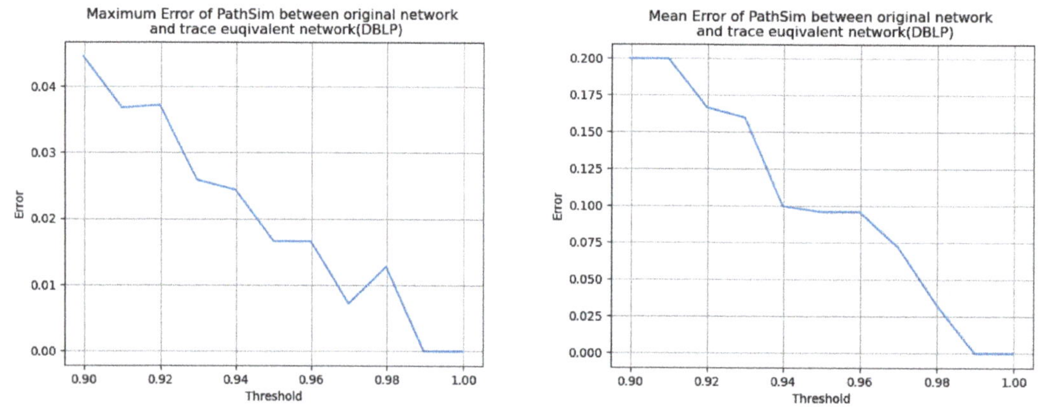

Figure 7. Trend of maximum error (**Left**) and mean error (**Right**) of PathSim on DBLP between original network and trace-equivalent network.

In conclusion, this subsection evaluated the maintainability of data mining algorithms in both the original network and its trace-equivalent network. The results showed that the degree of inconsistency increases as the threshold value decreases, with 100% consistency when the threshold value is set above 0.95 for ACM and 0.99 for DBLP. The findings confirmed the maintainability of data mining algorithms, demonstrating that the trace-equivalent network can serve as a reliable substitute for the original network while maintaining the accuracy and dependability of results obtained from algorithms. The results also highlighted the trade-off between network simplicity and consistency of results and the importance of considering the appropriate threshold value when evaluating trace-equivalent networks. Furthermore, the results also provide useful guidelines for network analysis. By demonstrating the maintainability of data mining algorithms on trace-equivalent networks, we can simplify large, complex networks without sacrificing the precision and reliability of results obtained from algorithms. This can greatly enhance the efficiency and scalability of network analysis, making it easier to gain valuable insights from large datasets.

Label Consistency. In addition to evaluating the maintainability of data mining algorithms, this study also explored the consistency of labels in the ACM and DBLP datasets. The nodes of the type author in these datasets were labeled for the purpose of machine learning and deep learning, and the labeled data were used to verify the consistency of the labels. The results, displayed in Table 5 and Figure 8, showed that as the threshold value increased, the degree of inconsistency in the labels decreased. It suggests that the larger the threshold gets, the less the inconsistency with which the label appears. Moreover, this also shows one possible future direction in which we can leverage trace equivalence to handle classification or clustering tasks. By leveraging trace equivalence to handle classification or clustering tasks, researchers and practitioners can simplify the network and reduce noise in the data, which can greatly enhance the accuracy and performance of machine learning and deep learning algorithms. Furthermore, these results suggest that trace equivalence can play a key role in improving the robustness of machine learning and deep learning algorithms in complex networked systems. By reducing noise and inconsistencies in the data, trace equivalence can help improve the performance and reliability of these algorithms, enabling them to produce more accurate and meaningful results. This finding has important implications for the application of trace equivalence in machine learning and deep learning.

Table 5. Statistics of node labels consistency on ACM and DBLP datasets under trace equivalence. TL: number of total nodes appear in trace equivalence classes, IC: number of nodes whose label is inconsistent in their trace equivalence class, T: threshold.

Datasets	TL	IC	T	Datasets	TL	IC	T
ACM	60	1	0.9	DBLP	16	2	0.9
	69	3	0.8		19	2	0.8
	95	19	0.7		31	2	0.7
	121	30	0.6		47	3	0.6
	148	48	0.5		61	4	0.5
	163	60	0.4		91	7	0.4
	213	99	0.3		128	10	0.3
	440	243	0.2		169	23	0.2
	1232	740	0.1		205	40	0.1

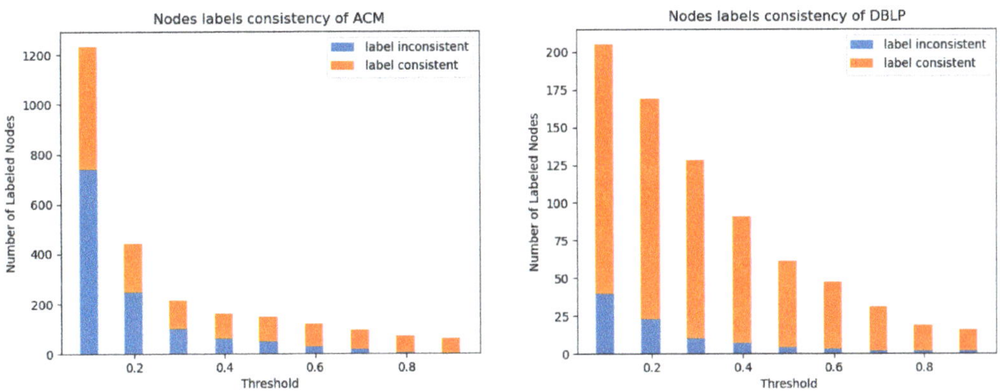

Figure 8. Histogram of node labels consistency on ACM (**Left**) and DBLP (**Right**) datasets under trace equivalence.

4. Conclusions and Future Directions

In this study, we propose the utilization of trace equivalence from the field of concurrent systems as a means to simplify information networks. By defining the concepts of trace and trace equivalence in information networks, we have developed a computational method for deriving trace-equivalent networks from original information networks. To evaluate the effectiveness of our approach, we conducted experiments on two widely used datasets, the ACM and DBLP networks. The results of our experiments showed that the use of trace equivalence reduced the number of nodes by up to 65.21% in ACM and 46.68%

in DBLP while maintaining the accuracy and reliability of the results obtained from data mining algorithms.

We applied the PathSim algorithm to both the original and trace-equivalent networks and compared the results to determine the consistency between the two. The analysis showed that when the threshold value was set above 0.95 for ACM and 0.99 for DBLP, the PathSim algorithms produced identical results on both networks, with 100% consistency. This shows that not only trace-equivalence networks but also approximate trace-equivalence networks can serve as a reliable substitute for the original network. However, as the threshold value decreased, the degree of inconsistency, as indicated by the mean error, increased. Our findings, which are further reinforced by the results of the labeled data of the datasets, demonstrate the effectiveness of using trace equivalence as a means of simplifying information networks while preserving their information content. These results hold significant implications for future research in the field and the practical application of trace equivalence in information networks.

In the future, we plan to further investigate the potential of other equivalence concepts from the process theory of concurrent systems and how they can be applied to information networks. This research has the potential to not only simplify large and complex networks, but also to enhance the efficiency and accuracy of data mining tasks. As such, we believe that the use of trace equivalence in information networks holds great promise for future research and practical applications.

Author Contributions: Conceptualization, R.L., J.W. and W.H.; methodology, R.L., J.W. and W.H.; software, R.L.; validation, R.L. and W.H.; formal analysis, R.L., J.W. and W.H.; investigation, R.L.; resources, R.L.; data curation, R.L.; writing—original draft preparation, R.L.; writing—review and editing, R.L., J.W. and W.H.; visualization, R.L.; supervision, J.W.; project administration, J.W.; funding acquisition, J.W. All authors have read and agreed to the published version of the manuscript.

Funding: This research was funded by the National Natural Science Foundation OF China grant number 12261027.

Data Availability Statement: The data presented in this study are openly available in OpenHGNN Public at https://doi.org/10.1145/3511808.3557664 (accessed on 21 October 2022) , reference number [28].

Conflicts of Interest: The authors declare no conflict of interest.

References

1. van Glabbeek, R.J. The linear time-branching time spectrum. In Proceedings of the 1th International Conference on Concurrency Theory (CONCUR'90), Amsterdam, The Netherlands, 27–30 August 1990; pp. 278–297.
2. Clarke, E.M.; Henzinger, T.A.; Veith, H.; Bloem, R. *Handbook of Model Checking*; Springer: Berlin/Heidelberg, Germany, 2018; Volume 10.
3. van Glabbeek, R.J. The Linear Time—Branching Time Spectrum I. In *Handbook of Process Algebra*; Bergstra, J., Ponse, A., Smolka, S., Eds.; Elsevier Science: Amsterdam, The Netherlands, 2001; pp. 3–99. [CrossRef]
4. van Glabbeek, R.J. The linear time-branching time spectrum II. In Proceedings of the 4th International Conference on Concurrency Theory (CONCUR'93), Hildesheim, Germany, 23–26 August 1993; pp. 66–81.
5. He, H.; Wu, J.; Xiong, J. Approximate Completed Trace Equivalence of ILAHSs Based on SAS Solving. *Information* **2019**, *10*, 340. [CrossRef]
6. Hoare, C. *A Model for Communicating Sequential Process*; Department of Computing Science Working Paper Series; University of Wollongong: Wollongong, NSW, Australia, 1980; Volume 80.
7. Mazurkiewicz, A. Trace theory. In *Petri Nets: Applications and Relationships to Other Models of Concurrency*; Brauer, W., Reisig, W., Rozenberg, G., Eds.; Springer: Berlin/Heidelberg, Germany, 1987; pp. 278–324.
8. Hoare, C.A.R. Communicating Sequential Processes. *Commun. ACM* **1978**, *21*, 666–677. [CrossRef]
9. Cheval, V.; Comon-Lundh, H.; Delaune, S. Trace Equivalence Decision: Negative Tests and Non-Determinism. In Proceedings of the 18th ACM Conference on Computer and Communications Security, Chicago, IL, USA, 17–21 October 2011; Association for Computing Machinery: New York, NY, USA, 2011; pp. 321–330. [CrossRef]
10. Wang, C. Polynomial Algebraic Event Structure and Their Approximation and Approximate Equivalences. Ph.D. Thesis, Beijing Jiaotong University, Beijing, China, 2016.
11. Baelde, D.; Delaune, S.; Hirschi, L. A Reduced Semantics for Deciding Trace Equivalence. *Log. Methods Comput. Sci.* **2017**, *13*, lmcs:3703. [CrossRef]

12. Zheng, X.; Liu, Y.; Pan, S.; Zhang, M.; Jin, D.; Yu, P.S. Graph Neural Networks for Graphs with Heterophily: A Survey. *arXiv* **2022**, arXiv:2202.07082. [CrossRef].
13. Xie, Y.; Yu, B.; Lv, S.; Zhang, C.; Wang, G.; Gong, M. A survey on heterogeneous network representation learning. *Pattern Recognit.* **2021**, *116*, 107936. [CrossRef]
14. Shi, C.; Yu, P.S. Recent Developments of Deep Heterogeneous Information Network Analysis. In Proceedings of the 28th ACM International Conference on Information and Knowledge Management, Beijing, China, 3–7 November 2019; Association for Computing Machinery: New York, NY, USA, 2019; pp. 2973–2974. [CrossRef]
15. Yang, C.; Zou, J.; Wu, J.; Xu, H.; Fan, S. Supervised contrastive learning for recommendation. *Knowl.-Based Syst.* **2022**, *258*, 109973. [CrossRef]
16. Zhou, J.; Cui, G.; Hu, S.; Zhang, Z.; Yang, C.; Liu, Z.; Wang, L.; Li, C.; Sun, M. Graph neural networks: A review of methods and applications. *AI Open* **2020**, *1*, 57–81. [CrossRef]
17. Yu, P.; Fu, C.; Yu, Y.; Huang, C.; Zhao, Z.; Dong, J. Multiplex Heterogeneous Graph Convolutional Network. In Proceedings of the 28th ACM SIGKDD Conference on Knowledge Discovery and Data Mining, Washington, DC, USA, 14–18 August 2022; Association for Computing Machinery: New York, NY, USA, 2022; pp. 2377–2387. [CrossRef]
18. Wu, S.; Sun, F.; Zhang, W.; Xie, X.; Cui, B. Graph Neural Networks in Recommender Systems: A Survey. *ACM Comput. Surv.* **2022**, *55*, 1–37. [CrossRef]
19. Bouritsas, G.; Frasca, F.; Zafeiriou, S.; Bronstein, M.M. Improving Graph Neural Network Expressivity via Subgraph Isomorphism Counting. *IEEE Trans. Pattern Anal. Mach. Intell.* **2023**, *45*, 657–668. [CrossRef] [PubMed]
20. Xie, Y.; Xu, Z.; Zhang, J.; Wang, Z.; Ji, S. Self-Supervised Learning of Graph Neural Networks: A Unified Review. *IEEE Trans. Pattern Anal. Mach. Intell.* **2022**, *45*, 2412–2429. [CrossRef] [PubMed]
21. Fu, X.; Zhang, J.; Meng, Z.; King, I. MAGNN: Metapath Aggregated Graph Neural Network for Heterogeneous Graph Embedding. In Proceedings of the Web Conference 2020, Taipei, Taiwan, 20–24 April 2020; Association for Computing Machinery: New York, NY, USA, 2020; pp. 2331–2341. [CrossRef]
22. Zhao, J.; Wang, X.; Shi, C.; Hu, B.; Song, G.; Ye, Y. Heterogeneous Graph Structure Learning for Graph Neural Networks. In Proceedings of the AAAI Conference on Artificial Intelligence, Virtually, 2–9 February 2021; Volume 35, pp. 4697–4705. [CrossRef]
23. Pang, Y.; Wu, L.; Shen, Q.; Zhang, Y.; Wei, Z.; Xu, F.; Chang, E.; Long, B.; Pei, J. Heterogeneous Global Graph Neural Networks for Personalized Session-Based Recommendation. In Proceedings of the Fifteenth ACM International Conference on Web Search and Data Mining, Tempe, AZ, USA, 21–25 February 2022; Association for Computing Machinery: New York, NY, USA, 2022; pp. 775–783. [CrossRef]
24. Lv, Q.; Ding, M.; Liu, Q.; Chen, Y.; Feng, W.; He, S.; Zhou, C.; Jiang, J.; Dong, Y.; Tang, J. Are We Really Making Much Progress? Revisiting, Benchmarking and Refining Heterogeneous Graph Neural Networks. In Proceedings of the 27th ACM SIGKDD Conference on Knowledge Discovery and Data Mining, Singapore, 14–18 August 2021; Association for Computing Machinery: New York, NY, USA, 2021; pp. 1150–1160. [CrossRef]
25. Singhal, A. Modern information retrieval: A brief overview. *IEEE Data Eng. Bull.* **2001**, *24*, 35–43.
26. Ozella, L.; Price, E.; Langford, J.; Lewis, K.E.; Cattuto, C.; Croft, D.P. Association networks and social temporal dynamics in ewes and lambs. *Appl. Anim. Behav. Sci.* **2022**, *246*, 105515. [CrossRef]
27. Sun, Y.; Han, J.; Yan, X.; Yu, P.S.; Wu, T. PathSim: Meta Path-Based Top-K Similarity Search in Heterogeneous Information Networks. *Proc. VLDB Endow.* **2020**, *4*, 992–1003. [CrossRef]
28. Han, H.; Zhao, T.; Yang, C.; Zhang, H.; Liu, Y.; Wang, X.; Shi, C. OpenHGNN: An Open Source Toolkit for Heterogeneous Graph Neural Network. In Proceedings of the 31st ACM International Conference on Information and Knowledge Management, Atlanta, GA, USA, 17–21 October 2022; Association for Computing Machinery: New York, NY, USA, 2022; pp. 3993–3997. [CrossRef]

electronics

Article

Handling Class Imbalance and Class Overlap in Machine Learning Applications for Undeclared Work Prediction

Eleni Alogogianni * and Maria Virvou

Department of Informatics, University of Piraeus, 80, M. Karaoli & A. Dimitriou str., 185 34 Piraeus, Greece
* Correspondence: alogogianni@unipi.gr; Tel.: +30-697-96-24-529

Abstract: Undeclared work is a composite socioeconomic matter severely affecting the welfare of workers, legitimate companies, and the state by issuing unfair competition in the labour market and causing considerable state revenue losses by tax evasion. Labour inspectorates are tasked to deal effectively with this issue but usually lack adequate resources and proper tools, yet they own large volumes of past inspection data that, if aptly processed through innovative machine learning techniques, may produce understandable insights into the extent and prevailing patterns of undeclared work and efficient tools to address it. Such datasets are typically imbalanced regarding undeclared work, and contain overlapping inspection discoveries, two issues that impede the learning process. This research points to the problems of class imbalance and class overlap in this domain and applies combinations of data engineering techniques to address them using a dataset of 16.7 K actual labour inspections. Three associative classification algorithms are employed, and multiple classifiers are built and assessed for their predictability and interpretability. The study indicates the overall benefits for the inspection authorities when integrating machine learning methods in targeting undeclared work and proves considerable prediction performance improvement when following data engineering approaches to address the class imbalance and class overlap issues.

Keywords: class imbalance; class overlap; data mining; machine learning; predictive modelling; undeclared work; labour inspectorate; public authority; informal economy; tax evasion

Citation: Alogogianni, E.; Virvou, M. Handling Class Imbalance and Class Overlap in Machine Learning Applications for Undeclared Work Prediction. *Electronics* **2023**, *12*, 913. https://doi.org/10.3390/electronics12040913

Academic Editor: Ping-Feng Pai

Received: 28 December 2022
Revised: 26 January 2023
Accepted: 6 February 2023
Published: 11 February 2023

1. Introduction

Undeclared work is a serious and complex problem that strongly impacts society and the economy. It is defined as paid activities that are lawful, as regards their nature, but are not declared to the public authorities to avoid tax and social security contribution payments and to bypass specific legal standards per labour law [1,2]. Consequently, undeclared work severely undermines the well-being of workers, who are usually paid below the minimum wages and may work under unsafe conditions; of the lawful businesses by introducing unfair competitiveness in the labour market; and of the state through significant losses in tax revenues and insurance contributions. This illegal employment pattern has several causes and features and displays considerable heterogeneity since it can be located in various work environments and business sectors, involving a labour force of different profiles and backgrounds [3]. In addition, it is inherently hidden, making its detection by the inspection authorities even more complicated, requiring more sophisticated approaches [4].

In particular, labour inspectorates are tasked to deal with this illegal phenomenon in the labour market, yet they often face practical issues, lacking the appropriate tools and resources to plan and coordinate effective deterrence and preventative measures. They usually perform random checks or ground their inspection scheduling in filed complaints or risk analysis tools that use red flag indicators, manually configured based on labour inspection expertise [5]. Yet, these high-risk indicators may contain a lot of bias and finally exclude specific groups of businesses from being inspected, or may trigger repetitive and redundant onsite inspections [6]. Hence, a shift towards innovative data-driven solutions is indispensable, even more so when large volumes of related data are available and may be appropriately processed and analysed [7]. Notably, data mining and machine learning applications can generate models trained on past inspection data, offering predictions on future checks and understandable knowledge regarding the most prevailing patterns of undeclared work and other labour law infringements. In addition, machine learning systems are convenient to use and maintain; they contain less prejudice and more justice [8], and can explain how predictions are made, raising the user's confidence in following them [9].

Undeclared work is comprehensively studied in the social and economic sciences, e.g., [2,10]; multiple surveys are conducted by the EC [1,11,12], targeting to expose its prevalence, nature, and specificities; and different organisations identify it as one of their major priorities for policy measures, such as the European Labour Authority (ELA) [13,14] and the European Platform Tackling Undeclared Work [15], the International Labour Organization (ILO) [3,4], and the Organization for Economic Cooperation and Development (OECD) [16]. Although the adverse effects and impact of informal employment on society and the economy are vastly recognised, not much research was published until recently related to applying data mining and machine learning techniques in its prediction and understanding [17]. This fact triggered our first research in the field [18], employing Association Rule Mining (ARM) [19] and a dataset of 2.5 K actual past inspections performed by the Hellenic Labour Inspectorate (HLI) in a specific area and period. The dataset instances were labelled per the inspection findings, taking values among four main categories of discoveries, one of which, undeclared work, had our primary interest. That research revealed the considerable advantages of using innovative data-driven techniques to produce understandable outcomes, exposing specific correlations of company and employment features with inspection outcomes that existed in the dataset but were previously unknown to the labour inspection experts of the authority. The study also identified the prospects of applying machine learning in undeclared work prediction and motivated further exploration by adopting interpretable classification modelling.

Thus, in [20], we applied Associative Classification (AC), which refers to supervised machine learning using ARM, generating classification models comprised of a set of interpretable class association rules (CARs), of the simple form of if-then rules, that meet the user-configurable support and confidence thresholds. Particularly, the Classification Based on Associations (CBA) [21] algorithm was used, which produces effective and maintainable classifiers, with a dataset of 18.5 K records of actual inspection outcomes coming from the inspections conducted by the Hellenic Labour Inspectorate in Attica in 2018–2019. In this initial application of an explainable classification method in this domain, the three main categories of violations (undeclared work, underdeclared work, and other infringements) were united in one, the infringement class (INFR); thus, the dataset was transformed into a binary (INFR/NO_INFR), and a relatively balanced one. The study was analysed per the CRISP-DM methodology [22], and the produced model accomplished an overall accuracy of over 65%, while also extracting interesting knowledge related to patterns of labour law compliance and noncompliance.

Yet, having all the violation types merged into one, the above study did not provide focused knowledge on the feature patterns associated specifically with undeclared work, nor any classification model distinguishing between the infringement categories. This deficiency prompted us for extended research [23], using two types of datasets: the same binary as above and the corresponding four-class dataset preserving the initial four-categories labelling based on the inspection findings. The application also embedded two different AC algorithms, CBA and CBA2 [24]; consequently, four distinct classifiers were generated and assessed per their prediction performance and knowledge provision. CBA2 is an enhanced version of CBA that deals with the class imbalance problem by splitting the user-defined minimum support value to the different classes according to their distribution in the dataset, hence allowing CAR generation for the minority classes, while also preventing redundant CAR generation for the majority class. This detailed application study followed the data mining project analysis phases per the CRISP-DM methodology in the business environment of a public authority responsible for facing undeclared work, the Hellenic Labour Inspectorate. It concluded by identifying different preferable models, one for maximum prediction yields, trained by the binary dataset, and one for providing focused insights per type of violation, trained by the four-class dataset.

This research also unveiled that the models generated using the dataset of four classes, one of which is undeclared work with a ratio of 4%, missed identifying those rare instances of unregistered employment adequately. The causes of this low performance in undeclared work prediction are identified in class imbalance and class overlap phenomena existing in the data space with a non-neglecting ratio.

Class imbalance is a usual problem in machine learning when actual data are used for training, where often the instances of one class, the majority class, predominate the instances of the other classes (minority classes), thus impeding the learning process and introducing a predictive tendency for the majority class [25,26]. In the application domain of undeclared work prediction, datasets of past inspection visits naturally display a considerable imbalance concerning undeclared work [20,23], since this unlawful phenomenon is multifaceted and not easily detected in onsite checks, and due to the authorities' limited resources, only a small percentage of businesses is inspected [4]. However, in machine learning applications, when the class of interest is the minority class, such as in fraud detection systems [27], intrusion detection [28], and undeclared work detection [23], predictive models favouring the majority class may bring adverse outcomes.

In addition, the prediction performance may further worsen if there are a considerable number of class overlaps in the dataset, i.e., data instances with the same or similar features but belonging to different classes, issuing the so-called class overlap problem [29]. In this application domain, using datasets with details of past inspections, class overlaps are expected to exist in the dataspace, since several actual checks with similar features may often conclude with different findings. When class imbalance and class overlap coexist in the dataspace and no actions are taken to deal with them, the produced predictive models prove poor performance [23,30,31].

Our latest research [32] focused on addressing these issues by following approaches at the data level [26] before building the classifiers. We used the same data of actual past inspections as in [20,23]; still, the dataset was here differently structured, with each tuple corresponding to an inspection case, and not to an inspection discovery, ending up containing, finally, 16.7 K inspection instances (an inspection may conclude with several findings). We applied three different data engineering techniques, in isolation and combination, generating several classifiers assessed in predicting undeclared work. We used again the CBA algorithm [21], that we also applied in [20,23], to enable the comparison of the produced prediction performance results with the previous studies and the identification of the impact of the suggested approaches on the models' predictability. This study proved that applying data engineering methods to solve the class imbalance and class overlap problems highly enhanced the efficiency of the classification models, raising the ratio of undeclared work prediction (recall) to more than 70% and still preserving the overall accuracy at 70%. In addition, with less imbalanced datasets of undeclared and underdeclared work, the models managed to predict more than 75% of the cases with violations.

The current research paper constitutes an extensive study of the latest one [32], further examining the challenges of class imbalance and class overlap in the application domain of undeclared work prediction by focusing and operating on the data and modelling levels.

We suggest and apply four different engineering techniques on the data level, starting with the complete initial dataset. By setting the target group of violations, we employ data reduction to create a separate binary final dataset per targeted group of infringements. In this way, we transform an imbalanced multi-class dataset into several binary datasets on the grounds of the decision-makers' targets, thus enhancing the models' predictability and eliminating the overlaps among the violation classes. Following this, we implement class overlap removal (COR) in the binary final datasets to deal with overlaps between the opposing classes, in isolation or combination with a data balancing method, random oversampling (ROS), or random undersampling (RUS) to handle the disparity between the class of violations and that of no infringements.

On the modelling level, we implement three AC algorithms, the CBA and CBA2, as used in [23] for results comparison, and the Classification based on Predictive Association Rules (CPAR) [33], an AC method that was not exploited before in this domain. CPAR utilises a greedy algorithm to generate rules directly from the training dataset instead of generating large candidate rules from frequent itemsets, as in the other two AC methods [34]. It is implemented here to assess its outcomes and sensitivity in class imbalance and class overlaps in this domain.

Multiple classifiers are built by combining the different modelling and data engineering techniques, tested, and evaluated for their predictability in this domain. In addition, this research study sheds light on the interpretability aspect of the produced results at both the global and local levels [9,35,36], as well as the adaptability of the suggested approaches in the business environment of an enforcement authority in charge of facing undeclared work.

The present study proves highly significant in multiple ways, mainly because (i) it demonstrates the application of one more AC method (CPAR) not used before in this application domain, (ii) it completes the research of our previous studies by illustrating through experimentation with actual data all combinations of the suggested data engineering and modelling techniques, thus enabling comparison and discussion of the results, and (iii) it also examines in detail the interpretability and adaptability aspects of the recommended approaches, which are highly significant when adopting machine learning techniques in a public institution environment.

2. Materials and Methods

2.1. Problem Description

As discussed, the application domain of the current study is the labour inspectorate, and the objective is to predict undeclared and underdeclared work using machine learning methods aiming to achieve high predictability, interpretability, and adaptability in the business environment of the enforcement authority. While undeclared work refers to work completely unrecorded and concealed from the state, underdeclared work concerns partially recorded labour, usually taking two forms; with fewer recorded working hours than actually performed and/or with less reported wages than in reality paid. This research focuses on addressing these two most severe types of infringement under labour relations law and uses data coming from the Hellenic Labour Inspectorate (HLI), yet the suggested approaches may well be applied to other kinds of violations, exploiting data from other enforcement authorities, such as the social security institutions or tax authorities.

The HLI is organised in 125 local offices countrywide and its central offices in the capital. It employs around 700 labour inspectors assigned with several duties, including onsite inspection visits, labour disputes mediation, advising employers and employees on applying labour law provisions, and investigation of work accidents. One of its primary tasks is to deal with undeclared and underdeclared work around the country, whose labour market consists of about 340 K companies and 2.1 M employees, significantly increasing in the summer months and displaying a large diversity in the different districts. Around 35 K inspection visits are dedicated to protecting employees' rights against these two illegal practices, and the selection is usually random or relies on filed complaints.

The inspectorate owns a risk assessment tool, which is a subsystem of its integrated information system, for inspection targeting and monthly planning, yet it is not often used for two main reasons; first, based on red flag indicators user-specified, it needs manual configuration and continuous update, which can be performed only at the central offices and by labour inspection and risk analysis experts; this task requires devoted and experienced analysts being in often contact with the local labour inspectors countrywide to achieve proper feedback collection and efficient tool configuration, which is not always feasible. Secondly, and as a result of the first deficiency, local labour inspectors are uncertain and distrustful in following a tool's suggestions when being mostly excluded by its configuration process and unaware of its specific features leading to its outcomes.

The inspection authority also owns the ERGANI information system, where all companies are obliged by law and on due dates to declare all their employment data and any changes made before these are applied. Labour inspectors have access to its data, which they may examine before, during, or after an inspection visit. However, investigations are made case by case, and no automated mechanism is available to identify and offer hints on high-risk businesses for targeted inspections.

Concluding the above, and given the availability of adequate and relevant data resources, applying innovative data analysis and machine learning methods for efficient inspection planning and meaningful knowledge provision rises as the optimum solution for achieving increased overall productivity and successful allocation of the inspectorate's resources.

2.2. Data Sources and Preprocessing

The present research study uses the data collected and appropriately integrated after a thorough investigation into the business needs and available data sources of the HLI, going through the business understanding and data understanding phases per the CRISP-DM methodology, extensively explained in [23] and summarised here for completeness.

As previously discussed, the HLI offers, through the ERGANI, digital services to employers to obligatorily use for all kinds of employment declarations, such as commencements and terminations of labour contracts, working day and hour schedules, annual leaves, overtime, etc. The labour inspectors investigate these declared employment data during or after an onsite inspection and, based on their findings, may ascertain labour law violations, such as undeclared or underdeclared work. Thus, since 2013, when this information system was established, it has gathered large volumes of valuable data on registered employment in the labour market countrywide.

Meanwhile, through its integrated information system (IIS), the HLI digitalised all its internal functioning, including registering and monitoring the inspection cases at the inspections subsystem. Hence, since 2018, when it was formally applied, all labour inspectors are mandated to record all their inspection details in the system and monitor their cases until they are finalised. In addition, one of the HLI internal processes is handling the complaints received through different channels; these are all recorded into the IIS and forwarded to the appropriate local labour inspection department for further examination and inspection planning.

Integrating inspection data with other details made known to the inspectorate before the inspections are performed, such as company characteristics and registered employment data coming from ERGANI, may well form a dataset, which, when labelled per the inspection discoveries and analysed with machine learning techniques, may provide predictions for future inspections and extract patterns linked with specific violations.

Following this approach and after the appropriate data cleaning and anonymisation, i.e., omission of records with no data at crucial features and exclusion of all features related to the identification of inspection cases, companies, or branches—such as case ID, tax number, name, address, etc.—we concluded with a dataset of 25 features. Subsequently, and in close cooperation with domain experts, we proceeded to a meticulous feature selection and feature construction based on their importance and relevance to the findings of an inspection, ending up with the set of 12 features illustrated in Table 1. For those taking numerical values, their range was discretised. For those taking values from a large set of categories, these were aggregated in fewer groups, ending at the categorical values per feature, as shown in the table. The last column illustrates the ratio of the number of records in the whole dataset with this categorical value at the specific feature. These steps relate to data preprocessing, a crucial stage in the data mining process, and require specialised knowledge in the application domain to lead to meaningful machine learning outcomes and avoid overfitting.

Table 1. Initial dataset: features, set of values per feature, and categorical values ratio in the dataset.

Group	Feature	Values	Description–Ranges	Ratio%
Inspection related features	Inspection Time zone	MORNING	06.01–14.00	68.7
		EVENING	14.01–22.00	29.77
		NIGHT	22.01–06.00	1.53
	Inspection Day	WEEKDAY	Monday–Friday	86.86
		WEEKEND	Saturday–Sunday	13.14
	Initiation Trigger	SCHEDULED	Scheduled or random	83.63
		COMPLAINT	Complaint or other info	16.37
Business related features	Legal Form	CORP	Corporation	62.57
		SOL_PROP	Sole proprietorship	37.43
	Business Sector	HORECA	Hotel/restaurant/catering	23.6
		PROD_CONSTR	Production/construction	10.51
		SALES	All kinds of sales	34.39
		SERVICES	All kinds of services	31.5
	Region	CENTRAL_ATHENS	Central part of Athens	28.02
		NORTH_ATHENS	North part of Athens	15.7
		SOUTH_ATHENS	South part of Athens	14.94
		WEST_ATHENS	West part of Athens	7.83
		PIRAEUS	Piraeus	14.42
		WEST_ATTICA	West part of Attica	6.98
		EAST_ATTICA	East part of Attica	12.11
Employment related features	Workplace Size	SMALL_SIZE	1–10 employees	48.1
		MEDIUM_SIZE	11–50 employees	28.16
		LARGE_SIZE	51–250 employees	13.09
		VERY_LARGE_SIZE	>251 employees	10.65
	Employment	LOW_EMPL	1–16 h/week	14.27
		MEDIUM_EMPL	17–32 h/week	29.31
		FULL_EMPL	33–40 h/week	56.42
	Payment	LOW_PAID	≤700 EUR/month	48.4
		MEDIUM_PAID	701–900 EUR/month	26.17
		HIGH_PAID	901–1100 EUR/month	11.1
		VERY_HIGH_PAID	>1100 EUR/month	14.33
	Frequency of working schedule changes	RARE_CHANGES	0–2.00 changes/employee	67.25
		MEDIUM_FREQ_CHANGES	2.01–4 changes/employee	12.57
		OFTEN_CHANGES	4.01–10 changes/employee	12.07
		VERY_ OFTEN_CHANGES	>10.01 changes/employee	8.11
Past inspections related feature	Past Compliance	UNINSPECTED	No past inspections	68.88
		COMPLIANT	No past violations	12.88
		LOW_DELINQ	Low delinquency: <40%	3.55
		MED_DELINQ	Medium delinquency: 40–100%	12.12
		HIGH_DELINQ	High delinquency: 100–300%	2.39
		VERY_HIGH_DELINQ	Very high delinquency: >300%	0.18
Outcome	Findings	UDW	Undeclared work	2.55
		UDW, UNDER_DW	Undeclared and underdeclared work	0.44
		UDW, OTHER_INFR	Undeclared work and other infringements	0.13
		UDW, UNDER_DW, OTHER_INFR	Undeclared and underdeclared work and other infringements	0.04
		UNDER_DW	Underdeclared work	30.71
		UNDER_DW, OTHER_INFR	Underdeclared work and other infringements	1.18
		OTHER_INFR	Other infringements	8.36
		NO_INFR	No infringements	56.59

Data preprocessing also includes data selection as per the objective of the application. Taking into account the diversity in the labour market affected by several locality and seasonality factors countrywide, as well as the hidden and multi-faceted nature of undeclared work, the dataset to be used for classification training should not include all the performed inspections by the HLI throughout the years because it would lead to generating models offering predictions based on the most dominating patterns of violations, thus still keeping the undeclared work concealed.

Under this given, for the purposes of experimenting with machine learning in this domain, the initial dataset is constructed to include the labour inspections performed in Attica in 2018–2019, counting in a total of 16,718 cases, hence studying undeclared work prediction in this district and period. Data from 2020 and thereafter were excluded from the dataset because employment was severely affected by the COVID-19 pandemic crisis, yet it is a factor falling outside the research of this study.

Consequently, each tuple in the initial dataset of Table 1 corresponds to an inspection case performed in Attica in 2018–2019, with its features including the time zone and day and its trigger to be either a complaint or monthly plan. The inspected business' characteristics comprise its legal form, economic sector, and the region of Attica where it is established. Additionally, the employment details of the inspected workplace include the size based on the number of employees, the type of employment as per the average weekly working hours, the payment level as per the monthly average wage, and the frequency of working schedule changes calculated averagely per employee and based on the declared changes in ERGANI in the last semester before the inspection visit. The past compliance of the inspected workplace is a constructed feature to indicate if and at what level prior inspections later affected the reviewed business' level of labour law compliance. It is calculated as the ratio of past violations, if any, to the total past inspections, if any. Last, the outcome of the inspection case is registered, which can be with no infringements, or it can take values among undeclared work, underdeclared work, other infringements, or a combination of them, i.e., it is defined by one of the eight distinct categories of inspection findings as described in Table 1.

Hence, by completing all the data collection, integration, and preprocessing steps, which include data selection, cleaning and anonymisation, feature selection and construction, and data discretisation and aggregation, we conclude with the dataset of Table 1, which is well-structured and contains a considerable number of inspection cases for models to learn from, yet it cannot be used as-is for classification training.

Indeed, if we take the findings feature as the class, since this is the characteristic that we wish to predict, and we use this dataset to train classification models, the produced classifiers would be of poor prediction performance for several reasons. First, it contains many (eight) class values, i.e., the categorical values of the findings feature; second, most of these values are severely underrepresented; third, it conceals multiple overlaps among the different classes. As also seen in [23], these three primary dataset deficiencies impede the machine learning process and generate poor classifiers; hence, we focus on addressing them by applying the techniques described in the following paragraphs.

2.3. Target Setting and Data Reduction

The first method applied to deal with the initial dataset complexity and handle uneven class distributions and class overlapping relates to data reduction reasoning, i.e., eliminating data irrelevant to the machine learning goal. To be reminded that the aim, in this application domain, is to effectively predict undeclared work and other labour law violations and then plan onsite inspections. Thus, all the violation types may be considered interesting for prediction by the authority. However, since the training of only one classification model with a dataset containing all infringement categories with irregular dispersion and overlaps proves inefficient, several different smaller and simpler datasets can be generated per type of violation that the inspectorate aims to address; hence, subsequently, simpler and more effective classifiers can be constructed.

Thus, by proceeding with target setting and data reduction, we practically reduce the data space and select that part that is relevant, each time, to the target of the inspections to be performed. In other words, for each different violation or group of violations the inspectorate wishes to target using deterrence or preventative measures, a separate final dataset is constructed to contain only those past inspection cases that discovered at least one of the target violations and be labelled as positives (P), and those past cases that found the inspected company compliant with the labour law provisions and be labelled as negatives (N). Following this approach, we aim at building a distinct classifier, using each of these final datasets, to identify the riskiest businesses for these violations.

In the present study, we are interested in undeclared and underdeclared work prediction, and for the purposes of testing and evaluation, we create three different final datasets: one for undeclared work, one for purely underdeclared work, and one to target both of these violations. Thus, we isolate from the initial dataset the inspection cases that discovered, among others, undeclared work to form the UDW group, those that discovered underdeclared work to build the UNDER_DW group, and those that revealed at least one of the two to create the UDW-or-UNDER_DW group; the cases that found no violations are gathered to the NO_INFR group. All data-instance groups and their ratios per feature value are illustrated in Table 2, where multiple preliminary understandings can be derived.

Table 2. Groups of inspection cases per targeting and their ratios per feature value.

Feature	Values	UDW	UNDER_DW	UDW-or-UNDER_DW	NO_INFR
Inspection Time	MORNING	64.20	59.96	60.38	72.79
	EVENING	31.44	36.88	36.35	26.59
	NIGHT	4.36	3.16	3.28	0.61
Inspection Day	WEEKDAY	82.01	84.39	84.32	87.00
	WEEKEND	17.99	15.61	15.68	13.00
Initiation Trigger	SCHEDULED	62.50	80.93	79.56	86.99
	COMPLAINT	37.50	19.07	20.44	13.01
Legal Form	CORP	47.16	59.63	58.58	64.38
	SOL_PROP	52.84	40.37	41.42	35.62
Business Sector	HORECA	31.82	35.88	35.44	17.40
	PROD_CONSTR	16.29	8.92	9.52	10.62
	SALES	22.16	25.26	25.02	42.33
	SERVICES	29.73	29.93	30.02	29.65
Region	CENTRAL_ATHENS	39.58	29.45	30.26	26.20
	NORTH_ATHENS	12.88	15.02	14.91	15.21
	SOUTH_ATHENS	10.98	16.65	16.18	14.45
	WEST_ATHENS	8.14	11.12	10.92	6.29
	PIRAEUS	10.98	11.83	11.71	16.68
	WEST_ATTICA	5.11	7.65	7.47	7.21
	EAST_ATTICA	12.31	8.28	8.55	13.96
Workplace Size	SMALL_SIZE	65.34	47.21	48.75	48.72
	MEDIUM_SIZE	28.41	35.55	34.80	22.98
	LARGE_SIZE	5.11	10.20	9.86	14.59
	VERY_LARGE_SIZE	1.14	7.04	6.59	13.72
Employment	LOW_EMPL	24.62	23.45	23.43	9.32
	MEDIUM_EMPL	33.14	33.39	33.38	26.97
	FULL_EMPL	42.23	43.16	43.19	63.70
Payment	LOW_PAID	57.58	56.65	56.60	44.32
	MEDIUM_PAID	27.08	23.84	24.13	27.73
	HIGH_PAID	6.25	7.61	7.54	13.06
	VERY_HIGH_PAID	9.09	11.90	11.72	14.88
Frequency of changes in the working schedule	RARE_CHANGES	85.98	76.37	77.06	59.42
	MEDIUM_FREQ_CHANGES	6.82	9.42	9.27	15.08
	OFTEN_CHANGES	3.60	8.24	7.85	15.52
	VERY_ OFTEN_CHANGES	3.60	5.97	5.82	9.98
Level of Past Compliance	UNINSPECTED	81.25	73.04	73.74	67.96
	COMPLIANT	6.06	8.19	8.00	16.41
	LOW_DELINQ	0.57	1.55	1.48	4.85
	MED_DELINQ	9.28	14.34	13.91	9.30
	HIGH_DELINQ	2.84	2.64	2.65	1.34
	VERY_HIGH_DELINQ	0.00	0.24	0.22	0.13
Total data instances		**528**	**5412**	**5860**	**9461**

By uniting each of the first three violation groups of Table 2, whose instances are labelled positive, with the fourth group of cases with no violations, whose records are labelled negative, three final datasets are built; the UDW dataset with 9989 records, the UNDER_DW dataset with 14,873 records, and the UDW-or-UNDER_DW dataset with 15,321 records. Figure 1a illustrates the class distribution of the initial dataset in the dataspace, where it is perceived that learning can be severely hindered by the obstacles we previously discussed. Figure 1b–d display the class distributions of the above final datasets.

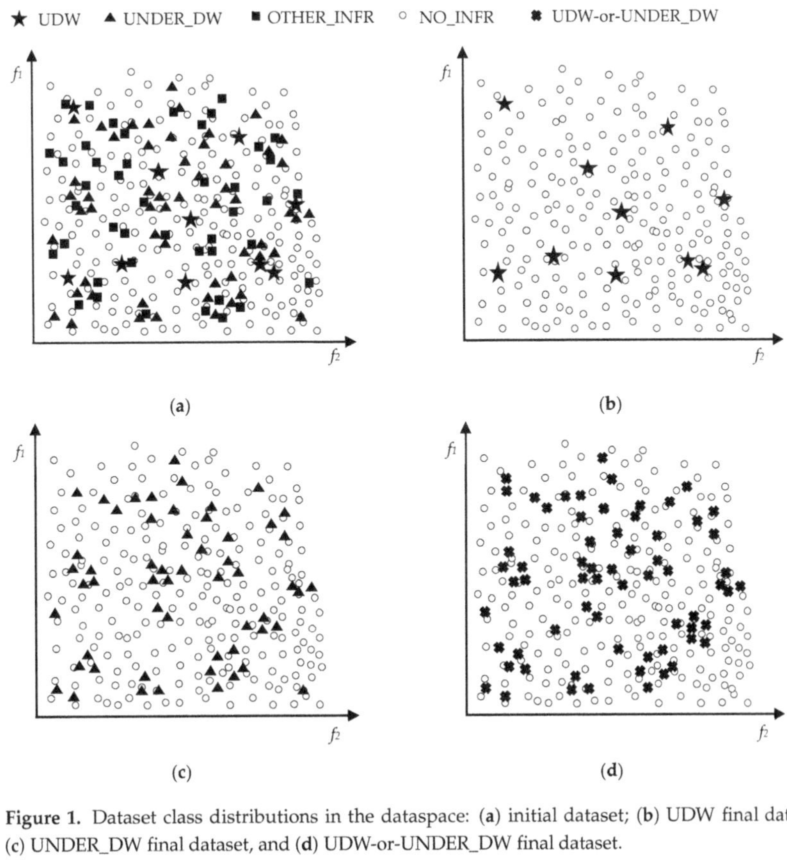

Figure 1. Dataset class distributions in the dataspace: (**a**) initial dataset; (**b**) UDW final dataset; (**c**) UNDER_DW final dataset, and (**d**) UDW-or-UNDER_DW final dataset.

As also observed in the figures, by applying targeting and data reduction, multi-class datasets are transformed into several binary ones on the basis of the infringements to be targeted, also achieving exclude overlaps among the different violation types. Yet, class overlap and imbalance issues still exist in the produced binary datasets.

Table 3 presents the rate of class imbalance and class overlap in the final datasets. The UDW dataset displays a considerable imbalance as regards undeclared work (5.29%), whereas, in all datasets, the overlap ratio, i.e., the percentage of negatives falling on positives, is non-neglectable, reaching more than 25%. To address these two machine learning obstacles and assist the generation of efficient classifiers, the following two data sampling approaches are proposed, which are applied in isolation and in combination in this study to evaluate their results in increasing prediction performance. Data sampling should be implemented only in the training part of the data, which is used to produce the classification models, whereas the testing instances should remain unchanged to avoid the data leakage phenomenon and extracting misleading and too optimistic prediction results.

Table 3. Imbalance and overlap ratios in the final datasets.

		UDW		UNDER_DW		UDW-or-UNDER_DW	
		Total	**Ratio**	**Total**	**Ratio**	**Total**	**Ratio**
Imbalance	**YES**	528	5.29%	5412	36.39%	5860	38.25%
	NO	9461	94.71%	9461	63.61%	9461	61.75%
Overlaps		2544	25.47%	4094	27.53%	4176	27.26%

2.4. Overlaps Handling

In application domains where the cost of misclassifying positives (minority class instances) is significantly higher than the cost of misclassifying negatives (majority class instances), class overlap existence in the dataset may result in models with low efficiency. Even more so in imbalanced datasets, where several negatives may fall over the rare positives in the dataspace, the classifiers trained with this dataset will probably have difficulty predicting future positive cases correctly.

In such situations, we need to create well-recognised class clusters in the training dataspace that can lead to generating explicit CARs and robust models with improved predictability. Thus, to foster the prediction of instances we especially wish to identify (the positives), we remove from the training data the less interesting cases (the negatives) that fall over them; i.e., when the testing and training samples are defined, and before the classifier is built, the class overlap removal (COR) function examines the training sample, and if it identifies two data instances as having the same value at all the features but belonging to opposing classes, it deletes from the training dataset the one labelled as negative. Even when several negative data instances have the same characteristics with one positive in the training sample, they are all removed, leaving only the positive case existing in that particular area of the dataspace, hence assisting the classification model recognising this area as positive.

Following this approach, the training data class distribution of the imbalanced UDW dataset displayed in Figure 2a is transformed into that of Figure 2b. Negatives that overlap positives are eliminated, and the learning process may now be more effective with respect to predicting undeclared work.

2.5. Data Balancing

Handling overlaps between negatives and positives may be combined with a data balancing technique to deal with the class imbalance issue. As observed in Figure 2b, the few positives are now clearly 'seen' in the dataspace, yet the negative class is highly dominant and may affect the classification training and the generation of an effective model. Hence, balancing the training data shall increase the produced classifiers' predictability of the positives.

In this research study, we employ two simple methods to obtain balanced training data, random oversampling (ROS) and random undersampling (RUS) with replacement. ROS suggests adding to the training data copies of randomly selected data instances from the minority class, while RUS refers to deleting from the training data randomly chosen majority class records. Both approaches aim at adjusting the training data class distribution to a user-defined balance and assist the machine learning process. They are implemented here to achieve an equal distribution of positive and negative training data samples for testing and assessment purposes.

Figure 2c,e illustrate the class distribution in the data space when ROS and RUS are applied correspondingly. If COR is also employed, which should be implemented before ROS or RUS, the dispersion of the classes in the training data is represented in Figure 2d,f accordingly.

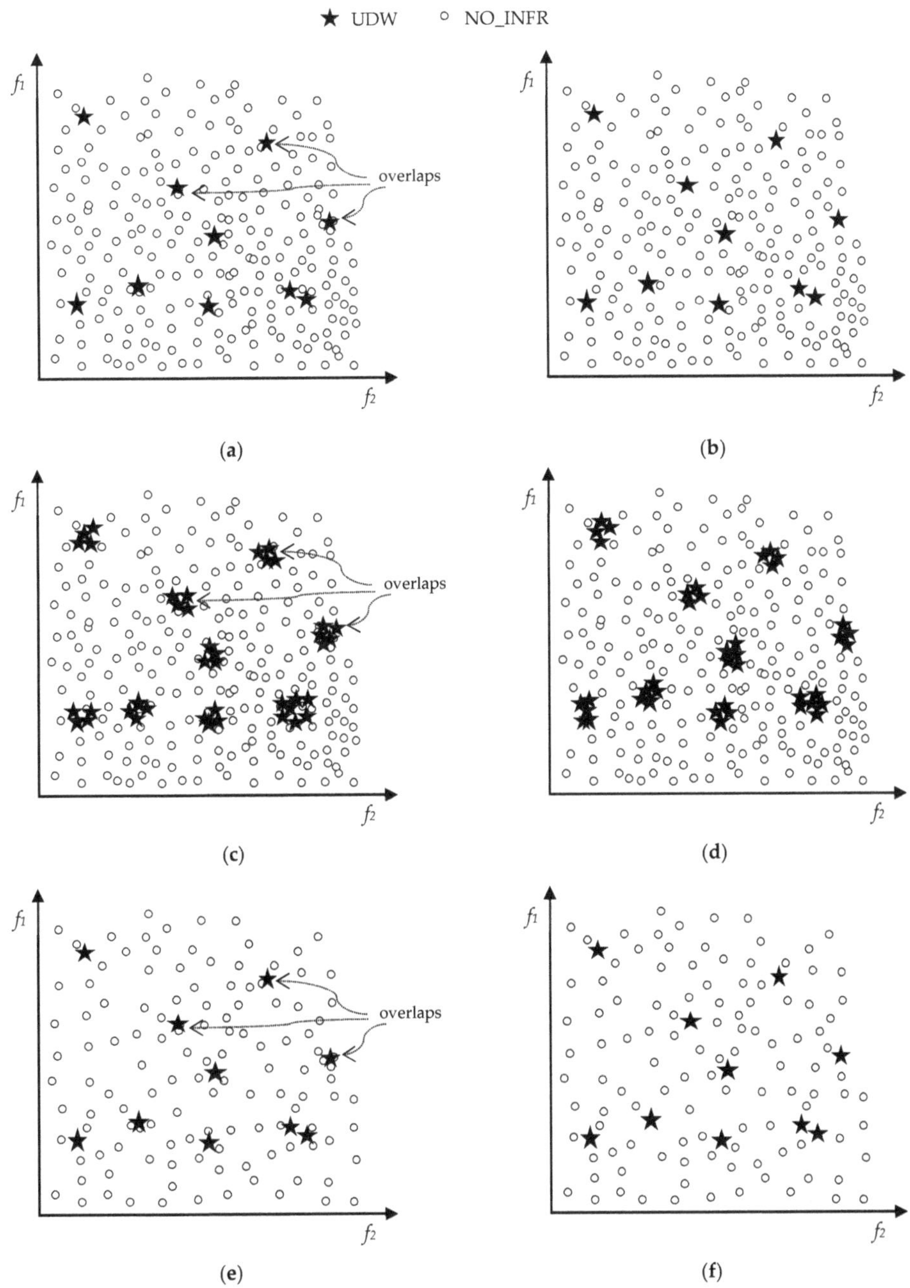

Figure 2. UDW training data class distributions in the dataspace: (**a**) final dataset (FD); (**b**) final dataset with applied class overlap removal (FD_COR); (**c**) final dataset with applied random oversampling (FD_ROS); (**d**) final dataset with applied class overlap removal and random oversampling (FD_COR_ROS); (**e**) final dataset with applied random undersampling (FD_RUS); and (**f**) final dataset with applied class overlap removal and random undersampling (FD_COR_RUS).

2.6. Modelling

As discussed, in the present research, we engage associative classification to build the classification models. AC was initially selected for application in this domain for two main reasons; first, several studies [33,37,38] evidenced that AC models achieve increased predictive accuracy than other interpretable machine learning methods, such as rule induction [39,40] and decision trees [41,42]. Indeed, AC can reveal further hidden knowledge often missed by other classification techniques due to its practices in extracting associations between feature values and classes. Secondly, interpretability is, as explained, of principle significance in this domain. AC generates models consisting of simple, of the type if-then, rules that are conveniently understandable and manually updated, if need be, by the domain users [37].

AC algorithms operate in three main phases; rule discovery, rule sorting and pruning to generate the classifier, and testing set prediction to evaluate its effectiveness [37]. Several algorithms exploit different methodologies at each step to improve their predictability. This research study tests and assesses the application of the CBA [21], CBA2 [24], and CPAR [33] algorithms in the domain of undeclared work prediction, with their parameters setting to follow the authors' recommendations.

CBA was used in [20,23,32] and CBA2 in [23]; hence, they were also applied here for results comparison and to enable distinguishing the prediction improvement brought by the suggested approaches. CBA was one of the first research studies that utilised ARM [19] for classification purposes, employing the Apriori algorithm for rule generation. Rule sorting is based on confidence, support, and the length of the rules' antecedent. Rule pruning uses the database coverage method that also includes a default class at the end of the classifier. Last, class prediction in CBA is based on one rule, the highest sorted rule that matches the test case body [37]. CBA2 is an enhanced version of CBA, as regards the class imbalance problem, differentiating only at the learning phase where the user-defined minimum support threshold is distributed to the different classes according to their frequency in the input dataset. CPAR, however, follows completely different techniques at all AC stages. In rule generation, it utilises an improved adaptation of the FOIL [40] algorithm, a greedy approach that generates rules directly from the training set [33,34]. In addition, it uses the Laplace accuracy measure for rule evaluation and pruning, as well as for class assignment to the test cases during prediction. CPAR generates much smaller classifiers than other AC algorithms [33]; yet, it proves, through various experimentations [33,37], that it is highly competitive concerning predictive accuracy compared to, e.g., CBA, hence its involvement in the present study. Using these three distinct AC algorithms in combination with the six types of training data class distributions, as illustrated in Figure 2, we produce eighteen different classification models per each final dataset (Figure 1b–d) and evaluate their prediction performance. Thus, in total, fifty-four models are created and assessed, as presented in the next section.

2.7. Performance Evaluation Metrics

To train and test each of the classifiers, the stratified 10-fold cross-validation method is followed, which divides the input data into ten stratified folds, with each fold maintaining the class distribution of the input dataset, and uses the nine folds for training and the tenth fold for testing. As explained, the data sampling techniques, COR, ROS, and RUS, are applied only in the training part of the data, i.e., the nine folds, keeping the testing fold unaffected.

The process iterates along the ten folds, employing each time a different fold for testing, i.e., another 10% of the data sample is classified by the model trained by the remaining 90% of the sample; thus, in the end, classification results are collected for all the instances of the input dataset and depicted in the confusion matrix of Table 4. True positives (TP) represent the positives (inspection cases with violations) correctly predicted by the model, while false negatives (FN) refer to their misclassifications. Similarly, true negatives (TN) are the negatives (inspections with no infringements) correctly identified by the classifier, whereas false positives (FP) correspond to their misidentifications. In addition, there can be cases of data instances remaining unclassified when the applied AC algorithm does not include a default class in its classifiers, such as CPAR. Hence, we denote UNP and UNN the unclassified positives and negatives accordingly.

Table 4. Confusion matrix.

		PREDICTED		UNCLASSIFIED
		Positives (P)	Negatives (N)	
ACTUAL	Positives (P)	TP	FN	UNP
	Negatives (N)	FP	TN	UNN

The confusion matrix values may be used to calculate various performance evaluation metrics, enabling the comparison between the produced classifiers and, also, with the results of the previous studies [23,32].

In the research area of classification problems and techniques, numerous and diverse assessment metrics are proposed [43], of which, the most used and easily perceived are employed here.

First, accuracy (*Acc*) (1) refers to the total prediction accuracy of the model, considering both the prediction correctness of positives and negatives, and is calculated as the ratio of correct classifications to the total instances.

$$Acc = (TP + TN)/(TP + FN + FP + TN + UNP + UNN) \quad (1)$$

Yet, when highly imbalanced datasets are involved, accuracy can be misleading when it may still offer very high yields, while the minority class remains hidden. Thus, two other metrics are considered, focusing on the minority class; precision (p) (2), which is the ratio of positives correctly classified to all predicted positives and indicates the model's exactness,

$$p = TP/(TP + FP), \quad (2)$$

and recall (r) (3), which is calculated as the ratio of positives rightly predicted to all actual positives, revealing the model's completeness,

$$r = TP/(TP + FN + UNP) = TP/P. \quad (3)$$

Precision and recall are complementary parameters; thus, we also utilise the weighted harmonic mean of these, F_β-*score* (F_β) (4), where β is defined by the user indicating the weight (importance) of recall in comparison to precision, in the domain of application.

$$F_\beta\text{-}score = ((1 + \beta^2) \times p \times r)/(\beta^2 \times p + r) \quad (4)$$

Last, specificity (s) (5) refers to the prediction of negatives and is calculated as the ratio of correctly identified negatives to all actual negatives, i.e.,

$$s = TN/(FP + TN + UNN) = TN/N. \quad (5)$$

Last, before we proceed with the performance assessment calculations, the β factor of the F_β-*score* must be defined for the current application domain. With respect to this, one needs to consider the cost of misclassifications for the inspectorate of positives and negatives.

False negatives correspond to inspection cases revealing violations, but the model fails to predict them as such; on the contrary, it classifies the cases as "labour law compliant", i.e., with no infringements. In such events, the inspectorate does not proceed to perform onsite inspections, but it allocates its resources toward checking other, predicted as riskier, businesses. Hence, it fails to detect these violations, leading to several negative consequences, such as, among others, significant losses in state revenues.

On the other hand, false positives refer to negative cases that are wrongly predicted as positives, thus triggering unnecessary onsite inspections, which, cost-wise, may be seen as human and financial resources of the inspectorate being wasted inefficiently. Thus, false negatives, in comparison to false positives, are a lot costlier for the state and society, leading to the pursuit of higher recall yields than precision.

Thus, based on the severity of each targeted group of violations, we define β to be five for undeclared work (UDW), three for underdeclared work (UNDER_DW), and four when targeting both (UDW-or-UNDER_DW).

Concluding with the methodology, Figure 3 illustrates all the steps followed in this study, starting with data collection and ending with the performance evaluation of the models.

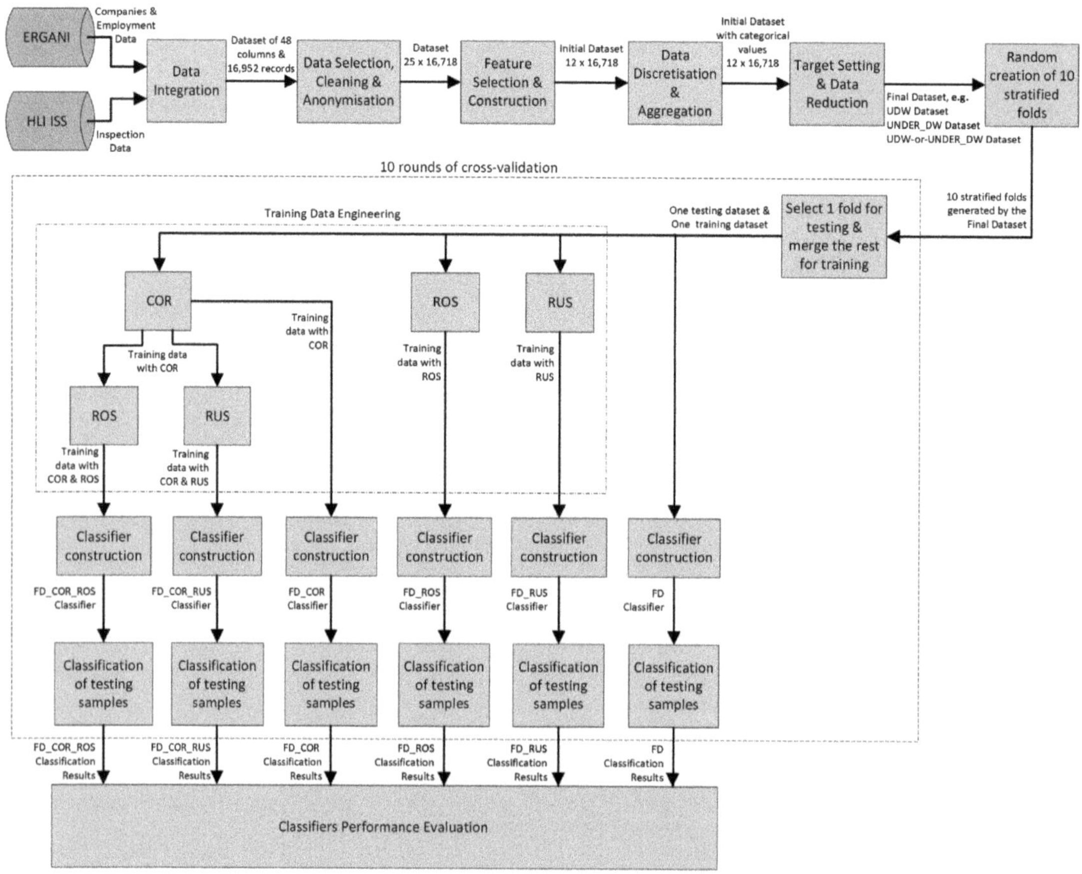

Figure 3. Methodology steps to create the initial dataset and then, after target setting, to construct a final dataset, e.g., the UDW dataset. From the same final dataset and using the same AC algorithm, six models are produced, based on the different training data class distributions, and evaluated.

3. Results

3.1. Classification Results

As described in Figure 3, six classifiers are produced correspondingly to the six different training data class distribution approaches using the same final dataset and AC algorithm, as summarised in Table 5. The first is the final dataset, produced from the initial dataset after the target setting. The rest are combinations of the data engineering methods COR, ROS, and RUS, as described in the previous section.

Table 5. Summary of the six class distributions induced by the application of training data engineering methods.

Training Data Engineering Method	Description	Class Distribution
FD	Final dataset. No training data engineering method applied.	Figure 2a
FD_COR	Final dataset with class overlap removal (COR) applied.	Figure 2b
FD_ROS	Final dataset with random oversampling (ROS) applied.	Figure 2c
FD_COR_ROS	Final dataset with class overlap removal (COR) and random oversampling (ROS) applied.	Figure 2d
FD_RUS	Final dataset with random undersampling (RUS) applied.	Figure 2e
FD_COR_RUS	Final dataset with class overlap removal (COR) and random undersampling (RUS) applied.	Figure 2f

For each of the three final datasets, UDW, UNDER_DW, and UDW-or-UNDER_DW, by combining the three AC algorithms of Section 2.6, i.e., CBA, CBA2, and CPAR, with the six different training sample class distributions of Table 5, eighteen models are produced using LAC [44], an associative classification java library. Their classification results are gathered and presented in the confusion matrixes illustrated in Tables 6–8 correspondingly.

Table 6. UDW classification results (confusion matrixes) per algorithm and training data engineering method.

UDW Dataset: P = 528/N = 9461								
		CBA		CBA2		CPAR		
Training Data Engineering Method		Predicted P	Predicted N	Predicted P	Predicted N	Predicted P	Predicted N	Unclassified
FD	P	32	496	23	505	219	164	145
	N	51	9410	16	9445	1115	6219	2127
FD_COR	P	76	452	70	458	282	137	109
	N	265	9196	310	9151	1801	5661	1999
FD_ROS	P	295	233	347	181	260	114	154
	N	1695	7766	3046	6415	1521	5355	2585
FD_COR_ROS	P	302	226	327	201	322	124	82
	N	2222	7239	2770	6691	2278	5477	1706
FD_RUS	P	372	156	350	178	288	113	127
	N	2873	6588	2820	6641	1804	5454	2203
FD_COR_RUS	P	370	158	354	174	333	103	92
	N	3342	6119	3211	6250	2375	5229	1857

Table 7. UNDER_DW classification results (confusion matrixes) per algorithm and training data engineering method.

UNDER_DW Dataset: P = 5412/N = 9461								
		CBA		CBA2		CPAR		
Training Data Engineering Method		Predicted P	Predicted N	Predicted P	Predicted N	Predicted P	Predicted N	Unclassified
FD	P	1774	3638	1776	3636	2541	2028	843
	N	966	8495	770	8691	2259	5844	1358
FD_COR	P	4133	1279	4117	1295	3773	1639	0
	N	4857	4604	4724	4737	4401	5060	0
FD_ROS	P	3457	1955	3451	1961	2805	1607	1000
	N	3055	6406	2934	6527	2506	5267	1688
FD_COR_ROS	P	4138	1274	4130	1282	3729	1683	0
	N	4850	4611	4702	4759	4372	5089	0
FD_RUS	P	3538	1874	3590	1822	2823	1650	939
	N	3148	6313	3205	6256	2617	5216	1628
FD_COR_RUS	P	4130	1282	4133	1279	3734	1678	0
	N	4804	4657	4686	4775	4394	5067	0

Table 8. UDW-or-UNDER_DW classification results (confusion matrixes) per algorithm and training data engineering method.

UDW-or-UNDER_DW Dataset: P = 5860/N = 9461								
		CBA		CBA2		CPAR		
Training Data Engineering Method		Predicted P	Predicted N	Predicted P	Predicted N	Predicted P	Predicted N	Unclassified
FD	P	1645	4215	1913	3947	2725	2056	1079
	N	782	8679	965	8496	2080	5690	1691
FD_COR	P	4691	1169	4630	1230	4124	1736	0
	N	5331	4130	5066	4395	4401	5060	0
FD_ROS	P	3815	2045	3726	2134	2971	1818	1071
	N	3170	6291	3041	6420	2391	5460	1610
FD_COR_ROS	P	4444	1416	4473	1387	3981	1879	0
	N	4824	4637	4742	4719	4212	5249	0
FD_RUS	P	3875	1985	3852	2008	2960	1746	1154
	N	3279	6182	3226	6235	2335	5343	1783
FD_COR_RUS	P	4461	1399	4475	1385	3986	1874	0
	N	4808	4653	4729	4732	4227	5234	0

Several preliminary conclusions may be derived by examining the results in Tables 6–8, identifying the most effective combinations of algorithms and training data sampling methods in increasing the true positives. However, for a thorough evaluation analysis, the performance evaluation metrics given in Section 2.7 are calculated and presented in the following subsection, while, at the same time, various application domain aspects are considered.

3.2. Performance Evaluation Results

Tables 9–11 illustrate the prediction performance measurements of all the models coming from the different combinations of the three AC algorithms and six data engineering methods using the three final datasets. They are calculated using the values in Tables 6–8 correspondingly.

Table 9. Classification assessment of the 18 models produced using the UDW dataset.

Prediction Performance Measurements of the 18 Models Produced Using the UDW Dataset						
AC Algorithm	**Data Engineering Method**	*Acc* %	*p* %	*r* %	F_5 %	*s* %
CBA	FD	94.52	38.55	6.06	6.26	99.46
	FD_COR	92.82	22.29	14.39	14.59	97.2
	FD_ROS	80.7	14.82	55.87	50.49	82.08
	FD_COR_ROS	75.49	11.97	57.2	49.94	76.51
	FD_RUS	69.68	11.46	**70.45**	**58.81**	69.63
	FD_COR_RUS	64.96	9.97	70.08	56.89	64.68
CBA2	FD	**94.78**	**58.97**	4.36	4.52	**99.83**
	FD_COR	92.31	18.42	13.26	13.40	96.72
	FD_ROS	67.69	10.23	65.72	54.38	67.8
	FD_COR_ROS	70.26	10.56	61.93	52.17	70.72
	FD_RUS	69.99	11.04	66.29	55.59	70.19
	FD_COR_RUS	66.11	9.93	67.05	54.90	66.06
CPAR	FD	64.45	16.42	41.48	39.18	65.73
	FD_COR	59.5	13.54	53.41	47.98	59.84
	FD_ROS	56.21	14.6	49.24	45.12	56.60
	FD_COR_ROS	58.05	12.38	60.98	52.98	57.89
	FD_RUS	57.48	13.77	54.55	48.97	57.65
	FD_COR_RUS	55.68	12.3	63.07	54.43	55.27

Table 10. Classification assessment of the 18 models generated using the UNDER_DW dataset.

Prediction Performance Measurements of the 18 Models Generated Using the UNDER_DW Dataset						
AC Algorithm	**Data Engineering Method**	*Acc* %	*p* %	*r* %	F_3 %	*s* %
CBA	FD	69.04	64.74	32.78	34.48	89.79
	FD_COR	58.74	45.97	**76.37**	**71.63**	48.66
	FD_ROS	66.31	53.09	63.88	62.61	67.71
	FD_COR_ROS	58.82	46.04	**76.46**	**71.72**	48.74
	FD_RUS	66.23	52.92	65.37	63.87	66.73
	FD_COR_RUS	59.08	46.23	**76.31**	**71.65**	49.22
CBA2	FD	**70.38**	**69.76**	32.82	34.66	**91.86**
	FD_COR	59.53	46.57	**76.07**	**71.54**	50.07
	FD_ROS	67.09	54.05	63.77	62.64	68.99
	FD_COR_ROS	59.77	46.76	**76.31**	**71.77**	50.3
	FD_RUS	66.2	52.83	66.33	64.68	66.12
	FD_COR_RUS	59.89	46.86	**76.37**	**71.85**	50.47
CPAR	FD	56.38	52.94	46.95	47.49	61.77
	FD_COR	59.39	46.16	69.72	66.33	53.48
	FD_ROS	54.27	52.81	51.83	51.93	55.67
	FD_COR_ROS	59.29	46.03	68.90	65.64	53.79
	FD_RUS	54.05	51.89	52.16	52.13	55.13
	FD_COR_RUS	59.17	45.94	68.99	65.70	53.56

Table 11. Classification assessment of the 18 models built using the UDW-or-UNDER_DW dataset.

Prediction Performance Measurements of the 18 Models Generated Using the UDW-or-UNDER_DW Dataset						
AC Algorithm	**Data Engineering Method**	*Acc* %	*p* %	*r* %	F_4 %	*s* %
CBA	FD	**67.38**	**67.78**	28.07	29.07	**91.73**
	FD_COR	57.57	46.81	**80.05**	**76.84**	43.65
	FD_ROS	65.96	54.62	65.1	64.37	66.49
	FD_COR_ROS	59.27	47.95	75.84	73.33	49.01
	FD_RUS	65.64	54.17	66.13	65.28	65.34
	FD_COR_RUS	59.49	48.13	76.13	73.61	49.18
CBA2	FD	**67.94**	**66.47**	32.65	33.66	**89.8**
	FD_COR	58.91	47.75	**79.01**	**76.08**	46.45
	FD_ROS	66.22	55.06	63.58	63.01	67.86
	FD_COR_ROS	60	48.54	76.33	73.84	49.88
	FD_RUS	65.84	54.42	65.73	64.94	65.9
	FD_COR_RUS	60.09	48.62	76.37	73.89	50.02
CPAR	FD	54.92	56.71	46.50	47.00	60.14
	FD_COR	59.94	48.38	70.38	68.54	53.48
	FD_ROS	55.03	55.41	50.70	50.95	57.71
	FD_COR_ROS	60.24	48.59	67.94	66.38	55.48
	FD_RUS	54.19	55.9	50.51	50.80	56.47
	FD_COR_RUS	60.18	48.53	68.02	66.45	55.32

In Tables 9–11, the highest values per performance evaluation metric are identified in bold, where one can realise that accuracy, precision, and sensitivity favour different models than recall and F-score. For instance, when targeting undeclared work (Table 9), the classifier generated by CBA2 with no engineering in training data (FD) achieves the highest accuracy, reaching 94.78%, precision at 58.97%, and sensitivity at 99.83%. However, it identifies only 4.36% of the cases with undeclared work (recall) and proves completely inefficient. Thus, for the reasons we explained previously, we mainly focus on the recall and F-score metrics to identify the most effective models per final dataset.

For undeclared work prediction (Table 9), the model produced by CBA and trained with RUS proves to be the most successful, identifying more than 70% (*r*) of the undeclared work cases while still attaining an overall accuracy and sensitivity near 70%. This is considered a significantly improved performance by the domain experts because, in practice, if this classifier were used for planning inspections against undeclared work, it would trigger only 32.48% of the total inspection cases ($TP + FP$) to reveal 70.45% of the existing undeclared work, raising the inspection yields (*p*) from the current ratio of 5.29% to 11.46%. Additionally, compared with the results of undeclared work prediction (*r*) by the CBA and CBA2 models trained with the four-class dataset in [23] being near 0% and 7.5%, respectively, the outcomes of the suggested approach to deal with class imbalance prove substantially improved.

Meanwhile, we should not neglect the performance of the CPAR algorithm in comparison with the other two when no data engineering is applied (FD) for undeclared work detection. Indeed, even in such a highly imbalanced dataspace (UDW) with more than 25% overlaps, this algorithm proves to perform well, identifying more than 41% (*r*) of the undeclared work cases while activating only 13.35% of the total inspections, thus tripling their gains to more than 16% (*p*). Conversely, CBA and CBA2 face difficulties with the class imbalance and display a disappointing prediction performance until this issue is solved, whereas eliminating the class overlap does not seem to improve the performance.

When less imbalanced datasets are involved (Tables 10 and 11) and no sampling methods are applied to handle class imbalance and class overlap (FD), CPAR again demonstrates a considerably improved performance compared to CBA and CBA2 in terms of predicting the cases with violations, succeeding to identify around 47% of them while keeping the precision to decent levels: at 53% for underdeclared work (Table 10) and 56.7% when both infringements are targeted (Table 11). CBA and CBA2 models, in these cases, trigger a small number of inspections whose accuracy, though, is very high, up to more than 67%, with the CBA2 model offering slightly increased yields compared to CBA. However, these models do not manage to identify a competent number of existing violations, discovering only around one-third of them. This deficiency originates, as verified, from the class overlap issue, which, when handled (as in FD_COR models), boosts the recall ratio to more than 76%, while maintaining the overall accuracy on average to 59–60%.

More specifically, when focusing on underdeclared work (UNDER_DW final dataset) or both undeclared and underdeclared work (UDW-or-UNDER_DW final dataset), the application of CBA using training data with no overlaps (FD_COR) produces the classifiers that identify most of the actual cases with violations, accomplishing a recall of 76.37% and 80.05%, accordingly. In this case, the success ratio (precision) rises from the present 36.39% (Table 3) to 45.97% (Table 10) for underdeclared work and from 38.25% (Table 3) to 46.81% (Table 11) for both violations. In the meantime, it is demonstrated that applying oversampling and undersampling techniques (ROS and RUS) does not enhance the models' prediction performance. Last, comparing these performance results for detecting underdeclared work with the outcomes of the CBA and CBA2 algorithms trained with the four-class dataset in [23] achieving a recall of 34.64% and 39.98%, respectively, one can recognise the substantive improvements of the proposed methods even when less rare (than undeclared work) violations are targeted.

Concluding, when highly imbalanced datasets are involved, such as the UDW with the minority class reaching only 5.29%, even if class overlaps coexist in the dataspace, it is the imbalance issue that mainly affects the CBA and CBA2 classifiers performance. Once RUS is applied, these models reach maximum recall.

On the other hand, as regards the other two less imbalanced datasets, it is the class overlap that impedes the CBA and CBA2 learning process, which is remarkably improved when the negatives falling on positives are eliminated from the training data. If balancing techniques are applied in such datasets, no further enhancements are observed.

Contrarywise, CPAR operates differently from CBA and CBA2 at all associative classification stages, hence its disparate behaviour per final dataset and data engineering method. As discussed, CPAR is not so sensitive to class imbalance and class overlap. It performs satisfactorily well, even with significantly uneven class distributions and/or a considerable ratio of overlaps. Yet, to maximise its prediction efficiency, it needs the application of both COR and RUS for the UDW dataset, whereas only COR is necessary for the other two final datasets. Compared to CBA and CBA2, though, when the appropriate data engineering methods are employed, CPAR is less successful in predicting violations.

3.3. Models Explainability

As initially discussed, being able to understand and interpret the outputs of a machine learning model is of major significance in the present application domain because, first, it will enhance the labour inspectors' knowledge about the most predominant attributes highly connected with each type of violation and, secondly, it will build their trust in the model's suggestions for onsite inspections.

In the current study, we integrate approaches to support the models' explainability on two levels. In data preprocessing, through cooperation with labour inspection experts, we create a set of domain-identifiable qualitative features taking values easily perceivable to the labour inspectors. Additionally, in modelling, we use associative classification algorithms, creating white-box models consisting of class association rules (CARs) of the if-then form that provide understandable results for experts in the domain. These approaches foster the interpretability of the produced classifiers at both the global and local levels. Global interpretations refer to a model's extractions explaining the general relationships it learned, such as the patterns associated with a predicted response. On the other hand, local interpretations focus on explaining specific predictions given by a model, such as the attributes and interactions that drove the particular prediction [36].

Table 12 summarises all the classification models produced by the three final datasets and the combinations of the three AC algorithms with the six class distributions of Table 5. The last column displays the average number of CARs contained in the models, calculated by the ten classifiers generated for each model during the 10-fold cross-validation method. CPAR is observed to create significantly smaller classifiers than the other two algorithms, with CBA2 models being, on average, ten times bigger. Additionally, differences are noticed between the models of the same dataset and algorithm but of different class distributions.

The AC classifiers use their CARs to predict an unseen data instance following their algorithm classification method. The rule, or rules, used for determining the class of a data instance also reveals the reasoning for this classification, i.e., the local explanations. Global explanations can be extracted by examining the high-order ranked rules of a classifier and summarising their attribute correlations most often seen.

Table 12. Classification models and the corresponding number of CARs.

Summary of the Generated Classification Models and Their Number of Class Association Rules (CARs)					
Final Dataset	**AC Algorithm**	**Data Engineering Method**	**No.**	**Classification Model**	**Num of CARs**
UDW	CBA	FD	1	UDW-CBA-FD	762
		FD_COR	2	UDW-CBA-FD_COR	679
		FD_ROS	3	UDW-CBA-FD_ROS	451
		FD_COR_ROS	4	UDW-CBA-FD_COR_ROS	483
		FD_RUS	**5**	**UDW-CBA-FD_RUS**	**265**
		FD_COR_RUS	6	UDW-CBA-FD_COR_RUS	269
	CBA2	FD	7	UDW-CBA2-FD	788
		FD_COR	8	UDW-CBA2-FD_COR	737
		FD_ROS	9	UDW-CBA2-FD_ROS	217
		FD_COR_ROS	10	UDW-CBA2-FD_COR_ROS	283
		FD_RUS	11	UDW-CBA2-FD_RUS	303
		FD_COR_RUS	12	UDW-CBA2-FD_COR_RUS	311
	CPAR	FD	13	UDW-CPAR-FD	76
		FD_COR	14	UDW- CPAR-FD_COR	71
		FD_ROS	15	UDW-CPAR-FD_ROS	129
		FD_COR_ROS	16	UDW-CPAR-FD_COR_ROS	118
		FD_RUS	17	UDW-CPAR-FD_RUS	46
		FD_COR_RUS	18	UDW-CPAR-FD_COR_RUS	49
UNDER_DW	CBA	FD	19	UNDER_DW-CBA-FD	893
		FD_COR	20	UNDER_DW-CBA-FD_COR	1069
		FD_ROS	21	UNDER_DW-CBA-FD_ROS	766
		FD_COR_ROS	22	UNDER_DW-CBA-FD_COR_ROS	1075
		FD_RUS	23	UNDER_DW-CBA-FD_RUS	726
		FD_COR_RUS	24	UNDER_DW-CBA-FD_COR_RUS	1062
	CBA2	FD	25	UNDER_DW-CBA2-FD	1394
		FD_COR	**26**	**UNDER_DW-CBA2-FD_COR**	**1574**
		FD_ROS	27	UNDER_DW-CBA2-FD_ROS	1376
		FD_COR_ROS	28	UNDER_DW-CBA2-FD_COR_ROS	1594
		FD_RUS	29	UNDER_DW-CBA2-FD_RUS	1220
		FD_COR_RUS	30	UNDER_DW-CBA2-FD_COR_RUS	1573
	CPAR	FD	31	UNDER_DW-CPAR-FD	121
		FD_COR	32	UNDER_DW-CPAR-FD_COR	93
		FD_ROS	33	UNDER_DW-CPAR-FD_ROS	145
		FD_COR_ROS	34	UNDER_DW-CPAR-FD_COR_ROS	96
		FD_RUS	35	UNDER_DW-CPAR-FD_RUS	109
		FD_COR_RUS	36	UNDER_DW-CPAR-FD_COR_RUS	99

Table 12. *Cont.*

Summary of the Generated Classification Models and Their Number of Class Association Rules (CARs)					
Final Dataset	**AC Algorithm**	**Data Engineering Method**	**No.**	**Classification Model**	**Num of CARs**
UDW-or-UNDER_DW	CBA	FD	37	UDW-or-UNDER_DW-CBA-FD	938
		FD_COR	38	UDW-or-UNDER_DW-CBA-FD_COR	1127
		FD_ROS	39	UDW-or-UNDER_DW-CBA-FD_ROS	744
		FD_COR_ROS	40	UDW-or-UNDER_DW-CBA-FD_COR_ROS	1118
		FD_RUS	41	UDW-or-UNDER_DW-CBA-FD_RUS	687
		FD_COR_RUS	42	UDW-or-UNDER_DW-CBA-FD_COR_RUS	1108
	CBA2	FD	43	UDW-or-UNDER_DW-CBA2-FD	1426
		FD_COR	44	UDW-or-UNDER_DW-CBA2-FD_COR	1670
		FD_ROS	45	UDW-or-UNDER_DW-CBA2-FD_ROS	1316
		FD_COR_ROS	46	UDW-or-UNDER_DW-CBA2-FD_COR_ROS	1688
		FD_RUS	47	UDW-or-UNDER_DW-CBA2-FD_RUS	1234
		FD_COR_RUS	48	UDW-or-UNDER_DW-CBA2-FD_COR_RUS	1608
	CPAR	FD	49	UDW-or-UNDER_DW-CPAR-FD	122
		FD_COR	**50**	**UDW-or-UNDER_DW-CPAR-FD_COR**	**96**
		FD_ROS	51	UDW-or-UNDER_DW-CPAR-FD_ROS	144
		FD_COR_ROS	52	UDW-or-UNDER_DW-CPAR-FD_COR_ROS	97
		FD_RUS	53	UDW-or-UNDER_DW-CPAR-FD_RUS	113
		FD_COR_RUS	54	UDW-or-UNDER_DW-CPAR-FD_COR_RUS	101

Rule ranking is a pre-processing phase in AC mining that sorts the generated rules based on specific criteria, which can be different per AC algorithm, and is later used in prediction [37]. CBA and CBA2 rank their classification rules based on their confidence, support, and antecedent length (shortest). In contrast, CPAR ranks its rules on the grounds of their expected accuracy, i.e., the probability that a test case satisfying the rule's body belongs to its class [33]. Thus, in any case, the highest-ordered CARs of a classifier have the strongest prediction power, revealing the most dominant attribute correlations with each class.

Aiming to exhibit and explain the interpretability aspect of the classifiers generated in this research study, we select one from each final dataset and different AC algorithm that accomplishes high recall yields and, in the following tables, we present the first high-ranked classification rules, thereby disclosing the most prevailing feature patterns of compliance and non-compliance as regards the violation they are targeting.

In particular, Table 13 illustrates the feature interactions associated with undeclared work and those with compliance, as identified by the UDW-CBA-FD_RUS classifier (No. 5, Table 12), which is built from the UDW dataset, using the CBA algorithm and applying RUS to training data to address the class imbalance. As per the recall and F_5 metric (Table 9), this is the most efficient classifier in undeclared work prediction revealing more than 70% of the actual cases. As previously explained, an inspection case from the testing set is classified as risky or non-risky (YES/NO) based on a prediction mechanism using the generated CARs; thus, one or more of these rules contributes to defining the most suitable class for the given test case body. This rule practically offers also the local interpretation for the given prediction. For instance, the second rule of Table 13 explains that if a complaint is filed for a company of the HORECA business sector making rare changes in the employees' working schedule and using low employment, then an onsite inspection shall most probably reveal undeclared work. On the other hand, the first rule says that if a scheduled audit is performed in a large-sized company in the sales sector with full-time employees, it will most likely find the employer labour law compliant.

Global interpretations may be derived for risky and non-risky businesses by examining the components of each group of rules predicting these two classes. In Table 13, the most dominant features are identified in bold, revealing that if at least three of these coexist, then there is a strong indication of undeclared work: filed complaint, performing an evening or night inspection, to a company of the HORECA sector, established in central Athens, using low employment, paying low wages, and making rare changes in the working schedule.

Table 13. Prevailing patterns of compliance and non-compliance as regards undeclared work.

Highest-Ranked Class Association Rules from the UDW-CBA-FD_RUS Model [1]		
No.	**Body/Feature Values**	**Class/Risky**
1	**SCHEDULED, LARGE_SIZE, FULL_EMPL, SALES**	NO
2	**COMPLAINT, RARE_CHANGES, LOW_EMPL, HORECA**	YES
3	**COMPLAINT, RARE_CHANGES, HORECA, CENTRAL_ATHENS**	YES
4	**SCHEDULED**, MORNING, **VERY_LARGE_SIZE, FULL_EMPL, CORP**	NO
5	MORNING, WEEKDAY, **VERY_LARGE_SIZE, FULL_EMPL, CORP**	NO
6	WEEKDAY, **VERY_LARGE_SIZE, FULL_EMPL, CORP**, SERVICES	NO
7	**COMPLAINT**, WEEKEND, **LOW_PAID**	YES
8	**COMPLAINT, RARE_CHANGES, LOW_EMPL, CENTRAL_ATHENS**	YES
9	WEEKDAY, LOW_PAST_INFR	NO
10	**SCHEDULED, OFTEN_CHANGES, FULL_EMPL**, MEDIUM_PAID	NO
11	**COMPLAINT, LOW_EMPL**, CORP	YES
12	**SCHEDULED, OFTEN_CHANGES**, MEDIUM_PAID, **CORP**	NO
13	**EVENING**, WEEKDAY, **RARE_CHANGES, HORECA, CENTRAL_ATHENS**	YES
14	**COMPLAINT**, SMALL_SIZE, **RARE_CHANGES, LOW_PAID**, SOL_PROP, **HORECA**	YES
15	**VERY_LARGE_SIZE**, NORTH_ATHENS	NO
16	**COMPLAINT, EVENING, RARE_CHANGES, LOW_EMPL**	YES
17	MEDIUM_SIZE, **RARE_CHANGES**, MEDIUM_PAID, **HORECA**	YES
18	**MEDIUM_FREQ_CHANGES, CORP**, NORTH_ATHENS	NO
19	**SCHEDULED, VERY_OFTEN_CHANGES, CORP, SALES**	NO
20	WEEKDAY, MEDIUM_SIZE, **LOW_EMPL, CENTRAL_ATHENS**	YES
21	**SCHEDULED**, WEEKDAY, **CORP, SALES**, NORTH_ATHENS	NO
22	**SCHEDULED**, MORNING, NO_PAST_INSP, **CORP, SALES**, EAST_ATTICA	NO
23	**SCHEDULED, MEDIUM_FREQ_CHANGES**, PIRAEUS	NO
24	**NIGHT, RARE_CHANGES**, NO_PAST_INSP	YES
25	**COMPLAINT**, MORNING, **LOW_EMPL, CENTRAL_ATHENS**	YES
26	**COMPLAINT**, MORNING, **HORECA, CENTRAL_ATHENS**	YES
27	**COMPLAINT**, MEDIUM_SIZE, **LOW_EMPL**	YES

[1] Classifier generated by the UDW final dataset, using the CBA algorithm, and applying RUS in the training data.

Non-risky businesses are recognised when combining three or more characteristics: scheduled inspection, to a sales business, of legal form corporation, of large or very large size, with full-time employees, making medium or often or very often changes in the working schedule.

Table 14 presents the ten top-ranked rules linked with underdeclared work and the corresponding ten high-ordered rules associated with compliance, generated by the UNDER_DW-CBA2-FD_COR classifier (No. 26, Table 12), which is built from the UNDER_DW dataset, using the CBA2 algorithm and COR implementation in training data. As per Table 10, this model is among the most successful ones in identifying underdeclared work. Here, from the extracted global interpretations, one may notice differences in the dominating features associated with this type of violation compared with those of undeclared work. For instance, underdeclared work is significantly revealed through scheduled inspections, whereas, as regards undeclared work prediction, this attribute was mainly linked with compliant businesses, as per the UDW classifier (Table 13). Additionally, underdeclared work is discovered primarily in companies that were never inspected before (NO_PAST_INSP). In contrast, businesses that were checked and found compliant with labour law (NO_PAST_INFR) will probably be found compliant again. These characteristics, though, did not appear in the rules of undeclared work prediction.

Table 14. Prevailing patterns of compliance and non-compliance as regards underdeclared work.

Highest-Ranked Class Association Rules from the UNDER_DW-CBA2-FD_COR Model [1]		
No.	**Body/Feature Values**	**Class/Risky**
1	**SCHEDULED**, MORNING, WEEKDAY, SMALL_SIZE, **RARE_CHANGES**, **LOW_PAID**, **NO_PAST_INSP**, CENTRAL_ATHENS	YES
2	**SCHEDULED**, WEEKDAY, MEDIUM_SIZE, **RARE_CHANGES**, **LOW_EMPL**, **LOW_PAID**, **NO_PAST_INSP**, HORECA	YES
3	**SCHEDULED**, MEDIUM_SIZE, **RARE_CHANGES**, **LOW_PAID**, MED_PAST_INFR, CORP, HORECA	YES
4	**SCHEDULED**, WEEKDAY, SMALL_SIZE, **RARE_CHANGES**, MEDIUM_EMPL, **LOW_PAID**, **NO_PAST_INSP**, SOL_PROP, SERVICES	YES
5	**SCHEDULED**, **RARE_CHANGES**, **LOW_EMPL**, **LOW_PAID**, **NO_PAST_INSP**, WEST_ATHENS	YES
6	**SCHEDULED**, MORNING, SMALL_SIZE, **RARE_CHANGES**, MEDIUM_EMPL, **LOW_PAID**, **NO_PAST_INSP**, SOL_PROP SALES	YES
7	**SCHEDULED**, MORNING, WEEKDAY, SMALL_SIZE, **RARE_CHANGES**, MEDIUM_EMPL, **LOW_PAID**, **NO_PAST_INSP**, SERVICES	YES
8	MORNING, SMALL_SIZE, **RARE_CHANGES**, **LOW_PAID**, **NO_PAST_INSP**, HORECA, CENTRAL_ATHENS	YES
9	**SCHEDULED**, MORNING, SMALL_SIZE, **RARE_CHANGES**, **LOW_PAID**, **NO_PAST_INSP**, SERVICES, CENTRAL_ATHENS	YES
10	EVENING, SMALL_SIZE, **RARE_CHANGES**, MEDIUM_EMPL, **LOW_PAID**, **NO_PAST_INSP**, CENTRAL_ATHENS	YES
11	MORNING, **FULL_EMPL**, **NO_PAST_INFR**, SALES PIRAEUS	NO
12	WEEKEND, **VERY_LARGE_SIZE**, **NO_PAST_INFR**	NO
13	**VERY_OFTEN_CHANGES**, **SALES**, PIRAEUS	NO
14	MORNING, **NO_PAST_INFR**, CORP, **SALES**, PIRAEUS	NO
15	SCHEDULED, WEEKEND, **VERY_LARGE_SIZE**, HIGH_PAID	NO
16	SCHEDULED, MEDIUM_SIZE, **OFTEN_CHANGES**, **NO_PAST_INFR**, CORP	NO
17	SCHEDULED, MORNING, RARE_CHANGES, **FULL_EMPL**, **NO_PAST_INFR**, PIRAEUS	NO
18	MORNING, **NO_PAST_INFR**, **SALES**, PIRAEUS	NO
19	MORNING, MEDIUM_FREQ_CHANGES, **FULL_EMPL**, **NO_PAST_INFR**, SALES	NO
20	MEDIUM_SIZE, **OFTEN_CHANGES**, **NO_PAST_INFR**, CORP	NO

[1] Classifier generated by the UNDER_DW final dataset, using the CBA2 algorithm, and applying COR in the training data.

These differences in the global interpretations extracted as regards the detecting, on the one, undeclared work and, on the other, underdeclared work, clearly show the effectiveness of the approach to create different final datasets per targeted violation. Not only did the prediction performance improve significantly, as previously explained, but the derived knowledge is now more precise for each targeted violation, as seen here.

Last, Table 15 illustrates the mined knowledge when targeting both undeclared and underdeclared work, coming from the first high-ranked rules for both classes of the UDW-or-UNDER_DW-CPAR-FD_COR classification model (No. 50, Table 12), generated by the UDW-or-UNDER_DW dataset, employing the CPAR method and applying COR in training data. According to the recall metric of Table 11, among the CPAR classifiers generated by this dataset, this model achieves the highest performance, reaching to more than 70%. In this set of rules, one may notice that the dominating feature patterns have different compositions, comprising combinations of characteristics prevailing in the previous two groups of global interpretations.

Table 15. Prevailing patterns of compliance and non-compliance as regards undeclared or underdeclared work.

Highest-Ranked Class Association Rules from the UDW-or-UNDER_DW-CPAR-FD_COR Model [1]		
No.	**Body/Feature Values**	**Class/Risky**
1	**RARE_CHANGES, LOW_EMPL, LOW_PAID, NO_PAST_INSP, HORECA,** PIRAEUS	YES
2	WEEKDAY, **RARE_CHANGES, LOW_EMPL, LOW_PAID, NO_PAST_INSP, HORECA, CENTRAL_ATHENS**	YES
3	**RARE_CHANGES, LOW_EMPL, LOW_PAID, NO_PAST_INSP, HORECA,** SOUTH_ATHENS	YES
4	MORNING, **RARE_CHANGES, LOW_PAID, NO_PAST_INSP, HORECA,** WEST_ATHENS	YES
5	**RARE_CHANGES, LOW_PAID, NO_PAST_INSP, HORECA**	YES
6	MORNING, MEDIUM_SIZE, **RARE_CHANGES, LOW_EMPL,** MED_PAST_INFR, CORP, **HORECA**	YES
7	**NIGHT, RARE_CHANGES,** PROD_CONSTR	YES
8	**NIGHT, RARE_CHANGES,** HIGH_PAID	YES
9	**RARE_CHANGES, LOW_EMPL,** HIGH_PAST_INFR, CORP	YES
10	MORNING, **FULL_EMPL,** MEDIUM_PAID, **NO_PAST_INFR, SALES,** PIRAEUS	NO
11	MEDIUM_SIZE, **OFTEN_CHANGES, FULL_EMPL, NO_PAST_INFR, SALES**	NO
12	WEEKEND, **OFTEN_CHANGES, FULL_EMPL, NO_PAST_INFR, SALES**	NO
13	**FULL_EMPL,** HIGH_PAID, **NO_PAST_INFR, SALES,** EAST_ATTICA	NO
14	**VERY_LARGE_SIZE, FULL_EMPL, NO_PAST_INFR,** EAST_ATTICA	NO
15	MORNING, **VERY_LARGE_SIZE, MEDIUM_FREQ_CHANGES, FULL_EMPL,** HIGH_PAID	NO
16	MORNING, **MEDIUM_FREQ_CHANGES, FULL_EMPL,** MEDIUM_PAID, EAST_ATTICA	NO
17	SMALL_SIZE, **OFTEN_CHANGES, FULL_EMPL,** HIGH_PAID, **SALES**	NO

[1] Classifier generated by the UDW-or-UNDER_DW final dataset, using the CPAR algorithm, and applying COR in the training data.

4. Discussion

In this research study, we discuss the impact of undeclared work on society and the economy and the problems the enforcement authorities face in addressing it. We investigate the business needs and available data sources of a labour inspectorate, a public institution responsible for dealing with this employers' illegal practice, and put forward the necessity for applying innovative machine learning methods towards improving its effectiveness in this direction. We use a large block of actual past inspection data and focus on the class imbalance and class overlap issues that naturally exist in such domain datasets, obstructing the machine learning process.

To overcome these issues, we propose and apply combinations of data engineering techniques. Initially, we use data reduction based on the decision makers' selections of the target group of violations. With the aim of testing, evaluation, and demonstration, we create three different final datasets per the inspectorate's priorities for deterring infringements; one solely for undeclared work, one for underdeclared work, and one for both of these severe violations. Then we implement the class overlap removal (COR) method, which deletes from the training data the negatives that fall on positives, either isolated or in combination with random oversampling (ROS) or random undersampling (RUS) that handle class imbalance in the datasets. Hence, we create six diverse training data class distributions per final dataset, which are then compounded with three different AC algorithms, the CBA, CBA2, and CPAR, to build multiple classifiers, which are subsequently evaluated in detecting the targeted violations.

Based on considerations regarding the costs of positive and negative misclassifications for the inspectorate, we focus on the recall assessment metric to identify the most effective classifier per targeted violation. We conclude that for undeclared work prediction involving highly imbalanced datasets, using CBA and applying random undersampling suffices to boost the recall from 6% to more than 70% while maintaining accuracy to 70%. When only underdeclared work or both violations are targeted, and less imbalanced datasets are related, removing the class overlapping achieves the highest recall at 76–80% with the same algorithm. CPAR is also introduced in this study, displaying less sensitivity in class imbalance and class overlap in this application domain, achieving good results in all final datasets, even without data engineering applications to training sets.

Overall, this machine learning application illustrates the outputs of fifty-four classification models derived by the combinations of the AC algorithms, the final datasets, and the data engineering techniques, enabling the comprehension of the strengths and weaknesses of each approach and the identification of the most suitable model per the needs and resources of the enforcement authority. Indeed, there is no best model for all required tasks of inspection planning and targeting violations; on the contrary, several considerations must always be taken into account, such as the available time and number of inspections that can be performed to achieve a specific goal.

For instance, the models that attain increased recall fall short on precision and specificity, i.e., they would trigger several inspections that would finally conclude with no violations (false positives). These models are appropriate when the inspectorate wishes to detect most of the actual fraudulent businesses, e.g., in a specific area and period and can allocate adequate resources to perform several onsite visits; such are the cases when the HLI runs an action plan targeting undeclared and underdeclared work in tourist places, and a group of inspectors visits an area for this purpose.

On the other hand, on occasions when limited resources and time are available and high inspection yields are sought, the experts should choose a model with increased precision that initiate few onsite visits yet their success rate is high, such as the CBA2-FD for targeting underdeclared work, reaching violation prediction success at 70% and specificity at 92%.

The present research paper is of significant value in this application domain, not only because of the detailed demonstration of the classifiers' prediction performance and methods for improvement, as previously discussed, but also due to presenting knowledge extraction, which is valuable to the domain users.

In particular, we follow different approaches to enhance the interpretability of the outcomes; we use qualitative features that take comprehensible (by the domain users) values; we employ associative classification algorithms that produce simple and understandable rules of the if-then form; also, we create different final datasets per targeted group of violations to build classifiers devoted to these violations and derive focused knowledge related to them.

Thereby, the domain users' benefit in enhanced knowledge is two-fold. First, they obtain understandable explanations (local interpretations) for each inspection case or business classified as risky or non-risky as per a particular classifier, e.g., a UDW classifier. Hence, they can perceive the reasoning and estimate the fairness of a model's suggestion and be involved in the decision-making process of inspection planning; thus, their trust and acceptance in the models' outputs are increased. Secondly, they gain insights into the predominant trends and attribute patterns associated with the targeted violations. Indeed, in this application, we showed that the global interpretations derived by the classifiers targeting undeclared work display some differences from those of underdeclared work, proving that the proposed approaches can unveil attribute associations with each type of infringement that would remain hidden otherwise.

5. Conclusions

In the previous section, we summarised the outcomes related to the predictability and interpretability aspects of the classification models produced through the methodology we introduced in this study, and we concluded with the substantial improvements they offer both in the area of inspection planning and also in the domain knowledge provision. However, an even more crucial aspect one needs to examine when integrating such innovative machine learning techniques into the routine processes of a public enforcement authority, such as the labour inspectorate, is the adaptability and the level of user acceptance. Several innovative systems introduced into public institutions ended up being of very limited use or abandoned mainly due to several adaptation complications in their working environment or poor user acceptance.

The proposed methods in the current study can be easily adapted in the working environment of an enforcement authority accountable to address undeclared work and other severe labour law violations. Figure 4 illustrates a machine learning system with the characteristics we described so far being integrated into the business cycle of a labour inspectorate, e.g., the HLI. It may be configured to periodically draw and incorporate data from databases containing past inspections and other relevant information, such as employment and company characteristics, and create or update datasets per the users' needs or the authority's targets, as we presented for the HLI. Through a simple user interface, the managers can make selections on the data areas and attributes to be included in the datasets, thus building distinct classifiers per targeted violation, business sector, region, etc. Following this, they can test and evaluate the models while including, if necessary, techniques to face class imbalance and class overlap, and finally select the most appropriate classifiers on each occasion while considering the available resources and other inspection planning details.

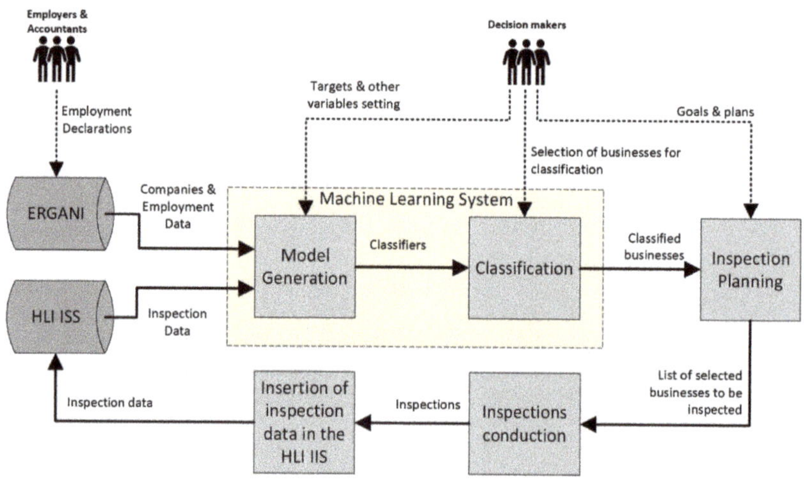

Figure 4. Adaptation of the proposed methodology in the business environment of a labour inspectorate.

No particular ICT or machine learning knowledge shall be necessary for the users to build different models per their needs in such a configurable system. The labour inspection managers are, thus, encouraged to actively engage in goal setting and inspection scheduling while exploiting the benefits of an innovative machine learning tool. Additionally, once the most successful classifiers are identified per the authority's goals and managers' needs and put to productive use, no manual feedback collection is necessary from the local labour inspectors regarding their findings to update the models. This task can be a system process scheduled to run periodically, automatically updating the classification models by integrating the new inspection data or other related details inserted into the databases, as depicted in Figure 4.

Concluding, an inspection recommendation system integrating interpretable machine learning techniques and the proposed approaches for class imbalance and class overlap may well adapt to the business environment of a labour inspectorate and be effortlessly accepted by the domain users, offering multiple benefits and solving all the deficiencies arising from a risk analysis tool manually configurable based on users' perceptions and experiences.

Our future research shall focus on designing an advanced integrated recommendation system that is flexible and adaptable to a labour inspectorate's changing goals and needs, needing to apply targeted preventative and deterrence measures to address severe labour law violations. Explorations on other machine learning techniques concentrating on achieving improved prediction performance and explainability of outputs at local and global levels shall also be included. Last, efforts shall be made to incorporate a scheduling module for targeted inspections per specific violations, areas, or business sectors, yet also considering other characteristics, such as the probability score of each classification and the cost of each suggested inspection based on local resources and attributes.

Author Contributions: Conceptualisation, E.A.; methodology, E.A.; software, E.A.; validation, E.A. and M.V.; formal analysis, E.A.; investigation, E.A.; resources, E.A.; data curation, E.A.; writing—original draft preparation, E.A.; writing—review and editing, M.V.; visualisation, E.A.; supervision, M.V.; project administration, E.A. and M.V. All authors have read and agreed to the published version of the manuscript.

Funding: This research received no external funding.

Data Availability Statement: The data presented in this study are available on request from the corresponding author. The data are not publicly available due to restrictions imposed by the public authority providing them for the present research study.

Acknowledgments: The authors thank the Hellenic Labour Inspectorate for providing the source data for the present research study.

Conflicts of Interest: The authors declare no conflict of interest.

References

1. European Commission, Directorate-General for Employment, Social Affairs and Inclusion. Special Eurobarometer 498 Report—Undeclared Work in the European Union. 2020. Available online: https://europa.eu/eurobarometer/surveys/detail/2250 (accessed on 18 December 2022).
2. Williams, C.C. Tackling Undeclared Work in the European Union: An Evaluation of Government Policy Approaches. *UTMS J. Econ.* **2019**, *10*, 135–147. Available online: http://www.utmsjoe.mk/files/Vol.%2010%20No.%202/UTMSJOE-2019-1002-01-Williams.pdf (accessed on 20 November 2022). [CrossRef]
3. International Labour Organization (ILO). Labour inspection in Europe: Undeclared Work, Migration, Trafficking. International Labour Organizatio—Geneva. January 2010. Available online: https://www.ilo.org/wcmsp5/groups/public/---ed_dialogue/---lab_admin/documents/publication/wcms_120319.pdf (accessed on 20 November 2022).
4. International Labour Organization (ILO). Labour Inspection and Undeclared Work in the EU. Geneva. 2013. Available online: https://www.ilo.org/wcmsp5/groups/public/---ed_dialogue/---lab_admin/documents/publication/wcms_220021.pdf (accessed on 20 November 2022).
5. Wu, R.-S.; Ou, C.; Lin, H.; Chang, S.-I.; Yen, D.C. Using data mining technique to enhance tax evasion detection performance. *Expert Syst. Appl.* **2012**, *39*, 8769–8777. [CrossRef]
6. West, J.; Bhattacharya, M. Intelligent financial fraud detection: A comprehensive review. *Comput. Secur.* **2016**, *57*, 47–66. [CrossRef]
7. Liao, C.-W.; Chiang, T.-L. Designing of dynamic labor inspection system for construction industry. *Expert Syst. Appl.* **2012**, *39*, 4402–4409. [CrossRef]
8. Dwork, C.; Hardt, M.; Pitassi, T.; Reingold, O.; Zemel, R. Fairness through awareness. In Proceedings of the ITCS'12: 3rd Innovations in Theoretical Computer Science Conference, Cambridge, MA, USA, 8–10 January 2012; pp. 214–226. [CrossRef]
9. Coussement, K.; Benoit, D.F. Interpretable data science for decision making. *Decis. Support Syst.* **2021**, *150*, 113664. [CrossRef]
10. Pfau-Effinger, B. Varieties of Undeclared Work in European Societies. *Br. J. Ind. Relat* **2009**, *47*, 79–99. [CrossRef]
11. European Commission, Directorate-General for Employment, Social Affairs and Inclusion. Special Eurobarometer 402 Report—Undeclared Work in the European Union. Publications Office. 2014. Available online: https://europa.eu/eurobarometer/surveys/detail/1080 (accessed on 18 December 2022).
12. European Commission, Directorate-General for Employment Social Affairs and Equal Opportunities. Special Eurobarometer 284 Report—Undeclared Work in the European Union. 2007. Available online: https://europa.eu/eurobarometer/surveys/detail/618 (accessed on 18 December 2022).
13. European Union. Regulation (EU) 2019/1149 of the European Parliament and of the Council of 20 June 2019 Establishing a European Labour Authority. 2019. Available online: https://eur-lex.europa.eu/legal-content/EN/TXT/?uri=CELEX%3A32019R1149 (accessed on 18 December 2022).

14. Cremers, J. The European Labour Authority and rights-based labour mobility. *ERA Forum* **2020**, *21*, 21–34. [CrossRef]
15. European Union. Decision (EU) 2016/344 of the European Parliament and of the Council of 9 March 2016 on Establishing a European Platform to Enhance Cooperation in Tackling Undeclared Work. 2016. Available online: https://eur-lex.europa.eu/eli/dec/2016/344/oj (accessed on 18 December 2022).
16. Organisation for Economic Co-operation and Development Staff, Informal Employment and Promoting the Transition to a Salaried Economy, OECD 2004. Organization for Economic Cooperation & Development. 2004. Available online: https://www.oecd.org/employment/emp/34846912.pdf (accessed on 18 December 2022).
17. de Wispelaere, F.; Pacolet, J.; Rotaru, V.; Naylor, S.; Gillis, D.; Alogogianni, E. Data Mining for More Efficient Enforcement: A Practitioner Toolkit from the Thematic Workshop of the European Platform Undeclared Work. Brussels. 2018. Available online: https://biblio.ugent.be/publication/8572421/file/8572424 (accessed on 20 November 2022).
18. Alogogianni, E.; Virvou, M. Association Rules and Machine Learning for Enhancing Undeclared Work Detection. In Proceedings of the 2020 11th International Conference on Information, Intelligence, Systems and Applications (IISA), Piraeus, Greece, 15–17 July 2020; pp. 1–8. [CrossRef]
19. Agrawal, R.; Imieliński, T.; Swami, A. Mining association rules between sets of items in large databases. In Proceedings of the 1993 ACM SIGMOD International Conference on Management of Data—SIGMOD'93, Washington, DC, USA, 25–28 May 1993; pp. 207–216. [CrossRef]
20. Alogogianni, E.; Virvou, M. Data Mining for Targeted Inspections Against Undeclared Work by Applying the CRISP-DM Methodology. In Proceedings of the 2021 12th International Conference on Information, Intelligence, Systems & Applications (IISA), Chania Crete, Greece, 12–14 July 2021; pp. 1–8. [CrossRef]
21. Liu, B.; Hsu, W.; Ma, Y. Integrating Classification and Association Rule Mining. In Proceedings of the 4th International Conference on Knowledge Discovery and Data Mining (KDD'98), New York, NY, USA, 27–31 August 1998; Available online: https://www.aaai.org/Papers/KDD/1998/KDD98-012.pdf (accessed on 20 November 2022).
22. Chapman, P.; Clinton, J.; Kerber, R.; Khabaza, T.; Reinartz, T.; Shearer, C.; Wirth, R. *CRISP-DM 1.0: Step-By-Step Data Mining Guide*; SPSS Inc.: Chicago, IL, USA, 2000; Volume 9, pp. 1–73.
23. Alogogianni, E.; Virvou, M. Addressing the issue of undeclared work—Part I: Applying associative classification per the CRISP-DM methodology. *Intell. Decis. Technol.* **2022**, *15*, 721–747. [CrossRef]
24. Liu, B.; Ma, Y.; Wong, C.-K. Classification Using Association Rules: Weaknesses and Enhancements. In *Data Mining for Scientific and Engineering Applications*; Massive Computing; Grossman, R., Kamath, C., Kegelmeyer, P., Kumar, V., Namburu, R.R., Eds.; Springer: Boston, MA, USA, 2001; Volume 2, pp. 591–605. [CrossRef]
25. He, H.; Garcia, E.A. Learning from Imbalanced Data. *IEEE Trans. Knowl Data Eng.* **2009**, *21*, 1263–1284. [CrossRef]
26. Haixiang, G.; Yijing, L.; Shang, J.; Mingyun, G.; Yuanyue, H.; Bing, G. Learning from class-imbalanced data: Review of methods and applications. *Expert Syst. Appl.* **2017**, *73*, 220–239. [CrossRef]
27. Baesens, B.; Höppner, S.; Verdonck, T. Data engineering for fraud detection. *Decis. Support Syst.* **2021**, *150*, 113492. [CrossRef]
28. Wang, M.; Zheng, K.; Yang, Y.; Wang, X. An Explainable Machine Learning Framework for Intrusion Detection Systems. *IEEE Access* **2020**, *8*, 73127–73141. [CrossRef]
29. Denil, M.; Trappenberg, T. Overlap versus Imbalance. In *Advances in Artificial Intelligence. Canadian AI 2010*; Lecture Notes in Computer Science; Springer: Berlin/Heidelberg, Germany, 2010; pp. 220–231. [CrossRef]
30. Santos, M.S.; Abreu, P.H.; Japkowicz, N.; Fernández, A.; Soares, C.; Wilk, S.; Santos, J. On the joint-effect of class imbalance and overlap: A critical review. *Artif. Intell. Rev.* **2022**, *55*, 6207–6275. [CrossRef]
31. Prati, R.C.; Batista, G.; Monard, M.C. *Class Imbalances versus Class Overlapping: An Analysis of a Learning System Behavior*; Springer: Berlin/Heidelberg, Germany, 2004; pp. 312–321. [CrossRef]
32. Alogogianni, E.; Virvou, M. Undeclared Work Prediction Using Machine Learning: Dealing with the Class Imbalance and Class Overlap Problems. In Proceedings of the 2022 13th International Conference on Information, Intelligence, Systems & Applications (IISA), Corfu, Greece, 18–20 July 2022; pp. 1–8. [CrossRef]
33. Yin, X.; Han, J. CPAR: Classification based on Predictive Association Rules. In Proceedings of the 2003 SIAM International Conference on Data Mining, San Francisco, CA, USA, 1–3 May 2003; pp. 331–335. [CrossRef]
34. Mattiev, J.; Kavsek, B. Coverage-Based Classification Using Association Rule Mining. *Appl. Sci.* **2020**, *10*, 7013. [CrossRef]
35. Du, M.; Liu, N.; Hu, X. Techniques for interpretable machine learning. *Commun. ACM* **2019**, *63*, 68–77. [CrossRef]
36. Murdoch, W.J.; Singh, C.; Kumbier, K.; Abbasi-Asl, R.; Yu, B. Definitions, methods, and applications in interpretable machine learning. *Proc. Natl. Acad. Sci. USA* **2019**, *116*, 22071–22080. [CrossRef] [PubMed]
37. Abdelhamid, N.; Thabtah, F. Associative Classification Approaches: Review and Comparison. *J. Inf. Knowl. Manag.* **2014**, *13*, 1450027. [CrossRef]
38. Li, W.; Han, J.; Pei, J. CMAR: Accurate and efficient classification based on multiple class-association rules. In Proceedings of the 2001 IEEE International Conference on Data Mining, San Jose, CA, USA, 29 November–2 December 2001; pp. 369–376. [CrossRef]
39. Cohen, W.W. Fast Effective Rule Induction. In *Machine Learning Proceedings 1995*; Elsevier: Amsterdam, The Netherlands, 1995; pp. 115–123. [CrossRef]
40. Quinlan, J.R.; Cameron-Jones, R.M. *FOIL: A Midterm Report*; Springer: Berlin/Heidelberg, Germany, 1993; pp. 1–20. [CrossRef]
41. Quinlan, J.R. Induction of decision trees. *Mach. Learn.* **1986**, *1*, 81–106. [CrossRef]

42. Salzberg, S.L. C4.5: Programs for Machine Learning. *Mach. Learn.* **1994**, *16*, 235–240. [CrossRef]
43. Tharwat, A. Classification assessment methods. *Appl. Comput. Inform.* **2021**, *17*, 168–192. [CrossRef]
44. Padillo, F.; Luna, J.; Ventura, S. LAC: Library for associative classification. *Knowl. Based. Syst.* **2020**, *193*, 105432. [CrossRef]

electronics

MDPI

Article

An Innovative Tool to Measure Employee Performance through Customer Satisfaction: Pilot Research Using eWOM, VR, and AR Technologies

Ioan-David Legman [1], Manuela Rozalia Gabor [2,*] and Mihaela Kardos [2]

[1] "George Emil Palade" University of Medicine, Pharmacy, Sciences and Technology of Targu Mures, 540142 Targu Mures, Romania

[2] Department ED1—Economic Sciences, Faculty of Economics and Law, "George Emil Palade" University of Medicine, Pharmacy, Sciences and Technology of Targu Mures, 540142 Targu Mures, Romania

* Correspondence: manuela.gabor@umfst.ro or rozalia_gabor@yahoo.com; Tel.: +40-265-262-275

Abstract: Recent research reflects the assessment of customer satisfaction from different perspectives, an important aspect in all sectors that must be expressed in measurable parameters of organization performance. By reviewing the literature, we noticed the lack of a specific indicator to quantify the tripartite relation: customer satisfaction—employee performance—company performance. Therefore, based on Six Sigma and Lean Six Sigma methods, the paper introduces an innovative measurement tool named the Spc indicator (The Assessment System of Employee Performance according to Customer Satisfaction) and the related implementation methodology (named ITA). The aim of the paper is to implement an innovative tool to improve the efficiency of employee performance assessment systems in relation to company performance in services and industry sectors through customer satisfaction assessment. By using AR and VR as implementation technologies, our present results extend and compare the results from other pilot research made by authors in the e-commerce sector. The results point out that mystery shoppers and electronic word-of-mouth (eWOM) applied in e-commerce are more efficient than AR and VR technologies applied in services and industry, as reflected in the company's performance. Furthermore, customer–employee interactions and communications with eWOM in e-commerce are more efficient than WOM used in services and industry. This paper contains both theoretical and practical contributions by offering a new, short-time innovative tool for the continuous improvement of the company with applications in different fields.

Keywords: e-commerce; electronic word-of-mouth (eWOM); company performance; cost reduction; continuous improvement

Citation: Legman, I.-D.; Gabor, M.R.; Kardos, M. An Innovative Tool to Measure Employee Performance through Customer Satisfaction: Pilot Research Using eWOM, VR, and AR Technologies. *Electronics* **2023**, *12*, 1158. https://doi.org/10.3390/electronics12051158

Academic Editors: Galina Ilieva and George A. Tsihrintzis

Received: 31 January 2023
Revised: 24 February 2023
Accepted: 24 February 2023
Published: 27 February 2023

1. Introduction

In the technology century, competitive advantages reflect an organization's ability to achieve high performance through proper, effective, and efficient management. These coordinates are fundamental in the current economic environment marked by increased *technological and informational complexity* and social changes with consequences on employees' and consumers' personalities [1]. Strategy can be customized, and each company utilizes the decisions considered most effective. Porter [2] has become a classic for the three types of strategies that companies can adopt to face competition:

- Concentrated effort strategy;
- Differentiation strategy through products, services, outlets, and prices [3];
- Strategy of global domination through costs.

The philosophy of any customer-centered company must be the customer before all. It must be based on the *continuous improvement* of both the products and services it provides regardless of the sector. From this philosophy, results the importance and necessity of customer satisfaction analysis. Recent research reflects the assessment of customer satisfaction from different perspectives, using quantitative, statistical, behavioral, qualitative, and intrinsic tools. Measuring customer satisfaction is one of the most important elements that has come to the attention of companies and organizations in all sectors [3]. Customer satisfaction must be expressed in measurable parameters as one of the key performance indicators (KPIs) of the companies. Customer satisfaction as a company performance indicator is difficult to achieve in terms of employee motivation and involves that all employees have direct contact with the customer, face-to-face or by electronic platforms (e-mail, chat, etc.). Customer satisfaction must motivate employees to achieve the highest standards and, in consequence, constantly increase labor productivity. In industrial sectors, the customer is not the direct consumer. Moreover, the purchasing process usually involves more people with different roles, each contributing to this final process.

Based on these considerations and using (as a starting point) the concepts of *Six Sigma* and *Lean Six Sigma*, this paper contributes (both theoretically and practically) to the development of international scientific literature by introducing a new and innovative measurement tool together with the specific implementation methodology. Our research is a complex one by presenting, comparatively, the results of its implementation in three different sectors:

- Online commerce;
- Package delivery services;
- Automotive industry.

These research results were obtained during the doctoral research of the first author under the coordination of the second author. The authors applied the proposed indicator and methodology as pilot research in e-commerce, the results being published in [4]. During the doctoral research, the authors extended the implementation of the indicator by adapting the implementation methodology for the automotive industry and service sectors to compare their continuous improvement processes, customer-oriented strategies, and the cost reduction management of these companies. The main scope was to develop and adapt the new indicator and the implementation methodology according to each sector's specificities. All the conditions and details about the implementation methodology are presented in the Material and Methods section.

The authors name the new indicator the **Spc**—*The Assessment System of Employee Performance according to Customer Satisfaction* [4]. The implementation method of the Spc indicator—is named **ITA Methodology** (*Initiation—Testing—Application*). They both directly ***contribute*** to sustainable company growth, as we further demonstrate through the performance indicators of the three companies from the research.

By conducting a literature review (detailed in the next section), we noticed the lack of a specific tool to quantify the tripartite relation *customer satisfaction—employee performance—company performance*; therefore, we consider our research results to be an important scientific contribution to the field, both *theoretically* (by introducing a new indicator Spc and a new implementation methodology, ITA) and *practically* (based on the results of their implementation in three different fields such as services, industry, and e-commerce). The proposed measurement tool, the Spc and its specific methodology (ITA methodology), fill a gap in the literature:

- They are the first measurement tools that simultaneously take into consideration: customer satisfaction, employee performance, and company performance.
- The implementation methodology used *new electronics technologies* and *information systems*, as follows: *augmented reality* (AR), *virtual reality* (VR) *Spectacles VR-BOX v2.0*, *electronic word-of-mouth* (eWOM), *VR glasses, chat, platform Warp Studio, OCS* (*Online Comments System*) *platform* and *Kahoot platform*.
- There are well-known tools for measuring service/product quality, customer satisfaction (e.g., SERVQUAL), and continuous company improvement (e.g., Six Sigma, Lean Six Sigma, EFQM Excellence Model of European Foundation Quality Model). These tools work separately from only one direction and from the QMS (Quality Management

System), not as an interface of *customer satisfaction—employee performance—company performance* as ***Spc*** and ***ITA methodology*** does.

- Our paper specifically corresponds to the new trends in the digital era and focuses on how *information technologies, electronic multimedia,* and *computer science* change business models and significantly affect companies' performance. The rapid penetration of information technologies brings new opportunities for innovation, continuously improving and increasing efficiency and identifying key applications of information technology in practice. In this context, our research contributes to investigating the application of such technologies and information systems as those mentioned above in the business area.

The *aim* of the paper is to analyze the efficiency increase in employee performance assessment systems in relation to performance economic indicators (KPIs) starting from customer satisfaction assessment based on the results of a pilot study in the e-commerce sector made by the authors during their doctoral research [4] by adapting them for package delivery services and the automotive industry by introducing ITA methodology and the Spc indicator.

As mentioned above, the Spc indicator and ITA methodology were **developed and proposed by the authors** and the ***information system*** and ***digital technologies*** were used for implementation: AR (augmented reality) and VR (virtual reality technologies) [5].

Our research is important from the perspective of the company's economic performance, which is often determined in economic terms [6]. Regarding these aspects, in the present research, KPIs were considered (Figure 1):

(1) *Decreasing the number of NRR (Negative Response Rate) followed by decreasing the number of dissatisfied customers* and the number of *dissatisfied employees;*
(2) *Total cost reduction;*
(3) *Waste reduction through economic efficiency of the yield of production factors* (Eeypf) and *economic efficiency on the consumption of production factors* (Eecpf);
(4) *Continuous improvement of the management process;*
(5) *Economic performance* measured by *turnover* and *profit.*

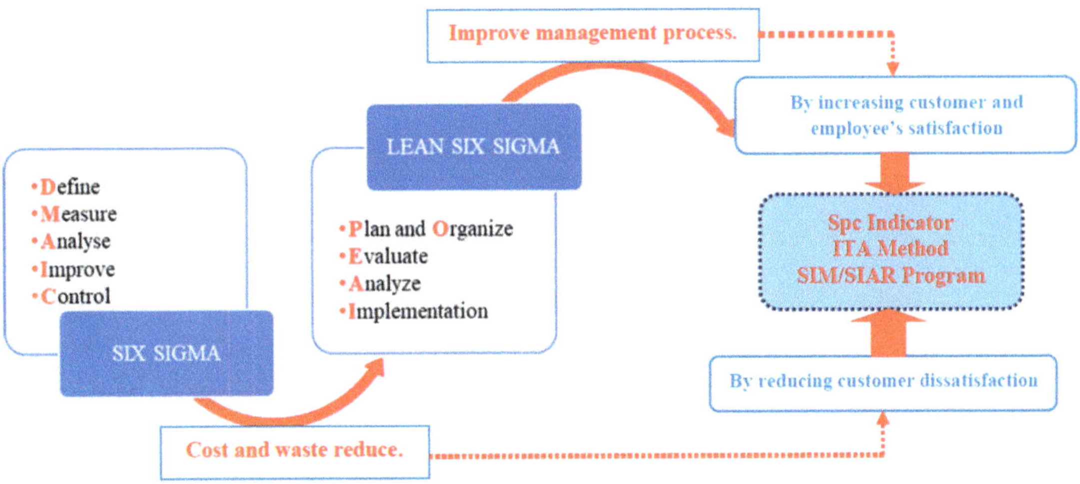

Figure 1. The conceptual framework of the research.

In our research, the element "key" from KPIs is considered the competitive advantage of the companies to have satisfied customers and implicitly satisfied employees. The "performance" element is given by all of the economic performance indicators mentioned above. The "indicator" is considered to be the moment *before implementing ITA Methodology* and *Spc* (considered M0) for each sector and the future corrections for more sectors. The conceptual framework is presented in Figure 1: the main concepts, Six Sigma and Lean Six Sigma, used as the reference for developing the method, the indicator, and the implementation program proposed by the authors, while the conceptual and methodological aspects are detailed in the following sections.

Customer satisfaction is most important because, without satisfied customers, many companies could not survive. Achieving success in business depends on many factors, mainly on participants' values [7]. Customer satisfaction is directly related to company performance. In modern marketing, customer satisfaction is considered a key element of business success [8]. Customer satisfaction also influences future purchasing decisions. Therefore, an important role is played by the quality of company products and services, their selling techniques, and employees' attitude toward customers. Companies strive for sustainable sales and profit increases, strengthening the relationship with their customers by expanding their loyal customers [9]. The strategy of maximizing customer satisfaction is based on the exploitation of potential sales for existing customers, most often considering price reductions, various bonuses, loyalty points, etc. [10]. However, we cannot talk about customer satisfaction if there is a complaint. Therefore, this aspect is another important starting point in our research by taking into consideration the NRR (negative response rate) indicator used by an e-commerce company as the initial analysis moment (M0-before implementing Spc and ITA methodology) and further as the implementation through SIM (**S**pc Indicator, **I**TA Methodology, and the **M**ystery Shopper) and SIAR (**S**pc indicator, **I**TA Methodology, and **AR** technology for services, respectively, VR technology for automotive industry) programs. Our research also considers the significant transition from physical oral communication (WOM—word-of-mouth) to *electronic oral communication* (eWOM), even more obvious since the beginning of the COVID-19 pandemic [11]. In the customer–employee direct relations, there are numerous differences between the two communication forms [12].

There are also situations when companies constantly increase customer satisfaction, but only a small fraction of the customers return. In our research, we take this aspect into consideration by measuring the rate of return (in percent) from each company because many companies lose customers continually, even if they have a high degree of customer satisfaction [9].

2. Literature Review

Because the present paper introduces a new measurement tool and a new methodology for implementing it, we present in the following subsections a short literature review for each theoretical concept that formed the basis of the conception of the *Spc indicator* and *ITA Methodology* following the conceptual framework of the research from Figure 1.

2.1. Six Sigma and Lean Six Sigma

Six Sigma is an applied methodology to improve business performance [13], minimize errors and defects [14,15], and maximize value [15]—basically the most effective method used to improve organization performance [16]. Six Sigma aims to satisfy the customer and earn their loyalty, and, for the success of these steps, the active involvement of employees is necessary, as in problems identified by the DMAIC (Define, Measure, Analyze, Improve, Control) method [13,17]. Any business can be improved by Six Sigma and Lean Six Sigma [18]. Six Sigma can facilitate the solving of company problems [19], adapted to the dynamics of current management [20] and on cost reduction [21,22].

Lean Six Sigma (LLS), introduced by George in 2002 [23], unlike Six Sigma, is a concept about process change and process improvement, eliminating and reducing the process variation [24] that directly involves employees in this process [25] for jointly developing a gradual solving strategy [26]. LLS is segmented into four phases, creating value [19] according to Figure 1, and has numerous benefits [27]: high quality and efficiency, increased employee motivation, improved customer relationships, improved response reaction, increased productivity and profit, etc. Although the pros regarding these methods' effectiveness are numerous, there are also opinions stating that these methods ignore the human factor [28].

Both methods help the company focus on issues that improve productivity, eliminating unnecessary processes and unusual activities that would be a barrier to increasing the company's economic efficiency and performance. Six Sigma is based on profit maximization and customer satisfaction, as most customers, when dissatisfied, share this dissatisfaction with other customers, thus boycotting the company's business [29]. Six Sigma tries to improve existing goods and services with better control over resources, optimizing costs, time, and product quality [30]. LSS is a technique that improves productivity and increases value, making improvements in terms of customer satisfaction, price level, quality, and other important aspects [31]. LSS starts with customers, with the main objective to eliminate any issues that would lead to customer dissatisfaction, offering an opportunity to develop the business, and creating a relationship between customer and company, by meeting its requirements today, not tomorrow [32]. Improving company procedures, LLS improves production, as reflected in the company revenues. LLS is more efficient by allowing an increase in production and customer satisfaction [33].

2.2. Customer Satisfaction—Short Evolution of Measurement Methods and Concepts

In the scientific literature, customer satisfaction has many definitions, the terms "consumer satisfaction" and "customer satisfaction" being synonymous [34], while important elements in defining customer satisfaction are [35]:

- Customer satisfaction is an affective or cognitive response that can vary in intensity;
- The response focuses on a specific element: product, expectations, services, etc.;
- The answer is specific only to a specific period: after the purchasing experience, after consumption, etc.

AT&T was the first company to introduce marketing research different from what had existed on the market in the 1970s, namely SAM—Satisfaction Attitude Measurement, carried out by mail [36], followed by the Cardozo model based on understanding the impact of customer satisfaction on its future purchases [36]. Howard & Seth's model is based on inputs that stimulate the purchasing process, perceptions, analysis, and outputs [37]. Day and Hunt's research [38], also in the 1970s, focused on the customer satisfaction—financial performance relation, while customer loyalty as company intangible assets was later developed and included [39]. However, customer satisfaction should not be used as a single indicator of loyalty [40,41] and must be analyzed in the customer–employee and customer–company relationships [42].

Numerous studies have shown that the main determinant of trust is satisfaction accumulated over time because of transactions carried out on the market [43]. Regardless of the variables in the measurement model or method, the possibility of its adjustment and adaptation must exist [36].

With the development of the *digital economy*, market and consumer trends have created a new approach regarding customer loyalty interpretation. The competitive dynamics of the competitive environment, the progressive saturation of many markets, and the structural changes in exchange processes induced by the emergence of the *digital economy* [44] have supported the progressive importance of customer satisfaction, leading to an increased interest in the interconnections between supply and demand. However, in recent years, the study of consumer behavior has shown that expanding the research on the customer–product interaction can reveal more information about customer loyalty [45]. In the 1980s, a new concept was introduced in measuring customer satisfaction, i.e., trust, being considered a determining factor in the customer–producer relationship [46].

The areas of research related to customer satisfaction are presented in Table 1.

Table 1. Customer satisfaction research—comparative table.

Field of Research	Author and Publication Year
Distribution channels	Andaleeb, 1992 [47] Anderson and Narus, 1990 [48] Anderson and Weitz, 1989 [49] Shurr and Ozanne, 1985 [50]
Consumer markets	Fletcher and Peters, 1997 [51] Gurviez, 1996 [52]
Services	Crosby, Evans, and Cowles, 1990 [53] Grayson and Ambler, 1999 [54] Moorman, Zaltman, and Deshpandé, 1992 [55] Moorman, Deshpandé, and Zaltman, 1993 [56]

2.3. *Interface Quality—Employees—Customers—Company Performance*

Technology has moved from the industrial to *digital area,* creating a deep impact on both producers' and consumers' behavior. The main aspects characterizing a business with quality products/services are high level of customer retention (loyalty), low costs, high profit rates, low staff fluctuation, staff motivation, etc., practically the Six Sigma concept.

A company's performance depends on several efficiency indicators, such as cost, profit, and productivity. Six Sigma's DMAIC (define, measure, analyze, improve, and control) elements are very important in increasing a company's economic efficiency [24].

An effective method for improving the quality of direct contacts between customers and employees is the *mystery shopper* [57], which, as well as Six Sigma, minimizes errors and maximizes value [15]. Some companies choose to become customer-centered companies, "earth's most customer-centric company".

The concepts of the Six Sigma method were applied to our pilot research in e-commerce. The information collected during mystery shopping is used to help a company better formulate its requirements for employees and improve the way customers are served [58]. The aim of a mystery shopper is not to penalize employees, but to identify certain problems and solve them to create an image of the customer's experience.

Employees must be permanently educated to have a responsible attitude and meet customers' demands [55], while education can be formal, informal, or non-formal [59]. The way a customer is served can be decisive in competition between companies. Whether it is the speed of service or the complementary services, all can add something to the direct customer–employee interaction. In order to be able to talk about employee loyalty to the company, it is preferable that, first, the organization shows its attachment to employees [60]. Furthermore, a powerful product on the market will create a strong image for the company [61].

The main company objective is to meet consumer needs. At some point, the company will have dissatisfied customers. Most of them, when expressing their discontent in the form of a complaint, have a state of disappointment and frustration [16], which can be solved by following essential rules in the employee–customer communication [62–64]. Today, customer satisfaction is no longer enough—it requires satisfying customers [65]. The company can create an advantage over the competition by identifying what is essential for customers, and one of the ways to obtain this information is directly from customers. Most of the time, this will not produce an immediate effect, but it is a gain, leading to results [66]. The continuous improvement of the employee–customer relationship can only bring benefits [67].

The increase in cognitive power and affirmation of individual consumption patterns, correlated with a gradual increase in customer expectations compared to market supply, has emphasized a dynamic relation between the business system and the customer [68]. The atmosphere created by the company during the purchase will influence future customer purchases in that company. Kim's conceptual model in 2006, developed by Chebat and

Morrin in 2007 [69], presents this connection between the store's atmosphere and emotional status [69].

Customers can purchase products both online and offline. Increased market volatility, uncertainty, and rapid changes characterizing economic and social environments and online environment development, different from traditional markets, have revealed some perspectives that are beneficial to classical markets in the acquisition process [70]. There may be several factors influencing this communication process between employee and customer (culture, employee/customer status, online/face-to-face dialogue environment, etc.). Adopting eWOM communication is a powerful mechanism for generating the response for a product [71]. The customer is stimulated through eWOM to express their opinions (positive or negative) so that the information can be processed [72]. This element is an important source of information for both the company and other customers [73]. Electronic WOM can increase a company's long-term profitability by collecting information about customers and accessing the company's platforms or other social media [74].

The purchasing atmosphere influences information processing, facilitating the orientation to negative information or the orientation of filters toward the perception of positive product elements [75]. Competition brings to market the same product at the same price, but customer service can place the company in a positive light [76] and can differentiate it from its competitors. Job satisfaction creates a positive atmosphere in any organization and leads directly to increasing individual attachment to an organization [77] alongside the existence of an organized environment [78]. Consumer utilitarian behavior is a rational approach involving an efficient purchase [79]. In this context, consumers can assess the experience as an achievement of the pursued objective.

3. Materials and Methods

In actual digital economies, information technologies, computer-based science, and electronic tools are intensively used as competitive advantages for companies. Therefore:

- The based concept of *Six Sigma* used in this research is about process change and process improvement [24], which directly involves the employee in this process [25], for a joint gradual solving strategy [26].
- The concept of *Lean Six Sigma,* referring to the main objective to reduce customer dissatisfaction [32], creates the possibility of adjustments and adaptation that must exist in a company [36].
- The necessity that employees must be permanently educated in order to have a responsible attitude and meet customers' demands [55] and the importance of the continuous improvement of the employee–customer relationship that could bring benefits to the company [67].

These points represent the main theoretical foundations for the first research hypothesis:

H1. *A growth and development program requires continuous improvements related, adapted, and updated to the period of time in which it is applied.*

For the second research hypothesis, the theoretical foundations are based on and starting from the fact that:

- Based on the *Six Sigma* principles, a company must adapt to the dynamic of current management [20] for a joint gradual solving strategy [26];
- Regarding the *customer satisfaction measurement* tool, a possibility of its adjustments and adaptations must exist in a competitive company [36];
- By ensuring the important *interface quality—employees—customers—company performance* for a competitive company, the education of the employee can be formal, informal, or non-formal [59].

Based on this theoretical framework, we formulated the second research hypothesis.

H2. *Performance evaluation systems require innovative adjustments by including elements from other sectors.*

Due to the novelty of the new measurement indicator (Spc), its implementation (ITA methodology), the aim and objectives of our research (the validation or invalidation of these results in other economic sectors: services and industry), the lack of similar studies in the literature, the theoretical and practical concepts from the literature review in the previous section directly linked to our research, we used as research hypotheses the same ones as in the pilot research applied in e-commerce during the doctoral research of one of the authors, and already published by the authors [4] as follows:

- H1: A growth and development program requires continuous improvements related, adapted, and updated to the period of time in which it is applied [24,26,32,36,55,67].
- H2: Performance evaluation systems require innovative adjustments by including elements from other sectors [20,26,36,59].

The research hypotheses were formulated in line with the references mentioned in the literature review section taking into consideration that the continuous improvement process plays a critical and strategic role for organizations with the final purpose of increasing company KPIs. Another scientific consideration for testing our research hypotheses is, according to the literature review, that the traditional methods for assessing company performance in the new digital economy era have deficiencies giving only a static and retrospective view. Therefore, in the digital economy and especially after the use of online communication in all domains after the COVID-19 pandemic, a modern and innovative measurement tool is necessary with the main scope to emphasize the need for both consumer and employee satisfaction.

Based on the conceptual framework described in Figure 1, data were collected between December 2018 and September 2020 in different time intervals depending on the sector. The research sample has a total of 121 subjects from the company's employees who directly interact with customers:

- 32 employees from an e-commerce company;
- 67 employees from a services company (parcel delivery);
- 22 employees from an automotive industry company.

For the calculus of the Spc indicator for each of the three companies, the following formula was used:

$$Spc = \frac{WmL \times Maps}{Cha \times t} \times \frac{\sum c}{1000} \quad (1)$$

where:

Spc = the Spc indicator;
WmL = average labor productivity;
Maps = weighted arithmetic average of customer satisfaction;
Cha = salary expenses per employee per hour (in Euro);
t = average time to solve a specific task;
Σc = total amount of contacts (employee effort).

The first element of the Spc indicator, *WmL* was collected differently according to the specific activity of the companies:

- For e-commerce, the *WmL* represents the average number of direct contacts resolved (customer—employee) per hour per employee by chat or/and phone;
- For parcel delivery services, the *WmL* represents the average number of packages delivered (voluminous or simple) per hour per employee;
- For the automotive industry, the *WmL* represents the average time to dismantle or deliver a part/piece.

For the *Maps* element, for all three companies, the same method was used to collect the information by an e-mail sent to all customers with a 5-point Likert scale questionnaire (1—totally disagree; ... 5—totally agree) immediately after the personal employee—customer contact to measure customer satisfaction. The *questionnaire* directly refers to order evaluation and contained four *items* regarding customer satisfaction: transport quality, communication quality with the company's employees, promptness of the employee to serve the customer, and company prices.

The *Cha* element has the same significance for all three sectors: the expenses per hour, in Euro, per employee.

For interpretation of the Spc indicator values for all three companies, a legend was established empirically (Table 2):

- For values 0.00–0.09, the Spc indicator shows poor employee efficiency;
- For values 0.10–0.19, it indicates a medium efficiency;
- For values 0.20–0.29, the Spc indicates a good efficiency of the employees;
- For values 0.30–0.39, the significance of the Spc is very good;
- Over or equal to 0.40, the Spc shows excellent employee efficiency.

Table 2. Comparative table for describing Spc indicator variables and implementation methodology.

Symbol from Spc Indicator Formula	Variable Name and UM	Company' Sector		
		E-Commerce (Pilot Research)	**Services**	**Industry**
$Spc = \frac{WmL \times Maps}{Cha \times t} \times \frac{\sum c}{1000}$	Employee performance assessment system based on customer satisfaction	0.0–0.09 0.10–0.19 0.20–0.29 0.30–0.39 ≥0.40	Legend for Spc values and interpretation:	Weak Medium Good Very good Excellent
WmL	Average labor productivity	Average number of contacts resolved (chat/phone)/hour/employee	Average number of packages (voluminous/simple) delivered/hour/employee	Average number of parts (dismem-bered/delivered)/hour/employee
Maps	Weighted arithmetic average of satisfaction	E-mail to the customer's address with 5-point Likert scale questionnaire (1—dissatisfied ft... 5—satisfied ft) completed by the customer after contact with the employee		
Cha		Salary expenses/employee/hour (euro)		
t	Average time to solve a task	Average time to resolve a contact with the customer (min)	Average time to deliver a package	Average time to dismantle/deliver a part
Σc	Total amount of contacts (employee effort)	Contacts taken over (telephone and chat)	Collets delivered	Delivered/disassembled parts
Method Used for Implementing Spc		**ITA Methodology (Initiation—Testing—Application) with the Following Steps for Implementing:**		
Step 1: Initiating: tools for preparation		The OCS (Online Comments System) platform used by the company	AR technology, Virtual Reality Spectacles VR-BOX v 2.0	VR technology: Platform Warp Studio (https://www.warpvr.com/ access on 1 June 2020)
Step 2: Testing method for employee		Mystery shopper and focus group	Mystery shopper, testing through contest on Kahoot platform, interview	Mystery shopper, testing through contest on Kahoot platform
Step 3: Application (Program used)		SIM (Spc Indicator—ITA method with Mystery Shopper)	SIAR (Spc Indicator—ITA method with **AR** technology)	SIAR (Spc Indicator—ITA method with VR technology)
		The companies KPIs were used: the turnover, the profit, the total costs (all in Euros), the number of employees, the Eeypf—Economic efficiency of the yield of production factors (the value must be over 1 unit), the Eecpf—Economic efficiency on the consumption of production factors (the value must be under 1 unit), Rate of return (in %).		
		Other Information		
Number of employees in study		32	67	22
Initial moment (before implementing Spc)—M0		December 2018	July 2020	April 2020
Implementation period (after implementing Spc) M1/M2/M3		January (M1)—February (M2)—March (M3) 2019	August (M1)—September (M2) 2020	May (M1)—June (M2) 2020
Customer service element used for each sector		NRR—Negative Response Rate	Complaint-receiving systems (free phone lines)	Complaint reception systems (forms)
Employee—client type of contact/communication		eWOM (electronic word-of-mouth) (chat and phone)	Face to face/WOM—Word-of-mouth	Face to face/WOM—Word-of-mouth

In Table 2, methodological information is structured regarding the Spc formula indicator [4], the elements, variables, implementation method and their description in the three sectors. In the column named *E-commerce (pilot study)* from Table 2, there are already published results [4] from the pilot study during the period December 2018–March 2019 on 32 employees using the SIM program (**S**pc indicator, **I**TA Methodology, and **M**ystery Shopper). These results were considered the starting point for the implementation in the next companies and the base for adapting the SIM program and transforming it into the SIAR program (**S**pc indicator, **I**TA Methodology, **AR** technology for services, VR technology for automotive industry).

For the first step of the ITA method implementation on the employees from each company, the initiation, different strategies, and tools for the employees' preparation were used according to the specific activities of the organizations from the study.

- For *electronic commerce*, the OCS (*online comment system*) platform of the company was used by the authors together with the company assistant;
- For the *package delivery services*, the authors used AR technology and VR Spectacles VR-BOX v 2.0 and VR glasses to optimize the storage and transport vehicle spaces;
- For the *automotive industry*, VR technology and Warp Studio Platform were used for initiating the employee.

For the second step of the ITA methodology, the Testing, also different strategies were used: the Mystery Shopper and the focus group for e-commerce, the Mystery Shopper and Kahoot platform for services and industry.

For the third step, to measure and assess the impact of the application of the Spc indicator and ITA methodology on the company's KPIs, the following economic indicators were used: the turnover, profit, total costs (all in Euros), number of employees, Eeypf (economic efficiency of the yield of production factors (the value must be over 1 unit)), Eecpf (economic efficiency on the consumption of production factors (the value must be under 1 unit)), and the rate of return (in %).

The **ITA** methodology (**I**nitiating—**T**esting—**A**pplication) of implementing the Spc indicator is based on management functions [80], as the main objective of this method is economic development. The first component of the method aims to increase company performance [81] and allows the employee to find solutions and make the change [82]. Employees operate in different environments; therefore, the training must be customized to the company specificities [83], an aspect which was also respected in the current research, being adapted for each of the three sectors. To see the readiness of employees to solve a problem requires testing [84]. This involves employee evaluation, i.e., measurement and quantitative assessment of training effects [85], and at the testing stage, it can be observed whether the employee is suitable for that position within the company [86] based on feedback received [87].

For calculus and graphical representation of data, Microsoft Excel was used.

4. Results

In this paragraph, we comparatively present the results from the three sectors: e-commerce published in the pilot research during the doctoral studies of one of the authors [4], courier services, and the automotive industry. The purpose of this paper is to analyze: (1) for which of the three sectors the indicator recorded the best values of KPIs, (2) the period of time when improvements were observed, and (3) their evidence in the company's performance. Thus, based on the information from Table 2, we present (Table 3) the average values for each moment (before and during the implementation of the ITA method and the Spc indicator), mentioning the interpretation of the Spc values.

Table 3. Average values for the elements of the Spc indicator before and after implementation.

Moment	Contacts Taken		Hours Worked/ Month	Cost/Hour /Employee (euro)	Maps	t	WmL	Σc	Σc/h	Average Value of Spc and Interpretation	
	Chat	Phone									
E-commerce (32 employees)											
M0	109	161.1	125.1	4.05	2.87	8.45	3.50	12,223	97.7	0.120	Medium
M1	116.9	275	129.2	4.05	3.72	7.46	3.00	12,557	97.3	0.158	Medium
M2	100.5	377	128.1	4.05	3.62	7.73	3.75	15,281	119.4	0.213	Good
M3	112.5	334	115.5	4.05	3.71	7.55	3.85	14,292	124.3	0.218	Good
Services (67 employees)											
M0	-	-	138.0	3.25	3.38	6.86	8.98	1206	9.00	0.105	Medium
M1	-	-	155.7	3.25	3.45	6.60	9.20	1422	9.20	0.132	Medium
M2	-	-	162.3	3.25	3.27	6.40	9.47	1535	9.46	0.140	Medium
Industry (22 employees)											
M0	-	-	175.5	4.15	3.07	7.21	8.38	1467	8.77	0.086	Weak
M1	-	-	173.9	4.15	3.44	6.95	8.70	1513	8.77	0.102	Medium
M2	-	-	175.0	4.15	3.63	6.41	9.43	1646	8.73	0.130	Medium

(Note: M0 represents the moment before implementation and from M1 to M2; M3 represents the moment after implementation).

According to the results from Table 3, in the *e-commerce* sector, the Spc indicator recorded higher values since the first month of implementation (M1), with an improvement in values from medium to good in the last 2 months (M2 and M3). It follows the same upward trend as the values of the Maps element even if, in the last month, the average number of hours worked/month is the lowest, which practically proves the effectiveness of the tool and the ITA implementation method. The same upward trend was also recorded for the average labor productivity and the number of contacts/hour.

For the *services* sector, the implementation results are not so spectacular, but it is important to notice the increase in the total number of contacts, the average number of contacts/hour, and the average labor productivity. The average values of the Spc indicator maintain an average level from the initial moment M0 until the end of the implementation period. The service company was the company with the biggest number of employees in the total research.

For the *automotive industry* sector, the Spc indicator has evolved from weak to medium, with an upward trend for the Maps variables, the average labor productivity, and the total number of dismembered parts and a relatively constant value over all three months for the average number of dismembered parts per hour by an employee.

In Figure 2, the average values of the Spc indicator are presented for the entire research period, comparatively for all researched sectors. The superiority of the values for e-commerce can be observed.

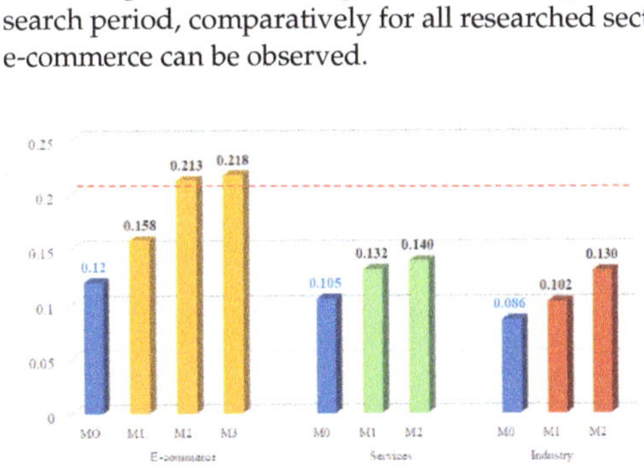

Figure 2. Average values of Spc indicator for each indicator before and after Spc implementation. (Note: M0 represents the moment before implementation (blue color) and from M1 to M2; M3 represents the moment after implementation: yellow for e-commerce, green for services and red for industry).

As major differences between employees in the same sector in terms of average labor productivity have been observed since the M0 moment of the research, in Figure 3, we represent the distribution and structure of the Spc indicator's ranges, highlighting the efficiency and performance of e-commerce, as the range of values is much more varied but also better positioned compared to the services and the industry sectors.

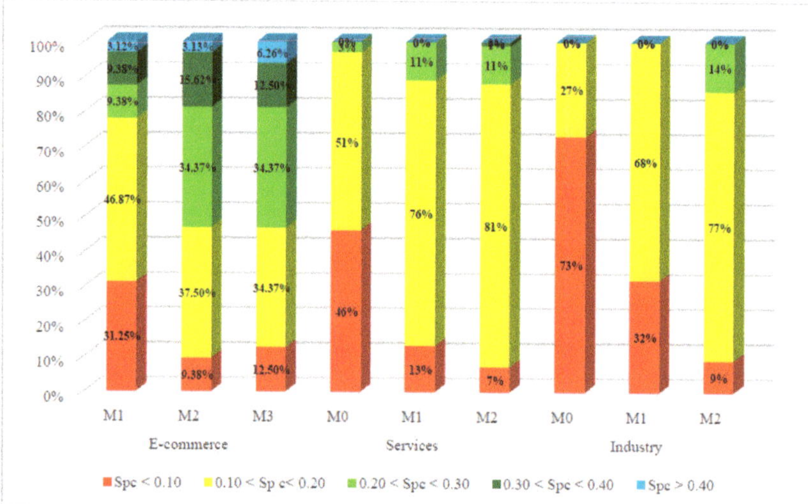

Figure 3. Spc structure on the three sectors for each moment (before/after implementation). (Note: M0 represents the moment before implementation and from M1 to M2; M3 represents the moment after implementation).

The main practical purpose of the research was to highlight the potential of different types of employee training and their effect on the company KPIs mentioned in Table 4 (turnover, profit, total costs, number of employees, Eeypf (economic efficiency on the yield of production factors (with super unit values)), Eecpf (economic efficiency on the consumption of production factors (with subunit values)), rate of return).

Table 4. The companies' KPIs before and after Spc implementation.

Performance Indicator	E-Commerce				Services			Industry		
	Before	After			Before	After		Before	After	
	M0	M1	M2	M3	M0	M1	M2	M0	M1	M3
Turnover (€)	97,470	96,248	101,744	97,470	106,988	44,630	45,728	1,305,669	1,286,323	1,299,307
Profit (€)	13,182	12,967	22,123	13,182	29,889	5219	5966	21,059	23,763	25,853
Total costs (€)	84,288	83,281	79,621	84,288	77,099	39,411	39,762	1,284,610	1,262,560	1,273,454
Number of employees	39	39	41	39	41	88	88	27	27	27
Eeypf [1]	1.16	1.16	1.28	1.16	1.39	1.13	1.15	1.02	1.02	1.02
Eecpf [2]	0.86	0.87	0.78	0.86	0.72	0.88	0.87	0.98	0.98	0.98
Rate of return %	15.64	15.57	27.79	15.64	38.77	13.24	15.00	1.64	1.88	2.03

[1] Economic efficiency on the yield of production factors (must be > 1). [2] Economic efficiency of production factor consumption (must be < 1). M0 represents the moment before implementation (grey column) and from M1 to M2; M3 represents the moment after implementation.

The positive results from Table 4 prove the effectiveness of the Spc indicator through ITA methodology during the SIM and SIAR implementation programs. The results indicate much better, the results being highlighted in the e-commerce sector.

Since both the Spc indicator values and the KPIs indicators from e-commerce had better evolutions compared to services and industry, Figure 4 are presented the mean, median, range, using the box-plot graph, comparatively to a threshold of 0.2 (representing good values), above the average of the Spc indicator. For all three sectors, the ascending evolution of the average values is visible, as well as the variations around the average for each moment (before or after implementation).

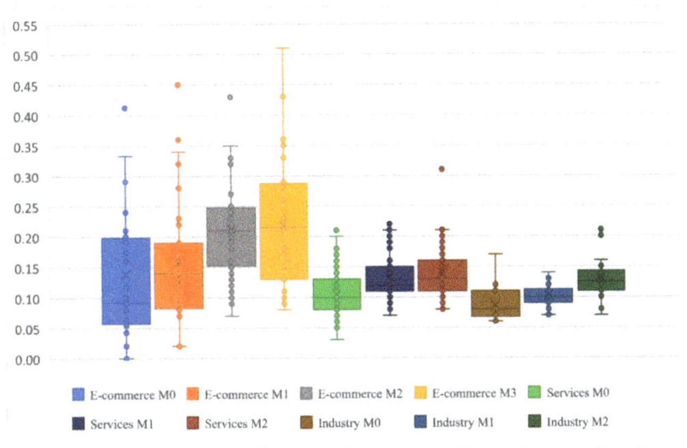

Figure 4. Box-plots for values of the Spc indicator for e-commerce, services, and industry.

Figure 5 shows the average values of each element of the Spc indicator formula by sector and by research moments (before and after implementation).

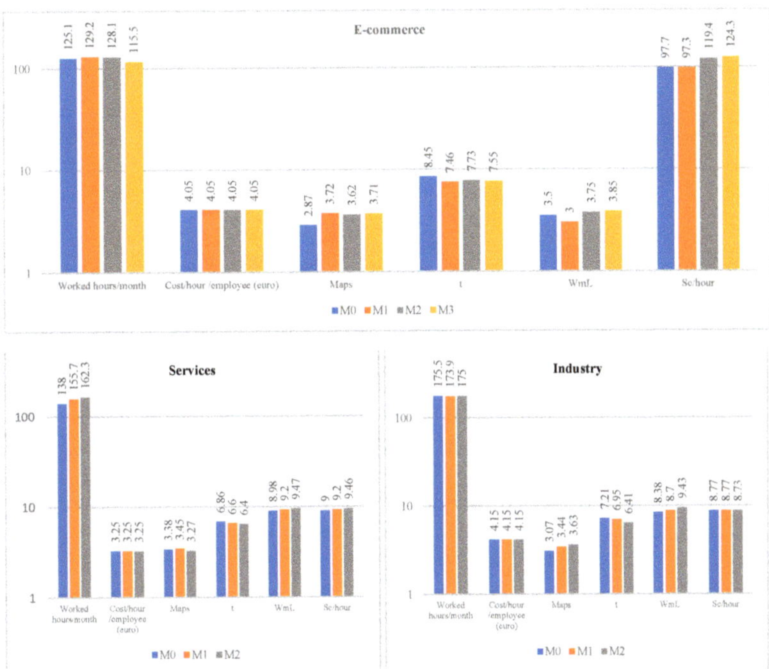

Figure 5. Evolution of the Spc indicator elements/variables—average values/moment for each sector.

5. Discussion

Our research results emphasize that in communication by phone with customers, the employee's tone is a decisive factor in solving their problems/complaints. Empathy can often make the difference between an amicable resolution of the case (considered a success when we have a satisfied customer) and failure (the loss of a customer) [88]. It depends on the company's orientation on how to solve the complaint or the customer–employee communication problem; repercussions might appear in future interactions between them, which is a risk for the company. It is essential that the customer is satisfied by its experience with the company, but this might lead to the emergence of a phenomenon called customer moral hazard (CMH). A favorable solution to a problem/complaint might place the customer in a risky situation, knowing that he is protected against risk and the company in question bears the cost. Customer purchasing decisions may also be influenced by consumer-to-consumer communication (C2C) in eWOM [89]. To prevent these abusive behaviors of customers, it is necessary to continuously educate and train both employees and customers [90].

Nowadays, *information technologies* and the electronic communication path with clients have taken over the daily system of each person, forming the basis of postmodern society [5]. There are several factors influencing the educational and learning environment within a company, such as organizational culture, technology, and economic aspects. Technology properly used and adapted to the needs of each sector could contribute to the development of the employer–employee–customer relationship and introduce new approaches in the process of employee improvement and cooperation between employees to provide access to diverse information. It is also used to adapt learning experiences with the stated purpose of satisfying requirements, real needs, and latent needs of customers [91].

The *Augmented Reality (AR)-based learning system* is a method allowing users of *computing technology* and *new digital tools* to directly contribute to the efficiency of the employee performance improvement processes [5,92,93] with direct effects on increasing customer satisfaction and company KPIs [5]. At the international level, several studies for and against the use of these innovative learning and evaluation methods of hard and soft skills have been carried out [84], and any improvement (soft skills) is based on formal education. Starting from employee training in development, assembly, quality control, and maintenance [94], all these company sectors benefit from AR implementation, primarily due to increased productivity and secondly due to reduced costs.

To be able to implement AR and VR technologies within an activity, a new attitude regarding the employee training process is necessary. For improved results, active training must first be developed. Active learning with AR and/or VR technologies can contribute to the continuous training of employees and the continuous improvement of the company.

Space, time, and contextualized understanding become part of a non-transferable learning experience. According to Gisbert, Esafe, and Camacho [95], the benefits of using AR and 3D worlds as training tools are multiple, such as being autonomous learning processes [96] and a useful tool in setting out prejudices and cultural barriers [97], as follows:

- Provide a unique learning and knowledge exchange environment;
- Provide opportunities for group interactions engaged in learning;
- Improve communication skills (so that trainees can easily transfer course knowledge to real-life situations);
- Support creativity, exploration, and identity development.

The Spc indicator uses, in addition to the classic economic indicators (cost, productivity, profit, etc.), new customer service items (such as the NRR—measured within the e-commerce company). This is the customer service model used as the pilot research for the Spc indicator implementation and development for other sectors such as service and industry.

Customer satisfaction must come first and must be considered an element that all employees should focus on. Moreover, placing the customer at the center of the company is very important, but also other elements regarding employee activity (productivity, involved costs, and other important company indicators) must be considered.

The application of the ITA methodology starts by identifying the elements considered for implementation, i.e., staff training. At this stage, two learning aspects were pursued: (1) the processing one, which comprises processes developed in a learning segment; (2) the motivational one, which refers to employee involvement in the learning activity.

Competition characterizes the market economy, sets the market in action, and continues to push participants in economic life toward permanent development [98]. Regardless of the sector, the Spc indicator reflects the real economic situation of the company in relation to its customers, as long as it is properly applied. From the applied research within the three companies, specific aspects related to the Spc indicator's implementation and adaptation in different companies from different sectors are highlighted.

The research results of the comparative analysis of the Spc indicator values and formula elements for e-commerce, services, and industry confirm the two holistic research hypotheses as follows:

1. H_1: A growth and development program requires continuous improvements related, adapted, and updated to the period of time in which it is applied;
2. H_2: Performance evaluation systems require innovative adjustments by including elements from other sectors.

The research hypotheses were formulated in line with the references mentioned in the literature review section and also considering that continuous improvement plays a critical and strategic role for the organizations, being known as an approach with the main purpose of enhancing organization performance [99,100]. Moreover, traditional methods and approaches to the evaluation of company performance are fundamental deficiencies in the fact that they provide only a retrospective view of the company's competitive position that existed at some point in the past [101]. Thus, in the process of a company's performance evaluation, modern and innovative performance evaluation methods (such as Spc and ITA methodology), combining financial and non-financial performance indicators and allowing the performance to be evaluated both quantitatively and qualitatively, should be used [102].

Finding new ways to train employees is more difficult than ever, especially when information technology, digital economy, and computer science have gained such momentum. *AR* and *VR technologies* are highly effective tools that can be applied in any sector. Skills developed using *AR technology* are essential, and they are designed to address the intense challenges of knowledge and digitalization society, which has emphasized the usefulness of both *AR/VR technologies* and the *internet of things* (IoT) concept. The main criteria for the evaluation of such technologies must be effectiveness and functionality. Managers often focus mainly on efficiency instead of customer satisfaction [103]. The application of information technologies should not only be on the mental level, but also on the physical level. These information technologies can be effectively used, especially for group learning [104].

These efforts have resulted in a key economic indicator, the profit, which is essential for any company in the market economy. Considering the customer at the heart of any successful economic activity, this research focus has been on its satisfaction and on how to increase it. Any company has both strengths and weaknesses, but it is essential that participants in the economic activity find competitive advantages over market competitors, identify new elements making the economic activity more efficient. Each of the three case studies reveals specific situations using the same application principles. To be fully efficient, the application of the SIAR program must be carried out from the employees' own initiative, without constraints, and they must be aware of their role in the company's growth.

The research subject refers to the issues of customer dissatisfaction increase following the interactions with company representatives, with direct consequences in decreasing the number of customers and implicitly reducing company performance. The causes of these situations lie in the absence of continuous employee training, stagnation of the training process, and thus limitation to routine work. Generally, these aspects of direct (by any means) employee–customer interactions are reflected in customer feedback, negatively affecting the company's market image. In this research, we used as a starting point the analysis of causes for employee–customer tensions, and we found out that many of these problems really start from the employee.

The research was carried out in three sectors, with a different number of employees, based on pilot research in e-commerce/by testing and subsequently adapted the methodology for services and industry. The employee—customer interaction in e-commerce is made by chat, phone, and e-mail. For services (courier company), the interaction is direct and face-to-face, while for industry (automotive company), it is both face-to-face and electronic channels.

The research subject is of high interest currently as companies are constantly looking to identify new ways for sustainable growth, both nationally and internationally. In the 21st century, the aim of a company is not only to obtain profit by any means, but also to build a lasting relationship with customers that needs to be continuously improved and strengthened so that the customer is aware of their role in company growth.

To highlight these, another author's contribution is identifying the need for a new measurement tool to establish and measure the tripartite relation: *customer satisfaction—employee performance—company performance.*

To achieve the research aim and objectives, both classical and innovative concepts were used: we have developed, tested, and proposed the introduction of an innovative tool for measuring employee efficiency determined by both employee activity and customer satisfaction regarding the purchased product or service.

The research results highlight the way in which information technology, electronic communication channels, and company KPIs can lead to positive and effective results within a company, regardless of its sector. The idea of developing this indicator is based on the concepts and objectives of the Six Sigma method in services, mainly to understand how certain errors occur in customer relations, specifically to identify customer dissatisfaction causes.

6. Conclusions

From the results presented above, we can conclude that the testing method using the Mystery Shopper of the ITA methodology applied in e-commerce is more efficient than AR and VR technologies applied in services and industry. Thus, efficiency is reflected in the Spc indicator evolution and, most importantly, in the evolution of the company performance indicators (KPIs).

We can also conclude that, given that the types of customer–employee interactions were different (eWOM in e-commerce and WOM in services and industry), in services and industry, customer feedback being perceived directly by the employee, eWOM communication is more efficient than WOM. The pilot research results in e-commerce highlighted employee aversion to risk. With this company's attitude toward employees, instead of the problems being solved, we concluded—with the help of the focus group—that the organizational structure actually made things worse and that taking risks was not rewarded by the company. Therefore, some strictness in setting certain objectives would prevent managers from achieving maximum efficiency as employees do not take risks [105]. A solution to this problem can be the formation of eight employee groups, in which the Spc indicator is taken as an average of the eight employees (i.e., a group evaluation, not an individual one).

Improving company performance is the main goal, but the context and method of action are much more complex. To achieve this goal, it is necessary to improve several economic indicators and continuously improve by re-educating/training employees in terms of attitude towards customers. This aspect is more important now, when loyalty and attraction of new customers are essential for business sustainability regardless of the sector.

A fundamental company policy is that customer satisfaction is the most effective indicator, but that it is not always enough. The idea of employees depending solely on customer satisfaction is a rather delicate one, as many of them felt discouraged. We consider that, besides this, the employee productivity indicators, hourly cost per employee, and duration of the solution (i.e., all elements underlying the Spc indicator design) are also important. The Spc indicator creates a real picture regarding customer satisfaction—employee performance relationship—as an important element in increasing company efficiency and performance.

Therefore, we consider this paper to contain *important scientific contributions both theoretically and practically*, as the application of the Spc indicator and the ITA methodology have led to evidence of the following real *advantages* for companies not only from e-commerce, service, and industry sectors but also from other fields. Our main *theoretical contribution* is linked to:

- Increasing labor productivity, followed by an increase in the number of contacts for an employee.
- Improving the cognitive process of employees within the company, which was directly reflected in the improvement of the company's economic and financial indicators.
- Improving the relationship between employees and customers, leading to increased satisfaction.
- Reorganization of the employee program resulting in increased staff efficiency.
- Better control over the operating parameters of each employee and the entire sector by introducing an SIM and SIAR program.

The paper presents important *practical contributions* for the stakeholders:

- The applied research presented in this paper reveals real situations at a national level in two sectors, one secondary and one tertiary; the latter being the most developed, not only at a national but also at a global level.
- The Spc indicator and ITA methodology introduced and implemented by the authors do not intend to eliminate the methods already used at the company level.
- The Spc indicator and ITA methodology introduced and implemented by the authors show that some aspects need to be continuously improved to increase the company's economic performance, which is often determined in economic terms [6].

Our results emphasize that electronic tools and digital technologies for communications, such as eWOM, chat, OCS platform, and e-mail, together with AR and VR technologies, improve customer—employee—company communication with the main impact on company KPIs.

The present research has *limits* linked to the relatively small number of subjects participating in the research due to the targeted SMEs from three different fields for implementations of the Spc and ITA methodology. This option was taken into consideration due to our presumed reluctance of the companies to participate in the research. Therefore, for *future research*, we intend to extrapolate the investigation to include medium-sized companies, both national and international.

The research subject is of high interest currently in the research field of customer satisfaction assessment as companies are constantly looking for new solutions to increase customer satisfaction.

Author Contributions: Conceptualization, I.-D.L. and M.R.G.; methodology, I.-D.L. and M.R.G.; validation, I.-D.L., M.R.G. and M.K.; formal analysis, I.-D.L. and M.R.G.; investigation, I.-D.L.; data curation, I.-D.L.; writing—original draft preparation, I.-D.L., M.R.G. and M.K.; writing—review and editing, M.R.G. and M.K.; visualization, I.-D.L., M.R.G. and M.K.; supervision, M.R.G. All authors have read and agreed to the published version of the manuscript.

Funding: This research received no external funding.

Data Availability Statement: Not applicable.

Conflicts of Interest: The authors declare no conflict of interest.

References

1. Alecu, C.; Gherasim, O. *Metode şi Tehnici Utilizate în Managementul Organizaţiei*; Pro Universitaria: Bucuresti, Romania, 2015; p. 81.
2. Porter, M. *Despre Concurenţă*; Meteor Press: Bucuresti, Romania, 2008.
3. Hill, N. *Customer Satisfaction*; Cogent: London, UK, 2007; p. 3.
4. Legman, D.I.; Gabor, M.R. New Optimization Technique for Sustainable Manufacturing: The Implementation of the Spc Indicator (System of Evaluating Employee Performance Depending on Customer Satisfaction) as an Important Element of Satisfaction Measurement. *Proc. MDPI* **2020**, *63*, 1–8.
5. Legman, D.I.; Gabor, M.R. Augmented Reality technology—A sustainable element for Industry 4.0. *Acta Marisiensis Oecon.* **2020**, *14*, 9–18. [CrossRef]
6. Drucker, P.F. *Managementul Strategic*; Teora: Bucureşti, Romania, 2001; p. 113.
7. Kaiser, S. *Sustainable Event Management*; Tirol: Kufstein, Austria, 2010; p. 35.
8. Morgeson, V.F.; Mithas, S.; Keiningham, L.T.; Aksoy, L. An Investigation of the Cross-National Determinants of Customer Satisfaction. *J. Acad. Mark. Sci.* **2011**, *39*, 198–215. [CrossRef]
9. Stauss, B. *Effective Complaint Management, The Business Case for Customer Satisfaction*; Springer: Cham, Switzerland, 2019; p. 6.
10. Butscher, S.A. *Customer Loyalty Programmes and Clubs*, 2nd ed.; Routledge: London, UK, 2016.
11. Wu, J.; Ding, F.; Xu, M.; Mo, Z.; Jin, A. Investigating the Determinants of Decision-Making on Adoption of Public Cloud Computing in E-government. *J. Glob. Inf. Manag.* **2016**, *24*, 71–89. [CrossRef]
12. Ray, N. *Managing Diversity, Innovation, and Infrastructure in Digital Business*; IGI Global: Hershey, PA, USA, 2019; p. 64.
13. Williams, B.; DeCarlo, N. *Six Sigma for Dummies*; Wiley Publishing Inc.: Hoboken, NJ, USA, 2005; p. 26.
14. Keki, B. *Ultimate Six Sigma: Beyond Quality Experience*; Emerald Group Publishing Limited: New York, NY, USA, 2001; p. 37.
15. Pai Bhale, N.G. Six Sigma in Service: Insights from Hospitality Industry. *Int. J. Adv. Res. Sci. Eng.* **2017**, *6*, 1–10.
16. Jones, P.; Robinson, P. *Operations Management*; Oxford University Press: Oxford, UK, 2012.
17. Larson, A. *Demystifying Six Sigma*; American Management Association: New York, NY, USA, 2003; p. 44.
18. Nelson, B.; Sproull, B. *The Critical Methodology for Theory of Constraints, Lean, and Six Sigma*; CRC Press: New York, NY, USA, 2016; p. 100.
19. Tetteh, E.G. *Lean Six Sigma Approaches in Manufacturing, Services and Production*; IGI Global: Hershey, PA, USA, 2015; p. 175.
20. Mockler, R. *Management Strategic Multinational*; Editura Economică: Bucureşti, Romania, 2001; p. 325.
21. Prahoveanu, E. *Economie politică—Fundamente de teorie economică*; Editura Eficient: Bucureşti, Romania, 1997; p. 150.
22. Legman, I.D.; Blaga, P. Six Sigma Method Important Element of Sustainability. *Acta Marisiensis Oecon.* **2019**, *13*, 37–68. [CrossRef]
23. George, M.L. *Lean Six Sigma: Combining Six Sigma Quality with Lean Production Speed*; McGraw-Hill Education: New York, NY, USA, 2002.
24. Kesterson, R.K. *The Intersection of Change Management and Lean Six Sigma*; CRC Press: Boca Raton, FL, USA, 2018; p. 30.
25. Bloom, D. *The Field Guide to Achieving HR Excellence through Six Sigma*; CRC Press: Boca Raton, FL, USA, 2016; p. 67.
26. Mihuţ, I. *Euromanagement*; Editura Economică: Bucureşti, Romania, 2002; p. 279.
27. Plenert, G.; Plenert, J. *Strategic Excellence in the Arhitecture, Engineering and Construction Industries*; Routledge: New York, NY, USA, 2018; p. 43.
28. Caroll, C.T. *Six Sigma for Powerful Improvement*; CRC Press: Boca Raton, FL, USA, 2013.
29. Wang, F.K.; Yen, C.T.; Chu, T.P. Using the design for Six Sigma approach with TRIZ for new product development. *Comput. Ind. Eng.* **2016**, *98*, 522–530. [CrossRef]
30. Ikumapayi, O.M.; Akinlabi, E. Six Sigma versus lean manufacturing? An overview. *Mater. Today-Proc.* **2020**, *26*, 3275–3281. [CrossRef]
31. Kaswan, M.S.; Rathi, R. Analysis and modeling the enablers of Green Lean Six Sigma implementation using Interpretive Structural Modeling. *J. Clean. Prod.* **2019**, *231*, 1182–1191. [CrossRef]
32. Hussain, K.; He, Z.; Ahmad, N. Green, lean, Six Sigma barriers at a glance: A case from the construction sector of Pakistan. *Build. Environ.* **2019**, *161*, 106225. [CrossRef]
33. Thomas, A.J. Implementing Lean Six Sigma to overcome the production challenges in an aerospace company. *Prod. Plan. Control* **2016**, *27*, 591–603. [CrossRef]
34. Kruger, F. *The Influence of Culture and Personality on Customer Satisfaction*; Springer Gabler: Cham, Switzerland, 2016.
35. Giese, J.L.; Cote, J.A. Defining Customer Satisfaction. *Acad. Mark. Sci. Rev.* **2000**, *1*, 14.
36. Siskos, Y. *Customer Satisfaction Evaluation*; Springer: New York, NY, USA, 2010; p. 10.
37. Jackson, T. Motivating Sustainable Consumption: A Review of Evidence on Consumer Behaviour and Behavioural Change. In *Centre for the Understanding of Sustainable Prosperity, the Social Psychology of Sustainable Consumption*; 2005; Available online: https://timjackson.org.uk/wp-content/uploads/2018/04/Jackson.-2005.-Motivating-Sustainable-Consumption.pdf (accessed on 10 July 2020).
38. Burgess, P. *Integrating the Packaging and Product Experience in Food and Beverages*; Elsevier: Cambridge, UK, 2016; p. 101.
39. Darroch, J. Knowledge management, innovation and firm performance. *J. Knowl. Manag.* **2005**, *9*, 101–115. [CrossRef]
40. Jones, T.O.; Sasser, E.W., Jr. Why Satisfied Customers Defect. 1995. Harvard Business Review. Available online: https://hbr.org/1995/11/why-satisfied-customers-defect (accessed on 1 July 2020).
41. Chandrashekaran, M.; Rotte, K.N.; Tax, S.S.; Grewal, R. Satisfaction strength and customer loyalty. *J. Mark. Res.* **2007**, *44*, 153–163. [CrossRef]

42. Yim, C.K.; Tse, D.K.; Chan, K.W. Strengthening customer loyalty through intimacy and passion: Roles of customer–firm affection and customer–staff relationships in services. *J. Mark. Res.* **2008**, *45*, 741–756. [CrossRef]
43. Parasuraman, A.; Zeithaml, V.A.; Berry, L.L. SERVQUAL: A multiple item scale for measuring consumer perceptions of service quality. *J. Retail.* **1989**, *64*, 12–40.
44. Gnyawali, D.R.; Fan, W.; Penner, J. Competitive actions and dynamics in the digital age: An empirical investigation of social networking firms. *Inform. Syst. Res.* **2010**, *21*, 594–613. [CrossRef]
45. Gijsbrechts, E.; van Heerde, H.J.; Pauwels, K. Winners and losers in a major price war. *J. Mark. Res.* **2008**, *45*, 499–518.
46. Andersen, P.H.; Kumar, R. Emotions, trust and relationship development in business relationships: A conceptual model for buyer-seller dyads. *Ind. Mark. Manag.* **2006**, *35*, 522–535. [CrossRef]
47. Andaleeb, S.S. The trust concept: Research issues for channel distribution. *Res. Mark.* **1992**, *11*, 1–34.
48. Anderson, J.; Narus, C.J.A. A model of distributor firm and manufacturer firm working partnership. *J. Mark.* **1990**, *54*, 42–58. [CrossRef]
49. Anderson, E.; Weitz, B. Determinants of continuity in conventional industrial channel dyads. *Mark. Sci.* **1989**, *8*, 310–323. [CrossRef]
50. Shurr, P.H.; Ozanne, J.L. Influence on exchange processes: Buyer's preconceptions of a seller's trustworthiness and bargaining toughness. *J. Consum. Res.* **1985**, *11*, 938–947. [CrossRef]
51. Fletcher, K.P.; Peters, L.D. Trust and direct marketing environments: A consumer perspective. *J. Mark. Manag.* **1997**, *13*, 523–539. [CrossRef]
52. Gurviez, P. The trust concept in the brand-consumer relationship. In Proceedings of the 25th EMAC Conference European Marketing Academy, Budapest, Hungary, 14–17 May 1996; Beràcs, J., Bauer, A., Simon, J., Eds.; Volume I, pp. 559–574.
53. Crosby, L.A.; Evans, K.R.; Cowles, D. Relationship quality in services selling: An interpersonal influence perspective. *J. Mark.* **1990**, *54*, 68–81. [CrossRef]
54. Grayson, K.; Ambler, T. The dark side of long-term relationships in marketing services. *J. Mark. Res.* **1999**, *36*, 132–141. [CrossRef]
55. Moorman, C.; Zaltman, G.; Deshpandè, R. Relationships between providers and users of market research: The dynamics of trust within and between organizations. *J. Mark. Res.* **1992**, *29*, 314–328. [CrossRef]
56. Moorman, C.; Deshpandè, R.; Zaltman, G. Factors affecting trust in market research relationship. *J. Mark.* **1993**, *57*, 81–101. [CrossRef]
57. Sabin, N. Cercetările de tip "clientul misterios"—Repere ale evolutiei marketingului modern/"Mystery Shoopper" Research—A Landmark of Modern Marketing. *Rev. Mark. Online (RMkO)* **2017**, *2*, 46–51.
58. PamInCa. *The Essential Guide to Mystery Shopping*; Happy About: Cupertino, CA, USA, 2009; p. 18.
59. Potolea, D. *Pregătire Psihopedagogică*; Polirom: Bucureşti, Romania, 2008; p. 85.
60. Fisher, C.D.; Schoenfeldt, L.F.; Shaw, J.B. *An Introduction to Human Resource Management*; Houghton Mifflin Company: Boston, MA, USA, 1996.
61. Kapferer, J.N. *The New Strategic Brand Management*; Kogan Page: London, UK, 2008; p. 238.
62. Cava, R. *Comunicarea cu Oamenii Dificili*; Curtea Veche Publishing: Bucureşti, Romania, 2012.
63. Murphy, H.A.; Hildebrandt, H.W. *Effective Business Communications*; McGraw-HILL: Singapore, 1991; p. 611.
64. Chiru, I. *Comunicarea interpersonală*; Tritonic: Bucureşti, Romania, 2003.
65. Chris, D. *Client o dată, client mereu: Cum să oferi servicii care iţi fidelizează clienţii*; Editura Publică: Bucureşti, Romania, 2008; p. 298.
66. von Weizsacker, E. *Factor Four, Doubling Wealth-Halving Resource Use*; Springer: New York, NY, USA, 2006; p. 64.
67. Lunt, P.K.; Livingstone, S. *Mass Consumption and Personal Identity: Everyday Economic Experience*; Open University Press: Buckingham, UK, 1992.
68. Srinivasan, S.; Hanssens, D.M. Marketing and firm value: Metrics, methods, findings, and future directions. *J. Mark. Res.* **2009**, *46*, 293–312. [CrossRef]
69. Chebat, J.C.; Morrin, M. Colors and cultures exploring the effects of mall décor on consumer perceptions. *J. Bus. Res.* **2007**, *60*, 189–196. [CrossRef]
70. Vrontis, D.; Thrassou, A. A new conceptual framework for business consumer relationships. *Mark. Intell. Plan.* **2007**, *25*, 789–806. [CrossRef]
71. Ismgilova, E.; Slade, E.; Rana, N.P.; Dwivedi, Y.K. The Effect of Electronic Word of Mouth Communication on Intention to Buy: A Meta-Analysis. *Inform. Syst. Front.* **2020**, *22*, 1203–1226. [CrossRef]
72. Ziegele, M. Example, please! Comparing the effects of single customer reviews and aggregate review scores on online shoppers' product evaluations. *J. Consum. Behav.* **2015**, *14*, 103–114. [CrossRef]
73. Zainal, N.T.A.; Harun, A. Examining mediating effect of attitude towards electronic words-of mouth (eWOM) on the relation between the trust in eWOM source and intention to follow eWOM among Malaysian travelers. *Asia Pacif. Manag. Rev.* **2017**, *22*, 35–44. [CrossRef]
74. Yen, C.L.; Tang, C.H. Hotel attribute performance, eWOM motivations and media choice. *Int. J. Hosp. Manag.* **2015**, *46*, 79–88. [CrossRef]
75. Mehrabian, A.; Russell, J.A. *An Approach to Environmental Psychology*; MIT Press: Cambridge, MA, USA, 1974.
76. PMP. Market Experts. Competition Analysis: Definition, Objective, Scope and the Most Common Mistakes. Available online: https://www.pmrmarketexperts.com/en/competition-analysis-definition-scope/ (accessed on 10 October 2020).

77. Backstrom, K. Understanding Recreational Shopping: A new approach. *Int. Rev. Retail. Distrib. Consum. Res.* **2006**, *16*, 143–158. [CrossRef]
78. Kaiser, S.; Ringlstetter, M.J. *Strategic Management of Professional Service Firms. Theory and Practice*; Springer: Cham, Switzerland, 2011; p. 49.
79. Babin, B.J.; Darden, W.R.; Griffin, M. Work and/or fun: Measuring hedonic and utilitarian shopping value. *J. Consum. Res.* **1994**, *20*, 644–656. [CrossRef]
80. Carter, N.M. General and Industrial Management by Henri Fayol. *Acad. Manag. Rev.* **1986**, *11*, 454–456. [CrossRef]
81. Livy, B. *Corporate Personnel Management*; Pitman Publishing: London, UK, 1988; p. 145.
82. Weiss, D. *Les Resources Humaines*; Editions d'Organisation: Paris, France, 1999; p. 442.
83. Cerdin, J.L.; Peretti, J.M. *The Success of Apprenticeships: Views of Stakeholders on Training and Learning*; Wiley: Hoboken, NJ, USA, 2020; p. 35.
84. Gabor, M.R.; Blaga, P.; Matiș, C. Supporting Employability by a Skills Assessment Innovative Tool—Sustainable Transnational Insights from Employers. *Sustainability* **2019**, *11*, 3360. [CrossRef]
85. Gadenne, V. *Theorie und Erfahrung in der psychologischen Forschung*; LIT Verlag: Münster, Germany, 1984.
86. Armin, T. *Human Resources Strategies*; Springer: Cham, Switzerland, 2020; p. 105.
87. Goffee, R.; Jones, G. *Why Should Anyone Be Led by You? What Takes to Be an Authentic Leader*; Harvard Business School Press: Boston, MA, USA, 2006.
88. Fader, P.S. *Customer Centricity: Focus on the Right Customers for Strategic Advantage*; Wharton Digital Press: Philadelphia, PA, USA, 2012.
89. Yang, H.; Morgan, S.; Wang, Y. *The Strategies of China's Firms: Resolving Dilemmas*; Elsevier–Chandos Publishing: Waltham, MA, USA, 2015.
90. Ştefănescu, F. *Dezvoltare Durabilă şi Calitatea Vieţii*; Editura Universităţii din Oradea: Oradea, Romania, 2007; p. 54.
91. Bîrsan, J.; Moldoveanu, F.; Moldoveanu, A.; Morar, A.; Butean, A. Immersive education in smart educational buildings. *eLearning Softw. Educ.* **2020**, *2*, 11–16.
92. Chung, S.; Kwon, S.; Moon, D.; Ko, T. Smart Facility Management Systems Utilizing Open BIM and Augmented/Virtual Reality. In Proceedings of the 35th International Symposium on Automation and Robotics in Construction (ISARC2018), Berlin, Germany, 22–25 July 2018; pp. 846–853.
93. Benko, H.; Jota, R.; Wilson, A. Mirage Table: Freehand interaction on a projected augmented reality tabletop. In Proceedings of the SIGCHI Conference on Human Factors in Computing Systems (CHI 12), Austin, TX, USA, 5–10 May 2012; ACM: New York, NY, USA, 2012; pp. 199–208.
94. Segovia, D.; Mendoza, M.; Gonzalez, E. Augmented Reality as a Tool for Production and Quality Monitoring. *Procedia Comput. Sci.* **2015**, *75*, 291–300. [CrossRef]
95. Gisbert, M.; Esteve, V.; Camacho, M. Delve into the deep: Learning potential in Metaverses and 3D worlds. *eLearning Pap.* **2011**, *25*, 1–8.
96. Heo, H.; Joung, S. Self-regulation strategies and technologies for adaptive learning management systems for web-based instruction. In Proceedings of the Association for Educational Communications and Technology, Chicago, IL, USA, 19–23 October 2004.
97. Zeki, S.; Bartels, A. The temporal order of binding visual attributes. *Vis. Res.* **2006**, *46*, 2280–2286.
98. Johns, G. *Comportament Organizational (Organizational Behaviour)*; Editura Economică: Bucureşti, Romania, 1998; p. 479.
99. Bond, T. The role of performance measurement in continuous improvement. *Int. J. Oper. Prod.* **1999**, *19*, 1318–1334. [CrossRef]
100. Gonzalez Aleu, F.; Van Aken, E.M. Systematic literature review of critical success factors for continuous improvement projects. *Int. J. Lean Six Sigma* **2016**, *7*, 214–232. [CrossRef]
101. Rosova, A. Methods and approaches to the evaluation of company performance. *Poprad Econ. Manag. Forum* **2017**, 31–36. Available online: https://www.pemf-conference.com/wp-content/uploads/2022/04/Proceedings_PEMF_2017.pdf (accessed on 1 May 2019).
102. Narkuniene, J.; Ulbinaite, A. Comparative analysis of company performance evaluation methods. *Entrep. Sustain.* **2018**, *6*, 125–138. [CrossRef]
103. Jivan, A. *Managementul Serviciilor*; Editura de Vest: Timişoara, Romania, 1998; p. 209.
104. Al-Azawi, R.; Albadi, A.; Moghaddas, R.; Westlake, J. *Exploring the Potential of Using Augmented Reality and Virtual Reality for Stem Education*; Springer International Publishing: Cham, Switzerland, 2019.
105. Kotter, J. *Ce fac liderii cu adevărat (What Leaders Really Do?)*; Meteor Press: Bucureşti, Romania, 2008; p. 97.

electronics

Article

Improving Multi-Class Motor Imagery EEG Classification Using Overlapping Sliding Window and Deep Learning Model

Jeonghee Hwang [1], Soyoung Park [2] and Jeonghee Chi [2,*]

1 Department of Computer Software, Namseoul University, Cheonan 31020, Republic of Korea
2 Department of Computer Science and Engineering, Konkuk University, Seoul 05029, Republic of Korea
* Correspondence: jhchi@konkuk.ac.kr; Tel.: +82-2-450-3350

Abstract: Motor imagery (MI) electroencephalography (EEG) signals are widely used in BCI systems. MI tasks are performed by imagining doing a specific task and classifying MI through EEG signal processing. However, it is a challenging task to classify EEG signals accurately. In this study, we propose a LSTM-based classification framework to enhance classification accuracy of four-class MI signals. To obtain time-varying data of EEG signals, a sliding window technique is used, and an overlapping-band-based FBCSP is applied to extract the subject-specific spatial features. Experimental results on BCI competition IV dataset 2a showed an average accuracy of 97% and kappa value of 0.95 in all subjects. It is demonstrated that the proposed method outperforms the existing algorithms for classifying the four-class MI EEG, and it also illustrates the robustness on the variability of inter-trial and inter-session of MI data. Furthermore, the extended experimental results for channel selection showed the best performance of classification accuracy when using all twenty-two channels by the proposed method, but an average kappa value of 0.93 was achieved with only seven channels.

Keywords: multi-class motor imagery; EEG classification; FBCSP; overlapping window; overlapping bandpass filter; LSTM

Citation: Hwang, J.; Park, S.; Chi, J. Improving Multi-Class Motor Imagery EEG Classification Using Overlapping Sliding Window and Deep Learning Model. *Electronics* **2023**, *12*, 1186. https://doi.org/10.3390/electronics12051186

Academic Editors: Galina Ilieva and George A. Tsihrintzis

Received: 24 January 2023
Revised: 18 February 2023
Accepted: 20 February 2023
Published: 1 March 2023

1. Introduction

Cognitive information and communication technology (CogInfoCom) is a technology used to facilitate interaction between humans and information and communication devices or robots. This technology employs various tools, including brain-computer interface (BCI), gesture control, and eye tracking [1]. BCI is a technology that measures and analyzes brainwave signals to recognize and control user intentions [2]. Ongoing research explores the use of BCI in areas such as behavioral analysis and improving the quality of life for individuals with cognitive impairments, with BCI being integrated with gesture control or eye tracking technologies for this purpose [3–5]. Furthermore, with the development of low-cost BCI devices, researchers are exploring the use of BCI to control robots in real-life situations [6,7] and for virtual reality-based education [8]. Brainwaves, which are now being integrated into various fields, are considered an important biological signal. However, BCI has the characteristic of being greatly influenced by vision, making it a field that requires delicate measurement and precise analysis [9–12].

The main objective of a BCI system is to detect specific brain activities and use signal patterns to command a computer to perform specific tasks [13–15]. The electroencephalogram (EEG) can be used to recognize a person's intention to control an external device [16]. When people imagine moving their hand or foot, a specific region of their cerebral cortex is activated, resulting in a decrease in amplitude of the EEG rhythm signal within a specific frequency band detected in that region. This is referred to as event-related desynchronization (ERD), while an increase in amplitude of the rhythm signal in other regions is called event-related synchronization (ERS). ERS and ERD are mainly characterized by mu (8–14 Hz) and beta wave (14–30 Hz) spectra, respectively. These imagination-based activities in BCI are referred to as motor-imagery (MI) [17–19], and EEG data for MI tasks in a BCI system are collected using electrodes attached to the scalp [17,20].

EEG signals are widely used as a major brain signal in the BCI system due to their non-invasive nature [21]. However, since brain activity can be affected by multiple sources of environmental, physiological, and activity-specific noise [22,23], it is important to consider the following properties of EEG signals. EEG signals are naturally non-stationary. Diverse behavioral and mental states continuously change the statistical properties of brain signals. Thus, it poses a problem that signals other than the information signals we want to obtain are always irregularly present [24]. In addition, EEG signals that are recorded often have a low signal-to-noise ratio (SNR) due to the presence of various types of artifacts, such as electrical power line interference, electromyogram (EMG), and electrooculogram (EOG) interference [25]. To improve the signal-to-noise ratio and eliminate artifacts from the EEG signals, effective preprocessing is necessary before feature extraction [26]. Furthermore, EEG reveals inherent inter-subject variability in brain dynamics, which can be attributed to differences in physiological artifacts among individuals. This phenomenon can significantly impact the performance of learning models [27].

To address these problems, many researchers have implemented various feature extraction techniques for MI classification. The most important thing in the MI-based BCI system is to extract discriminative characteristics of the EEG signals that affect system performance. Common spatial pattern (CSP) is a popular method of extracting different MI features. The CSP spatial filtering method well represents the spatial characteristics of the EEG signal for each motion image. However, the CSP algorithm has limitations in that the frequency band, acquisition time, and the number of source signals must be determined in advance [28,29]. To solve this problem, an FBCSP method [30] that divides the EEG signal into several narrow frequency bands and extracts features by applying different CSP filters to each of the divided signals has been proposed. However, there are limitations in selecting the signal acquisition time or the number of spatial features to be extracted [31].

Recently, many studies have been proposed for automatic feature extraction and classification using deep learning methods such as CNN, LSTM, and restricted Boltzmann machine (RBM). The results of these approaches have shown that it reduces the time-consuming preprocessing and achieves a higher accuracy [32,33]. A RBM with a four-layer neural network was applied to accomplish better performance for motor imagery classification in [32]. Zhang et al. proposed a hybrid deep network model based on CNN and LSTM to extract and learn the spatial and temporal features of the MI task [33]. CNN combined with short-time fourier transformation (STFT) was applied for two-class MI classification in [34]. In another study [35], LSTM using dimension-aggregate approximation (1d-AX) channel weighting technique to extract features from EEG is proposed to enhance classification accuracy. In [36], EEG signals were classified by constructing a convolutional neural network (CNN) using an image-based approach. Meanwhile, some studies [33,37–41] have suggested adding time segments based on FBCSP, but the performance improvement in accuracy was not significant. The authors of [37] showed that multiple time segments by sliding windows from a continuous stream of EEG can extract more discriminable features. In [38], regularized CSP algorithms were proposed to promote the learning of good spatial filters, including extracting features from a fixed time segment of 2s. Moreover, Zhang et al. developed a hybrid deep learning method to extract discriminative features, combining the time domain method and the frequency domain method for a four-class MI task [33]. In [41], to address the issue of nonstationary EEG signals, sliding window-based CSP methods have been proposed to consider session-to-session and trial-to-trial variability. Experimental results showed that the sliding window-based methods outperformed the existing models for both healthy individual and stroke patients. EEG signals are sequential data, and a recurrent neural network (RNN) is one of the architectures to train the sequential processing, demonstrating good performance in time-series signals analysis. The most popular type of RNN is the long short-term memory (LSTM) network [33,42]. Although many EEG classification methods based on neural network have been proposed, there are a few studies that applied LSTM to multi-class MI task.

In this study, a framework is presented to improve the classification accuracy of four-class MI EEG signals using an LSTM-based classification method for extracting temporal features from time-varying EEG signals. We apply an overlapping sliding window approach not only to augment training data sets, but also to acquire time series data of EEG signals. Moreover, considering that the phenomena of ERD and ERS appearing in the sensorimotor cortex during motion imagination occur in different frequency bands for each subject, an overlapping band-based FBCSP is used to extract the subject-specific spatial features. In addition, to explore the effectiveness of channel selection processing, we investigate whether feature extraction from channels filtered by channel correlation affects the classification accuracy of MI task.

The rest of this paper is organized as follows. Section 2 provides a review of related work. Section 3 describes the proposed LSTM-based method with or without channel selection for four-class MI EEG classification. The experimental results and analysis are discussed in Section 4, and Section 5 concludes the paper.

2. Related Work

The extraction of discriminative features from EEG signals is an important factor affecting the performance of BCI systems in classifying MI tasks. Feature extraction is carried out in the spatial, time, and frequency domains [26].

2.1. Feature Extraction and Classification Techniques

CSP is generally used as a spatial domain feature extraction method for MI EEG classification [26]. CSP aims to learn a spatial filter that maximizes the variance of spatially filtered data in one class while minimizing the variance of filtered data in another class [28,43]. This approach has shown a noticeable effect in two-class EEG signals classification. Furthermore, various CSP-based algorithms including FBCSP [29,44–46], an improved version of CSP algorithm, have been proposed to extract spatial patterns from EEG signals. In [44], regularization on the CSP filter coefficients was proposed to deal with CSP problems using many electrodes, and this study has shown that the number of electrodes can be reduced with little performance loss. Arvaneh et al. [45] proposed a sparse multi-frequency band CSP (SMFBCSP) algorithm that was optimized using a mutual information-based approach. Their proposed method achieved better performance than other methods based on CSP, sparse CSP, and FBCSP. In a study [46], they suggested a method to select the most discriminative filter banks by using mutual information of features extracted channels. They employed CSP features extracted from multiple overlapping sub-bands, and classification was performed using a support vector machine. Spatial domain approach can be combined with temporal domain approach to enhance the classification performance [27,47]. Ai et al. [43] introduces a new method to combine the features by the CSP and local characteristic-scale decomposition (LCD) algorithms to extract multiscale features of MI EEG signals. To archive high-classification accuracy and low-computational cost, they considered that EEG signals represent brain activity by fusing features extracted from the associated brain regions. Hamedi et al. [48] explored the use of neural network-based algorithms with EEG time-domain features. This work used multilayer perceptron and radial basis function neural networks for feature classification. Lu et al. [32] used the restricted Boltzmann machine (RBM) for EEG classification, where frequency domain representations of EEG signals were pretrained using fast Fourier transform (FFT) and wavelet packet decomposition (WPD) in stacked RBMs. They achieved better performance over other state-of-the-art methods in experimental results. In [49], Park et al. presented a new method to avoid overfitting problems and improve performance of MI BCIs, using wavelet packet decomposition CSP and kernel extreme learning machine. The proposed method outperformed existing methods in terms of classification accuracy. Tabar et al. [50] proposed a deep network, combining CNN and stacked autoencoders

(SAE) to classify EEG motor imagery signals. They used the short-time Fourier transform (STFT) to construct 2D images for training their network. The features extracted by the CNN are classified through the deep network SAE. Lee et al. proposed a classification approach utilizing the continuous wavelet transform (CWT) and a CNN [51]. The CWT was utilized to generate an EEG image that incorporates time-frequency and electrode location information, resulting in a highly informative representation.

Recently, many researchers have utilized neural network techniques as an effective architecture for classifying MI tasks. These techniques combine all three phases of extraction, selection, and classification into a single pipeline [27,35]. Several studies have employed deep learning frameworks to classify EEG signals, and these have shown improvements in classification accuracy. Dai et al. used a CNN with hybrid convolution scale and experimented with different kernel sizes to obtain high classification accuracy [29]. They demonstrated that using a single convolution scale limits the classification performance. Sakhavi et al. introduced a temporal representation of the EEG to preserve information about the signal's dynamics and used a CNN for classification [52]. Moreover, a hybrid deep learning scheme that combines CNN and LSTM has been proposed, where CNN extracts spatial information and LSTM processes temporal information. Zhang et al. developed a deep learning network based on CNN-LSTM for four-class MI, which was trained using all subjects' training data as a single model [33]. This study showed a better result than an SVM classifier. They also proposed a hybrid deep neural network with transfer learning (HDNN-TL) in [53], which aimed to improve classification accuracy when dealing with the individual differences problem and limited training samples. RNN (recurrent neural network) is a type of ANN whose computing units are connected in a directed graph along a sequence, making it a popular choice for analyzing time-series data in various applications, including speech recognition, natural language processing, and more [35,42,47]. The most popular type of RNN is the LSTM network, which is an excellent way to expose the internal temporal correlation of time series signals [27,53]. Zhou et al. applied wavelet envelope analysis and LSTM to consider the amplitude modulation characteristics and time-series information of MI-EEG [54]. In [55], a RNN-based parallel method was applied to encode spatial and temporal sequential raw data with bidirectional LSTM (bi-LSTM), and its results showed superior performance compared to other methods.

2.2. Channel Selection Approach

EEG signal processing, scalp regions where the signal recordings are collected, are called channels or electrodes [56]. High-density EEG electrodes reveal more information about the underlying neuronal activity, but increase redundancy due to noise, and generate high-dimensional data. Therefore, it is crucial to have efficient channel selection methods that can identify optimal channels and reduce system complexity [56–58].

Several studies have used channel selection algorithms to enhance system performance, in which some channels are generally selected, considering channel location, dependency, and redundancy [56,59]. An improved binary gravitation search algorithm (IBGSA) is used for detecting effective channels for MI classification [57]. In this study, the results showed that detecting effective channels can obtain a better performance. In [56], an optimization-based channel selection method was proposed for MI tasks to reduce the computational complexity associated with the large number of channels. The proposed method initializes a reference candidate solution and then iteratively identifies the most relevant EEG channels. Yang et al. utilized a filtering technique in channel selection, where the most correlated channels are selected based on the consideration of mutual information and redundancy between channels [59]. In [60], to obtain high classification accuracy, a filtering method has been proposed to reduce the number of channels by iteratively optimizing the number of relevant channels. In another study [61], an optimization method using channel contribution score was used for channel selection, resulting in an average accuracy of 90% with only seven channels. To represent the brain functional relationships for MI tasks, Ma et al. [62] used the correlation matrix that expresses the functional relevance between channels. The proposed method showed MI decoding performance of above 87.03%. Li et el. [63] proposed an EEG decoding framework to consider spatial dependency and temporal scale information for MI classification. In this study, they extracted both spatial features by channel projection and temporal features, and then applied CNN to classify EEG tasks.

3. Improving Multi-Class MI Classification

The proposed method performs feature extraction based on overlapping band-based FBCSP (Filter Bank Common Spatial Pattern) and performs classification based on LSTM. This section describes the preprocessing for feature extraction and then explain classification using overlapping band-based FBCSP and LSTM.

3.1. Prepocessing

The proposed method utilized the publicly available BCI competition IV dataset 2a [64], which was recorded using twenty-two EEG channels ($C = 22$) and three EOG channels at a sampling rate of 250 Hz ($R = 250$). The EEG channels represent brain waves, and the EOG channels represent eye blink signals. Figure 1 shows the window determination process for feature extraction from a single-trial EEG. We used data collected from twenty-two EEG channels for 3 seconds (3s), starting 1 s after the cue sign, after removing three EOG channels from the BCI dataset. That is, the number of samples, n_i, acquired in a single trial of the ith subject is as follows.

$$n_i = 3_S * R * C \tag{1}$$

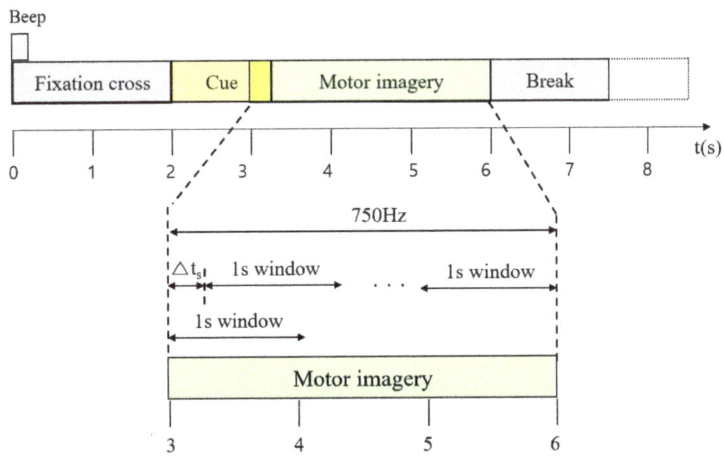

Figure 1. Feature extraction from a single-trial EEG.

If the number of valid trials after removing rejected trials generated during EEG data measurement is V, the total number of data N_i acquired from the ith subject is as follows.

$$N_i = n_i * V_i \tag{2}$$

EEG signals require extraction of many features in a single session. The number of features extracted from overlapping windows is much greater than the number of features extracted from non-overlapping windows, and the shorter the length of the sliding window, the more features that can be extracted. Therefore, in this study, an overlapping window of 1 s from 1 s after the cue sign was applied and an interval of 0.1 s was placed between consecutive sliding windows to extract more distinguishable features from EEG signals and improve classification accuracy. The number of samples included in the 1 s window is $R*C$. Furthermore, it is essential to extract more features within a session rather than extract features from three 1 s windows due to the inherent non-stationarity in the EEG data. Therefore, we performed feature extraction while moving the 1 s window by Δts. As a result, the number of samples, n_i, extracted from a single trial from the ith subject is shown in Equation (3).

$$n_i = \left(\frac{R}{(R * \Delta t_s)} - 1 \right) * R * C \quad (3)$$

Therefore, the total samples, N_i, that can be obtained from the ith subject is shown in Equation (4).

$$N_i = \left(\frac{R}{(R * \Delta t_s)} - 1 \right) * R * C * V_i \quad (4)$$

3.2. LSTM-Based FBCSP with Overlapped Band

After determining the window for feature extraction, feature extraction was performed. We used the overlapping band-based FBCSP algorithm in this study. This algorithm, like the conventional FBCSP, consisted of four steps: bandpass filtering, spatial filtering using CSP, feature selection, classification. Figure 2 shows the general framework for the proposed approach.

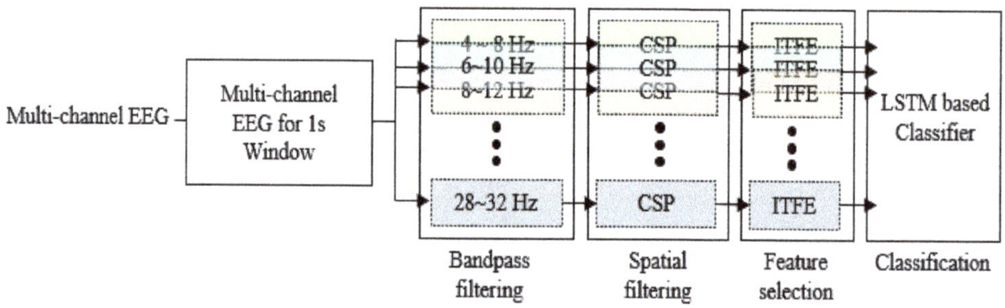

Figure 2. Processing steps of the filter bank common spatial pattern.

A filter bank that decomposes the EEG into multiple frequency passbands was employed in the first step, starting from 4 to 32 Hz with the bandwidth of 4 Hz and overlap of 2 Hz. A total of 13 bandpass filters were used, namely, 4–8, 6–10, 8–12, 10–14, . . . , 28–32 Hz due to the overlapping between two frequency bands. The signals were bandpass filtered by Chebyshev type II filter. As suggested by many studies [33,52,53], CSP features extracted from overlapping sub-bands led to an improved performance of motor imagery EEG-based BCI systems. Inspired by these research results, we used multiple overlapping filter bands to achieve higher classification accuracy.

In the second step, filtered signals were transformed to spatial subspace using CSP algorithm for feature extraction, and CSP features in each frequency band were extracted. In the third step, the discriminative features were selected from the filter bank which consisted of overlapping frequency bands, using the ITFE algorithm [65] which optimized the approximation of mutual information between class labels and extracted EEG/MEG components for multiclass CSP. The fourth step employed two-stacked LSTM layers to classify the selected CSP features. Thus, the selected features were then fed into LSTM networks.

LSTM network is an advanced RNN that allows information to persist. It can handle the vanishing gradient problem of RNN [33,42]. The key to LSTM is cell state, which consists of three gates. The forget gate decides to remember or forget the previous time step's information. The input gate attempts to learn new information, while the output gate transmits the updated information from the current time step to the next. At last, in the output gate, the cell passes the updated information from the current time step to the next time step. In other words, LSTM can control important information to be retained and unrelated information to be released by using three gates. Therefore, LSTM is an excellent way to reveal the internal temporal correlation of time series signals and can learn one time step at a time from EEG channels, so we adopt LSTM to extract discriminative features of time-varying EEG signals.

As mentioned above, we employ an overlapping bandpass filter as well as overlapping window-based feature extraction method to further improve classification accuracy of four-class MI EEG signals. Moreover, LSTM is used for classification that enables better quality learning by storing the correlation information from EEG signals through time. In this scenario, we anticipate that our approach will provide us more discriminative information for feature extraction from EEG signals.

3.3. LSTM Based FBCSP with Overlapped Band Applying Channel Selection

EEG is measured by a BCI device with many channels. To explore the effectiveness of channel selection, we first carried out the channel selection task by correlation between channels and then performed feature extraction and classification with only selected channels among multiple channels. Figure 3 shows the EEG classification processing step including the channel selection step.

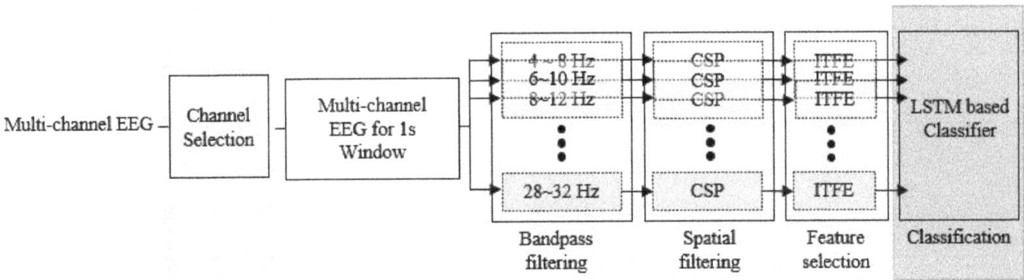

Figure 3. Processing steps of the FBCSP with channel selection.

Pearson's correlation coefficient is used to find channel correlation for subject's MI in channel selection task. We calculated the correlation coefficient between channels for each MI and determined that the correlation between the two channels was high when the absolute value of the correlation coefficient is greater than 0.8. $MICoeff_{j,k,l}$, which stores high correlation information between channels for each MI, is calculated by Equation (5) and stores 1 if the correlation between channel j and channel k in the lth motion is high or 0 otherwise, where l is the lth MI for each subject and j and k mean the jth and kth channels.

$$MICoeff_{j,k,l} = \begin{cases} 1 & if\ coeff\left(C_{j,k,l}, C_{j,k,l}\right) \geq 0.8 \\ 0 & otherwise \end{cases} \tag{5}$$

where j and $k = 0, \ldots, 21$, and $l = 1, \ldots, 4$.

Figure 4 shows an example of *MICoeff* showing high correlation by channel during one trial for several subjects. That is, channels having a high inter-channel correlation for each MI are shown. For example, for subject1, channel 0 showed high correlation with channels 2, 3, and 4 in all motions but high correlation with channel 7 only in right motions. Channels with high correlation for all MIs can interfere with unambiguously determining the class in MI classification, thus those channels were removed. That is, channels with high correlation between channels for each MI of all subjects are checked, and the high correlation between all channels is ranked, eliminating the channels in order of maximum correlation. Thus, only channels that allow the subject MI to be discriminated are selected.

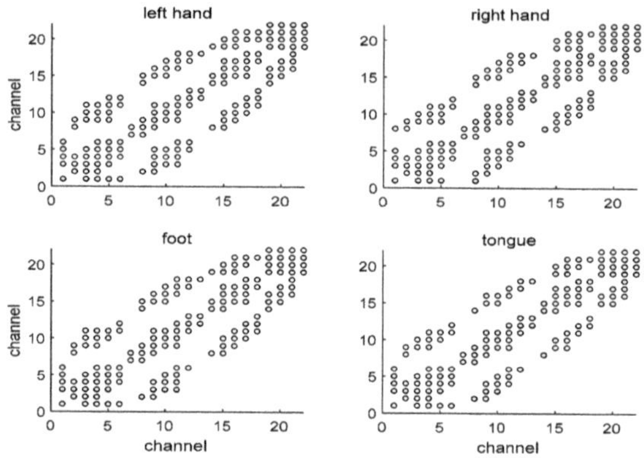

(a)

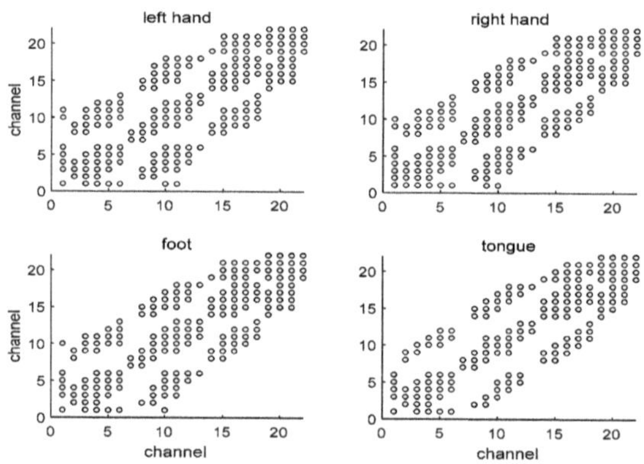

(b)

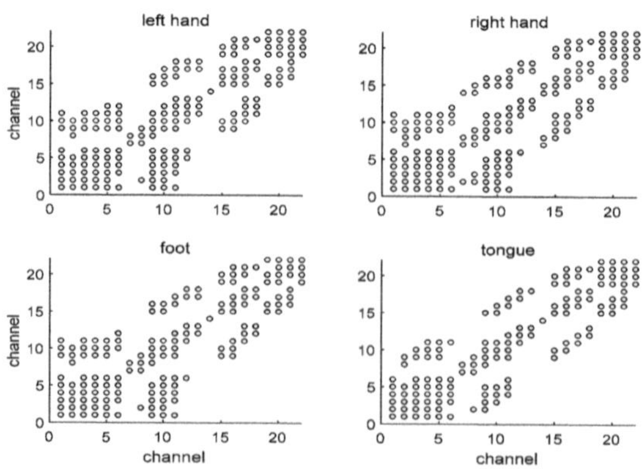

(c)

Figure 4. Correlation between channels for each MI. The circle (o) represents a high correlation between two channels. (**a**) Subject 1; (**b**) Subject 3; (**c**) Subject 8.

4. Experimental Results

4.1. Dataset and Experimental Environment

In this study, we used the BCI competition IV-2a dataset [64]. This dataset was collected while imagining movements of the left hand, right hand, feet, and tongue from twenty-two EEG electrodes and three EOG channels with a sampling frequency of 250 Hz and a bandpass filtered between 0.5 Hz and 100 Hz from nine subjects. All experiments were carried out using Python in an Intel i9-7920X CPU and an Nvidia GTX 1080 Ti GPU environment. The window size for feature extraction was set to 750 (750win) and 250 (250win); 750win is a window without applying window sliding, and the window movement time Δts of 250win with window sliding was set to 0.1 s. Subject-specific features were extracted using FBCSP in each channel except for the EOG channel. 250win-OB is a technique that extracts features by applying an overlapped band in FBCSP to 250win. The overlap size applied to the bandpass filter was set to two. In FBCSP, the classifier used two-layer-stacked LSTM. Of the total trials for each user, 80% was used as a training dataset and 20% as a testing dataset, and the epoch was set to 400. We evaluated the proposed method based on various evaluation metrics such as accuracy, kappa coefficient, precision, recall, and the results of all the evaluation metrics were represented as the average value of 10 repetitions. The kappa value was mainly used as the evaluation metric for comparison evaluation with previously proposed algorithms. The kappa value is a scale that reflects the classification accuracy by correcting the classification results caused by chance, and the BCI competition committee that provides the data used in this experiment also recommends this scale [64,66].

4.2. Experimental Evaluation

We first compared the kappa values of 750win, 250win, and 250win-OB. As shown in Figure 5, in subject7 with the highest kappa value, 750win was 0.82, whereas 250win was 0.97 and 250win-OB was 0.98. In subject6 with the lowest kappa value, the kappa value was 0.19 for 750win, while it was 0.90 for 250win and 0.94 for 250win-OB. The average kappa value of all subjects in 750win was 0.54, whereas it was 0.92 in 250win and 0.95 in 250win-OB. These results show that the window size, application of a sliding window, and overlap of the bandpass filter greatly affect MI EEG classification results.

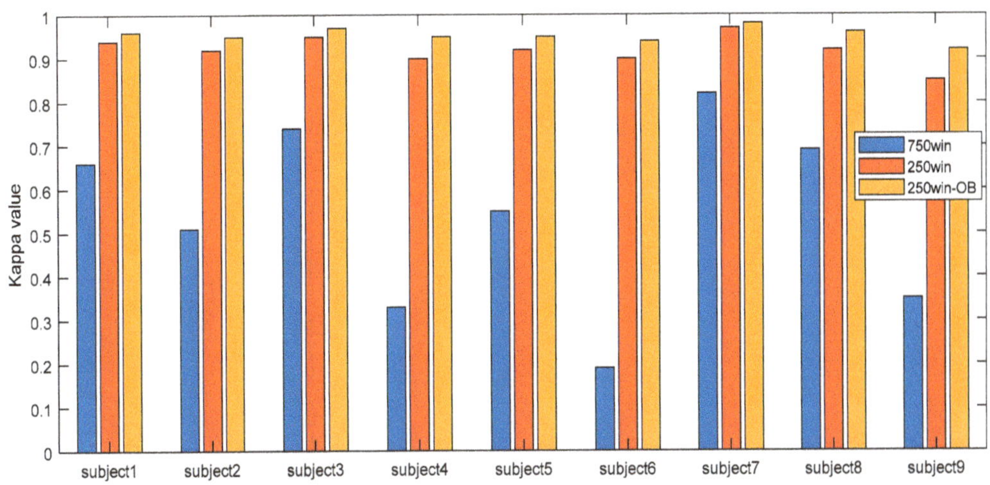

Figure 5. Kappa value according to window size.

Figure 6 shows the results of an MI EEG classification of 250win-OB. All indicators for subject3 and subject7 appeared higher than other subjects, and subject9 showed lower indicators than other subjects. The average index of all subjects showed 0.97 in accuracy, precision, and recall, and a slightly lower kappa value of 0.95. These results have shown that the algorithm proposed in this study classifies the MI EEG of various subjects quite well.

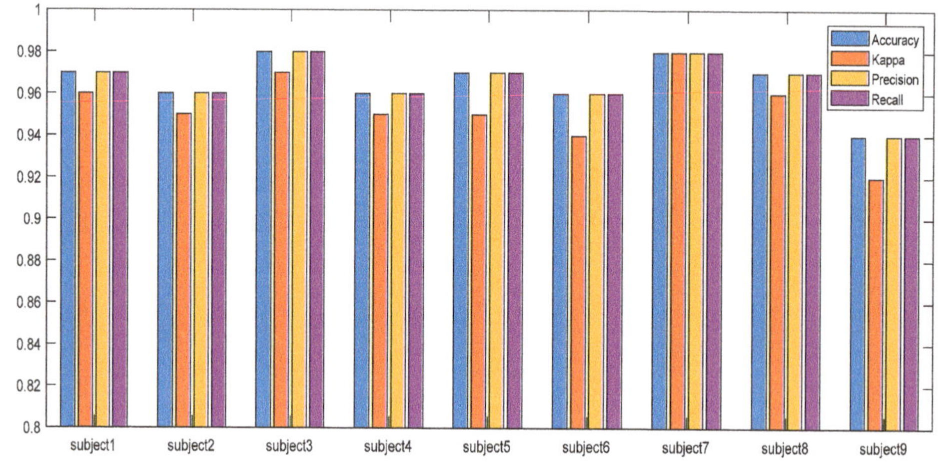

Figure 6. Index of classification result of 250win-OB.

We compared the performance of the existing methods and the 250win-OB method proposed in this study. Figure 7 shows the results of the comparison by kappa value. Through this result, the 250win-OB method shows better performance than other previously proposed methods. Existing techniques showed a large difference in the kappa value according to the subject, whereas the 250win-OB maintained a significantly high value for all subjects. In more detail, FBCSP [30] had an average kappa value of 0.57 and a standard deviation of 0.18 for each subject, SRLDA [67] showed 0.74 and 0.17, shared network [33] showed 0.81 and 0.12, and HDNN-TL [53] showed 0.81 and 0.10. On the other hand, the method proposed in this work showed an average of 0.95 and a standard deviation of 0.02. Therefore, through this comparison, it was shown that the proposed method is more suitable for the MI EEG classification of various subjects than existing algorithms.

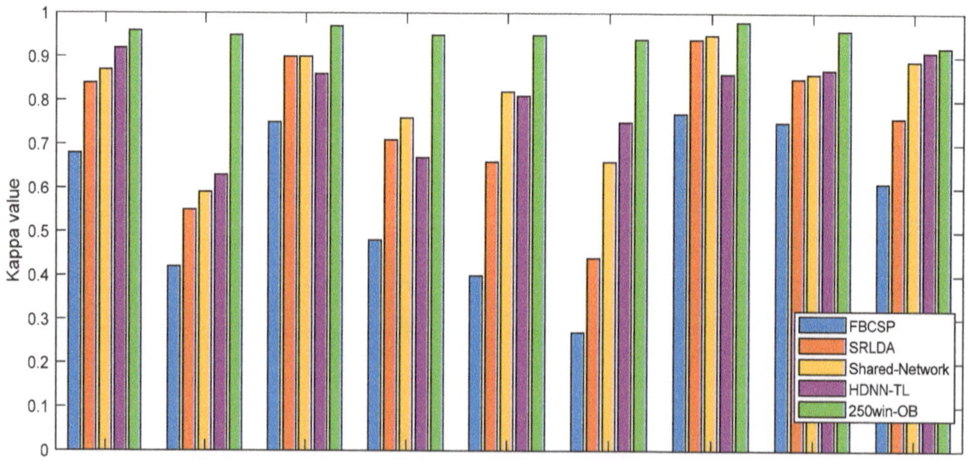

Figure 7. Performance comparison between existing methods and the proposed method.

In addition, the experimental results showed differences in classification results for each algorithm. In FBCSP, SRLDA, and 250win-OB, subject7 had the highest kappa value, while subject1 had the highest in HDNN-TL. The subject with the lowest kappa value was subject6 in FBCSP and SRLDA, whereas subject2 had the lowest in shared network and HDNN-TL, and the 250win-OB showed the lowest result in subject9. The lowest kappa value of 250win-OB also improved by about 340.7% from 0.27 to 0.92 compared to FBCSP, and by about 68.5% from 0.63 to 0.92 compared to HDNN-TL, which showed the best performance among existing techniques.

Figure 8 shows the comparison of classification accuracy with existing techniques. A-SVM [68] and BLRDLPP [69] are techniques that extract features and use the machine learning algorithm SVM for classification, while TCANET [70] is a new CNN-based classification technique. The experimental results show that the proposed method in this paper, 250win-OB, which extracts detailed features and learns through deep learning classification, outperforms A-SVM or BLRDLPP techniques that classify with machine learning algorithms after feature extraction, as well as TCANET, which learns with overall deep learning. Through such experiments, our findings showed that the suggested algorithm outperforms other existing algorithms in classifying the four-class MI EEG.

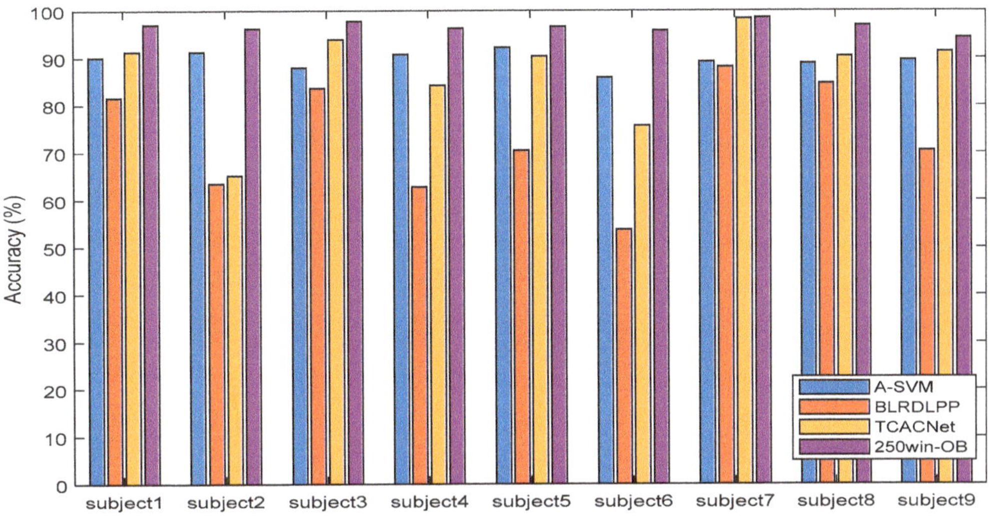

Figure 8. Comparison of accuracy with existing methods and the proposed method.

The correlation coefficients between channels are calculated to conduct channel selection for classifying EEG. Figure 9 shows a heat map of the correlation between channels for each user. As shown in the experimental results, the channel correlation coefficient values for each user showed a lot of variation. Subject3 and subject5 show a much higher correlation between channels than other subjects, whereas subject6 and subject9 show a relatively low correlation compared to other subjects. Overall, there are differences in the value of cumulative correlation, but channels with high inter-channel correlation showed high correlation in most subjects.

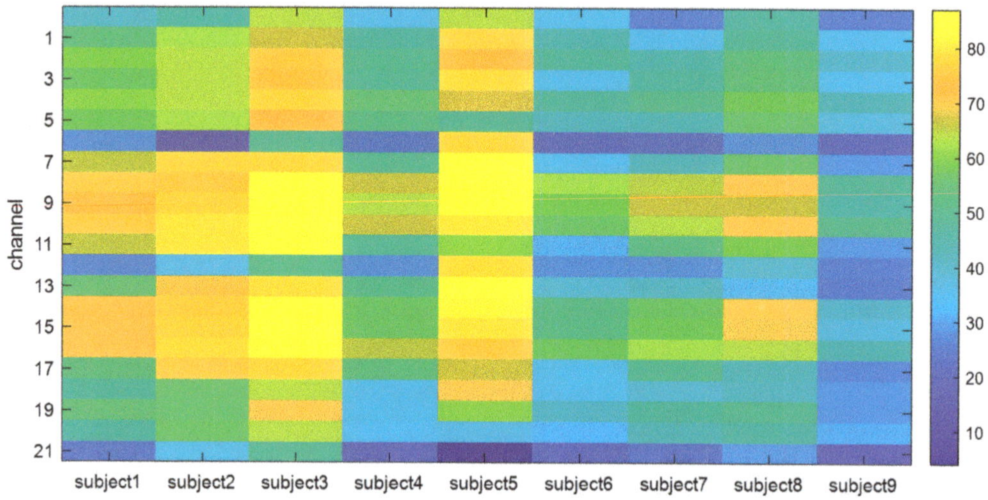

Figure 9. Cumulative channel correlation heatmap by subject. The heatmap is based on the cumulative value of the number of times the correlation between channels is greater than 0.8.

To analyze the effect of the number of channels on the classification accuracy, the results using all 22 channels and the results after removing channels with high correlations were compared. The number of channels to be removed can be specified, and in this experiment, the results after removing 5, 10, and 15 channels were compared with the results using all channels, and the results are shown in Figure 10 with the comparison of kappa values. The proposed 250win-OB method was used in the experiments.

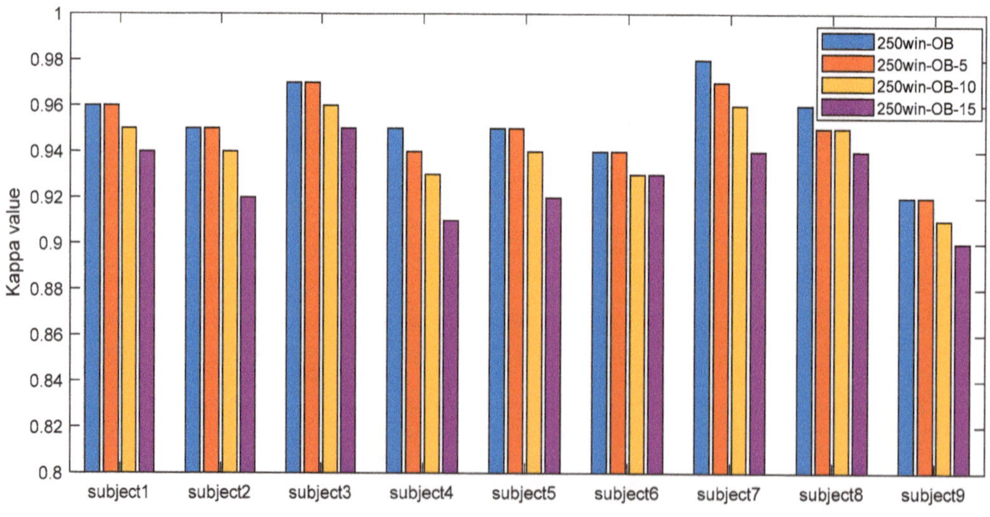

Figure 10. Change of kappa value according to channel removal.

When five channels with high correlation were removed, subject4, subject7, and subject8 showed slightly lower results than 250win-OB with all channels, but with these exceptions, most subjects showed the same performance as 250win-OB. In the case of 250win-OB-10 with 10 channels deleted, the average performance was lowered by 1.35%

compared to 250win-OB. In the case of 250win-OB-15, using only seven channels after deleting fifteen channels, it showed 2.87% lower performance than 250win-OB. Experimental results showed that classification was best performed when all twenty-two channels were used, but an average kappa value of 0.93 was maintained even when only seven channels were used.

5. Conclusions

The EEG used in the BCI system has a problem in that end-to-end learning is difficult because it is greatly affected by noise and has a great effect on performance depending on the frequency range used. To classify the four-class MI EEG for each subject, we proposed an overlapped band-based FBCSP with an LSTM classifier. The proposed algorithm applied a sliding window for each channel, tried to overcome the dependence on frequency band by extracting features for each window using FBCSP-based on overlapped band, and tried to classify features over time using LSTM. Through experiments, we showed that the algorithm proposed in this study can classify the four-class MI EEG of all subjects better than other existing algorithms. In future work, we plan to conduct a study on selecting the minimum required number of channels based on the set accuracy and finding the channel selection threshold for choosing the number of channels. Based on the findings of this paper, we believe that our research can be extended to EEG-based emotion recognition, preference recognition in neuromarketing and game control, and so on.

Author Contributions: Conceptualization, J.H. and J.C.; methodology, J.C.; software, S.P. and J.C.; validation, J.H. and J.C.; formal analysis, J.H. and J.C.; investigation, J.H.; writing—original draft preparation, J.H. and J.C.; writing—review and editing, J.H., S.P. and J.C.; supervision, J.C. All authors have read and agreed to the published version of the manuscript.

Funding: Funding for this paper was provided by Namseoul University.

Data Availability Statement: https://www.bbci.de/competition/iv/ (accessed on 18 February 2023).

Conflicts of Interest: The authors declare no conflict of interest.

References

1. Katona, J. A Review of Human–Computer Interaction and Virtual Reality Research Fields in Cognitive InfoCommunications. *Appl. Sci.* **2021**, *11*, 2646. [CrossRef]
2. McFarland, D.J.; Wolpaw, J.R. Brain-computer interfaces for communication and control. *Commun. ACM* **2011**, *54*, 60–66. [CrossRef] [PubMed]
3. Izso, L. The significance of cognitive infocommunications in developing assistive technologies for people with non-standard cognitive characteristics: CogInfoCom for people with non-standard cognitive characteristics. In Proceedings of the 2015 6th IEEE International Conference on Cognitive Infocommunications (CogInfoCom), Gyor, Hungary, 19–21 October 2015; pp. 77–82.
4. Eisapour, M.; Cao, S.; Domenicucci, L.; Boger, J. Virtual Reality Exergames for People Living with Dementia Based on Exercise Therapy Best Practices. *Proc. Hum. Factors Ergon. Soc. Annu. Meet.* **2018**, *62*, 528–532. [CrossRef]
5. Amprimo, G.; Rechichi, I.; Ferraris, C.; Olmo, G. Measuring Brain Activation Patterns from Raw Single-Channel EEG during Exergaming: A Pilot Study. *Electronics* **2023**, *12*, 623. [CrossRef]
6. Katona, J.; Ujbanyi, T.; Sziladi, G.; Kovari, A. Speed control of Festo Robotino mobile robot using NeuroSky MindWave EEG headset based brain-computer interface. In Proceedings of the 2016 7th IEEE International Conference on Cognitive Infocommunications (CogInfoCom), Wroclaw, Poland, 16–18 October 2016; pp. 000251–000256. [CrossRef]
7. Stephygraph, L.R.; Arunkumar, N. Brain-Actuated Wireless Mobile Robot Control through an Adaptive Human–Machine Interface. In Proceedings of the International Conference on Soft Computing Systems: ICSCS 2015; Advances in Intelligent Systems and Computing. Springer: New Delhi, India, 2015; Volume 1, pp. 537–549. [CrossRef]
8. Markopoulos, E.; Lauronen, J.; Luimula, M.; Lehto, P.; Laukkanen, S. Maritime safety education with VR technology (MarSEVR). In Proceedings of the 2019 10th IEEE International Conference on Cognitive Infocommunications (CogInfoCom), Naples, Italy, 23–25 October 2019; pp. 283–288.
9. Spaak, E.; Fonken, Y.; Jensen, O.; de Lange, F.P. The Neural Mechanisms of Prediction in Visual Search. *Cereb. Cortex* **2015**, *26*, 4327–4336. [CrossRef]
10. de Vries, I.E.; van Driel, J.; Olivers, C.N. Posterior α EEG dynamics dissociate current from future goals in working memory-guided visual search. *J. Neurosci.* **2017**, *37*, 1591–1603. [CrossRef]

11. Qian, L.; Ge, X.; Feng, Z.; Wang, S.; Yuan, J.; Pan, Y.; Shi, H.; Xu, J.; Sun, Y. Brain Network Reorganization During Visual Search Task Revealed by a Network Analysis of Fixation-Related Potential. *IEEE Trans. Neural Syst. Rehabil. Eng.* **2023**, *31*, 1219–1229. [CrossRef]
12. Liu, Y.; Yu, Y.; Ye, Z.; Li, M.; Zhang, Y.; Zhou, Z.; Hu, D.; Zeng, L.-L. Fusion of Spatial, Temporal, and Spectral EEG Signatures Improves Multilevel Cognitive Load Prediction. *IEEE Trans. Human-Mach. Syst.* **2023**, 1–10. [CrossRef]
13. Yusoff, M.Z.; Kamel, N.; Malik, A.; Meselhy, M. Mental task motor imagery classifications for noninvasive brain computer interface. In Proceedings of the 2014 5th International Conference on Intelligent and Advanced Systems (ICIAS), Kuala Lumpur, Malaysia, 3–5 June 2014; pp. 1–5.
14. Djemal, R.; Bazyed, A.G.; Belwafi, K.; Gannouni, S.; Kaaniche, W. Three-Class EEG-Based Motor Imagery Classification Using Phase-Space Reconstruction Technique. *Brain Sci.* **2016**, *6*, 36. [CrossRef]
15. Wolpaw, J.; Birbaumer, N.; Heetderks, W.; McFarland, D.; Peckham, P.; Schalk, G.; Donchin, E.; Quatrano, L.; Robinson, C.; Vaughan, T. Brain-computer interface technology: A review of the first international meeting. *IEEE Trans. Rehabil. Eng.* **2000**, *8*, 164–173. [CrossRef]
16. Kaiser, V.; Bauernfeind, G.; Kreilinger, A.; Kaufmann, T.; Kübler, A.; Neuper, C.; Müller-Putz, G.R. Cortical effects of user training in a motor imagery based brain–computer interface measured by fNIRS and EEG. *Neuroimage* **2014**, *85*, 432–444. [CrossRef]
17. Pfurtscheller, G.; Neuper, C. Motor imagery activates primary sensorimotor area in humans. *Neurosci. Lett.* **1997**, *239*, 65–68. [CrossRef] [PubMed]
18. Pfurtscheller, G.; Neuper, C. Motor imagery and direct brain-computer communication. *Proc. IEEE* **2001**, *89*, 1123–1134. [CrossRef]
19. Siuly, S.; Li, Y.; Wen, P. Modified CC-LR algorithm with three diverse feature sets for motor imagery tasks classification in EEG based brain–computer interface. *Comput. Methods Programs Biomed.* **2014**, *113*, 767–780. [CrossRef]
20. Pfurtscheller, G.; Neuper, C.; Flotzinger, D.; Pregenzer, M. EEG-based discrimination between imagination of right and left hand movement. *Electroencephalogr. Clin. Neurophysiol.* **1997**, *103*, 642–651. [CrossRef]
21. He, B.; Baxter, B.; Edelman, B.J.; Cline, C.C.; Ye, W.W. Noninvasive Brain-Computer Interfaces Based on Sensorimotor Rhythms. *Proc. IEEE* **2015**, *103*, 907–925. [CrossRef] [PubMed]
22. Barbati, G.; Porcaro, C.; Zappasodi, F.; Rossini, P.M.; Tecchio, F. Optimization of an independent component analysis approach for artifact identification and removal in magnetoencephalographic signals. *Clin. Neurophysiol.* **2004**, *115*, 1220–1232. [CrossRef]
23. Ferracuti, F.; Casadei, V.; Marcantoni, I.; Iarlori, S.; Burattini, L.; Monteriù, A.; Porcaro, C. A functional source separation algorithm to enhance error-related potentials monitoring in noninvasive brain-computer interface. *Comput. Methods Programs Biomed.* **2020**, *191*, 105419. [CrossRef]
24. Shenoy, P.; Krauledat, M.; Blankertz, B.; Rao, R.P.N.; Müller, K.-R. Towards adaptive classification for BCI. *J. Neural Eng.* **2006**, *3*, R13–R23. [CrossRef]
25. Nicolas-Alonso, L.F.; Gomez-Gil, J. Brain computer interfaces, a review. *Sensors* **2012**, *12*, 1211–1279. [CrossRef]
26. Dai, G.; Zhou, J.; Huang, J.; Wang, N. HS-CNN: A CNN with hybrid convolution scale for EEG motor imagery classification. *J. Neural Eng.* **2019**, *17*, 016025. [CrossRef]
27. Alzahab, N.A.; Apollonio, L.; Di Iorio, A.; Alshalak, M.; Iarlori, S.; Ferracuti, F.; Porcaro, C. Hybrid deep learning (hDL)-based brain-computer interface (BCI) systems: A systematic review. *Brain Sci.* **2021**, *11*, 75. [CrossRef] [PubMed]
28. Müller-Gerking, J.; Pfurtscheller, G.; Flyvbjerg, H. Designing optimal spatial filters for single-trial EEG classification in a movement task. *Clin. Neurophysiol.* **1999**, *110*, 787–798. [CrossRef]
29. Wang, Y.; Gao, S.; Gao, X. Common spatial pattern method for channel selection in motor imagery based brain-computer interface. In Proceedings of the Annual International Conference of the IEEE Engineering in Medicine and Biology—Proceedings, Shanghai, China, 31 August–3 September 2005; Volume 7, pp. 5392–5395. [CrossRef]
30. Ang, K.K.; Chin, Z.Y.; Zhang, H.; Guan, C. Filter bank common spatial pattern (FBCSP) in brain-computer interface. In Proceedings of the 2008 IEEE International Joint Conference on Neural Networks (IEEE World Congress on Computational Intelligence), Hong Kong, China, 1–8 June 2008; pp. 2390–2397.
31. Ma, Y.; Ding, X.; She, Q.; Luo, Z.; Potter, T.; Zhang, Y. Classification of Motor Imagery EEG Signals with Support Vector Machines and Particle Swarm Optimization. *Comput. Math. Methods Med.* **2016**, *2016*, 4941235. [CrossRef]
32. Lu, N.; Li, T.; Ren, X.; Miao, H. A Deep Learning Scheme for Motor Imagery Classification based on Restricted Boltzmann Machines. *IEEE Trans. Neural Syst. Rehabil. Eng.* **2016**, *25*, 566–576. [CrossRef] [PubMed]
33. Zhang, R.; Zong, Q.; Dou, L.; Zhao, X. A novel hybrid deep learning scheme for four-class motor imagery classification. *J. Neural Eng.* **2019**, *16*, 066004. [CrossRef]
34. Shovon, T.H.; Al Nazi, Z.; Dash, S.; Hossain, M.F. Classification of motor imagery EEG signals with multi-input convolutional neural network by augmenting STFT. In Proceedings of the 2019 5th International Conference on Advances in Electrical Engineering (ICAEE), Dhaka, Bangladesh, 26–28 September 2019; pp. 398–403. [CrossRef]
35. Wang, P.; Jiang, A.; Liu, X.; Shang, J.; Zhang, L. LSTM-based EEG classification in motor imagery tasks. *IEEE Trans. Neural Syst. Rehabil. Eng.* **2018**, *26*, 2086–2095. [CrossRef] [PubMed]
36. Yang, T.; Phua, K.S.; Yu, J.; Selvaratnam, T.; Toh, V.; Ng, W.H.; So, R.Q. Image-based motor imagery EEG classification using convolutional neural network. In Proceedings of the 2019 IEEE EMBS International Conference on Biomedical & Health Informatics (BHI), Chicago, IL, USA, 19–22 May 2019; pp. 1–4.

37. Blankertz, B.; Tomioka, R.; Lemm, S.; Kawanabe, M.; Muller, K.-R. Optimizing Spatial filters for Robust EEG Single-Trial Analysis. *IEEE Signal Process. Mag.* **2007**, *25*, 41–56. [CrossRef]
38. Lotte, F.; Guan, C. Regularizing Common Spatial Patterns to Improve BCI Designs: Unified Theory and New Algorithms. *IEEE Trans. Biomed. Eng.* **2010**, *58*, 355–362. [CrossRef]
39. Ang, K.K.; Chin, Z.Y.; Zhang, H.; Guan, C. Mutual information-based selection of optimal spatial–temporal patterns for single-trial EEG-based BCIs. *Pattern Recognit.* **2012**, *45*, 2137–2144. [CrossRef]
40. Yahya-Zoubir, B.; Bentlemsan, M.; Zemouri, E.T.; Ferroudji, K. Adaptive time window for EEG-based motor imagery classification. In Proceedings of the International Conference on Intelligent Information Processing, Security and Advanced Communication, Batna, Algeria, 23–25 November 2015; pp. 1–6.
41. Gaur, P.; Gupta, H.; Chowdhury, A.; McCreadie, K.; Pachori, R.B.; Wang, H. A Sliding Window Common Spatial Pattern for Enhancing Motor Imagery Classification in EEG-BCI. *IEEE Trans. Instrum. Meas.* **2021**, *70*, 4002709. [CrossRef]
42. Liu, Y.; Huang, Y.-X.; Zhang, X.; Qi, W.; Guo, J.; Hu, Y.; Zhang, L.; Su, H. Deep C-LSTM Neural Network for Epileptic Seizure and Tumor Detection Using High-Dimension EEG Signals. *IEEE Access* **2020**, *8*, 37495–37504. [CrossRef]
43. Ai, Q.; Chen, A.; Chen, K.; Liu, Q.; Zhou, T.; Xin, S.; Ji, Z. Feature extraction of four-class motor imagery EEG signals based on functional brain network. *J. Neural Eng.* **2019**, *16*, 026032. [CrossRef] [PubMed]
44. Farquhar, J.; Hill, N.J.; Lal, T.N.; Schölkopf, B. Regularised CSP for Sensor Selection in BCI. In Proceedings of the 3rd International BCI workshop, Graz, Austria, 21–24 September 2006; pp. 1–2.
45. Arvaneh, M.; Guan, C.; Ang, K.K.; Quek, C. Multi-frequency band common spatial pattern with sparse optimization in Brain-Computer Interface. In Proceedings of the 2012 IEEE International Conference on Acoustics, Speech and Signal Processing (ICASSP), Kyoto, Japan, 25–30 March 2012; pp. 2541–2544. [CrossRef]
46. Kumar, S.; Sharma, A.; Tsunoda, T. An improved discriminative filter bank selection approach for motor imagery EEG signal classification using mutual information. *BMC Bioinform.* **2017**, *18*, 125–137. [CrossRef]
47. Al-Saegh, A.; Dawwd, S.A.; Abdul-Jabbar, J.M. Deep learning for motor imagery EEG-based classification: A review. *Biomed. Signal Process. Control.* **2020**, *63*, 102172. [CrossRef]
48. Hamedi, M.; Salleh, S.-H.; Noor, A.M.; Mohammad-Rezazadeh, I. Neural network-based three-class motor imagery classification using time-domain features for BCI applications. In Proceedings of the 2014 IEEE REGION 10 SYMPOSIUM, Kuala Lumpur, Malaysia, 14–16 April 2014; pp. 204–207. [CrossRef]
49. Park, H.-J.; Kim, J.; Min, B.; Lee, B. Motor imagery EEG classification with optimal subset of wavelet based common spatial pattern and kernel extreme learning machine. In Proceedings of the 2017 39th Annual International Conference of the IEEE Engineering in Medicine and Biology Society (EMBC), Jeju, Korea, 11–15 July 2017; pp. 2863–2866. [CrossRef]
50. Tabar, Y.R.; Halici, U. A novel deep learning approach for classification of EEG motor imagery signals. *J. Neural Eng.* **2016**, *14*, 016003. [CrossRef]
51. Lee, H.K.; Choi, Y.-S. Application of Continuous Wavelet Transform and Convolutional Neural Network in Decoding Motor Imagery Brain-Computer Interface. *Entropy* **2019**, *21*, 1199. [CrossRef]
52. Sakhavi, S.; Guan, C.; Yan, S. Learning Temporal Information for Brain-Computer Interface Using Convolutional Neural Networks. *IEEE Trans. Neural Netw. Learn. Syst.* **2018**, *29*, 5619–5629. [CrossRef]
53. Zhang, R.; Zong, Q.; Dou, L.; Zhao, X.; Tang, Y.; Li, Z. Hybrid deep neural network using transfer learning for EEG motor imagery decoding. *Biomed. Signal Process. Control.* **2020**, *63*, 102144. [CrossRef]
54. Zhou, J.; Meng, M.; Gao, Y.; Ma, Y.; Zhang, Q. Classification of motor imagery eeg using wavelet envelope analysis and LSTM networks. In Proceedings of the 2018 Chinese Control and Decision Conference (CCDC), Shenyang, China, 9–11 June 2018; pp. 5600–5605. [CrossRef]
55. Ma, X.; Qiu, S.; Du, C.; Xing, J.; He, H. Improving EEG-based motor imagery classification via spatial and temporal recurrent neural networks. In Proceedings of the 2018 40th Annual International Conference of the IEEE Engineering in Medicine and Biology Society (EMBC), Honolulu, HI, USA, 18–21 July 2018; pp. 1903–1906.
56. Handiru, V.S.; Prasad, V.A. Optimized Bi-Objective EEG Channel Selection and Cross-Subject Generalization with Brain–Computer Interfaces. *IEEE Trans. Hum.-Mach. Syst.* **2016**, *46*, 777–786. [CrossRef]
57. Ghaemi, A.; Rashedi, E.; Pourrahimi, A.M.; Kamandar, M.; Rahdari, F. Automatic channel selection in EEG signals for classification of left or right hand movement in Brain Computer Interfaces using improved binary gravitation search algorithm. *Biomed. Signal Process. Control.* **2017**, *33*, 109–118. [CrossRef]
58. Baig, M.Z.; Aslam, N.; Shum, H.P.H. Filtering techniques for channel selection in motor imagery EEG applications: A survey. *Artif. Intell. Rev.* **2019**, *53*, 1207–1232. [CrossRef]
59. Yang, H.; Guan, C.; Wang, C.C.; Ang, K.K. Maximum dependency and minimum redundancy-based channel selection for motor imagery of walking EEG signal detection. In Proceedings of the 2013 IEEE International Conference on Acoustics, Speech and Signal Processing, Vancouver, BC, Canada, 26–31 May 2013; pp. 1187–1191. [CrossRef]
60. Shenoy, H.V.; Vinod, A.P. An iterative optimization technique for robust channel selection in motor imagery based Brain Computer Interface. In Proceedings of the 2014 IEEE International Conference on Systems, Man, and Cybernetics (SMC), San Diego, CA, USA, 5–8 October 2014; pp. 1858–1863. [CrossRef]
61. Li, M.; Ma, J.; Jia, S. Optimal combination of channels selection based on common spatial pattern algorithm. In Proceedings of the 2011 IEEE International Conference on Mechatronics and Automation, Beijing, China, 7–10 August 2011; pp. 295–300. [CrossRef]

62. Ma, X.; Qiu, S.; Wei, W.; Wang, S.; He, H. Deep Channel-Correlation Network for Motor Imagery Decoding from the Same Limb. *IEEE Trans. Neural Syst. Rehabil. Eng.* **2019**, *28*, 297–306. [CrossRef] [PubMed]
63. Li, Y.; Zhang, X.-R.; Zhang, B.; Lei, M.-Y.; Cui, W.-G.; Guo, Y.-Z. A Channel-Projection Mixed-Scale Convolutional Neural Network for Motor Imagery EEG Decoding. *IEEE Trans. Neural Syst. Rehabil. Eng.* **2019**, *27*, 1170–1180. [CrossRef]
64. Brunner, C.; Leeb, R.; Müller-Putz, G.; Schlögl, A.; Pfurtscheller, G. *BCI Competition 2008–Graz Data Set A*; Laboratory of Brain-Computer Interfaces, Institute for Knowledge Discovery, Graz University of Technology: Graz, Austria, 2008; Volume 16, pp. 1–6.
65. Grosse-Wentrup, M.; Buss, M. Multiclass Common Spatial Patterns and Information Theoretic Feature Extraction. *IEEE Trans. Biomed. Eng.* **2008**, *55*, 1991–2000. [CrossRef] [PubMed]
66. Schlögl, A.; Lee, F.; Bischof, H.; Pfurtscheller, G. Characterization of four-class motor imagery EEG data for the BCI-competition 2005. *J. Neural Eng.* **2005**, *2*, L14–L22. [CrossRef]
67. Nicolas-Alonso, L.F.; Corralejo, R.; Gomez-Pilar, J.; Alvarez, D.; Hornero, R. Adaptive Stacked Generalization for Multiclass Motor Imagery-Based Brain Computer Interfaces. *IEEE Trans. Neural Syst. Rehabil. Eng.* **2015**, *23*, 702–712. [CrossRef]
68. Antony, M.J.; Sankaralingam, B.P.; Mahendran, R.K.; Gardezi, A.A.; Shafiq, M.; Choi, J.-G.; Hamam, H. Classification of EEG Using Adaptive SVM Classifier with CSP and Online Recursive Independent Component Analysis. *Sensors* **2022**, *22*, 7596. [CrossRef]
69. Zhu, J.; Zhu, L.; Ding, W.; Ying, N.; Xu, P.; Zhang, J. An improved feature extraction method using low-rank representation for motor imagery classification. *Biomed. Signal Process. Control.* **2023**, *80*, 104389. [CrossRef]
70. Liu, X.; Shi, R.; Hui, Q.; Xu, S.; Wang, S.; Na, R.; Sun, Y.; Ding, W.; Zheng, D.; Chen, X. TCACNet: Temporal and channel attention convolutional network for motor imagery classification of EEG-based BCI. *Inf. Process. Manag.* **2022**, *59*, 103001. [CrossRef]

electronics

MDPI

Article

IoT Data Sharing Platform in Web 3.0 Using Blockchain Technology

Abdul Razzaq [1,*], Ahmed B. Altamimi [2,*], Abdulrahman Alreshidi [3], Shahbaz Ahmed Khan Ghayyur [4], Wilayat Khan [5] and Mohammad Alsaffar [3]

1 Ocean Technology and Engineering, Ocean College, Zhejiang University, Zhoushan 316021, China
2 Department of Computer Engineering, University of Ha'il, Ha'il 81481, Saudi Arabia
3 Department of Information and Computer Science, University of Ha'il, Ha'il 81481, Saudi Arabia
4 Department of Computer Science and Software Engineering, International Islamic University, Islamabad 44000, Pakistan
5 Department of Electrical and Computer Engineering, COMSATS University Islamabad, Wah Cantt 47010, Pakistan
* Correspondence: 11934071@zju.edu.cn (A.R.); altamimi.a@uoh.edu.sa (A.B.A.)

Abstract: As Internet of Things (IoT)-based systems become more prevalent in the era of data-driven intelligence, they are prone to some unprecedented challenges in terms of data security and systems scalability in an era of context-sensitive data. The current advances in IoT-driven data sensing and sharing rely on third-party sources of information (TTPs) that gather data from one party, then transmit it to the other. As a result of TTPs' involvement, such IoT systems suffer from many issues including but not limited to security, transparency, trust, and immutability as a result of the involvement of the company. Moreover, a multitude of technical impediments, such as the computation and storage poverty of IoTs, privacy concerns, and energy efficiency, enhances the challenges for IoTs. To address these issues of IoT security, we propose a blockchain-enabled open IoT data-sharing framework based on the potential of the interplanetary file system (IPFS). We have used a case study-based approach to evaluate the proposed solution. It is submitted that the proposed scenario is implemented by building smart contracts in Solidity and deploying them on the local Ethereum test network, using the Solidity programming language. With the implementation of smart contracts on the blockchain for access roles in IoT data sensing, the proposed solution advocates for a blockchain-based approach to data security for IoT systems that makes use of smart contracts for access roles.

Keywords: Web 3.0; Internet of Things; blockchain; smart contract; distributed storage; IPFS; data sharing

Citation: Razzaq, A.; Altamimi, A.B.; Alreshidi, A.; Ghayyur, S.A.K.; Khan, W.; Alsaffar, M. IoT Data Sharing Platform in Web 3.0 Using Blockchain Technology. *Electronics* **2023**, *12*, 1233. https://doi.org/10.3390/electronics12051233

Academic Editors: Galina Ilieva and George A. Tsihrintzis

Received: 25 January 2023
Revised: 26 February 2023
Accepted: 27 February 2023
Published: 4 March 2023

1. Introduction

In an Internet of Things (IoT), physical objects (things) that are connected to the internet are equipped with software and sensors which allow them to exchange data with the rest of the world's systems and devices by means of the internet. The recommended method for secure data sharing fails in these circumstances because of the volume of data created, different devices [1], lack of confidence as well as participants, and the lack of openness in data management.

The information interconnection of the entire production process is the key component of Industry 4.0. In order to transition industry production to the industry 4.0 age, information physics system development must be accelerated. In each stage of production, businesses use a sizable number of sensors and actuators, but each one can only affect the subsystem to which it belongs. The Internet of Things' effectiveness is constrained by the close coupling of components [2,3].

The first version of the internet, known as Web 1.0, denotes the beginning of the internet in the late 1980s. Only static "read-only" messages created by a small number of users were included. The development of web 2.0, which placed a strong emphasis on enhancing user engagement and interaction, was then observed around the world. Users were able to create accounts using a variety of Web 2.0 apps, allowing them to establish distinctive online personas. With the advent of web 3.0, the globe is now moving toward the most recent paradigm in the web's evolution. What benefits does the new internet have to offer, then? Let us learn more about the new way of looking at the internet and the technologies which will be key in igniting this new revolution.

In essence, interconnection and interoperability are two key qualities that the IoT inevitably requires [4]. While interoperability refers to how IoT devices may swap information and utilize that information to carry out data analytics [5], interconnection refers to how these devices are connected to one another through ubiquitous networks with high-speed transmission. In other words, to break the data isolation in IoTs, which also supports decision-making capability at the system level [6,7] for an extensive range of industrial architectures, seamless data exchange among multiple industrial sectors and their systems, such as carriers, suppliers, and manufacturers, is necessary. For instance, logistics companies can optimize the schedule of delivering packages in order to cut down the delivery time [8] and significantly reduce delivery costs when they receive road conditions and provided real-time traffic information from the industry.

Blockchain technology has emerged as a potential solution in several distributed applications where trust and transparency are essential aspects. As a result, it is not unexpected that both businesses and academia are debating how to effectively merge IoT systems with blockchains. To address the issue of secure data interchange, a number of research projects suggest directly connecting IoT systems to a blockchain platform [9,10]. The vast majority use hybrid storage strategies like a provider who keeps the data current, while the blockchain offers benefits such as integrity and reliable distribution [11]. Authors propose, for example, storing access control strategies that the storage provider queries as it receives an access request. As a result, the storage provider operates as a hub for making and enforcing policy decisions, while the blockchain safeguards policy integrity and enables open audits of policy changes.

The research community has made technical advances in the past decade to support data-sharing methodologies. Collaboration and wise judgments can help research-based activities develop in this way. Data sharing is a necessary step in maximizing the benefits of scientific advances [12]. However, it is critical to understand when the best moment is to share the data. Before beginning the data exchange procedure, these questions must be answered completely. By employing the resources of blockchains [13], this research allows for protected data sharing and sale. In the realm of information technology, blockchain, or a distributed ledger, is a novel trend. Blockchains have been used in several financial and non-financial applications.

The centralized authorities known as cloud servers store a vast amount of data [14]. A single-point failure is one of the potential hazards associated with a dominant authority. To avoid any catastrophe, data backup services from third parties are used. The issue is that network nodes have storage and processing constraints. A peer-to-peer framework named IPFS is being used for this purpose [15].

Among peer-to-peer protocols, IPFS is content-based, and assigns a cryptographic hash to each IoT data file. The hash is targeted to make the text unchangeable [16]. By cutting bandwidth costs, speeding up IoT data downloads, and sharing vast volumes of data without duplication, IPFS allows storage savings. Up to 256 KB of unstructured binary data can be stored in a single IPFS object. If the data is over 256 KB, it is split up and stored as IPFS objects with one empty object connecting the IoT data files. The IPFS storage system is therefore an immutable storage system since, if a file's hash value is modified, it will affect the hash value of the file. The IPFS data transport protocol supports hash string routes. Encrypted data and additional information can be stored in it.

The system architecture design is shown in Figure 1, which is intended to guide system developers in maintaining the layer of abstraction that is maintained throughout the system development process. As a result, there are three layers which are all interconnected. The first layer consists of a deployed sensor system, where all of the sensors are deployed and all of them produce data in package form. The second layer is a data processing algorithm, and the third layer is a data analytics system that provides readable data to be analyzed. During the cryptographic process, the blockchain ledger receives data from the IoT data server, which stores all the data generated by the sensors. Some of the contributions that this study can provide include the following:

- Enable trust-based access management—implemented via smart contracts—to enable access control and authorization for IoT-based security-critical data.
- Modularize the solution with algorithmic implementation that automates and customizes the solution with parameterized input from the users.
- Validate the solution via a scenario-driven approach to assess system performance based on algorithmic execution and query response times.

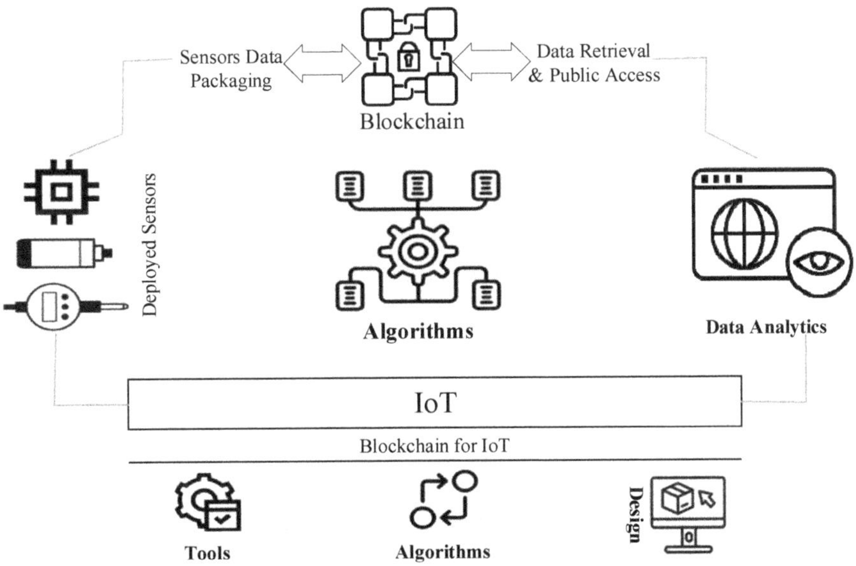

Figure 1. Overview of the recommended Model.

Paper Organization

As for the remainder of the paper: Section 2 presents the state-of-the-art, while Section 3 presents the rationale and problem description. In Section 4, we examined the algorithmic design, technology implementation, and system model of the proposed scheme and smart contracts. Section 5 contains details about the evaluation and simulation results. The last section, Section 6, concludes the paper.

2. Existing Work and Technical Challenges

This section provides background information to assist in putting the components of a blockchain-based IoT data-sharing system into perspective. Additionally, we review and impartially contrast the most pertinent studies that are currently available in order to support the contributions and scope of the proposed model.

Despite its promising qualities, a security problem [17] will always exist which prevents open data sharing in the IoT. After shared information has been received by numerous recipients, the data owner has little control over who can view the information. In most data-sharing situations, the sender merely permits the recipient to make use of the provided data, and does not let the recipient divulge the shared data to other parties or the general public without authorization for the goal of profit or other self-interest. It is essential that if there is a data leakage incident, the sending party should be found and held accountable, regardless of whether the data leakage occurred intentionally or accidentally (for example, if the sending party is aware of the data breach and had obtained the leaked data through the Internet).

For auditable private data sharing, Kokoris-Kogias et al. [18] introduced CALYPSO, where access control laws are enacted, and data is stored on-chain by a collective authority made possible by the blockchain. The massive amounts of IoT data generated by numerous IoT devices in real-world systems are too much for this method to manage. A system for exchanging time-series IoT data was developed by Shafagh et al., and it requires data owners to make transactions in order to set policies each time the data is shared with a new party. After that, only the proprietor is allowed to make changes to the policy [19].

To get the most out of the research's capabilities, data exchange is essential. The literature proposes and discusses a variety of data exchange strategies. There is not enough research on incentive mechanisms to encourage data sharing. To address these flaws, the authors of [20] performed a study of health and medical data in order to find incentive processes and compare pre- and post-empirical outcomes. According to the survey, the rate of data sharing for a single reward for medical and health data is being analyzed. As a result, it is argued that further incentive-based research is required to stimulate data collection.

The Internet of Things significantly enables in the automation of our everyday lives (IoT). Information is frequently shared and exchanged between electronic devices online [21]. A system must be created to ensure data integrity and digital device authentication due to security and privacy concerns. The authors of [22] proposed a decentralized blockchain-based scenario called a "bubble of trust." However, the suggested technique has certain drawbacks, such as the inability to adjust to a real-time setup, the need for an initiation step, and the lack of discussion of cryptocurrency rate progression.

The blockchain-based IoT data-sharing schemes have drawbacks, including security concerns, high maintenance costs, and the monitoring of enormous amounts of data coming from IoT networks [23]. The output of smart industries depends on data collected from IoT devices or their DTs. The data that is gathered may come from erroneous sensors, RFID, actuators, or their DTs, which introduce inaccurate data for analysis and action [24,25]. The authors proposed a secure fabric-based data transport system as a solution to these problems. Data is stored using a data consensus technique through a dynamic linked-assisted storage system. But power data security is neglected, and this technology is only suggested for modest uses [26].

The blockchain has a substantial storage problem, particularly when large volumes of data must be retained on network nodes. Because it does not support the storage of very large files, terminal node storage capacity is constrained. This conundrum leads to several problems, such as the need for great computing power and the high computational cost for vast amounts of data. In response to these problems, Stiechen et al. [27] presented an IPFS-based decentralized storage technique. The files are segmented on each node; on the other hand, until users are granted the proper rights, a file cannot be seen. This is a clever tactic for protecting sensitive information. The suggested schemes encounter latency when downloading files from the server because of blockchain interaction, and they do not provide real-time data saving.

Table 1 lists the benefits and drawbacks of centralized and decentralized identity management systems. To demonstrate the differences between current blockchain-based systems and old central systems, we provided four major aspects.

Table 1. Comparison between centralized and decentralized.

Acreage	Conventional Systems	Blockchain Systems
1- Control	Centralized	Decentralized
2- Identity Change	Simple to alter details on the server.	History is unchangeable and secure to alter.
3- Storage	Centralized servers	Distributed Nodes.
4- Freedom	Identity theft is a possibility for users.	Ownership of the data is returned to the users.

3. Research Methodology and Motivational Consequence of Solution

We now present the research methodology that gives the details of the design for a proposed solution. An overview of the research method is presented in Figure 2 which is based on four steps, following an incremental mechanism to analyze, design, implement, and validate the solution, as detailed below.

Figure 2 is the visualized overview of our research methodology and is divided into four different modules. In the first module of literature analysis, we conducted a critical analysis of the available literature of published research including a road map of technology and technical reports. We followed the recommendations to perform the literature analysis [28]. Prior to implementation, the solution is discussed in the second module of design. The third module of implementation has a thorough discussion of how the answer is implemented using computational and storage-intensive methods.

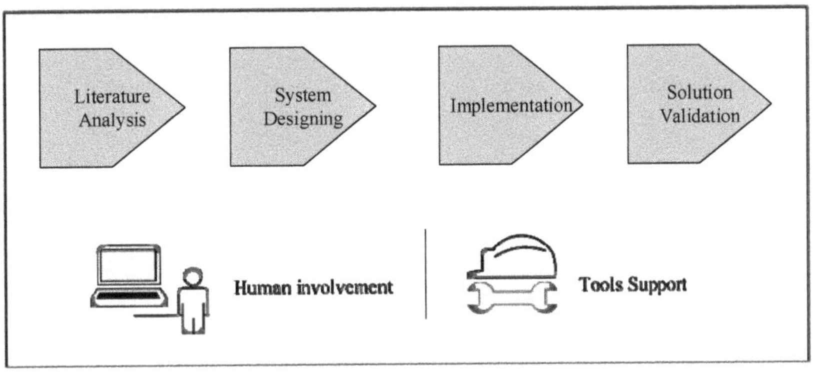

Figure 2. Illustration of Research Methodology.

The suggested system is summarized at an abstract level in Figure 3, where the module flow is shown. It is intended that all modules and stakeholders will communicate. Every component of the system design demonstrates the usage of data to illustrate the IoT idea. For instance, the data sensing module deals with gathering and representing data that is gathered from sensors, transmitted to the server, and stored in the database. System design helps programmers create and improve systems while abstracting away some implementation specifics that can be supplied with the right tools.

According to Figure 3, this system is composed of four layers: the sensing layer, the storage layer, the processing and blockchain layer, and the user layer. In addition to reading data from sensors, the sensing layer is responsible for packaging the sensing information for sending to the second layer of IoT storage for further processing. As part of layer 2, the data from all deployed sensors' data is stored in detail, the details of the sensing. The processing Blockchain layer 3 is used to save the transaction for each data-sharing action with the required detail. The fourth layer is the user interface layer used to share data.

We have obtained inspiration to work on digital data exchange utilizing blockchain based on the current research stated above. Although most researchers have worked in comparable areas, there is a great room to improve and alter previous work in order to assist the research community.

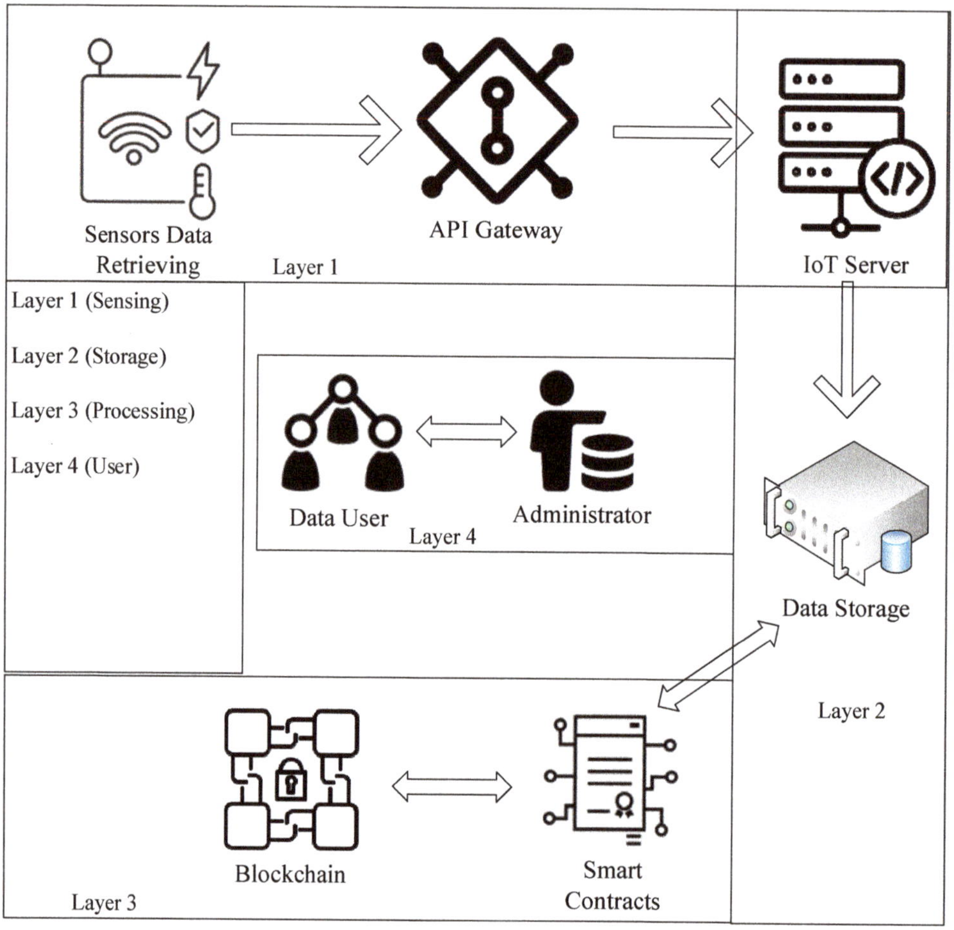

Figure 3. Overview of the proposed solution.

Figure 4 shows the flow of getting IoT data and storing it in a blockchain using a smart contract as the method for storing IoT data. The package file of IoT data is uploaded and saved the transaction record by the hash key when uploaded to IPFS. It is transferred to the DApp and uploaded. There are two kinds of uploading classifications in the DApp: one is carried out manually by the admin, and the other is carried out instantly by the system. The admin gets the hash key from the blockchain along with other necessary data and manually uploads the available package file of IoT data to IPFS. In other kinds, the system uploads immediately after receiving a fresh package file from the IoT server. Using the path, the system downloads the file from the IoT server, uploads it to IPFS, and then retrieves the back file hash that is recorded in the blockchain along with other information. Both execution processes are the same, but one is manual uploading by a user and the second is auto uploading by the system.

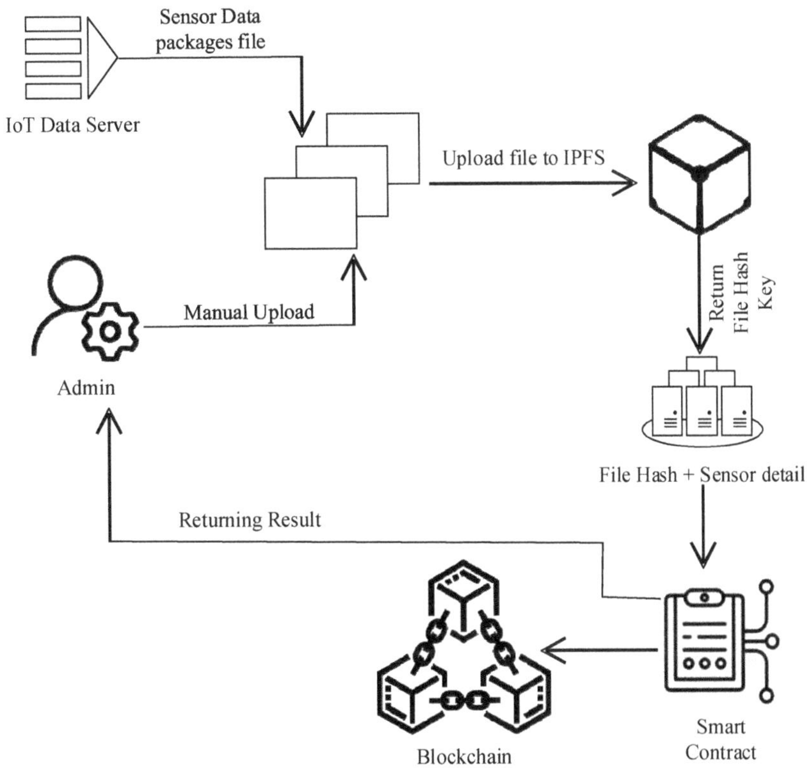

Figure 4. Data storing process.

The manual or system starts the digital data-sharing process by creating metadata for the original file. The metadata would contain details about the file's name, category, description, and size. Once finished, the information and the entire data file are uploaded to IPFS. Here is an illustration of a file transfer to IPFS (see in Listing 1):

Listing 1. Function source for uploading the data into IPFS and return hash.

```
//var UploadingType = ReactSession.get("uploadingType");
var func1 = performance.now();
console.log(func1);
var loc = document.getElementById("locationid"); //
locationid.options[locationid.selectedIndex].value;
var location = loc.options[loc.selectedIndex].text;
const sensor = this.sensorid.value;
const description = this.descriptionid.value;
ipfs.add(this.state.buffer, (error, result) => {
console.log('Ipfs result', result)
if(error) {
console.error(error)
return
}
sm1 = performance.now();
this.props.AddDataPackegeRecord(sensor, location, result [0].hash, description, 'Admin')
sm2 = performance.now();
})
```

When a file is uploaded to IPFS, it generates hashes of the contents and sends them back to the admin or system. When IPFS sends the hash to the admin or system, it maps the available parameters with the hash key. If this process is started by the admin (manually), admin will select the package file of IoT data and upload it manually to IPFS through the given system, and IPFS returns a hash key. The admin will map the required parameters (sensor, location, description) through the available input form and submit it to a smart contract where all data will be saved in the blockchain. The same execution process will be started for system uploading. The system will fetch the latest last uploaded file from the IoT data server by the given path; it will be uploaded by the system directly to IPFS, retrieve the hash key which will be mapped with available information, and stored in the blockchain through a smart contract. See the next code snippet (see in Listing 2):

Listing 2. Smart Contract Function to Record the Transaction in Blockchain Ledger.

```
function AddDataPackegeRecord(uint _sensorId, string memory _location, string memory
_hashKey,
string memory _desc, string memory _uploadingType) public{
dataUploadCount ++;
GetDataList[dataUploadCount] = DataUpload(dataUploadCount, _sensorId, _location,
_hashKey, _desc, _uploadingType, now);
GetData_sid[_sensorId] = DataUpload(dataUploadCount, _sensorId, _location, _hashKey,
_desc, _uploadingType, now);
GetData_date[now] = DataUpload(dataUploadCount, _sensorId, _location, _hashKey, _desc,
_uploadingType, now);
GetData_loc[_location] = DataUpload(dataUploadCount, _sensorId, _location, _hashKey,
_desc, _uploadingType, now);
GetData_sid_loc[_location][_sensorId] = DataUpload(dataUploadCount, _sensorId, _location,
_hashKey, _desc, _uploadingType, now);
emit DataUploadCreated(dataUploadCount, _sensorId, _location, _hashKey, _desc,
_uploadingType, now);
}
```

Phase 1 is a part of the sensors' data in IoT. There are also several sorts of sensor data. The data is packaged in a file for a certain time period, such as an IoT data package for 10 min, though it might be less or more. The gateway service sends this packet of IoT data to the IoT server. As an IoT server where all the data is processed of the deployed sensors, MSSQL is used in the same server to store the data.

Phase 2 is part of the system's service. There are two sorts of IoT data uploading categories in the DApp. Manually uploading and using a system, we have created a service called system service or auto uploading service for system uploading. The system service runs on the server's backend and makes a request to the IoT server to obtain the most up-to-date package file containing IoT data. The system service grabs the package file from the server and uploads it to an IPFS server, which then returns the hash of the file to the system. The smart contract performs the function to save the data in the blockchain by receiving the file hash and other necessary parameters from the system service. This service cycle of actions repeatedly occurs after a predetermined amount of time or is started by getting a package file of IoT data from the server.

Phase 3 is part of the manual uploading category by Admin; the technique for uploading a package file of IoT data to IPFS and storing it on the blockchain through a smart contract is the same, with the exception that this activity is conducted by the admin (manually).

Phase 4 is for accessing the existing data publicly. Users can view and download all IoT data packages for free from this open-access platform. By using a web portal, users can view the IoT data. The user will be able to access the data in a variety of ways, depending on their needs.

$$Failed_{\_Transactions} = \sum_{i=1}^{n} Total_{Requests} - \sum_{i=1}^{j} Accepted_{Requests} \tag{1}$$

In order to determine the number of failed transactions, we take the number of accepted requests and subtract them from the total number of requests in the equation (i).

$$Successful_{\_Transactions} = \sum_{i=1}^{n} Total_{Requests} - \sum_{i=1}^{j} Rejected_{Request} \quad (2)$$

Using Equation (2) and subtracting the number of rejected requests from the total number of requests, one can obtain the number of successful transactions.

4. Algorithms and Technologies for Solution Implementation

The specifics of the implementation are given in this section. A private network of the Ethereum blockchain makes up the proposed solution. Solidity is effectively used by the open-source distributed network Ethereum, a computer language that enables the creation of smart contracts.

4.1. Overview of System

- A lightweight cross-platform code editor called Visual Studio Code is available in the Microsoft Visual Studio Code product family. VSC is a lightweight code editor for a wide variety of operating systems [29].
- An emulator that works on a blockchain can be used to run a wide range of kinds of tests and commands by utilizing Ganache, a blockchain-assisted emulator. In order to run tests, deploy apps, and establish contracts, you can use a personal Ethereum blockchain called Ganache that you can access throughout the browser [30].
- A browser extension known as Metamask is used to connect to dispersed web pages by connecting to the Internet. Rather than running the complete Ethereum node in the browser, it runs Ethereum decentralized apps that are run in the browser [31].
- A hash string path can be used to transfer files using the distributed open storage system IPFS. It is employed to keep protected data that includes other data. The pathways work in a manner comparable to the traditional web URI. As a result, using their hash, all IoT data can be viewed at any time.

4.2. Proposed Solution—Algorithms

The Algorithms' Interpretation: the computational stages, data storage operations, and algorithm flow. By mapping the processes with algorithmic steps, the consistency between the proposed solution (Figure 5) and algorithmic specifications (Algorithm 1) is preserved.

Algorithm 1 Contract Creating

Input: σ, L, $h(\gamma\wp)$, Δp, ψ, ρD, Φp Sensor, Location, Hash, Description
Uploading Type, Date, Blockchain Address
Output: bool
procedure SMARTCONTRACT
if msg.sender is not Φp **then** Get Blockchain address to execute the smart contract
throw;
end if
mapping $h(\gamma\wp)$ to (σ / L / ρD) Map with each parameter
end procedure

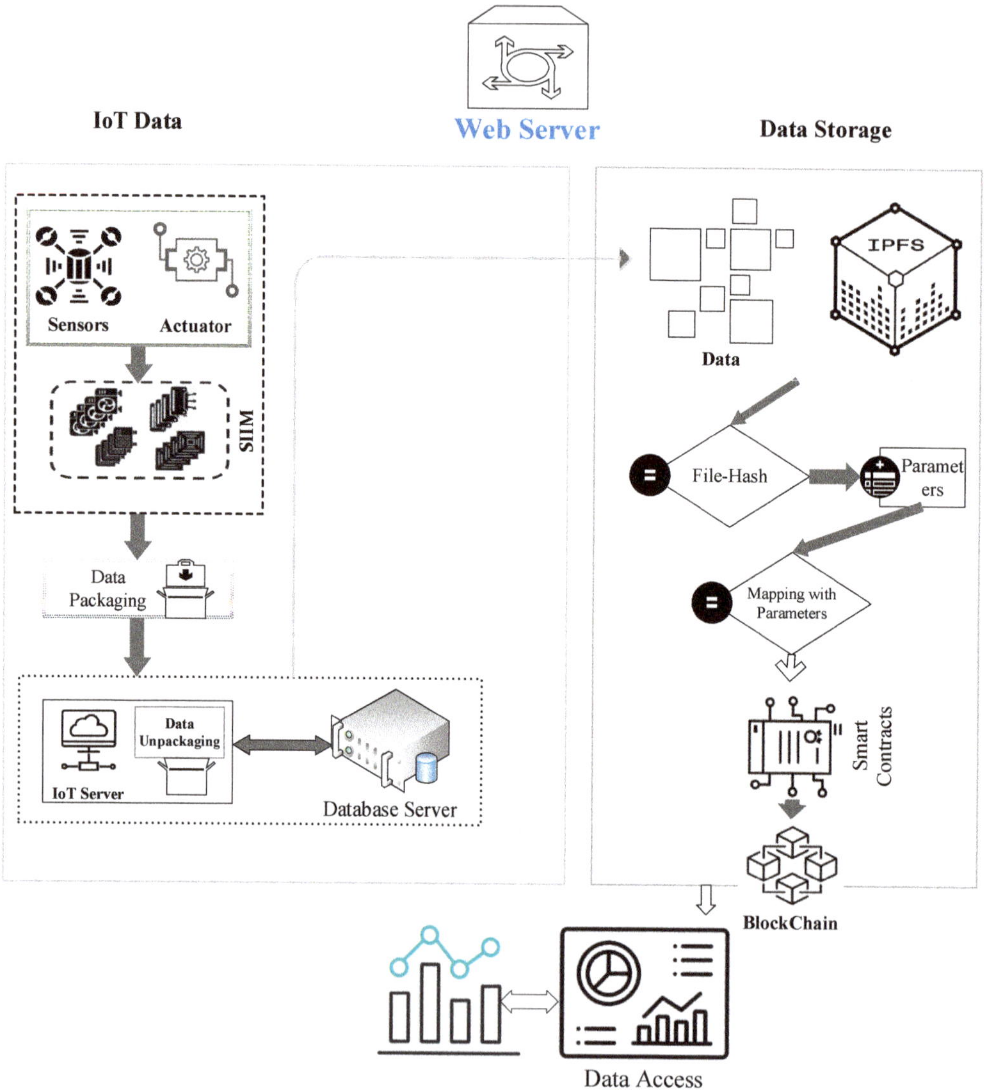

Figure 5. Overview of the detailed solution.

The functionality for uploading data is described in this section and seen in Algorithm 2. The technique is used to save the file hash and mapping of some other attributes in a smart contract and upload the data to IPFS. With a hash of the uploaded data, various parameters are mapped (date, uploading type, location, sensor, and description).

- Input(s): The input to the algorithm is used to map the parameters with a hash key.
- Processing: IoT data is read from the file and converted into a buffer, which is then uploaded to IPFS as an IoT data file and gives the hash key. A smart contract is used to record the uploaded data's hash key in the blockchain along with the extra attributes like sensor, location, description, uploading type, and date.
- Output: To save the mapped data in the blockchain is the result.

Algorithm 2 Uploading Data

Input: σ, L, Δp, ψ, ρD, $\Theta\lambda$ Sensor, Location, Description
Uploading Type, Date, Meta Data File
Output: R Uploading Message
procedure DATAUPLOADINGMODULE Event based function
if ψ == User | | ψ == System **then** Uploading by User OR System
FS $\leftarrow$ File($\Theta\lambda$) Get File stream
FB $\leftarrow$ *Buffer.form* (FS) Convert to Buffer
FH $\leftarrow$ *IPFS.Add* (FB) Get Hash of Uploaded Data
R $\leftarrow$ SBC(σ, L,FH, Δp, ψ, ρD) Store Data to Blockchain with file hash
end if
end procedure

The data accessing functionality is validated in Algorithm 3 and specified in this section. Data from the blockchain is accessed using the protocol and made publicly accessible to users. In accordance with the necessary criteria, the user can obtain the data from the blockchain. There are different types for accessing the data. A user can access the data based on sensor, location data, and sensor with location mapping.

- Input(s): The parameters used to obtain the data are mapped using the algorithm's input.
- Processing: The data could be accessed from the blockchain based on different selections such as sensor, location, date, and sensor mapping with a location.
- Output: The output is available mapped data to public access.

Algorithm 3 Data Access

Input: σ,L,ρD Sensor, Location, Date
Output: R, μ
procedure INTERFACEMODULE
if $\sigma == N$ **then**
$\mu \leftarrow$ *GetData*(σ) Get Data against Sensor
$\rho D == N$
$\mu \leftarrow$ *GetData*(ρD) Get Data against given Date
L == N
$\mu \leftarrow$ *GetData*(L) Get Data against Location
σ == N && L == N
$\mu \leftarrow$ *GetData*(σ,L) Get Data against Sensor Location
end if
R $\leftarrow$ UpdateDashboard(μ) Update available data on user screen
end procedure

The platform where all scenarios are successfully executed is shown in Figure 7 of the case study we are about to give, which includes the developed algorithms. Figure 6 shows how stakeholders submit the IoT dataset to IPFS's decentralized storage, and that data is then published to IPFS. The from date, to date, list of sensors, and list of locations where all the sensors are deployed are some of the custom parameters used by the custom query. Figure 7 depicts the internal blockchain ledger where we store the IPFS dataset, uploading information together with the dataset hash. Several sensors have been deployed in the area, and some of these include temperature, salinity, and pH sensors.

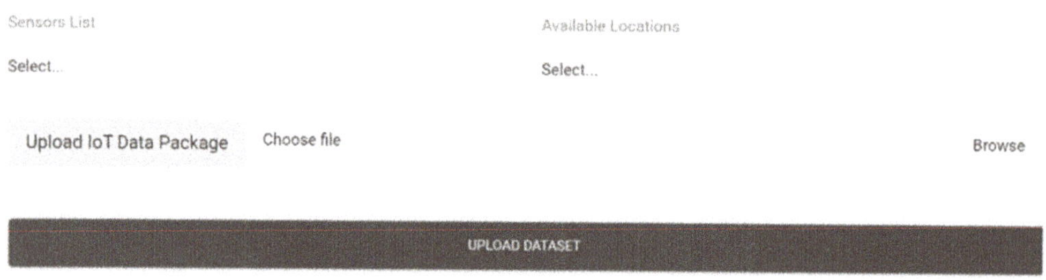

Figure 6. Case Study Trail Performed.

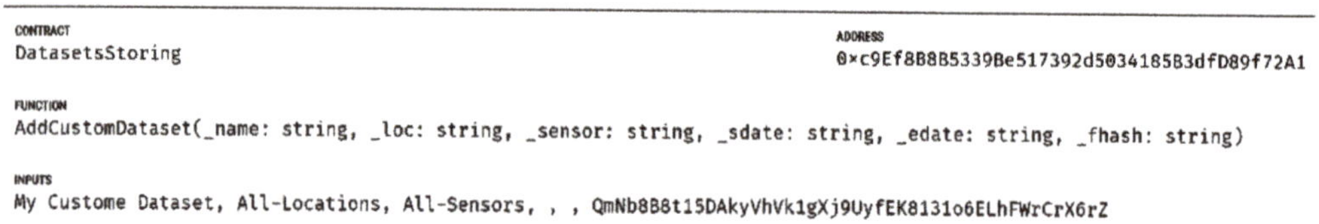

Figure 7. Data in the blockchain ledger.

4.3. Algorithmic Execution of Tools and Technologies

This section summarizes how relevant technologies and tools complement the suggested solution. In this debate, readers are encouraged to gain a better understanding of technology in general. A stack of technologies and tools is depicted in Figure 8. For instance, the sensor data is put into a CSV file and then encrypted and posted to the IPFS network, producing a hash key. The NodeJS framework has several tools that are utilized to generate a server-side application. We used VSC to start the NodeJS application. To rapidly build a personal Ethereum blockchain that you can use to run tests, issue commands, and examine the state while controlling how the chain functions, we used the Ganache Truffle Suite package.

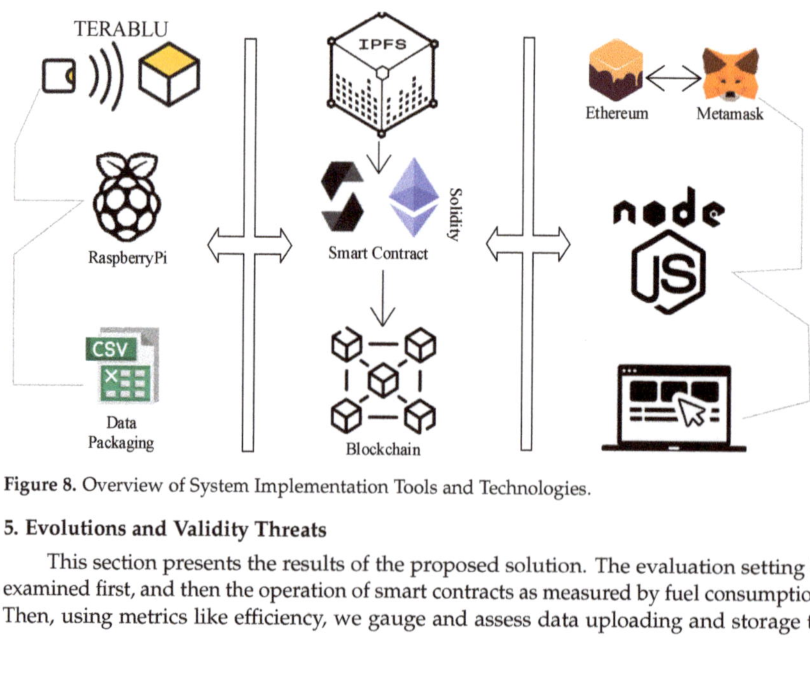

Figure 8. Overview of System Implementation Tools and Technologies.

5. Evolutions and Validity Threats

This section presents the results of the proposed solution. The evaluation setting is examined first, and then the operation of smart contracts as measured by fuel consumption. Then, using metrics like efficiency, we gauge and assess data uploading and storage to the blockchain as well as query answer, including performance and algorithmic execution. Using the ISO/IEC-9126 model as the basis for the assessment criteria [32], In software-intensive systems, it is often necessary to use a quality evaluation tool to assess their performance. Additionally, a risk of the validity of this study is discussed, as well as possible limitations that must be taken into account in future research.

5.1. Evaluation Environment

Hardware and Software

A collection of hardware and software resources is used in the evaluation environment in order to run the solution, which can also be used to keep track of every step of execution and the result of the solution. Evaluation tests were conducted on the hardware side using both manual user input and automatic IoT data uploading via the Windows Platform (core i7 with 16 GB of runtime memory). Through execution evaluation, also referred to as evaluation scripts in the world of software, system testing is automated. Similar NodeJS scripts written in the ReactJS programming language were executed in Visual Studio Code. Additionally, the review process makes use of a variety of already-existing libraries, containing but not limited to ipfs.http, web3, and react. Using a JavaScript performance library script, for example, the CPU consumption of data is monitored when data is being uploaded to IPFS and placed on a blockchain, as well as when it is being retrieved from the blockchain using a JavaScript performance library script. To create a local Ethereum blockchain environment, a Ganache suit is employed, and a browser extension called Metamask is used to enable connections to distributed websites. In order to make use of gas transaction fees for the purpose of carrying out system functions, the Ganache suit and Metamask extension are linked to local Ethereum accounts.

Without paying for gas, the Ethereum smart contract cannot be carried out. In order to compare the fuel needed for the two methods of uploading the data, the fuel utilized to upload the original data was measured. The smallest unit of Ethereum money, the Gwei, is used to quantify fuel consumption. 10^9 Wei is referred to as Gwei.

The price of contract migration execution is indicated in our proposed system (see Table 2). The price is specified in ether and includes the gas utilized. The amount of gas consumed multiplied by the price of gas equals one unit of ether. In this arrangement, the gas spent stands in for the continuous cost of computing. The value variations of ether in the account, the network has changed the price of gas [33].

Table 2. Analyse of the costs associated with data storage.

Execution Type	Gas Used	Cost in Ether
Contract Creation	2,027,188	0.04054376
Contract Migration Call	27,363	0.0054726
Initial Contract	225,237	0.0450474
Initial Migration Call	42,363	0.0084726

In the working prototype of our system, we automatically establish a gas restriction. The cost of creating the contract is 0.04054376 in ether, and the total amount of gas utilized is 2,027,188. The migration requires the establishment of contracts, which has a relatively low cost of 0.0027363 (ether) and uses only 27,363 of gas. If the input data is little in size, the general costs can be decreased even more.

The duration of time required for users to share data with others was the final test item. Data sharing time is a measurement of the overall amount of time spent reading, recalling, and sharing data. The outcomes of several sets of trials we ran with an average data size are displayed in Figure 9. A 450-byte upload consumes an average of 671,807 gas; a 1500-byte storage consumes an average of 1,942,901 gas. The data size increases with fuel consumption. When IoT data was transferred to IPFS using the suggested system, there was no discernible difference in fuel consumption despite the increased quantity of data.

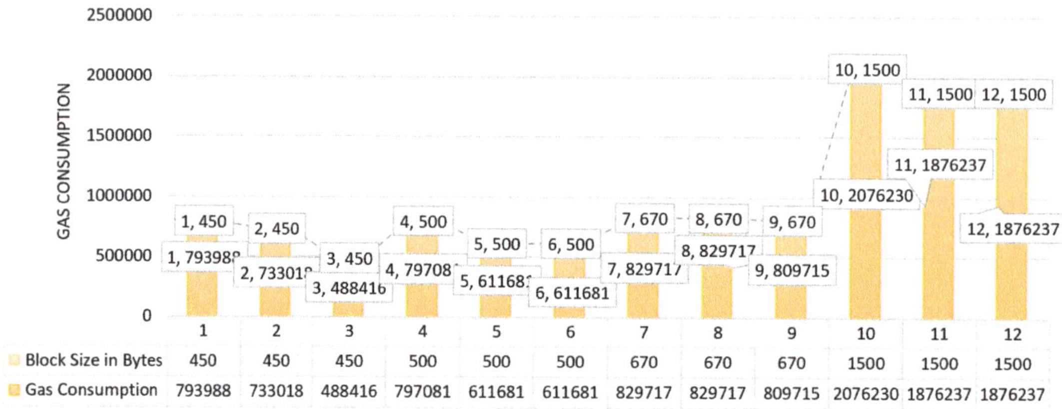

Figure 9. Gas consumption is based on transaction count and block size.

All of the network's entities and their interactions are depicted in a sequence diagram in Figure 10. Five distinct entities exist. Only the administrator, who has direct access to the dataset, uses the manual uploading entity. The dataset-based time cycle in the system is uploaded using a system uploading entity. Any stakeholder with public access might be a user entity and could access the data using their own custom queries. For the purpose of illustrating how the system works, Figure 9 depicts the execution flow.

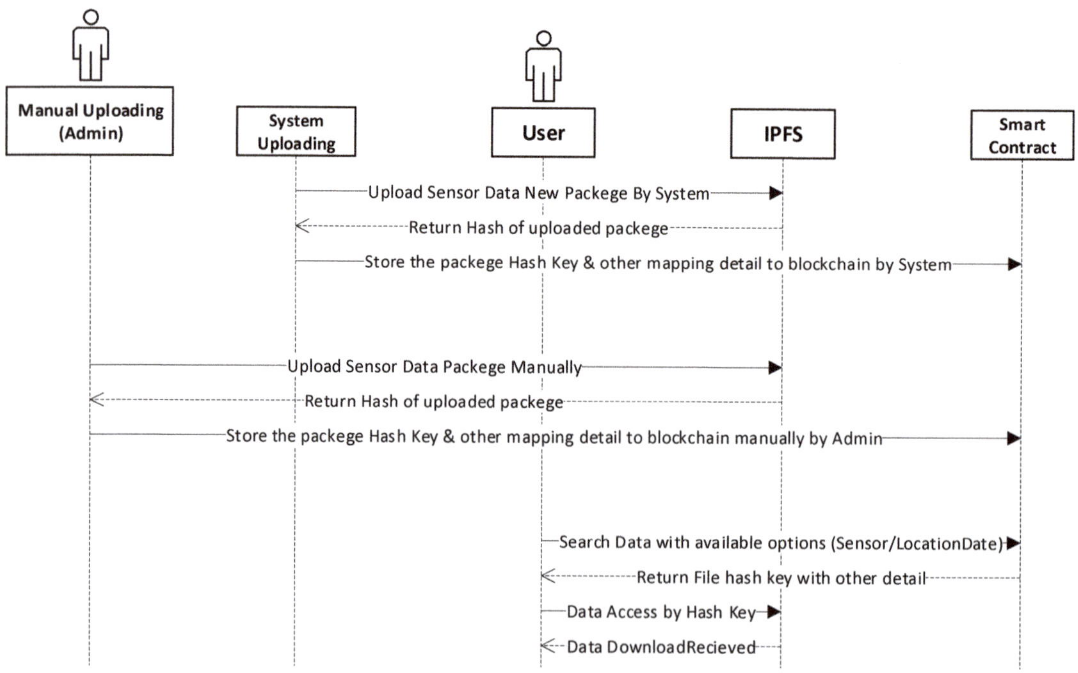

Figure 10. Data sharing process.

5.2. Evaluations of Query Response Time

Data querying is the key entity needed to store IPFS data packages and chain the details of IoT records. The performance of the solution in terms of storing and retrieving data from the blockchain may be evaluated using the query response time. Test results were conducted on two different methods: IPFS for IoT data storage and blockchain for file hashes. According to Figure 11, the horizontal axis indicates the two different execution functions, while the vertical axis is the response time as measured in milliseconds. As you can see from the title "Complete function", it explains how the entire method will be implemented from the moment the IoT data package is stored in IPFS to the point the record details are saved to the blockchain using the file hash that was created. "Smart Contract Function" shows the delay because of the Smart Contract execution call through Metamask. During the execution of a collection of functions using smart contracts, we also evaluate the performance of CPU consumption (see Figure 12). As with the data exchange, we assessed each stage of every strategy. There are several approaches, including calling encryption of the dataset, storing data in the blockchain ledger, and uploading it to IPFS storage.

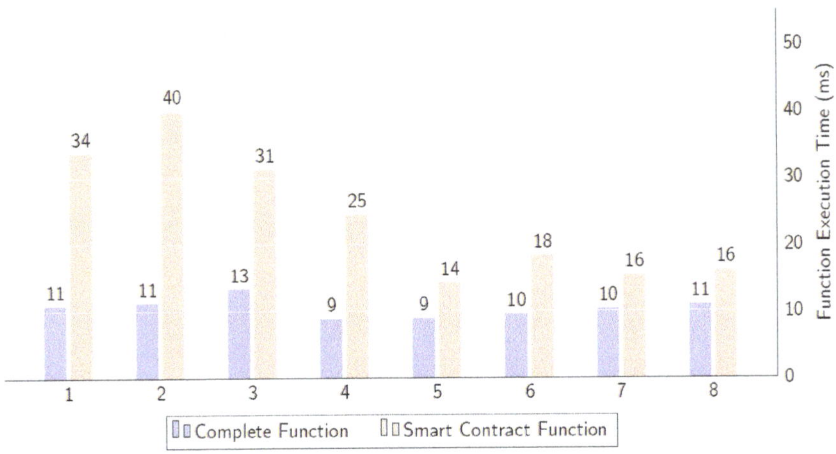

Figure 11. The time required to execute a function and keep the data in IPFS and Blockchain.

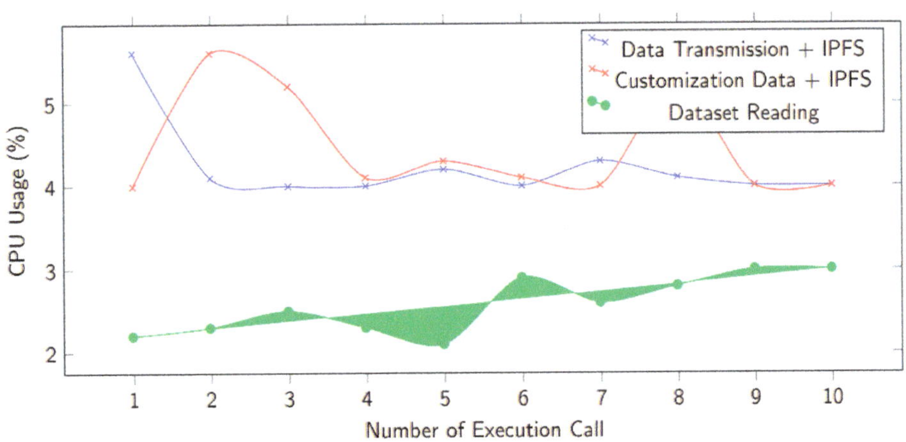

Figure 12. CPU time spent performing calculations.

6. Conclusions and Future Work

Typically, Internet of Things systems refer to a group of pervasive systems that take advantage of embedded sensors, applications, and networks in order to provide intelligent surroundings and systems. In order to make IoT data sharing and storage effective, it is crucial that a framework is put in place that enables IoT data storage in impromptu, unsafe settings. During the development of a reliable and distributed access control system, we looked into blockchain technology, specifically Ethereum smart contracts, which can be used for sharing data from IoT devices. To provide a distributed and reliable access control mechanism, we used Ethereum smart contracts to share IoT data in a distributed and secure manner. The solution described in this article combines IPFS and the Ethereum blockchain to store IoT data securely. Users may save and manage access roles for their IoT data more easily with the use of smart contracts. The suggested workaround logs the hash value along with other information in a blockchain ledger and encrypts IoT data provided to IPFS' decentralized storage. As part of this experiment, data lengths of different sizes were used to assess the performance of data uploading and access. It was found that the higher the size of the data, the more efficient and faster the process of uploading can be achieved. The researchers have further established that the upload technique that uses the system costs the same amount of gas regardless of the size of the data when it comes to the consumption of fuel, even when the data size increases.

Author Contributions: Conceptualization, A.R. and A.A.; methodology, A.R., S.A.K.G. and A.B.A.; resources, W.K. and M.A. writing—original draft preparation, A.R.; writing—review and editing, A.R., M.A., A.A. and W.K.; Supervision, A.B.A.; funding acquisition, A.B.A. All authors have read and agreed to the published version of the manuscript.

Funding: This research has been funded by Scientific Research Deanship at University of Ha'il-Saudi Arabia through project number RG-22020.

Institutional Review Board Statement: Not applicable.

Informed Consent Statement: Not applicable.

Data Availability Statement: Not applicable.

Conflicts of Interest: The authors declare no conflict of interest.

References

1. Shafiq, M.; Gu, Z.; Cheikhrouhou, O.; Alhakami, W.; Hamam, H. The Rise of "Internet of Things": Review and Open Research Issues Related to Detection and Prevention of IoT-Based Security Attacks. *Wirel. Commun. Mob. Comput.* **2022**, *2022*, 8669348. [CrossRef]
2. Fahmideh, M.; Ahmad, A.; Behnaz, A.; Grundy, J.; Susilo, W. Software Engineering for Internet of Things: The Practitioners' Perspective. *IEEE Trans. Softw. Eng.* **2021**, *48*, 2857–2878. [CrossRef]
3. Alreshidi, A.; Ahmad, A. Architecting software for the internet of thing based systems. *Future Internet* **2019**, *11*, 153. [CrossRef]
4. Liu, C.H.; Lin, Q.; Wen, S. Blockchain-enabled data collection and sharing for industrial IoT with deep reinforcement learning. *IEEE Trans. Ind. Informat.* **2019**, *15*, 3516–3526. [CrossRef]
5. Razzaq, A.; Mohsan SA, H.; Ghayyur SA, K.; Alsharif, M.H.; Alkahtani, H.K.; Karim, F.K.; Mostafa, S.M. Blockchain-Enabled Decentralized Secure Big Data of Remote Sensing. *Electronics* **2022**, *11*, 3164. [CrossRef]
6. Shafiq, M.; Tian, Z.; Bashir, A.K.; Jolfaei, A.; Yu, X. Data mining and machine learning methods for sustainable smart cities traffic classification: A survey. *Sustain. Cities Soc.* **2020**, *60*, 102177. [CrossRef]
7. Shafiq, M.; Tian, Z.; Sun, Y.; Du, X.; Guizani, M. Selection of effective machine learning algorithm and Bot-IoT attacks traffic identification for internet of things in smart city. *Future Gener. Comput. Syst.* **2020**, *107*, 433–442. [CrossRef]
8. Ahmad, A.; Khan, A.A.; Waseem, M.; Fahmideh, M.; Mikkonen, T. Towards process centered architecting for quantum software systems. In Proceedings of the 2022 IEEE International Conference on Quantum Software (QSW), Barcelona, Spain, 11–15 July 2022; pp. 26–31.
9. Chen, Y.; Hu, B.; Yu, H.; Duan, Z.; Huang, J. A Threshold Proxy Re-Encryption Scheme for Secure IoT Data Sharing Based on Blockchain. *Electronics* **2021**, *10*, 2359. [CrossRef]
10. Razzaq, A.; Mohsan, S.A.H.; Li, Y.; Alsharif, M.H. Architectural Framework for Underwater IoT: Forecasting System for Analyzing Oceanographic Data and Observing the Environment. *J. Mar. Sci. Eng.* **2023**, *11*, 368. [CrossRef]

11. Xia, Q.I.; Sifah, E.B.; Asamoah, K.O.; Gao, J.; Du, X.; Guizani, M. MeDShare: Trust-less medical data sharing among cloud service providers via blockchain. *IEEE Access* **2017**, *5*, 14757–14767. [CrossRef]
12. Razzaq, A. Blockchain-based secure data transmission for internet of underwater things. *Cluster Comput.* **2022**, *25*, 4495–4514. [CrossRef]
13. Shrestha, A.K.; Vassileva, J. Blockchain-Based Research Data Sharing Framework for Incentivizing the Data Owners. In *Blockchain—ICBC 2018, Proceedings of the International Conference on Blockchain, Seattle, WA, USA, 25–30 June 2018*; Springer: Cham, Switzerland, 2018; pp. 259–266.
14. Fahmideh, M.; Grundy, J.; Ahmad, A.; Shen, J.; Yan, J.; Mougouei, D.; Peng, W.; Ghose, A.; Gunawardana, A.; Aickelin, U.; et al. Engineering Blockchain Based Software Systems: Foundations, Survey, and Future Directions. *ACM Comput. Surv.* **2022**, *55*, 1–44. [CrossRef]
15. Benet, J. Ipfs-content addressed, versioned, p2p file system. *arXiv* **2014**, arXiv:1407.3561.
16. Benet, J. IPFS—Content Addressed, Versioned, P2P File System(DRAFT 3). 2014. Available online: https://arxiv.org/abs/1407.3561 (accessed on 14 March 2021).
17. Ahmad, A.; Malik, A.W.; Alreshidi, A.; Khan, W.; Sajjad, M. Adaptive security for self-protection of mobile computing devices. *Mob. Netw. Appl.* **2019**, 1–20. [CrossRef]
18. Kokoris-Kogias, E.; Ceyhun Alp, E.; Gasser, L.; Jovanovic, P.; Syta, E.; Ford, B. Calypso: Auditable Sharing of Private Data Over Blockchains. Cryptology ePrint Archive, Report 2018/209, 2018. Available online: https://eprint.iacr.org/2018/209 (accessed on 25 February 2023).
19. Shafagh, H.; Burkhalter, L.; Hithnawi, A.; Duquennoy, S. Towards blockchain-based auditable storage and sharing of IoT data. In Proceedings of the 2017 on Cloud Computing Security Workshop, CCSW '17, Dallas, TX, USA, 30 October–3 November 2017; ACM: New York, NY, USA, 2017; pp. 45–50.
20. Rowhani-Farid, A.; Allen, M.; Barnett, A.G. What incentives increase data sharing in health and medical research? *A systematic review. Res. Integr. Peer Rev.* **2017**, *2*, 4.
21. Razzaq, A. A Systematic Review on Software Architectures for IoT Systems and Future Direction to the Adoption of Microservices Architecture. *SN Comput. Sci.* **2020**, *1*, 350. [CrossRef]
22. Hammi, M.T.; Hammi, B.; Bellot, P.; Serhrouchni, A. Bubbles of Trust: A decentralized blockchain-based authentication system for IoT. *Comput. Secur.* **2018**, *78*, 126–142. [CrossRef]
23. Alsamhi, S.H.; Shvetsov, A.V.; Shvetsova, S.V.; Hawbani, A.; Guizan, M.; Alhartomi, M.A.; Ma, O. Blockchain-empowered security and energy efficiency of drone swarm consensus for environment exploration. *IEEE Trans. Green Commun. Netw.* **2022**, *7*, 328–338. [CrossRef]
24. Sahal, R.; Alsamhi, S.H.; Brown, K.N.; O'shea, D.; McCarthy, C.; Guizani, M. Blockchain-empowered digital twins collaboration: Smart transportation use case. *Machines* **2021**, *9*, 193. [CrossRef]
25. Alsamhi, S.H.; Almalki, F.A.; Afghah, F.; Hawbani, A.; Shvetsov, A.V.; Lee, B.; Song, H. Drones' edge intelligence over smart environments in B5G: Blockchain and federated learning synergy. *IEEE Trans. Green Commun. Netw.* **2021**, *6*, 295–312. [CrossRef]
26. Liang, W.; Tang, M.; Long, J.; Peng, X.; Xu, J.; Li, K.C. A Secure Fabric Blockchain-based Data Transmission Technique for Industrial Internet-of-Things. *IEEE Trans. Ind. Inform.* **2019**, *15*, 358–3592. [CrossRef]
27. Steichen, M.; Fiz Pontiveros, B.; Norvill, R.; Shbair, W. Blockchain-Based, Decentralized Access Control for IPFS. In Proceedings of the 2018 IEEE International Conference on Blockchain (Blockchain-2018), Halifax, NS, Canada, 30 July 2018–3 August 2018; pp. 1499–1506.
28. Kitchenham, B.; Brereton, O.P.; Budgen, D.; Turner, M.; Bailey, J.; Linkman, S. Systematic literature reviews in software engineering a systematic literature review. *Inf. Softw. Technol.* **2009**, *51*, 7–15. [CrossRef]
29. Truffle Suite. Available online: https://www.trufflesuite.com/guides/configuring-visual-studio-code.html (accessed on 15 March 2021).
30. Truffle Suite. Available online: Https://truffleframework.com/docs/ganache/overview (accessed on 15 March 2021).
31. MetaMask. Available online: https://metamask.io/ (accessed on 15 March 2021).
32. Estdale, J.; Georgiadou, E. Applying the iso/iec 25010 quality models to software product. In Proceedings of the Systems, Software and Services Process Improvement, European Conference on Software Process Improvement, Bilbao, Spain, 5–7 September 2019; Springer: Cham, Switzerland, 2018; pp. 492–503.
33. Wood, G. Ethereum: A Secure Decentralised Generalised Transaction Ledger. Available online: https://gavwood.com/paper.pdf (accessed on 20 March 2021).

electronics

MDPI

Article

Oracles Integration in Blockchain-Based Platform for Smart Crop Production Data Exchange

Ivan Popchev [1], Irina Radeva [2,*] and Lyubka Doukovska [2]

[1] Bulgarian Academy of Sciences, 1040 Sofia, Bulgaria; ivan.popchev@iict.bas.bg
[2] Intelligent Systems Department, Institute of Information and Communication Technologies, Bulgarian Academy of Sciences, 1113 Sofia, Bulgaria; l.doukovska@mail.bg
* Correspondence: irina.radeva@iict.bas.bg

Abstract: Blockchain oracles are an intermediary designed to connect external non-deterministic information and real-world data to the blockchain digital infrastructure. The variety of proposed solutions and purposes are of great variety and suggest that it is necessary to take into account different features of the process and specifically define the required functionalities. The purpose of this paper is to present the integration of oracles into an EOSIO blockchain-based platform for smart crop production data exchange by smart contracts. The functions of two oracles are presented. Their integration is described at the design level and at the implementation of the smart contracts. The design level is illustrated by workflow diagrams of internal processes between oracle applications and the blockchain smart contract and by external processes in the oracles' smart contracts. The implementation level is illustrated by oracle application configuration files and elements of C++ smart contracts, such as constant and variable declarations, multi-index tables, internal contract functions, and actions called by other contracts and external programs. As results of the oracles' operation, a report on the detected emergency failures and an estimate of the cost of ram resource are presented.

Keywords: blockchain oracle; blockchain-based platform; smart contracts; smart crop production; EOSIO/Antelope; C++; Swift

Citation: Popchev, I.; Radeva, I.; Doukovska, L. Oracles Integration in Blockchain-Based Platform for Smart Crop Production Data Exchange. *Electronics* **2023**, *12*, 2244. https://doi.org/10.3390/electronics12102244

Academic Editor: Juan M. Corchado

Received: 13 April 2023
Revised: 9 May 2023
Accepted: 13 May 2023
Published: 15 May 2023

1. Introduction

Blockchain oracles are an intermediary designed to connect external non-deterministic real-world information with the blockchain digital infrastructure through smart contracts. The definitions found in different sources are varied, but taken together, a trend is revealed in which oracles seem to cover a vast spectrum of characteristics and functions. Blockchain oracles are a *service* that requests and transfers data off-chain to smart contracts on the blockchain [1]; a *device or entity* that connects a deterministic blockchain with off-chain data [2]; an *element for the blockchain ecosystem* as they enable smart contracts to operate in a broader capacity [3]; a *complex computerized systems* that connect data from the outside world to the blockchain world; an *Application Programming Interface* (API) [4]; *third-party information service providers* that send external data to a blockchain protocol and are able to secure, verify, and validate the data that the blockchain network receives and uses; an *application* that retrieves, verifies, and transmits external information (i.e, information stored off-chain) to smart contracts; a *mechanism to trigger smart contract* functions using off-chain data [5]; a *Web 3.0 ecosystem method* of connecting to existing systems, data sources, and advanced computing [6].

Regardless of whether oracles are defined as a device, element, complex computerized systems, API, service provider, mechanism, or Web 3.0 method, their main purpose is related to blockchain ecosystems and, in their predominant implementation, is associated with use of smart contracts.

The concept of the smart contract is proposed by Nick Szabo [7]. Smart contracts are a self-executing, fully programmable, and automated agreement intended to implement trusted transactions when predetermined conditions are met, which usually works on a blockchain. The blockchain is a decentralized infrastructure software which supports a distributed digital ledger of cryptographically signed transactions that are grouped into blocks [8]. Analysing the current status of blockchain smart contract applications in [9], it is concluded that smart contract technology is promising but still in initial stages and has many drawbacks: the lack of strong data processing capacity, insufficiently effective management by the main blockchain systems, the insouciantly advanced contract language development, vulnerability scanning and processing techniques, low level of support, security vulnerabilities, etc.

The design, implementation, and integration of blockchain oracles is closely related to the blockchain platforms for which they are intended and their specific application. The blockchain platforms provide a digital infrastructure for development, deployment, and management of decentralized applications. Examples of such platforms are Ethereum, Quorum, Hyperledger Fabric, IBM Blockchain, R3 Corda, Tezos, Hyperledger Sawtooth, Stellar, and EOSIO.

The wide variety of solutions based on different blockchain platforms raises the question of their interoperability. In [10] these challenges are analysed, but it is found that in order to be trusted the oracles must either be managed by a trusted third party or have cryptographic attestation. The authors acknowledge that *oracles can make blockchains compatible with non-blockchain systems*.

In [11] the various approaches proposed for implementing blockchain oracles are explored. The authors conclude that oracles are key to the scalability and interoperability of blockchains. The solutions offered can be centralized or decentralized, and the main categories that oracles fall into are *data feed oracles* and *computation oracles*. The first category acts as an intermediary that submits external data to smart contracts on demand. The second category performs user-defined off-chain computational tasks for blockchains.

A blockchain oracle framework proposed in [12] covers key features such as *origin of data, type of oracles,* and *type of blockchains, encryption method, oracle data source, data validation,* and *oracle integration method.* Smart contracts are considered one of the most applied methods for integrating oracles into blockchain-based solutions. These guidelines of oracle's framework are used in the current paper.

From a technical point of view blockchain oracles are software, therefore their integration is the process of combining separate software programs or elements into a single system. The operation of oracles is described in [13]. Generally, there is an oracle's smart contract and a blockchain smart contract that need to use off-chain data. Then five steps are performed: first step—the blockchain smart contract sends an action to the oracle's smart contract specifying the required off-chain data and the request's *id* to the oracle's smart contract (usually done by passing a URL that is an API endpoint); second step—the oracle scans the blockchain for incoming actions to its smart contract; third step—the incoming request is extracted from the blockchain transaction and executed; forth step—the server invokes a sanction on the blockchain smart contract with the response data and respective *id*, making the result available on the chain; and fifth step—the oracle's smart contract matches the *id* to the blockchain's smart contract request and calls a call-back function.

This paper is a continuation of research on the application and implementation of blockchain technologies in the National Research Program "Smart crop production" (https://rst-tto.com/rsttakt/index.php/newsroom/news-releases/50-nrp-scp (accessed on 4 May 2023) and "BG PLANTNET establishment of national information network genebank—plant genetic resources" (http://delc.space/genbank/ (accessed on 4 May 2023)). The framework of the projects are presented in [14]. Part of the tasks in the projects are dedicated to blockchain applications and implementations in smart crop production and more specifically to the identification of appropriate applications of the blockchains, to the building of pilot blockchains for selected areas, and to the analysis and development of models for efficient blockchains solutions for smart crop production.

Some of the results achieved so far involve different aspects of these problems. The main elements of the technology, the definitions, the focus areas in risk management, and the implications for internal audit and control procedures in companies that adopt blockchain in intelligent agriculture are discussed in [15].

The algorithms and solutions for multi-criteria selection of blockchain software и IoT platforms in agriculture are presented in [16]. In [17] the most widely used IoT platforms in agriculture are analysed and compered. A multi-criteria framework for selection of an IoT solution in a fuzzy environment is proposed. In this framework as a decision analysis method has been presented as a new modification of Multi-Attribute Border approximation Area Comparison (MABAC) method with a specific distance measure via intuitionistic fuzzy values.

A blockchain-enabled supply-chain model for a smart crop production framework and blockchain-based GenBank store system model are presented in [18–20]. In [21,22] the blockchain applications in cyber–physical–social space and experiments with supervised and unsupervised learning tools related to smart crop production and analyses with different classification, regression, and clustering algorithms are presented.

A framework of the blockchain-based platform for smart crop production data exchange is proposed is [23]. The prototype of the platform, its architecture design, topology, core functionalities, and tests are presented in [24]. The platform is based on private blockchain and distributed file system networks. It aims to support the integration of information exchange resulting from the use of various technologies in smart agriculture which generate a large amount of data, require processing, analysis, and have to be reliable in terms of quality and sources. A scheme of the building phases of the platform is presented in Figure 1.

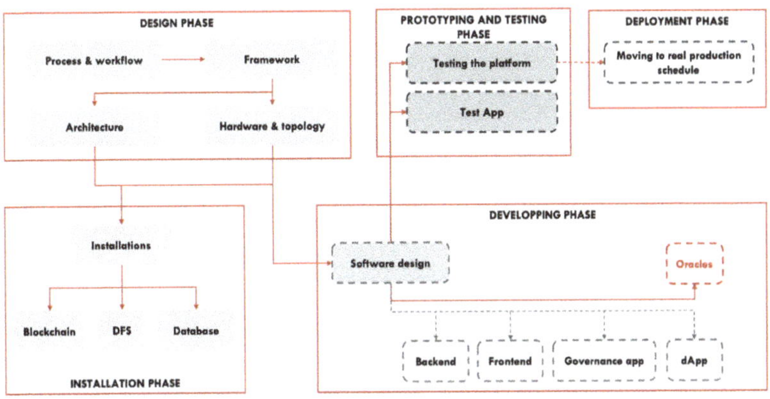

Figure 1. Building phases scheme.

The descriptions of business processes, workflows, the general concept of the framework, and the architecture of the platform are defined for the design phase. The installation phase includes the blockchain, the distributed file system networks, and the database deployment. The development phase includes the preparation of all software solutions, including blockchain oracles, frontend and backend, and the test application that will later run as a dApp (decentralized application). The prototyping and testing phase is designed to check the functionality of the platform and various experiments. The last phase is planned for the implementation of the platform in real operation. All elements in the diagram that are marked with dashed lines are under development or testing.

The purpose of this paper is to present the design framework and oracles' integration by smart contracts in an *EOSIO* blockchain-based platform for smart crop production data exchange.

Further, this paper is organized as follows: In Section 2 the types of blockchain oracles are presented. The Section 3 describes the infrastructure of the blockchain-based platform, the framework, and functions of two oracles. The Section 4 describes the integration of oracles and workflow diagrams of the internal and external processes between blockchain's and oracles' smart contracts. In Section 5 examples of implementation of oracles' functions using smart contracts are presented. The Section 6 is the discussion and future development.

2. Types of Blockchain Oracles

The diversity of types of oracles found in various sources [4–6,25,26], allows a preliminary orientation in their capabilities, methods of their integration, and implementation in the blockchain networks for which they are intended. Oracles can be classified according to origin data, data direction, the trust, data source, and trust models. They can also be distinguished based on whether they extract external data from on-chain contracts, send information from the blockchain to off-chain applications, or perform off-chain computational tasks.

Outbound oracles bring blockchain data to the outside world. They allow smart contracts to send commands to off-chain systems to prompt them to perform certain actions.

Inbound oracles bring off-chain—or real-world data—to the blockchain. The imported information can represent almost anything. Inbound oracles are the most widely recognized oracle that gathers off-chain data and delivers it onto the blockchain network for smart contract consumption. They reflect scenarios such as "if this happens, then do this" or "if the price of the asset reaches/falls to a certain value, then trigger a sale/purchase".

Cross-Chain oracles exchange information between different blockchain networks. They enable interoperability between blockchains, such as using data from one blockchain to trigger an action on another, or linking assets between different blockchains so that they can be used outside of the one where they were issued.

Software oracles are one of the most common types. They interact with online sources of information and transmit it to the blockchain. Information can originate from online databases, servers, or websites—basically any data source on the web—and provide information to smart contracts in blockchain networks in real time.

Hardware oracles provide and transmit information through camera motion sensors, radio frequency identification (RFID) sensors, thermometers, and barcode scanners.

Human oracles are individuals with specialized knowledge in a particular field who serve as oracles. These specialists investigate and verify the authenticity of information and confirm their identity through cryptography. It is assumed that fraud, falsification of their identity, or provision of corrupted data is relatively unlikely.

Centralized oracles are controlled by a single entity and act as a single data provider for smart contracts. Therefore, the parties must have significant trust in this one entity, which is seen as a potential problem. Additionally, they represent a single point of failure that can potentially compromise the security of the smart contract, and a compromised oracle means a compromised smart contract. By presumption, oracles are supposed to enforce contracts between untrustworthy parties, but if they are over-centralized, they can become the intermediary they were meant to replace. This is known as the "oracle problem".

Decentralized oracles (also called consensus oracles) have goals similar to those of public blockchains—avoiding counterparty risk. In these, to determine the validity and accuracy of the data, the smart contract queries multiple oracles. However, as yet, decentralized oracles do not completely remove trust but rather distribute it among many participants. Decentralized oracle networks (DONs) enable the deployment of hybrid smart contracts in which off-chain infrastructure and on-chain code are connected to provide decentralized applications (dApps) that respond to real-world events and interact with traditional systems.

Contract-specific oracles are designed to be used by a single smart contract. This means that if one wants to implement several smart contracts, a proportional number of contract-specific oracles must be developed. This type of oracle is considered very time consuming and expensive to maintain. On the other hand, oracles can be designed from scratch to serve a specific use case, and developers have a flexibility to tailor them to specific requirements.

Figure 2 illustrates one possible interpretation of the types of oracles in terms of the three areas—physical, digital, and blockchain ecosystems—that define their characteristics and purpose.

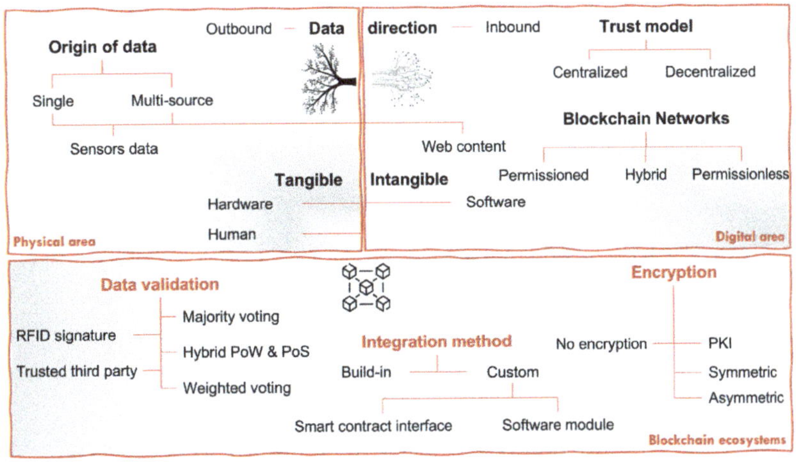

Figure 2. Blockchain oracle types.

The origin of the data can be from the physical or digital area. In the first case, data could be generated by sensors or hardware (tangible objects). The so-called "human" oracles are also a source of data in the physical area, although their functions could be expanded to more specific applications. The origin of the data may also be from web content (intangible sources from the digital area), for example financial information, sports scores, weather updates, operational data, and user data, which are categorized under general http(s) data.

The direction of the information can be towards physical area (inbound oracles) or towards digital area (outbound oracles).

The digital area relates to the type of blockchain networks (permissionless, permissioned, or hybrid) and to the trust model (centralized or decentralized) for both—blockchain networks and oracles. Public blockchain networks are generally considered to be decentralized, while private blockchains are primarily centralized. For the most part oracles are developed as centralized, but there are a number of solutions with decentralized oracle networks that are actively gaining popularity.

Data validation, encryption methods, and integration methods refer entirely to blockchain ecosystem areas. Data validation (RFID signature, majority voting, weighted voting, hybrid PoW and PoS, or trusted third party) depends on whether the data provided by the external system is true, comes from the original source, and has not been altered. The most common approach is to rely on trusted data providers when oracles do not use any data validation method. Such a strategy is applicable if the data source is reliable.

Encryption methods refer to the confidentiality of data that is transferred from external data sources to the oracles and from the oracles to the blockchain. It is the cryptographic technology used to secure communication between two entities. A distinction must be made between encryption methods and techniques. The latter are the protocols themselves, cryptographic algorithms, and data transmission security schemes. The most commonly used encryption method is Public Key Infrastructure (PKI).

Oracle integration is the method of connecting an oracle to a blockchain in order to provide data. These can be smart contracts, software modules, custom solutions, and embedded solutions. The most common method is using a smart contract. A pair of smart contracts, one on-chain and one off-chain, can be used to integrate decentralized web applications (dApps). There is a variant of integration through software modules that are used to communicate between physical devices communicating and the blockchain, where the module is an intermediary agent that manipulates (according to certain rules) the incoming data before sending it to the oracle.

Oracle types discussed in this paper are illustrated in Figure 3. They could be classified as multi-source inbound centralized software oracles running on a permissioned blockchain with no encryption and data validation from a trusted third party. The applied integration method is a custom smart contract interface.

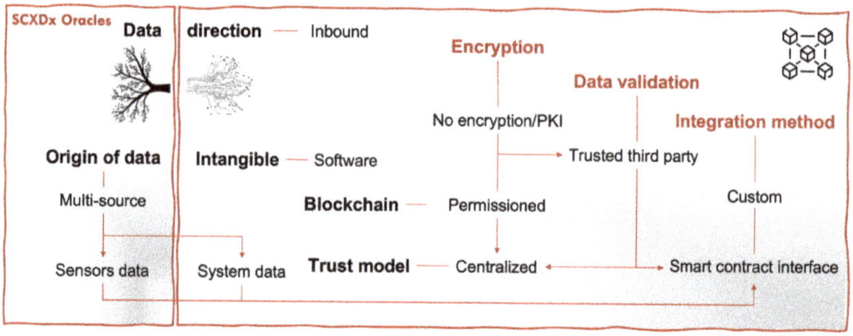

Figure 3. SCPDx oracle types.

The data are retrieved from a sensor network. A server oracle application accesses the data through an API with a predefined username and password. A PKI is about to be introduced in future developments, most likely based on the ECC standard.

3. The Infrastructure of the Platform and Oracles' Framework

The working name of the blockchain-based platform is SCPDx. It is based on an *EOSIO* blockchain (EOSIO 2.1.0) and distributed file system (IPFS 0.13.0 for MAC and IPFS 0.11.0 for Ubuntu). The infrastructure is presented in Figure 4. It is deployed on four virtual machines (vm_s) with the following configurations: vm_1—Intel Xeon configuration, 32 cores, 32 GB ram, 1TB hdd, 100 GB NET LAN, Ubuntu 20.04 OS (EOSIO node 1, EOSIO node 2, ipfs node 1, dApp, and an Oracle/Oracle API); vm_2—Intel i9, 16 cores, 16 GB ram, 1TB hdd, 100 GB NET LAN, Ubuntu 20.04 OS (Ipfs node 2); vm_3—Intel i9, 16 Cores, 16 GB ram, 1TB hdd, 100 GB NET LAN, Ubuntu 20.04 OS (Ipfs node 3); vm_4—Mac M1, 8 cores, 16 GB ram, 512 GB hdd, 100 MB NET Wi-Fi, OSX 13.4 (EOSIO node 3).

The blockchain and distributed file networks are set as private. Since private blockchains are always permissioned, it differs from the public blockchain in terms of infrastructure requirements. At this stage, to achieve transaction processing performance, the platform does not require significant computing power. The private blockchain is deployed on traditional servers that are part of the partners' infrastructure. Blockchain nodes are located in different geographical locations, on different networks, and exchange data over the Internet. Currently, network delays and periodic outages have not significantly affected consistency of data.

The *partners' infrastructure* is not a single and coherent one; however, any member who requested access can use the data exchange services through a test application (Test App) and public/private keys access. At a later stage, the functionality of the Test App will be transferred to a dApp. The *users' infrastructures* are considered external for the platform.

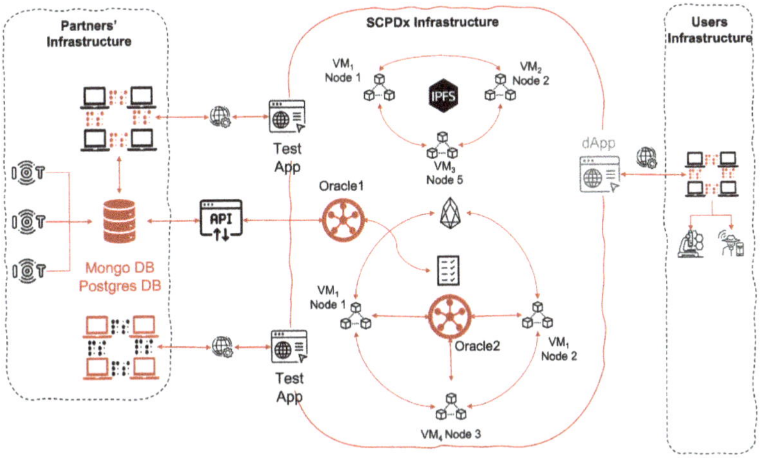

Figure 4. SCPDx infrastructure.

Databases store transaction statistics, raw IoT (sensor) data, file catalogues, and more. In addition to various other purposes, raw IoT data are intended to be used by oracles in automated actions in smart contracts.

All partners/members are considered users. A *user* is a member in the role of a publisher or reader of data. A *publisher* is enabled broader rights of sharing and service access related to the copyright and tracking activity of provided data. A *reader* has more limited access to the specific contents on the platform. The user's data and files could be uploaded to the platform either by API, if it is on a database, or directly through a Test App installed on a PC. Users are partners—scientific and educational institutes—participants in the National Scientific Program "Smart crop production".

The oracles' framework and interactions between sensors, blockchain networks, and oracles are presented in Figure 5. There is an existing IoT network that takes periodic measurements of various parameters. The measured parameters are recorded in a Postgres database on a server using API [27].

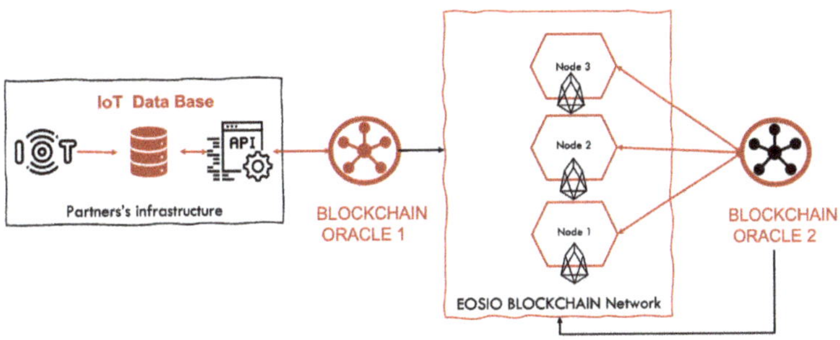

Figure 5. The oracles' framework.

Oracle1 is intended to retrieve temperature and humidity readings from the sensor network every 60 min and to calculate and record daily min, max, mean, variance, and standard deviation of all readings every 24 h. It is also used to upload historical data to the blockchain. For 60 min readings and 24 h data, *oracule1* connects to an API and writes the data to the blockchain.

Oracle2 performs two functions. The first function is system support, management, and maintenance of the blockchain. It queries the current status of each blockchain node every 60 min and receives the result as a Boolean flag. In the case where it cannot establish a connection with any of the nodes, this event is recorded in the blockchain, and a notification is sent to the system administrator by email. The second function is to retrieve the current market quote of the *ram* resource price for the public *EOSIO* blockchain and for the platform's blockchain every 60 min. These data are collected as statistics, and if necessary, the price of the *ram* resource for the private blockchain can be as well.

This functionality is developed regarding the evaluation of resources consumed by the users of the platform. Due to the specifics of the *EOSIO* blockchain, *ram* is the only non-renewable resource and must be provided by purchase from the system account. Since the blockchain network is installed as private, the system account is owned by the developer. At this stage the operations are free for all users. When opening the platform to users external to the research project, it is necessary to provide the mechanism for sharing maintenance and operation costs among all participants. From the developer's point of view, it is important to set a fair price for using the platform and to bind all transactions to system and/or custom tokens. How this is solved at the prototype stage is described in [24].

In summary, *oracle1* is a server-based software oracle running on a private permissioned blockchain that extracts readings from multiple sensor sources. The data are not encrypted; validation is by a trusted third party; the integration method applied is a custom smart contract interface; the sensor data are accessed via an API with a predefined username and password; and its functions are as follows:

(1) To retrieve and upload real-time temperature and humidity readings from two sensor networks;
(2) To process and upload daily min, max, average, variance, and standard deviation for all retrieved data readings;
(3) To upload historical data.

Oracle2 is also a server-based software oracle that extracts data from the private blockchain and the public *EOSIO* blockchain. The data are not encrypted; validation is by a trusted third party; the applied integration method is a custom smart contract interface; data from the private blockchain are accessed via an API with a predefined blockchain account and corresponding private key; data from the public *EOSIO* blockchain are publicly available and are retrieved via an API, which does not require the use of a user account or keys; and its functions are as follows:

(1) The monitoring, management and system maintenance of the blockchain;
(2) The registration and monitoring of the used *ram* resources.

4. Integration of Oracles

Each oracle consists of an oracle application (*oracle app*), an *oracle account*, and *a smart contract*. The *oracle app* is an application installed on a server and provides a connection to external data. The *oracle account* is a blockchain account with a smart contract installed to communicate with the outside environment and/or other smart contracts.

The access to on-chain data is possible by a *user application* as well. In this case it is necessary to develop this user application according to the oracle's smart contracts technical specifications and to set respective permissions. Such an application is not yet available since SCPDx prototype is in the development stage.

The oracles' workflow diagram is shown in Figure 6. The *oracle app1* and the *oracle app2* are respective applications for *oracle1* and *oracle2*. Basically, those applications could be web-based or server-based. In this implementation, the installations are on external servers 1 and 2 with MAC OS. The *oracle apps* are written in Swift version 5.7 [28].

All communication and data exchange between *oracle app1*, *oracle app2*, the *oracles' smart contracts*, and the *user application* are parallel and independent. The *oracles' smart contracts* contain multi-index tables for storing the data and performing an external (for the blockchain) and internal (for the blockchain account) request.

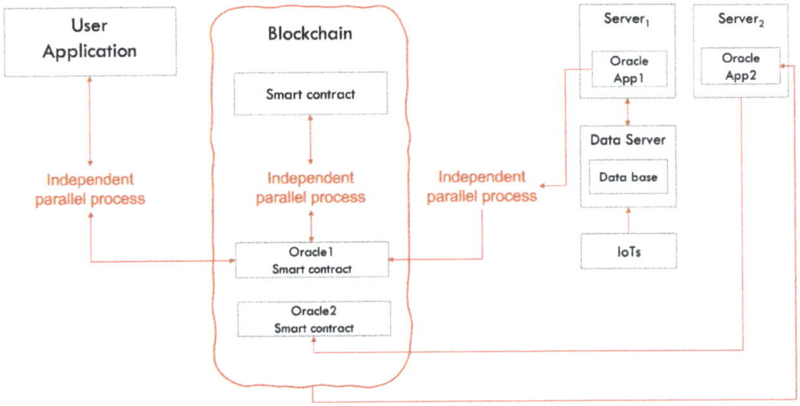

Figure 6. Oracles' workflow diagram.

Access to the data stored in the *EOSIO* multi-index tables is possible in several ways.

The first way is through a smart contract action executed by the same or another (call-back) smart contract in the blockchain.

The second is from an external application by executing a request to the blockchain API. This is possible if the address of the blockchain and the account to which the multi-index table belongs are known, as well as an appropriate software library.

The third way is by running the *cleos* command from the command line with the appropriate parameter format. In this case, if the blockchain address and the account of the multi-index table it belongs to are known, no blockchain account is even required. It is exactly what ensures the transparency and auditability of data in the blockchain, as it can be easily verified by an independent third party. This, of course, applies to public networks, but it is also valid for private ones, provided that no access restrictions are imposed (by IP address or otherwise). Additionally, depending on how the primary and secondary indexes of the multi-index table are defined, data can be filtered by a selected indicator (by dates, by sensor id, by indicators and their values, etc.).

The second and third ways are implemented here. For the first variant, a technical specification for the call-back procedure is provided below.

The oracles discussed here are identical in the way they work and implement their smart contracts, although the data they collect has a different purpose. The difference is in the formats of the multi-index tables and the syntax of the actions. For this reason, only one smart contract is described, since the second one has similar programming code.

4.1. Oracle1 Integration

The *oracle app1* is developed to retrieve data from databases that contain sensor reading data. The main functions of the application are as follows:

(1) To retrieve real-time data from sensor readings and upload it on a blockchain;
(2) To process statistical data of sensor readings and upload it on a blockchain;
(3) To statistically process historical data of sensor readings and upload it on a blockchain.

It is necessary to emphasize that the functions of the oracle are performed by its application and its corresponding smart contract. The oracle application is responsible for the interaction with the external data and the smart contract for the operations in the blockchain. This is the reason that the functions of the oracles described in the previous section are the same as those of their applications.

The *oracle1 smart contract* contains two multi-index tables for the sensor's raw data readings and daily processed statistics. There are three types of operations used: *add*—allows the *oracle app1* to add records; fetch 1 (*getlastiorec*)—allows external applications that have the appropriate permissions to fetch data (e.g., the most recent value, the arithmetic mean of data over a period); fetch 2 (*getlastrec*)—allows another smart contract action (from the same blockchain) that has the appropriate permissions to fetch data (call-back).

Within one blockchain, multiple accounts can exist to retrieve data recorded in the *oracle1 smart contract* multi-index table and to perform calculations and/or make decisions on this basis. This is realized by using the so-called call-back convention.

Figure 7 describes a communication scheme of a user's blockchain account, a smart contract (blockchain smart contract), and an *oracle account* (oracle1); i.e., *oracle1 smart contract* internal interactions. The user account with a smart contract can be any account that contains a call-back action according to the oracle smart contract technical specifications and with the necessary permissions granted.

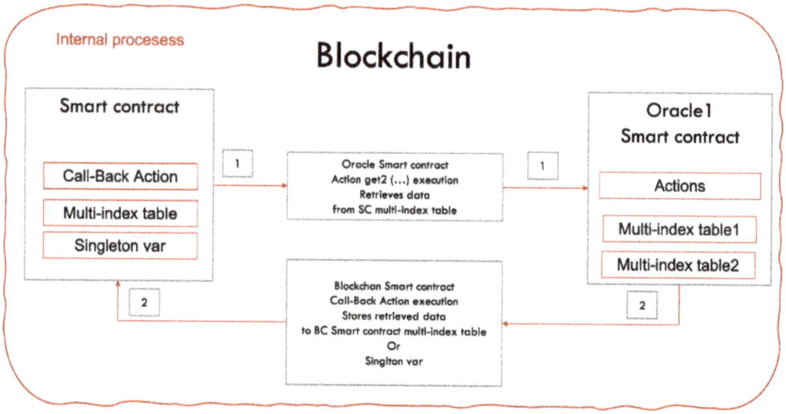

Figure 7. *Oracle1* and blockchain smart contract interactions.

The internal processes for *oracle2* coincide in structure with that of *oracle1* (Figure 7).

The interactions between sensors, database, database API, *oracle app1*, *oracle1 smart contract*, and *user application* are presented in Figure 8. These are the communication processes between external components and the blockchain network. The internal component is only the *oracle1 smart contract*.

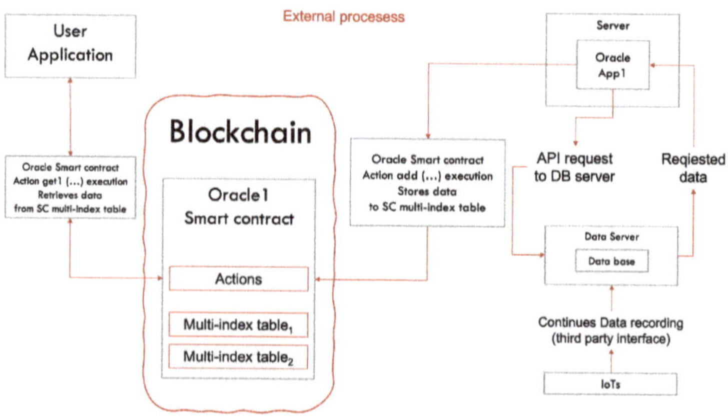

Figure 8. *Oracle1 smart contract* external processes.

4.2. *Oracle2 Integration*

The *oracle app2* main functions are as follows:

(1) Monitoring the operation of blockchain nodes.

The addresses of all blockchain nodes, the checking interval of their status, and email addresses of the system administrators are set in the application's configuration file. In this particular implementation, the nodes are checked every hour. The result as a true/false flag is recorded in a multi-index table of the application's smart contract. In case a given node is not active, a problem email message is sent. Based on the results of the checks, statistics are extracted for the number of failures in the network as well as for the time to restore the working capacity of the nodes. This information can also be accessed by another smart contract in the private network using a call-back functionality.

(2) Periodic creation of a snapshot file, which is used to restore the operation of a blockchain node after an emergency shutdown.

In our case, this is done every 24 h for each of the nodes, and this parameter is set in the configuration file. The size of these files is negligible (about 10 MB) and does not affect the disk space of the servers in the network. This is done by executing a POST request to the *EOSIO nodeos* API.

(3) Retrieving current blockchain *rammarket* table of the *EOSIO system account* by executing the *cleos* command with the appropriate parameters [29].

The application retrieves the necessary data and calculates the current value every 60 min. This parameter is set in the configuration file. The data are recorded in the multi-index of the smart contract. The information is used to estimate the cost of the blockchain resources used for tests or particular blockchain accounts. The data can also be accessed from another smart contract in the private network using call-back functionality. The application retrieves similar data about the *rammarket* data from the public EOSIO blockchain as well and records it in a multi-index table of the smart contract. These data are used for comparison of the cost of resources on the private network versus the public EOSIO network and is available from another smart contract using call-back functionality.

The interactions between an *oracle app2, oracle2 smart contract, private blockchain nodes,* and *EOSIO public blockchain* are presented in Figure 9. These are the processes between external components and the blockchain networks.

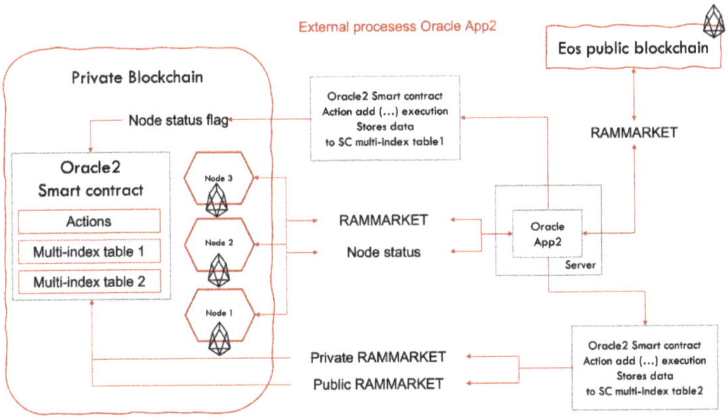

Figure 9. *Oracle2 smart contract* external processes.

5. Oracles' Smart Contracts Implementation

Each smart contract contains the following basic components:

- Declarations of the libraries used—they can be standard (built-in) in *EOSIO* or custom;
- Data declarations—constants, variables, structures, or multi-index tables;
- Declarations of functions that are used inside the contract;

- Declarations of actions—the functions that are called by other contracts or external programs.

The used libraries in the smart contracts are the *EOSIO* build-in.

As examples of the oracles' smart contracts implementation, this section demonstrates only some parts of the smart contracts' program code, its syntax, declarations, and the configuration files of the server applications. As a result of oracles' functions, a summary table of failures statistics, *ram* price estimations, and generated reports about status of the used resources are presented.

The *oracles* use specialized *smart contracts*, written on C++, custom interface, and a dedicated *oracle blockchain account*.

The complete source code of the smart contracts is available in the GitHub repository: https://github.com/scpdxtest/SCPDx.git (accessed on 13 April 2023).

For *oracle app1* settings (parameters), a JSON (JavaScript Object Notation) configuration file is used with sensor's *id* (included in API's path), the type of measured data (for example, temperature), and the interval for data retrieval in seconds.

```
{
    "9" : [
        {
          "iotPath" : "https://<api endpoint>/v1.1/Datastreams(903)/Observations",
          "indicator" : "tempreture",
          "checkInterval" : 3600.0,
        }
    ],
    "7" : [
        {
          "iotPath" : "https://<api endpoint>/v1.1/Datastreams(703)/Observations",
          "indicator" : "tempreture",
          "checkInterval" : 3700.0,
        }
    ]
}
```

The *oracle2* JSON configuration file contains a name of the blockchain network, addresses of the individual blockchain nodes, addresses of the system administrators, node status check interval in seconds, *ram* resource cost extraction interval in seconds, and interval of the snapshot file.

```
{
    "scpdx" : [
        {
          "chainName" : "scpdx",
          "chainPoints" : [
              {"node" : "<node1.endpoint>"},
              {"node" : "<node2.endpoint>"},
              {"node" : "<node3.endpoint>"}
          ],
          "alertAddresses" : [
              {"address" : "<system administrator 1 mail address>"},
              {"address" : "<system administrator 2 mail address>"}
          ],
          "checkInterval" : 3600.0,
          "ramCheckInterval" : 3700.0,
          "snapshotInterval" : 86400.0
        }
    ],
    "eosiopublic" : [
        {
          "chainName" : "eosiopublic",
          "chainPoints" : [
              {"node" : "https://eos.api.eosnation.io"}
          ],
          "alertAddresses" : [
          ],
          "checkInterval" : 0.0,
          "ramCheckInterval" : 3900.0,
          "snapshotInterval" : 0.0
        }
    ]

}
```

The snapshot file is used when restoring the operation of a blockchain node after an emergency stop.

5.1. Upload Real-Time Sensor Readings

For uploading real-time sensor readings, the following actions are used from the *oracle1 smart contract* and a corresponding *multi-index table*.

A structure that is passed as input parameters to the ***add*** action and syntax:

```
struct iot_res {
  double value;
  string date_str;
};

ACTION add (name creator, uint64_t iotid, name type, std::vector<iot_res> results)
```

Oracle1 smart contract multi-index table (IoT registry) format:

```
TABLE t_reg {
  uint64_t id;
  uint64_t iot_id;
  double value;
  eosio::time_point_sec reg_at;
  name type;

  uint64_t primary_key() const { return id; }
  uint64_t by_iot() const { return iot_id; }
  uint64_t third_key() const { return reg_at.sec_since_epoch(); }
  double fourth_key() const { return value; }
  uint128_t by_type() const { return ((uint128_t)type.value << 64) + id; }
};
```

The *user application* and *oracle1 smart contract* can retrieve the data recorded in the *multi-index table* by action ***getlastiorec*** *input/output parameters* format:

```
struct getLast {
  time_point_sec date;
  double value;
};

[[eosio::action]] getLast getlastiorec (name actor, uint64_t iot_id)
```

With the given example, the extraction of the last recorded value from a specific sensor is implemented. Depending on the required functionalities, other algorithms for data extraction, for example, the arithmetic mean value of measured parameters for a certain period of time, the last three measured values, or others, can be used.

In this particular implementation the used action in the *oracle1 smart contract* is:

```
ACTION getLast getlastrec (name actor, uint64_t iot_id)
```

In general, when a smart contract has to receive data from another smart contract, the so-called *call-back* convention is used. The *oracle smart contract* developer must provide a sample of the *call-back action* in order for it to be implemented in the *user's smart contracts* to which data will be provided.

The *call-back action* sample in the *user's smart contract*:

```
// call-back function sample
  ACTION callback (const name& caller, const double& value, const string& timestamp) {
    string tm = timestamp;
    double val = value;
    print("According to myOracle at ", tm, " ", " value is ", val);
// implement your decision making algorithm here ...
  }
```

The *oracle1 smart contract* uses *id* to match the request coming from the *user smart contract* and then invokes a *call-back action* on it with the response. It suggests that the *user's smart contract* has two actions.

In step 1, the *user's smart contract* calls (executes) the action from the *oracle1 smart contract* and defines the request to receive data.

In step 2, the *oracle1 smart contract* calls (executes) the *call-back action* in the *user's smart contract* that has a predefined interface (defined by the operator/owner of the *oracle smart contract*). The *call-back action* records the received data in a predefined *multi-index table* (Figure 6).

The other way to store data instead of in multi-indexes tables is a *singleton*. The difference is that singletons can only store a single data record and therefore don't need a primary key which makes access easier. Singletons are usually used to store global configuration data for the smart contract or data for subsequent calculations.

The maximum execution time of a smart contract action is 140 ms. For input–output operations, the actions should be allocated, for example, 20% of the time. The remaining time is translated into processor cycles for a particular processor (clock speed, performance, etc.).

5.2. Registration and Monitoring of the RAM Resource

The resources in *EOSIO* blockchain are *net*, *cpu*, and *ram*. *Net* is average consumption in bytes over the last 3 days. *Cpu* is the processing power of an account measured in microseconds over the last 3 days as well. *Ram* is the information that is accessible from application logic. It limits the maximum space that can be occupied to store permanent data. *Cpu* price is measured in SYS Token/ms/Day, *net* price in SYS Token/KiB/Day, 1 KiB = 1024 bytes, and *ram* in SYS/1 byte.

An account can exchange *net* and *cpu*, but must buy *ram*, because it is not freed automatically. The only way to free up *ram* is to delete the data that is using the account (multi-index tables). Freed unused *ram* can be sold and purchased at the market price, which is determined by the Bancor algorithm [29,30]. The utility token in this private blockchain is SYS.

The data on the registration and monitoring of the *ram* resource is recorded in the blockchain. It can also be treated as raw data from a website source.

The *ram* price is extracted from the *rammarket* table of the *EOSIO system account* or by executing the *cleos* command with the corresponding parameters:


```
"rows": [{
    "supply": "10000000000.0000 RAMCORE",
    "base": {
      "balance": "68581458306 RAM",
      "weight": "0.50000000000000000"
    },
    "quote": {
      "balance": "1002012.4747 SYS",
      "weight": "0.50000000000000000"
    }
  }
```


Based on the Bankor algorithm, Table 1 presents the results for the price of a *ram* resource as of 4 April 2023.

Table 1. SCPDx *ram* and EOS *ram* prices.

Description	Value	Units
RAM Market price SCPDx blockchain	1.463	SYS/MiB
Public EOS price	1.19	USD

It is possible to compare the *ram* resource price and the public *EOSIO* blockchain (EOS RAM Token quote in USD) at https://bloks.io/ (accessed on 4 April 2023).

5.3. Statistical Processing of Sensor Data

The data are statistically processed and uploaded on the blockchain. It can be historical or daily aggregated from the real-time sensor readings. Here, historical data from a sensor group installed in a greenhouse located in Maritsa Vegetable Crops Research Institute (MVCRI), Plovdiv (https://izk-maritsa.org/en/home/ (accessed on 12 May 2023)) was statistically processed and uploaded to the blockchain. The raw data are the temperature and humidity readings of five sensors over an eight-month period and comprised about 380,000 records or 10.9 Mb. The processed data uploaded on the blockchain constituted a volume of about 500 KB (0.5 MB). For the statistical calculations, a standard built-in array processing functions in Swift 5.7 is used.

A structure that is passed as input parameters in an *oracle1 smart contract* to the action ***addmar***:

```
struct mar_res {
  uint64_t iot_id;
  double t_min;
  double t_max;
  double t_avg;
  double t_std;
  double t_var;
  double h_min;
  double h_max;
  double h_avg;
  double h_std;
  double h_var;
  string date_str;
};

ACTION addmar (name creator, std::vector<mar_res> results)
```

A *multi-index table* (sensors registry) format:

```
TABLE m_reg {
  uint64_t id;
  uint64_t iot_id;
  double t_min;
  double t_max;
  double t_avg;
  double t_std;
  double t_var;
  double h_min;
  double h_max;
  double h_avg;
  double h_std;
  double h_var;
  eosio::time_point_sec reg_at;

  uint64_t primary_key() const { return id; }
  uint64_t by_iot() const { return iot_id; }
  uint64_t third_key() const { return reg_at.sec_since_epoch(); }
};
```

A reference to the memory used to upload the processed data is obtained from the command line: *cleos -u http://<blockchain endpoint> get account iotoracle*:

Resources status before uploading data to the *oracle1 smart contract*:

```
memory:
     quota:         12 MiB    used:     9.242 MiB

net bandwidth:
     staked:        1000.0000 SYS          (total stake delegated from account to self)
     delegated:        0.0000 SYS          (total staked delegated to account from others)
     used:              25.53 KiB
     available:         575.9 MiB
     limit:             575.9 MiB

cpu bandwidth:
     staked:        1000.0000 SYS          (total stake delegated from account to self)
     delegated:        0.0000 SYS          (total staked delegated to account from others)
     used:              33.74 ms
     available:         57.56 sec
     limit:             57.59 sec
```

Resources status after data upload:

```
memory:
     quota:          12 MiB     used:      9.787 MiB

net bandwidth:
     staked:         1000.0000 SYS           (total stake delegated from account to self)
     delegated:         0.0000 SYS           (total staked delegated to account from others)
     used:            134.5 KiB
     available:       575.8 MiB
     limit:           575.9 MiB

cpu bandwidth:
     staked:         1000.0000 SYS           (total stake delegated from account to self)
     delegated:         0.0000 SYS           (total staked delegated to account from others)
     used:            124.4 ms
     available:       57.47 sec
     limit:           57.59 sec
```

The comparison shows that about 500 KiB of *ram* is used to upload the historical data. Based on the data collected by *oracle2*, its value can be estimated for any date. In the current example, at 04/04/23 (Table 1), it is 500 KiB (=0.5 MiB) × 1.463 SYS/MiB = 0.7315 SYS. Assuming 1 SYS = 1 EOS, the price in USD is USD 1.19 × 0.7315 = USD 0.87. Therefore, a user must purchase a *ram* of this value, provided he wants to store such a volume of data in the blockchain.

Assuming that this is historical data for 8 months from five sensors that measure two parameters, it can be found that the monthly cost to upload statistically processed data is USD 0.108. These are operational costs that would have to be paid by the user. The presented calculation should be interpreted as an isolated example of the cost of the resource for using the blockchain and cannot serve as a criterion for the cost of maintenance of the platform.

5.4. Monitoring and Maintaining the Blockchain Network

The monitoring and maintenance of the blockchain network enables real-time monitoring of the state of nodes, immediate action in case of failure, and collection of statistics on the frequency of failures and recovery.

Table 2 is a summary of the data generated by *oracle2*.

Table 2. Blockchain network failure statistics.

Parameters	
Starting date	August 2022
Number of nodes:	3
OS	1 × OSX, 2 × UBUNTO 20.04
Total number of failures	29
Average node recovery time	up to 2 h
Maximum node recovery time	6 h
Minimum node recovery time	up to 1 h

The redistricted emergency failures are mainly due to the following:

- Interruption and breakdowns of Internet providers;
- Power failure;
- Disk memory overflow—only once, due to a wrong configuration of the node.

Since all interruptions are due to failures of the nodes' external infrastructure, it can be concluded that from a software perspective, the *eos.io* blockchain ecosystem is rather reliable. The statistics show that from the point of view of system administration, the chosen notification approach is efficient enough. The time it takes for the nodes to get back up and running varies and very much depends on how long the outage was.

6. Discussion and Future Development

This paper commented, analysed, and presented an integration of two server-based blockchain oracles into a blockchain-based platform for smart crop production data exchange by smart contracts.

Oracle1 is intended to retrieve and upload, on blockchain real-time data, readings from two sensor networks, to process and upload daily readings statistics, and to upload historical data as needed. Currently, the oracle work is stable, and no gaps have been reported when collecting the data. The resources used fully correspond to the expected parameters. However, a comprehensive assessment of its performance cannot be provided as new sensor networks are yet to be connected. In addition, the need to store historical data is currently incidental and it is difficult to determine the load on the blockchain network and its performance at higher transaction intensity.

Oracle2 is developed for system functions. The monitoring of the operation of blockchain nodes facilitates the work of the system administrator. With the inevitable scaling of the blockchain network, it is assumed that the system functions will evolve, and the analysis of the collected statistics will optimize the operation of the entire platform. For about eight months of operation, the oracle has detected all emergency interruptions of the blockchain nodes. On this basis the maximum, average, and minimum nodes' recovery time and the main reasons for those failures are identified. From this data, it can be concluded that the interruptions in the work of the blockchain nodes are mainly due to external factors such as interruptions in Internet connections, power outages, and unplanned server software updates. The notification that the *oracle* sends to the system administrator significantly reduces the recovery time of the nodes.

The *oracle2* also allows assessment of the *ram* resource cost for uploading processed historical data. Since these results are obtained on the basis of very little data and low-intensity transactions, this functionality remains to be further tested under more active exchange, volume, and type of data. At the current load of the platform, the cost of the *ram* resource used is relatively low. A possible increase of the *ram* price may occur when increasing the frequency of measurements from the sensor network or a rise in the number of sensors. The fact that the blockchain network is private has no effect on the cost of *ram* resources, only on who covers this cost.

Both *oracles'* integration is described at the design level and through particular implementation of smart contracts. The oracles' functions are performed by an *oracle application* and a corresponding *oracle smart contract*. The first is responsible for the interaction with the external data, and the second is responsible for the operations in the blockchain. The concrete solution is illustrated by oracles' workflows, the internal processes between the *oracle applications* and the *blockchain smart contract*, and the external processes of the *oracle smart contracts*. The main functions are illustrated by examples of the configuration files of the server applications (oracle applications), elements of the C++ smart contracts representing constants and variables declarations, multi-index tables, internal functions in the contracts, and actions called by other contracts and external programs.

There are a number of potential fallacies in developing and setting software blockchain oracles. They mainly refer to the implementation and used protocols. Regardless of the fact that authors and developers propose their own solutions, the implementation and integration approaches can be different and should be tailored to the particular tasks and specifics of the information systems and infrastructure used.

The main criterion of whether an oracle is properly designed is whether it achieves its predefined functionality. This process is measurable and testable. After almost 10 months of operation, the current implementation of blockchain oracles meets the set goals and is sufficiently stable from an operational point of view.

The presence of a single point of failure is always a threat for any information system, regardless of whether it is based on blockchain technology or not. The mitigation of this risk could be achieved by duplicating the infrastructure components—IoT networks, by adding a group or groups of sensors measuring the same parameters (but this leads to an increase in the cost/investment when building the IoT component of the platforms), or by duplicating the software component; for example, by installing a group of oracles on different servers to retrieve data from the same IoT sensors. A mixed approach is also applicable. The second option is probably more cost-effective, while the first increases the reliability of the obtained data from the physical world. In this particular implementation, the second option is more appropriate. It is planned to add one or more software oracles installed on independent servers. This is a subject for future development.

Verification of external data sources is of particular importance for the reliability of the information received. It is customary to work with verified information providers (fixed IP addresses, data encryption, etc.). In the case presented in this paper, the data comes from sensor IoT networks of a partner's organization. The entire information infrastructure is under the management of the project members, and the data are assumed to be from a reliable and verified source. In the next stages of development of the platform, encryption of the data received from the IoT sensor networks is envisaged by using public/private key technology—the same principle that is used for the authentication of users in the EOSIO blockchain network (ECC keys).

From a cybersecurity perspective, which is beyond the scope of this paper, oracles introduce a degree of risk, but it is a manageable process. At this stage of implementation standard means and security measures are provided, such as access to the server and blockchain infrastructure through encrypted connections, using digital certificates, limiting access to networks only through a list of user IP addresses, and installing all software components on their own information resources. The management is centralized and is entirely under the control of the project's members. Complementing and expanding the functionality of the platform, or in the case of opening it to public access, more significant cybersecurity measures must be taken.

The oracles are particularly valuable in terms of transferring data from the physical world to information systems. The safe and reliable transfer of digitized information intended for process management and/or decision making is extremely important in the development and operation of information systems/platforms. Basing such platforms on blockchain technologies increases their reliability in terms of immutability, auditability, and transparency of stored information and performed transactions. From a software point of view, blockchain oracles are not very different from any other application (server or WEB based). For this reason, the risks when integrating them into software platforms, including blockchain-based ones, are of a general nature. With an appropriate risk management plan, which includes access control, use of complex hardware and software approaches for cyber security protection of information and network resources and infrastructure, centralized management, and continuous control of activities, the risks are manageable.

The future development of oracles' integration could go in several directions. First, given that the main public blockchain networks based on *EOSIO* technology have made a hard fork, a private blockchain network operating under the management of the *Antelope.io* software is going to be installed [31], and upcoming tests for compatibility, data portability and performance, etc. are going to be performed. This hard fork added a number of new functionalities. For example, Ethereum VM (EVM) support, which allows existing applications running on Ethereum blockchain to be migrated onto the new version of Antelope.io, better management of resources and access to on-chain data (permissioned access to multi-index tables, extracting information about transactions), extended options for authentication, integration with most available wallets (hardware, web, and software), which makes it suitable for the implementation of dApps and web3 applications, and the possibility of using Solidity for smart contracts and transactions migration features.

A second direction is expanding the scope of access to various external data sources and the integration of oracles with other smart contracts that have decision-making functions.

A third direction is experiments to integrate the functions of intelligent personal assistants into the oracles' smart contracts. The characteristics of an intelligent agent, such as autonomy, reactivity, and proactivity in communication with an external environment and virtual infrastructures, whether it is a virtual educational space [32,33] or other domain, in principle do not differ significantly from the purpose of a smart contract. Implemented in decentralized applications, such oracles would enable significant customization of data exchange services and decision support in smart crop production.

Another future development is oracles' integrations in risk assessment and management framework [34,35] of the platform. This is a sufficiently specific topic that implies expanding and detailing the functions of the system oracle in the direction of identifying, registering, processing, and signalling about external environment risk events to security systems or platform administrators to take appropriate actions.

Author Contributions: Conceptualization, I.P. and I.R.; methodology, I.R.; software, I.R.; validation, I.P. and L.D.; formal analysis, I.P.; investigation, I.R. and L.D.; resources, I.R.; data curation, L.D.; writing—original draft preparation, I.R.; writing—review and editing, I.P. and I.R.; visualization, I.R.; supervision, I.P. and L.D.; project administration, L.D. and I.R.; funding acquisition, L.D. All authors have read and agreed to the published version of the manuscript.

Funding: This work was supported by the Bulgarian Ministry of Education and Science under the National Research Program "Smart crop production" approved by Decision of the Ministry Council No. 866/26.11.2020 and by the Scientific Research Fund "BG PLANTNET establishment of national information network genebank—plant genetic resources", project KP-06-N36.

Data Availability Statement: https://github.com/scpdxtest/SCPDx.git (accessed on 13 April 2023).

Conflicts of Interest: The authors declare no conflict of interest.

References

1. Blockchain Oracle | Article about Blockchain Oracle by The Free Dictionary. Available online: https://encyclopedia2.thefreedictionary.com/blockchain+oracle (accessed on 17 March 2023).
2. What Is a Blockchain Oracle? *What Is the Oracle Problem? Why Can't Blockchains Make API Calls? This Is Everything You Need to Know about Off-Chain Dat | Better Programming.* Available online: https://betterprogramming.pub/what-is-a-blockchain-oracle-f5ccab8dbd72 (accessed on 17 March 2023).
3. Blockchain Oracles Explained. Available online: https://wirexapp.com/blog/post/blockchain-oracles-explained-0512 (accessed on 17 March 2023).
4. Oracles and Blockchain: DeFi Oracles Examined | Gemini. Available online: https://www.gemini.com/cryptopedia/crypto-oracle-blockchain-overview#section-blockchain-oracles-explained-why-do-we-need-oracles (accessed on 17 March 2023).
5. Oracles | ethereum.org. Available online: https://ethereum.org/en/developers/docs/oracles/ (accessed on 17 March 2023).
6. What Is a Blockchain Oracle and How Does It Work? Available online: https://cointelegraph.com/blockchain-for-beginners/what-is-a-blockchain-oracle-and-how-does-it-work (accessed on 17 March 2023).
7. Szabo, N. Smart Contracts: Building Blocks for Digital Markets. 1996. Available online: https://www.fon.hum.uva.nl/rob/Courses/InformationInSpeech/CDROM/Literature/LOTwinterschool2006/szabo.best.vwh.net/smart_contracts_2.html (accessed on 3 April 2023).
8. Yaga, D.; Mell, P.; Roby, N.; Scarfone, K. *Blockchain Technology Overview*; National Institute of Standards and Technology: Gaithersburg, MD, USA, 2018. [CrossRef]
9. Taherdoost, H. Smart Contracts in Blockchain Technology: A Critical Review. *Information* **2023**, *14*, 117. [CrossRef]
10. Inclusive Deployment of Blockchain for Supply Chains: Part 6—A Framework for Blockchain Interoperability | World Economic Forum. Available online: https://www.weforum.org/whitepapers/inclusive-deployment-of-blockchain-for-supply-chains-part-6-a-framework-for-blockchain-interoperability (accessed on 4 April 2023).
11. Ezzat, S.K.; Saleh, Y.N.M.; Abdel-Hamid, A.A. Blockchain Oracles: State-of-the-Art and Research Directions. *IEEE Access* **2022**, *10*, 67551–67572. [CrossRef]
12. Mammadzada, K.; Iqbal, M.; Milani, F.; García-Bañuelos, L.; Matulevičius, R. Blockchain Oracles: A Framework for Blockchain-Based Applications. In *Business Process Management: Blockchain and Robotic Process Automation Forum*; Asatiani, A., García, J.M., Helander, N., Jiménez-Ramírez, A., Koschmider, A., Mendling, J., Meroni, G., Reijers, H.A., Eds.; Springer International Publishing: Cham, Switzerland, 2020; pp. 19–34.
13. Michel, C. Learn EOS Development. The Complete Guide to Dapps on the EOS Blockchain. 2019. Available online: https://learneos.dev (accessed on 28 February 2023).
14. Doukovska, L. Artificial intelligence to support bulgarian crop production. *Eng. Sci.* **2021**, *LVIII*, 30–48. [CrossRef]
15. Radeva, I. Blockchains: Practical approaches. *Eng. Sci.* **2022**, *LIX*, 3–23. [CrossRef]
16. Ilieva, G.; Yankova, T.; Radeva, I.; Popchev, I. Blockchain Software Selection as a Fuzzy Multi-Criteria Problem. *Computers* **2021**, *10*, 120. [CrossRef]
17. Ilieva, G.; Yankova, T. IoT System Selection as a Fuzzy Multi-Criteria Problem. *Sensors* **2022**, *22*, 4110. [CrossRef] [PubMed]

18. Krasteva, I.; Glushkova, T.; Moraliyska, N.; Velcheva, N. A Blockchain-Based Model of GenBank Store System. In Proceedings of the IEEE 10th International Conference on Intelligent Systems (IS'20), Varna, Bulgaria, 28–30 August 2020; pp. 606–611. [CrossRef]
19. Krasteva, I.; Glushkova, T.; Stoyanova-Doycheva, A.; Moralivska, N.; Doukovska, L.; Radeva, I. Blockchain-based approach to supply chain modeling in a smart farming system. In Proceedings of the Big Data, Knowledge and Control Systems Engineering (BdKCSE'21), Sofia, Bulgaria, 28–29 October 2021; pp. 1–6. [CrossRef]
20. Radeva, I.; Popchev, I. Blockchain-Enabled Supply-Chain in Crop Production Framework. *Cybern. Inf. Technol.* **2022**, *22*, 151–170. [CrossRef]
21. Orozova, D.; Popchev, I.; Baltov, M. Cyber-Physical Social Space towards Blockchain and Smart Specialisation Solutions. In Proceedings of the 22nd International Symposium on Electrical Apparatus and Technologies (SIELA), Bourgas, Bulgaria, 1–4 June 2022; pp. 1–4. [CrossRef]
22. Popchev, I.; Orozova, D. Algorithms for Machine Learning with Orange System. *Int. J. Online Biomed. Eng. IJOE* **2023**, *19*, 109–123. [CrossRef]
23. Popchev, I.; Doukovska, L.; Radeva, I. A framework of blockchain/IPFS-based platform for smart crop production. In Proceedings of the International Conference Automatics and Informatics, Varna, Bulgaria, 6–8 October 2022; IEEE: Piscataway, NJ, USA, 2022; pp. 265–270. [CrossRef]
24. Popchev, I.; Doukovska, L.; Radeva, I. A Prototype of blockchain/distributed file system Platform. Presented at the IEEE International Conference on Intelligent Systems IS'22, Warsaw, Poland, 12–14 October 2022; IEEE: Piscataway, NJ, USA, 2022; pp. 1–7. [CrossRef]
25. Curran, B. What Are Oracles? Smart Contracts, Chainlink & "The Oracle Problem". *Blockonomy* **2018**. Available online: https://blockonomi.com/oracles-guide/ (accessed on 28 February 2023).
26. Al Breiki, H.; Rehman, M.H.U.; Salah, K.; Svetinovic, D. Trustworthy Blockchain Oracles: Review, Comparison, and Open Research Challenges. *IEEE Access* **2020**, *8*, 85675–85685. [CrossRef]
27. Terziyski, A.; Tenev, S.; Jeliazkov, V.; Jeliazkova, N.; Kochev, N. METER. AC: Live Open Access Atmospheric Monitoring Data for Bulgaria with High Spatiotemporal Resolution. *Data* **2020**, *5*, 36. [CrossRef]
28. The Swift Programming Language | Documentation. Available online: https://docs.swift.org/swift-book/documentation/the-swift-programming-language (accessed on 28 March 2023).
29. Binesh, A. EOS Resource usage. *Medium*, 6 May 2019. Available online: https://medium.com/shyft-network/eos-resource-usage-f0a8098827d7 (accessed on 2 March 2023).
30. Rosenfeld, M. Formulas for Bancor System. Available online: https://drive.google.com/file/d/0B3HPNP-GDn7aRkVaV3dkVl9NS2M/view?resourcekey=0-mbIgrdd0B9H8dPNRaeB_TA (accessed on 4 April 2023).
31. Home—Antelope. Available online: https://antelope.io/ (accessed on 4 April 2023).
32. Todorov, Y.; Valkanov, V.; Popchev, I. Intelligent Personal Assistant for Aiding Students. Presented at the John Atanasoff Celebration Days—111th Anniversary Sofia, Sofia, Bulgaria, 4–6 October 2017; pp. 283–286.
33. Todorov, Y.; Popchev, I.; Radeva, I. Personal Assistant Architecture in Virtual Educational Space. *Inf. Technol. Control* **2019**, *2*, 20–26. [CrossRef]
34. Popchev, I.; Radeva, I.; Velichkova, V. Blockchains in Enterprise global risk management. In Proceedings of the 2021 International Conference Automatics and Informatics (ICAI), Varna, Bulgaria, 30 September–2 October 2021; pp. 282–287. [CrossRef]
35. Popchev, I.; Radeva, I.; Nikolova, I. Aspects of the evolution from risk management to enterprise global risk management. *Eng. Sci.* **2021**, *LVII*, 16–30. [CrossRef]

electronics

MDPI

Systematic Review

Investigating the Factors Influencing the Adoption of Blockchain Technology across Different Countries and Industries: A Systematic Literature Review

Agostino Marengo [1,*] and Alessandro Pagano [2]

1 Department of Human Science, University of Foggia, 71122 Foggia, Italy
2 Department of Economics, University of Bari, 70121 Bari, Italy; alessandro.pagano@uniba.it
* Correspondence: agostino.marengo@unifg.it

Abstract: Despite the reported disruptive nature of blockchain technology in the extant literature, its adoption is slower than its potential. This difference between the technology's promises and its current adoption has sparked interest in understanding the factors impeding widespread adoption. This systematic literature review (SLR), drawn from 1786 studies published between 2008 and May 2023, seeks to address this gap. Specifically, our research explores the influence of factors and their differences and commonalities on blockchain adoption. The SLR, examining individual and organisational perspectives, identifies 152 unique factors influencing 25 industries across 21 countries. This review also highlights distinct commonalities and variations in these factors across industries and countries. For instance, while regulatory issues and costs were universal concerns, the importance of technical understanding diverged between industries. Furthermore, country-specific factors, including local regulations and cultural aspects, emerged as significantly influenced insights that provide a comprehensive perspective on the dynamics of blockchain adoption, offering valuable guidance to industry practitioners and researchers striving to navigate the complexities of blockchain integration.

Keywords: blockchain; adoption; factors; countries; literature; industries

Citation: Marengo, A.; Pagano, A. Investigating the Factors Influencing the Adoption of Blockchain Technology across Different Countries and Industries: A Systematic Literature Review. *Electronics* **2023**, *12*, 3006. https://doi.org/10.3390/electronics12143006

Academic Editor: Juan M. Corchado

Received: 12 June 2023
Revised: 4 July 2023
Accepted: 7 July 2023
Published: 9 July 2023

1. Introduction

The Industrial Revolution brought about several emerging technologies, leading to significant changes across many industries. Among these technologies, blockchain technology (BCT) has captured the attention of many, becoming one of the most unique, disruptive technologies of the 21st century. Introduced initially in the form of Bitcoin by Satoshi Nakamoto [1], blockchain has shown to be a vast and multifaceted technology, with Bitcoin representing just one of many possible applications [2].

Blockchain is a distributed and decentralised technology that uses cryptographic measures to securely store data in interconnected blocks, forming a transparent, immutable, and decentralised network [3]. The advent of this technology has presented the world with new methods of transaction and data management that are expected to revolutionise conventional processes.

The inherent characteristics of blockchain, such as its decentralised nature, fewer intermediaries, proof of work (POW), proof of stake (POS), cryptographic security, audibility, and near real-time update capabilities, present a significant shift from traditional centralised systems [4,5]. Furthermore, the types of blockchains, like permissioned, permissionless, centralised, decentralised, and hybrid, propose profound implications on how trust, accountability, and efficiency are established in systems involving peer-to-peer transactions [6]. They are also why blockchain technology holds such tremendous potential for transforming operations across various industries, from finance to healthcare, supply chain management, and beyond [7–9].

Despite this broad applicability and potential, blockchain technology's actual adoption and application exhibit significant variation across industries and countries [10].

Previous research into this field has primarily been industry specific or country specific, limiting our understanding of blockchain adoption from a global and cross-sectoral perspective [11,12]. This fragmented knowledge, combined with the nascent state of technology, has created a research gap, emphasising the need for a more comprehensive, cross-sectoral, and global study.

This knowledge gap is significant given the scale of investments flowing into blockchain technologies. Between 2009 and 2018, over USD 13.1bn was invested in blockchain startups, with the USA, China, and the European Union being the most prominent contributors [13–15]. While these figures speak to the increasing recognition of the technology's potential, they also underscore the critical need for an improved understanding of the factors influencing its adoption.

Past studies have identified key factors influencing blockchain adoption, such as perceived trust, perceived usefulness, and organisational readiness [16,17]. These findings have significantly contributed to understanding the factors driving blockchain adoption decisions. Moreover, many studies have employed robust research methodologies, including surveys, case studies, and experiments, to provide empirical evidence supporting their findings [18–20]. This empirical basis enhances the validity and reliability of the research outcomes. However, the existing body of the literature has certain limitations and weaknesses. One notable limitation is the lack of generalizability of findings due to the narrow focus of many studies on specific industries or countries. While these studies offer valuable insights within their respective contexts, it is imperative to consider a broader range of industries and countries to ensure a comprehensive understanding of blockchain adoption across diverse settings [20,21].

Additionally, some studies have heavily relied on self-reported data, which may introduce response biases or subjective interpretations of the factors influencing blockchain adoption. To minimise the biases, explicit and systematic methods can be used by reviewing articles and all available evidence. This leads to reliable findings from which conclusions can be drawn and decisions made [22]. Therefore, this paper offers a systematic review of the literature exploring the factors influencing blockchain adoption across various industries and countries. Unlike past studies that merely identify the factors, this study also explains how the factors influence blockchain adoption. Specifically, the purpose of this study is to find answers to the following research questions:

RQ 1: *How do the factors influence blockchain adoption across industries and countries?*

RQ 2: *How do the commonalities and differences influence blockchain adoption across different industries and countries?*

The rest of this paper proceeds as follows: Section 2 outlines the materials and methods, Section 3 presents the results, Section 4 describes the discussion, and Section 5 presents this study's conclusions, limitations, and future directions.

2. Materials and Methods

To answer the research questions, this present study conducted a systematic literature review to identify the factors influencing the adoption of blockchain technology across different countries and industries. This study followed the guidelines outlined by Okoli [23] and Kitchenham and Brereton [24]. The review process was conducted in stages: search strategy, inclusion and exclusion criteria, screening and selection, and data extraction and analysis. Here, we provide further details for each stage.

2.1. Search Strategy

A comprehensive search of electronic databases was conducted for peer-reviewed articles published between 2009 (the year of the introduction of blockchain) and May 2023. This study chose widely used databases in information systems research, which include, Table 1,

Google Scholar, ScienceDirect, Web of Science, Scopus, IEEE Xplore, Springer, Emerald, and the ACM Digital Library. This study used multiple databases because searching multiple databases can maximise available data and consider all relevant literature. According to Ewald and Klerings [25], searching two or more databases decreased the risk of missing relevant studies.

Table 1. Number of articles retrieved from databases.

Database	Number of Articles
Scopus	51
IEEE Xplore	7
Springer	656
Web of Science	35
Google Scholar	1020
Emerald	5
ACM	2
Science Direct	7
Total	1783

The search terms combined relevant keywords about blockchain technology, e.g., "blockchain", "distributed ledger technology", "adoption", "diffusion", acceptance", "factor", "determinants", and "elements", using Boolean operators like AND, OR. The search was performed in the articles' titles, abstracts, and keywords. The following table shows the number of papers retrieved from each database.

We used advanced research; Springer and Google Scholar returned the most irrelevant papers.

2.2. Inclusion and Exclusion Criteria

Specific inclusion and exclusion criteria were applied to ensure the selected articles' quality and relevance. Only articles that met the following criteria were included in this review:

Written in English: Since English is the primary language of scientific communication, articles written in English were considered for comprehensively analysed text articles and were preferred to ensure a comprehensive analysis of the factors influencing blockchain adoption. We refer to full-text articles that have complete content and open-access articles. This includes open-access articles and articles that may require a subscription or access to academic libraries.

Empirical investigation: Only articles that empirically investigated the factors influencing the adoption of blockchain technology were included. This criterion aimed to focus on studies that provided improvidence and insights.

Published in journal and conference papers: Articles published in reputable journals and conference proceedings are included to capture diverse research outputs.

Articles were excluded if they met any of the following criteria:

Non-English language: Articles written in languages other than English were excluded due to language limitations.

Focus on cryptocurrency without a clear link to blockchain technology: Articles solely focused on cryptocurrency without a clear connection to blockchain technology were excluded, as the objective was to focus on factors specific to blockchain adoption.

Lack of specific address to adoption factors: Articles that did not specifically address the factors influencing blockchain adoption were excluded to ensure the relevance and focus of this review.

2.3. Screening and Selection

We employed a systematic process for identifying and removing duplicates. Initially, we used EndNote 20 software to remove exact duplicates based on title and author information. Subsequently, we manually reviewed the remaining articles to ensure that no duplicates were overlooked. The remaining articles were then selected for a full-text review based on the inclusion and exclusion criteria. Any disagreements about inclusion were resolved via discussion until consensus among authors was reached.

2.4. Data Extraction and Analysis

Data extraction was conducted from the included articles to capture key information, including the country, industry, and key findings related to the adoption of blockchain technology. The factors influencing blockchain adoption were identified and categorised into main groups based on recurring themes and patterns, as discussed in Section 3.2.

To ensure the rigour of our systematic review, we followed the PRISMA (Preferred Reporting Items for Systematic Reviews and Meta-Analyses) guidelines as incorporated in the review on blockchain technology by Sahoo, Kumar [26]. This measure enhanced the reliability and validity of the findings [27]. In light of PRISMA guidelines, Figure 1 demonstrates the number of articles included in this study.

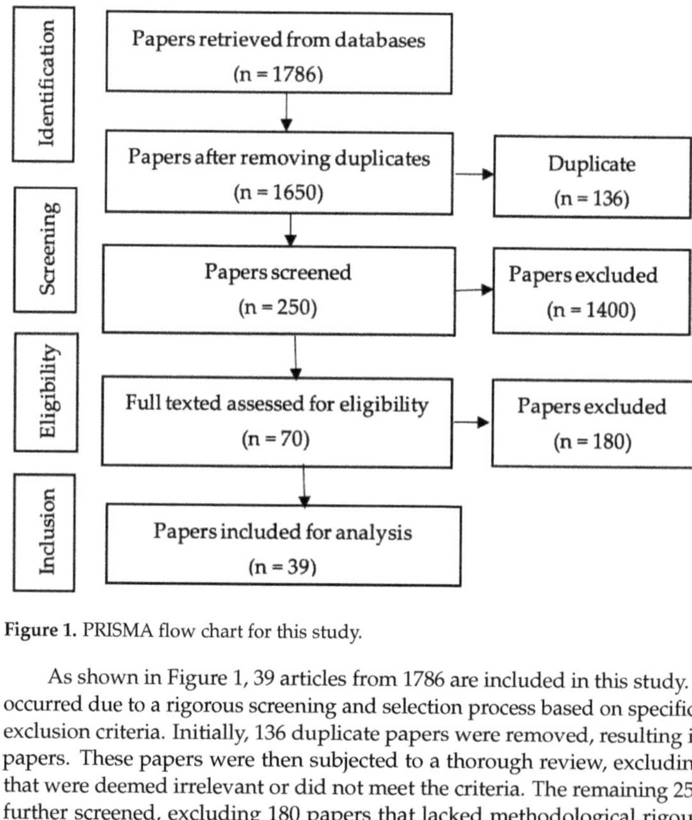

Figure 1. PRISMA flow chart for this study.

As shown in Figure 1, 39 articles from 1786 are included in this study. The reduction occurred due to a rigorous screening and selection process based on specific inclusion and exclusion criteria. Initially, 136 duplicate papers were removed, resulting in 1650 unique papers. These papers were then subjected to a thorough review, excluding 1400 papers that were deemed irrelevant or did not meet the criteria. The remaining 250 papers were further screened, excluding 180 papers that lacked methodological rigour or relevance to the research objectives. Finally, the remaining 70 papers underwent a comprehensive analysis, including 39 papers that provided substantial insights into the factors influencing blockchain adoption.

3. Results

This section presents detailed results of our analysis of the factors influencing blockchain adoption across different industries and countries. We organise the results into different tables based on the research questions.

RQ 1: *What factors influence blockchain adoption across different industries and countries?*

3.1. Factors for Industries and Countries

Drawing upon 39 diverse studies, the analysis provides a comprehensive understanding of factors influencing the adoption of blockchain technology. These studies cover a wide range of 25 distinct industries and 21 countries and report 152 unique factors. The most frequently studied industry appears to be the "supply chain", which underscores the significance of blockchain in enhancing transparency and efficiency in this industry. "India" surfaces as the country with the most studies, reflecting the growing interest and application of blockchain technology in this country. Regarding influencing factors, common themes across the studies include "perceived ease of use", "perceived usefulness", and "top management support", all of which indicate the crucial role of user perception and organisational backing in facilitating blockchain adoption. Table 2 summarises the factors identified in this SLR for different industries and countries.

Table 2. Factors affecting the adoption of blockchain technology.

Source	Factors	Industry	Country
[28]	Perceived trust, perceived ease of use, autonomous motivation, perceived usefulness	Taxing System	Bangladesh
[29]	Perceived ease of use, government support, vendor support, adoption intention, perceived usefulness, security concerns, top management support, technology readiness, the complexity of technology, technology compatibility, relative advantage, cost concerns	Supply chain	India
[30]	Optimism, innovativeness, discomfort, insecurity, perceived ease of use, perceived usefulness	Intelligence communities	Malaysia
[31]	Perceived ease of use, output quality, trust, perceived usefulness, information quality	crowdsourcing platform	China
[32]	Disintermediation, traceability, trust, coordination/control, compliance, price of technology products/services	Agriculture food supply chain	India
[33]	Perceived usefulness, trialability, relative advantage, compatibility, perceived ease of use	Education	Malaysia
[34]	Technology characteristics, task characteristics, inter-organisational trust, technology trust, user satisfaction, service quality, information quality, system quality, intention to adopt blockchain, blockchain efficiency, social influence, facilitating conditions, efforts expectancy, performance	Supply chain	Australia
[35]	Customer satisfaction, cost saving, favourable economy, increased use of technological devices, government support	Insurance	Malta

Table 2. *Cont.*

Source	Factors	Industry	Country
[36]	Transparency, smart contracts, shared database, secured database, reduced settlement lead times, reduced transaction cost, improved risk management, decentralised database, auditability, privacy, anonymity, immutability, provenance, traceability	Supply chain	India
[37]	Perceived usefulness, individual technology fit, task technology fit, perceived safety, network externality, perceived ease of use	Logistics	Taiwan
[38]	Strategic orientation, social influence, innovativeness, perceived ease of use, perceived usefulness, self-efficacy, complexity, security	Tourism	Taiwan
[39]	Facilitating conditions, performance expectancy, social influence, effort expectancy, trust	Supply Chain	Brazil
[40]	Regulatory support, competitive pressure, market dynamics, cost, upper management support, complexity, relative advantage	Supply chain	Malaysia
[41]	disintermediation, relative advantage, maturity, smart contact coding, data security, compatibility, complexity, perceived benefits, blockchain knowledge, participation incentives, innovativeness, technology readiness, business model readiness, organisational size, top management support, organisational readiness, critical user mass, trading partner support, business use cases, government support, industry pressure, market dynamics, regulatory environment	SMEs	Ireland
[42]	Increase in data availability, reduction in information, asymmetry, easy verification of transactions, comprehensibility of the transaction, data accuracy and reliability, data inalterability, exclusion of false information from contractual information, hacking attempts system denials, high-security encryption, cost reduction via the exclusion of intermediaries, contract conclusion with a reasonable fee, cost reduction due to process efficiency	Real Estate	Kosovo
[43]	Sufficient capital, staff training, support from the senior management, ease of local legislation, support from the shipping community, professional consultation, and assistance	Maritime	Singapore

Table 2. *Cont.*

Source	Factors	Industry	Country
[44]	Complexity, ease of use, lack of interoperability and standardisation, lack of scalability and system speed, huge resource (energy, infrastructure), initial capital requirement, lack of government regulation, lack of trust among agro-stakeholders	Agriculture	India
[21]	Cost, governance, perceived compatibility, perceived ease of use, perceived usefulness, privacy, observability, security, trialability, people's readiness, process readiness, technology readiness, top management enthusiasm, top management expertise, top management support, competitive pressure, customer's influence, connection with ICT providers	Supply chain	Europe
[45]	Budget availability, financial risk and uncertainty, cost saving, talent and knowledge acquisition, stakeholder's awareness and acceptance, blockchain ecosystem, disintermediation and business process, infrastructure and platform integration, standardisation, security and privacy, blockchain maturity and use case, management support, training and skills, HIT strategy, regulation compliance, regulatory uncertainty and governance, incentives availability	Health	USA
[46]	Regulatory governance and industry standards, technological improvements, and optimisation on efficiency, tracking and tracing, digitalised management, air traffic management	Aviation	Republic of Korea
[47]	Relative advantage, upper management support, human resources, compatibility, cost, complexity, technological infrastructure, and architecture.	Supply Chain	Sri Lanka
[48]	Perceived benefits, complexity, compatibility; organisational readiness, top management support, organisational size, regulatory environment, market dynamics, transparency, integrity of data, immutability	Government organisations	Malaysia
[49]	Organisational readiness, trading partner pressure, perceived benefits, complexity, top management support, compatibility	SMEs	South Africa

Table 2. *Cont.*

Source	Factors	Industry	Country
[50]	trialability, relative advantage, competitive advantage, compatibility	Construction	UK
[51]	Management/leadership buy in, transaction cost efficiency, transaction storage/energy efficiency, scalability, security and integrity, user data privacy, user engagement and desirability, ease of local and international legislation and regulation, personnel training, availability of funds for implementation, professional consultation and advisory capability, blockchain talent availability, integration with other cloud services/e-commerce platforms, incentives for miners, smart contract robustness and business case deployability, interoperability and standardisation, technology investment and maturity	Banking	India
[52]	Relative advantage, compatibility, observability, complexity, trialability	Education	Saudi Arabia
[53]	Perceived usefulness, trading partners' pressure, and competitive pressure	Manufacturing	Bangladesh
[54]	food quality control, provenance tracking and traceability, and partnership and trust	Agri Food	India
[55]	facilitating conditions, performance expectancy, and initial trust	Banking	India
[56]	Infrastructure and competencies, organisation characteristics, organisation readiness, organisation size, industry and market environment, support environment, regulatory environment	Cyber Security	South African
[57]	perceived efficiency, transparency, standardisation and platform development and traceability	Food industry	Russia, Estonia
[58]	Efficiency and security, perceived usefulness	SMEs	Italy
[59]	Security risk, regulatory support, technology latency, and technology complexity	Banking	Malaysia
[60]	Relative advantage, compatibility, perceived trust, top management considerations, absorptive capacity, information sharing, collaborative culture, trading partners' influence, regulatory support	Apparel	Bangladesh
[61]	Perceived benefits, perceived usefulness, perceived ease of use, subjective norms, perceived behavioural control, attitude, firm size	SME	Italy

Table 2. *Cont.*

Source	Factors	Industry	Country
[62]	Trust, load shedding, unemployment/layoffs, current infrastructure, useful life and educational campaigns	Clearing and settlement industry	South Africa
[63]	Task characteristics, technology characteristics, perceived ease of use, perceived usefulness, security concerns, government support	Blood bank	India
[64]	Close relationship with supplier, close relationship with the customer, just-in-time (JIT), strategic planning, many suppliers outsourcing, e-procurement, third party logistics (3 PL), subcontracting, reduced lead time, flexibility, forecasting, cost saving, resource planning, reduced inventory level	Oil industry	Pakistan
[65]	Inter-organisational, trust, relational governance, data transparency, data immutability, interoperability, product type	Supply Chain	India

The articles reported in Table 2 were categorised into main groups based on recurring themes and patterns found in the literature. The categories and how the factors in each category influence blockchain adoption are explained below.

3.1.1. Technological Factors

Technological factors encompass various aspects related to blockchain technology itself [45]. This includes evaluating the technological characteristics of blockchain, such as its scalability, consensus mechanisms, and transaction speed. Compatibility with existing systems and infrastructures is another crucial consideration, as organisations need to assess how well blockchain integrates into their current technologies. Complexity and scalability issues are essential to evaluate whether the blockchain system can handle the expected transaction volume and future growth [51]. Interoperability and standardisation play a role in facilitating seamless integration and communication between different blockchain networks and systems.

3.1.2. Organisational Factors

Organisational factors focus on the internal dynamics of an organisation and its readiness for blockchain adoption [59]. Top management support is crucial for driving organisational change and securing the necessary resources for implementing blockchain solutions [60]. Organisational readiness and culture influence the organisation's ability to adapt to new technologies and embrace change. Factors such as resource availability and allocation, including budget and skilled personnel, play a significant role in successful implementation [64]. The size and structure of the organisation can also influence the adoption process, with larger organisations potentially facing additional complexities in coordination and decision making.

3.1.3. Regulatory and Legal Factors

Regulatory and legal factors are essential considerations for blockchain adoption. Organisations must navigate the regulatory environment and ensure compliance with applicable laws and regulations [61]. This includes understanding the implications of blockchain technology on existing legal frameworks, such as contract law and data protection regulations [48]. Data privacy and protection are particularly critical in industries dealing with sensitive or personal information. Intellectual property rights related to blockchain innovations and patents must also be considered to protect the organisation's intellectual assets.

3.1.4. Trust and Security Factors

Trust and security factors are vital for successfully adopting blockchain technology [25]. Perceived trust in blockchain technology, including its immutability and resistance to tampering, is crucial for organisations and individuals to have confidence in using it. Addressing security concerns and implementing robust security measures is essential to protect sensitive data and prevent unauthorised access [45]. User privacy and anonymity are also important considerations, particularly in industries where privacy regulations are strict. According to Ghode, Yadav [65], building trust among stakeholders and ensuring the security of blockchain systems are critical for adoption.

3.1.5. Economic and Financial Factors

Economic and financial factors focus on adopting blockchain technology's potential economic benefits and financial implications [35]. Organisations consider the cost savings and efficiency gains that can be achieved via process optimisation, reduced intermediaries, and streamlined operations [45]. Evaluating the blockchain implementation's return on investment (ROI) is necessary to justify the costs involved. Financial risks and uncertainties, such as market volatility and regulatory changes, must be assessed. Adoption incentives and subsidies provided by governments or industry associations can also influence the decision to adopt blockchain [41].

3.1.6. User-Related Factors

User-related factors refer to the usability and acceptance of blockchain technology by users. Perceived ease of use is crucial to ensure users can interact with blockchain systems without significant barriers or complexities [63]. The perceived usefulness and benefits of blockchain technology play a role in user acceptance, as users need to see tangible advantages in adopting the technology. User training and support are necessary to ensure users have the skills and knowledge to utilise blockchain effectively [43]. User acceptance and potential resistance to change also need to be addressed with effective change management strategies.

3.1.7. Stakeholder Factors

Stakeholder factors recognise the importance of various stakeholders in the blockchain adoption process. This includes stakeholder involvement and participation, as the success of blockchain projects often relies on the collaboration and engagement of different stakeholders. Inter-organisational trust is crucial when multiple organisations or entities are involved in a blockchain network or consortium. Social influence and norms can shape the perception and adoption of blockchain technology within a specific industry or community [29,30]. The influence of trading partners and industry peers also plays a role, as organisations may adopt blockchain to align with industry standards or meet the expectations of their business partners [49].

3.1.8. Industry-Specific Factors

Industry-specific factors acknowledge that different industries' unique characteristics and requirements impact blockchain adoption. Supply chain dynamics, such as complex value chains or regulatory pressures, can drive the need for enhanced transparency, traceability, and coordination, making blockchain adoption more appealing [27,40,57]. Market characteristics, including competition and customer demands, can influence the urgency for blockchain implementation. Understanding the unique challenges and opportunities within a specific industry helps tailor blockchain solutions to address industry-specific needs [49].

3.2. Factors for Countries

The SLR comprehensively analyses factors influencing blockchain adoption across different countries. Key factors include perceived ease of use and usefulness, trust, government and upper management support, security concerns, and relative advantage observed in countries like Bangladesh, India, and Malaysia. In addition, technological characteristics, service quality, customer satisfaction, and cost-saving measures are crucial in countries like Australia, Malta, and the USA. Countries like Taiwan and Singapore emphasise technological fit, social influence, sufficient capital, and professional assistance. For European nations and the Republic of Korea, governance, compatibility, privacy, and regulatory standards play pivotal roles. Infrastructure readiness and organisational characteristics appear vital for countries like Sri Lanka and South Africa. Lastly, countries like Italy and Pakistan highlight efficiency, perceived benefits, strategic planning, and supplier relationships as significant factors for blockchain adoption. The common factors among countries are presented in Table 3.

Table 3. Factors influencing blockchain adoption across countries.

Country	Factors
Bangladesh	Perceived trust, perceived ease of use, autonomous motivation, perceived usefulness, trading partners' pressure, and competitive pressure
India	Perceived ease of use, government support, vendor support, adoption intention, perceived usefulness, security concerns, disintermediation, traceability, trust, complexity, ease of use, management/leadership buy in, transaction cost efficiency
Malaysia	Optimism, innovativeness, discomfort, insecurity, perceived ease of use, perceived usefulness, perceived usefulness, trialability, relative advantage, compatibility
China	Perceived ease of use, output quality, trust, perceived usefulness, information quality
Australia	Technology characteristics, task characteristics, inter-organisational trust, technology trust, user satisfaction, service quality
Malta	Customer satisfaction, cost saving, favourable economy, increased use of technological devices, government support
Taiwan	Perceived usefulness, individual technology fit, task technology fit, perceived safety, network externality, perceived ease of use, strategic orientation, social influence, innovativeness, perceived ease of use, perceived usefulness, self-efficacy, complexity, security
Brazil	Facilitating conditions, performance expectancy, social influence, effort expectancy, trust
Ireland	Disintermediation, relative advantage, maturity, smart contact coding, data security, compatibility, complexity, perceived benefits
Kosovo	Increase in data availability, reduction in information, easy verification of transactions
Singapore	Sufficient capital, staff training, support from the senior management, ease of local legislation, support from the shipping community, professional consultation, and assistance
Europe	Cost, governance, perceived compatibility, perceived ease of use, perceived usefulness, privacy, observability, security, trialability
USA	Budget availability, financial risk and uncertainty, cost saving, talent and knowledge acquisition, stakeholder's awareness and acceptance
Republic of Korea	Regulatory governance and industry standards, technological improvements, and optimisation on efficiency, tracking and tracing, digitalised management, air traffic management
Sri Lanka	Relative advantage, upper management support, human resources, compatibility, cost, complexity, technological infrastructure, architecture

Table 3. *Cont.*

Country	Factors
South Africa	Infrastructure and competencies, organisation characteristics, organisation readiness, organisation size, industry and market environment, support environment, regulatory environment, trust, load shedding, unemployment/layoffs, current infrastructure, useful life and educational campaigns
Saudi Arabia	Relative advantage, compatibility, observability, complexity, trialability
Russia, Estonia	Perceived efficiency, transparency, standardisation and platform development and traceability
Italy	Efficiency and security, perceived usefulness, perceived benefits, perceived usefulness, perceived ease of use, subjective norms, perceived behavioural control
Pakistan	Close relationship with the supplier, close relationship with the customer, just-in-time (JIT) strategic planning, many suppliers outsourcing, e-procurement, third party logistics (3 PL), subcontracting, reduced lead time, flexibility, forecasting, cost saving, resource planning, reduced inventory level
UK	Trialability, relative advantage, competitive advantage, compatibility

3.3. *Factors for Industries*

The analysis reflects an extensive array of factors influencing blockchain adoption across various industries. Perceived ease of use and perceived usefulness are common factors across most industries, like taxing systems, supply chains, education, intelligence communities, crowdsourcing platforms, logistics, and more. In addition, government and top management support are particularly significant for industries such as the supply chain, insurance, and banking. Some unique factors for industries include autonomous motivation for taxing systems, disintermediation for agriculture food supply chain, customer satisfaction for insurance, and individual technology fit for logistics. Moreover, the adoption in the banking industry shows a complexity of factors ranging from security and integrity to regulation and legislation compatibility. For certain industries like the food industry and agri-food, elements like food quality control, provenance tracking, and traceability also play a crucial role. In essence, blockchain adoption is influenced by a multifaceted mix of factors, varying significantly across different industries, emphasising the importance of customisation and specificity in blockchain implementation strategies. Table 4 shows the factors found to be common among industries while adopting blockchain technology.

Table 4. Factors influencing blockchain adoption across industries.

Industry	Factors
Taxing System	Perceived trust, perceived ease of use, autonomous motivation, perceived usefulness
Supply Chain	Government support, vendor support, adoption intention, perceived usefulness, security concerns, top management support, technology readiness, complexity of technology, technology compatibility, relative advantage, cost concerns, transparency, smart contracts, shared database, secured database, reduced settlement lead times, reduced transaction cost, improved risk management, decentralised database, auditability, privacy, anonymity, immutability, provenance, traceability, facilitating conditions, performance expectancy, social influence, effort expectancy, trust, regulatory support, competitive pressure, market dynamics, cost, upper management support, complexity, relative advantage, perceived compatibility, perceived ease of use, perceived usefulness, privacy, observability, security, trialability, people's readiness, process readiness, technology readiness, top management enthusiasm, top management expertise, top management support, competitive pressure, customer's influence, connection with ICT providers

Table 4. *Cont.*

Industry	Factors
Intelligence communities	Optimism, innovativeness, discomfort, insecurity, perceived ease of use, perceived usefulness
Crowdsourcing platform	Perceived ease of use, output quality, trust, perceived usefulness, information quality
Agriculture food supply chain	Disintermediation, traceability, trust, coordination/control, compliance, price of technology products/services
Education	Perceived usefulness, trialability, relative advantage, compatibility, perceived ease of use
Insurance	Customer satisfaction, cost saving, favourable economy, increased use of technological devices, government support
Logistics	Perceived usefulness, individual technology fit, task technology fit, perceived safety, network externality, perceived ease of use
Tourism	Strategic orientation, social influence, innovativeness, perceived ease of use, perceived usefulness, self-efficacy, complexity, security
SMEs	Disintermediation, relative advantage, maturity, smart contact coding, data security, compatibility, complexity, perceived benefits, blockchain knowledge, participation incentives, innovativeness, technology readiness, business model readiness, organisational size, top management support, organisational readiness, critical user mass, trading partner support, business use cases, government support, industry pressure, market dynamics, regulatory environment, organisational readiness, trading partner pressure, perceived benefits, complexity, top management support, compatibility
Real Estate	Increase in data availability, reduction in information, asymmetry, easy verification of transactions, comprehensibility of the transaction, data accuracy and reliability, data inalterability, exclusion of false information from contractual information, hacking attempts system denials, high-security encryption, cost reduction via the exclusion of intermediaries, contract conclusion with a reasonable fee, cost reduction due to process efficiency
Maritime	Sufficient capital, staff training, support from the senior management, ease of local legislation, support from the shipping community, professional consultation, and assistance
Agriculture	Complexity, ease of use, lack of interoperability and standardisation, lack of scalability and system speed, huge resource (energy, infrastructure), initial capital requirement, lack of government regulation, lack of trust among agro-stakeholders
Health	Budget availability, financial risk and uncertainty, cost saving, talent and knowledge acquisition, stakeholder's awareness and acceptance, blockchain ecosystem, disintermediation and business process, infrastructure and platform integration, standardisation, security and privacy, blockchain maturity and use case, management support, training and skills, HIT strategy, regulation compliance, regulatory uncertainty and governance, incentives availability
Aviation	Regulatory governance and industry standards, technological improvements, and optimisation on efficiency, tracking and tracing, digitalised management, air traffic management
Government organisations	Perceived benefits, complexity, and compatibility, organisational readiness, top management support, and organisational size, regulatory environment and market dynamics, transparency, integrity of data, immutability
Construction	Trialability, relative advantage, competitive advantage, compatibility

Table 4. *Cont.*

Industry	Factors
Banking	Management/leadership buy in, transaction cost efficiency, transaction storage/energy efficiency, scalability, security and integrity, user data privacy, user engagement and desirability, ease of local and international legislation and regulation, personnel training, availability of funds for implementation, professional consultation and advisory capability, blockchain talent availability, integration with other cloud services/E-commerce platforms, incentives for miners, smart contract robustness and business case deployability, interoperability and standardisation, technology investment and maturity, facilitating conditions, performance expectancy, and initial trust, security risk, regulatory support, technology latency, and technology complexity
Manufacturing	Perceived usefulness, trading partners' pressure, and competitive pressure
Agri-Food	Food quality control, provenance tracking and traceability, and partnership and trust
Cyber Security	Infrastructure and competencies, organisation characteristics, organisation readiness, organisation size, industry and market environment, support environment, regulatory environment
Food industry	Perceived efficiency, transparency, standardisation and platform development and traceability
Clearing and settlement industry	Trust, load shedding, unemployment/layoffs, current infrastructure, useful life and educational campaigns
Blood bank	Task characteristics, technology characteristics, perceived ease of use, perceived usefulness, security concerns, government support
Oil industry	Close relationship with supplier, close relationship with customer, just-in-time (JIT) strategic planning, many suppliers outsourcing, E-procurement, third party logistics (3 PL), subcontracting, reduced lead time, flexibility, forecasting, cost saving, resource planning, reduced inventory level

RQ 2: *What are the commonalities or differences in the factors across different industries and countries?*

3.4. Factors Common among Countries

Upon analysing the data, it is evident that several factors commonly influence blockchain adoption across a range of countries. The most prevalent factors include "perceived ease of use" and "perceived usefulness", which resonate with eight and seven countries, respectively, highlighting the importance of user perception and the utility of the technology in facilitating adoption. Another significant factor is "government support", underlined in six different countries, indicating the role of regulatory bodies in fostering the adoption of blockchain. "Top management support" also emerged as a notable factor across six countries, reflecting the crucial role of organisational leadership in driving technological adoption. Other recurring factors like "trust", "complexity", "compatibility", and "security concerns" also significantly influence the adoption of blockchain, as these factors appeared in five different countries each. Table 5 demonstrates the common factors among countries.

Table 5. Common factors influencing blockchain adoption across countries.

Factor	Countries
Perceived ease of use	Bangladesh, India, Malaysia, China, Taiwan, Sri Lanka, Saudi Arabia, Italy
Perceived usefulness	Bangladesh, India, Malaysia, China, Taiwan, Italy
Government support	India, Malta, Ireland, India, Sri Lanka, Malaysia
Top management support	India, Ireland, Europe, India, South Africa, Italy
Trust	Bangladesh, China, India, Brazil, South Africa
Complexity	India, Taiwan, Europe, India, South Africa
Compatibility	Malaysia, Europe, Sri Lanka, South Africa, Italy
Security concerns	India, Taiwan, Europe, USA, India
Technology readiness	India, Ireland, Europe
Perceived benefits	Ireland, Malaysia, Italy
Relative advantage	Malaysia, Sri Lanka, UK, Saudi Arabia, Bangladesh

3.5. Factors Common among Industries

Some prominent commonalities were observed in assessing the factors influencing blockchain adoption across various industries. As shown in Table 6, key factors such as perceived ease of use and perceived usefulness appeared to be universally relevant, cutting across a broad array of industries, including supply chain, taxing system, intelligence communities, crowdsourcing platforms, education, logistics, SMEs, maritime, agriculture, government organisations, banking, manufacturing, agri-food, cyber security, apparel, clearing and settlement industry, blood bank, and the oil industry. Trust also emerged as a significant factor in industries ranging from supply chain to real estate and banking. Other recurring factors, such as government support, compatibility, security concerns, and top management support, were significantly prevalent in specific industries, demonstrating their unique impact in shaping blockchain adoption within those industries.

Table 6. Common factors influencing blockchain adoption across industries.

Factor	Industries
Perceived ease of use	Supply chain, taxing system, intelligence communities, crowdsourcing platform, education, logistics, SMEs, maritime, agriculture, government organisations, banking, manufacturing, agri-food, cyber security, apparel, clearing and settlement industry, blood bank, oil industry
Perceived usefulness	Supply chain, taxing system, intelligence communities, crowdsourcing platform, education, logistics, SMEs, maritime, agriculture, government organisations, banking, manufacturing, agri-food, cyber security, apparel, clearing and settlement industry, blood bank, oil industry
Trust	supply chain, taxing system, crowdsourcing platform, agriculture, food, insurance, real estate, SMEs, construction, banking, manufacturing, apparel
Government support	Supply chain, insurance, SMEs, maritime, agriculture, SMEs, banking
Compatibility	supply chain, SMEs, construction, banking, education, apparel
Security concerns	Supply chain, logistics, maritime, agriculture
Top management support	Supply chain, education, SMEs, banking
Complexity	Supply chain, intelligence communities, tourism, SMEs, agriculture, banking

4. Discussion

Some prominent commonalities were observed in assessing the factors influencing blockchain adoption across various industries and countries. Key factors such as perceived ease of use and perceived usefulness appeared to be universally relevant, cutting across a broad array of industries, including supply chain, taxing system, intelligence communities, crowdsourcing platforms, education, logistics, SMEs, maritime, agriculture, government organisations, banking, manufacturing, agri-food, cyber security, apparel, clearing and settlement industry, blood bank, and the oil industry. These factors are consistently highlighted in the literature as foundational pillars for blockchain adoption. Trust also emerged as a significant factor in industries ranging from supply chain to real estate and banking. Other recurring factors, such as government support, compatibility, security concerns, and top management support, were significantly prevalent in specific industries, demonstrating their unique impact in shaping blockchain adoption within those industries.

Exploring the factors influencing blockchain adoption across different industries and countries provides comprehensive insights into the evolving blockchain landscape. Our analysis of 39 studies encompassing 21 countries and 25 industries identified 152 distinct factors, giving an overarching picture of the commonalities and disparities in blockchain adoption drivers.

Interestingly, while certain factors were reported universally, suggesting their foundational role in blockchain adoption, regardless of industry or geographical area, it is essential to note that the factors influencing blockchain adoption are predominantly universal phenomena with widespread implications [28,31,32]. Perceived usefulness and perceived ease of use are the most frequently noted in the literature, underpinning blockchain adoption across industries and countries [28–31,33,37,38]. As a pivotal factor, trust underscores the importance of transparency and security in blockchain technology. These findings align with previous research highlighting the importance of perceived ease of use and usefulness in technology adoption [66], emphasising the enduring influence of these fundamental principles even in emerging technologies like blockchain. The significance of trust also echoes findings from research on technology adoption, where user trust significantly influences adoption decisions [67].

However, while these general trends emerged, the importance of specific factors in certain industries and countries was also evident. For example, the banking industry emphasises transaction cost efficiency, security and integrity, and user data privacy [51,55,59]. This reflects the banking industry's unique needs and challenges, particularly in ensuring security and reducing operational costs. It highlights the importance of considering industry-specific studies to gain a more nuanced understanding, as advocated by previous researchers [46].

From a country perspective, factors like regulatory support and technology characteristics were more prominent in specific countries such as India and Malaysia [29,30,33,40,44,48,51,59,63,65]. This suggests that the country's contextual factors can significantly shape blockchain adoption, emphasising the need for localised strategies to promote its acceptance. Policymakers and industry leaders can develop targeted initiatives to support blockchain adoption within their regions by considering country-specific factors.

Our findings have practical implications for policymakers and industry leaders as they elucidate key considerations for fostering blockchain adoption. Our research serves as a robust starting point, setting the stage for more detailed and context-specific studies in this burgeoning field. It calls for strategies that address both universal and specific factors influencing adoption, recognising the importance of understanding the intricacies of blockchain adoption factors for successful implementation. By incorporating a comprehensive analysis of the pros and cons of related prior research, as suggested by the reviewer, we can provide a more balanced overview of the state of research and contribute to a deeper understanding of the factors driving blockchain adoption.

5. Conclusions

This study conducts a systematic literature review of the factors influencing blockchain adoption across various industries and countries. Several factors are identified after analysing 39 studies published between 2008 and May 2023. This study also identifies the factors that are common among countries and industries. However, the findings also highlighted the importance of industry-specific and country-specific factors, underlining the need for a context-specific approach. This study contributes significantly to the literature on technology adoption and provides valuable insights for practitioners and researchers alike.

Limitations and Future Directions

This study provides a comprehensive review of the existing empirical studies, many opportunities exist to explore the adoption of blockchain technology further. Some of the opportunities are explained below.

Future studies can focus on exploring the interactions and relationships between different factors identified in this research. This can involve examining how factors interact and influence each other in the context of blockchain adoption.

While this study covers a range of countries and industries, future research can further expand the understanding of blockchain adoption by exploring more diverse contexts, such as emerging economies, which can provide unique insights into the challenges and opportunities faced in these dynamic environments. Additionally, focusing on the factors for the industries like non-profit / charity that have not been extensively examined in relation to blockchain adoption can provide a more comprehensive understanding of the technology's potential.

Most of the published research on the adoption of blockchain is cross-sectional. Conducting longitudinal studies can provide a deeper understanding of the dynamics of blockchain adoption over time. By tracking the progress of organisations and industries in their adoption journey, researchers can identify patterns, changes, and trends in the factors influencing adoption. Longitudinal studies can also shed light on the long-term impacts of blockchain adoption and the evolution of best practices.

This study does not differentiate the adoption of blockchain technology at the organisational or individual level. Future research with the questions outlined in this study for each of the adoption levels can provide insights into the specific motivations, challenges, and adoption drivers experienced by individuals and organisations, enabling targeted strategies and interventions for successful adoption.

Although a systematic literature review approach has been used in this study, there still exists a possibility that some papers may be missed due to strictly following the research purpose.

Author Contributions: Conceptualization, A.M.; methodology, A.M. and A.P.; validation, A.M. and A.P.; formal analysis, A.M.; investigation, A.M. and A.P.; data curation, A.P.; writing—original draft preparation, A.M. and A.P.; writing—review and editing, A.M. All authors have read and agreed to the published version of the manuscript.

Funding: This research received no external funding.

Data Availability Statement: Data available on request by the authors.

Conflicts of Interest: The authors declare no conflict of interest.

References

1. Nakamoto, S. Bitcoin: A Peer-to-Peer Electronic Cash System; *Satoshi Nakamoto Institute*. 2008. Available online: https://nakamotoinstitute.org/bitcoin/ (accessed on 6 July 2023).
2. Taherdoost, H.; Madanchian, M. Blockchain-Based New Business Models: A Systematic Review. *Electronics* **2023**, *12*, 1479. [CrossRef]
3. Vu, N.; Ghadge, A.; Bourlakis, M. Blockchain adoption in food supply chains: A review and implementation framework. *Prod. Plan. Control* **2023**, *34*, 506–523. [CrossRef]

4. Mahmudnia, D.; Arashpour, M.; Yang, R. Blockchain in construction management: Applications, advantages and limitations. *Autom. Constr.* **2022**, *140*, 104379. [CrossRef]
5. Zheng, X.R.; Lu, Y. Blockchain technology–recent research and future trend. *Enterp. Inf. Syst.* **2022**, *16*, 1939895. [CrossRef]
6. Sabry, S.S.; Kaittan, N.M.; Majeed, I. The road to the blockchain technology: Concept and types. *Period. Eng. Nat. Sci.* **2019**, *7*, 1821–1832. [CrossRef]
7. Merlo, V.; Pio, G.; Giusto, F.; Bilancia, M. On the exploitation of the blockchain technology in the healthcare sector: A systematic review. *Expert Syst. Appl.* **2022**, *213*, 118897. [CrossRef]
8. Boakye, E.A.; Zhao, H.; Ahia, B.N.K. Emerging research on blockchain technology in finance; a conveyed evidence of bibliometric-based evaluations. *J. High Technol. Manag. Res.* **2022**, *33*, 100437. [CrossRef]
9. Yaqoob, I.; Salah, K.; Jayaraman, R.; Al-Hammadi, Y. Blockchain for healthcare data management: Opportunities, challenges, and future recommendations. *Neural Comput. Appl.* **2021**, *34*, 11475–11490. [CrossRef]
10. AlShamsi, M.; Al-Emran, M.; Shaalan, K. A systematic review on blockchain adoption. *Appl. Sci.* **2022**, *12*, 4245. [CrossRef]
11. Rana, R.L.; Adamashvili, N.; Tricase, C. The Impact of Blockchain Technology Adoption on Tourism Industry: A Systematic Literature Review. *Sustainability* **2022**, *14*, 7383. [CrossRef]
12. Casino, F.; Dasaklis, T.K.; Patsakis, C. A systematic literature review of blockchain-based applications: Current status, classification and open issues. *Telemat. Inform.* **2019**, *36*, 55–81. [CrossRef]
13. Gartner.com. *Predicts 2019: Blockchain Business*; Gartner: Stamford, CT, USA, 2018.
14. Wang, T.; Lund, B.D.; Marengo, A.; Pagano, A.; Mannuru, N.R.; Teel, Z.A.; Pange, J. Exploring the Potential Impact of Artificial Intelligence (AI) on International Students in Higher Education: Generative AI, Chatbots, Analytics, and International Student Success. *Appl. Sci.* **2023**, *13*, 6716. [CrossRef]
15. Marengo, A.; Pagano, A. Training Time Optimization through Adaptive Learning Strategy. In *2021 International Conference on Innovation and Intelligence for Informatics, Computing, and Technologies, 3ICT 2021*; IEEE: Piscataway, NJ, USA, 2021; pp. 563–567. [CrossRef]
16. Wang, X.; Liu, L.; Liu, J.; Huang, X. Understanding the Determinants of Blockchain Technology Adoption in the Construction Industry. *Buildings* **2022**, *12*, 1709. [CrossRef]
17. Kamble, S.S.; Gunasekaran, A.; Kumar, V.; Belhadi, A.; Foropon, C. A machine learning based approach for predicting blockchain adoption in supply Chain. *Technol. Forecast. Soc. Chang.* **2021**, *163*, 120465. [CrossRef]
18. Balasubramanian, S.; Shukla, V.; Sethi, J.S.; Islam, N.; Saloum, R. A readiness assessment framework for Blockchain adoption: A healthcare case study. *Technol. Forecast. Soc. Chang.* **2021**, *165*, 120536. [CrossRef]
19. Malik, S.; Chadhar, M.; Vatanasakdakul, S.; Chetty, M. Factors affecting the organizational adoption of blockchain technology: Extending the technology–organization–environment (TOE) framework in the Australian context. *Sustainability* **2021**, *13*, 9404. [CrossRef]
20. Amico, C.; Cigolini, R. Improving port supply chain through blockchain-based bills of lading: A quantitative approach and a case study. *Marit. Econ. Logist.* **2023**, 1–31. [CrossRef]
21. Lanzini, F.; Ubacht, J.; De Greeff, J. Blockchain adoption factors for SMEs in supply chain management. *J. Supply Chain Manag. Sci.* **2021**, *2*, 47–68.
22. Snyder, H. Literature review as a research methodology: An overview and guidelines. *J. Bus. Res.* **2019**, *104*, 333–339. [CrossRef]
23. Okoli, C. A guide to conducting a standalone systematic literature review. *Commun. Assoc. Inf. Syst.* **2015**, *37*. [CrossRef]
24. Kitchenham, B.; Brereton, P. A systematic review of systematic review process research in software engineering. *Inf. Softw. Technol.* **2013**, *55*, 2049–2075. [CrossRef]
25. Ewald, H.; Klerings, I.; Wagner, G.; Heise, T.L.; Stratil, J.M.; Lhachimi, S.K.; Hemkens, L.G.; Gartlehner, G.; Armijo-Olivo, S.; Nussbaumer-Streit, B. Searching two or more databases decreased the risk of missing relevant studies: A metaresearch study. *J. Clin. Epidemiol.* **2022**, *149*, 154–164. [CrossRef] [PubMed]
26. Sahoo, S.; Kumar, A.; Mishra, R.; Tripathi, P. Strengthening Supply Chain Visibility With Blockchain: A PRISMA-Based Review. *IEEE Trans. Eng. Manag.* **2022**, 1–17. [CrossRef]
27. Hölbl, M.; Kompara, M.; Kamišalić, A.; Nemec Zlatolas, L. A systematic review of the use of blockchain in healthcare. *Symmetry* **2018**, *10*, 470. [CrossRef]
28. Kabir, M.R. Behavioural intention to adopt blockchain for a transparent and effective taxing system. *J. Glob. Oper. Strateg. Sourc.* **2021**, *14*, 170–201. [CrossRef]
29. Kumar Bhardwaj, A.; Garg, A.; Gajpal, Y. Determinants of blockchain technology adoption in supply chains by small and medium enterprises (SMEs) in India. *Math. Probl. Eng.* **2021**, *2021*, 5537395. [CrossRef]
30. Razali, N.A.M.; Wan Muhamad, W.N.; Ishak, K.K.; Saad, N.J.A.M.; Wook, M.; Ramli, S. Secure Blockchain-Based Data-Sharing Model and Adoption among Intelligence Communities. *IAENG Int. J. Comput. Sci.* **2021**, *48*, 18.
31. Liu, N.; Ye, Z. Empirical research on the blockchain adoption–based on TAM. *Appl. Econ.* **2021**, *53*, 4263–4275. [CrossRef]
32. Saurabh, S.; Dey, K. Blockchain technology adoption, architecture, and sustainable agri-food supply chains. *J. Clean. Prod.* **2021**, *284*, 124731. [CrossRef]
33. Ullah, N.; Mugahed Al-Rahmi, W.; Alzahrani, A.I.; Alfarraj, O.; Alblehai, F.M. Blockchain technology adoption in smart learning environments. *Sustainability* **2021**, *13*, 1801. [CrossRef]

34. Alazab, M.; Alhyari, S.; Awajan, A.; Abdallah, A.B. Blockchain technology in supply chain management: An empirical study of the factors affecting user adoption/acceptance. *Clust. Comput.* **2021**, *24*, 83–101. [CrossRef]
35. Grima, S.; Spiteri, J.; Romānova, I. A STEEP framework analysis of the key factors impacting the use of blockchain technology in the insurance industry. *Geneva Pap. Risk Insur.—Issues Pract.* **2020**, *45*, 398–425. [CrossRef]
36. Kamble, S.; Gunasekaran, A.; Arha, H. Understanding the Blockchain technology adoption in supply chains-Indian context. *Int. J. Prod. Res.* **2019**, *57*, 2009–2033. [CrossRef]
37. Lian, J.-W.; Chen, C.-T.; Shen, L.-F.; Chen, H.-M. Understanding user acceptance of blockchain-based smart locker. *Electron. Libr.* **2020**, *38*, 353–366. [CrossRef]
38. Nuryyev, G.; Wang, Y.-P.; Achyldurdyyeva, J.; Jaw, B.-S.; Yeh, Y.-S.; Lin, H.-T.; Wu, L.-F. Blockchain technology adoption behavior and sustainability of the business in tourism and hospitality SMEs: An empirical study. *Sustainability* **2020**, *12*, 1256. [CrossRef]
39. Queiroz, M.M.; Fosso Wamba, S.; De Bourmont, M.; Telles, R. Blockchain adoption in operations and supply chain management: Empirical evidence from an emerging economy. *Int. J. Prod. Res.* **2021**, *59*, 6087–6103. [CrossRef]
40. Wong, L.-W.; Leong, L.-Y.; Hew, J.-J.; Tan, G.W.-H.; Ooi, K.-B. Time to seize the digital evolution: Adoption of blockchain in operations and supply chain management among Malaysian SMEs. *Int. J. Inf. Manag.* **2020**, *52*, 101997. [CrossRef]
41. Clohessy, T.; Acton, T. Investigating the influence of organizational factors on blockchain adoption: An innovation theory perspective. *Ind. Manag. Data Syst.* **2019**, *119*, 1457–1491. [CrossRef]
42. Hoxha, V.; Sadiku, S. Study of factors influencing the decision to adopt the blockchain technology in real estate transactions in Kosovo. *Prop. Manag.* **2019**, *37*, 684–700. [CrossRef]
43. Zhou, Y.; Soh, Y.S.; Loh, H.S.; Yuen, K.F. The key challenges and critical success factors of blockchain implementation: Policy implications for Singapore's maritime industry. *Mar. Policy* **2020**, *122*, 104265. [CrossRef]
44. Yadav, V.S.; Singh, A.R.; Raut, R.D.; Govindarajan, U.H. Blockchain technology adoption barriers in the Indian agricultural supply chain: An integrated approach. *Resour. Conserv. Recycl.* **2020**, *161*, 104877. [CrossRef]
45. Alzahrani, S.; Daim, T.; Choo, K.-K.R. Assessment of the blockchain technology adoption for the management of the electronic health record systems. *IEEE Trans. Eng. Manag.* **2022**, *70*, 2846–2863. [CrossRef]
46. Li, X.; Lai, P.-L.; Yang, C.-C.; Yuen, K.F. Determinants of blockchain adoption in the aviation industry: Empirical evidence from Korea. *J. Air Transp. Manag.* **2021**, *97*, 102139. [CrossRef]
47. Paththinige, P.; Rajapakse, C. Evaluating the Factors that Affect the Adoption of Blockchain Technology in the Pharmaceutical Supply Chain-A Case Study from Sri Lanka. In Proceedings of the 2022 International Research Conference on Smart Computing and Systems Engineering (SCSE), Colombo, Sri Lanka, 1 September 2022; pp. 363–370.
48. Kamarulzaman, M.S.; Hassan, N.H.; Bakar, N.A.A.; Maarop, N.; Samy, G.A.N.; Aziz, N. Factors Influencing Blockchain Adoption in Government Organization: A Proposed Framework. In Proceedings of the 2021 International Conference on Computer & Information Sciences (ICCOINS), Kuching, Malaysia, 13–15 July 2021; pp. 366–371.
49. Molati, K.; Ilorah, A.I.; Moeti, M.N. Determinant Factors Influencing the Adoption of Blockchain Across SMEs in South Africa. In Proceedings of the 2021 15th International Conference on Advanced Technologies, Systems and Services in Telecommunications (TELSIKS), Nis, Serbia, 20–22 October 2021; pp. 265–269.
50. Marengo, A.; Pagano, A.; Ladisa, L. Towards a mobile augmented reality prototype for corporate training: A new perspective. In Proceedings of the 14th International Conference on Mobile Learning 2018, Lisbon, Portugal, 14–16 April 2018; pp. 129–135.
51. Mishra, R.; Singh, R.K.; Kumar, S.; Mangla, S.K.; Kumar, V. Critical success factors of Blockchain technology adoption for sustainable and resilient operations in the banking industry during an uncertain business environment. *Electron. Commer. Res.* **2023**, 1–35. [CrossRef]
52. Alalyan, M.S.; Jaafari, N.A.; Hussain, F.K. Technology Factors Influencing Saudi Higher Education Institutions' Adoption of Blockchain Technology: A Qualitative Study. In Proceedings of the Advanced Information Networking and Applications: Proceedings of the 37th International Conference on Advanced Information Networking and Applications (AINA-2023), Juiz de Fora, Brazil, 29–31 March 2023; Volume 1, pp. 197–207.
53. Tasnim, Z.; Shareef, M.A.; Baabdullah, A.M.; Hamid, A.B.A.; Dwivedi, Y.K. An Empirical Study on Factors Impacting the Adoption of Digital Technologies in Supply Chain Management and What Blockchain Technology Could Do for the Manufacturing Sector of Bangladesh. *Inf. Syst. Manag.* **2023**, 1–23. [CrossRef]
54. Shardeo, V.; Patil, A.; Dwivedi, A.; Madaan, J. Modelling of critical success factors for blockchain technology adoption readiness in the context of agri-food supply chain. *Int. J. Ind. Syst. Eng.* **2023**, *43*, 80–102. [CrossRef]
55. Jena, R.K. Examining the factors affecting the adoption of blockchain technology in the banking sector: An extended UTAUT model. *Int. J. Financ. Stud.* **2022**, *10*, 90. [CrossRef]
56. Mulaji, S.M.; Roodt, S. Factors Affecting Organisations' Adoption Behaviour toward Blockchain-Based Distributed Identity Management: The Sustainability of Self-Sovereign Identity in Organisations. *Sustainability* **2022**, *14*, 11534. [CrossRef]
57. Dehghani, M.; Popova, A.; Gheitanchi, S. Factors impacting digital transformations of the food industry by adoption of blockchain technology. *J. Bus. Ind. Mark.* **2022**, *37*, 1818–1834. [CrossRef]
58. Sciarelli, M.; Prisco, A.; Gheith, M.H.; Muto, V. Factors affecting the adoption of blockchain technology in innovative Italian companies: An extended TAM approach. *J. Strategy Manag.* **2022**, *15*, 495–507. [CrossRef]
59. Basori, A.A.; Ariffin, N.H.M. The Adoption Factors of Two-Factors Authentication in Blockchain Technology for Banking and Financial Institutions. *Indones. J. Electr. Eng. Comput. Sci.* **2022**, *26*, 1758–1764. [CrossRef]

60. Nath, S.D.; Khayer, A.; Majumder, J.; Barua, S. Factors affecting blockchain adoption in apparel supply chains: Does sustainability-oriented supplier development play a moderating role? *Ind. Manag. Data Syst.* **2022**, *122*, 1183–1214. [CrossRef]
61. Prisco, A.; Abdallah, Y.O.; Morande, S.; Gheith, M.H. Factors affecting blockchain adoption in Italian companies: The moderating role of firm size. *Technol. Anal. Strateg. Manag.* **2022**, 1–14. [CrossRef]
62. Dowelani, M.; Okoro, C.; Olaleye, A. Factors influencing blockchain adoption in the South African clearing and settlement industry. *S. Afr. J. Econ. Manag. Sci.* **2022**, *25*, 11. [CrossRef]
63. Kuberkar, S.; Singhal, T.K. Factors Influencing the Adoption Intention of Blockchain and Internet-of-Things Technologies for Sustainable Blood Bank Management. *Int. J. Healthc. Inf. Syst. Inform. (IJHISI)* **2021**, *16*, 1–21. [CrossRef]
64. Aslam, J.; Saleem, A.; Khan, N.T.; Kim, Y.B. Factors influencing blockchain adoption in supply chain management practices: A study based on the oil industry. *J. Innov. Knowl.* **2021**, *6*, 124–134. [CrossRef]
65. Ghode, D.; Yadav, V.; Jain, R.; Soni, G. Adoption of blockchain in supply chain: An analysis of influencing factors. *J. Enterp. Inf. Manag.* **2020**. [CrossRef]
66. Davis, F.D. Perceived usefulness, perceived ease of use, and user acceptance of information technology. *MIS Q.* **1989**, 319–340. [CrossRef]
67. Mayer, R.C.; Davis, J.H.; Schoorman, F.D. An integrative model of organizational trust. *Acad. Manag. Rev.* **1995**, *20*, 709–734. [CrossRef]

MDPI
St. Alban-Anlage 66
4052 Basel
Switzerland
www.mdpi.com

Electronics Editorial Office
E-mail: electronics@mdpi.com
www.mdpi.com/journal/electronics

www.ingramcontent.com/pod-product-compliance
Lightning Source LLC
Chambersburg PA
CBHW061818210926
51850CB00006B/743
9783036595689